Information Technology Law

INFORMATION TECHNOLOGY LAW

Fourth edition

Ian J Lloyd

Professor of Information Technology Law and
Director of the Centre for Law, Computers
and Technology, University of Strathclyde, Glasgow

OXFORD
UNIVERSITY PRESS

OXFORD
UNIVERSITY PRESS

Great Clarendon Street, Oxford OX2 6DP

Oxford University Press is a department of the University of Oxford.
It furthers the University's objective of excellence in research, scholarship,
and education by publishing worldwide in

Oxford New York

Auckland Bangkok Buenos Aires Cape Town Chennai
Dar es Salaam Delhi Hong Kong Istanbul Karachi Kolkata
Kuala Lumpur Madrid Melbourne Mexico City Mumbai Nairobi
São Paulo Shanghai Taipei Tokyo Toronto

Oxford is a registered trade mark of Oxford University Press
in the UK and in certain other countries

Published in the United States
by Oxford University Press Inc., New York

© Oxford University Press

British Library Cataloguing in Publication Data
Data available

Library of Congress Cataloging in Publication Data
Data available

ISBN 0 406 97578 7

1 3 5 7 9 10 8 6 4 2

Typeset in Sabon
by Doyle & Co, Colchester

Printed in Great Britain
on acid-free paper by
The Cromwell Press, Trowbridge, Wilts

Preface

Ten years have passed since the first edition of this book was published. One of the themes which has been stressed throughout the decade has been the difficult relationship between fast moving computer technology and the slow, deliberate pace of most legislative developments. The relationship between law and technology continues to be a difficult one, littered with false dawns and dead ends. In some areas the picture is a depressing one for laws and lawyers. In the second half of the 1990s the application of intellectual property law to the Internet appeared set to be a major topic. Issues such as the legality of hypertext linking and the extent to which copyright protected the look and feel of software dominated the legal landscape but have subsequently disappeared almost without trace. The relationship between domain names and trade mark law surfaced briefly in the courts but has subsequently been taken over by alternative forms of dispute resolution operated by the Internet industry. Even in the field of software and audio piracy which continues to be headline news, the copyright owner's response relies more on the application of established principles than reliance upon new forms of copyright legislation. Changes in market practice such as the Apple music downloading service also provide an extra legal response.

If developments such as these give rise to a degree of scepticism concerning the value of the law, the events of September 11 continue to reverberate. Faced with unprecedented terrorist threats, information is rightly regarded as a critical weapon in the government's armoury. Reliance upon information technology as a basis for surveillance does entail processing of vast amounts of data about millions of individuals whose abhorrence of terrorism is as great as any politician's. Striking a successful balance between personal privacy and state security is likely to be one of the most challenging tasks facing governments in the coming years. There is no doubt that the vast majority of people would give up much if not all of their right to privacy rather than die in a terrorist attack. This is certainly a valid concern but as with any survey of public opinion, the answer may be influenced by the form of the question. If asked whether law enforcement agencies should be able to access credit card records if this would prevent terrorist attacks, most people would agree. If the question is couched in terms whether the government should know everything that everyone does, the response might be different. There are few simple answers to questions which are fundamental to the shape of the society in which we will live. If the law has perhaps been marginalised in areas such as trademarks and domain names, the establishment of appropriate regimes has never been more important in these areas. Regulation of the use of information technology continues to be a massive challenge for us all.

As always, thanks are due to very many colleagues and friends working in the field. In particular I would like to express my gratitude to colleagues at Strathclyde, Denise Bula, Catherine Colston, Carol Hutton, Chirsty McSween, Janet Riddell and Jeremy Warner. To those also who have helped with our LLM course in Information Technology and Telecommunications Law, Francis Aldhouse, Olson Alleyne, Neil Bruce, Neville Cordell, Peter Davies, Gabriela Kennedy, Ian King, Matthias Klang, Ray London, Linda McPherson David Mellor, Ramsay Milne, Andrew Murray, Steven Saxby and Scott Singer. Thanks are due also to all of our students working with whom continues to be a real pleasure. It would generally be unfair to name names but I would like to pay a small tribute to Hugh McTaggart, a student on the course in session 2002-3 who died in a house fire earlier this year.

In previous editions, my greatest appreciation has been reserved for Moira Simpson. This time, Moira has to share my thanks with our son Thomas John to whom this book is dedicated with all our love.

Ian Lloyd
August 2004

Contents

Contents

Contents

Table of statutes

Table of statutory instruments

Table of European legislation

Table of conventions and other enactments

Table of conventions and other enactments

List of cases

List of cases

Chapter 1

The emerging information society

The development of information technology

From calculating machine to the microchip

1.1 The use of mechanical devices to aid mathematical calculations dates back some 5,000 years to the invention of the abacus in Asia Minor.[1] Moving forward several millennia, more complex mechanical devices capable of being programmed to perform a range of different tasks were designed by pioneers such as Pascal and Leibniz working in the seventeenth and early eighteenth centuries, Babbage and the Countess of Lovelace in the nineteenth century and Hollerith, whose invention of a mechanical device to process US census returns in 1890 was one of the most successful mechanical processing devices.[2] Although the work of these pioneers anticipated many of the features of modern computers, the technology of the day proved incapable of putting their ideas into practical effect[3] and it was only with the invention of the electronic valve, which substituted for mechanical components, that the programmable computer became a practical possibility. Much pioneering work was carried out during the Second World War in connection with the Allies' attempts to break the cryptographic systems employed by the Germans and Japanese by use of the computing device known as Colossus.[4] In essence, however, Colossus was a machine designed for one specific purpose, and the work of John von Neumann was required to enable computers to act upon a variety of programs to perform a range of tasks. The first computer with the capability of performing a range of tasks in accordance with specific sets of instructions (programs) was the ENIAC (Electronic Numerical Integrator and Calculator) machine developed in the US in 1947.[5]

[1] See http://www.digitalcentury.com/encyclo/update/comp_hd.html.
[2] See http://www.comlab.ox.ac.uk/archive/other/museums/computing/pioneers.html for a series of links to information on these and many other computing pioneers.
[3] A recent biography suggests that what we might now refer to as human factors was as significant a cause of Babbage's failure. The inventor, it was suggested, was himself a difficult person who related in an uneasy manner with civil servants who understood little and feared the application of technology. See D Swade *The Cogwheel Brain* (2000, Little Brown).

4   See http://www.cranfield.ac.uk/CCC/BPark/colossus.
5   See http://www.seas.upenn.edu/~museum/.

Four generations of computer technology

1.2 Taking pioneering machines such as ENIAC as representing the first generation of computing technology, initial estimates as to the market for computers now appear ludicrously low – one pioneer suggested that a single machine would satisfy the computing needs of the UK, whilst the Chairman of IBM considered that there might be a world market for five machines.[1] Given the limited nature of the functions carried out by the original machines, these estimates were perhaps not as short-sighted as hindsight might suggest. The invention of the transistor in 1948 transformed the situation, and by the second half of the 1950s computers were beginning to become established in commercial and public sector organisations. This second generation of computers can be dated from around 1956–63. Although use of transistors increased the reliability and decreased the size of computers, the mainframe machine remained supreme until the invention of the semiconductor chip brought about a new age of miniaturisation and a third generation of computers. Dating from about 1964, this third generation dominated the market until 1971, when the first large-scale integrated chips signalled the advent of the fourth generation of computers and, with it, the era of the personal computer.[2] Whilst the original semiconductor chips were able to fit three components onto a piece of silicon, large scale integrated chips increased this into the hundreds. Since then, Very Large Scale Integration (VLSI) and Ultra Large Scale Integration (ULSI) brought further increases into the hundreds of thousands and then the millions. Despite major research activities, especially in Japan, we await the arrival of the next generation of computers whose defining characteristic has been identified as human-like intelligence.

1   C Evans *The Mighty Micro* (1980, Coronet).
2   See http://www.digitalcentury.com/encyclo/update/comp_hd.html.

Computers and law today

The pace of technological change

1.3 If significant legal changes can be identified over the past 30 years, comparison between computer technology in 1970 and 2004 indicates a pace of development so rapid as almost to defy comprehension. In 1970, the first man had just landed on the moon. Although much stress was placed at the time on the role played by computers in guiding the lunar module to Tranquillity Base, a typical motor car of the 2000s possesses many times the computing power of the Apollo spaceship, whilst a desktop personal computer (PC) exceeds the total processing capability of the serried ranks of computers which featured prominently in television coverage from 'Mission Control'. A further example of developments in processing power, which may provide little comfort to nervous flyers, is that

2

the processing power of the mainframe computers installed a decade ago by the US air traffic control authorities would not suffice to run a flight simulator program used on a PC.[1] The processing power of computers is widely estimated as doubling every two years, an exponential increase which shows no sign of slackening. Today, microprocessors outnumber humans on the planet, and it is estimated that by the year 2010, 95% of telecommunications traffic will be between machines.

[1]   G Stix 'Aging Airways' *Scientific American*, May 1994, p 70.

1.4   In the 1970s, the remoteness and mysterious nature of the operations of computers was regarded as forming part of the public concern at the implications of their operations. In the UK, the 1975 White Paper *Computers and Privacy* asserted that because 'data are stored, processed and often transmitted in a form which is not directly intelligible, few people may know what is in the records or what is happening to them'. In 1970, Alan Westin, one of the early authorities on the topic of privacy and the computer, wrote to the effect that 'you do not find computers on street corners or in free nature, you find them in big powerful organisations'.[1] Today, computers *are* found on street corners, controlling traffic lights and the increasingly omnipresent closed-circuit television cameras. It is a rare form of human activity which is not affected in some way by the ubiquitous machine. As far back as 1994, it was estimated that two-thirds of the economy of developed countries was either dependent on or at least reliant upon some form of information technology.[2] In its 1995 Green Paper, *Copyright and Related Rights in the Information Society*,[3] the European Commission indicates that 'activities covered by copyright and related rights account for an estimated 3–5% of Community gross domestic product'. As we move further into the 'information society', these figures can only increase.

[1]   A Westin *Privacy and Freedom* (1970, Bodley Head).
[2]   European Commission Green Paper on Information Security (This document was prepared by the then DG XIII in 1994 but was not formally published).
[3]   http://www.ispo.cec.be/infosoc/legreg/com95382.doc.

1.5   The computer is at the core of information technology activities. In many instances, the terms can be regarded as synonymous. Although it is difficult to think of an aspect of life which has not been affected by the all-pervasive machine, a satisfactory definition of the beast has proved elusive. Faced with the problem, Parliament's normal response has been to decline to attempt the task. In perhaps the most blatant example, the Computer Misuse Act 1990, uses the word 'computer' on 41 occasions, whilst the words 'program' and 'data' are used 29 and 25 times respectively. None of these words is afforded any definition in the legislation.

The legal response to the computer

1.6   The quarter century between 1945 and 1970 can be seen as the first stage in the evolving relationship between law and computer (now generally referred to as 'information') technology. Whilst legal issues relating to computers had been raised, the first article on a computer law topic appearing in 1960,[1] the subject was generally relegated to the periphery of legal consciousness.

[1] The first article is generally regarded as being Roy Freed's 'Legal Implications of Computer Use' published in 1962 (5(12) Comm ACM 607) The text of this historic article can be downloaded from the ACM Digital Library site at http://portal.acm.org. It is typical of the situation at the time that an article on legal issues should have been published in a technical rather than a purely legal publication.

1.7 Although early uses of computers were mainly mathematical, we have moved a very long way from the notion of the computer as a calculating machine. The scope of the machine's capabilities has expanded to the extent that virtually any item of information, sound, pictures, text or graphics may be transformed into digital format, effectively represented as a series of zeros and ones. Thus, the letter 'A' is represented in ASCII[1] by the figures 11000001, whilst its lower case equivalent is 10000001. Again, the music blasting out of a compact disc (CD) player represents the processing by the equipment of a vast series of zeros and ones, the results of the processing of the sounds of the original performance. Increasingly, digitisation is becoming a feature of films and television productions, allowing special effects which would have been unthinkable in previous eras. The film 'Toy Story 2' was claimed to be the first movie to exist purely within a digital environment. The characters were all digitally created with no film being used in the course of production. A more recent and more widely known example of the application of digital technology was in the production of 'The Lord of the Rings' where the character of Gollum was a largely digital creation.

[1] American Standard Code for Information Interchange. The series of eight digits is referred to as a byte.

1.8 One aspect of the phenomenon of digitisation which carries considerable legal significance is that data becomes an almost totally pliable commodity. As the expanding market for multimedia products demonstrates, a single CD may contain recordings of sound, text, music and still and moving images. The particular form of storage device is becoming a matter of limited significance. We are all familiar with musical CDs and electronic encyclopaedias such as *Microsoft Encarta* or *Britannica Online*. The latter example may serve to illustrate one of the major economic aspects of digitisation. A full set of the encyclopaedia in paper format costs £995. The CD equivalent costs £60. Access is also available over the Internet on a subscription basis at a cost for domestic users of around £40 per year.[1] Beyond issues of cost, the Internet is based around the transfer of information in digital format and as transmission speeds increase, so more and more complex and substantial forms of data may be transmitted online. It is now commonplace for individuals or undertakings to purchase and download copies of software from a remote site (normally making payment by means of a credit card number). Until recently, it was not considered viable to transmit music or video programs of more than a few seconds in length over the Internet. Developments in the technology of compressing data, coupled with increased transmission capacity, are changing the situation. The MP3 system allows music to be transmitted over the Internet in real time, a prospect which is causing considerable concern to the owners of copyright in musical works and which is driving significant changes in laws relating to both the extent and the enforcement of copyright.[2]

1   See http//www.britannica.com.
2   See para 21.33 below.

1.9   As indicated above and as will be discussed in more detail in the remainder of this book, many Internet-based activities challenge the continuing relevance and effectiveness of traditional legal provisions. Beyond reform of areas of the law, per se, the notion of convergence is assuming increasing importance in the development of regulatory policy. Traditionally, technologies such as the telephone, broadcasting, cinema and the printed word have been considered discrete and subject to quite different regulatory regimes. The technologies are converging and it is increasingly argued that regulatory regimes should also move together. The most notable application of the principle can be seen in the Communications Act 2003 which replaces regulatory bodies (and many aspects of substantive law) in the fields of telecommunications and broadcasting with a single regulator in the form of the Office of Communications (OFCOM).[1]

1   The regulators replaced are the Office of Telecommunications (OFTEL), the Broadcasting Standards Commission, the Radio Authority (which was responsible for the auction of third generation (3g) mobile telephony frequencies which raised some £23bn for public funds in 2000) and the Independent Television Commission.

The beginnings of computer-specific legislation

1.10   The world's first computer-specific statute was enacted in 1970, by the German state of Hesse, in the form of a Data Protection Act. Prompted in large measure by memories of the misuse of records under the Nazi regime, the legislation sought to assuage public concern about the use of computers to store and process large amounts of personal data. Such concerns remain significant and have even grown in the post-11 September 2001 environment, following the terrorist attacks in the US (hereafter 'September 11'), and the concept of data protection remains one of the most significant legal responses to the computer revolution. Following the Hessian example the first wave of national data protection statutes were enacted in European states in the 1970s. Computer crime statutes can be dated from the early 1980s with the US taking the lead here through the enactment of the Computer Fraud and Abuse Act in 1984. Specific intellectual property provisions designed to deal initially with the copyright status of computer programs date from the mid-1980s. Today, in addition to amending and developing the scope of laws in the above fields, much legislative attention is aimed at ensuring the development of effective regulatory regimes, both for e-commerce and for the relationships between individuals and companies and government agencies.

1.11   Given the international nature of the topic, it is not surprising that many of the activities in the field of information technology law have been initiated by international organisations. The EU has been a major influence on UK developments in the fields of data protection, intellectual property law and electronic commerce. Other governmental agencies, such as the Council of Europe, the Organisation for Economic Cooperation and Development and the United Nations, have also played important roles. Significant also has been the work of non-governmental agencies such as the International Chamber of Commerce (ICC) and the World Intellectual Property Organization, (WIPO) together with an almost baffling range of agencies (and acronyms) which has contributed to the development and organisation of the Internet and World Wide Web (WWW).

Premises for computer-specific legislation

1.12   To date, most computer-specific statutes have been justified on the basis that their enactment is necessary to bring computer-related activities unequivocally within the ambit of existing provisions of law. Thus, in considering the application of the provisions of the English Criminal Damage Act 1968 to instances of computer hacking where the damage suffered was to the intangible contents of a computer system rather than any physical components, the Law Commission argued that although there had been a number of successful prosecutions under this statute, there remained:

> ... recurrent (and understandable) difficulty in explaining to judges, magistrates and juries how the facts fit in with the present law of criminal damage.[1]

[1]   *Computer Misuse* (Law Com no 186) para 2.31. See also discussion at para 13.61 below.

1.13   As will be discussed,[1] this approach has not been an unqualified success. The principal danger is that computer-specific statues might be regarded as isolated and compliance a matter of little importance. This difficulty has perhaps befallen the concept of data protection within the UK system. In the absence of any general right to privacy, the enactment of a statute providing for such protection in a computer context has lacked solid legal foundations.

[1]   See Chapter 11 below.

1.14   Even where it has been possible to bring computer-related activities within established legal concepts difficulties and tensions are often becoming apparent. An excellent example can be seen in the field of intellectual property law. Here statutes such as the Copyright (Computer Software) (Amendment) Act 1985 provided that computer programs should be classed as literary works and protected as such under the copyright regime.[1] It is certainly the case that computer code can have the appearance of a form of literary work and the extension of the legislation to such works has proved reasonably successful. The essence of intellectual property law as it has developed over a period of centuries has been to confer a basket of exclusive property rights on the right-holder. Where copyright works were limited to books and similar works no particular tension between the wish of a legitimate holder to use (read) the work and that of the right-holder to prevent the making of further copies. In the digital environment use becomes inextricably linked with the act of copying. Although recent legislative reforms creating specific or sui generis rights in fields such as the legal protection to be afforded to databases adhere to the basic structure of copyright law, tensions continue to grow between the absolute nature of intellectual property rights and the distributive nature of the Internet. It may be argued that legislative efforts have provided a sticking plaster to wounds which require more radical medical or surgical treatment. The emergence of the Internet, it may be suggested, challenges at an individual the continuing validity of established notions of ownership and possession whilst at a national level, concepts of national territorial jurisdiction are increasingly challenged by global communications networks.

[1] Section 1(1).

The impact of the Internet and the emergence of cyberspace

1.15 The expanding corpus of computer-specific law, coupled with the societal and economic impact of computing and a substantial body of case law, spawned a vast range of articles and books on the topic of computer or information technology law. Almost all of the focus, however, was on the computer as a stand-alone machine. Effectively avoiding the notice of lawyers,[1] the Internet was emerging as a powerful force. Like love, the WWW is changing everything. The second stage of legal development was characterised by the attempt to shoehorn computer-related conduct into existing legal concepts. In many respects also, as epitomised by the concept of data protection, a goal of legislation was to restrict or control the uses to which technology could be put. Increasingly, it is becoming apparent that more radical reform is required. Just as the Industrial Revolution rendered obsolete aspects of law based on notions of an agrarian society, so a legal system focusing on issues of ownership, control and use of physical objects must re-orientate itself to suit the requirements of an information society.

[1] In the first edition of this book, which was published in 1993, the word Internet appears twice, both times in a footnote and there is no mention whatsoever of the WWW.

1.16 The word 'cyberspace' was coined by William Gibson in his science fiction novel *Necromancer*, published in 1984. It has subsequently become widely used as a means of denoting the apparent – or virtual – location within which electronic activities are undertaken. To take the example of a telephone call: although each party's words will be received by the other, and although legal provisions exist to resolve issues such as the time and place when a contract may be considered to have been made, the overall conversation does not occur at either end of the connection. As was stated by Beldam LJ in the case of *Re Levin*:[1]

> ... the operation of the keyboard by a computer operator produces a virtually instantaneous result on the magnetic disk of the computer, even though it may be 10,000 miles away. It seems to us artificial to regard the act as having been done in one rather than the other place.

The imaginary location where the words of the parties meet in conversation is what is referred to as cyberspace.

1   (1996) Times, 11 March.

1.17 From a legal perspective, the term and the concept of a quasi-physical territory is helpful in attempting to analyse the issues involved with computer communications. The geographical location where conduct occurs is one of the major factors determining which country's laws apply to activities. As has been discussed in other contexts, the operations of global networks pay little heed to national boundaries, and one of the arguments frequently mooted is that there is need for a new legal regime in cyberspace. In the context of ecommerce, comparison is sometimes made with the development of the Law Merchant in the Middle Ages – a body of law and courts developed and administered by those responsible for commercial transactions, and which provided a consistent legal basis for international trade, avoiding the vagaries and discrepancies of national legal systems.[1] Although there is a clear role for some forms of industry self-regulation, this technique leaves unrepresented the vast numbers of individuals who deal with Internet Service Providers (ISPs) and the increasing numbers of organisations offering goods or services over the Internet.

1   This suggestion is put forward in D Johnson and D Post 'Law and Borders – The Rise of Law in Cyberspace' (1996) Stan LR 1367. Note, however, the emphatic rejection of the notion of a discrete community of Internet users in the case of *US v Thomas* 1997 US App LEXIS 12998, discussed at para 15.33ff below.

1.18 This is not, however, to suggest that cyberspace is presently unregulated. Indeed, one of the problems involved in assessing the topic is that there is a surfeit of regulation. Laws relating to broadcasting, the media, data protection, evidence, contract, tort, defamation and intellectual property all have a role to play, as do provisions of criminal law. Indeed, the inhabitants of cyberspace may be, at least in theory, the most massively regulated individuals in the world in that, depending upon the nature of their activities, they may theoretically be subject to the jurisdiction of virtually all of the world's legal systems. Theory and practice are greatly divergent, and the challenge of developing effective mechanisms for law enforcement is substantially greater than that of identifying relevant legal provisions. In its 1988 Green Paper on *Copyright and the Challenge of Technology*,[1] the Law Commission suggested that '(t)hese new technologies have entailed the de facto abolition of national frontiers and increasingly make the territorial application of national copyright law obsolete'. Such comments have equal validity with respect to other areas of the law, and consideration needs to be given to the uneasy relationship between terrestrial boundaries and the claim to jurisdiction of the courts of a particular country, and the operation of worldwide communications networks such as the Internet.

1   COM (88) 72 final.

The development of communications and the emergence of regulation

1.19 The ability to communicate is a basic requirement both of human society and, increasingly so, in what is generally referred to as the 'information society'. Communication can, of course, take a variety of forms. One of the major features distinguishing homo sapiens from other forms of life has been the ability to communicate other than through sounds or the use of body language. Cave paintings, dating back to around 25000 BC mark the oldest recorded form of non-verbal communication with the first forms of writing being found in Sumeria around 3500 BC. The Sumerian system of writing, referred to as cuneiform because characters were created through the use of a wedge-shamed implement, used some 2,000 different signs. The Egyptian system of hieroglyphics (writing of the Gods) introduced a basic system of 24 symbols corresponding to what we would now term as the letters of the alphabet. This trend was developed by the Greeks with the word 'alphabet' being derived from the first two letters *alpha* and *beta*.

1.20 The invention of the printing press in the fifteenth century created the potential for creating multiple copies of a work quickly and relatively cheaply. Dissemination, however, remained a relatively slow process being limited effectively to the speed of rider on horseback. Such delay had implications for the feasibility of what would today be regarded as shared or contemporaneous events. It was (and remains) the case that public intimation of the dissolution of Parliament and the calling of a general election is given in Edinburgh several days after the it is declared in London, the delay reflecting the time taken for news to travel between the two capitals.

1.21 The coming of the railways speeded the communication of information and brought with them massive societal changes including new perspectives on the nature of time itself. Although the needs of mariners to be able to establish location with a degree of accuracy had led to the development of accurate clocks and the concept of a standard time based on the Royal Observatory in Greenwich as far back as the eighteenth century, it remained the practice for towns to maintain their own system of time based on the rising and setting of the sun. This produced variations of 1 minute for every 12.5 miles travelled along an east-west axis.

1.22 Such relatively small discrepancies mattered little at a time when it was relatively rare for individuals to move more than 20 miles from their birthplace. With the coming of the railways it became possible for journeys of hundreds of miles to be made in the course of a few hours and the need was identified for a more standardised system of time. In the UK the maritime standard was widely adopted in the 1840s, often under the heading of 'railway time' although formal recognition had to wait until 1880 with the enactment of the Definition of Time Act. In 1884, following the International Meridian Conference held in Washington, Greenwich Mean Time (GMT) was recognised as the basis from which other time zones would be derived. Since 1972, although Greenwich remains the location of the prime meridian, the terminology of Coordinated Universal Time (UTC) has been adopted since the 1970s as the base unit of time measurement.

Towards electronic communications

1.23   The next radical change in the world of communications came with the invention of the telegraph in the nineteenth century. For the first time, messages could be transmitted over long distances at something approaching real time. In part the need of the railways for a speedy mechanism of communication in order to regulate the movement of trains acted as a catalyst for developments and the first UK telegraph line was a 1.5-mile system on the railway from London to Camden in 1837. The coverage of the telegraph network expanded rapidly. Between 1846 and 1852 the size of the US network expanded 600 fold prompting the journal *Scientific American* to comment that:

> The spread of the telegraph is about a wonderful a thing as the noble invention itself.[1]

---

[1]   Cited in T Standage *The Victorian Internet* (1998, Weidenfeld and Nicolson). This book provides an excellent account of the development of the telegraph network and its societal impact.

1.24   A number of significant parallels can be drawn between the original telegraph systems and the modern communications market. The system has indeed been described as 'The Victorian Internet'. The key element of the telegraphy system was that text would be converted into long and short electrical impulses in the form of what is generally referred to as 'dots and dashes'. A dash would be three times the length of a dot with particular combinations corresponding to numbers and to the letters of the alphabet. Initially, a range of codes was adopted in different countries with incompatibilities making international traffic problematic. A message had to be sent to the national border, deciphered, carried physically across the border and retransmitted by the authorities of the next state. It was estimated that a message sent from Madrid to Berlin would require to be deciphered and retransmitted on no fewer than 19 occasions. In addition to causing delay, repeated deciphering and retransmission afforded obvious potential for errors to creep into a message.

1.25   From the 1850s, Morse code became accepted as an international standard and an increasing number of bilateral agreements were entered into between states to allow direct international connections. In the attempt to rationalise the situation the International Telegraph Union (ITU) was established in 1865 following a meeting of 20 European states. Perhaps surprisingly, but providing an early indication of the global nature of electronic communications, the ITU was established nine years before the Postal Union Convention was signed by 22 countries to establish the Universal Postal Union. With the substitution of the word 'Telecommunications' for 'Telegraph', the ITU remains a major global player in the communications sector and depending upon developments in the sector may take on more direct regulatory responsibilities in the area of the Internet.

The development of the telephone system

1.26   Although the telegraph provided almost instantaneous communication between sending and receiving stations, the need to transcribe and decode messages meant that, although generally faster than surface mail, delivery of messages to a particular addressee required the employment of delivery staff who would take a message from the telegraph office and cycle through the streets to the recipient's address. The telephone provided a more direct form of communication between individuals.

1.27 Credit for the invention of the telephone is generally given to Alexander Graham Bell. He was, however, not the only person to have been researching in the field. In one of history's 'strange but true' events, Elisha Grey also developed a working telephone system and sought a patent for his invention. The patent system essentially works on the basis of 'first come, first served'. Bell arrived at the US Patent Office a matter of hours before Grey. Bell was, in 1878, granted a patent (174465) which in a mere six pages specified what are recognisably still the key features of the telephone system. The patent system works effectively on the basis of first come, first served and confers a monopoly on the successful applicant. Bell was awarded a patent and entered the history books, Elisha Grey was consigned to little more than a footnote in dull legal text books.

1.28 Superlatives almost become exhausted in describing Bell's patent. It was the most heavily litigated award of all time with more than 600 law suits raised challenging its validity. Perhaps the most serious challenge was raised by the Western Union Telegraph Company which held a dominant position in the telegraph sector. This claim was settled in 1879. Other challenges persisted but in what was the second most significant event in the memorable year of 1888[1] its validity was upheld by the US Supreme Court,[2] in what is reportedly the longest judgment delivered in US patent history (some 197,000 words). The patent has frequently been described as the most valuable grant of all time.

[1]   The most memorable event of the year 1888 was undoubtedly the formation of Glasgow Celtic Football Club.
[2]   *The Telephone Cases* 1888 US 1.

1.29 From Bell's invention the telephone network spread rapidly. In the US the monopoly conferred on Bell by his patent meant that the Bell Telephone Corporation had a period of some 20 years to develop its network free from competition. Even when the patents expired, Bell's dominance, subsequently through the vehicle of the American Telephone and Telegraph Company (AT&T) remained substantial until landmark antitrust actions in the 1970s sought to break up the market. From a relatively early stage, however, the telephone system was subject to regulation with the establishment of the Interstate Commerce Commission in 1887 and more significantly the Federal Communications Commission (FCC) in 1934. This can be considered the world's first telecommunications regulatory agency and in many respects it has served as a prototype for subsequent developments in Europe and elsewhere over the last 20 years.

The development of the Internet

1.30 The concept of a decentralised computer network had been considered in a number of countries, including the UK, but it was with the provision of substantial funding from the Advanced Research Projects Agency (ARPA)[1] in 1964 that a practical implementation was developed. The project was based upon ideas drawn up by Paul Baran of the RAND Corporation, an organisation described as 'America's foremost Cold War think-tank'. Its genesis lay in the desire to find a method of enabling the US military and government to maintain communications after a nuclear war. The assumption was that telecommunication control centres would be a leading target for attack and that traditional telecommunications networks would be rendered unusable. The solution lay in reversing the conception that a telecommunications network should seek to be as reliable as possible by building in the assumption of unreliability. From this starting point, the system should be designed in such a way as to enable messages to overcome obstacles. The system would link a number of computers or 'nodes'. Every message would be divided up into a number of segments called 'packets'. Each packet would be labelled with its intended destination and with information as to its position in the message as a whole. The packets would be sent on their way and would pass from node to node until all arrived at the intended destination, where they would be reassembled to indicate the complete message. Although packets would be forwarded in approximately the correct direction, the particular route taken by a packet would be dependent upon chance and network availability. If one section of the network had been damaged, the packets would be routed via other sections. A helpful illustration might be to analogise the system with the road network of the UK. The motorway network might be compared with a telecommunications network. It provides high-capacity and (the M25 possibly excepted) high-speed transport links. Disruption at a few key locations – by nuclear attack or less dramatic incidents – would render the system unusable. The Internet might be compared with the non-motorway road network. Travel may be slower and more circuitous, but the sheer variety of routes would make total disruption of service a most unlikely event.

[1]   ARPA was established under the auspices of the Department of Defense, with a remit of establishing US leadership in areas of science and technology which might possess military applications

1.31   The initial network, ARPANET, which was named after its sponsors, was installed in 1969 with four nodes. By 1972, this figure had grown to 37. One of the next major developments was the evolution of the communication standard Transmission Control Protocol/Internet Protocol (TCP/IP). The TCP component is responsible for converting messages into streams of packets, whilst the IP is responsible for addressing and routing the packets to their intended destination. The TCP/IP protocols were developed in the 1970s, but it was with their adoption as the basis for ARPANET on 1 January 1983 that the Internet[1] could be said to have originated.

[1]   The word 'Internet' has been defined in a 1995 resolution of the US Federal Networking Council as follows: 'Internet refers to the global information system that (i) is logically linked together by a globally unique address space based on the Internet Protocol (IP) ... (ii) is able to support communications using the Transmission Control Protocol/Internet Protocol (TCP/IP) suite ... and (iii) provides, uses or makes accessible, either publicly or privately, high level services layered on the communications and related infrastructure described herein.'

1.32 A feature of the TCP/IP protocols is that they enable any user to connect to the Internet. There are no social or political controls over the making of such a connection and the cost implications are minimal. It is somewhat ironic that a system which was designed to enable the authorities to retain control over a nuclear wasteland should have metamorphosed into a system which is almost a byword for anarchy.

1.33 Although the size and usage of the Internet grew very significantly in the 1970s and 1980s, it remained predominantly a tool for the academic community. Although effective as a mechanism for transferring large amounts of data, its use, in common with most computers of the time, required a considerable degree of technical competence. In the early 1990s, more user-friendly navigational tools were introduced in the form of Archie, Gopher and Veronica. The most significant technical innovation was undoubtedly the introduction of the World Wide Web (WWW) in 1992. Developed by Tim Berners-Lee, a physicist at the nuclear physics research centre, CERN, the WWW uses the system known as hypertext to create links between documents. A user need only 'click' on a marked link to move to the other document. The addition of browsers such as Mosaic, Netscape Navigator and Microsoft Explorer served to complete the transformation of the Internet from a text-based network of elusive resources to what has been described as 'a multimedia tapestry of full-color information'.[1]

[1] The Internet Time Line at http://www.discovery.com/DCO/doc/1012/world/technology/internet/inet2.html.

1.34 In essence, the WWW is a triumph of form over function. The file transfer facilities associated with the WWW have been available virtually since the inception of the Internet, and even more readily to those willing to master the complex hierarchies and functions of navigational tools such as the gopher, an electronic creature who, it is appallingly punned, is now living on burrowed time. Just as the development of graphical user interfaces such as the Macintosh operating system and Microsoft Windows made computing attractive to the masses, so the WWW makes computer networks a more user-friendly species.

1.35 Cyberspace has developed with almost incredible speed, certainly when compared with other forms of communication technologies. In 1876 Alexander Graham Bell was awarded a patent for the telephone. Its impact on the world has been massive but 74 years were to elapse before 50 million subscribers were connected. Radio took 38 years to reach the same figure. With the PC only 16 years elapsed. From its inception in 1993, the WWW required only four years to acquire 50 million users. In terms of statistics, in 1989, the Internet had some 100,000 host computers. By 1992, this figure had climbed to 1,000,000. In 1997 the figure had increased to some 13 million sites with the Internet maintaining a 100% annual growth rate through much of the decade. More recently the rate of growth has slowed, not surprisingly given the fact that continuation of the earlier rate of expansion would have seen the number of computers connected to the Internet exceeding the human population of earth by August 2003. Taking figures as of early 2004, there are estimated to be some 233 million Internet sites in the world[1] and 605 million persons in more than 200 countries are estimated to have access to the Internet and WWW.[2] For users in the developed world, the Internet is becoming a feature of our everyday lives. It is rare to find a newspaper which does not contain some feature on the Internet. Most newspapers, and many television and radio programmes, maintain an electronic presence on the Internet. Many advertisements and publicity documents refer readers to an Internet site for further information.

1   http://isc.org.
2   www.nua.com.

A history of UK communications regulation

1.36   As communications technologies have developed the issue how they are to be controlled by law has assumed significance. It has always tended to be the case that specific legal regulation has followed some time beyond the introduction of the technology. In Chapter 2 consideration will be given to the emerging attempts to provide for a measure of Internet governance. This chapter will examine issues of communications regulation in a more general sense focusing on the lessons which previous attempts at regulation may provide for what is a topical and increasingly heated debate on how Internet-related conduct should be regulated. Parallels with previous forms of electronic communication in the form of the telegraph and the telephone are of limited significance in that the main task of the law in the earlier examples was to regulate the networks themselves whereas with the Internet it is the nature of the conduct carried out over the networks which is the main topic of interest. Nonetheless, certain elements of commonality can be identified which may serve as both prediction and warning. Following initial laissez faire policies towards both the telegraph and the telephone, the legislative response was to restrict access to the sector, effectively providing that only one provider (in the case of the UK, the state itself and in the US, private sector monopolists) could operate in respect of major areas of activity.

Postal regulation

1.37   The postal system provided the earliest form of communications regulation. For a period of centuries although the term Royal Mail was used, this meant just that, the communications network used for transporting the Royal mail. Other persons had to rely upon a range of message services operated by institutions such as trades guilds and monasteries. During the Middle Ages access to the facilities of the Royal Mail was made available to a wider range of users but it was only in the reign of Charles I that the Royal mail was opened for public use with the establishment of the 'Letter Office of England and Scotland'. It was with the restoration of King Charles II that a state monopoly was established under the auspices of the General Post Office. This monopoly was established in part because of security concerns and the wish to exercise controls to dissuade or detect seditious correspondence. Initially, the Post Office delivered only to 'general letter offices' rather than individual homes a system analogous to the more recent *poste restante* service whereby letters can be addressed to and received from a post office. In 1680 William Dockwra established a system of individual delivery within areas of London. Upon its success, the operation was taken over by the Post Office in 1682 'on the prompting of the Duke of York, later King James II, who was greedy for the large profits it made'.[1] Although the extent of the monopoly was diluted significantly over the course of time, it was only with the passage of the Postal Services Act 2000, itself prompted by European legislation relating to the liberalisation of communications services, that a licensing system was introduced as the basis for operation of postal services. As will be discussed, licensing has come to constitute one of the most important, albeit transitory, regulatory tools in the telecommunications sector.

[1]   http://www.bathpostalmuseum.org/Museum/41500_-1700/41500_-1700.html.

Regulation of the telegraph system

1.38   In the nineteenth century, the nature of the messages transmitted over the telegraph network drew comparison with the postal system. Just as in the twentieth century computer programs were classed as literary works for the purpose of the law of copyright, so telegraph messages were sufficiently literary in character to be classed as letters. Although the telegraph network was originally established by private companies, once the commercial and social impact of the telegraph was recognised the view was taken that telegrams should fall within the scope of the Postmaster General's monopoly. A number of companies were licensed by Special Act of Parliament to provide telegraph services. A series of Telegraph Acts enacted in the 1860s laid down a legislative framework for the operation of the telegraph system. The Telegraph Act 1863 was concerned with topics which remain relevant to this day, encompassing issues such as the confidentiality of messages transmitted over the network and the ability of telegraph operators to enter private property to develop and maintain their infrastructure. Further statutes effectively nationalised the networks. The Telegraph Act 1868 authorised the Postmaster General to acquire by agreement the telegraph operations of any company providing such service in the UK. The Telegraph Act 1869 took matters further and enacted provisions analogous to those applying to the mail whereby the Postmaster General was to have the:

> exclusive privilege of transmitting messages or other communications transmitted, or intended for transmission, by any wire or wires used for the purpose of telegraphic communication, with any casing, coating, tube, or pipe inclosing the same, and any apparatus connected therewith for the purpose of telegraphic communication, or by any apparatus (other than such wire) for transmitting messages or other communications by means of electric signals.[1]

[1]   Telegraph Act 1869, s 4.

The emerging information society

1.39   Although it is tempting to consider the telegraph as outdated technology it may be noted that whilst the first transatlantic telegraph link was established in 1858 it was not until 1952 that telephone calls could make the same journey. For a period of nearly a century, data traffic dominated the world's networks. Although the period from the 1960s to the 1990s saw voice traffic achieving superiority, the emergence of the Internet has, mobile phone revolution notwithstanding, brought about a situation where the bulk of communications traffic involves data exchange between computers. In another indication of the re-emergence of data traffic an estimated 69 million text messages are sent in the UK every day with 111 million messages being transmitted on New Year's Eve 2003.[1]

[1]   www.bbc.co.uk.

Regulation of the telephone system

1.40   Although Alexander Graham Bell was awarded the main US telephone patent, other inventors and corporations also secured awards. In the UK, one of the pioneers was the Edison Telephone Company which, having secured UK patents in respect of 'improvements in instruments for controlling by sound the transmission of electric currents, and the reproduction of corresponding sounds at a distance', commenced business in 1879 and offered telephone services in areas of London 'between the hours of 9 A.M. and 6 P.M., Sundays excepted'.

1.41   Litigation was not far behind. The case *A-G v Edison Telephone Co of London*[1] was concerned with the issue whether telephone services should be regulated under the Telegraph Acts and therefore fall within the scope of the Postmaster General's exclusive rights as established under the Telegraph Act 1879. The statute made no mention of the telephone. On behalf of the company it was argued that the Telegraph Acts applied only to the transmission of text messages and that voice traffic therefore was not regulated by the statute.

[1]   (1880) 6 QBD 244.

1.42   The case is interesting in a number of aspects. It demonstrates that the law's problems in dealing with new forms of technology are not restricted to the late twentieth and twenty-first centuries. The notion of convergence of technologies can also be seen in operation here with the same basic infrastructure being used for the transmission of voice and data traffic. After extensive debate the court concluded that that a telephone conversation should be classed as a telegram under the provisions of the Telegraph Act 1879 and the network itself regarded a telegraph. In reaching this conclusion the court sought to consider what constituted the substance of the communications involved and concluded that:

> it does not appear to us that the fact, if it is a fact, that sound itself is transmitted by the telephone establishes any material distinction between telephonic and telegraphic communication, as the transmission if it takes place is performed by a wire acted on by electricity. We are of opinion, then, that, fully admitting

16

all that has been, or indeed can be said as to the novelty and value of the telephonic transmitter and receiver, the whole apparatus, transmitter, wire and receiver, taken together form 'a wire used for the purpose of telegraphic communication, with apparatus connected therewith, for the purpose of telegraphic communication' – that is, they are a telegraph within the definition of the Act of 1863 [Telegraph Act 1863], which is embodied by reference in the Act of 1869 [Telegraph Act 1869]. The wire is a wire. The transmitting and receiving instruments are apparatus connected therewith for the purpose of conveying information by electricity; and this, as it seems to us, is telegraphic communication. Indeed, though for scientific purposes it may, no doubt, be necessary to distinguish between telegraphs and telephones, it seems to us that the word 'telegraph,' as defined in the Telegraph Acts, is (to use Professor Stokes's words) 'wide enough to cover every instrument which may ever be invented which employs electricity transmitted by a wire as a means for conveying information.' Indeed, looking to the extension of the definition inserted in the Act of 1869, the words 'transmitted by a wire' might probably be left out of this definition.

Given the recent emergence of satellite and mobile mobile telephony, this last point was undoubtedly justified. The court continued:

Of course no one supposes that the legislature intended to refer specifically to telephones many years before they were invented, but it is highly probable that they would, and it seems to us clear that they actually did, use language embracing future discoveries as to the use of electricity for the purpose of conveying intelligence. The great object of the Act of 1863 was to give special powers to telegraph companies to enable them to open streets, lay down wires, take land, suspend wires over highways, connect wires, erect posts on the roofs of houses, and do many other things of the same sort. The Act, in short, was intended to confer powers and to impose duties upon companies established for the purpose of communicating information by the action of electricity upon wires, and absurd consequences would follow if the nature and extent of those powers and duties were made dependent upon the means employed for the purpose of giving the information. Suppose a company found it essential to erect posts along a highway, and suppose the body having control of the highway gave their consent, would the validity of the consent, and therefore the liability of the parties concerned to an indictment for obstructing the highway, notwithstanding such consent, be dependent on the question whether the messages were sent by an Edison's transmitter or by a Morse key?[1]

[1]   *A-G v Edison Telephone Co of London* (1880) 6 QBD 244 at 253-254.

1.43   With the conclusion that telephone communications fell under the telegraph regime and thereby were subject to the Postmaster General's exclusive privileges it was recognised that operators would require to be licensed in order to operate lawfully. Initially the view was taken that licences would be issued only in areas where services were not being provided by the Post Office. This policy was changed in 1882 with the Postmaster General declaring that it would 'not be in the interests of the public to create a monopoly in relation to the supply of telephonic communication' and that a licence would be granted to all responsible applicants. Licenses were issued to a number of existing private companies, most significantly the National Telephone Company which operated most of the trunk network, for periods of 31 years but subject to the right of the Postmaster General to acquire the business at the end of 10, 17 or 24 years. A licence fee of 10% of gross income was payable to the Postmaster General, a rate considerably higher than that charged for licences under the Telecommunications Act 1984 where prior to the removal of the licensing system, fees were capped at a maximum of 0.08% of turnover.

1.44 The Telegraph Act 1899 made provision for local authorities to operate telegraph (and telephone) services and six local authorities were licensed to this end. Within a fairly short period of time concerns were raised that the existence and growth of a private telephone network might affect adversely the publicly owned telegraph network. The failure of competing operators to provide for interconnection was also a cause for concern and, in a manner similar to that followed in the telegraph sector a process of creeping nationalisation occurred. As early as 1892 the long-distance or trunk network had been acquired from the National Telephone Company and at the start of the twentieth century the intention was indicated to nationalise the remainder of the networks. This occurred through the relatively simple expediency of acquiring the assets of companies upon the termination of their licenses. By 1912, the General Post Office was the only provider of telephone services with the exception of the city of Kingston upon Hull whose licence was due to expire in 1914. With the onset of the First World War the existence of the anomaly was perhaps a matter of little concern and the licence was renewed subject to the condition that the authority ensure satisfactory interconnection with the remainder of the network.

1.45 From 1914 until 1980 the telecommunications sector virtually disappeared from the legal landscape. Services were operated by the General Post Office with virtually no specific legal authority. The one exception was the Telephone Act 1951. This marked the first time in which the word 'telephone' appeared in the title of a UK statute.[1] Until 1951 telephone services were supplied to customers on the basis of a contract with the Postmaster General. The Act conferred a power on the Postmaster General, with the consent of the Treasury, to make regulations prescribing the terms under which the telephone service could be used including charges and conditions of service. A similar change can be seen in the more recent move from reliance on individual licences as the basis for provision of services to the requirement being one of compliance with general terms laid down by statute or statutory instrument.

[1] The only subsequent use of the word is in the Mobile Telephones Re-Programming Act 2002. This statute makes it an offence to change the identifying details of a mobile phone –normally subsequent to the theft of the instrument.

1.46 From the 1950s it became increasingly clear that this method of organisation had major defects. In the decade 1955–65 the percentage of households possessing a television set increased from 40 to 88%, washing machines from 20 to 56% and refrigerators from 10 to 39%. In respect of telephones the decade brought an increase of only 1%, from 21 to 22%. The Post Office Act 1969 abolished the office of Postmaster General and established the Post Office as a public corporation. At governmental level the Postmaster General was replaced by the Minister of Posts and Telecommunications but the Act essentially freed the organisation from government control over its day-to-day operations. The Post Office was divided into two divisions concerned with postal and telecommunications services. By s 27 of the Post Office Act 1969, the Post Office was empowered to grant licences to other operators with the approval of the Minister of Posts and Telecommunications. Evidencing the proposition that turkeys seldom vote for Christmas, with the exception of licensing the continuing activities of Kingston upon Hull, this power was never exercised.

1.47 In 1977 the report of the Carter Committee recommended that the Post Office should be split into two separate corporations. Acting on this, the British Telecommunications Act 1981 established British Telecom (BT) as a public corporation in its own right. The Act also made a number of significant changes to the manner in which telephone services were provided. Until its entry into force the Post Office's exclusive privilege to provide telecommunications services extended to the supply (on a rental basis) of all equipment required by customers. In large part the approach was justified by reference to fears that the connection of unsuitable equipment would damage the stability of the entire network. Experience has suggested that these fears were exaggerated although similar arguments have more recently been put forward as a ground for resisting the installation of third-party equipment in telephone exchanges in connection with the, so-called, unbundling of the local loop.[1] As a first step, the Act provided that the BT monopoly was limited to the provision of the first telephone receiver in any premises. Customers could then obtain further receivers or other items of equipment from other suppliers. Subsequently even this restriction was lifted.

[1]   Unbundling involves a telecommunications network provider, almost always BT within the UK, allowing other providers access to its telephone exchanges in order to install and maintain equipment necessary to allow the other provider to make broadband facilities available to its own customers.

1.48 Whilst the British Telecommunications Act 1981 transferred the privilege of operating a telecommunications network to the new corporation a significant change was made to the licensing provisions. Whilst previously it had been for the Post Office to decide whether and upon what terms a licence might be granted to another operator, the 1981 Act stated that this power could be exercised by the Secretary of State. Effectively, the political decision had been taken that the telephone market should be opened to competition and, giving effect to this, a further licence was issued in 1982 when Mercury Communications was established as a telecommunications network provider. Discounting the role of Kingston upon Hull, this can be seen as the start of what is generally referred to as the liberalisation of telecommunications – the opening up of a previously monolithic market to at least a measure of competition.

1.49 Initially competition was limited, it being announced in 1983 that no further fixed-line network licences would be issued to long-distance, fixed-link operators for a period of seven years. This was on the basis that in order to encourage Mercury to invest in the development of a network, it would require assurance of a stable competitive environment. Even at this stage it was recognised that the emerging market in mobile communications would provide alternatives to traditional fixed-link operations. The first licences for the creation of mobile networks were granted to Cellnet and Vodafone in 1983.

1.50 The, so-called, duopoly, ended in 1990 when additional licences were issued. By the end of the decade, matters moved on to the extent that the OFTEL draft work programme for 1999 stated that:

> The UK now has over 200 licensed operators which include 5 national carriers, 4 mobile operators and over 60 companies licensed to operate international facilities.

The role of licences

1.51 Reference has been made above to the award of licences to those providing telecommunications services and facilities. Licensing, sometimes also referred to under headings such as authorisation or registration,[1] has been a pivotal feature of communications regulation both in the telecommunications and in the broadcasting sector although the emergence of digital technology is serving the challenge some of the rationale behind the approach.

[1] Terminology in the field is somewhat confused and confusing. Although semantically the expressions convey different meanings, they have tended to used interchangeably within legislation. Eligibility to obtain a television licence, for example, requires nothing more than the ability to pay the fee required. Applications for registration under the Data Protection Act 1984 could be refused if the Data Protection Registrar was satisfied that the conduct of an applicant would be likely to contravene statutory requirements.

1.52 The word 'licence' is generally defined in the sense of conferring some form of official permission to undertake an activity which would otherwise be unlawful. An obvious example can be seen in the field of motoring where a criminal offence is committed by a person who drives a vehicle without possessing an appropriate driving licence. A range of considerations can be seen as underpinning the operation of a licensing system. In some cases, as epitomised in the driving licence example, an element of quality control operates to try to ensure that those participating in the activity possess an appropriate degree of skill or expertise. In more commercial fields of activity the qualitative requirement is often expressed in terms that the licensee should be a 'fit and proper person' to be permitted to engage in an activity. An amalgam of financial, technical and personnel factors may be taken into account in deciding whether this criterion is satisfied by a particular applicant.

1.53 The initial licences awarded to BT and Mercury were extremely substantial documents running to several hundred pages of text. The effect of a licence is to define closely the rights, privileges and obligations granted to or imposed upon the licence holder. These were especially onerous in the case of BT and were designed specifically to require it to refrain from exercising rights or market power in such a way as to deter or eliminate competition. This might even be used to prevent the exercise of rights conferred under the general law. An example of such use of licensing terms can be seen in relation to the provision of telephone directories. Although the point has not been definitely resolved, it seems that the UK's copyright system, almost alone in the world, would provide protection to alphabetical listings of names, addresses and telephone numbers. Given its dominant position in the domestic telephone market, this permitted BT an effective monopoly concerning the provision of telephone directories and information services. During the 1990s number of companies indicated plans to publish collections of directories, typically on CD, only to be faced with the threat of legal action by BT alleging infringement of copyright. Although such a course of action was quite lawful, access to directory information was liberalised by means of an amendment made to BT's licence requiring that it:

> shall ... on request by any person make available to him for the purpose of enabling him to provide directories or a directory information service
> (a)   the contents of the database, in machine readable form, which the Licensee uses to compile directories ... and
> (b)   on-line access (including a search facility) to the database which the Licensee uses to provide a Directory Information Service.

1.54   One of the prime purposes of licensing in the early days of liberalisation was to place limits on the commercial freedom of BT where this might adversely impact upon competition. This was especially evident in respect of obligations to conclude interconnection and access agreements.

1.55   Beyond controlling the behaviour of licensees, licences have also been used as a means for allocating scarce resources. The allocation of licences in respect of the, so called, 3g mobile licences constitutes an topical illustration of this point. A limited number of radio frequencies exist which require to be shared between all regions of the world. The allocation process is conducted under the auspices of the International Telecommunications Union. Licences to operate mobile networks had previously been issued following what was referred to as a 'beauty contest' in which competing operators sought to persuade the regulatory authorities that their proposals offered the optimum benefit. For the 3g licences, a new approach was adopted it being argued that:

> Auctions are a fast, transparent, fair and economically efficient way of allocating the scarce resource of radio spectrum. Government should not be trying to judge who will be innovative and successful.

1.56   At least in the short term the auction proved enormously successful from a governmental perspective, raising some £22.5bn. By way of comparison and to demonstrate the growth in the telecommunications sector, the initial sale of 51% of BT in 1984 raised some £3.2bn.

1.57 The availability of radio spectrum will continue to be constrained. The move from analogue to digital transmission systems does ease significantly resource constraints. This has been especially noticeable in the field of broadcasting where a situation where only five channels, each of which was subject to licensing controls, could broadcast has been revolutionised with the arrival of literally hundreds of channels available over satellite and cable systems. The legal consequences have been and remain profound. It has increasingly been recognised that the notion of exerting regulatory control prior to an undertaking being permitted to conduct activities in a sector such as telecommunications, data processing or broadcasting is technically unnecessary and of limited social value. As will be discussed in various contexts throughout this book, there has been a move away from prior or ex ante regulation towardss reliance upon controlling substantive activities. A perhaps more significant consequence of the digital technological revolution has been the phenomenon generally referred to as convergence.

Regulation of the Internet

1.58 Historically, as indicated above, we have had varying control regimes over all forms of communications technology. These have varied from fairly minimal controls prior to publication in the case of printed works to stringent requirements for the grant of a licence prior to commencing activities in the broadcasting and telecommunications sector.

1.59 An initial question concerns the location of the Internet within the various regulatory regimes. As users of the system will be aware, the Internet crosses many traditional boundaries. It can be used to publish text and visual materials. Many radio programmes can be listened to over the Internet and, as bandwidth constraints lessen, a similar trend can be seen with television broadcasts. With the use of software packages such as MP3, the Internet is being used for the dissemination of audio works, to the extent that some involved in the music industry have predicted the demise of CDs and High Street record stores. The Internet is also being used increasingly as a channel for voice telephony. The nature of its structure means that calls to anywhere in the world will be charged on the same basis as local telephone calls. Although the quality of performance may still be a little inferior to that attainable using traditional telephone networks, the gap is closing whilst cost savings are very substantial.

1.60 The seemingly remorseless advance of the Internet (and the WWW) is challenging many existing models of society and forms of regulation. For the first time, there exists a global communications network which is in large measure outwith the control of national authorities, and certainly does not fit into many existing regulatory schema. Whilst it is emphatically not the case that Internet-based activities are not subject to legal regulation, it is equally clear that no single state can exert control over the Internet as a whole. Although some states make considerable efforts to control Internet access and use, it is unclear also how effective such controls can be. The Internet, it is said, interprets censorship as a form of damage and seeks to find ways around it. That said, a considerable number of agencies can be identified as playing significant roles in determining the destiny of the Internet. The nature and legal status of these will be considered in subsequent chapters. What may be said at this stage is that the Internet is at an important stage in its organisational history. From its beginnings as an adjunct to US defence policy, it has expanded into the academic sphere and, increasingly, into the commercial world. The largest single sector of the Internet is now represented by the domain name '.com' (commercial).[1] Differing demands and expectations of users means that the notion of a set of shared and common values is no longer applicable. From a situation where all network nodes were located in the US, its tentacles have spread to the furthest corners of the world. Recent estimates suggest that some 40% of Internet sites are located outwith the US. Control mechanisms developed in an era of US hegemony may not be appropriate for application in other political and social cultures. It has been said that:

> In principle, any node can speak as a peer to any other node, as long as it obeys the rules of the TCP/IP protocols, which are strictly technical, not social or political.[2]

[1] http://www.limitless.co.uk/ewos61016.html.
[2] 'A Brief History of the Internet', by Bruce Sterling published at http://www.vir.com/Demo/tech/SterlingBrief.html.

1.61 The existence of the Internet is having profound changes on all aspects of society, and has also changed dramatically the nature of the computer revolution. A report produced to mark the completion of the ARPANET commented that:

> ... the promise offered by the computer as a communications medium between people, dwarfs into relative insignificance the historical beginnings of the computer as an arithmetic engine.[1]

[1] ARPANET *Concluding Report* (1989) III-24.

1.62 The history of the Internet may suggest that predictions are dangerous, but the Internet's move into the mainstream of world affairs makes social and political, economic and legal factors of nearly as much importance as the original technical specifications. The first telegraph message transmitted by Marconi across the Atlantic Ocean consisted of the text 'What hath God wrought?' The task of answering this question has occupied law makers ever since. The same will surely apply also to the Internet.

1.63 One of the more noticeable phenomena of the information society is that of convergence of technologies. A website may contain attributes of all three models. In a decision of the Court of Session,[1] albeit issued only in the course of an action seeking an interim interdict (interlocutory injunction), it was held that in terms of the copyright legislation, a website should be classed as a cable programme service. The massive investment currently being undertaken to create cable networks in the UK means that television programmes are carried over the same wires as telephone calls. Trials have been conducted to establish the feasibility of introducing systems of 'video on demand', where the contents of a film or other programme will be transmitted to a viewer using the telephone system. Even television transmissions may soon become more interactive, so that, for example, a viewer will be able to place an order for goods or services advertised on television by pressing a few buttons on a television remote control device. As technologies converge, so pressures have emerged for the law to take a similar approach. Both the European Commission[2] and the Department of Trade and Industry[3] have published Green Papers on the topic. The latter document states that:

> Digital technology is rapidly being adopted for the reproduction, storage and transmission of information in all media. This means that any form of content (still or moving pictures, sound, text, data) can be made available via any transmission medium, eroding the traditional distinctions between telecommunications and broadcasting. Already it is possible to receive television or radio over the Internet, while digital televisions will have some of the capabilities we currently find only in computers.
>
> The greatly increased capacity and versatility of networks provides opportunities to improve the delivery of existing services and to create new ones. Consumers will have easier access to a wider range of content through various transmission media. They will be able to select the services they want at a time convenient to them and to benefit from enhanced two-way communication (including on-line purchases) through interactivity. The potential benefits to the citizen/consumer, to business and to government are significant.

It continues:

> Our system of regulation faces new challenges as delivery systems adopt a common technology and assume common capabilities. Some new services fall within the remit of more than one regulator, creating a risk of excessive and/or inconsistent regulation. Where an identical service is transmitted over different delivery systems, it may be subject to different regulatory regimes. The development of new services, and their wide availability, must not be jeopardised by such regulatory overlaps and anomalies.[4]

---

[1]   *Shetland Times v Willis* 1997 SLT 669.
[2]   Green Paper on the Convergence of the Telecommunications, Media and Information Technology Sectos and the Implications for Regulation. Towards and Information Society Approach. COM 97 (623) Available from http://www.ispo.cec.be/convergencegp/greenp.html.
[3]   'Regulating Communications. Approaching convergence in the information age.' CM 4022 Available from http://www.dti.gov.uk/converg/index.htm.
[4]   Executive Summary.

1.64   Within Europe, the Commission publishes an annual survey of progress in the field of telecommunications law. This has traditionally been regulated by means of a large number of directives applying to specific aspects of telecommunications. Significantly, the 1999 review saw a change in title to

Review of Communications Policy,[1] together with the indication of a substantial change in regulatory policy towards a more generalist and minimalist approach. This was implemented in 2000 with the adoption of a new regulatory regime whereby five directives replaced more than 20 existing directives and a small host of other legislative and quasi-legislative measures such as recommendations.

[1] Available from http://www.ispo.cec.be/infosoc/telecompolicy/review99/review99en.pdf.

1.65 As indicated above, much of the impetus for change has come from the EU. In part, this is reflective of another aspect of the technological changes. Although there would inevitably be an area of overlap in border regions, broadcasting was largely a national phenomenon. Regulation could thus be enforced effectively at a national level. Similar factors would have applied to the telecommunications networks. Although gateways would have facilitated international telephone calls, the need for a massive infrastructure again made national control a practical proposition. These situations are changing. Satellite broadcasting does not respect national boundaries, whilst cellular telephones offer the potential for a worldwide network. National regulatory techniques can only survive in the context of international harmonisation and agreement. Convergence of laws will become as important an element of the new environment as that of technologies. In respect of national initiatives, a Commission communication[1] has advocated that Directive 83/189/EEC,[2] which establishes a procedure for the exchange of information between member states and the Commission regarding proposed technical standards and regulations, should be extended to include proposed 'rules on Information Society Services'. The term 'Information Society Services' is defined in the document *Europe's Way to the Information Society: an action plan* as encompassing 'the various services which will be carried on the information superhighways'.[3]

[1] Communication ... concerning regulatory transparency in the internal market for information society services, COM (96) 392 final.
[2] OJ 1993 L 109/8.
[3] COM (94) 347 final.

1.66 The key initial document in European moves towards the information society is the report of Commissioner Bangemann's 'group of prominent persons' to the meeting of the European Council in Corfu in June 1994.[1] Entitled *Europe and the global information society*, the Bangemann Report added a political dimension to previously technically driven moves towards convergence. Three topics are identified in the report as requiring legislative action:

- intellectual property rights;
- privacy; and
- security of information (encryption and information security).

[1] http://www.ispo.cec.be/infosoc/backg/bangeman.html.

1.67 As well as providing for development of the infrastructure, areas of law can be identified where action is required. Given the economic importance of information, the establishment of appropriate forms of intellectual property rights is essential. The concept of the exclusive right of the copyright owner to control the reproduction of a work sits uneasily with the nature of computer operations and the evolving culture of the WWW. In a similar vein, the increasing trade in information products and services may require changes to principles of contractual and non-contractual liability which, developed in the industrial age, are perhaps more suited for regulating rights and obligations in respect of physical or tangible products.

1.68 The Bangemann Report makes no mention of the topic of ecommerce. Rather than standing as a criticism of the document, this should perhaps be taken as an indication of the pace of technical change and the need for rapid legal response. Existing law-making mechanisms may not be well suited to the task. Although, in cases of emergency, it has been known for the process to be compressed into one or two days (often demonstrating the truth of the adage 'act in haste, repent at leisure'), a period of six to eight months is normally required. In the parliamentary session 1998–99, 35 Acts of Parliament became law. Most of these were brought forward on behalf of the government, although each year some time is allocated for Bills proposed by individual Members of Parliament. The Computer Misuse Act 1990, which constitutes the major legal response to activities such as computer hacking, was such a measure.

1.69 For most areas of law, major statutory reform occurs at lengthy intervals. In the field of intellectual property, for example, only three major copyright statutes were enacted in the twentieth century (in 1911, 1956 and 1988).[1] Although smaller pieces of legislation have been introduced in the field, there is an increasing perception that aspects of the law are ill suited for the needs of the information society. The validity of this perception will be considered in more detail in the remaining chapters of this book, but the point may be noted that relatively few statutes can be enacted in any year and that considerable time may pass before any amendments can be made. The challenge for the future will relate not merely to what the law says in relation to the information society, but how it is made. With increasing moves towards globalisation, the question will also increasingly be: by whom are laws to be made? Even in these early days, it is significant to note the increasing involvement of bodies such as the World Trade Organization in areas of law, such as intellectual property and data protection, which had not previously been seen as a significant component of international trade.

[1] Copyright Act 1911, Copyright Act 1956 and Copyright, Designs and Patents Act 1988.

Chapter 2

Internet regulation and the rise, fall and rise of .com

Introduction

2.1 Chapter 1 laid emphasis on the vital importance of the Internet for the information society. This chapter will attempt to address some of the legal implications arising both from the emergence of the Internet and the uses to which it may be put. As stated, the communications sector has always been regulated and the Internet is no exception. In some respects it may be argued that the Internet is the most heavily regulated electronic communications network in that activities carried out over it are subject, in theory if not always in practice, to a mass of legal regulation. When it comes to the issue of regulation of the overall network, reference to specific legal provisions is limited. Reference to the Internet is entirely lacking in the Communications Act 2003 and, indeed, government ministers were at pains on numerous occasions to point out that the measure was not intended to regulate the Internet. Communications regulation has tended to operate at a national level with international agencies such as the International Telecommunications Union operating at a functional rather than a policy level in respect of international communications. Almost from its outset, the Internet has functioned on an international basis and the question who controls it is assuming considerable political and legal importance. Depending on the perspective of the commentator, for most of its existence, the Internet could be described either as being governed on the basis of consensus amongst Internet users or directed by an unelected, self-perpetuating clique. Regulatory structures have tended to evolve rather than develop in any structured manner, and a baffling range of organisations and acronyms need to be confronted in any attempt to understand the manner in which the Internet operates and is controlled. This chapter will initially describe the nature of the organisations which have been involved in Internet regulation and seek to analyse the legal basis for their activities.

2.2 In its early days, Internet-based operations made little impact upon the average person. Whilst its initial status as almost a form of private members' club continues to influence debate as to the future shape and form of regulation, with some users calling for the law to provide the same freedom for internal self-regulation as is afforded to voluntary organisations, the prevailing view is that the Internet's effect on the wider world is such as to call for a greater degree of legal involvement. One of the major forces for change has undoubtedly been the increasing use of the Internet for commercial purposes. At the beginning of the twenty-first century there seemed to be no limits to the potential growth of commercial activities on the Internet. Investors rushed to take a stake in any and every form of business and share values soared to dizzy levels. In November 1999, *Fortune* magazine reported that the Internet bookseller Amazon's share capital was 17 times greater than that of the world's largest 'bricks and mortar' book chain, Barnes and Noble, and that it had a market value five times greater than Barnes and Noble. The, so called, dot com phenomenon was widely seen as an unstoppable force which would revolutionise the world of commerce. Contemporaneously with a more general fall in worldwide share values, what has come to be referred to as ecommerce saw its progress come to a halt with many of the pioneering ventures finding their future in the bankruptcy courts rather than in the company of established retail giants. More recently, there has been something of a renaissance in the scale and perceived utility of ecommerce as organisations have come to realise where the strengths and weaknesses of this form of activity lie. It has been suggested that ecommunications involve a switch from 'bricks and mortar' to 'clicks and mortar' and the true value of ecommerce lies in the facility to provide information-based products and services. This definition encompasses subjects such as airline tickets where leading budget airlines provide figures showing that more than 90% of flights are purchased over the Internet. Even more traditional airlines are moving to systems of electronic ticketing although the increased security requirements being imposed on airlines in the aftermath of September 11 are making paperless travel a largely unattainable goal. Whilst some product retailers continue – such as Amazon which has recently announced its first trading profits – these do tend to operate in either niche markets or in fields where the value of goods is primarily determined by content rather than by weight. The second section of the chapter will consider the nature and legal implications of applications of ecommerce.

A short history of communications regulation

2.3 As described in Chapter 1, traditionally, all forms of communication have been subject to some form of official control. Often, the initial response has been to attempt to operate a strict system of licensing. When the printing press was first introduced, for example, in the sixteenth century, the initial reaction of the UK authorities was to require that those operating a press should be licensed. Licensing even extended to each individual document printed. The controls over the printed word have been weakened very significantly in the intervening centuries and, although legal actions may be brought in respect of the contents of publications, there is no requirement to seek authorisation in advance of publication.

2.4   As other forms of recording and communication technologies have developed, systems of licensing have tended to follow within a short period of time. Radio, television and cinematographic films are all subject to statutory controls. As well as seeking to regulate content, a prime purpose of licensing has been to ration access to and use of scarce resources. In the days of analogue broadcasts emanating from terrestrial transmitters, limitations on the range of frequencies available justified the operation of a strict system of licensing of operators. As developments in broadcasting technology have occurred, the rationing rationale has been steadily eroded. Another factor which is becoming increasingly relevant is the growth in satellite broadcasting. With terrestrial systems, broadcasts can be confined broadly within national boundaries. Although there will always be an overlap in border regions, the range of transmitters is generally limited. Although international agreements exercise some control, satellite broadcasts pay little regard to national boundaries. What is occurring is a shift from nationally based broadcasting systems to global operations, with limited prospect of national regulatory controls proving effective. In a number of cases, the UK authorities have attempted to prevent satellite broadcasts containing hard-core pornography. One well-publicised case concerned a satellite channel 'Red Hot Dutch'. Here, an order was made under the provisions of the Broadcasting Act 1990 which had the effect of prohibiting the supply of the decoders necessary to receive the offending signals. Enforcement problems are compounded by the fact that, in many respects, the UK's legal controls are more restrictive than those applied in other states, including some which are members of the EU. Where material would be lawful in its country of origin, it is difficult to see how effective enforcement might be undertaken against its producer or disseminator.

The emergence of Internet regulation

2.5   It is often stated that the person who controls access to files and records is the most powerful individual in any organisation or, indeed state. In large part, Internet traffic is carried over communications networks owned and controlled by a range of public and private sector communications providers. The decision of the European Commission prohibiting a proposed merger between the US-based telecommunications companies MCI/Sprint and Worldcom provides much useful information about the nature of the technology underpinning the Internet. Although frequently viewed as a network in which all users are equal, the Commission decision shows that this is far from the case at the level where individuals and Internet Service Providers (ISPs) are connected to the global network. As the decision states:

> The Internet is an interconnected 'networks of networks' that carries bits of data between two or more computers through thousands of interconnected networks. Approximately 300 networks providing Internet connectivity operate long distance transmission networks that, together, form the global Internet's international 'backbone'. A handful of these operate networks that

connect to multiple countries in more than one region. It is estimated that the ten largest Internet connectivity providers control 70 percent of international Internet bandwidth. Below the top tier providers are a number of Internet connectivity providers that operate at regional level (Europe, USA and Asia).[1]

---

[1]   Case no COMP/M.1741-MCI at para 16.

2.6   Whilst communications companies may carry traffic, for any form of two-way communication it is a basic necessity that the parties should be able to identify each other. Once there is a movement from direct contact to the involvement of some form of intermediary to act as a conduit for the transmission of a message there is need for some unique and individual form of identification. This may take the form of indicators both of individual identity and of geographical location. An obvious example is that of a postal address. As time has moved on, so there has been a move from emphasis on names to one where numbers become the prime identifier. From house names the vast majority of addresses are now identified by some form of number, whether identifying the location of a flat within a larger building or a particular house in a street. Above all, perhaps, the ubiquitous postcode serves as one of the closest equivalents to an identity card in current British society.

2.7   From a human perspective, names offer many benefits, especially in the form of ease of recognition and recollection. Perhaps indicative of human limitations, the average person has a greater facility for remembering words rather than numbers. From an efficiency standpoint, however, numbers possess overwhelming advantages. Names may often be duplicated so that there are, for example, towns called Glasgow in Jamaica, South Africa and Zimbabwe. In the US there are Glasgows in Alabama, Minnesota, Delaware, Iowa, California, Georgia, Illinois, Missouri, Ohio, Oregon, West Virginia, Kentucky, Missouri, Montana, North Carolina, Virginia and Pennsylvania.[1] There is, however, only one city of Glasgow with the telephone dialling code 0141.

---

[1]   http://bmcphee.com/glasgow_places.htm.

2.8   Until the 1960s most telephone exchanges were referred to using an abbreviated form of the area covered. Telephone numbers for the town of Kirkintilloch, for example, would use the code KIR.[1] In reality, of course, as those familiar with sending text messages on mobile phones will be aware, the letters matched to numbers on the telephone dial or keypad.[2] Given that each number typically occupies the space associated with three or four letters the number of memorable combinations was severely limited even at the national level. The *Oxford English Dictionary*, for example, references some 290,000 words and 615,000 word forms. As the telephone network expanded and as it became possible for users to dial directly on an international basis so the complexity of numbers increased. Clearly there cannot be enough memorable words to go around as telephone identifiers and for the last 30 years the UK telephone system has worked on the basis solely of numbers.

¹ For more information on old dialling codes, see http://www.telephonesuk.co.uk/
   old_dialing_codes.htm#ODC.
² Recently, a number of companies have sought to obtain telephone numbers which relate to
   letters in such a way as to promote their business. In evidence before the Select Committee
   on Trade and Industry in 1999, the Director General of Telecommunication cited the case
   of a travel agency called Boomerang Travel whose telephone number translated to '4
   Australia'. Two practical problems were identified with this technique. First, many fixed
   line phones are marked solely with numbers. Secondly, even when letters are used, the
   Director reported there are four different variations in the manner the letters ABCDEF are
   presented. Depending on the pattern used, the consequence might be a wrong number.

2.9 In some ways the emergence of the Internet has seen a reversion towards names as a means of identifier. Although at the technical level the Internet functions exclusively through the processing of IP numbers, the system of domain names has been adopted as a more 'user friendly' form of identifier. In similar manner to the system of telephone names, letters are effectively translated into numbers although unlike telephone dials, there is no direct correlation between letter and number.

2.10 The TCP/IP protocols referred to at para 1.30 above enable any user to connect to the Internet. There are no social or political controls over the making of a connection and cost implications are minimal. All computers linked to the Internet are allocated a unique identifier known as an IP number. At present these are 32 binary digits in length (normally in the region of eight or nine decimal numbers). Just as Oftel required to insert an extra '1' into all UK telephone numbers in 1994 in order to secure what appears to be temporary relief from a shortage of available numbers, so the exponential rate of growth in Internet usage, compounded by the increasing availability of Internet access via mobile phones and has led to the introduction of a new numbering system known as IP V6. An increase in number length to 128-bit numbers is calculated to provide capacity for some 340 billion, billion, billion, billion computers. Even at the Internet's (and mobile phone networks) current rates of expansion, this should be sufficient for the foreseeable future!

2.11 The issuance of IP numbers is a relatively non-problematic task. As with phone numbers, although some combinations might be more memorable than others this is a matter of limited importance. Initially all Internet connections were referred to solely by IP number. As the number of users increased, so pressure grew for a more memorable means of identification. In 1987 the system of domain names came into effect. Typically users will seek to use some form of name which has a connection with their real-life existence. In the educational sector, for example, most institutions will make use of some form of abbreviation of their name. Strathclyde University, for example, uses the designator 'strath' whilst Southampton can be found at 'soton'. With the increasing commercialisation of the Internet, firms will also wish to have their real-life identity mirrored in their Internet address.

2.12 At the outset it should be stressed that for the working of the Internet, it is a user's IP number which is critical. Typing an address such as http://

itlaw.law.strath.ac.uk in a web browser initiates a process of trying to match the name with the appropriate IP number. Initially the attempt will be made by the ISP's own equipment. If it fails to make a match, the query will be passed on to more comprehensive name servers, a process know as domain name resolution. The definitive tables of names and numbers are maintained on what are referred to as root servers. There are 13 of these machines. Ten are located in the US with the remaining three in England, Japan and Sweden. The key root server is maintained by Network Solutions with the other servers downloading information about new domains from this server on a daily basis. Although very many ISPs will maintain their own Domain Name Server, the information on this will invariable have been copied, perhaps with a delay of a few days, from the root servers. In order to be accessible to the Internet world, therefore, it is imperative that a user be issued with an IP number and that the registered name and domain be accepted by the Network Solutions root server.

2.13   Whilst, as discussed above, the supply of IP numbers is virtually inexhaustible, words are in rather shorter supply. A typical directory might contain in the region of 200,000 words. At the level of personal names large numbers of individuals co-exist happily under the same identifiers. The Glasgow telephone directory, for example, lists some 20 pages of McDonalds. Because each domain name has to be mapped with a specific IP number, the Internet is not nearly as flexible. Although, as will be discussed below, the domain name structure offers a range of categories based both on national origin and nature of activity, the issue of allocation of and rights to particular domain names remains one of the most problematic aspects of the Internet and its regulation.

The domain name structure

2.14   Two initial categories of domain name can be identified – generic and country code. There are currently ten generic domain names, some widely available but others limited to fairly narrow categories of users. Technical support for each domain name is provided by an organisation known as a registry. Effectively, each registry will maintain the definitive database of all names allocated and their associated IP numbers:

- .aero – (restricted to certain members of the global aviation community) sponsored by Societe Internationale de Telecommunications Aeronautiques SC (SITA);
- .biz – (restricted to businesses) operated by NeuLevel;
- .com – operated by Verisign Global Registry Services;
- .coop – (restricted to co-operatives) sponsored by Dot Cooperation LLC;
- .info – operated by Afilias Limited;
- .museum – (restricted to museums and related persons) sponsored by the Museum Domain Management Association (MuseDoma);
- .name – (restricted to individuals) operated by Global Name Registry;
- .net – operated by Verisign Global Registry Services;

- .org – operated by Public Interest Registry; and
- .pro – (restricted to licensed professionals) operated by RegistryPro.

These names carry no indication of country of origin. Although it is sometimes assumed that the names 'belong' to the US,[1] this is not the case and many companies operating on an international basis see value in possessing a non-country specific identifier. British Airways, for example, have a website at http://www.britishairways.com.

[1] Two other generic codes, .gov and .mil are restricted to US governmental and military organisations. A further code, .edu, is primarily although not exclusively used by US educational establishments.

2.15 There exists also what are referred to as country code domain names. Based on ISO standard 3166, these consist of a two-letter denominator for every country in the world. The UK, for example, is referred to as .uk, France as .fr and Germany as .de. It should be noted that there is no requirement that a company be established or operate in a particular country in order to register a domain name in that location. One country domain name with an interesting tale is that of Tuvalu. Tuvalu is a collection of nine small coral atolls in the Pacific Ocean close to Fiji. It is classed as a 'Least Developed Country' with a population of around 10,000 and GDP of $11m. Its only export is copra. It has one computer connected to the Internet. It also 'possesses' the ISO code TV and in 1998 entered into a deal worth $50m with a Canadian company to licensing rights to the domain .tv. The company planned to sell domain names to television companies wishing to establish a web presence. Sadly for the Tuvaluans, the deal fell through when the company failed to make payments although it has recently been announced that a similar, albeit less valuable, agreement has been concluded. Other locations which have proved popular 'homes' for websites are Tonga whose ISO code is .to and Italy with the designator .it.

2.16 In most countries, there is a further indicator of the nature of the business. In the UK domain names may be registered in the following categories:

Name	Intended usage
ac.uk	Academic
co.uk	Commercial
gov.uk	Governmental
ltd.uk	Limited liability companies
mod.uk	Ministry of Defence
net.uk	Internet networks
nhs.uk	National Health Service
plc.uk	Public limited companies
police.uk	Police
sch.uk	Schools

Administration of domain names

2.17   The allocation of IP numbers was initially administered by an organisation, the Internet Assigned Numbers Authority (IANA), which is part of the Information Science Institute within the University of Southern California. Its web page[1] proclaims that it is: 'Dedicated to preserving the central co-ordinating functions of the global Internet for the public good.'

[1]   http://www.iana.org/.

2.18   Initially IANA also allocated domain names but from 1993, although it continued to play what has described as a co-ordinating role, the task has been conducted by a range of domain name registries. Whilst some of these are based in the public sector, the majority are private sector companies. In respect of most of the generic domain names, the US National Science Foundation, which sponsored much of the pioneering development work on the Internet, entered into a five-year contract with a commercial organisation, Network Solutions Inc,[1] for the management of most of the generic domains.

[1]   http://www.networksolutions.com/.

2.19   The operation of the system of domain names has been the source of much controversy and some litigation in recent years. As indicated above, although we are all used to domain names such as strath.ac.uk, there is no technical reason why this is required, the name being merely an alias for the critical IP number. Some organisations have sought to set up alternative domain structures. One such company is Name.Space which offers no fewer than 517 top-level domains including such delights as .beer and .president.[1] The main problem that the company has faced has been the refusal of the keepers of the Internet root servers to include details of its users on their machines. Effectively, this limits significantly the range of persons with whom their users can communicate.

[1]   See http://namespace.autono.net/.

2.20   Faced with this refusal to include its details, a lawsuit was raised, *PG Media, Inc D/B/A Name.Space v Network Solutions Inc and the National Science Foundation*.[1] The basis for the complaint was that the defendants were in breach of US anti-trust law and by preventing the claimant and its customers using such names as they wished were in violation of the US Constitution's guarantee of free speech. The claims were dismissed by the US district court in March 1999 and a subsequent appeal was also rejected.

[1]   202 F 3d 573 (2000).

2.21   Although the district court upheld the role of Network Solutions and the National Science Foundation, changes have been occurring from other directions. Concern at the working of the system of internet domain names had been arising, not least prompted by the limited number of domains creating scarcity of what were perceived as suitable domain names. To give an example, the domain name *aba.com* is registered to the American Bankers Association, *aba.org* to the

America Birding Association and *aba.net* to a company, Ansaback, which provides email auto-respond services. All appear bona fide organisations, but there is no room left for the perhaps better known (at least to lawyers) American Bar Association whose WWW site has to use the less intuitive domain name *abanet.net*.

National domain names

2.22 The situation with regard to the national domains is rather more complex with a mix of public and private sector organisations playing the role of domain name registry. In the UK this role is played by a non-profit making company Nominet.[1] As with much of the Internet, the legal basis for its actions is unclear, it being stated that:

> Nominet UK derives its authority from the Internet industry in the UK and is recognised as the UK registry by the Internet Assigned Numbers Authority (IANA) in the USA.

[1] http://www.nic.uk/.

Reform of Internet regulation

2.23 Given the increasing economic importance of the Internet, concern grew from the mid-1990s concerning the somewhat nebulous legal status under which it operated. Concerns were also expressed at the extent of US dominance over the working of what was becoming a vital global communications network. This was especially noticeable in the field of domain names dispute resolution policies. Network Solutions, which possessed a monopoly concerning the registration of names in the .com domain, adopted a range of procedures which afforded greater weight to US trademark rights than to those emanating from other jurisdictions.

2.24 The Internet International Ad Hoc Committee (IAHC) was established in 1996 'at the initiative of the Internet Society, and at the request of the Internet Assigned Numbers Authority', with the remit to:

> resolve a difficult and long-standing set of challenges in the Domain Name System, namely enhancing its use while attempting to juggle such concerns as administrative fairness, operational robustness and protection of intellectual property.

2.25 The IAHC recommended that administration of the .com domain should be removed from the sole control of Network Solutions and made available to a number of competing registries. It recommended also, as described at para 2.14 n 1 above, an expansion in the number of generic domains. At the conclusion of its work, the IAHC put forward for signature by the various interest groups a Generic Top Level Domain Memorandum of Understanding. The work of the

IAHC culminated in the conclusion of a Generic Top Level Domain Memorandum of Understanding (gTLD-MoU). The Memorandum, which is published in the name of the 'Internet Community' endorsed the final report of the IAHC which recommended expansion of the number of generic top level domains and adopted a set of six principles:

- the Internet Top Level Domain (TLD) name space is a public resource and is subject to the public trust;
- any administration, use and/or evolution of the Internet TLD space is a public policy issue and should be carried out in the interests and service of the public;
- related public policy needs to balance and represent the interests of the current and future stakeholders in the Internet name space;
- the current and future Internet name space stakeholders can benefit most from a self-regulatory and market-oriented approach to Internet domain name registration services;
- registration services for the gTLD name space should provide for global distribution of registrars;
- a policy shall be implemented that a second-level domain name in any of the CORE-gTLDs which is identical or closely similar to an alphanumeric string that, for the purposes of this policy, is deemed to be internationally known, and for which demonstrable property rights exist, may be held or used only by, or with the authorization of, the owner of such demonstrable intellectual property rights. Appropriate consideration shall be given to possible use of such a second-level domain name by a third party that, for the purposes of this policy, is deemed to have sufficient rights.

2.26 In January 1998 the US Department of Commerce published a Green Paper, *A proposal to Improve Technical Management of Internet Names and Addresses*.[1] This proposal studiously avoided making any reference to the work of the IAHC and the Global Memorandum of Association. It received a lukewarm response from the EU which commented that the Paper appeared to be seeking to retain US dominance over the Internet. A further US White Paper, *Management of Internet Names and Addresses*,[2] published in June 1998 moved much closer to the proposals of the IAHC and the terms of the Global Memorandum and drew the speedy response from the Commission that it:

> can now confirm that the EU should act to participate fully in the process of organization and management of the Internet that has been launched by the US White Paper.[3]

1   Available from http://www.ntia.doc.gov/ntiahome/domainname/dnsdrft.htm.
2   Available from http://www.ntia.doc.gov/ntiahome/domainname/6_5_98dns.htm.
3   http://www.ispo.cec.be/eif/dns/com98476.html.

2.27 Ultimately, agreement was reached that yet another new body, the Internet Corporation for Assigned Names and Numbers (ICANN), was established in October 1998. It is described as:

> a non-profit, private sector corporation formed by a broad coalition of the Internet's business, technical, and academic communities. ICANN has been

designated by the U.S. Government to serve as the global consensus entity to which the U.S. government is transferring the responsibility for coordinating four key functions for the Internet: the management of the domain name system, the allocation of IP address space, the assignment of protocol parameters, and the management of the root server system.[1]

[1]   http://www.icann.org/general/fact-sheet.htm.

2.28   Following this quite precise job description, there is a reversion to platitude with the comment that:

ICANN is dedicated to preserve the operational stability of the Internet; to promote competition; to achieve broad representation of the global Internet community; and to coordinate policy through private-sector, bottom-up, consensus-based means.

In terms of legal status, ICANN is a company registered under the law of California.

2.29   Effectively ICANN has taken over the role of IANA by means of a Memorandum of Understanding[1] and subsequently a contract entered into with the US government[2] and also removes the monopoly of Network Solutions in respect of the .com domain. Whilst the first part of the process was carried out smoothly, negotiations with Network Solutions were more difficult with legal action being threatened by Network Solutions on more than one occasion. Agreement was eventually reached in November 1999 and at the time of writing 32 organisations were accredited to act as registries for the .com domain.[3] In order to qualify to act as a registrar,[4] an organisation must provide evidence of financial and technical stability.

[1]   Available from http://www.icann.org/general/icann-mou-25nov98.htm.
[2]   See http://www.icann.org/general/iana-contract-09feb00.htm.
[3]   For an up-to-date list see http://www.icann.org/registrars/accredited-list.html.
[4]   For full details of the accreditation process see http://www.icann.org/registrars/accreditation.htm.

2.30   Given an increasing number of registries located throughout the world, the possibility for domain name disputes is exacerbated. In an effort to control the problem, all registrars are obliged to operate the ICANN Uniform Domain Name Dispute Resolution Policy.[1] This obliges applicants to agree that any disputes will be adjudicated by an approved dispute resolution service. At present three organisations operate such services:

- the World Intellectual Property Organization;[2]
- E-Resolution;[3] and
- the National Arbitration Forum.[4]

[1]   Available from http://www.icann.org/udrp/udrp.htm.
[2]   http://arbiter.wipo.int/domains/.
[3]   http://www.eresolution.ca/.
[4]   http://www.arbforum.com/domains/.

2.31 A considerable number of cases have already been referred to these agencies.[1] In addition to providing for a degree of priority to be given to trade mark owners provision is made also for names to be withdrawn when a party registers the name in bad faith. Bad faith will be evidenced by:

(i) circumstances indicating that you have registered or you have acquired the domain name primarily for the purpose of selling, renting, or otherwise transferring the domain name registration to the complainant who is the owner of the trademark or service mark or to a competitor of that complainant, for valuable consideration in excess of your documented out-of-pocket costs directly related to the domain name; or

(ii) you have registered the domain name in order to prevent the owner of the trademark or service mark from reflecting the mark in a corresponding domain name, provided that you have engaged in a pattern of such conduct; or

(iii) you have registered the domain name primarily for the purpose of disrupting the business of a competitor; or

(iv) by using the domain name, you have intentionally attempted to attract, for commercial gain, Internet users to your web site or other on-line location, by creating a likelihood of confusion with the complainant's mark as to the source, sponsorship, affiliation, or endorsement of your web site or location or of a product or service on your web site or location.[2]

[1] For a complete list see http://www.icann.org/udrp/proceedings-list-name.htm.
[2] ICANN Uniform Domain Name Dispute Resolution Policy, para 4b.

2.32 These provisions will allow action to be taken against the activity generally described as 'cybersquatting' and against other improper uses of the domain name system. An example of an action brought under these proceedings is a dispute heard before the WIPO panel involving the mark ABTA.[1] Generally associated with the Association of British Travel Agents who own trade marks in the acronym the domain name, ABTA.net was registered by a hotelier. In the event the WIPO panel found for ABTA on a range of grounds, including use of a mark 'identical or confusingly similar' to a trade mark. The Panel also found in favour of ABTA on the bad faith issue. Key elements here were that the name was not being used and that the holder had not evidenced any plans to make use of the name. 'The concept of a domain name being used in bath faith' it was held, 'is not limited to positive action: inaction is within the concept'.

[1] http://arbiter.wipo.int/domains/decisions/html/d2000-0086.html.

The future of ICANN and Internet regulation

2.33 At the time of its establishment, ICANN was seen in some quarters as providing a blueprint for a more democratic form of Internet regulation. Provision was made for a number of its directors to be elected by those Internet users. In the hard light of experience these hopes were unrealistic and the work of ICANN has been subject to considerable criticism.

2.34 At a basic level, ICANN was established by unilateral action on the part of the US government, albeit with the tacit support of the European Commission. As Internet penetration has increased in other areas of the world, this narrow focus has been a cause for complaint. ICANN's role is in respect of the generic domain name codes but in more recent times country-level codes have begun to assume greater importance and the relationship between ICANN and the agencies responsible for the administration of country codes has at times been difficult.

2.35 In Autumn 2002, the initial contract between the US Department of Commerce expired. It was extended for a further year[1] but on condition that ICANN introduced substantial reforms to its procedures and on the understanding that its progress would be closely monitored. In an accompanying statement[2] the Department expressed concern that:

> ICANN has been troubled by internal and external difficulties that have slowed its completion of the transition tasks and hampered its ability to garner the full support and confidence of the global Internet community.

It continued:

> ICANN's reputation in the Internet community has suffered. In particular, ICANN has been criticized for over-reaching, arbitrariness, and lack of transparency in its decision making. Concerns have been raised about ICANN's lack of accountability and that it is inserting itself too much into the pricing and nature of services offered by, and business practices of, domain name companies. Some consider ICANN too slow to act on various issues, especially the roll-out of new gTLDs. There has also been growing concern that ICANN's structure, processes, and inability to make progress on other key DNS issues have undermined its effectiveness and legitimacy. Not surprisingly, many in the Internet community have called for ICANN to review its mission, structure, and processes for efficacy and appropriateness in light of the needs of today's Internet.

[1] http://www.ntia.doc.gov/ntiahome/domainname/agreements/Amend5_09192002.htm.
[2] http://www.ntia.doc.gov/ntiahome/domainname/agreements/docstatement_09192002.htm.

2.36 Extensive reforms have been put in place by ICANN but the future of the organisation remains uncertain. Given the importance of the Internet for all aspects of modern life it cannot be considered satisfactory that a central co-ordinating body should continue in existence on a year-by-year basis and longer-term resolution is required. It may be that for the longer term, an agency similar to the International Telecommunications Union should assume responsibility for the technical aspects of the work. Although the Union's structures might themselves be criticised as providing excessive weight to governmental interests in an era of increasing private sector involvement in the communications sector, its deliberations do bring together public and private sector interests.

From Armageddon to cyberspace – the growing commercialisation of the Internet

2.37 Until 1991, the Internet remained the exclusive province of the academic/ military/governmental sectors. The prime justification for this approach was that the infrastructure used for data transmission was funded by the public sector. Aspects of the technology have been used in the private sector for a number of years. The computerised legal information retrieval service 'Lexis', for example, began operations in 1973. Services such as 'CompuServe' and 'America Online' also began operations in the 1980s, using proprietary communications software and operating over the normal telephone network. Effectively, this would mean that a CompuServe member could send emails to another member, but not to a subscriber to another service.

2.38 In 1991, the decision was taken in the US to allow commercial users to access the Internet. Almost without exception, organisations such as CompuServe and America Online have migrated to the Internet through the adoption of the TCP/IP standards, and have been joined by many thousands of other organisations offering individual subscribers the possibility of Internet access. At the time of writing, there are around 150 ISPs operating in the UK. The range of services provided by these organisations varies significantly. Some provide significant value added services. These might include technical help desks and access to proprietary information services as well as access to the Internet. Users pay fees, generally based upon the level of usage. More recently, a large number of operators have come into the market offering free Internet access (except for the telephone charges incurred by the user whilst online). A number of ISPs are now offering free connections (by means of an 0800 number) to the Internet at evenings and weekends. At present, it is estimated that around 18% of local telephone calls are made for the purpose of establishing connection with the Internet, a figure which is likely to rise significantly. It is perhaps not surprising that domestic Internet usage is considerably higher in the US, where local telephone calls are generally free of charge.

Why is the Internet valuable for commercial users?

2.39 Today, the .com domain, which hosts websites of commercial relevance, is the largest single Internet domain, with some 12 million hosts. Eighty-four per cent of sites registered in 1998 were in the .com domain.[1] In the UK domain, however, the academic domain .ac.uk remains the largest sector, with slightly over 700,000 hosts as opposed to 585,000 in .co.uk.

[1]   http://www.domainstats.com/.

2.40 A number of elements can be identified which make the Internet valuable for the commercial sector. As many users of email will be aware, the Internet provides marketers with a cheap promotional device, albeit referred to under the derogatory epithet of 'spamming'. Also, from the marketing perspective, the owner of a website can, through the judicious use of 'cookies', obtain a considerable amount of information about those visiting the site. More directly, of course, the Internet can be used for the conclusion of contracts for the sale and supply of goods and services.

2.41   One of the most notable aspects of ecommerce has been the facility it offers for relatively small and newly established companies to establish what is effectively a global presence. An excellent example is the electronic bookshop Amazon.com. Located in Seattle (chosen because this city is home to some of the biggest book wholesalers in the US), Amazon originally consisted of little more than a computer and small warehouse. It can compete, however, with more traditional booksellers around the globe and, in November 1999, towards the height of the 'dot com' boom, *Fortune* magazine reported that Amazon's share capital was 17 times greater than that of the world's largest bricks and mortar book chain, Barnes and Noble, and that it had a market value five times greater than Barnes and Noble. At a more basic level, many small businesses which would never previously have contemplated international trade are now in a position to do so. An example, close to the heart of the author, is the company miracleblanket.com which from its base in Oregon supplied a wonderfully successful baby swaddling blanket to very appreciative parents in Glasgow.

2.42   In discussing this aspect of the Internet's role, a distinction can be drawn between three forms of transaction. In the first category, as epitomised by the online sale of books, Internet businesses allow contracts of sale to be entered into electronically, with the goods involved being delivered using traditional mechanisms. Such transactions can be equated with existing forms of catalogue system and, save for the introduction of an international dimension, raise few novel legal issues. A second category relates to the provision of services. As with the previous situation, the contract will be concluded electronically but there will remain some element of physical performance of the contract. Perhaps the best example, and one of the major sectors of ecommerce, concerns the sale of aeroplane tickets. Most airlines now operate a system of online booking of aeroplane tickets. Such a facility can provide considerable cost benefits to the airline, which will require to employ and support fewer reservations staff and, in a number of cases, passengers are offered a discount for ordering online. In many cases, the next step is for the airline to post tickets to the customer, who then completes the journey in the normal manner. There is increased reliance, however, on what are referred to as electronic tickets. On receiving electronic confirmation of a successful booking, the customer will receive a booking number. No ticket will be issued and, on arrival at the airport, the customer need only quote the booking number in order to receive a boarding pass for the flight. Many 'low cost' airlines such as Ryanair and Easyjet actively promote themselves as ticketless carriers although increased security demands in the aftermath of September 11 have brought with them requirements that passengers carry some official form of photographic identification such as a passport or driving licence. Similar cost benefits to the service provider can be identified in many sectors. A recent survey by Salomon, Smith Barclay has suggested that the costs to a bank of an average transaction carried out within a branch is 67.5p; with telephone banking the cost is reduced to 37p; and with Internet banking there is a further reduction to 2p. It is scarcely surprising that many banks are promoting the merits of this form of service.

2.43   The trend towards increasing dematerialisation of the contract performance phase reaches its ultimate in the third category of contracts. The phenomenon of digitisation is concerned with the practice where information is recorded in digital format. Any form of information, images, sound or text may be recorded in this way. In addition to software itself, we are all familiar with musical CDs and electronic encyclopaedias such as *Microsoft Encarta* or *Britannica Online*.

The scale of Internet commerce

2.44   Increasingly, ecommerce is being conducted over the Internet, with websites offering a range of products and services. As the range of services expands, so, it appears, does the number of estimates as to its scale. It been estimated by the Interactive Media in Retail Group, whose members include companies such as Tesco, Argos, IKEA and lastminute.com, that 20 million UK consumers will engage in some form of Internet-based shopping during 2004. The value of these transactions is estimated to amount to £17bn, a figure which it is predicted will rise to £80bn.[1]

[1]   www.imrg.org.

2.45   Whilst impressive in terms of raw number, these figures represent a relative small portion of total retail transactions currently amounting to perhaps £300 for every person in the country. In further figures published in 2002 by the Office of National Statistics it was suggested that:

> (b)usinesses are continuing to experience difficulties in providing estimates of online sales. The value of orders received over the Internet by UK non-financial sector businesses increased by 39 per cent between 2001 and 2002, from £16.8bn to £23.3bn (1.2% of total economic activity in the sectors).[1]

[1]   Value of e-trading by non-financial sector businesses.

2.46   Some 27% of this figure represented transactions between business and consumers, generally referred to as B-C transactions. This sector, then, is a small albeit increasing sector of the ecommerce economy with the bulk of transactions relating to contracts between businesses, referred to as B-B. The largest sector (66%) of this relates to the supply of physical goods with the electronic component effectively operating as a contracting and ordering mechanism. Twenty-nine per cent of transactions related to the supply of services with 5% relating to 'digitised products'. Although small, this represented a fivefold increase on figures for the previous year and given the growth in sectors such as online audio supply sites likely to have increased further in subsequent years.

Conclusions

2.47 The Internet has developed to an extent which could never have been foreseen in the pioneering days of the 1970s. In little more than a quarter of a century, it has become an essential component of the global economy. Even so, however, it continues to defy definition. We can identify individual attributes, but the overall picture remains elusive.

2.48 Any predictions are dangerous, but the notion of convergence discussed in this chapter and Chapter 1 perhaps offers a hint of where the future lies. The Internet is about communications and, from a stage where differing forms of communication were transmitted over different media and regulated in different ways, we can predict a single, all-purpose network, to the extent that it will be impossible to tell when a database ends and a newspaper begins or when a video film transforms into a television broadcast.

2.49 Regulation will increasingly be the critical issue. With the emergence of organisations such as ICANN, the regulation of the network has been put on a rather more solid legal foundation. The problem, however, is not so much the technology. The TCP/IP protocols are essentially neutral. As will be discussed in the remaining chapters of this book, the key issue for the law is to regulate activities carried out in the context of networked technologies.

Chapter 3

Privacy, technology and the law

Introduction

3.1   Privacy is an elusive concept. It appears to be universally valued with a wide range of surveys of public opinion showing strong support for the protection of privacy. Although much of this material originates from the US and has been conducted by or on behalf of interest groups,[1] in the UK, the Information Commissioner (formerly Data Protection Commissioner) has conducted surveys of public opinion. A number of these have been published in the Commissioner's annual reports which can be obtained from the Information Commissioner's Office website.[2] The following passages are taken from the Commissioner's report for the year 2000.

> On a spontaneous level, as is the case every year, there is little understanding of the rights that people have which reinforce their personal privacy – more importantly the level of understanding of anything has fallen significantly with the best response being 23% who know it exists but little else and only 19% knowing about subject access rights.

However, although individuals may not have been aware of the nature and extent of their legal rights, the report continued:

> Respondents were read a list of issues and asked to say how important they think each is. The proportion who thought that protecting peoples' rights to personal privacy was very important increased but not significantly from 73% to 75%. In terms of people's hierarchy of priorities the issue remains extremely important. Again only Crime Prevention and Improving Standards of Education are thought to be more important issues by the public.

[1]   You will find a very extensive collection of links to surveys on privacy on the Electronic Privacy Information Center (EPIC) website, http://www.epic.org/privacy/survey/default.html.

[2]   http://www.dataprotection.gov.uk/dpr/dpdoc.nsf. Another useful resource is maintained by Roger Clark. In addition to containing links to surveys conducted around the world, it also has much useful and interesting material on the general topic of privacy.

3.2 Privacy is generally accepted to be a fundamental human right and as this concept moves to the centre of the UK's legal stage so it might be that the perceived importance of and reliance upon principles of data protection may increase.

3.3 Although almost everyone will claim to value privacy, matters become more difficult. Once the attempt is made to turn debate from the most general and abstract level, discussion inevitably becomes lost in a quagmire of competing claims and expectations and varying social and cultural experiences. Different people and, indeed, different societies have different views what aspects of life belong in the public and the private domain. Celebrities may court and value a greater degree of attention than the average person would find tolerable. At a societal level, the UK is noted for attaching great value to privacy in respect of dealings with the tax system. In Sweden, by way of contrast, information about tax returns is a matter of public record. This is reported to have produced problems for the authorities at the time when the pop group Abba was at the height of its fame. Many thousands of fans discovered that they could readily obtain copies of their idols' tax returns (which included a photograph). Dealing with the demand for copies is claimed to have brought the system close to meltdown. Again, it is possible to buy a directory in Swedish bookstores. This is similar in format to a telephone directory containing details of name, address and a string of numbers. In this case, however, the digits represent the subject's declared income for the tax year in question. Even in the age of freedom of information legislation it is difficult to envisage such a scenario being acceptable to the average British citizen.

3.4 Again, although individuals may claim to value privacy, they frequently appear to do little to protect themselves. Hundreds of thousands of individuals have applied for supermarket 'loyalty cards'. Such cards provide an invaluable point of linkage between details of individual transactions and the more generic stock management computer systems which have long been a feature of retail life. The seller now knows not only what has been bought but also who has bought it; when; in conjunction with what other products; and what form of payment has been tendered. Analysis of the information will reveal much about the individual's habits and life style which may be used as the basis for direct marketing targeted at the individual customer.[1] Recent developments might suggest that the benefits of loyalty cards to retailers have been overstated with one major UK operator discontinuing the system.[2] More recently, however, a new scheme, Nectar, has been introduced by eight major operators with the declared aim of attracting 50% of UK consumers.[3] All too often, it would appear, we are willing to sell our electronic souls for a can of beans.

[1] For an excellent collection of links to materials on this topic see http:/www.amadorbooks. com/nocardsg.htm.
[2] http://news.bbc.co.uk/hi/english/business/newsid_735000/735835.stm.
[3] http://www.nectar.com/html/index.htm.

Privacy and the law

3.5   The classical legal definition of privacy is attributed to a US judge, Judge Cooley, who opined that it consists of 'the right to be let alone'. A considerable number of other definitions have been formulated over the years. A number of these were cited in the Report of the Committee on Privacy.[1] The essential component, at least for the purposes of the present book, may be stated in terms that an individual has the right to control the extent to which personal information is disseminated to other people. This notion, which is often referred to as involving 'informational privacy', has two main components. The first concerns the right to live life free from the attentions of others, effectively to avoid being watched. This perhaps is the essence of privacy as a human condition or state. Once a third party has information, the second element comes into play with the individual seeking to control the use to which that information is put and, in particular, its range of dissemination. The first component might prohibit entry to private property whilst the second has been illustrated in a number of recent high-profile cases concerning the freedom of newspapers and magazines to publish information about the lives of celebrities.

[1]   Available from http://itlaw.law.strath.ac.uk/readingqxq/infosec/commitee.html.

3.6   The dual nature of the concept of privacy is reflected in the wording of the European Convention on Human Rights which refers to the need to have respect for 'private life'. The provisions of the Convention will be discussed in more detail below but at this introductory stage it is important to note that the right to privacy – in common with most forms of human rights – cannot be absolute. Indeed, as a former Italian Data Protection Commissioner Stefano Rodata has commented:

> the right to be let alone can acquire a heavily negative meaning when this implies a disregard for the conditions of the less wealthy, abandoning the weakest to social violence.[1]

[1]   S Rodata in 'Policy Issues in Data Protection and Privacy', Proceedings of an OECD seminar, Paris, 24–26 June 1974, OECD 1976, p 133.

3.7   Traditionally this comment has referred to the ability of the well-to-do to live in protected communities free from the impact of the poverty and violence of areas of society around them. It is also appropriate for the information age where those with resources and a good credit history will have access to credit facilities either denied to poorer individuals or, and perhaps more damagingly, available only at an extortionate cost. In the field of communications and data privacy, access to secure encrypted communications may be accessible only to an elite whilst reference to the small but growing number of privacy-related cases brought before the UK courts shows that the claimants are, by and large well resourced, including luminaries such models,[1] actors[2] and premiership footballers.[3]

[1]   *Campbell v MGN Ltd* [2004] UKHL 22, [2004] 2 WLR 1232.
[2]   *Douglas v Hello!* [2001] QB 967.

³   *A v B (a company)* [2002] EWCA Civ 337, [2003] QB 195. It would appear that cases involving 'ordinary' individuals are more likely to be ventilated before the European Court of Human Rights. In the recent case of *Peck v United Kingdom* (2003) 36 EHRR 41, the complainant's art 8 rights were held to have been violated by the broadcasting of CCTV footage which showed him making an attempt to kill himself.

The post-Second World War emergence of rights to privacy

3.8   Notions of a right to privacy have formed a feature of many domestic laws for decades and even centuries. In the aftermath of the Second World War the concept of human rights began to be recognised at an international level. These developments have been especially significant for the UK, where the courts and Parliament have been reluctant to recognise or create a specific and legally protectable right to privacy.

3.9   In 1948, the General Assembly of the United Nations adopted the Universal Declaration of Human Rights. This proclaimed in art 12 that:

> No one shall be subjected to arbitrary interference with his privacy, family, home or correspondence, nor to attacks upon his honour and reputation. Everyone has the right to the protection of the law against such interference or attacks.

3.10   Although influential, the Universal Declaration has no binding legal force. Such an instrument was not long delayed. In 1949 the Council of Europe was established by international treaty. Its stated goals include the negotiation of agreements with the goal of securing 'the maintenance and further realisation of human rights and fundamental freedoms'.¹ One of the first actions undertaken within the Council was the negotiation of the Convention for the 'Protection of Fundamental Rights and Fundamental Freedoms' (ECHR). The ECHR was opened for signature in November 1950 and entered into force in September 1953.

¹   Statute of Council of Europe, art 1.

3.11   As the Preamble to the ECHR states, the signatory states reaffirmed:

> ... their profound belief in those fundamental freedoms which are the foundation of justice and peace in the world and are best maintained on the one hand by an effective political democracy and on the other by a common understanding and observance of the human rights upon which they depend ...

3.12   Of the many rights conferred by the ECHR, art 8 is of particular relevance in the present context. This provides that:

> 1   Everyone has the right to respect for his private and family life, his home and his correspondence.
>
> 2.   There shall be no interference by a public authority with the exercise of this right except such as is in accordance with the law and is necessary in

a democratic society in the interests of national security, public safety or the economic well-being of the country, for the prevention of disorder or crime, for the protection of health or morals, or for the protection of the rights and freedoms of others.

3.13 Although the second paragraph of the ECHR, art 8 is couched in terms relating to interference by public authority, the jurisprudence of the European Court of Human Rights has established that the obligation imposed upon member states is to ensure that private and family life is protected by law against intrusions by any person or agency whether within the public or the private sector.[1]

[1] In the case of *Hatton v United Kingdom* (Application No 36022/97) (2003) 15 BHRC 259 the court referred to the existence of 'a positive duty on the State to take reasonable and appropriate measures to secure the applicants' rights under Article 8 § 1 of the Convention'. It is noteworthy that in its initial Recommendations, (73)22 and (74)29, on the processing of personal data, issued in 1973 and 1974, the Council of Europe drew a distinction between processing in the public and the private sector. Whilst the recommendation for action in the former was based specifically on art 8, in respect of private sector processing it was commented that: 'It is also doubtful whether the European Convention on Human Rights, of which Article 8 (1) guarantees to everyone "the right to respect for his private and family life, his home and his correspondence", offers satisfactory safeguards against technological intrusions into privacy. The Committee of Experts on Human Rights has noted, for example, that the Convention takes into account only interferences with private life by public authorities, not by private parties.'

3.14 The concept of privacy has been discussed and developed extensively within the US. Although lacking specific reference in the Constitution, the right of privacy has been seen as emerging from a range of constitutionally guaranteed protections. As was stated by Mr Justice Douglas in the case of *Griswold v Connecticut*:

Various guarantees create zones of privacy. The right of association contained in the penumbra of the First Amendment is one, as we have seen. The Third Amendment in its prohibition against the quartering of soldiers 'in any house' in time of peace without the consent of the owner is another facet of that privacy. The Fourth Amendment explicitly affirms the 'right of the people to be secure in their persons, houses, papers, and effects, against unreasonable searches and seizures.' The Fifth Amendment in its Self-Incrimination Clause enables the citizen to create a zone of privacy which government may not force him to surrender to his detriment. The Ninth Amendment provides: 'The enumeration in the Constitution, of certain rights, shall not be construed to deny or disparage others retained by the people.'[2]

[1] (1965) 381 US 479 at 484.

3.15 This expansive basis for the right to privacy has resulted in the doctrine being applicable to an extensive range of situations, including forming the basis of the seminal Supreme Court ruling in the case of *Roe v Wade*[1] which established a constitutional right to abortion. Within Europe, although the legal basis for the doctrine is rather more precise, the provisions of the ECHR, art 8 have also been held applicable in a wide range of situations. In a recent case before the

European Court of Human Rights, complaints argued that the British government was in breach of its obligations under art 8 by reason of a failure to impose adequate controls over night flights into Heathrow airport, thereby depriving them of the opportunity of a full night's sleep.[2] Although initially successful,[3] the finding of a breach of art 8 was reversed on appeal by a majority judgment of the Grand Chamber.

1   410 US 113.
2   *Hatton v United Kingdom* (Application No 36022/97) (2003) 15 BHRC 259.
3   Case No 36022/97, 21 October 2001.

3.16   It should be stressed once again that the obligation imposed on states is to secure respect for private life. This may involve establishing a specific right to privacy or, as is currently the case, may be secured under a number of other legal headings. Although of perhaps peripheral relevance to this book, the decision of the High Court in the case of *Douglas v Hello!*[1] is of some interest as illustrating the current UK position. The well known actors Michael Douglas and Catherine Zeta Jones succeeded, at least in part, in arguing that the publication of unauthorised photographs of their wedding reception violated their art 8 rights. The remedy provided by the courts (in the form of an award of damages) lay principally, however, under the long-established law of breach of confidence.

1   [2001] QB 967.

3.17   Although the second paragraph of the ECHR, art 8 is couched in terms relating to interference by public authority, the jurisprudence of the European Court of Human Rights has established that the obligation imposed upon member states is to ensure that private and family life is protected by law against intrusions by any person or agency whether within the public or the private sector. In the case of *Hatton v United Kingdom*,[1] the court referred to the existence of 'a positive duty on the State to take reasonable and appropriate measures to secure the applicants' rights under Article 8 § 1 of the Convention' and it is now recognised that states must provide protection against invasive conduct perpetrated by private sector agencies.

1   (Application No 36022/97) (2003) 15 BHRC 259.

3.18   The European notion of private life is less tied to physical objects and, may protect individuals in respect of their activities in the public arena. Publishing photographs of celebrities has, for example, been considered to amount to a breach of ECHR, art 8 even though the pictures may have been taken in a public place. See, for example, the case of *Campbell v MGN Ltd*[1] where the publication of a photograph of a well-known fashion model taken leaving a meeting of a drug user support group was held to constitute a breach. Although the decision was reversed on appeal[2] on the basis that in the particular case, the newspaper's art 10 right of freedom of expression should prevail over the claimant's art 8 rights, the trial judge's ruling was reinstated by a narrow (3-2) majority of the House of Lords.[3] Of greater significance in the present context is the fact the court has interpreted the right to respect for private life in an active sense to encompass the grant of access to at least some forms of personal data. In the case of *Gaskin v United Kingdom*,[4] the complainant, whose childhood had been spent in the care of Liverpool City Council sought in adulthood access to a wide range of social work and medical records compiled during these years. At the time the request was made the Data Protection Act 1984 provided a right of subject access only in respect of data held in electronic format. Although the Council took significant steps to assist the complainant, in particular by seeking the consent of all those responsible for creating records to their disclosure, access was denied save where positive consent was obtained.[5] Recognising that the grant of access to records containing personal data was an integral part of the requirements of art 8, the court held that the UK was in breach of its obligations by failing to establish an appropriate mechanism for determining the extent to which access should be granted.

[1]   [2002] EWHC 499 (QB).
[2]   [2002] EWCA Civ 1373, [2003] QB 633.
[3]   [2004] UKHL 22.
[4]   (1990) 12 EHRR 36.
[5]   In some cases, consent was refused but in a majority of cases the original author either could not be traced or failed to respond to the request. Effectively, silence was regarded as constituting refusal.

3.19   As demonstrated in *Gaskin*,[1] although the breadth of art 8 rights offer benefits for individuals, it also suffers from an inevitable lack of precision, especially in situations where conflict arises between competing claims. Building on the general principles, a trend emerged within Western Europe during the last third of the twentieth century for the introduction of data protection laws concerned specifically with the issues arising from the processing of personal data. One of the major concerns was that the capability of the computer to store, process and disseminate information posed significant threats to the individual's ability to control the extent to which personal information was disseminated and the uses to which it might be put. A linkage has frequently been drawn between the general right to privacy and the notion of informational privacy. This is clearly seen both in the Council of Europe Convention on the Automated Processing of Personal Data and more recently and extensively in the text of the EC Directive 'on the protection of individuals with regard to the processing of personal data and on the free movement of such data',[2] which makes no fewer than 14 references to the noun 'privacy'. Article 1 of the Directive is explicit:

> 1. In accordance with this Directive, Member States shall protect the fundamental rights and freedoms of natural persons, and in particular their right to privacy with respect to the processing of personal data.

The scope of these measures will be discussed in more detail in the following chapters.

[1]   *Gaskin v United Kingdom* (1990) 12 EHRR 36.
[2]   Directive 95/46/EC, OJ 1995 L 281/31 (the Data Protection Directive).

Privacy and surveillance

3.20   One of the main ways in which privacy can be threatened is by the act of placing an individual under surveillance. Surveillance can take a variety of forms. Physical surveillance is as old-established as society. At an official level, it might involve placing individuals suspected of criminal conduct under surveillance, whilst at the private level, reference can be made to the nosy neighbour looking at life through the corner of a set of lace curtains. In some instances, the success of surveillance may depend on its existence being unknown to its target. In other cases, the fact that conduct may be watched is itself used as an instrument for social control. As George Orwell wrote in his novel *1984*:

> There was of course no way of knowing whether you were being watched at any given moment. How often, on what system, the Thought Police plugged in on any individual wire was guesswork. It was even conceivable that they watched everyone all the time. But at any rate they could plug in your wire whenever they wanted to. You had to live – did live, from habit that became instinct – in the assumption that every sound you made was overheard and, except in darkness, every movement scrutinised.

The development of infra-red camera technology might render George Orwell's vision almost too optimistic.

3.21   In 1971 Alan Westin in his seminal work, *Information Technology in a Democracy*,[1] identified three forms of surveillance:

* physical;
* psychological; and
* data.

At that time, it may be suggested, clear distinctions could be drawn between the three categories.

* *Physical surveillance*, as the name suggests, involves the act of watching or listening to the actions of an individual. Such surveillance, even making use of technology, has tended to be an expensive undertaking capable of being applied to a limited number of individuals. It has been estimated, for example, that a team of eight people would be required to place an individual under discrete surveillance on a 24-hour basis.
* Examples of *psychological surveillance* include forms of interrogation or the use of personality tests as favoured by some employers. Once again, logistical and cost constraints have served to limit the use of these techniques. The end product of any form of surveillance is data or information.
* With both physical and psychological surveillance, an active role is played by the watcher. *Data surveillance* involves a different, more passive, approach. Every action of an individual reveals something about the person. Very few actions do not involve individuals in giving out a measure of information about themselves. This may occur directly, for example, in filling in a form, or indirectly, as when goods or services are purchased.

The essence of data surveillance lies in the collection and retention of these items of information.

1   Harvard University Press.

3.22   With the ability to digitise any form of information, boundaries between the various forms of surveillance are disappearing with the application of information technology linking surveillance techniques into a near seamless web of surveillance. Developments in data processing suggest that the distinction between informational and physical privacy is becoming more and more flimsy. The reach of systems of physical surveillance has been increased enormously by the involvement of the computer to digitise and process the information received. Concern at these privacy implications of information technology was expressed by Lord Hoffmann delivering his judgment in the House of Lords in the case of *R v Brown*:

> My Lords, one of the less welcome consequences of the information technology revolution has been the ease with which it has become possible to invade the privacy of the individual. No longer is it necessary to peep through keyholes or listen under the eaves. Instead, more reliable information can be obtained in greater comfort and safety by using the concealed surveillance camera, the telephoto lens, the hidden microphone and the telephone bug. No longer is it necessary to open letters, pry into files or conduct elaborate inquiries to discover the intimate details of a person's business or financial affairs, his health, family, leisure interests or dealings with central or local government. Vast amounts of information about everyone are stored on computers, capable of instant transmission anywhere in the world and accessible at the touch of a keyboard. The right to keep oneself to oneself, to tell other people that certain things are none of their business, is under technological threat.[1]

1   [1996] 1 All ER 545 at 555-556.

Examples and consequences of data surveillance

3.23   As far back as 1972 in considering the threats to privacy resulting from computerised data processing, the Committee on Privacy identified the prospect that:

> Because the data are stored, processed and often transmitted in a form which is not directly intelligible, few people may know what is in the records or what is happening to them.[1]

1   *Report of the Committee on Privacy* (Cm 5012, 1972) at para 130.

3.24   In an information-based society extensive details concerning the most trivial actions undertaken are recorded. In the context of ecommerce, an online bookshop will know, at least once customers have bought goods and accepted the presence of cookies on their computers, the title of every book which is examined and the nature of catalogue searches made. This can be linked to name and address details. Even in the physical environment, trials are being conducted with image recognition systems linked to CCTV cameras[1] which can monitor the movements of specific individuals. One of the most extensive systems has been installed in the London Borough of Newham.[2] Here it has been reported that images from 150 cameras are compared:

> ... with a database of known criminals stored on computer at the council's headquarters. Information is then passed to police.
>
> The makers say the system is sophisticated enough to take into account light conditions, whether the suspect is wearing glasses, makeup or earrings, the expression and even the ageing process.
>
> Growing a beard or trying some other disguise will apparently not fool the camera because it can see through it.
>
> If the system, known as Mandrake, recognises a crook, it sounds the alarm and displays a code number. A council operator, who never knows the identity of the suspect, then phones police, who have their own screens.[3]

Images of around 60–100 convicted criminals are maintained on the system, which claims an accuracy rate of around 75%. The downside, of course, is that 25% of innocent people will be viewed with suspicion because of a false identification. Given further estimates that the average person is 'captured' on a CCTV system 200 times a day, the statistics become rather more worrying.

[1]   As was reported in the *Independent*, 12 January 2004, more than 4 million CCTV cameras are in use in the UK. At a ratio of one camera to 15 people this, it is claimed, makes the UK the 'most-watched nation in the world'.
[2]   http://www.bbc.co.uk/londonlive/news/july/cctv_170701.shtml.
[3]   *Daily Mail*, 15 October 1998.

3.25   Intelligent systems are also being installed in shops.[1] Surveillance devices in the workplace allow employers to monitor the activities and efficiency of individuals. Even the Internet and WWW which are often touted as the last refuge of individualism might equally accurately be described as a surveillance system *par excellence*. An individual browsing the Web leaves electronic trails wherever he or she passes. A software program can transmit a tracer known as a 'cookie'[2] from a website to the user's computer. The cookie remains there until the site is next accessed at which time details of the user and previous visits to the site can be automatically recalled (and sent to a third party).[3]

[1]   *Sunday Herald*, 26 August 2001. Text available from http://www.sundayherald.com/18007.
[2]   For information about the nature of these devices see http://www.cookiecentral.com/faq.htm.
[3]   A Report on Privacy on the Internet has been prepared for the European Commission Working Party on Data Protection and gives some interesting insights into the topic. The report is available from http://www.europa.eu.int/comm/internal_market/privacy/docs/wpdocs/2000/wp37en.pdf.

3.26   In terms of goods themselves, the ubiquitous barcode which contains facilitates identification of the product and its price at the checkout may be replaced by radio frequency identification tags (RFID). RFID tags, which are essentially a form of microchip, are capable of transmitting information both prior to and after the point of sale. This would, for example, enable movement of the object to be tracked both in the store and also externally. One possibility which has been canvassed is that future generations of banknotes will have RFID tags embedded in order to enable movements of cash to be tracked with a view to countering money laundering. In respect of motor cars, the European Commission has launched a programme designed to specify standards for electronic vehicle identification (EVI). The programme, it is stated aims to develop:

> an *electronic, unique identifier for motor vehicles*, which would enable a wealth of applications, many of them of crucial importance for the public authorities to combat congestion, unsafe traffic behaviour and vehicle crime on the European roads. It is clear that such an identifier as well as the communication means to remotely read it should be standardised and *interoperable* all over Europe.[1]

In the UK it has been reported in a similar context that:

> Government officials are drawing up plans to fit all cars in Britain with a personalised microchip so that rule-breaking motorists can be prosecuted by computer.
>
> Dubbed the 'Spy in the Dashboard' and 'the Informer' the chip will automatically report a wide range of offences including speeding, road tax evasion and illegal parking. The first you will know about it is when a summons or a fine lands on your doormat.
>
> The plan, which is being devised by the government, police and other enforcement agencies, would see all private cars monitored by roadside sensors wherever they travelled.[2]

[1] http://europa.eu.int/comm/transport/road/roadsafety/its/evi/index_en.htm (emphasis in original).
[2] *Sunday Times*, 24 August 2003.

3.27 Examples of thickening information threads and trails are legion. Barely ten years ago, the only records compiled by UK telephone companies regarding telephone usage concerned the number of units (an amalgam of the time of day when a call is made, its duration and its identification as local, long-distance or international). Today, it is near universal practice to present users with itemised bills. These may provide considerable assistance to the person (or company) responsible for paying the bill in monitoring and controlling usage but does also provide useful marketing information to the service provider as well as raising issues concerning the privacy of other persons who might make use of the facility. Recent research conducted on behalf of BT illustrates well the issues involved. 15,000 calls an hour, it is reported, are made from work phones to sex or chat telephone lines.[1] With mobile phones, even more data is recorded with location data enabling the movements of the phone to be tracked with ever greater precision. Again, the widespread use of cash-dispensing machines allows the withdrawals of bank customers to be tracked on a real-time basis both nationally and internationally.

[1] Cited on Ceefax (an electronic information service broadcast by the BBC), 21 July 2003.

3.28 There is no doubt that the world we inhabit today has changed and is changing with considerable speed. As well as being a commodity in its own right, data is the motor and fuel which drives the information society. A database with no data is a poor creature indeed and with the development of more and more sophisticated search engine technologies, the value of a database lies increasingly in the amount of data held rather than the thought which lies behind the selection and organisation of material. The Internet and its use in academic life provides a very apposite example. There is no doubt that it provides teachers and students with access to a massively increased range of data. An author trying to track down a missing citation need often require only to submit a few words to a search engine such as 'Google' to be presented with the answer in seconds. More, however, does not always mean better. Excessive use of electronic resources will cause traditional research skills to atrophy, the availability of 100 electronic articles saying the same thing adds little to the reader's understanding of a topic – even making the charitable assumption that the articles are accurate in what they say. The tendency is to seek to find the answer before one has understood the question.

3.29 Similar issues arise in the wider world. Information is replacing knowledge and the change in terminology indicates also reliance on a more mechanistic and statistical based view of the world. An example can be seen in the increasing use of DNA technology for crime detection purposes. In the UK, aided by a policy of taking and retaining samples from everyone charged and convicted of even the most minor offence, the national police DNA database now contains more than 2 million entries. This tool, as with most forms of scientific evidence, is based upon calculations of probability. Recent high-profile cases in the UK have shown up some of the failings of such an approach and, in particular, that technology is as effective only as those applying it. The consequences for those wrongly identified and convicted on the basis of misunderstanding of statistics has been profound and tragic.

3.30 Although we may challenge the efficacy of some of the models, there is no doubt that the underlying principles of data protection matter more today than ever before. With developments in data processing and other forms of technology there is the potential for every movement we make to be tracked and recorded. There is a well-established tradition of providing for necessary exceptions from the strict application of data protection principles in the context of national security and crime prevention and detection. These have been applied in the context of specific investigations and with the attempt made to secure a reasonable balance between the interests of the state and of individuals. With a move towards reliance upon databases, whether of DNA samples or other forms of information, there has been a significant shift in the nature of policing, from the attempt to find evidence linking an individual with an offence to one where an individual is sought whose profile fits that of a suspected offender. In many cases such an approach is justified but, as will be discussed in the final section of this chapter, the perceived need to defeat terrorism is leading to the removal of some data protection safeguards with little being put in place to replace these. As with all aspects of design, unless components are included at an early stage, it is more difficult and expensive to incorporate them at a later stage.

3.31 Many of the recorded instances of the misuse of information have occurred not as part of the original design but as a by product of the fact that the information is available. The story has been told how the elaborate population registers maintained by the Dutch authorities prior to the Second World War (no doubt with the best possible motives) were used by the invading Germans to facilitate the deportation of thousands of people.[1] In this case, as in any similar case, it is clear that it was not information per se that harmed individuals, rather it was the use that was made of it. In this sense information is a tool; but a very flexible tool, and whenever personal information is stored the subject is to some extent 'a hostage to fortune'. Information which is freely supplied today, and which reflects no discredit in the existing social climate, may be looked upon very differently should circumstances change. It may, of course, be questioned how far any legal safeguards may be effective in the situation of an external invasion or unconstitutional usurpation of power. In discussion of this point in Sweden it has been suggested that:

> Under a threat of occupation there may be reason to remove or destroy computer installations and various registers in order to prevent the installations or important information from falling into enemy hands. An enemy may, for example, wish to acquire population registers and other records which can assist his war effort. There may be reason to revise the plans as to which data processing systems should be destroyed or removed in a war situation.[2]

[1]   Hondius *Emerging Data Protection in Europe* (1975, North Holland).
[2]   Transnational Data Report, vol 1, no 5, p 17.

3.32 Whilst such plans and procedures might appear to afford protection against the possibility of outside intervention it must be recognised that, in the past, the use of personal information as a weapon against individuals has not been the exclusive province of totalitarian states. Again, during the Second World War, the US government used information supposedly supplied in confidence during the census to track down and intern citizens of Japanese ancestry.[1] More recently, it has been reported that the US Selective Service system purchased a list of 167,000 names of boys who had responded to a promotion organised by a chain of ice-cream parlours offering a free ice-cream on the occasion of their eighteenth birthday. This list of names, addresses and dates of birth was used in order to track down those who had failed to register for military service.[2] Such practices illustrate, first, the ubiquitous nature of personal information and, secondly, that no clear dividing line can be drawn between public and private sector users, as information obtained within one sector may well be transferred to the other. At a slightly less serious level, it was reported in the UK that information supplied in the course of the 1971 census describing the previous occupations of respondents was passed on to health authorities, who used it to contact retired nurses with a view to discovering why they left the profession and to encourage them to consider returning to work.[3] Whilst it may be argued that no harm was caused to the individuals concerned by the use to which this information was put, it provides further evidence of the ubiquitous nature of information, and of the ease with which information supplied for one purpose can be put to another use.

1   Petersen *Japanese Americans* (1971, Random House).
2   Transnational Data Report, vol 10, no 4, p 25.
3   Madgwick and Smythe *The Invasion of Privacy* (1974, Pitman).

3.33   The potential dangers were described by Browne-Wilkinson VC in *Marcel v Metropolitan Police Commissioner*.[1] Documents belonging to the plaintiff had been seized by the police in the course of a criminal investigation. Civil proceedings were also current in respect of the same incidents, and a subpoena was served on behalf of one of the parties to this litigation seeking disclosure of some of these documents. Holding that the subpoena should be set aside, the judge expressed concern that:

> ... if the information obtained by the police, the Inland Revenue, the social security offices, the health service and other agencies were to be gathered together in one file, the freedom of the individual would be gravely at risk. The dossier of private information is the badge of the totalitarian state.[2]

Although this ruling was overturned in the Court of Appeal, Nolan LJ expressed agreement with the proposition that 'strict limits must be placed upon the use to which the seized documents can properly be put by the police'.

1   [1992] Ch 225.
2   [1992] Ch 225 at 240. This quotation is also of considerable relevance to the emerging practice of data matching which is considered more fully at para 5.16 below.

Does informational privacy have a future after September 11?

3.34   Great and tragic events invariably carry a lasting legacy and aftershocks from the events of September 11 continue to reverberate around the globe. The perception, true or false, that the Internet and forms of electronic communications are linked with the spread of global terrorism has impacted significantly on governmental attitudes to many of the issues discussed in this chapter and, indeed, throughout the whole of the field of information technology law. Of particular relevance to the present discussion is the extent to which changes have been, and are being, made to the delicate balance between personal privacy and the interests of the government and also, of course, society at large in preventing the commission of terrorist offences. Many of the legislative responses to the threat of global terrorism, especially those within the UK, have been enacted with great speed, driven by perceived necessity but carrying with them also the risk of creating a chasm between those whose primary interest is in law enforcement and individuals and bodies concerned with the protection and promotion of individual rights and freedoms. Creative tension between different interest groups is inevitable and when there is a degree of acceptance that each group is acting in good faith, can produce benefits. When creation turns to destruction, everyone loses and in many respects the present debate between civil libertarian lobbyists and government has become sterile. Possible consequences are that individuals may lose some of the major elements of protection introduced and developed over the past decades whilst governments risk losing popular legitimacy if they are seen as unconcerned with and threatening towards the rights of citizens.

3.35 Many significant legislative moves have been made in order to enhance the powers of law enforcement and national security agencies in the aftermath of September 11. Many of the aspects, such as increased powers of arrest and detention, are outside the scope of this book. For present purposes, the most important changes relate to increased rights of access to personal data.

3.36 The start point of the analysis should be the EC Directive on Privacy and Electronic Communications.[1] As originally drafted this Directive provides individuals with extensive guarantees of privacy in respect of data pertaining to their electronic communications. At a very late stage in the legislative process, however, and following the events of September 11, an amendment was accepted by the European Parliament permitting member states to 'adopt legislative measures providing for the retention of data for a limited period justified on the grounds laid down in this paragraph'.[2] The grounds referred to include the safeguarding of 'national security ... defence, public security, and the prevention, investigation, detection and prosecution of criminal offences or of unauthorised use of the electronic communication system'. Even prior to the entry into force of the Directive, this power has been extensively used within the UK.

[1]   Directive 2002/58/EC, OJ 2002 L 201/37.
[2]   Article 15.

3.37 Initial legislative provisions date back to the Regulation of Investigatory Powers Act 2000 which empower a senior police office to require a communications provider to disclose any communications data in its possession where this is considered necessary in the interests of national security, the prevention or detection of crime or a number of other situations.[1] The term' communications data' is defined broadly to include traffic and location data although as has been stated by the Home Office:

> It is important to identify what communications data does include but equally important to be clear about what it does *not* include. The term communications data in the Act does not include the content of any communication.[2]

[1]   Section 22.
[2]   Consultation paper on a Code of Practice for Voluntary Retention of Communications Data (March 2003).

3.38 The Regulation of Investigatory Powers Act 2000 did not require that providers retain data although concerns had been expressed that mobile phone operators were retaining customer records for a period of months and in some cases years.[1] The conformity of this practice with the requirements of the Data Protection Act 1998 that:

> Personal data processed for any purpose or purposes shall not be kept for longer than is necessary for that purpose or those purposes,[2]

had been doubted. The passage of the Anti-Terrorism, Crime and Security Act 2001, which was rushed through Parliament in a matter of weeks, provided a legal basis for the retention of data. The Act conferred power on the Secretary of State to draw up a code of practice specifying periods of time during which communications providers would be required to retain communications data.[3] Although the Secretary of State is granted legislative power, it was envisaged that a voluntary code would be agreed between government and the communications industry. To date, however, negotiations have not produced agreement with industry concerns centring in large part on the cost implications of retaining large amounts of data. The leading service provider AOL, for example, has estimated that it would require 36,000 CDs in order to store one year's supply of communications data relating to its customers with set-up costs of £30m and annual running costs of the same amount.

[1] See, for example, 'Liberties Fear Over Mobile phone details' *Guardian*, 27 October 2001, reporting that the mobile network Virgin has retained all data from the establishment of its network in 1999.
[2] Schedule 1, fifth data protection principle.
[3] Section 102.

3.39 Initial proposals by the government for the establishment of a code of practice received heavy criticism both in terms of the period of time within which data might require to be retained and also the range of government agencies which might be granted access to this data. An initial draft code was withdrawn in July 2002 and a further draft was published in March 2003.[1] This restricted the range of agencies who might seek access to data but retains the requirement that data be retained for a period of 12 months.

[1] Available from http://www.homeoffice.gov.uk/docs/consult.pdf.

Conclusion

3.40 Almost 60 years ago the world was recovering from the trauma of global conflict. The negotiation of the Universal Declaration and the European Convention on Human Rights was seen as a major legislative component of the road to recovery. The enhancement of individual rights was seen as the best response to the trauma of global terror. Today, the view appears to be that rights need to be restricted in order to defeat terror. Whilst it may, of course, be argued that a closer parallel is with the enactment of emergency legislation in time of war, the present situation is perhaps more akin to the image portrayed in George Orwell's novel *1984* where a condition of perpetual and undeclared war existed between three power blocks with shifting alliances and battles generally fought far from home but used as justification for repressive domestic policies.

3.41 Few issues in the field admit of easy answers. Any attempt to strike a balance between competing interests is difficult, especially in a fast-changing environment. Most would agree that law enforcement agencies should be provided with the best possible tools to enable them to perform their vital tasks. Data can constitute an extremely valuable investigative tool but the whole premise of data protection legislation over the decades has been that the potential for misuse is considerable. At least within a UK context, the main problem is perhaps a lack of awareness. Alexander Solzhenitsyn once wrote:

> As every man goes through life he fills in a number of forms for the record, each containing a number of questions ... There are thus hundreds of little threads radiating from every man, millions of threads in all. If these threads were suddenly to become visible, the whole sky would look like a spider's web, and if they materialized as rubber bands, buses, trams and even people would all lose the ability to move, and the wind would be unable to carry torn-up newspapers or autumn leaves along the streets of the city. They are not visible, they are not material, but every man is constantly aware of their existence ... Each man, permanently aware of his own invisible threads, naturally develops a respect for the people who manipulate the threads.[1]

[1]   *Cancer Ward, Dial Press, New York* (New York, 1968) p 221.

3.42 If data were nuclear particles or perhaps even genetically modified foodstuffs, people would be aware of and respectful of the dangers involved in their use and transportation. The danger today is that data flows are invisible and when society becomes aware of the potential for misuse, it may be too late to put this technological genie back in a bottle.

Chapter 4

The emergence of data protection

Introduction

4.1 As indicated in Chapter 3, a variety of concerns about the potential use and misuse of computers spawned a growing call for legislative intervention in the latter part of the twentieth century. Two general approaches can be identified. The first, as applied within the US and perhaps a majority of countries in the world, adopts a sectoral approach, with a range of statutes being enacted to regulate specific forms of information handling. US examples include the Fair Credit Reporting Act 1970, which gives a right of access to information held by credit reference agencies, and the Privacy Act 1974, giving a right of access to certain records held by public agencies and placing restrictions on the use to which data may be put by these agencies. A considerable number of more sector-specific statutes also exist at both federal and state level. On occasion, these statutes have been adopted in response to a specific instance involving misuse of data. Thus, the Video Privacy Protection Act 1970 was enacted following an incident when the publication of video rental records indicating a penchant for pornographic films proved extremely damaging to the subject, a judge who had been nominated for appointment to the Supreme Court.[1]

1   See discussion in *Dirkes v Borough of Runnemede* (1996) 936 F Supp 235.

4.2 A different approach has prevailed within Europe, where the tendency has been to enact omnibus data protection statutes regulating all (or almost all) instances where personal data is processed by computer. In addition to covering a broader range of activities than is the case in US statutes, a feature of the data protection model has been the appointment of a supervisory agency, generally independent of government, to monitor the activities of those processing personal data and to intervene to support individuals concerned at the possible misuse of their data. Such a bureaucratic structure, which is seldom found in the US model, is a cause for continuing debate and disagreement between the EU and the US, a topic that will be discussed in more detail in Chapter 10.

4.3   The term 'data protection' made its first appearance in legislation in 1970 and, although it has been criticised as conveying the impression that the information, rather than its subjects, is to be protected, the phrase has been widely copied. The world's first data protection statute was enacted in the German state of Hesse in 1970, with the first national statute being the Swedish Data Protection Act 1973. The fact that data protection laws were first introduced in these two countries may not be entirely a matter of coincidence, and also illustrates what might be classed as the positive and negative aspects of the system. In the case of Germany, there had been experience of totalitarian regimes and of the ease with which personal data might be misused. In seeking to place limits on the ability of public and private sector bodies to process personal data, the law can be seen as acting primarily in a defensive or negative manner. The Swedish situation was very different. There was no background of totalitarianism, but instead a more than two-century long tradition of freedom of information, under which almost any item of official information was considered to be in the public domain. By conferring rights on individuals to access information held on computer, data protection could be seen as extending some of the concepts of freedom of information into the private sector.

International data protection initiatives

4.4   Although the first data protection laws were enacted on a national basis, even prior to these interventions, pressure had been exerted for international action in this field. In addition to a concern over the extent to which the application of computer technology could serve to threaten human rights, the justification for the intervention of international agencies was seen as being twofold. First, it was recognised that, given the scale of the international trade in computerised information, impossible burdens could be placed upon multinational enterprises should they be required to comply with differing standards in every country in which they acquired, stored, processed or even transferred data. A second factor lies in the realisation that, in the information age, national boundaries have become almost redundant. One nation's efforts to protect its citizens' liberties by placing restrictions upon the forms of data processing that may be carried out could easily be nullified were the data to be transferred abroad for processing. From the standpoint of data users, it would not be surprising if undertakings were to seek to base their processing in that country or those countries whose laws placed the fewest restrictions on their activities, ie which were willing to provide a data haven. It has, for example, been reported that a 'diversified consumer products company rented a house which straddled the border of two European countries to maintain the option of having computer tapes in the venue most expedient to management purposes'.[1] Fear of the establishment of data havens undoubtedly prompted much international action in this field and, as will be discussed, the issue of the control of transborder data flows has proved to be one of the most controversial aspects of the European Directive of 24 October 1995 on 'the protection of individuals with regard to the processing of personal data and on the free movement of such data'.[2]

1   B Patrick (1981) 21 Jurimetrics J 405 at 406.
2   Directive 95/46/EC, OJ 1995 L 281/31 (the Data Protection Directive).

4.5   During the 1970s and 1980s, most of the international initiatives in the data protection field were pursued within the Council of Europe and the Organisation for Economic Cooperation and Development (OECD). The following sections will consider the major activities carried out under the auspices of these organisations. Brief attention will also be paid to the work of the United Nations. During the 1990s, much of the focus switched to work within the EU and the slow progress towards the adoption of the Data Protection Directive.[1]

1   Directive 95/46/EC.

The Council of Europe

4.6   In 1968, the Parliamentary Assembly of the Council of Europe addressed a request to the Committee of Ministers that they consider the extent to which the provisions of the European Convention on Human Rights safeguarded the individual against the abuse of modern technology. The assembly noted particular concern at the fact that the European Convention, together with its United Nations predecessor, the Universal Declaration of Human Rights, had been devised before the development and widespread application of the computer.

4.7   The Committee of Ministers passed this request to its Committee of Experts on Human Rights, which in 1970 reported the view that the protection offered under existing conventions was inadequate. In particular, it was pointed out that the European Convention on Human Rights and similar documents were based largely on the premise that individuals' rights might be infringed by the actions of public authorities. The development of the computer placed a significant weapon in the hands of private agencies.[1]

1   Cf the concerns identified above regarding the restriction of the Committee on Privacy's remit to the private sector.

4.8   Whilst identifying the dangers of computer abuse, the Committee's report also drew attention to a paradox which remains unresolved to this day. Data protection seeks to give an individual a greater measure of control over personal information and to place controls over the dissemination of this information. This approach may conflict with another individual's claim to be allowed access to information under the European Convention on Human Rights. Here it is provided that: '(e)veryone has the right to freedom of expression. This shall include freedom to hold opinions and to receive and impart information and ideas without interference by public authority and regardless of frontiers.'[1] The issue is similar to that discussed above relating to the exercise and extent of the right of privacy. In 1986, the Parliamentary Assembly of the Council of Europe approved a Recommendation on Data Protection and Freedom of Information.[2] This advocated that the Committee of Experts on Data Protection be instructed 'to identify criteria and principles according to which data protection and access to official information could be reconciled'.[3] Although data protection and freedom of information are not inherently opposed, in that both concepts seek to improve the position of individuals against those organisations which hold information of relevance to aspects of their life, to date, no action has been taken under this recommendation.

[1]   Article 10.
[2]   Recommendation 1037/1986.
[3]   Paragraph 10.

4.9   Acting upon the Committee's report, two separate resolutions were adopted by the Committee of Ministers, dealing with the private and the public sectors. The differences between the two sets of recommendations are comparatively minor, and for both sectors it was recommended that national laws should ensure that:

1.   The information stored should be accurate and kept up to date. In general information relating to the intimate private life of persons or information which might lead to unfair discrimination should not be recorded or, if recorded, should not be disseminated.
2.   The information should be appropriate and relevant with regard to the purpose for which it has been stored.
3.   The information should not be obtained by fraudulent or unfair means.
4.   Rules should be laid down or specify the periods beyond which certain categories of information should no longer be kept or used.
5.   Without appropriate authorisation, information should not be used for purposes other than those for which it has been stored, nor communicated to third parties.
6.   As a general rule, the person concerned should have the right to know the information stored about him, the purpose for which it has been recorded, and particulars of each release of this information.
7.   Every care should be taken to correct inaccurate information and to erase obsolete information or information obtained in an unlawful way.
8.   Precautions should be taken against any abuse or misuse of information. Electronic data banks should be equipped with security systems which bar access to the data held by them to persons not entitled to obtain such information, and which provide for the detection of misdirections of information, whether intentional or not.
9.   Access to the information should be confined to persons who have a valid reason to know it. The operating staff of electronic data banks should be bound by rules of conduct aimed at preventing the misuse of data and, in particular, by rules of professional secrecy.
10.   Statistical data should be released only in aggregate form and in such a way that it is impossible to link the information to a particular person.[1]

[1]   Resolution (73)22.

4.10   The initial Council of Europe resolutions did not attempt to prescribe the means by which member states should give effect to the principles contained therein. As more and more countries enacted data protection legislation during the 1970s, so the problems resulting from the international trade of information, frequently referred to as transborder data flows, became acute. In an effort to minimise restrictions on the free flow of information, and in the hope of preventing major discrepancies between the national data protection laws, the Council of Europe moved beyond its earlier recommendations to sponsor, in 1981, the Convention for the Protection of Individuals with Regard to the Automatic Processing of Personal Data (hereafter 'the Convention').

4.11 The Convention can be seen as offering a carrot and threatening a stick to member states. In its Preamble, the Convention reaffirms the Council of Europe's commitment to freedom of information regardless of frontiers, and explicitly proceeds to prohibit the erection of national barriers to information flow on the pretext of protecting individual privacy.[1] This prohibition extends, however, only where the information is to be transferred to another signatory state. Impliedly, therefore, the Convention permits the imposition of sanctions against any non-signatory state whose domestic law contains inadequate provision regulating the computerised processing of personal data. A recalcitrant state could effectively be placed in data quarantine. The standards required of domestic laws are laid down in Chapter 2 of the Convention, and its requirements will be considered in detail when considering the substantive aspects of data protection.

[1]   Article 12(2).

4.12 The Council of Europe's activities in the field of data protection have not ceased with the entry into force of the Convention. A substantial number of recommendations have been addressed to member states concerning the interpretation and application of the Convention principles in particular sectors, and in respect of particular forms of processing. Table 1 gives details of these instruments.[1]

Table 1

Recommendation No R(2002) 9 on the protection of personal data collected and processed for insurance purposes (18 September 2002)

Recommendation No R(99) 5 for the protection of privacy on the Internet (23 February 1999)

Recommendation No R(97) 18 on the protection of personal data collected and processed for statistical purposes (30 September 1997)

Recommendation No R(97) 5 on the protection of medical data (13 February 1997)

Recommendation No R(95) 4 on the protection of personal data in the area of telecommunication services, with particular reference to telephone services (7 February 1995)

Recommendation No R(91) 10 on the communication to third parties of personal data held by public bodies (9 September 1991)

Recommendation No R(90) 19 on the protection of personal data used for payment and other operations (13 September 1990)

Recommendation No R(89) 2 on the protection of personal data used for employment purposes (18 January 1989)

Recommendation No R(87) 15 regulating the use of personal data in the police
  sector (17 September 1987)
Recommendation No R(86) 1 on the protection of personal data for social security
  purposes
Recommendation No R(85) 20 on the protection of personal data used for the
  purposes of direct marketing (25 October 1985)
Recommendation No R(81) 1 on regulations for automated medical data banks
  (23 January 1981)
Recommendation No R(2002) 9 on the protection of personal data collected and
  processed for insurance purposes (18 September 2002)

¹   The text of all these instruments can be obtained from http://www.coe.int/T/E/Legal_affairs/
    Legal_co-operation/Data_protection/Documents/International_legal_instruments/
    2CM.asp.

The Organisation for Economic Co-operation and Development

4.13   Although the Convention provides that the Committee of Ministers may
invite 'any State not a member of the Council of Europe to accede to this
Convention',¹ no external states have attempted to exercise this option. The
work of the Council of Europe has been viewed with considerable suspicion by
a number of countries, including the US. The difference in regulatory philosophy
between the US sectoral and the European omnibus approach has been identified
above. In one respect, statutes such as the Privacy Act 1974, the Fair Credit
Reporting Act 1970 and state legislation such as the Californian Information
Practices Act 1977 offer wider protection to the individual, as legislation typically
applies to all records coming within a specified category regardless of whether
the information is held on computer or in manual form. Against this, the
individual's rights are dependent upon whether a law has been promulgated in a
particular area.

¹   Article 23.

4.14   Faced with this divergence of approach, the view has been expressed by
several US commentators that the provisions of the Convention were motivated
more by considerations of commercial expediency and economic protectionism
than by a genuine concern for individual privacy. In the course of a meeting of
the Committee of Experts, the US observer contrasted the sectoral approach
adopted in that country with the omnibus data protection legislation envisaged
under the Convention, and concluded that:

> ... the draft convention appears to regulate a function, that is, it appears to
> regulate automated or electronic data processing and what the automated
> data processing industry may do with records about individuals. To our mind
> the draft convention is, in essence, a scheme for the regulation of computer
> communications technology as it may be applied to personal data record-
> keeping. The establishment and exercise of individual rights and the privacy of
> the individual seem to be treated in a secondary fashion ... I would note
> particularly that the word 'privacy' is rarely mentioned in the Convention and
> is not included in its title.¹

¹ Text of US Department of State telegram, quoted in Transnational Data Report, vol 1, no 7, p 22.

4.15 The difference in approach between the Council of Europe and the OECD approaches has been explained in terms of the differences in approach existing between the civil and common law systems of law. Thus, it has been stated that:

> In the final result, although substantially similar in core principles, the Convention and the Guidelines could be analogised, albeit in a rough fashion, to the civil and common law approaches, respectively. Common law systems proceed pragmatically formulating the rules of legal behaviour as they acquire experience, while the civil law tradition tends to rely upon codification of rules in advance of action.¹

¹ L Kirsch (1982) 1 Legal Issues of European Integration 21 at 45.

4.16 Although a representative of the US was afforded observer status at the meetings of the Council of Europe's committee of experts, its major input in this area has been through its involvement in the activities of the OECD. This organisation's efforts in the field of data protection parallel those of the Council of Europe and, in 1980, the Council of the OECD agreed 'Guidelines Concerning the Protection of Privacy and Transborder Flows of Personal Data' (hereafter 'the Guidelines'). As approved, the Guidelines are broadly in line with proposals submitted by the US delegation. At first glance, the scope of the Guidelines appears wider than that of the Convention. The latter applies only in the situation where personal information is subjected to automatic processing whilst the latter are to:

> ... apply to personal data, whether in the public or the private sectors, which, because of the manner in which they are processed, or because of their nature or the context in which they are used, pose a danger to privacy and individual liberties.¹

¹ Paragraph 2.

4.17 Despite this discrepancy, in so far as substantive provisions are concerned there is a considerable degree of overlap between the Convention and the Guidelines. Almost invariably, however, the particular provisions of the Guidelines are less precise than their equivalents in the Convention. Thus, in relation to the question of transparency of data processing, the Convention provides that:

> Any person shall be enabled ... to establish the existence of an automated data personal data file, its main purposes, as well as the identity and habitual residence or principal place of business of the controller of the file.¹

whilst the Guidelines merely advocate that:

> There should be a general policy of openness about developments, practices and policies with respect to personal data. Means should be readily available of establishing the existence and nature of personal data, and the main purposes of their use, as well as the identity and usual residence of the data controller.²

¹ Article 8.
² Paragraph 12.

4.18 In addition to its work in producing legal texts, the OECD has also sponsored the development of what is referred to as a privacy generator. This online package is intended to be used by web site developers and others to incorporate procedures and safeguards to ensure that sites operate in conformity with the principles laid down in the Guidelines.[1]

[1] http://cs3-hq.oecd.org/scripts/pwv3/pwhome.htm.

4.19 A further Declaration on Transborder Data Flows was adopted by the OECD in April 1985. This made reference to the fact that:

> Flows of computerised data and information are an important consequence of technological advances and are playing an increasing role in national economies. With the growing economic interdependence of Member countries, these flows acquire an international dimension.

and indicated its signatories' intention to:

1.   *Promote* access to data and information and related services, and avoid the creation of unjustified barriers to the international exchange of data and information.
2.   *Seek* transparency in regulations and policies relating to information, computer and communications services affecting transborder data flows.
3.   *Develop* common approaches for dealing with issues related to transborder data flows and, when appropriate, develop harmonized solutions.
4.   *Consider* possible implications for other countries when dealing with issues related to transborder data flows.

4.20 It is clear from these objectives that commercial and trading interests provide at least as significant a force for action as do concerns for individual rights. Although the Declaration commits its member countries to conduct further work relating to specific types of transborder data flows, especially those accompanying international trade, marketed computer services and computerised information services and intra-corporate data flows, no further measures have been adopted.

The United Nations

4.21 On 20 February 1990, the United Nations' Economic and Social Council agreed 'Guidelines Concerning Computerised Personal Data Files'.[1] These identify ten principles which, it is stated, represent the 'minimum guarantees that should be provided in national legislation'. The principles follow what might be regarded as the standard model, but there are two features of these Guidelines which justify mention at this point. First, they make provision for the application of the principles by international agencies,[2] bodies which might fall outside national laws. Secondly, the United Nations Guidelines provide the option for the extension of the principles both to manual files and to files held concerning legal persons.[3]

[1] E/CN.4/1990/72.

2   Part B.
3   Paragraph 10.

Data protection in the UK

4.22   As with many inventions, the UK could claim credit for some pioneering developments in the field of data protection, failed to develop these and subsequently had to act in response to external pressures. Whilst it is not intended to present an exhaustive survey of the historical development of data protection legislation in general, and the background to the UK Data Protection Act 1998 in particular, many of the aspects of the current legislation can be understood only in terms of their historical context. In particular, the lack of either of the historical motivations of the Germans or Swedes (or indeed of many of the European states which adopted data protection laws in the 1970s) has resulted in a situation where the concept has been seen as somewhat isolated. This chapter will essay an account of the major factors prompting both the introduction and the format of legislation.

The Report of the Committee on Privacy

4.23   As far back as 1969 a Data Surveillance Bill was introduced in the House of Commons by Kenneth Baker MP. If matters had been different, the UK would have possessed the world's first data protection law but, in common with most private member's initiatives, this failed to make significant progress. In the following session, a further Private Member's Bill was introduced by Brian Walden MP. This sought to establish a statutory right to privacy. In a manner which has not changed through a range of governments over the past 34 years, ministers expressed reluctance to establish what would necessarily be a rather vague right. An agreement was made with the Bill's sponsor that in return for its withdrawal, the government would establish the Committee on Privacy.[1] Chaired by Sir Kenneth Younger, the Committee was established in 1970 in return for the agreement by Brian Walden MP to withdraw his Private Member's Bill. The Committee's remit was to:

> ... consider whether legislation is needed to give further protection to the individual citizen and to commercial and industrial interests against intrusions into privacy by private persons or by companies and to make recommendations.

1   Cmnd 5012, 1972.

4.24   Despite two attempts by the Committee to persuade the Home Office to extend its remit to the public sector, the Committee's remit remained restricted to the private sector. Given the fact that many of the most sensitive aspects of data processing (for example, concerned with criminal records and intelligence and medical data) take place primarily in the public sector, this omission weakened the impact of the Committee's work.

4.25 In its report, the Committee devoted a chapter to the implications of the computer. After receiving evidence as to the nature and scale of processing activities, it concluded that '(w)e cannot on the evidence before us conclude that the computer as used in the private sector is at present a threat to privacy'.[1] Despite this, the Committee identified the computer's capacity to store and process large amounts of personal information, to develop personal profiles and to allow remote access to databases as factors causing legitimate public concern. In order to prevent potential dangers from becoming real, ten data protection principles were formulated, which it was recommended should be observed by users on a voluntary basis:

- Information should be regarded as held for a specific purpose and not be used, without appropriate authorisation, for other purposes.
- Access to information should be confined to those authorised to have it for the purpose for which it was supplied.
- The amount of information collected and held should be the minimum necessary for the achievement of the specified purpose.
- In computerised systems handling information for statistical purposes, adequate provision should be made in their design and programs for separating identities from the rest of the data.
- There should be arrangements whereby the subject could be told about the information held concerning him.
- The level of security to be achieved by a system should be specified in advance by the user and should include precautions against the deliberate abuse or misuse of information.
- A monitoring system should be provided to facilitate the detection of any violation of the security system.
- In the design of information systems, periods should be specified beyond which the information should not be retained.
- Data held should be accurate. There should be machinery for the correction of inaccuracy and the updating of information.
- Care should be taken in coding value judgments.[2]

[1]   Cmnd 5012, para 619.
[2]   Cmnd 5012, paras 592–600.

4.26 The notion that generalised statements of acceptable practice should be incorporated in legislation is one which has been widely accepted in European data protection statutes, although there has also been a developing recognition of the need for the principles to be interpreted in the context of particular forms of data processing. The Committee next considered the need to establish machinery to ensure the observance of the above principles. The possibility of introducing a system of self-regulation was considered, but rejected as impractical in view of the scale and diversity of computer applications. Perhaps with an eye to the wider usage of computers, the Committee recommended that the matter be kept under review and, specifically, that:

> ... the Government should legislate to provide itself with machinery for keeping under review the growth in and techniques of gathering personal information and processing it with the help of computers. Such machinery should take the

form of an independent body with members drawn from both the computer world and outside.[1]

[1]   Cmnd 5012, para 621.

4.27 The Committee's report was published in July 1972. Its contents and recommendations were debated in the House of Commons one year later, in July 1973. Speaking in this debate, the Home Secretary studiously avoided expressing any views on the Younger proposals on computers, but announced the publication, later that year, of a White Paper describing computer practices in the public sector and outlining the government's response to the Younger recommendations.[1] In fact, setting a precedent which was to become depressingly familiar, the White Paper, entitled *Computers and Privacy*, was not published until some two-and-a-half years later, in December 1975.[2] As indicated, the White Paper's coverage extended into the public sector with a supplement detailing the extent of government computer usage.

[1]   859 HC Official Report (5th series) col 1956, 13 July 1973.
[2]   Cmnd 6353.

4.28 Whilst the White Paper reiterated the finding of the Younger Committee that there was little concrete evidence of computer abuse, its conclusion was rather different. The potential dangers were considered so substantial that:

> In the Government's view the time has come when those who use computers to handle personal information can no longer remain the sole judges of whether their own systems adequately safeguard privacy.[1]

[1]   Cmnd 6353, para 30.

4.29 Having announced the intention to legislate in the field of data protection, the White Paper indicated that legislation should have two principle components. First, it would lay down standards and objectives to be met by those handling personal information. In determining the content of these, it was suggested that the principles suggested by the Younger Committee would serve as the 'starting point'.[1] Secondly, moving beyond the recommendations of the Younger Committee, machinery should be provided to ensure compliance with the statutory requirements. It was further recognised that the topic was a novel one and that statements of general principles would require considerable extension and specification. Accordingly, it was announced that a Data Protection Committee was to be established, with a remit to make detailed recommendations as to the scope and extent of data protection legislation and as to the form of supervisory mechanism which should be introduced.

[1]   Cmnd 6353, para 33.

The Committee on Data Protection

4.30 With hindsight, the publication of the 1975 White Paper can be seen as marking a high-water point in governmental enthusiasm for the concept of data protection. This enthusiasm was certainly matched by that of the Data Protection Committee, which, under the chairmanship of Sir Norman Lindop, presented its voluminous report in June 1978.[1] This remains the most comprehensive and detailed survey of the impact of data processing activities upon the rights and liberties of the individual conducted in the UK. It proposed that a multi-membered Data Protection Authority should be established. Anyone using a computer to handle personal information would be obliged to register details of their activities with this authority, which would also be charged with ensuring compliance with seven data protection principles. These should be divided into three categories, designed to safeguard the interests of individuals, of those holding information and, finally, the wider interests of society. Thus, it was proposed, legislation should provide that:

In the interests of data subjects:

(1) Data subjects should know what personal data relating to them are handled, why those data are needed, how they will be used, who will use them, for what purpose and for how long.

(2) Personal data should be handled only to the extent and for the purposes made known when they are obtained, or subsequently authorised.

(3) Personal data handled should be accurate and complete, and relevant and timely for the purpose for which they are used.

(4) No more personal data should be handled than are necessary for the purposes made known or authorised.

(5) Data subjects should be able to verify compliance with these principles.

In the interests of users:

(6) Users should be able to handle personal data in the pursuit of their lawful interests or duties to the extent and for the purposes made known or authorised without undue extra cost in money or other resources.

In the interests of the community at large:

(7) The community at large should enjoy any benefits, and be protected from any prejudice, which may flow from the handling of personal data.[2]

[1] Cmnd 7341.
[2] Cmnd 7341, para 21.09.

4.31 In terms of their content, these principles are not dissimilar from those advocated by the Younger Committee and indeed those which form the cornerstones of modern data protection statutes. Noteworthy, however, is the grouping of the principles into three categories: those designed to safeguard the interests of those who handle data; its subjects; and, more novel, those of society as a whole. Such an approach provides explicit recognition of the validity of the various claims and interests involved in this area, and attempts to provide a framework for the resolution of any conflicting claims.

4.32 Recognising the nebulous nature of these broad statements of principle, the Committee recommended that they should be supplemented by the creation of a number, estimated at around 50, of statutory codes of practice targeted at, and providing detailed provisions relating to, particular users or categories of user.[1] Although the notion of statutory codes was initially rejected by the government, these instruments are likely to play a significant role in the 1998 data protection regime.

[1]   Cmnd 7341, para 19.26.

4.33   The Lindop Committee's report was published towards the end of 1978. In early 1979, a general election saw a change of government with the arrival of a Conservative party pledged to reduce bureaucracy. Particularly, given the lack of any evidence of misuse of personal data or tradition of freedom of information, data protection was initially regarded as an unnecessary and unwanted expense and it appeared that little action would be taken. International developments were, however, to bring about a change of mind. During the 1970s, the lack of data protection law could be seen as a factor which would make the UK attractive to companies wishing to establish a European data processing centre. Unlike the situation in other countries, no formal or procedural requirements would limit the nature of the processing which could be conducted. As communications technologies developed to facilitate the international transfer of data, the possibility that national controls might be evaded was not lost on countries possessing data protection laws. Controls over the export of data were introduced. In commending the first Data Protection Bill to the House of Commons, the then Home Secretary commented that it was designed 'to meet public concern, to bring us into step with Europe and to protect our international, commercial and trading interests'.[1] Whilst undoubtedly civil libertarian concerns are fundamental to the concept of data protection, it is significant that these represented only one out of five interests identified and that, at least numerically, commercial and trading factors assumed greater significance. At least one reason for this can be seen in a letter to *The Times* from a leading industrialist arguing that:

> Lack of computer privacy legislation may seriously affect our overseas trade. Of the nine EEC countries only Italy, Ireland and the UK have no laws or firm legislative programme. Britain is regarded as becoming a 'pirate offshore data haven' by countries that have legislated on computer privacy.[2]

Continuing, concern was expressed at the possibility that privacy considerations might serve as a smokescreen for the imposition of data sanctions against the UK.

> It is difficult to distinguish between private and commercial data when it is being transmitted between countries. It would be all too easy for foreign data inspection boards to forbid export or import of data ostensibly to protect its citizen's privacy but in reality to protect employment or revenue by restricting trade with Britain.

[1]   HC Official Report (6th series) col 562, 11 April 1983.
[2]   *The Times*, 3 March 1980.

4.34   The validity of this observation is demonstrated by several well-documented instances in which British companies had been prevented from carrying out data processing or related activities on behalf of Swedish companies, owing to the Swedish authorities' concern at the lack of legislative safeguards.[1]

1   See, for example, J Bing *A Decade of Computers and Law* (1980, Universitetsforlaget) pp 70–71, describing the loss of contracts involving the processing of financial and medical data because of these concerns.

The Data Protection Act 1984

4.35   In March 1981, in response to a parliamentary question as to the government's intentions, the Home Secretary announced that: 'The Government has decided in principle to introduce legislation for this purpose when an opportunity occurs.'[1] In keeping with many developments in the field, opportunity was to be some time in coming. The report of the Committee on Data Protection was largely ignored and, in particular, the Home Secretary announced that instead of establishing an independent data protection authority, responsibility for the operation of the data protection regime would be vested in the Home Office.

1   HC Official Report (6th series) col 161, 19 March 1981.

4.36   This element of the government's response produced considerable criticism, with sceptical commentators expressing doubts as to whether the Home Office, which enjoys at least a measure of responsibility for some of the most sensitive computerised informational practices involving the police and national security agencies, could constitute a satisfactory public guardian against any abuse emanating from these quarters.

4.37   Following a further round of consultations, a further White Paper was published in April 1982.[1] By this time, the Lindop Report was reduced to the status of 'very helpful background information'. In one fundamental respect, however, the government view had changed. Following sustained criticism of its proposal that the Home Office should operate the registration scheme, the need for independent supervision of data users was recognised. The Lindop suggestion of a multi-membered Data Protection Authority was not, however, accepted; instead it was proposed to appoint a single Data Protection Registrar.

1   Cmnd 8539.

4.38   A Data Protection Bill, based on the provisions of the White Paper, was introduced in the House of Lords in November 1982. It successfully passed through that House, but fell at the committee stage in the House of Commons when Parliament was dissolved prior to the 1983 general election. An amended Bill was speedily introduced by the incoming government, receiving the Royal Assent on 12 July of the Orwellian year, 1984.

4.39   Given that the Data Protection Act 1984 was replaced in its entirety by the Data Protection Act 1998 detailed consideration of its contents is outside the scope of this book. Many of its provisions do, of course, remain applicable under the current regime and decisions made by the courts and the Data Protection Tribunal which was established as an appellate body continue to be cited as valid precedent. A few general comments concerning and a brief assessment of the impact of the 1984 Act may be helpful in providing initial comment on the impact and relevance of data protection within a UK context.

4.40   As indicated above the legislation was introduced not out of any genuine enthusiasm by the (Conservative) government of the day. Time after time *Hansard* reports comments from ministers to the effect that the legislation was being introduced for commercial reasons in order to enable the UK to ratify the Council of Europe Convention. This was to be done at the most minimal level. On every occasion where the Convention prescribed minimal standards but left the way open for signatories to provide additional protection in national legislation, the UK Data Protection Act 1984 remained conspicuously silent. Moving ahead some 15 years to the introduction of the Data Protection Act 1998 *Hansard* reports on the debates are replete with comments from (Labour) ministers to the effect that the legislation was being introduced reluctantly in order to comply at a minimal level with European requirements, this time in the form of European Directive 95/46. It is tempting to suggest that the Conservative ministers of the 1980s could have succeeded in an action alleging breach of copyright in their speeches.

4.41   Lack of governmental commitment to the concept has been a factor which bedevils data protection to this day. A decision that the concept should not impose any financial burdens on the taxpayer led to the introduction of an outdated and bureaucratic system of registration whereby anyone involved in processing personal data was obliged to register details of their activities and pay a fee. Failure so to do constituted a criminal offence. Beyond providing the supervisory agency's only significant source of revenue, it is difficult to identify any significant benefits arising from the concept. The financial straight-jacket imposed in the Data Protection Act 1984 continues under the Data Protection Act 1998 with the consequence that whilst terminology changes from registration to notification,[1] the requirement to pay what is effectively a tax associated with computer ownership remains. The 1984 Act might fairly be described as an unwanted and somewhat neglected statute. Over the years research has been carried out on behalf of the Data Protection Registrar (now Information Commissioner) seeking to ascertain public awareness of the Data Protection Acts and of related issues. The following passages are taken from the Commissioner's report for the year 2000.

> On a spontaneous level, as is the case every year, there is little understanding of the rights that people have which reinforce their personal privacy – more importantly the level of understanding of anything has fallen significantly with the best response being 23% who know it exists but little else and only 19% knowing about subject access rights.

[1]   See para 6.17 below.

4.42   Even when individuals were prompted awareness of the existence of the legislation has been limited.

Table 2

	1992	1993	1994	1995	1996	1997	1998	1999	2000
	%	%	%	%	%	%	%	%	%
Prompted awareness of Data Protection Act 1998	38	38	47	44	48	62	67	59	69
Semi-prompted awareness of Data Protection Act 1998	34	35	45	42	40	30	38	44	40

These results coupled with other evidence from the survey concerning awareness of the existence of the Office of Data Protection are disappointing. Although evidence is scanty it does appear that very little use is made of the rights, in particular that of subject access, conferred upon individuals by the Data Protection Act 1998.

4.43 Recent events such as the attempt by police forces to blame data protection requirements for failure to pass on information which may have prevented the Soham murders suggests that data protection retains a role as a scapegoat for organisational failings. Given, as was discussed in the Chapter 3, the increasing role and importance of information in our everyday lives, it is disappointing and perhaps even dangerous that there should continue to be such limited understanding what data protection is and is not about.

The EU Directive and the Data Protection Act 1998

4.44 Until the early 1990s, the EU had played a peripheral role in the data protection arena. This could be ascribed to two main causes. First, the limited nature of the legislative competencies conferred by the establishing treaties gave rise to doubts as to whether, and to what extent, the EC was empowered to act in this field. Although the increasing importance of information as a commodity within the Single Market has provided a basis for European action, the exclusion of matters coming within the ambit of national security and, to a partial extent, criminal and taxation policy, has served to limit the scope of the EU's intervention.

4.45 A second factor influencing work in this field had been a reluctance on the part of the Commission to duplicate work being conducted under the auspices of the Council of Europe. In 1979, the European Parliament's Legal Affairs Committee published a report 'on Community activities to be undertaken or continued with a view to safeguarding the rights of the individual in the face of developing technical progress in the field of automatic data processing'.[1] In it, the Committee recognised both the dangers to individual privacy resulting from computer databases and also the implications of divergent national provisions for the Community's competition policy and for the creation of a common market in data processing. Accordingly, it proposed that a Community directive be prepared 'on the harmonization of legislation on data protection to provide citizens of the Community with the maximum protection'. In the parliamentary debate which followed the publication of this report, the Commission representative expressed his sympathy with the motives behind the proposals, but argued that no Community action should be taken until there was a clearer indication of progress at the Council of Europe. In 1981, the Commission addressed a Recommendation to member states that they sign and ratify the Convention.[2]

---

[1]   PE 56.386/fin Doc 100/79.
[2]   OJ 1981 L 246/31.

4.46   By 1990, the Convention had been signed by all the Community member states, but ratified only by six.[1] As will be described, the Convention affords considerable discretion to signatories regarding the manner in which they comply with their obligations. The instrument also establishes minimum standards. A number of member states, such as Germany and Sweden, had enacted laws which were considerably in advance of the Convention's minimum standards, whilst others, such as the UK, had openly indicated an intention to do the bare minimum necessary to satisfy obligations under that instrument. By 1990, Commission concern at the effect discrepancies in the member states' laws and regulations might have on inter-community trade resulted in proposals being brought forward for a directive 'on the protection of individuals with regard to the processing of personal data and on the free movement of such data'.[2] The objective of the proposal was stated to be to harmonise the data protection laws of the member states at a 'high level'.[3] The Community legislation, it was further stated, would 'give substance to and amplify'[4] the provisions of the Convention.

---

[1]   Denmark, France, Germany, Luxembourg, Spain and the UK.
[2]   OJ 1990 C 277/03.
[3]   OJ 1990 C 277/03, Preamble, para 7.
[4]   OJ 1990 C 277/03, para 22.

4.47   The Commission proposal for a general directive in the area of data protection was accompanied by a further proposal for a directive 'concerning the protection of personal data and privacy in the context of public digital telecommunications networks'.[1] Following a five-year journey through the EU's legislative process, the Data Protection Directive was adopted on 24 October 1995[2] with a requirement that it be implemented within the member states by 24 October 1998. The Telecoms Directive – which for a while appeared to have been dropped from the legislative agenda – resurfaced, to be adopted in December 1997.[3] It also required to be implemented by October 1998. The, so called, Telecoms Data Protection Directive proved to be a somewhat short-lived measure. In conjunction with a much broader reform of the European telecommunications regulatory regime, the directive was replaced by the Directive 'concerning the processing of personal data and the protection of privacy in the electronic communications sector'[4]. This required to be implemented in the member states by 31 October 2003. The provisions of the communications directive will be discussed in more detail in Chapter 9.

1   OJ 1990 C 277/12.
2   Directive 95/46/EC, OJ 1995 L 281/31.
3   Directive 97/66/EC concerning the protection of personal data and privacy in the context of public digital telecommunications networks. OJ 1998 L 24.
4   Directive 2002/58/EC, OJ 2002 L 201/37 (Privacy and Electronic Communications Directive).

4.48   The timetable set for implementation of the general data protection directive was not to be widely met. Although the UK Data Protection Act 1998 received the Royal Assent in July 1988, this essentially constituted only a framework statute. It was provided that the substantive provisions of the Act would not come into force until a date to be fixed by regulation. This was to allow time for the drafting of necessary items of secondary legislation. This task proved more complex than initially foreseen, and it was not until 1 March 2000 that the new legislation entered into force. In its failure timeously to implement the Data Protection Directive,[1] the UK was joined by a majority of the member states. Legal action was raised by the Commission against Denmark, France, Germany, Ireland, Luxembourg and the Netherlands, alleging a continuing failure to implement the directive although in the case of every state except Luxembourg, the belated implementation of the directive resulted in the legal proceedings being abandoned.[2]

1   Directive 95/46/EC.
2   For current information on the status of implementation, see http://europa.eu.int/comm/internal_market/en/media/dataprot/law/impl.htm.

4.49   Although changes were made to the Data Protection Directive[1] during its prolonged passage through the EU's legislative process, its basic formulations are now ten years old. In the world of information technology, ten years is a long time and there is a real risk that developments such as the Internet and WWW will render elements of the new data protection regime obsolete before they even enter into force. The very right of the EU to legislate in the data protection field has not gone unchallenged. As discussed above, the limited legislative competence possessed by the EU institutions posed some difficulties for the UK at the time of the passage of the Data Protection Act 1998.

1   Directive 95/46/EC.

4.50   The legal basis for the Data Protection Directive[1] is stated to lie in the provisions of art 100A of the Treaty of Rome. This provides that the Community's law-making bodies may:

> adopt the measures for the approximation of the provisions laid down by law, regulation or administrative action in Member States which have as their object the establishing and functioning of the internal market.

Reliance upon art 100A has a further significant consequence in that any harmonising measures introduced under its authority have to secure 'a high level of protection'. Effectively, therefore, the Directive has to secure a level of protection equivalent to the highest currently available in the member states. It is unclear how effective the Directive has been in this regard, with complaints being aired from countries such as Germany that implementation might dilute their existing regimes, especially in respect of transborder data flows. For the UK, implementation of the Directive required significant change and expansion to the Data Protection Act 1984. A Consultation Paper was published by the Home Office in March 1996, seeking views on the implementation of the directive and indicating a preference for a minimalist approach to law reform:

> Over-elaborate data protection threatens competitiveness, and does not necessarily bring additional benefits for individuals. *It follows that the Government intends to go no further in implementing the Directive than is absolutely necessary to satisfy the UK's obligations in European law. It will consider whether any additional changes to the current data protection regime are needed so as to ensure that it does not go beyond what is required by the Directive and the Council of Europe Convention.*[2]

[1] Directive 95/46/EC.
[2] Paragraph 1.2 (emphasis in original).

4.51 In particular, the Home Office expressed an initial preference for implementing the requirements of the directive by statutory instrument under the authority of the European Communities Act 1972. Although such an approach would have the benefit of enabling the speedy introduction of the required changes, such legislation is limited to matters falling within the competence of the EU. The Preamble to the Data Protection Directive[1] recognises that:

> Whereas the activities referred to in Titles V and VI of the Treaty on European Union regarding public safety, defence, State security or the activities of the State in the area of criminal laws fall outside the scope of Community law, without prejudice to the obligations incumbent upon Member States under Article 56(2), Article 57 or Article 100A of the Treaty establishing the European Community; whereas the processing of personal data that is necessary to safeguard the economic well-being of the State does not fall within the scope of this Directive where such processing relates to State security matters.

Whilst art 1(2) provides that the Directive is not to apply to processing:

> ... in the course of an activity which falls outside the scope of Community law, such as those provided for by Titles V and VI of the Treaty on European Union and in any case to processing operations concerning public security, defence, State security (including the economic well-being of the State when the processing operation relates to State security matters) and the activities of the State in areas of criminal law, (or) ...by a natural person in the course of a purely personal or household activity.

[1] Directive 95/46/EC.

4.52   More recently the scope of the Data Protection Directive[1] was at issue in the case of *Bodil Lindqvist*[2] which was referred by the Swedish courts to the European Court of Justice for a preliminary ruling concerning a number of questions relating to the scope and impact of the Directive in the context of a home page set up on the Internet by a Swedish citizen in connection with her voluntary work for the Swedish Lutheran church.

¹   Directive 95/46/EC.
²   Case 101/01 [2004] QB 1014.

4.53   The substantive issues at stake in the case will be considered in more detail in subsequent chapters. On the jurisdictional point, however, it was argued on behalf of Mrs Lindqvist that her conduct, which related to the processing of personal data for charitable and religious purposes, fell outside the EU's legislative competence. This contention was supported by the Advocate General who pointed out that the Data Protection Directive¹ had been adopted under the authority of art 100A of the Treaty of Rome which empowers harmonisation measures where this is necessary for the attainment of the single market. The argument, effectively, is that the maintenance of different standards of data protection within the member states constitutes an impediment to the free movement of data. The Directive, essentially, sought primarily to overcome barriers to the free movement of personal data between the member states which might otherwise arise because of discrepancies between national data protection laws. In the present case, he argued:

> the home page in question was set up by Mrs Lindqvist without any intention of economic gain, solely as an ancillary activity to her voluntary work as a catechist in the parish community and outside the remit of any employment relationship. The processing of the personal data in question was therefore carried out in the course of a non-economic activity which had no connection (or at least no direct connection) with the exercise of the fundamental freedoms protected by the Treaty and is not governed by any specific rules at Community level.

¹   Directive 95/46/EC.

4.54   The European Court of Justice disagreed. Referring to its previous decision in the case of *Österreichischer Rundfunk*¹ it held that the specific limitations on the Data Protection Directive's² application – to activities provided for by Titles V and VI of the Treaty on European Union and processing operations concerning public security, defence, state security and activities in areas of criminal law – were restricted to activities on the part of state authorities and were not connected to the actions of individuals. It may be queried whether this view is accurate. At least for the UK many data controllers have registered or notified the intent to process personal data for crime prevention detection or persecution purposes, a fact which can be validated by the act of studying a few of the myriad notices on display in every High Street describing the rationale for the use of CCTV systems in shops and other private premises.

¹   *Rechnungshof v Österreichischer Rundfunk* Joined Cases C-465/00, C-138/01 and C-139/01 [2003] ECR I-1489.
²   Directive 95/46/EC.

4.55   Significant aspects of the Data Protection Act 1984 concern activities coming under these headings, in particular, where the processing activities of the police or Inland Revenue are concerned. These would have remained subject to the 1984 regime whilst other forms of activity would have been subject to the new regulatory schema. Responses to the Home Office Consultation Paper indicated a strong preference for the introduction of new primary legislation and, perhaps influenced also by a change of government, the intent to proceed on this basis was announced in the Queen's Speech in June 1997. Following a further consultation exercise,[1] the Data Protection Bill was introduced into the House of Lords in January 1998. Its progress through Parliament was relatively uncontroversial, with only one division being required throughout its parliamentary passage.[2] The major feature of the Bill's progress was the very large number, more than 200 in total, of amendments tabled by the government. The Act received the Royal Assent on 16 July, although, as indicated above, its entry into force was delayed pending the drafting of what proved to be 17 items of secondary legislation.

[1]   *Data protection. The Government's Proposals.*
[2]   This was in relation to proposals in the Bill to provide ministers with wide-ranging powers to exempt processing activities from the subject access provisions. The House of Lords voted to remove these powers from the Bill. A more closely defined provision was introduced in the House of Commons.

The Data Protection Act 1998 and its relationship with the Directive

4.56   As an initial comment, it may be noted that the Data Protection Act 1998 is considerably larger than its predecessor. The Data Protection Act 1984 has 43 sections and 6 Schedules; the 1998 statute has 75 sections and 16 Schedules. To an extent greater than its 1984 precursor, the Act provides only a framework, with significant matters remaining to be determined by statutory instruments. Although this approach will allow easier modification and updating of the legislation than was possible with the 1984 Act, significant issues relating to the identification of those data controllers who may be exempted from the notification requirement are not covered in the Act.

4.57   Given that the Data Protection Act 1998 is intended to implement a European Directive,[1] account has to be taken of the provisions of the latter. In *Campbell v MGN Ltd*,[2] Lord Phillips of Worth Matravers MR, stated:

> In interpreting the Act it is appropriate to look to the Directive for assistance. The Act should, if possible, be interpreted in a manner that is consistent with the Directive. Furthermore, because the Act has, in large measure, adopted the wording of the Directive, it is not appropriate to look for the precision in the use of language that is usually to be expected from the parliamentary draftsman. A purposive approach to making sense of the provisions is called for.

The European Court of Justice has also held in *Österreichischer Rundfunk*[3] that at least some of the provisions of the Directive are sufficiently precise to be relied upon directly by individuals within the member states.

[1]   Directive 95/46/EC.

2   [2002] EWCA Civ 1373, [2003] QB 633 at [96].
3   Joined Cases C-465/00, C-138/01 and C-139/01 [2003] ECR I-4989.

4.58 The Data Protection Act 1998 will extend significantly the area of application of the legislation, including regulating some systems of manual records. In the accompanying Explanatory and Financial Memorandum, it is estimated that compliance with the new regime will result in start-up costs to private sector data users of some £836m, with recurring costs of £630m. The start-up costs for the public and voluntary sectors are estimated at £194m and £120m respectively, with recurring costs of £75m and £37m. These figures are in addition to the costs incurred in complying with the present data protection regime, although no evidence has been published as to the scale of the present costs. The Home Office Regulatory Appraisal and Compliance Cost Assessment makes it clear that estimates are based upon a very small sample of users. Only four large and three small manufacturers were surveyed, for example, and although much publicity has been given to headline figures of a £1bn cost arising from implementation, the assessment document itself highlights the need to approach these estimates with caution. The Registrar has also questioned the accuracy of the financial calculations,[1] suggesting that this may have resulted from misunderstandings as to the nature of the Data Protection Directive's[2] requirements.

1   Press Release, 28 January 1998.
2   Directive 95/46/EC.

4.59 To date, it does not appear that data protection has had a significant impact on public consciousness. To justify costs of some £20 for every inhabitant of the UK, it is to be hoped that the new legislation, perhaps coupled with other legislative initiatives in the field of human rights and freedom of information, will provide the basis for enhanced public awareness of the crucial importance of information in modern society, and the need to secure an appropriate balance between those who hold and use data and those who may be affected by such activities.

Data protection in the wider context

4.60 Although a right of access to information held by credit reference agencies had been available since 1976 under the provisions of the Consumer Credit Act 1974, the Data Protection Act 1984 has been seen as a somewhat isolated measure. In particular, the lack of anything approaching a right to privacy has deprived the legislation of solid legal foundations, whilst criticism has been voiced by the Registrar that inadequate account has been taken of data protection issues in formulating other statutes, such as those concerned with the community charge or poll tax, which involve the obtaining and use of personal data.[1]

1   See the Fourth Annual Report of the Data Protection Registrar (1989).

4.61   The situation in 1998 is significantly different, and the new Data Protection Act 1998 should be seen as one of a trilogy of measures operating in the same general field. The Human Rights Act 1998 incorporates the European Convention on Human Rights into domestic law. Of particular relevance to data protection are the provisions of arts 8 and 10. Article 8 provides that 'everyone has the right to respect for his private and family life, his home and his correspondence'. Any interference with such rights by a public authority must be sanctioned by law and be:

> ... necessary in a democratic society in the interests of national security, public safety or the economic well being of the country, for the prevention of disorder or crime, for the protection of health or morals, or for the protection of the rights and freedoms of others.[1]

In its jurisprudence, the European Court of Human Rights has interpreted art 8 liberally to include rights of access to personal data. Indeed, following the decision of the court in the case of *Gaskin v UK*,[2] changes have required to be made to statutory provisions relating to subject access.

[1]   Article 10(2).
[2]   (1990) 12 EHRR 36.

4.62   Perhaps the most controversial aspect of the interface between the Human Rights Act 1998 and the Data Protection 1998 concerns the activities of the media. Article 10 of the European Convention on Human Rights guarantees the right to freedom of expression. Once again, this may be subject to derogation on conditions similar to those applying to respect for private and family life. Clearly, media activities, especially in the field of investigative journalism, may conflict with art 8 rights. Both the Data Protection 1998 and the Human Rights Act 1998 contain provisions and procedures for seeking to resolve such conflicts. Rather surprisingly, these differ in certain respects with the former statute's provisions, receiving a considerably warmer reception from media representatives than those found in the human rights legislation.[1]

[1]   See Chapter 9.

4.63   A second area where the Data Protection Act 1998 may have to relate with other measures is connected with the introduction of freedom of information legislation. A White Paper, *Your Right to Know*, was published in December 1997,[1] and a Bill was introduced into Parliament in 1999, receiving Royal Assent in 2000 but not entering into force until January 2005.[2] There is clear overlap between the two concepts and the Information Commissioner has responsibility in respect of both statutes. In other countries which have freedom of information legislation, it has been estimated that some 80% of requests relate to the inquirer's own personal data. In respect of this issue, freedom of information legislation may well supplement rights under the Data Protection 1998 by extending these to a wider range of manual records, but, with proposals for significant variations in access rights and exceptions thereto, the prospect arises of what the House of Commons Select Committee on Public Administration described as a 'confusing and messy patchwork of different provisions under which one may obtain access to one's own file'.[3] Even more significantly, however, there will be the potential for conflict between the aims and objectives of the statutes where personal data relates to a party other than the inquirer. Here, whilst freedom of information may give priority to openness and accessibility, data protection seeks to protect individual privacy and confidentiality.

1   Cm 3818.
2   Separate legislation applies within Scotland.
3   *Third Report from the Select Committee on Public Administration* (HC Paper 398/1 (1997–98)), para 17.

4.64 In many respects, it might have been desirable had reform to the Data Protection 1998 proceeded in parallel with freedom of information legislation. The Select Committee, whilst welcoming the prospect of freedom of information legislation, has commented critically on the possibility for overlap and conflict between the two systems. It noted also the fact that the Data Protection Registrar had not been consulted prior to the publication of the White Paper.[1] It is perhaps ironic that whilst the prospect of the European Directives adopted was used to justify much needed reform of the UK system during the first half of the 1990s, the desire to comply with the timetable for its implementation resulted in the 1998 Act being brought forward in isolation rather than as part of a comprehensive and coherent strategy governing access to information. To compound the irony, of course, the delay in formulating necessary items of secondary legislation meant that the UK ultimately failed to meet the European deadline.

1   *Third Report from the Select Committee on Public Administration* (HC Paper 398/1 (1997–98)), para 21.

Chapter 5

The scope of data protection

Introduction

5.1   As described in the previous chapters, the prime purpose of data protection legislation is to guard against some of the dangers identified as arising from the involvement of the computer in the record-keeping process. The Data Protection Directive provides that:

> Member States shall protect the fundamental rights and freedoms of natural persons, and in particular their right to privacy with respect to the processing of personal data.[1]

The word privacy appears on a dozen occasions in the legislation. Not surprisingly, given its very limited recognition in the UK's general law, the 'p' word does not appear at all in the Data Protection Act 1998 but there is clear recognition in the case law, perhaps most notably the decision of the Court of Appeal in the case of *Durant v Financial Services Authority*[2] that this is the purpose behind the statute. As was stated by Lord Justice Buxton:

> The guiding principle is that the Act, following Directive 95/46, gives rights to data subjects in order to protect their privacy.[3]

[1]   Directive 95/46/EC, art 1.
[2]   [2003] EWCA Civ 1746.
[3]   [2003] EWCA Civ 1746 at [79].

5.2   Neither the Data Protection Act 1998 nor the Data Protection Directive[1] makes any attempt to define the technologies involved in data processing. The practice of providing for what is generally known as technical neutrality is of long standing. When the Police and Criminal Evidence Act 1984, a measure including provisions relating to the admissibility of computer-generated documents as evidence in the course of criminal proceedings, was before Parliament, an attempt to include a definition of the word 'computer' was opposed by the Minister of State on the ground that:

Ossifying a definition of 'computer' on the face of a bill at the present stage of technological development might in the medium term, and possibly in the short term, be more of a nuisance than an advantage. [2]

[1] Directive 95/46/EC.
[2] HC Official Report, SC E (Police and Criminal Evidence Bill), col 1759, 6 March 1984.

5.3 Rather than defining the equipment involved, both the Data Protection Act 1998 and the Data Protection Directive[1] lay stress upon the activity of processing personal data. Article 3 of the Directive provides that it is to apply:

to the processing of personal data wholly or partly by automatic means, and to the processing otherwise than by automatic means of personal data which form part of a filing system or are intended to form part of a filing system.

A number of important points arise from this definition. The first, and the subject of recent judicial attention in the UK is the question what elements of data are to be considered as personal to a particular subject. Next comes the issue what forms of activity constitute processing. In the situation where this is carried out by 'automatic means', effectively through the use of some form of computer equipment, there are few areas of difficulty although, as will be discussed below, the concept of processing is exceptionally wide ranging. More contentious is the extent to which the legislation applies to the processing of data 'otherwise than by automatic means', that is as part of some system of paper based or manual files. The following sections in this chapter will describe and assess the key definitions in the legislation.

[1] Directive 95/46/EC.

Personal data

5.4 The premise underlying data protection legislation is that the processing of data relating to individuals constitutes a threat to the subject's rights and freedoms. If an individual cannot be identified from the manner in which data is collected, processed or used, there can be no significant threat to privacy and no justification for the application of legislative controls. The question may arise, however, when an individual may be identified. In one of the leading international cases in data protection, the German Constitutional Court held unlawful on data protection grounds a proposal for a national census. Amongst other issues concerned with the use to which the census data might be put, concern was expressed that although data would be published only in aggregated format, modern data processing techniques might permit the de-anonymisation of census data.[1]

[1] 'The Census Decision' (1984) 5 HRLJ 94.

5.5 The Data Protection Directive is stated as applying to the processing of:

... any information relating to an identified or identifiable natural person (data subject); an identifiable person is one who can be identified directly or indirectly, in particular by reference to an identification number or to one or more factors specific to his physical, psychological, mental, economic, cultural or social identity.[1]

The Preamble to the Directive states additionally that in order 'to determine whether a person is identifiable, account should be taken of all the means likely reasonably to be used either by the controller or by any other person to identify the said person'.[2]

[1]   Directive 95/46/EC, art 2(a).
[2]   Recital 26.

5.6   A number of member states, including the UK, have departed from the exact wording used in the Data Protection Directive.[1] Some member states (not including the UK) have chosen to extend the scope of their national laws to data relating to deceased persons, whereas the majority of member states have chosen to limit protection to information relating to living individuals. In implementing these provisions, the Data Protection Act 1998 provides that personal data:

> ... means data which relates to a living individual who can be identified—
> (a)   from those data; or
> (b)   from those data and other information which is in the possession of, or is likely to come into the possession of, the data controller,
> and includes any expression of opinion about the individual and any indications of the intentions of the data controller or any other person in respect of the individual.[2]

[1]   Directive 95/46/EC.
[2]   Section 1(1).

5.7   The decision as to whether an individual is identifiable has to be made by reference to information available to the data user. Clearly, where the data is directly linked to the name of an individual, this criterion will be satisfied. A statement that 'Ian Lloyd is the author of *Information Technology Law*' will be classed as personal data. The Data Protection Act 1998 provides that the individual may be identified from the personal data held and from 'other information which is in the possession of, or is likely to come into the possession of, the data controller'. This other information need not be held on computer. An example of the application of this provision might be seen in the case of a computer system which is designed to log telephone calls. It is likely that the record will indicate only the instrument from which the call emanated, together with details of the destination and duration of the call. No reference will be made to any individual, but possession of a telephone directory will enable the person responsible for the call to be identified. Where the data is transferred to a third party, the Act will not regulate the transaction where the additional key necessary to identify data subjects is not also transferred or disclosed.[1]

[1]   Section 1(9).

Relating to the data subject

5.8 In the example cited above there is no doubt that all of the data relates to a single data subject. In other situations matters may not be so straightforward and the determination whether and to what extent data relates to a particular data subject may be critical to questions relating to the application of the Data Protection Act 1998, especially perhaps in the context of a request for subject access. This point was discussed extensively in the case of *Durant v Financial Services Authority*.[1]

[1]   [2003] EWCA Civ 1746.

5.9   The appellant had been involved in a protracted dispute with Barclays Bank. This had resulted in unsuccessful litigation in 1993 and a continuing course of complaints to the industry regulatory body, the Financial Services Authority. The present case arose from a request from the appellant for access to a range of computerised and manual records which it was claimed came under the ambit of the subject access provisions of the Data Protection Act 1998. Although some information was supplied access to other records was provided only in partial form through the concealment or redaction of information which it was considered related to third parties. Other records were withheld on the ground either that the information contained therein did not constitute personal data relating to the appellant or, in the case of a number of records which were maintained in manual filing systems, that the system did not come within the concept of a relevant filing system as defined in the legislation.

5.10   Although there was no doubt that much if not all of the data in question had been generated following complaints from the appellant, the critical issue was whether it related to him. Counsel for Durant argued that the term 'relate to' should be interpreted broadly to encompass any data which might be generated following a search of a database made by reference to an individual's name. Thus, for example, a document describing the action which had been taken in response to a complaint from the appellant would be classed as personal data by virtue merely of the fact that his name would appear within the text. Counsel for the respondent advocated a more restrictive approach making reference to the *Shorter Oxford English Dictionary* which contained two definitions of the term, a broad reference to having 'some connection with, be connected to' and a more restrictive notion that there should be reference to or concern with a subject, 'implying, in this context, a more or less direct connection with an individual'. The latter approach was, it was suggested, consistent with the dicta of Lord Hoffmann in the case of *R v Brown*[1] decided under the Data Protection Act 1984 where it was stated that personal data was data 'concerning a living individual'.

[1]   [1996] AC 543.

5.11   This more restrictive interpretation was adopted by the Court of Appeal. The purpose of the subject access provisions in the legislation was, it was stated:

to enable him to check whether the data controller's processing of it unlawfully infringes his privacy and, if so, to take such steps as the Act provides, for example in sections 10 to 14 [of the Data Protection Act 1998], to protect it. It is not an automatic key to any information, readily accessible or not, of matters in which he may be named or involved. Nor is to assist him, for example, to obtain discovery of documents that may assist him in litigation or complaints against third parties.

...

It follows from what I have said that not all information retrieved from a computer search against an individual's name or unique identifier is personal data within the Act. Mere mention of the data subject in a document held by a data controller does not necessarily amount to his personal data. Whether it does so in any particular instance depends on where it falls in a continuum of relevance or proximity to the data subject as distinct, say, from transactions or matters in which he may have been involved to a greater or lesser degree. It seems to me that there are two notions that may be of assistance. The first is whether the information is biographical in a significant sense, that is, going beyond the recording of the putative data subject's involvement in a matter or an event that has no personal connotations, a life event in respect of which his privacy could not be said to be compromised. The second is one of focus. The information should have the putative data subject as its focus rather than some other person with whom he may have been involved or some transaction or event in which he may have figured or have had an interest, for example, as in this case, an investigation into some other person's or body's conduct that he may have instigated. In short, it is information that affects his privacy, whether in his personal or family life, business or professional capacity.[1]

[1] *Durant v Financial Services Authority* [2003] EWCA Civ 1746 at paras 27-8.

5.12 This approach adopts, it is suggested, an overly restrictive view of the rationale of data protection laws. Whilst determining the legality of data processing and correcting errors certainly constitute important elements, equally important is the ability to become aware what data is held. Much of the Data Protection Directive[1] and Data Protection Act 1998's requirements relating to the factors legitimising data processing stress the importance of the data subject being aware what is happening with regard to personal data. As was stated by the German Constitutional Court in the 1980s:

The possibilities of inspection and of gaining influence have increased to a degree hitherto unknown and may influence the individual's behaviour by the psychological pressure exerted by public interest ... if someone cannot predict with sufficient certainty which information about himself in certain areas is known to his social milieu, and cannot estimate sufficiently the knowledge of parties to whom communication may possibly be made, he is crucially inhibited in his freedom to plan or to decide freely and without being subject to any pressure/influence.[2]

[1] Directive 95/46/EC.
[2] 'The Census Decision' (1984) 5 Human Rights Law Journal 94.

5.13   Such factors support the adoption of an expansive definition of the scope of personal data. The court continued to make the important point that the individual's right under the Data Protection Act 1998 is to have details of personal data held communicated to him in intelligible. The right is not to a copy of any document although obviously this will in many cases represent the easiest means for a data controller to comply with an access request. In a case such as the present, it may well be that personal data in the form of an individual's name or other identifying data makes a peripheral appearance in a record. Rather than arguing that the appearance of the data does not come within the scope of the Act, it might be preferable to focus upon the extent of the information which might be supplied. Whilst the court was clearly concerned that the data protection legislation was being invoked in the present case in the attempt to obtain discovery of documents and data that could not be obtained though other legal channels it might have been preferable to have laid greater stress on the limited nature of the information which would be classed as personal data.

5.14   In supporting its conclusion, the court placed some stress upon the specific provision in the Data Protection Act 1998 that the definition of personal data extended to:

> any expression of opinion about the individual and any indication of the intentions of the data controller or any other person in respect of the individual;

This, it was argued:

> supports an otherwise narrow construction. If the term had the broader construction for which Miss Houghton contended, such provision would have been otiose.[1]

---

[1]   *Durant v Financial Services Authority* [2003] EWCA Civ 1746 at para 29.

5.15   Whilst there is considerable semantic logic behind this approach, the specific reference to ideas and intentions is not found in the Data Protection Directive[1] and represents perhaps an unfortunate legacy from the original UK Data Protection Act 1984. This included a widely criticised distinction between statements of opinion, which were classed as personal data and statements of intention which were not. The argument put forward by the government of the day was that statements of intention were personal to the data holder rather than to the subject. This is certainly argument but the point applies with equal if not greater validity with regard to statements of opinion. Even the then Data Protection Registrar was moved to comment to the effect that he found the distinction unclear and the provision in the Data Protection Act 1998 should perhaps be seen as a measure to remove what had generally been considered an unsatisfactory distinction rather than a conscious effort to limit the scope of the definition of personal data.

---

[1]   Directive 95/46/EC.

Data matching

5.16   In the situation where data is held solely by one data controller, the question of whether an individual is identifiable may readily be resolved. We live, however, in the age of the computer network. Distributive computing, epitomised at its most extensive by the Internet, renders the issue of physical possession of data secondary to the question of access. Practices such as data matching allow controllers to trawl across the contents of a wide range of computers. The term 'data matching' has been defined as involving:

> The comparison of data held by different data users (or by the same data user in different contexts). The aim of the comparison is not primarily the creation of a larger file of information about the data subject but the identification of anomalies and inconsistencies within a single set of data or between two or more different sets.[1]

[1]   Office of the Data Protection Registrar *A Guide to Developing Codes of Practice on Data Matching* (1998).

5.17   Operating principally in the public sector, the concept of data matching can be seen as an equivalent to some of the direct marketing techniques described above, but with the essential difference that it involves searches across a range of databases controlled by different government departments. In the past, strict controls have limited or, in many cases, prevented the exchange of data held by different departments, but provisions in the Social Security (Administration) Fraud Act 1997 provide a statutory basis for the exchange of information between the Department of Social Security and a range of other departments, including the Inland Revenue, for the purpose of detecting fraud.[1] Information may also be exchanged with local authorities responsible for the administration of various housing and council tax benefits, with the view to identifying inconsistencies. With the development of computer networks, it is a comparatively simple matter for such exchanges to take place automatically, so that although there may not be a single massive computer database, the effect may be chillingly similar.

[1]   Sections 1–3. The Anti-terrorism, Crime and Security Act 2001 authorises the widespread exchange of data between government departments.

5.18   Although the application of data matching is a new phenomenon for the UK, the technique has been applied in a number of other countries including Australia, New Zealand and the US. In New Zealand, the practice has been attacked by the Privacy Commissioner, who has challenged both the ethics of placing innocent individuals under surveillance and the benefits obtained by government. Many calculations, it was suggested, were 'based on frankly heroic assumptions'.[1] Further support for scepticism comes from the US, where a General Accounting Office report on the practice:

> ... found many problems with implementation of (statutory provisions regulating data matching) including poor quality or non-existent analyses. In 41 per cent of cases, no attempt was made to estimate costs or benefits or both. In 59 per cent of cases where costs and benefits were estimated, the GAO found that not all reasonable costs and benefits were considered ...[2]

1   *Dominion* (Wellington), 5 December 1996.
2   S Davies *Big Brother* (1996, Pan) p 86.

5.19   Indications of the scale which data matching activities can assume come from Australia, where a programme similar to that introduced under the Social Security (Administration) Fraud Act 1997 anticipates between 375–750 trillion attempted file matches each year. Vast to human eyes, these figures are eminently manageable using computer technology.[1] The Australian figures illustrate a further consequence of the activity. Almost no one can escape being the subject of data matching. Every database contains errors and the inevitable consequence is that suspicion of wrongdoing may fall upon innocent individuals.

1   S Davies *Big Brother* (1996, Pan) p 86.

5.20   Data matching can, of course, be put to positive as well as negative uses. In Parliament, during the passage of the Social Security Administration (Fraud) Act 1997, the suggestion was made that data matching techniques could be used to identify individuals who were entitled to benefit but had not submitted a claim. In terms of data protection, the exemptions from the non-disclosure principles are sufficiently broad to justify most of the disclosures of data which would occur in the context of data matching. Following the expression of concerns by the Data Protection Registrar at the privacy implications of the new provisions,[1] the government agreed to enter into discussions with a view to compiling a code of practice, and offered an undertaking that data matching would not commence until this work had been completed. The Code was introduced in October 1998,[2] preceded by a Foreword from the Registrar, who commented that:

> This Code is a positive move towards implementing best data protection practice in the DSS and its executive agencies. Openness is an important feature in providing public reassurance and the Department's commitment to include appropriate notifications to individuals on its forms and other relevant documents is helpful. The Code also includes systematic guidance on ensuring appropriate levels of data quality and periods of record retention. The inclusion of requirements for matches to be referred to trained staff, and for individuals to be given opportunities to explain discrepancies before action, are notable safeguards, as is the intention to review matching criteria in the light of experience.[3]

1   Thirteenth Report of the Data Protection Registrar (1997) p 36.
2   Available from http://www.dss.gov.uk/hq/pubs/datamatch/index.htm.
3   http://www.dss.gov.uk/hq/pubs/datamatch/foreword.htm.

5.21   The Registrar's Fourteenth Annual Report published in 1998 was slightly less laudatory, commenting that:

> We continue to have reservations about its scope, in particular that it is confined to data matching conducted by the DSS using powers created by the Social Security Administration (Fraud) Act 1997 but ignores similar exercises conducted by local authorities based upon the same Act and, in many cases, using the same sets of data.

5.22 It is not just in the more formal instances of data matching that there might be a number of separate data controllers. In the case of the Internet, the proliferation of search tools, such as Alta Vista and Dejavu News, allows users to scan thousands of sites to develop profiles of individual's postings to newsgroup discussions. Anyone placing material on the Internet, an act which will constitute processing as defined in the Data Protection Act 1998, should be aware that third parties may engage in such forms of processing. A scenario might be postulated whereby individual A posts data on a website, individual B controls an Internet search engine which is used by individual C to compile a collection of personal data, including elements originating from A's website. It is likely in such situations that there may be a plurality of data controllers, with resolution of relative areas of responsibility being a task of great complexity.

5.23 The Data Protection Directive's[1] approach is more extensive and the question may arise whether the Data Protection Act 1998 fully meets its requirements. Recital 26 refers to the identification being made by the data controller or by 'any other person'. It may be, for example, that aggregate data on individuals, resulting, for instance, from a census, may make no reference to individuals, but that these could be identified by third parties linking the original data with other sources of information in their possession. Although this approach is to be welcomed as preventing data users colluding so as to evade the legislation by arranging for different users to control data and means of identifying, it will also oblige data controllers to consider what forms of processing may be carried out by third parties. The operator of a website, for example, may put information online including stories or reports produced by a particular author. Assuming no further processing was carried out, it is unlikely that the operator would be regarded as a data user under the existing UK legislation. It is possible, however, that other web users could, through the application of search engines, conduct searches by reference to the author and by doing so compile a list of online publications and citations. A recent newsgroup posting illustrates the possibilities (with identities concealed for purposes of privacy protection):

> Subject: Is it a privacy issue
>
> From: T ... @reporters.net
>
> Date: Thu, 20 Jun 1996 13:26:50 +0100
>
> In article <F4Tf... yxEwv7@reporters.net> ... @reporters.net writes: For a magazine article I've been commissioned to write by a United Kingdom business journal, I need to talk with anyone with experience of employers or recruitment agencies searching Web search databases such as DejaNews for the writings and comments and other information about potential employees. I also need to talk to employers and recruitment agencies who have done such searches or are contemplating doing so. Anonimity [sic] is possible. Please reply to me at xxxt@xxx.demon.co.uk.

---

[1]   Directive 95/46/EC.

Sensitive data

5.24 The extent to which certain forms of data can be classed as especially sensitive and deserving of special protection has long been a contentious issue. During the passage of the Data Protection Act 1984, the attempt to identify sensitive data was compared, somewhat scornfully, by government ministers with the quest for the unicorn. Both were considered mythical creatures. In the case of personal data, the context in which data was held or used was considered far more important than the data itself. A list of names and addresses, for example, would not normally be considered sensitive, but this view might change if it referred to details of prominent persons and was in the hands of a terrorist organisation. Whilst this view is not without merit, it seeks to transform the exceptional into the norm. Ultimately, it was accepted that there are certain categories of information which would generally be regarded as possessing a degree of sensitivity and in respect of which, substantial numbers of data subjects might wish to be assured that dissemination would be limited and controlled.

5.25 As enacted, the Data Protection Act 1984 provided that regulations might be made to strengthen the data protection principles in respect of data relating to racial origin, political opinions, religious or other beliefs, physical or mental health, sexual life or criminal convictions.[1] This power was never exercised. The Data Protection Act 1998 brings the treatment of sensitive data within the heart of the legislation and subjects its processing to more extensive requirements than is the case with other forms of data. The definition of what constitutes sensitive data is broader than under the 1984 Act referring to:

(a) the racial or ethnic origin of the data subject;
(b) his political opinions;
(c) his religious beliefs or other beliefs of a similar nature;
(d) whether he is a member of a trade union;
(e) his physical or mental health or condition;
(f) his sexual life;
(g) the commission or alleged commission by him of any offence; or
(h) any proceedings for any offence committed or alleged to have been committed by him, the disposal of such proceedings or the sentence of the court in such proceedings.[2]

Specific provisions defining the circumstances under which sensitive data might be processed are contained in Sch 3. Opening with a general prohibition against the processing of such data, a number of exceptional situations are identified which may justify processing. These will be discussed in more detail in Chapter 7.

[1] Section 2(3).
[2] Section 2.

5.26 The scope of the concept of sensitive data has been interpreted broadly by the courts. In *Bodil Lindqvist*,[1] one particular item of information on the web page which was the cause of specific investigation was the indication that a named person had injured her foot and as a consequence was able to work only on a part-time basis. The Data Protection Directive[2] provides for additional controls to be imposed concerning the processing of special categories of data defined as that which is capable of:

> revealing racial or ethnic origin, political opinions, religious or philosophical beliefs, trade-union membership, and the processing of data concerning health or sex life.

The question for the court was whether the information regarding the foot injury came within the category of data concerning the subject's health life? The court's reply was succinct:

> In the light of the purpose of the directive, the expression data concerning health used in Article 8(1) thereof must be given a wide interpretation so as to include information concerning all aspects, both physical and mental, of the health of an individual.

[1]   Case 101/01, [2004] QB 1014.
[2]   Directive 95/46/EC.

5.27   When proposals for the introduction of categories of sensitive data were being debated in the UK Parliament prior to the enactment of the Data Protection Act 1984, a government minister compared the task of defining sensitive data with a hunt for a unicorn. Both were, it was suggested mythical creatures which did not exist outside the realm of fairy stories. That may be an extreme view but a fairer analogy may be with the response to a request for a definition of an elephant in terms that 'I don't know what it is but I know one when I see it'. Accepting the problem of reaching a clear definition the criteria supplied appears too wide. A reference to the fact that an athlete was unable to compete in a race because of a broken leg, for example, does not seem to be possessed of a sufficient degree of sensitivity to justify the imposition of additional controls.

The concept of processing

5.28   Under the Data Protection Act 1984, processing was defined as encompassing the acts of:

> ... amending, augmenting, deleting or re-arranging the data or extracting the information constituting the data and, in the case of personal data, means performing any of these operations by reference to the data subject.[1]

[1]   Section 1(7).

5.29   Although seemingly broad, this definition was found wanting in the case of *R v Brown*.[1] Here, a police officer had caused data relating to individuals to be displayed on a terminal attached to the police national computer. Beyond being seen and noted, it was not alleged that any further use had been made of the data. The defendant was charged under the Data Protection Act 1984 with the wrongful use of data contrary to the provisions of s 5 of the Act and was convicted at trial. Overturning the convictions, the House of Lords held by a majority that a distinction had to be drawn between the activities of processing and of use. As was stated by Lord Hoffmann:

> In my view, however, the scheme of the Act as a whole does not permit the phrase 'use [personal] data' to be constructed as including its retrieval. This is because the Act quite carefully uses a number of different words to describe various things which can be done to personal data. These include holding, using, disclosing, transferring, obtaining and, for present purposes most significantly, 'processing'.[2]

[1] [1996] 1 All ER 545.
[2] [1996] 1 All ER 545 at 560.

5.30 Accepting that the defendant's activities constituted processing, the question was posed whether it also amounted to using the data. Lord Hoffmann continued:

> I do not think that it can. The Act treats processing differently from using ... So it seems to me that 'using personal data' was not intended to include the various operations within the computer which fall within the definition of 'processing'.[1]

The concept of 'use', it was concluded, had to be interpreted in line with the normal meaning of the word and would require that some action be taken on the data. The consequence was that unfair or even unlawful processing of data will not constitute a criminal offence under the Data Protection Act 1984 in the absence of evidence that some further use is made of the data.[2]

[1] [1996] 1 All ER 545.
[2] There would appear little doubt, as indeed was suggested in the House of Lords, that a prosecution on the basis of an attempt to make unauthorised use of data would have been successful.

5.31 The definition in the Data Protection Act 1998 is very much broader, providing that:

> ... 'processing', in relation to information or data, means obtaining, recording or holding the information or data or carrying out any operation or set of operations on the information or data, including—
>
> (a) organisation, adaptation or alteration of the information or data;
> (b) retrieval, consultation or use of the information or data;
> (c) disclosure of the information or data by transmission, dissemination or otherwise making available; or
> (d) alignment, combination, blocking, erasure or destruction of the information or data.[1]

[1] Section 1(1).

5.32 It might be suggested, with little element of exaggeration, that whilst the act of dreaming about data will not constitute processing, any further activities will bring a party within the scope of the legislation. This is, of course, always subject to the requirement that the processing relates to personal data. Not all data will be so classed and it has been estimated that personal data accounts for only some 2–5% of all data which is subject to automated processing.[1]

---

[1]   M Briant in P Hansen et al *Freedom of Data Flows and EEC Law* (1988, Kluwer) p 47.

5.33 A further problem which may remain under the Data Protection Act 1998 concerns the interpretation of the word 'recorded'. This is not specifically defined in the Act, but in the case of *R v Gold*,[1] the House of Lords held that for the purposes of the Computer Misuse Act 1990, the word 'recorded' required 'the preservation of the thing which is the subject matter of them for an appreciable period of time with the object of subsequent retrieval or recovery'.[2] As the Data Protection Registrar has commented, many modern computer systems require that data be held in the system for only a short period of time.[3] The development of the Internet and WWW means that the availability of access to data is becoming an acceptable substitute for its possession. In *R v Gold*, for example, the particular data was retained for less than one second. The issue may assume considerable importance where data is being transferred from one user to another. Direct communications between computers may allow large amounts of data to be transmitted and received in a very short period of time. Once again, the issue might more properly be considered as one of control rather than the strict application of the legislation.

---

[1]   [1988] 1 AC 1063. See discussion at para 12.30ff below.
[2]   [1988] 1 AC 1063 at 1073, per Lord Brandon.
[3]   'What are your views?' Consultation Paper p 38.

5.34 Although not yet at issue before a UK court, the question what acts constitute processing was raised before the European Court in *Bodil Lindqvist*.[1] An initial issue concerned the question whether the mention of a person on a web page constituted processing of personal data as defined in the Data Protection Directive.[2] Two issues arose in this context, first whether the data on Mrs Linqvist's web page included personal data. The court's reply was unequivocal:

> The term undoubtedly covers the name of a person in conjunction with his telephone coordinates or information about his working conditions or hobbies.[3]

---

[1]   Case 101/01, [2004] QB 1014.
[2]   Directive 95/46/EC.
[3]   Case 101/01, [2004] QB 1014, para 24.

5.35 Equally clear and unsurprising was the court's determination that processing had taken place. The Swedish government, argued for a broad approach suggesting that 'as soon as personal data are processed by computer, whether using a word processing programme or in order to put them on an internet page, they have been the subject of processing'. Although counsel for Mrs Lindqvist argued that something more was needed beyond compilation of what was effectively a word processed document and that only metatags and other technical means used to assist with the compilation of indexes and retrieval of information would suffice, the court agreed with the Swedish government's submission:

According to the definition in Article 2(b) of Directive 95/46, the term processing of such data used in Article 3(1) covers any operation or set of operations which is performed upon personal data, whether or not by automatic means.[1]

¹ Case 101/01, para 25

5.36 Although all forms of processing are potentially covered by the Data Protection Directive,[1] the most stringent controls apply in the case of processing by automatic means. It is arguable that any use of a computer to create a document comes within the scope of this criterion as there is no direct physical link between the author pressing a key and a letter or symbol appearing on screen. The act of loading a page onto a web server involved a number of operations some at least of which are performed automatically.

¹ Directive 95/46/EC.

Extension to manual records

5.37 Under the Data Protection Act 1984, access was strictly limited to data which had been the subject of some form of automated processing. Although the definition of processing was somewhat general, the legislative intention was to restrict access to data which was held on computer. The Data Protection Directive,[1] based in large part on existing provisions of the German data protection law, required an extension to certain forms of manual records. Article 2 of the Directive provides that its scope is to extend to any 'personal data filing system' defined in terms of:

any structured set of personal data which are accessible according to specific criteria, whether centralised, decentralised or dispersed on a functional or geographical basis.

¹ Directive 95/46/EC.

5.38 By omitting any reference to automated processing the effect is clearly to encompass manual record keeping systems. Whilst, reflecting the ease with which modern retrieval systems can perform full text searches of vast collections of data in accordance with criteria determined by a user, every automated system is covered by the legislation, not every manual system is to be included. Recital 15 of the Data Protection Directive[1] explains that:

Whereas the processing of such data is covered by this Directive only if it is automated or if the data processed are contained or are intended to be contained in a filing system structured according to specific criteria relating to individuals, so as to permit easy access to the personal data in question;

Recital 27 continues the story:

Whereas the protection of individuals must apply as much to automatic processing of data as to manual processing; whereas the scope of this protection must not in effect depend on the techniques used, otherwise this would create a serious risk of circumvention; whereas nonetheless, as regards manual processing, this Directive covers only filing systems, not unstructured files; whereas, in particular, the content of a filing system must be structured according to specific criteria relating to individuals allowing easy access to the personal data; whereas, in line with the definition in Article 2(c), the different criteria for determining the constituents of a structured set of personal data, and different criteria governing access to such a set, may be laid down by each Member State; whereas files or sets of files as well as their cover pages, which are not structured according to specific criteria, shall under no circumstances fall within the scope of the Directive.

[1]   Directive 95/46/EC.

5.39   This provision clearly leaves considerable scope for member states to determine the extent to which manual records should be brought within the scope of their implementing legislation. The Data Protection Act 1998 utilises the concept of a 'relevant filing system' as the vehicle for this endeavour. The statutory definition is somewhat complex, in large part because the legislation seeks to co-exist with a range of earlier statutes which had provided for a right of access to certain medical, educational, social work and credit reference files. In its essential element, however, it provides that:

> 'relevant filing system' means any set of information relating to individuals to the extent that, although the information is not processed by means of equipment operating automatically in response to instructions given for that purpose, the set is structured, either by reference to individuals or by reference to criteria relating to individuals, in such a way that specific information relating to a particular individual is readily accessible.[1]

[1]   Section 1(1).

5.40   The extension to some forms of manual records has been the cause of considerable controversy with some estimates putting the cost of compliance in the region of £2bn. Costs of some £100m were estimated for the banking sector alone.[1] Such figures are likely to prove an exaggeration. The Data Protection Registrar has commented that there appears to have been an unrealistic assumption made that those keeping manual files will need to check every file for accuracy.[2] Whilst there will certainly be requirements to take reasonable steps to ensure that information is accurate and to correct any errors which come to light, no requirement for individual verification applies in respect of computerised records, and there is no good reason why the situation should be different with manual files. It should be noted, however, that the Consumer Credit Act 1974 and the Access to Health Records Act 1990 provide for access to credit and medical records irrespective of the format in which these are stored, whilst the Local Government (Access to Information) Act 1985 and the Open Government Code of Practice provide extensive rights of access to information. As the Data Protection Registrar has commented:

Experience elsewhere indicates that in practice, in many cases, information provided in response to Freedom of Information requests will relate to the individual making the request.[3]

1   Press Association Newsfile, 11 November 1993.
2   Briefing Note, 28 January 1998. This cites research carried out at Aston Business School and the Universities of Tilburg and Leiden which concluded that the 'financial impact of the proposed Directive will be very small for the majority of organisations studied in the public and private sectors in the UK and the Netherlands'.
3   Our Answers 1998, para 3.8

5.41   In determining what manual records will be covered, the question when information should be considered 'readily accessible' is of critical importance. In discussion of the extent of the provision in Parliament, it was suggested that it would not be sufficient that information about an individual should be located in a single place, for example, a manila folder containing all of an employee's work records. In order for the records to be covered, it would additionally be required that the information within the folder should be held in a structured format so that individual items might readily be extracted. Speaking during the Bill's Report stage in the House of Lords, Lord Williams stated that:

> Our intentions are clear. We do not wish the definition to apply to miscellaneous collections of paper about individuals, even if the collections are assembled in files with the individual's name or other unique identifier on the front, if specific data about the individual cannot be readily extracted from that collection.
>
> An example might be a personnel file with my name on the front. Let us assume that the file contains every piece of paper or other document about me which the personnel section has collected over the course of my career and those papers are held in the file in date order with no means of readily identifying specific information about me except by looking at every document. The Government's clear intention is that such files should not be caught.[1]

1   587 HL Official Report (5th series) col 467, 16 March 1998.

5.42   The Data Protection Registrar, however, commented that:

> It has ... been put to us that 'particular information' refers to information of a very specific nature. On this analysis information held in a file relating to an immigration application would arguably be covered as all the information in the file will, or should, be directly pertinent to that application. However, it has been argued that information held in a normal personnel file will not be 'particular information' as there will be a range of information concerning such matters as sickness absence, performance, pay, next of kin. We find this distinction unconvincing. The range of information in a personnel file may be wide because there is a wide range of information relevant to an individual's employment. Nevertheless the information is 'particular' in that it is all information held for, and relevant to, employment.[1]

1   Briefing Note, 29 January 1998.

5.43   Some answers to the issues raised can be found in the Court of Appeal decision in *Durant v Financial Services Authority*[1] discussed at para 5.8ff above.

In what was the key element of the dispute, the appellant sought access to four sets of manual files was at issue. As the judgment states:

> The first was the Major Financial Groups Division systems file ('the MFGD Systems file'). It was a file, in two volumes, relating to the systems and controls that Barclays Bank was required to maintain and which was subject to control by the FSA. The file, which was arranged in date order, also contained a few documents relating to part of Mr. Durant's complaint against the Bank, which concerned such systems and controls.
>
> The second category of file was 'the MFGD Complaints file' – relating to complaints by customers of Barclays Bank about it to the FSA – the sub-dividers being ordered alphabetically by reference to the complainant's name, containing behind a divider marked 'Mr. Durant' a number of documents relating to his complaint, filed in date order.
>
> The third category of file was the Bank Investigations Group file ('the B.I.G file'), maintained by the FSA's Regulatory Enforcement Department, relating and organised by reference to issues or cases concerning Barclays Bank, but not necessarily identified by reference to an individual complainant. It contained a sub-file marked 'Mr. Durant', containing documents relating to his complaint. Neither the file nor the sub-file was indexed in any way save by reference to the name of Mr. Durant on the sub-file itself.
>
> The fourth category of file was the Company Secretariat papers, a sheaf of papers in an unmarked transparent plastic folder held by the FSA's Company Secretariat, relating to Mr. Durant's complaint about the FSA's refusal to disclose to him details and the outcome of its investigation of his complaints against Barclays Bank, not organised by date or any other criterion.[2]

[1]   [2003] EWCA Civ 1746.
[2]   [2003] EWCA Civ 1746 at paras 13-16.

5.44   It was accepted by the FSA that all of these files contained some information which related to the appellant. The degree and level of identification varied with some files identifying him 'by reference to specific dividers within the file'. Files also contained a range of documents including copies of telephone attendance notes,

> a report of forensic examination of documents, transcripts of judgments, hand-written notes, internal memoranda, correspondence with Barclays Bank, correspondence with other individuals and correspondence between the FSA and him.[1]

[1]   *Durant v Financial Services Authority* [2003] EWCA Civ 1746 at para 17.

5.45   Discounting the issue whether data might be regarded as personal, the court considered the extent to which the records in question could be considered to constitute a relevant file:

> The parliamentary intention to which Mr. Sales referred, is, in my view, a clear recognition of two matters: first, that the protection given by the legislation is for the privacy of personal data, not documents, the latter mostly retrievable by a far cruder searching mechanism than the former; and second, of the practical reality of the task that the Act [Data Protection Act 1998] imposes on

all data controllers of searching for specific and readily accessible information about individuals. The responsibility for such searches, depending on the nature and size of the data controller's organisation, will often fall on administrative officers who may have no particular knowledge of or familiarity with a set of files or of the data subject to whose request for information they are attempting to respond. As (counsel for the respondent) pointed out, if the statutory scheme is to have any sensible and practical effect, it can only be in the context of filing systems that enable identification of relevant information with a minimum of time and costs, through clear referencing mechanisms within any filing system potentially containing personal data the subject of a request for information. Anything less, which, for example, requires the searcher to leaf through files to see what and whether information qualifying as personal data of the person who has made the request is to be found there, would bear no resemblance to a computerised search. And, as (counsel for the respondent) also pointed out, it could, in its length and other costs, have a disproportionate effect on the property rights of data controllers under Article 1 of the First Protocol to the ECHR, who are only allowed a limited time, 40 days, under section 7(8) and (10) of the Act to respond to requests, and are entitled to only a nominal fee in respect of doing so.

[1] *Durant v Financial Services Authority* [2003] EWCA Civ 1746 at para 45.

5.46 In conclusion it was stated that:

As to the 1998 Act [Data Protection Act 1998], to constitute a 'relevant filing system' a manual filing system must: 1) relate to individuals; 2) be a 'set' or part of a 'set' of information; 3) be structured by reference to individuals or criteria relating to individuals; and 4) be structured in such a way that specific information relating to a particular individual is readily accessible ... It is not enough that a filing system leads a searcher to a file containing documents mentioning the data subject. To qualify under the Directive [Data Protection Directive[1]] and the Act, it requires ... a file to which that search leads to be so structured and/or indexed as to enable easy location within it or any sub-files of specific information about the data subject that he has requested.[2]

[1] Directive 95/46/EC.
[2] *Durant v Financial Services Authority* [2003] EWCA Civ 1746 at para 46.

5.47 It is often stated that hard cases make bad laws. It may also be the case that bad cases make hard laws. These is no doubt that the judges in *Durant*[1] were extremely wary of what was regarded as an attempt to invoke the provisions of the Data Protection Act 1998 for purposes beyond those envisaged by the legislature. Perhaps the most intractable problem facing the courts in a case such as this is that there is the clear signal, not least from the Data Protection Directive,[2] that the legislation is concerned with protection of the right to privacy yet, as discussed extensively elsewhere, this remains something which is not explicitly protected in the UK. The content of the right to privacy has long evaded precise definition. The classic formulation, however, refers to the right 'to be left alone' whilst references to the concept of informational privacy lay stress on the ability to control the storage and dissemination of personal data. If the right to exercise at least a measure of control over the collection and use of personal data is to have any meaning, knowledge of the nature and extent of the information which is held must be a necessary concomitant. In adopting a restrictive view of the scope of relevant filing systems the court pays insufficient regard to the concept of informational privacy.

1   *Durant v Financial Services Authority* [2003] EWCA Civ 1746.
2   Directive 95/46/EC.

5.48 There is no doubt that compliance with a request for subject access may be difficult and expensive for the controller involved. As the court stated:

> The responsibility for such searches, depending on the nature and size of the data controller's organisation, will often fall on administrative officers who may have no particular knowledge of or familiarity with a set of files or of the data subject to whose request for information they are attempting to respond.[1]

It may, of course, be argued that exactly the same considerations will apply where a request is made for access to data held in automated systems. Especially with the proliferation of personal computers in every workplace it may often be impossible for a person charged with ensuring compliance with access requests made under the Data Protection Act 1998 to be aware of the totality of information which is held. It is entirely justifiable that a line has to be drawn in respect of the amount of time and effort which requires to be expended in dealing with an access request. It could not seriously be suggested, for example, that every piece of paper within an organisation should be scrutinised against the eventuality that a data subject is referred to. When files do exist in structured form there is a stronger case for requiring that relevant personal data be identified. The argument that the nature of file structures makes fair processing difficult is a well-established one and was explicitly rejected in the credit reference agency cases brought before the Data Protection Tribunal. Adopting a reasonably expansive view of the scope of access rights might serve to encourage data controllers to develop and maintain efficient and effective filing systems, a restrictive approach might have the opposite effect.

1   *Durant v Financial Services Authority* [2003] EWCA Civ 1746 at para 45.

Data protection actors

5.49 Under the Data Protection Act 1984, the data protection world was inhabited by data users, computer bureaux and data subjects. Operating under the supervision of the Data Protection Registrar and Tribunal (whose functions will be considered in the Chapter 6), these played roles related to the processing of personal data. Although the basic structure remains, the Data Protection Act 1998 makes changes to terminology and, more significantly, changes related to the substance of key definitions and requirements. In particular, whilst under the 1984 Act a requirement to register was a prerequisite for the application of the substantive provisions of the legislation, the 1998 Act provides for the breakage of this link.[1]

1   See para 6.18 et seq below.

The scope of data protection

Data controllers

5.50 The Data Protection Act 1984 regulated the activities of data users. In order to be classed as a data user, a party would need to be able to control the contents and use of personal data.[1] The term 'data controller' is substituted in the new legislation with little apparent change in extent. An individual or undertaking will be classed as a data controller when it:

> ... (either alone or jointly or in common with other persons) determines the purposes for which and the manner in which personal data are, or are to be processed.[2]

[1]   Section 1(5).
[2]   Section 1(1).

5.51 It is quite possible for persons to be classed as data users or controllers even though they do not own a computer. An example might concern the owner of a small business who records details of transactions on pieces of paper which are stored in the archetypal shoe box. Once a year, the shoe box may be collected by an accountant who transfers the data to computer in order to prepare a set of accounts. Assuming that some of the data in the accounts relate to individual creditors and debtors, all the criteria necessary for the application of the legislation will be satisfied and, doubtless much to their surprise, the business person will be classed as a data user/controller. In such a situation, the accountant will also be so regarded, the Divisional Court confirming in the case of *Data Protection Registrar v Griffin*[1] that anyone who processed data on behalf of clients would be regarded as a data user when he or she possessed any control or discretion concerning the manner in which the processing was carried out.

[1]   (1993) Times, 5 March.

5.52 A similar situation is postulated in the Data Protection Directive:

> ... where a message containing personal data is transmitted by means of a telecommunications or electronic mail service, the sole purpose of which is the transmission of such messages, the controller in respect of the personal data contained in the message will normally be considered to be the person from whom the message originates, rather than the person offering the transmission services; whereas, nevertheless, those offering such services will normally be considered controllers in respect of the processing of the additional personal data necessary for the operation of the service.[1]

[1]   Directive 95/46/EC, Recital 41.

Data processor

5.53 As in the example given above, some data controllers may seek to have processing carried out on their behalf by a third party. This was perhaps more prevalent in the early days of computing than is the case today, although one aspect which remains significant is where undertakings make arrangements as part of a disaster recovery plan, to obtain access to external processing facilities in the event of some interruption to service. The Data Protection Act 1984 made provision to regulate the activities of computer bureaux. The essence of such an organisation was that:

(a) as agent for other persons he causes data held by them to be processed ... or

(b) he allows other persons the use of equipment in his possession for processing.[1]

[1] Section 1(6).

5.54 Mirroring once again the terminology of the Data Protection Directive,[1] the Data Protection Act 1998 substitutes the term 'data processor' for 'computer bureau'. The term data processor is defined to encompass:

... any person (other than an employee of the data controller) who processes the data on behalf of the data controller.[2]

The phrase in brackets was included to avoid the possibility that employees engaged in processing in the course of their employment might be regarded as data processors. Given the expanded definition of processing adopted in the 1998 Act,[3] it will be the case that anyone who collects data for the processor – perhaps by conducting market research surveys – will be classed as a processor.

[1] Directive 95/46/EC.
[2] Section 1(1).
[3] See para 5.28 et seq above.

5.55 Although a greater range of persons may be classed as data processors, the requirements imposed on them are limited. Under the Data Protection Act 1984, those operating computer bureaux were required to register details of their activity[1] and subsequently to comply with the eighth data principle relating to the maintenance of adequate security measures.[2] It was also possible that an aggrieved individual might bring an action for compensation against a computer bureau.[3] The situation is somewhat different under the Data Protection Act 1998. Data processors will not be subject to the notification requirements,[4] whilst, in respect of the requirement to maintain appropriate security (now found in the seventh principle), the onus is placed upon the data controller for whom processing is conducted. The controller is responsible for selecting a processor who can provide satisfactory guarantees regarding security.[5] A written contract must also be entered into obliging the processor to act only on instructions from the controller in respect of the processing carried out, and also to comply with the requirements of the seventh principle.[6] Further, it is only the data controller who may be liable to compensate data subjects for losses arising from processing.[7]

[1] Section 5(1).
[2] Schedule 1.
[3] Section 23.
[4] Section 17, which provides for notification refers only to this obligation being imposed upon data controllers.
[5] Schedule 1, Pt 2, para 11.

6   Schedule 1, Pt 2, para 12.
7   Section 13.

Data subject

5.56   The terminology of data subject remains unchanged, as does its definition as 'an individual who is the subject of personal data'.[1] It would be a unique individual who is not to be classed as a data subject – many times over. In contrast to the situation with data controllers and processors, where the focus is very much on the obligations imposed under the legislation, for data subjects, the purpose of the statute is to confer rights. The most important right for data subjects is undoubtedly that of obtaining access to data held by controllers and of securing the correction of any errors contained therein.

1   Section 1(1). Section 1(4) contains the equivalent provision in the Data Protection Act 1984.

Jurisdictional issues

5.57   The Data Protection Act 1984 'applies to all data users who control the contents and use of personal data from within the United Kingdom'.[1] In part, this approach was necessary in order to comply with the Council of Europe's provisions regarding mutual assistance. In the situation where data is processed in the UK relating to, for example, French or German data subjects, the Data Protection Act will apply, with the main issue being the identification of the data user. The question whether an undertaking can be considered resident in the UK is one which arises in a number of contexts and which may produce different results. As the Registrar has commented, a company could be regarded as resident in the UK for the purpose of the Data Protection Act but not for taxation purposes. In the event that the company is not considered resident, it may be that it will be represented in the UK by a 'servant or agent' who will be classed as a data user for this purpose. It may also be the case that the undertaking which carries out the processing may be regarded as a computer bureau for the purpose of the legislation.

1   Section 39.

5.58   Similar problems arise when data relating to UK data subjects is processed abroad. In many instances, the data will remain under the legal control of the UK-based user, who will therefore be subject to the legislation. The view has been taken by the Registrar that jurisdiction will be claimed even where all aspects of the processing are carried out abroad but where it is intended that the data will be used in the UK – regardless of the form in which it is imported. The correctness of this interpretation has not been tested before the courts or the Data Protection Tribunal.

5.59 In the Data Protection Directive[1] it is provided that member states are to apply national laws where processing 'is carried out in the context of the activities of an establishment of the controller on the territory of the Member State'. Such a formulation may lead to extra-territorial application of national laws. Article 28(6) provides further that:

> Each supervisory authority is competent, whatever the national law applying to the processing in question, to exercise, on the territory of its own Member State, the powers conferred on it (to investigate suspected violations of the law and to intervene by legal or administrative measures to terminate breaches). Each authority may be requested to exercise its powers by an authority of another Member State.

[1] Directive 95/46/EC.

5.60 There is potential for overlapping jurisdiction in the situation where multinational undertakings process personal data in a variety of member states. In its Consultation Paper, the Home Office asserts that:

> While some of the provisions relating to geographical extent are clear enough, others are obscure and potentially ambiguous. There is, therefore, the potential for inconsistent approaches being adopted in different Member States. The danger is that this could make it possible for the national law of *more* than one Member State to apply to a single processing operation, or for *no* Member State's law so to apply.[1]

[1] 'Data protection. The Government's Proposals' (1997) para 2.27.

5.61 The multiple jurisdiction situation would appear to be an inevitable consequence of the free movement of data within the EU. Given that a major purpose of the Data Protection Directive[1] is to harmonise the laws of the member states, such a result should not be excessively burdensome for data users and, indeed, corresponds to the UK Registrar's interpretation of the existing situation under domestic law. It is difficult to envisage that a reasonable interpretation of the Directive's terms could produce a situation where no national law applied. In implementing the directive's provisions, the Data Protection Act 1998 will apply where:

(a) the data controller is established in the UK and the data are processed in the context of that establishment; or

(b) the data controller is established neither in the UK nor in any other EEA state but uses equipment in the UK for processing the data otherwise than for the purposes of transit through the UK.[2]

An example of the latter situation might be where equipment forming part of a computer network, perhaps involving an ISP, is located in the UK but managed from the US.

[1] Directive 95/46/EC.
[2] Section 5(1).

5.62 The question of establishment is defined more precisely than under the Data Protection Act 1984. The criteria adopted are that the controller satisfies one of the following criteria:

1. The controller is an individual who is ordinarily resident in the UK.
2. The controller is a body incorporated under UK law.
3. The controller is a partnership or unincorporated association subject to UK law.
4. The controller is a person maintaining an office, branch agency or regular practice in the UK.[1]

[1]   Data Protection Act 1998, s 5(3).

5.63 For multinational companies, it is the case that they will be regarded as established in every country in which they operate. The geographical location of any data processing operation will not be relevant. A company established, for example, in France, Germany and the UK will need to comply with the national laws of each of these states. The effect will be that the Data Protection Commissioner would be obliged to assist any inquiries made by the German supervisory authority regarding processing relating to German citizens carried out in the UK and to apply German law in determining the legality of this processing. The Data Protection Act 1998 provides that an Order may be made by the Secretary of State relating to the manner in which these functions might be exercised.[1]

[1]   Section 51(3). The Data Protection (Functions of Designated Authority) Order 2000, SI 2000/186, makes provisions for the Commissioner to co-operate with, and seek the co-operation of, other member state supervisory authorities in such matters. This provision is discussed in more detail below.

Conclusions

5.64 Given the expanded nature of some of its basic definitions, there is little doubt that the Data Protection Act 1998 will govern a greater range of activities than was the case under the Data Protection Act 1984. In addition to legal changes, developments in technology, such as permitting the automatic identification of individuals whose images are captured on video camera or, indeed, car number plates, will mean that many of these forms of surveillance will also be governed by the legislation. The scope of the legislation has begun to be examined by the courts. In *Bodil Linqvist*,[1] the European Court adopted an expansive view of the scope of the legislation. In *Durant v Financial Services Authority*,[2] the Court of Appeal took a rather more restrictive approach. It may well be that further decisions of the European Court will be necessary in order to provide a comprehensive and consistent approach to the scope of the Data Protection Directive[3] across the member states.

[1]   Case 101/01, [2004] QB 1014.
[2]   [2003] EWCA Civ 1746.
[3]   Directive 95/46/EC.

5.65   It clearly is the task of the courts to apply legislative provisions at issue before them. The courts have perhaps been ill served by the legislature which has promulgated laws which are rather imprecise. In *Campbell v MGN*,[1] Lord Phillips of Worth Matravers MR said:

> In interpreting the Act it is appropriate to look to the Directive [Data Protection Directive[2]] for assistance. The Act [Data Protection Act 1998] should, if possible, be interpreted in a manner that is consistent with the Directive. Furthermore, because the Act has, in large measure, adopted the wording of the Directive, it is not appropriate to look for the precision in the use of language that is usually to be expected from the parliamentary draftsman. A purposive approach to making sense of the provisions is called for.[3]

Even the most purposive form of interpretation cannot and should not provide an excuse for unfettered judicial decision making. Beyond issues of ambiguity and lack of precision in the drafting of the legislation, the Directive and the Act are to a considerable extent surviving dinosaurs from the age when computers were mainly free-standing machines, used almost exclusively by businesses and large organisations but with limited networking capabilities. The world has moved on and whilst the European Court was undoubtedly correct in determining that the development of a web page constituted processing as defined in the legislation, it is difficult to see that this, and a myriad of other pages maintained by individuals effectively by way of a hobby, constitute a sufficiently serious threat to the rights and freedoms of other individuals to justify the imposition of criminal sanctions. As will be discussed in the Chapter 6, the legislation does not apply where processing is for social or domestic purposes. The problem, which arises also in the context of copyright infringement, is that what used to be clear-cut distinctions, not least in terms of the scale of activities possible, are no longer applicable. The old models are broken but the form of their replacements has yet to be resolved in a satisfactory manner.

[1]   [2002] EWCA Civ 1373, [2003] QB 633.
[2]   Directive 95/46/EC.
[3]   [2002] EWCA Civ 1373, [2003] QB 633 at [96].

Chapter 6

Supervision of data users

Introduction

6.1   The notion that a specialised agency should be established with responsibility for action in the field of data protection is one which is common to virtually all European systems and marks a major point of divergence from the approach adopted in the US. One commentator has suggested that:

> data protection presupposes ... the establishment of an independent control authority. Experience confirms what was already stated in the earliest debates: It is not enough to trace a mandatory framework for data processing. The legislator must also secure the monitoring of the processing conditions. Neither the participation of the data subject not any of the traditional means of control guarantees, however, adequate supervision. Even if the data subject is entrusted with a series of rights he remains an outsider, deprived of the necessary information permitting him to analyze and evaluate the activities of the various public and private agencies.[1]

By way of contrast, it has been suggested that the:

> US approach towards privacy protection is designed to put the individual in the centre of the action, to let him have a large voice in decisions as to what information will be collected, used and disseminated about him. The Europeans take a paternalistic approach choosing to vest enforcement in bureaucracy.[2]

[1]   S Simitis 'Data Protection – Experiences and Tendencies' (1985) 3 Law/Technology at 11–12.

[2]   L Hummer in 'Transnational Data Regulation, The Realities' (1979) Online Conferences.

6.2   The establishment of a supervisory agency was not originally a requirement of the Council of Europe Convention, which requires signatories merely to 'designate one or more authorities' who will, at the request of another designated authority, furnish information on national laws and administrative practices, provide factual information related to specified automated files and undertake any investigations related to the request in conformity with national legal provisions.[1] Additionally, the designated authority may be required to provide assistance to individuals resident in the territory of another signatory state.[2] The Data Protection Directive[4] is more prescriptive, requiring the establishment of an independent supervisory authority (or authorities).[4] It specifies in Recital 62 that the establishment of independent supervisory authorities is an essential component of the protection of individuals with regard to the processing of personal data, and therefore provides under Article 28 that:

> Each Member State shall provide that one or more public authorities are responsible for monitoring the application within its territory of the provisions adopted by the Member States pursuant to this Directive.
>
> These authorities shall act with complete independence in exercising the functions entrusted to them.

[1]   Article 13(2).
[2]   Article 14.
[3]   Directive 95/46/EC.
[4]   Article 28.

6.3   Amendments to the Council of Europe Convention now make similar provision.[1] It may also be noted that the Treaty of Amsterdam, which made significant changes to the treaties establishing the EU, provides that independent supervisory agencies are to be established in respect of the Community institutions.[2]

[1]   Article 1 of the Additional Protocol
[2]   Article 2, inserting a new art 213B into the Treaty of Rome. A proposal for a regulation 'on the protection of individuals with regard to the processing of personal data by the institutions and bodies of the Community and on the free movement of such data' was presented by the Commission in July 1999. The text is available from http://europa.eu.int/comm/internal_market/en/media/dataprot/news/286en.pdf. It provides in art 1 for the appointment of an independent supervisory board, to be known as the European Data Protection Supervisor, to monitor the application of the directive within the Community institution.

6.4   Although independence is a key component of the regulatory structure it has been described by the ITU as a 'complex and widely misunderstood concept'.[1] The key element in the definition is that there is to be a distinction between the regulatory authority and those involved in the provision of telecommunications services. This is a matter which is easy to stipulate but harder to achieve in real life. Particular problems arise in respect of public sector processing especially given that the supervisory authorities tend to be funded directly or indirectly from the public purse.

6.5   In addition to requiring the establishment of a supervisory agency or agencies, the Data Protection Directive[1] prescribes also the basic powers to be vested in supervisory agencies. These agencies are to be afforded:

–   investigative powers, such as powers of access to data forming the subject-matter of processing operations and powers to collect all the information necessary for the performance of its supervisory duties;

- effective powers of intervention, such as, for example, that of delivering opinions before processing operations are carried out, in accordance with art 20, and ensuring appropriate publication of such opinions, of ordering the blocking, erasure or destruction of data, of imposing a temporary or definitive ban on processing, of warning or admonishing the controller, or that of referring the matter to national parliaments or other political Institutions; and

- the power to engage in legal proceedings where the national provisions adopted pursuant to this directive have been violated or to bring these violations to the attention of the judicial authorities ...[2]

It is further provided that:

Each supervisory authority shall hear claims lodged by any person, or by an association representing that person, concerning the protection of his rights and freedoms in regard to the processing of personal data. The person concerned shall be informed of the outcome of the claim.[2]

[1]   Directive 95/46/EC.
[2]   Article 28(3).
[3]   Article 28(4).

6.6   Under the UK's Data Protection Act 1984, the office of Data Protection Registrar was created. In addition to the Registrar, the Act provided for the establishment of a Data Protection Tribunal. The sole function of the Data Protection Tribunal was to hear appeals brought by data users or computer bureaux against decisions taken by the Registrar which directly affect them. The Tribunal could uphold the Registrar's original ruling, reverse it or, where the Registrar's act involved the exercise of a discretion, substitute its own ruling.

6.7   The Tribunal's status was unaffected by the Data Protection Act 1998. The Data Protection Registrar, however, became the Data Protection Commissioner. This change was at her suggestion, the argument being that the title Registrar placed undue emphasis on one, rather bureaucratic, aspect of her role, that of compiling and maintaining a register of data users. With the enactment of the Freedom of Information Act 2000, the Commissioner became responsible also for the operation of that legislation. Recognising this fact there has been a further change in nomenclature to Information Commissioner.[1] At the same time the title of the Tribunal was changed to that of the Information Tribunal.

[1]   Introduced by s 18 of the Freedom of Information Act 2000.

Forms of supervisory agency

6.8   One of the key decisions which needs to be made concerns the structure of the regulatory agency. Many options are available but the key choice lies perhaps between the appointment of a single regulator, albeit supported by what may be a substantial staff, or vesting authority in a multi-membered commission or authority. Trends have fluctuated with the early agencies such as the US Federal Communications Commission favouring a favouring the multi-member approach, a shift during the 1990s towards the single regulator model and a more recent move, driven perhaps by the notion of convergence towards the multi-member approach.

6.9 In part the choice whether to appoint a single regulator or a commission is influenced by national traditions. Historically, the UK has favoured the appointment of a single official. Examples include the Information Commissioner, the Director General of Fair Trading and the regulators for the privatised gas, electricity and railway industries. For the telecommunications sector, the Telecommunications Act 1984 established the post of Director General of Telecommunications. More recently, however, the Communications Act 2003 provided for the establishment of the Office of Communications (OFCOM) as a multi-membered regulatory body to take over the functions of the Director General of Telecommunications

6.10 The relative merits of single and multiple regulators have been ventilated in many other areas. A single regulator may well be able to bring a more focused and consistent approach to regulation although much will obviously depend upon the personality and abilities of the post holder. With a collegiate body, there is more potential for internal dissent but it is also likely that a wider range of interests and expertise may be represented with the consequence that decisions, when reached, may carry greater weight.

6.11 In many respects the debate concerning the leadership of the regulatory agency is made redundant by virtue of the fact that the organisations are frequently very large. The Information Commissioner, for example, employs more than 100 people.

The Information Commissioner and Tribunal

6.12 In large measure, the Data Protection Directive's[1] requirements relating to the establishment of an independent supervisory authority were satisfied by the establishment of the Data Protection Registrar under the Data Protection Act 1984. The first Data Protection Registrar, Mr Eric Howe, was appointed in 1984, and after serving two terms of office was replaced in 1994 by Mrs Elizabeth France who retired from the post in 2003 to become Telecommunications Ombudsman. In her Twelfth Annual Report, the Registrar indicated concern that the title of Registrar placed undue emphasis on one (rather bureaucratic) aspect of her role and suggested that with the introduction of a new Data Protection Act there should be a change in nomenclature so that her office should be described as Privacy Protection Commissioner. This request was accepted in part, although the Data Protection Act 1998, in common with the 1984 Act, eschewed any mention of the word 'privacy'. From the date of the 1998 Act's entry into force, it provided that the 'Data Protection Registrar ... shall continue in existence by the name of the Data Protection Commissioner.[2]

1   Directive 95/46/EC.
2   Schedule 5.

6.13   The Data Protection Act 1998 specifies the terms and conditions under which the Commissioner is to be appointed. This is to be for a fixed term not exceeding five years. Within this period, the Commissioner might be removed from office only following a resolution passed by both Houses of Parliament, a status equivalent to that of High Court judges. One change made from the Data Protection Act 1984 is the provision that a Commissioner may only serve for two terms, save where special circumstances make a continuation of appointment 'desirable in the public interest'.[1] Under the 1984 Act, there was no limit on the number of terms which an individual could serve. Concern has been expressed in the past that the government's role in deciding whether to continue an appointment might deter the supervisory agency from investigating public sector data processing. One incident has been reported from Germany when a state Data Protection Commissioner's appointment was not continued shortly after the individual concerned had been involved in a well-publicised disagreement concerning governmental data processing practices. Although the matter is not likely to be of significance in the near future, it might be considered unfortunate that the default has effectively been switched from the assumption that the Commissioner might continue in the post for more than two terms to the assumption that this will not be the case.

1   Data Protection Act 1998, Sch 5, para 2.

6.14   Under the Data Protection Act 1984, the Registrar possessed considerable discretion as to the manner in which statutory functions were performed. The role might fairly be described as one involving many powers but few duties. In many cases, the statute contained provisions such as 'the Registrar may'. Even where a provision opens with a prescriptive, 'the Registrar shall', this is almost invariably qualified by the phrase 'where he considers it appropriate'. This has been a source of some criticism as causing the effectiveness of the role to be very dependent upon the diligence of the Registrar. The Data Protection Act 1998 retains this basic approach whilst placing the Commissioner under a general duty to:

> ... promote the following of good practice by data controllers and, in particular, so to perform his functions under this Act as to promote the observance of this Act by data controllers.[1]

It is difficult to see how this duty can be enforced against the Commissioner in any meaningful way.

1   Section 51.

6.15   Inevitably, the operation of such a substantial organisation requires considerable resources. The issue of how the supervisory agency's work should be funded has been at the core of many of the debates about the format of the legislation. Although the Data Protection Act 1998 makes provision for public funds to be used to meet the Commissioner's expenses, it is the intention that his or her office should be largely self-financing.[1] This decision drives many others concerning the scope of the Act and the obligations imposed upon data users. The major source of income is from the fees payable by data users in connection with the Act's registration procedures. Clearly, maximisation of the numbers of those classed as data users will have a similar effect upon the income of the Commissioner, whilst any significant reduction in the numbers of those liable to register would have significant implications, either for the financial burdens imposed on those remaining subject to a registration requirement or for the Commissioner's income stream.

[1] In the *Eighth Report of the Data Protection Registrar* (1992) p 47 the then Registrar expressed concern that cuts in the level of government funding are compromising his ability to fulfil basic functions.

6.16 Initially, this chapter will focus on the establishment and maintenance of the Data Protection Register and the obligations imposed on data controllers. Attention will then be paid to the investigative and enforcement powers conferred on the Commissioner before concluding with an account of the remaining powers and duties imposed on the Commissioner.

From registration to notification

6.17 In terms of specific tasks, the major obligation imposed under the Data Protection Act 1984 was to compile and maintain a register of data users and computer bureaux. The Data Protection Register is the result of this activity. This is a publicly available document which can now be accessed over the Internet.[1] It is unclear, however, how valuable the information contained on the Register may be to the average data subject. In part, this is due to a somewhat idiosyncratic indexing system. A search for entries maintained by the University of Glasgow, for example, found some under this heading but others under that of Glasgow University. Even if the subject identifies the appropriate entry, many of these are substantial documents in their own right. A printout of the University of Strathclyde's entry in respect of its Central and Academic Services (one entry out of six) extends to 40 pages of text. The main purpose for which individuals might wish to consult the Register might be to find out who holds information on them. Given the size of the Register (211,000 entries in 2003 according to the Commissioner's annual report), unless a subject knows of a particular organisation, it is unlikely that consulting the register will produce much by way of enlightenment.

[1] http://www.dpr.gov.uk/search.html.

6.18 A feature of many of the early data protection statutes was the imposition of a system of licensing of data users. Effectively, this required users to demonstrate fitness to be permitted to process personal data. Although terminology in the field is somewhat inconsistent, the procedure might be analogised to the obtaining of a licence for the possession of a gun or the driving of a motor vehicle. With the massive increase in the number of computers, the impossibility of exercising effective control in this manner has been widely recognised. An initial step, which was implemented in the Data Protection Act 1984, saw the introduction of a system of registration of data users. Registration as applied in the Data Protection Act 1998 retains qualitative criteria, but switches the onus to the supervisory agency to indicate cause why an application should be rejected. The 1998 Act sees a further move away from the concept of prior control of processing with a move to a system whereby data controllers are required to notify details of their processing activities. The Data Protection Register will continue as the location within which the information supplied at notification is made accessible to the public.

6.19   Under the system of registration in the Data Protection Act 1984, acceptance of an application was not automatic. Applications might be rejected on three grounds. First that, in the Registrar's opinion, 'the particulars proposed for registration ... will not give sufficient information as to the matters to which they relate'.[1] An application may also be refused if the Registrar is satisfied that the applicant is likely to contravene any of the data protection principles[2] and, finally, if the Registrar:

> ... considers that the information available to him is insufficient to satisfy him that the applicant is unlikely to contravene any of those principles.[3]

The onus was on the Registrar to justify rejection of an application and only a tiny number of applications were formally refused. The latest figures indicate that 32 applications were refused in the year 1994–95, 31 in 1995–96 and none in subsequent years.[4] Even at the 'higher' levels, this translated into a refusal rate of one in every 2,650 applications made in the particular year – just under 0.04%.

[1]   Section 7(2)(a).
[2]   Section 7(2)(b).
[3]   Section 7(2)(c).
[4]   *Fifteenth Report of the Data Protection Registrar* (1999) chapter 5.

6.20   The effectiveness of the registration process adopted in the Data Protection Act 1984 was criticised from the outset. More recent statutes, such as the German Data Protection Act 1990, moved away from the requirements of universal registration exempting large numbers of data controllers from any procedural requirements. Even where users remain subject to a requirement to record details of their processing, systems of declaration or notification have been adopted. The Data Protection Directive follows this model. It provides initially that:

> Member States shall provide that the controller or his representative, if any, must notify the supervisory agency ... before carrying out (processing of personal data).[1]

Notification is very much a procedural requirement. Although it was suggested initially that the Commissioner might retain some power to reject or flag notifications which were considered to be unsatisfactory, the Act confers no such power.

[1]   Directive 95/46/EC, art 18(1).

6.21 Having established the principle of notification, the Data Protection Directive[1] continues to provide that simplification or exemption from notification may be offered:

> ... for categories of processing operations which are unlikely, taking account of the data to be processed, to affect adversely the rights and freedoms of data subjects.

subject to conditions being imposed on the kinds of data to be processed, the persons to whom it is to be disclosed and the length of time the data are to be stored. A range of other possible exemptions are identified in the Directive, some of which are adopted in the Data Protection Act 1998.[2]

[1]   Directive 95/46/EC.
[2]   Article 18(2).

6.22 When initial consultations on the implementation of the Data Protection Directive[1] began, the Data Protection Registrar was an advocate of the view that the powers to grant exemption should be used widely to remove thousands of data controllers from the bureaucratic burdens associated with the registration/ notification process. Such an approach would find support in a significant difference between the approach of the Data Protection Act 1984 and that of the Directive and the Data Protection Act 1998 towards the effect of exemption. Exemption under the 1984 Act removed a data user from all aspects of the legislation whilst exemption under the 1998 Act is, with two exceptions, merely from the requirement to notify details of processing. The first exception applies where data is processed solely for the purposes of an individual's 'personal, family or household affairs'.[2] The second exception applies where data is processed for the purpose of safeguarding national security.[3] This restates the position adopted in the 1984 Act although, as will be discussed below,[4] there are more stringent provisions allowing the Information Tribunal to quash a certificate issued by the Secretary of State certifying that data is processed for national security purposes. In all other cases, controllers who are exempt from the requirement to notify will remain subject to the substantive provisions of the legislation, with the requirements, for example, that data be processed fairly and that subject access requests be acceded to.

[1]   Directive 95/46/EC.
[2]   Section 36.
[3]   Section 28.
[4]   See para 8.28 below.

Exemptions from the requirement to notify

6.23 Under the Data Protection Act 1984, the list of categories of exempt processing was defined exhaustively in the statute.[1] The new approach promises to bring a greater measure of flexibility to the determination of what activities should be exempt from notification. Again, unlike the situation in the 1984 Act, where the Registrar had no formal role to play in the making of any statutory instruments, the Data Protection Act 1998 provides that the responsibility for drafting the notification regulations is to lie with the Commissioner who is, 'as soon as practicable after the passing' of the Act, to submit 'proposals as to the provisions to be included in the first notification regulations'.[2] The Commissioner is charged with the duty of keeping the working of the regulations under review and may submit further proposals to the Secretary of State.[3] The Secretary of State may also require the Commissioner to consider specific topics and make proposals.[4] Although the regulatory power remains with the Secretary of State, there is a statutory duty to consider proposals made by the Commissioner and, more generally, to consult with her before making use of any regulatory power conferred under the legislation.[5]

[1] Sections 32, 33.
[2] Section 25(1).
[3] Section 25(2).
[4] Section 25(3).
[5] Section 67(3).

6.24 As with the Data Protection Directive,[1] the Data Protection Act 1998 imposes a general requirement to notify details of processing:

> Subject to the following provisions of this section, personal data must not be processed unless an entry in respect of the data controller is included in the Register maintained by the Commissioner.[2]

Breach of this provision constitutes an offence. Unlike the situation under the Data Protection Act 1984, where liability was strict, a defence of 'due diligence' is available to data controllers. This may be justified on account of the wider range of exceptions potentially available from notification and the fact that controllers under the mistaken impression that they are so exempt will nonetheless be required to comply with the substantive requirements of the legislation.

[1] Directive 95/46/EC.
[2] Section 17(1).

6.25 In respect of the exemptions to be made available to controllers, the Data Protection Act 1998 provides that:

> If it appears to the Secretary of State that processing of a particular description is unlikely to prejudice the rights and freedoms of data subjects, notification regulations may provide (for exemption from notification).[1]

In initial consultation exercises concerning the extent of exemptions, the Registrar advocated that extensive use should be made of this provision in order to exclude 'potentially hundreds of thousands of data controllers from notification'. Subsequent events saw a substantial withdrawal from this position. In part, this can be traced to definitional problems. In proposals submitted in 1999, the Registrar commented:

> We consider it important that exemptions from notification must not have the effect of increasing administrative costs either for data controllers or for the Commissioner. This means that if there are to be exemptions, boundaries between the exempt and the non-exempt should be clear. It also means that in

exempting certain processing operations, the objective should be to exempt certain categories of data controller as a whole. There is little point in creating exemptions for certain processing operations if, by and large, data controllers still have to notify because other common processing operations are not exempt.

Accepting this in principle is easy; the difficulty is in the detail. It is not simply a question of saying that certain types of business, categorised, for example, by the number of employees or by turnover are exempt. The exemptions have to be formulated in terms which satisfy Article 18.2 of Directive 95/46/EC. That is, '*the purposes of the processing, the data or categories of data undergoing processing, the category or categories of data subject, the recipients or categories of recipient to whom the data are to be disclosed and the length of time the data are to be stored' all have to be specified*'.[2]

and it was concluded that no data controllers, other than those processing for social or domestic purposes, should be exempted from the requirement to notify. As will be discussed, however, a number of purpose related exemptions do apply.

[1] Section 17(3).
[2] Proposals for Notification Regulations (1999).

6.26 Definitional problems apart, pragmatic considerations undoubtedly also served to limit the numbers of those exempted from the requirement to notify details of processing. The fees obtained from those submitting applications for registration/notification constitute virtually the only source of income for the Registrar/Commissioner. The Data Protection Act 1998 provides that, in fixing the level of fees, 'the Secretary of State shall have regard to the desirability of securing that the fees payable to the Commissioner are sufficient to offset' the costs of running the Commissioner and Tribunal's statutory activities.[1] A significant reduction in the level of those requiring to notify will inevitably increase the level of fees for those remaining subject to the requirement.

[1] Section 26(2). It was indicated in Parliament that the cumulative deficit on the Registrar's activities since 1986 is some £4.5m. The Act further provides that account may be taken of the amount of any outstanding deficit when fixing fees. The Act contains a further provision allowing different levels of fees to be charged to different categories of controller (s 26(1)).

6.27 The Data Protection (Notification and Notification Fees) Regulations 2000[1] (the 'Notification Regulations') provide the basis for the new regime. They provide for a limited number of data controllers to be exempted from the notification requirement (whilst remaining subject to the substantive requirements of the legislation). The exemptions can be placed into two categories, the first relating to particular forms of processing and the second to specific categories of data controller. Especially in respect of the first category, it should be noted that whilst some forms of processing need not be notified, in the (likely) event that a controller engages in additional and notifiable forms of processing, a choice will be given either to notify everything or to include an indication in the Register entry to the effect that:

This data controller also processes personal data which is exempt from Notification.

The purpose of this is to put data subjects on notice that the entry on the Register will not give a complete picture of the controller's activities. Whilst the same argument could also have been advanced under the 1984 regime, the more limited scope of exemption warrants a change from previous practice.

¹ SI 2000/188.

Optional notification

6.28 Although it might appear logical for a data controller to seek to benefit from any exemption which might be on offer, the reality may be more complex. Where details of processing are held on the Register, the controller is under no further obligation to inform data subjects as to these matters. A controller whose details do not appear is required to supply the information otherwise required at registration within 21 days of receiving a request from any person. Failure to reply timeously will constitute an offence.[1] Responding to a single request may be as burdensome as making notification to the Registrar. Given the nature of this obligation, it is perhaps not surprising that the Data Protection Act 1998 provides that a normally exempt data controller may voluntarily notify details of processing activities.[2]

¹ Data Protection Act 1998, s 24.
² Section 18.

Exempt forms of processing

6.29 The Notification Regulations[1] provide for exemption in respect of three forms of processing, involving what has been referred to by the Commissioner as 'core business activities'.[2] It is stressed, however, that the conditions attached to the exemptions are, in common with similar provisions found in the Data Protection Act 1984, likely to ensure that they are of value only to small businesses. In addition to the purpose-related exemptions, a further exemption applies in respect of certain forms of processing conducted by non-profit making organisations.

¹ SI 2000/188.
² *Notification Exemptions. A Self Assessment Guide*, available from http://www.dpr.gov.uk/notify/self/index.html.

Staff administration

6.30 Although the concept of staff administration sounds relatively broad, the scope of the exemption is much more narrowly circumscribed. The activity of staff administration is defined as involving the purposes of:

> Appointments or removals, pay, discipline, superannuation, work management or other personnel matters.[1]

Data held may relate to past, present or potential employees or to 'any person, the processing of whose personal data is necessary for the exempt purposes'. This latter category might include, for example, the processing of data relating to the partner of an employee who will be entitled to pension or other benefits in the event of the employee's death. The data may consist of names, addressees and other identifiers as well as information relating to:

(i)   qualifications, work experience or pay; or
(ii) other matters the processing of which is necessary for the exempt purposes.

[1]   SI 2000/188, Sch, para 2.

6.31 Two further requirements will also need to be satisfied for an exemption to be available. First, the data must not be disclosed to third parties except with the consent of the data subject or where this is necessary for the exempt purposes. An example within the latter category would concern the transfer of data to the Inland Revenue for the purpose of operating the system of PAYE. Secondly, the data must not be retained for longer than is necessary for the exempt purposes. In most cases, this might be taken to mean that data may not be retained once an employee has left employment.[1]

[1]   SI 2000/188, Sch, para 2(d).

6.32 The word 'necessary' has been quoted on several occasions in the previous paragraphs and is used extensively throughout the provisions relating to exemption. The dictionary definition of the adjective 'necessary' refers to concepts such as:

> Unavoidable, indispensable, enforced, that which cannot be left out or done without.

The restrictions imposed by these definitions should be borne in mind when considering all of the exemptions. An employer might, quite reasonably, seek to maintain a record of employees' next of kin. This will be of obvious benefit in the event of an accident or illness occurring at work. It is more arguable, however, whether the holding of such data is necessary for staff administration purposes. The same caveat may be lodged in respect of most of the exemptions described below.

Advertising, marketing and public relations

6.33 This exemption applies when processing is:

> For the purpose of advertising or marketing the data controller's business, activity, goods or services and promoting public relations in respect of that business or activity or those goods or services.[1]

Whilst the purpose is broad, the exemption is subject to limitations largely similar to those described above in relation to the nature of the data which may be processed, the range of disclosure and period of retention. The exemption applies only in respect of the marketing of the controller's own goods or services.

¹   SI 2000/188, Sch, para 3(a).

Accounts and records

6.34   This exemption is couched in terms very similar to those applying under the Data Protection Act 1984. Exemption is offered in respect of processing conducted:

> ... for the purposes of keeping accounts relating to any business or other activity carried on by the data controller, or deciding whether to accept any person as a customer or supplier, or keeping records of purchases, sales or other transactions for the purpose of ensuring that the requisite payments and deliveries are made or services provided by or to the data controller in respect of those transactions, or for the purpose of making financial or management forecasts to assist him in the conduct of any such business or activity.¹

Data must be limited to personal identifiers, together with information about the financial standing of the data subject and any other information necessary to conduct the exempt processing.

¹   SI 2000/188, Sch, para 4(1)(a).

6.35   The exemption is somewhat broader than that previously provided for under the Data Protection Act 1984, but once again the requirement to show that data must necessarily be processed will constitute a significant limitation.

Non-profit making organisations

6.36   Under the Data Protection Act 1984, exemption was offered in respect of the activities of 'unincorporated members clubs'. This proved to be a difficult concept to define and the Notification Regulations provide for exemption for non-profit making organisations. The concept is undoubtedly broader than applying under the 1984 Act but, as with the other exceptions discussed above, only a limited range of activities will be covered. Processing is exempt in so far as it:

(a)   is carried out by a data controller which is a body or association which is not established or conducted for profit; and

(b)   is for the purposes of establishing or maintaining membership of or support for the body or association, or providing or administering activities for individuals who are either members of the body or association or have regular contact with it.¹

¹   SI 2000/188, Sch, para 5.

6.37   The data processed may relate only to limited categories of individuals, principally present, past or prospective members of the organisation and be limited to identifiers together with such information as is necessary for the purposes of the organisation, for example, data relating to subscription records. In common with the other exemptions, the data may be disclosed to third parties only with the consent of the data subject or where this is necessary for the exempt purpose.

Information to be supplied on notification

6.38   The Data Protection Act 1998 specifies the information – the 'registrable particulars' – which must be supplied to the Commissioner.[1] This is broadly equivalent to the information currently required at registration relating to the identification of the controller and the purposes for which the data is held, used and disclosed. Notice must also be given of the 'names or a description of, any countries outside the European Economic Area to which the data may be directly or indirectly transferred'. Two further items of information are novel. As mentioned above, where portions of the data held by the controller are exempt from notification, an indication of this fact must be given. A second item has proved more controversial. Controllers are required to give:

> ... a general description of measures to be taken for the purpose of complying with the seventh data protection principle.[2]

[1]   Section 16(1).
[2]   Section 18(2)(b).

6.39   The seventh principle[1] relates to the requirement to maintain appropriate data security measures. Whilst the making of such a statement has been a feature of the German legislation for a number of years, opponents have suggested that to publish such information in a public document might give assistance to hackers and others seeking to obtain unauthorised access to the data. Emphasis may, however, reasonably be put on the phrase 'general description' and a statement that security complies with, for example, a relevant British or international information security standard should comply with the obligation.

[1]   See para 7.114 below.

6.40   The notification procedures require that all data controllers provide a security statement, details of which will not appear on the Register. The Commissioner has identified four matters which require to be addressed:

- A statement of information security policy.
- Control of physical security (restrictions on access to sites and equipment).
- Controls on access to information (anti-hacking measures such as the use of passwords and encryption).
- A business continuity plan (disaster recovery).

Specific reference and endorsement is made to BS 7799, the British Standard on Information Security Management, and to the certification scheme 'c:cure' associated with it.[1]

¹   Data Protection Commissioner *Notification Handbook* (2000) para 3.2.3, available from
    http://www.dpr.gov.uk/notihand.doc.

Format of notifications

6.41   Whilst the Data Protection Act 1998 specifies the categories of information
which must be supplied, it is intended to allow flexibility as to the level of detail
which may be required. The lack of such flexibility has been identified as a
weakness of the 1984 regime. The Commissioner is required 'as soon as
practicable after the passing of this Act' to submit proposals to the Secretary of
State 'as to the provisions to be included in the first notification regulations'.¹
Aspects of these regulations, the Data Protection (Notification and Notification
Fees) Regulations,² have been referred to already. In respect of procedural aspects
they provide that:

> ... the Commissioner shall determine the form in which the registrable
> particulars (within the meaning of section 16(1) of the Act) and the description
> mentioned in section 18(2)(b) of the Act are to be specified, including in
> particular the detail required for the purposes of that description and section
> 16(1)(c), (d), (e) and (f) of the Act.³

¹   Section 25(1).
²   SI 2000/188.
³   SI 2000/188, reg 4.

6.42   The Notification Regulations make provision for all matters concerned
with notification. Initially, they seek to resolve two problem areas which were
identified under the Data Protection Act 1984. The first relates to data held by
schools. In many cases, responsibility for the data will be shared between the
head teacher and the Board of Governors and, as a consequence, schools have
tended to need to maintain two separate entries on the Register. A similar problem
has concerned partnerships where there may be a division between the individual
partners and the firm. It is now provided that a single registration is to be made
in the name of the school¹ and the partnership respectively.²

¹   SI 2000/188, reg 6.
²   SI 2000/188, reg 5.

6.43   Notifications may be made in two ways. A copy of the notification form
can be accessed over the Internet and completed online.¹ Users are guided on a
step-by-step basis through the form but, in a reversion to more old-fashioned
technology, there is no provision for the completed form to be submitted
electronically; instead, the controller is required to print out the completed form
and post it to the Commissioner. An alternative approach is to make contact by
telephone. After giving details of the nature of the organisation and the forms of
processing conducted, a form will be completed and posted to the controller
who may then make any necessary changes before returning it to the
Commissioner.

¹   http://www.dpr.gov.uk/notify/1.html.

6.44   In cases where a notification form is transmitted by recorded post, it will become valid from the day after posting. In other cases, it will be valid from the date it is received by the Commissioner.¹ Under the Data Protection Act 1984, an entry on the Data Protection Register was valid for three years unless the data user requested a shorter period of validity. At the end of this period, the user had to re-apply for registration. This system changed under the Data Protection Act 1998. Once made, notification will be valid indefinitely (subject to an obligation to notify changes in any of the registered particulars),² subject to payment of an annual fee. This fee may be collected by automatic mechanisms such as direct debit.

¹   SI 2000/188, reg 8.
²   SI 2000/188, reg 12.

6.45   Under the Data Protection Act 1984, the fee for registration rose in stages to stand at £75 by the end of the regime. The notification fee has been fixed at £35.¹ Whilst as a headline figure this marks a reduction, the reduced period of validity means that most data controllers will be faced with an increase of £30 over a three-year period. One further change may reduce the financial burden associated with registration, albeit at the cost of additional complexity in responding for requests for subject access. Under the 1984 system, a data user could choose to register different processing applications separately. A university, for example, might register separately processing in respect of present, former and prospective students and members of staff. In the event a request for access was received, the subject could be required to indicate which entry on the Register the request related to. In the event more than one entry was potentially relevant, a separate access fee could be charged in respect of each. Under the new system, each controller will have only one entry on the Register.

¹   SI 2000/188, reg 7.

Preliminary assessments

6.46   In most cases, once notification of processing is submitted, processing operations may commence. Certain forms of processing may, however, be subject to additional controls. The Data Protection Directive obliges member states to:

> Determine the processing operations likely to present specific risks to the rights and freedoms of data subjects and shall check that these processing operations are examined prior to the start thereof.¹

As implemented in the Data Protection Act 1998, regulatory power is conferred on the Secretary of State to determine categories of processing, referred to as 'assessable processing', which appear particularly likely:

(a)   to cause substantial damage or substantial distress to data subjects; or
(b)   otherwise significantly to prejudice the rights and freedoms of data subjects.²

To date, no order has been made specifying the form of processing which will be subject to preliminary assessment. It has been indicated that few forms of processing will be covered by such regulations. In Parliament, specific reference was made to activities involving data matching, genetic data and private investigations.[3]

1   Directive 95/46/EC, art 20.
2   Section 22(1).
3   HC Official Report, SC D (Data Protection Bill), cols 160–161, 19 May 1998.

6.47   Where processing comes within the ambit of such regulations, the controller may not commence activities until an assessment of its compliance with the data protection principles has been made by the Commissioner. The timetable for the Commissioner to act is a tight one. When receiving notification from any data controller, the Commissioner is to consider whether any of the processing activities described involve assessable processing[1] and, if so, whether the processing is likely to comply with the requirements of the statute. Such notice is to be given within ten days from receipt of the notification. The Commissioner is then required to give notice of his or her opinion to the controller within 28 days from the date of receipt of notification, which period might, in special circumstances, be extended by a further 14 days.[2] Processing must not be carried on during this period. In the event the Commissioner's assessment is that the processing would be unacceptable, there would not appear to be any mechanism to prevent the controller continuing with the plans, although it might be expected that an enforcement notice would be served in short order should this occur.

1   Data Protection Act 1998, s 18(2).
2   Section 18(3).

Independent data protection supervisors

6.48   Under the German data protection law, it is common practice for data controllers to appoint 'in house' data protection supervisors. Provided that such supervisors possess sufficient independence, this will exempt the controller from the requirement to notify the Federal Data Protection Commissioner. The Data Protection Directive also sanctions the adoption of such an approach,[1] and the Data Protection Act 1998 provides that the Secretary of State may make an order enabling controllers to appoint a data protection supervisor who will 'monitor in an independent manner the data controller's compliance' with the legislation. Any order will also specify the extent to which such action will exempt the controller from the notification requirement.[2]

1   Directive 95/46/EC, art 18(2).
2   Section 23.

6.49   In debate on this provision, the government pointed out that when such an option had been outlined in the consultation exercise preceding the introduction of the legislation, it had received some expressions of interest but little active support. It was indicated that, given the workload involved in implementing the new legislation, the making of any enabling regulations would not be seen as a priority issue.[1]

[1]   HC Official Report, SC D (Data Protection Bill), cols 165–166, 19 May 1998.

Enforcement of the Data Protection Act 1998

6.50   Having established a Register of those processing personal data, the ongoing task for the supervisory agency is to seek to ensure that controllers remain within the scope of their entries on the Register and that in general processing complies with the substantive requirements of the legislation. The nature of these requirements, principally in the form of the data protection principles, will be considered in Chapter 7. Failures on the part of controllers may constitute an offence and will also expose them to a range of sanctions made available to the Commissioner.

Powers of entry and inspection

6.51   Section 50 of and Sch 9 to the Data Protection Act 1998 provide that the Commissioner may approach a circuit judge (or in Scotland, a sheriff) seeking a warrant to enter and search any premises. The warrant will be granted if the judge is satisfied that a data controller is in breach of one or more of the principles or has committed an offence under the Act, and that evidence to that effect is to be found at the address specified. The warrant will empower the Commissioner or his or her staff to:

> Inspect, examine, operate and test any equipment found there which is intended to be used for the processing of personal data and to inspect or seize any document or other material found there.[1]

[1]   Schedule 9, para 1(3).

6.52   Procedures for the award of the warrant are similar to those found in the Data Protection Act 1984, although one significant loophole has been closed. Under the earlier Act, if the Registrar had sought entry to premises, been granted admission only for the occupier to refuse to co-operate further with inquiries, it was not subsequently possible in England to obtain a search warrant. The Data Protection Act 1998 now provides that a warrant may be sought in the situation where:

> Although entry to the premises was granted, the occupier unreasonably refused to comply with a request by the Commissioner or any of the Commissioner's officers or staff to (perform any of the acts which might be permitted in the execution of a search warrant).[1]

Apart from delaying action, there will be little benefit to a data controller in exercising evasionary tactics of the kind identified.

[1]   Schedule 9, para 2(1)(b)(ii).

Enforcement notices

6.53   Under the Data Protection Act 1984, the Registrar possessed power to serve enforcement, deregistration and transfer prohibition notices. With the departure from the much criticised system of (near) universal registration, the role for a deregistration notice (which has never been served) disappears. Again, as will be discussed in Chapter 10, changes in the rules relating to transborder data flows render redundant the notion of transfer prohibition notices (only one of which has been served).[1] The Data Protection Act 1998 does, however, retain the existing format of enforcement notices.[2] Under these, the Commissioner may serve notice on data controllers where he or she is satisfied that a breach of one or more of the data protection principles has occurred. The notice will identify the act or omission complained of and specify the steps that require to be taken to put matters right. Failure to comply with an enforcement notice constitutes an offence.[3] As with all other forms of notice served by the Commissioner, the recipient data controller may appeal to the Information Tribunal. Save in exceptional circumstances, the lodging of an appeal will suspend the operation of the notice.

[1]   See para 10.6 below.
[2]   Section 40.
[3]   Section 47.

6.54   Experience under the Data Protection Act 1984 indicated that a period of years might elapse between the initial moves to serve an enforcement notice and the completion of appeal proceedings. To date, there has been no appeal from a Tribunal decision to the courts, a step which would extend the length of the process even further. Little can be done to speed up the process itself, but one of the problems identified under the previous regime was that the passage of time might render all or part of the terms of an enforcement notice of dubious relevance. The Data Protection Act 1998 establishes a more flexible approach, providing that the Commissioner may, if he or she considers that all of its provisions need not be complied with in order to ensure compliance with the principles, vary or cancel an enforcement notice.[1] The recipient controller may also make written request to the Commissioner for variation or cancellation on the ground that a change of circumstances means that compliance with its terms is not necessary to secure compliance with the principles.[2] In order to avoid the possibility of a double appeal, such a request may only be made after the time available for submitting an appeal to the Tribunal has elapsed.

[1]   Section 41(1).
[2]   Section 41(2).

Information notices

6.55 Although the Data Protection Act 1984 empowered the Registrar to seek and execute search warrants in the event a breach of the principles was suspected,[1] that statute conferred no general investigative power and placed data users under no obligation to co-operate with any inquiries made by the Registrar. The Data Protection Act 1998 stops short of providing a general investigative power, but confers a new power on the Commissioner to serve an 'information notice' requiring the supply within a specified time of specified information relating to the matter under investigation.[2] An appeal against service of an information notice will lie to the Data Protection Tribunal and, save in exceptional circumstances, this act will suspend the operation of the notice.[3] Failure to comply with an information notice will constitute an offence, as will the reckless or intentional provision of false information in response to an information notice.[4]

[1] Section 16.
[2] Section 43(1).
[3] Section 43(4)–(5).
[4] Section 47.

6.56 An information notice may be served either on the Commissioner's own initiative, when he or she considers that information is reasonably required in order to determine 'whether the data controller has complied or is complying with the data protection principles',[1] or following a complaint from a data subject. In this latter respect, the Data Protection Act 1998 provides that any person may contact the Commissioner seeking an assessment whether it is likely that personal data has been or is being processed lawfully.[2] The Commissioner is obliged to consider the request and determine an appropriate response taking into account, inter alia, whether the data subject could have obtained the information by means of a request for subject access.[3]

[1] Section 43(1).
[2] Section 42(1).
[3] Section 42(7).

6.57 Although the information notice does constitute a new weapon in the Commissioner's armoury, it may be queried how useful the power will be in practice. The notice may be served when the Commissioner reasonably requires information to determine whether the principles are being observed, rather than the requirement for service of an enforcement notice that the Commissioner be satisfied that a breach has occurred. Beyond this, however, the appeal procedures are identical. Whilst it may be expected that many controllers will be happy to respond to an information notice in order to clarify what might be a misunderstanding of the nature of their processing activities, the possibility for appeals may persuade less scrupulous controllers to prevaricate in their response. Even if the Data Protection Tribunal ultimately upholds the information notice and the Commissioner obtains information indicating that a breach of the principles has occurred, no action can be taken until an enforcement notice, with its own appeal procedures, has been served.

Assessment of processing

6.58   Another new power conferred under the Data Protection Act 1998 enables the Commissioner, with the consent of the data controller involved, to assess any processing 'for the following of good practice and shall inform the data controller of the results of the assessment'.[1] Such action may provide a data controller with reassurance concerning the legality of current or proposed processing, thereby minimising the possibility that more formal enforcement measures, such as service of an enforcement or information notice, will be taken at some stage in the future.

[1]   Section 51(7).

Dissemination of information

6.59   The remaining powers of the Commissioner follow in large part those established under the Data Protection Act 1984. The Commissioner is to disseminate information giving guidance about good practice under the Data Protection Act 1998.[1] Good practice is defined as:

> Such practice in the processing of personal data as appears to the Commissioner to be desirable having regard to the interests of data subjects and others and includes (but is not limited to) compliance with the requirements of this Act.[2]

Under the 1984 Act, a wide range of material was published, perhaps most notably the series of Guidelines giving information about the Registrar's interpretation of the legislation. Members of the Registrar's office were also frequent speakers at conferences. It is likely that these activities will continue. The 1998 Act does give a new power to the Commissioner to levy fees for any matters concerned with the exercise of her powers.[3] It was indicated in Parliament that income from publications and presentations might account for 10% of the Commissioner's income.[4]

[1]   Section 51(1).
[2]   Section 51(9).
[3]   Section 51(8).
[4]   HC Official Report, SC D (Data Protection Bill), col 253, 2 June 1998.

Codes of practice

6.60   Provision relating to codes of practice was inserted into the Data Protection Act 1984 at a late stage during its parliamentary passage by a somewhat reluctant government, which pointed to the nebulous legal status of these documents. Under the 1984 regime, the Registrar's role is limited to encouraging 'trade associations or other bodies' to prepare and disseminate codes of practice.[1] The decision of the Data Protection Tribunal in the case of *Innovations (Mail Order) Ltd v Data Protection Registrar*[2] lends support to this view. Here, the Tribunal held that the appellant was in breach of the data protection principle relating to the fair obtaining of data, even though its conduct complied with a relevant industry code of practice.

1   Section 36(4).
2   Case DA/92 31/49/1, discussed in more detail at para 7.13ff below.

6.61   In spite of doubts concerning their legal status, a considerable number of codes were adopted under the Data Protection Act 1984. The Data Protection Directive also envisages a substantial role for both national and Community codes, providing that:

1.   The Member States and the Commission shall encourage the drawing up of codes of conduct intended to contribute to the proper implementation of the national provisions adopted by the Member States pursuant to this Directive, taking account of the specific features of the various sectors.
2.   Member States shall make provision for trade associations and other bodies representing other categories of controllers which have drawn up draft national codes or which have the intention of amending or extending existing national codes to be able to submit them to the opinion of the national authority.
3.   Member States shall make provision for this authority to ascertain, among other things, whether the drafts submitted to it are in accordance with the national provisions adopted pursuant to this directive. If it sees fit, the authority shall seek the views of data subjects or their representatives.
4.   Draft Community codes, and amendments or extensions to existing Community codes, may be submitted to the Working Party referred to in Article 29. This Working Party shall determine, among other things, whether the drafts submitted to it are in accordance with the national provisions adopted pursuant to this Directive. If it sees fit, the authority shall seek the views of data subjects or their representatives. The Commission may ensure appropriate publicity for the codes which have been approved by the Working Party.[1]

The major novelty for the UK is the provision in the Directive that supervisory agencies should take a view on the conformity of a draft code with statutory requirements. This is coming close to giving an unelected agency law-making powers – a practice which traditionally has been resisted in the UK.

1   Directive 95/46/EC, art 27.

6.62   The Data Protection Act 1998 establishes two roles for the Commissioner in respect of codes of practice. Acting either on his or her own initiative or under the direction of the Secretary of State, and after consulting with relevant trade associations and representatives of data subjects, the Commissioner may 'prepare and disseminate codes of practice for guidance as to good practice'.[1] Any code of practice prepared following directions from the Secretary of State is to be laid before Parliament, either in its own right or as part of another report by the Commissioner to Parliament.[2]

1   Section 51(3).
2   Section 52(3).

6.63 As with the procedure under the Data Protection Act 1984, the Commissioner is also under a duty to encourage the adoption and dissemination of codes by relevant trade associations. Additionally, however, it is provided that:

> ... where any trade association submits a code of practice to him for his consideration, consider the code and, after such consultation with data subjects or persons representing data subjects as appears to him to be appropriate, notify the trade association whether in his opinion the code promotes the following of good practice.[1]

In many respects, this provision formalises practice under the 1984 Act where many of the codes adopted contain a foreword from the Registrar indicating her views on the appropriateness of the code.

[1]   Data Protection Act 1998, s 51(4)(b).

International co-operation

6.64   As was the case under the Data Protection Act 1984, the Commissioner is the UK agency responsible for liaison with other data protection agencies under the auspices of the Council of Europe Convention.[1] The Commissioner is also responsible for working with the various Committees and Working Parties established at EU level[2] by the Data Protection Directive.[3] Such bodies have a particularly important role to play in determining whether third countries provide an adequate level of protection for personal data. The Commissioner is charged with the duty of disseminating information about any such findings and seeking to implement these within the UK.[4]

[1]   The Data Protection (Functions of Designated Authority) Order 2000, SI 2000/186.
[2]   Data Protection Act 1998, s 54(1).
[3]   Directive 95/46/EC.
[4]   Data Protection Act 1998, s 51(6).

6.65   The Data Protection Directive[1] also contains provisions requiring national supervisory agencies to co-operate with each other. In particular, '(e)ach authority may be requested to exercise its powers by an authority of another Member State'. The Data Protection Act 1998 provides that the Secretary of State may make an order relating to such tasks and specifying, in particular, the approach to be taken when a request for assistance relates to processing which is exempt under the UK legislation but is included in the national law of the requesting state.[2] The Data Protection (International Co-operation) Order 2000[3] makes appropriate provision. Article 5 applies in the situation where processing is taking place in the UK but where the provisions of s 5 would normally exclude jurisdiction – principally where the controller is not established in the UK.[4] Where the processing is subject to the jurisdiction of a supervisory authority from another member state, the Commissioner may, in responding to a request for assistance from that authority, act as if the processing were subject to the 1998 Act. Article 6 of the Order provides that the Commissioner may make a similar request for assistance to another supervisory authority in respect of processing subject to UK jurisdiction which is being carried out in another member state.

1   Directive 95/46/EC.
2   Section 54(2).
3   SI 2000/190.
4   See para 5.3ff above.

Professional secrecy

6.66   In addition to providing that powers be conferred on supervisory agencies, the Data Protection Directive requires also that:

> Member States shall provide that members and staff of the supervisory authority, even after their employment has ended, are to be subject to a duty of professional secrecy with regard to confidential information to which they have access.[1]

1   Directive 95/46/EC, art 28(7).

6.67   The Data Protection Act 1998's interpretation of this provision was the cause of a degree of controversy, and indeed has been criticised by the Commissioner as likely to impede the effective performance of her duties. It is provided that an offence will be committed where information obtained in the course of employment and relating to an 'identified or identifiable individuals or business' is disclosed by past or present Commissioners or members of staff without lawful authority.[1] The term 'lawful authority' is defined as requiring the consent of the individual, the availability of statutory authority, necessity for the performance of functions under the Act, compliance with Community obligations or in the course of legal proceedings. Finally, and most significantly, it is provided that 'having regard to the rights and freedoms or legitimate interests of any person, the disclosure is necessary in the public interest'.[2]

1   Section 59(1).
2   Section 59(2).

6.68   Although it is clearly reasonable that confidential information relating to a data controller should not be disclosed, the effect of this provision might be, for example, to prevent the Commissioner from publicising the fact that data controllers have been served with enforcement notices. It was indicated in Parliament that the government has 'found it difficult to get the provision right' and that the issue might be revisited in the context of freedom of information legislation.[1] The format finally adopted is less restrictive than that originally proposed, which would have empowered disclosure only when 'necessary for reasons of substantial public interest', but it remains unclear how extensively it might be interpreted. One possible compromise was suggested in Parliament, that notification regulations may require controllers to include information regarding enforcement notices (or other notices) as part of their entry on the Register.[2]

1   316 HC Official Report (6th series) cols 603–604, 2 July 1998.
2   316 HC Official Report (6th series) col 602, 2 July 1998.

The Information Tribunal

6.69 Reference has been made above to the appellate role of this body. The Tribunal was established under the Data Protection Act 1984 and little change is made to its make-up.[1] The Tribunal's membership consists of a Chairman and a number of Deputy Chairmen.[2] These appointees are to be barristers, advocates or solicitors of at least seven years' standing.[3] Additionally, a number of other members may be appointed by the Secretary of State representing the interests of data users and of data subjects.[4] A panel of three members will be convened to hear particular appeals.

1   Section 6 and Sch 5, Pt 2.
2   The number of deputy chairmen is to be at the discretion of the Lord Chancellor.
3   Section 3(4).
4   Section 3(5).

6.70 Under the Data Protection Act 1984, the Tribunal's sole function was to hear appeals brought by data users (or computer bureaux) against decisions by the Registrar adverse to their interests. The only notable change introduced by the Data Protection Act 1998 is that in very limited cases concerned with the application of the exemption for data processed for national security purposes, a data subject will, for the first time, have the right to bring a case before the Tribunal.[1] The procedures to be followed before the Tribunal are specified in detail in the Data Protection Tribunal (Enforcement Appeals) Rules 2000.[2] More specialised rules are prescribed for proceedings involving national security. Here the provisions of the Data Protection Tribunal (National Security Appeals) Rules 2000[3] will apply. The Tribunal may uphold the Registrar's original ruling, reverse it or, where the Registrar's act involves the exercise of a discretion, substitute its own ruling.[4] Tribunal decisions may be appealed on a point of law to the High Court, or the Court of Session.[5]

1   Section 28.
2   SI 2000/189.
3   SI 2000/206.
4   Section 14(3)–(4).
5   Section 14(5).

Conclusions

6.71 Throughout the currency of the Data Protection Act 1984, the Data Protection Registrars proved vigilant in pursuing the interests of the data subjects.

The Data Protection Tribunal demonstrated also a determination to interpret the data protection principles in an expansive and subject-friendly fashion. This element of the supervisory authority's work will be considered in more detail in Chapter 7. The new provisions do confer additional powers upon the Data Protection Commissioner and, as such, are to be welcomed. Less satisfactory, perhaps, is the fact that financial factors appear to have dictated the continuance of a system of near universal notification. Although much has been done to make the system as user-friendly as possible, it is difficult to avoid the conclusion that notification and the associated fee represents nothing more than a tax on computer owners.

6.72 As indicated at the beginning of this chapter, the notion that supervisory authorities are to be independent is integral to the Data Protection Directive's approach.[1] Successive Registrars and Commissioners have shown a willingness to become involved in debate on the role of data protection in modern society. Given the developments subsequent to September 11 attention has increasingly focused on activities within the public sector. In evidence before the House of Commons Home Affairs Committee the Information Commissioner recently expressed strong reservations concerning the privacy implications of Home Office proposals for the introduction of identity cards. This in turn produced comments from a Home Office spokesperson suggesting that the Commissioner was engaging in 'grandstanding'.

[1]   Directive 95/46/EC.

6.73 Many of the legislative responses to the threat of global terrorism, especially those within the UK, have been enacted with great speed, driven by perceived necessity but carrying with them also the risk of creating a chasm between those whose primary interest is in law enforcement and individuals and bodies concerned with the protection and promotion of individual rights and freedoms. Creative tension between different interest groups is inevitable and when there is a degree of acceptance that each group is acting in good faith, can produce benefits. When creation turns to destruction, everyone loses and in many respects the present debate between civil libertarian lobbyists and government has become sterile. Possible consequences are that individuals may lose some of the major elements of protection introduced and developed over the past decades whilst governments risk losing popular legitimacy if they are seem as unconcerned with and threatening towards the rights of citizens. For data protection supervisory authorities, the danger is that as the debate focuses increasingly on public sector processing, independence may become equated with impotence.

Chapter 7

The data protection principles

Introduction

7.1 Whilst notions of the form of supervision of data users have changed significantly over the years, the substantive requirements of acceptable processing practice have remained more stable. The formulation of general statements of acceptable processing practice has been a feature of data protection legislation from the earliest days. The role of such principles may fairly be analogised to that of the Ten Commandments; both establish general formulations of good conduct, but require to be interpreted and expanded in the context of specific activities and circumstances. The Data Protection Act 1984 and Data Protection Act 1998 each define eight data protection principles. Given the pivotal role of the principles, it is perhaps surprising that in both statutes, these should be relegated to a Schedule rather than, as in the Data Protection Directive[1] and Council of Europe Convention, being integrated into the body of the text. The 1984 principles required that:

1. The information to be contained in personal data shall be obtained, and personal data shall be processed, fairly and lawfully.
2. Personal data shall be held only for one or more specified and lawful purposes.
3. Personal data held for any purpose or purposes shall not be used or disclosed in any manner incompatible with that purpose or those purposes.
4. Personal data held for any purpose or purposes shall be adequate, relevant and not excessive in relation to that purpose or those purposes.
5. Personal data shall be accurate and, where necessary, kept up to date.
6. Personal data held for any purpose or purposes shall not be kept for longer than is necessary for that purpose or those purposes.
7. An individual shall be entitled—
   (a) at reasonable intervals and without undue delay or expense—
      (i) to be informed by any data user whether he holds personal data of which that individual is the subject; and
      (ii) to access to any such data held by a data user; and

(b)   where appropriate, to have such data corrected or erased.

8.   Appropriate security measures shall be taken against unauthorised access to, or alteration, disclosure or destruction of, personal data and against accidental loss or destruction of personal data.[2]

---

[1]   Directive 95/46/EC.
[2]   Schedule 1.

7.2   The Data Protection Directive also prescribes five 'principles relating to data quality', requiring member states to ensure that personal data is:

(a)   processed fairly and lawfully;

(b)   collected for specified, explicit and legitimate purposes and not further processed in a way incompatible with those purposes;

(c)   adequate, relevant and not excessive in relation to the purposes for which they are collected and/or further processed;

(d)   accurate and where necessary, kept up to date; every reasonable step must be taken to ensure that data which are inaccurate or incomplete, having regard to the purposes for which they were collected or for which they are further processed, are erased or rectified; and

(e)   kept in a form which permits identification of data subjects for no longer than is necessary for the purposes for which the data were collected or for which they are further processed.[1]

---

[1]   Directive 95/46/EC, art 6.

7.3   For the Data Protection Act 1998, the decision was taken to retain the number of principles at eight although these differ somewhat from their 1984 equivalents. It is now provided that:

1.   Personal data shall be processed fairly and lawfully and, in particular, shall not be processed unless—
     (a)   at least one of the conditions in Schedule 2 is met, and
     (b)   in the case of sensitive personal data, at least one of the conditions in Schedule 3 is also met.

2.   Personal data shall be obtained only for one or more specified and lawful purposes, and shall not be further processed in any manner incompatible with that purpose or those purposes.

3.   Personal data shall be adequate, relevant and not excessive in relation to the purpose or purposes for which they are processed.

4.   Personal data shall be accurate and, where necessary, kept up to date.

5.   Personal data processed for any purpose or purposes shall not be kept for longer than is necessary for that purpose or those purposes.

6.   Personal data shall be processed in accordance with the rights of data subjects under this Act.

7.   Appropriate technical and organisational measures shall be taken against unauthorised or unlawful processing of personal data and against accidental loss or destruction of, or damage to, personal data.

8.   Personal data shall not be transferred to a country or territory outside the European Economic Area unless that country or territory ensures an adequate level of protection for the rights and freedoms of data subjects in relation to the processing of personal data.[1]

---

[1]   Schedule 1.

7.4 As with the Ten Commandments, few would disagree with the contents of the principles. It is difficult, for example, to object to a requirement that data be processed fairly. The determination of what is fair may be a more difficult task. Detailed guidance concerning the application of the principles can be taken from a variety of sources. No fewer than four Schedules to the Data Protection Act 1998 expand upon the interpretation of the principles, whilst provisions in the body of the statute make additional provisions, often in the form of providing exceptions from their application. Again, in some instances it may be considered necessary to restrict or exclude the application of one or more of the principles giving priority to other interests, for example, the prevention or detection of crime. As with other statutes, further guidance on issues of interpretation will become available through decisions of the courts and Data Protection Tribunal resolving actual cases. A number of decisions of the Tribunal made under the Data Protection Act 1984 will remain of considerable relevance. Finally, a significant role is envisaged for sector-specific codes of practice, with the 1998 Act providing for these to receive an enhanced legal status compared with their 1984 forbears.

7.5 The data protection principles cover all aspects of data processing, from the initial step of collecting information through to its final disposal. For the purposes of the present work, the sixth (subject information) and eighth (transborder data flow) principles will be considered separately. Focusing on the remaining principles, this chapter will consider to what extent and under what conditions a data controller may lawfully process personal data. An obvious starting point is with the manner in which data is obtained. This will then be processed and put to use within the context of the controller's own activities. In some circumstances, the data may also be disclosed to third parties. Although no longer specifically covered in the principles, the Data Protection Act 1998 retains provisions defining circumstances in which data may be disclosed to third parties. Use may take a variety of forms and will include disclosure of data to a third party. Finally, this chapter will consider the operation of the seventh data protection principle, requiring that users adopt appropriate security measures.

Obtaining data

7.6 Both the first and the second data protection principles are relevant to the determination whether data has been obtained fairly and lawfully. After specifying that data is to be processed fairly and lawfully, the first principle refers to the need for the data controller to bring activities within one of a set of conditions laid down in Schs 2 and 3 to the Data Protection Act 1998. In both Schedules, the first condition is that the data subject should have consented to the processing.

7.7 It may be relatively straightforward to determine whether information has been obtained lawfully, but the criterion of fairness raises more subjective issues. In determining whether information has been obtained fairly, the Data

Protection Act 1998's interpretation of the first data protection principle provides that:

> ... regard shall be had to the method by which it was obtained, including in particular whether any person from whom it was obtained was deceived or misled as to the purpose or purposes for which it is to be held, used or disclosed.[1]

¹   Schedule 1, Pt II, para 1.

7.8   The second data protection principle requires that:

> Personal data shall be obtained only for one or more specified and lawful purposes and shall not be processed further in any manner incompatible with that purpose or those purposes.

In interpreting this principle, it is provided that the purposes for which data are to be processed may be specified either by the giving of notice to the data subject or in a notification given to the Commissioner.

The role of subject consent

7.9   Where data is collected from the data subject, it is provided that, save where this is already known, information must be given as to the identity of the controller, the purposes for which the data are intended to be used and any recipients of the data. The Data Protection Act 1998 indicates also that the subject must be supplied with:

> ... any further information which is necessary, having regard to the specific circumstances in which the data are or are to be processed, to enable processing in respect of the data subject to be fair.[1]

This requirement is not specified further in the Act. The Data Protection Directive, however, states that subjects must also be informed whether providing answers to any questions is voluntary or compulsory and as to the possible consequences of a failure to reply.[2] Notice must also be given of the right of subject access. This information must be supplied at the time the data is first processed. As in the *Innovations* case,[3] delay in giving the information will result in a breach of the principles. Where data is obtained from a third party, notice of the factors given above must be supplied at the time the data is recorded or disclosed to a third party.[4]

¹   Schedule 1, Pt II, para 3.
²   Directive 95/46/EC, art 10(c).
³   *Innovations (Mail Order) Ltd v Data Protection Registrar* Case DA/92 31/49/1.
⁴   Schedule 1, Pt II, para 2.

7.10   The first data protection principle requires that data be processed fairly and lawfully. The Data Protection Act 1984 contained a similar provision, although no further statutory guidance was given concerning its application. The provisions of the Data Protection Act 1998 are much more expansive and place the onus on the data controller to evidence justification for processing. In the case of general data, processing will be permitted only where the controller can demonstrate compliance with one of a list of conditions laid down in Sch 2. For sensitive data, Sch 3 provides a more restrictive set of qualifying conditions. In both Schedules, the list of legitimising factors begins with the notion of subject consent. Reference has been made above to this concept in the context of the act of obtaining data. The issue is a complex and somewhat controversial one, with a particular problem concerning the question of whether consent might be implied from the fact that a subject does not object to proposed processing, generally referred to as an 'opt-out' approach, or whether a positive act of assent is required, an 'opt-in' system.

7.11 Schedule 2 to the Data Protection Act 1998 provides that processing will be lawful when 'the data subject has given his consent to the processing'. Schedule 3 requires that the subject gives 'explicit consent'. Neither phrase is defined in the Act. The Data Protection Directive is a little more helpful, providing that:

> ... the data subject's consent shall mean any freely given specific and informed indication of his wishes by which the data subject signifies his agreement to personal data relating to him being processed.[1]

To complicate matters, however, the Directive also makes reference to the concepts of unambiguous and explicit consent without offering any indication as to how these terms differ from the above definition.

1   Directive 95/46/EC, art 2(h).

7.12 It may be taken that the requirements for mere 'consent' will be somewhat less than for explicit consent and that the system prevalent with many forms of transaction, where a customer is informed of the fact that data supplied may be used for specific purposes and, given the opportunity to object to this system, would be compatible with the requirements. The essence of the above requirements is that the subject must be given reasonable notice regarding the purposes for which data is obtained. In many instances, the requirement moves beyond mere knowledge to require the controller to demonstrate that the subject has consented to the processing.

7.13 Although the 1998 principles appear broader than their 1984 predecessors, decisions of the Data Protection Tribunal in cases brought under the earlier statute have interpreted these broadly. The Tribunal decision in the case of *Innovations (Mail Order) Ltd v Data Protection Registrar*[1] is therefore of considerable relevance to the present discussion.

1   Case DA/92 31/49/1.

Reasonable expectations concerning the use of data

7.14   The appellant operated a mail order business. It solicited custom in a variety of ways, including the distribution of catalogues and the placing of advertisements in various media, including newspapers, radio and television. Customer orders might be placed either in writing or over the telephone. In order to secure the delivery of goods, it is clearly necessary that customers provide details of their name and address, and it was accepted that there was no need specifically to inform them that the information would be used for this purpose. It was accepted also that customers should realise that their details would be retained by the appellant and used as the basis for future mailings of its catalogues. In addition to using the information to solicit further custom from the individuals concerned, however, the appellant made the information available to other organisations, a practice known as 'list broking'.

7.15   The appellant's catalogues gave customers notice of this possibility and its order forms offered customers the opportunity to exclude use of their data for broking purposes. Some adverts, especially those appearing on radio or television, did not make mention of the possibility and in the event that catalogue orders were placed by telephone, no mention would be made of this secondary purpose. An acknowledgment of order would, however, be sent and this would convey the message:

> For your information. As a service to our customers we occasionally make our customer lists available to carefully screened companies whose products or services we feel may interest you. If you do not wish to receive such mailings please send an exact copy of your address label to ...

7.16   The Registrar took the view that notification of the intended use came too late in the contractual process and served an enforcement notice alleging a breach of the first data protection principle and requiring, inter alia, that where notice was not given in promotional material, the subject's positive consent must be secured prior to the data being used for list-broking purposes. Effectively, therefore, the system would become one of 'opting in' rather than 'opting out'.

7.17   A number of arguments were put forward by the applicant as justifying their practices. It was suggested that, at the time of placing an order, customers would be concerned primarily with obtaining the goods and that a notice along the lines referred to above would have limited impact. Where orders were made by telephone, giving specific notice would increase the length of the call, thereby increasing costs for both the supplier and the customer. It was also pointed out that the details would not be used for list-broking purposes until 30 days from the date the acknowledgment or order was sent. This, it was suggested, allowed ample time for the customer to opt out. It was also pointed out that the appellant's practices were in conformity with an industry code of practice and the Council of Europe's Recommendation on the protection of personal data used for the purposes of direct marketing.[1]

[1]   Recommendation 85/20.

7.18 Notwithstanding these factors, the Tribunal upheld the Registrar's ruling. Use of the data for list-broking purposes, it was held, was not a purpose which would be obvious to the data subjects involved. Fair obtaining required that the subject be told of the non-obvious purpose before the data was obtained. Whilst a later notification might 'be a commendable way of providing a further warning', it could not stand by itself. Where prior notification might not be practicable, the Tribunal ruled 'the obligation to obtain the data subject's positive consent for the non-obvious use of their data falls upon the data user'.

7.19 The question what are obvious and non-obvious purposes will require to be made in the context of particular applications. It might be considered that, given the amount of junk mail received by the average person, an awareness might be assumed that customer details would be made available to other organisations for this purpose. The decision indicates, however, that a restrictive interpretation will be applied and data controllers may safely assume only that the most obvious and direct purposes need not be specifically drawn to the subject's attention.

7.20 The decision of the Tribunal in the *Innovations* case[1] was affirmed by a differently composed Tribunal in the case of *Linguaphone Institute v Data Protection Registrar*.[2] Once again, the conduct complained of lay in obtaining information from customers, or potential customers, inquiring about the appellant's products and services without disclosing at the time of obtaining that the information might also be used for list-broking purposes. In view of the decision in *Innovations*, there was no doubt that this conduct was unlawful. By the time of the Tribunal hearing, the appellant had modified its advertising to include a notice:

> (Please) tick here if you do not wish Linguaphone to make your details available to other companies who may wish to mail you offers of goods or services.

1   *Innovations (Mail Order) Ltd v Data Protection Registrar* Case DA/92 31/49/1.
2   Case DA/94 31/49/1.

7.21 The Tribunal expressed concern that:

> ... the opt-out box appears in minute print at the bottom of the order form. In the Tribunal's view the position, size of print and wording of the opt-out box does not amount to a sufficient indication that the company intends or may wish to hold, use or disclose that personal data provided at the time of enquiry for the purpose of trading in personal data. The Tribunal relies upon the Data Protection Registrar to agree a wording which should ensure that a proper explanation is given in all future advertisements.

7.22 In situations such as that at issue in *Innovations*,[1] it is relatively simple for data controllers to give notice of proposed forms of processing. A more difficult situation arises where changing circumstances see controllers seeking to use data which has been obtained for one purpose for another purpose. The decision of the Data Protection Tribunal in the case of *British Gas Trading Ltd v The Data Protection Registrar*[2] provides a good illustration of such a situation.

1   *Innovations (Mail Order) Ltd v Data Protection Registrar* Case DA/92 31/49/1.
2   The case is reported in the Fifteenth Report of the Data Protection Registrar (1999).

7.23   Under the provisions of the Gas Act 1972, the British Gas Corporation was established and granted the exclusive right to supply gas within the UK. The Gas Act 1986 opened the way for the introduction of competition into the gas market and transformed the British Gas Corporation into British Gas plc. Following further statutory amendments in the form of the Gas Act 1995, British Gas plc was turned into two companies: Transco, which was responsible for the transportation of gas, and the appellant (hereafter referred to as BGTL), which was involved in the supply of gas to domestic and business customers. From 1996, other companies were permitted to compete in the market for gas supply.

7.24   Given its previous monopoly situation, one of BGTL's major assets was a massive database relating to the accounts of some 19 million customers. Whilst the existence of this database and its transfer from British Gas to BGTL conformed with the Data Protection Act 1984, objection was raised to the manner in which the data was proposed to be used. In particular, in the new competitive market for gas and other utilities, BGTL proposed to use their database to promote its services in respect of gas and other products such as the 'Goldfish' credit card. Using its database records, BGTL sent leaflets (accompanying the quarterly gas bill) to all its customers. The leaflet was entitled 'Your Data Protection Rights – the right to choose the information you need'. It stated:

> We would like to write to you from time to time about our current range of products and services, as well as those we will be developing in the future. Also, we would like to send you information about products and services offered by other reputable organisations. In addition, we would like to pass on information about you to the other companies within our group in order that you may receive information about their products and services directly from those companies.

The leaflet continued:

> If you do not wish to receive information from us about products and services which we think will be of interest to you or do not consent to our passing information about you to other companies within our group, please complete and return the coupon below to: ...

7.25   A freepost address and a freephone telephone number were given to customers and the leaflet additionally gave the address of the Data Protection Registrar. No direct marketing material was enclosed with the leaflet, but the Registrar took the view that the use of the database for marketing purposes would constitute unfair processing and that the act of sending the leaflet, albeit informing customers of their rights under the Data Protection Act 1984, evidenced an intention to engage in unfair processing. After negotiations between the parties failed to reach an agreed solution, an enforcement notice was served requiring cessation of the practice.

7.26 Initial reference was made to the fact that the use of data for marketing purposes was included in BGTL's entry on the Data Protection Register. It was submitted that as the data had been fairly obtained and was being used for a registered purpose, there could be no question of unfair processing. The Tribunal disagreed:

> It is, we consider, necessary to look to see what was intended when the processing took place and for what purpose. The fact that processing when undertaken could be used for a registered purpose does not in our view render the processing fair when it is established it was not in fact carried out for a purpose to which a data subject had agreed. For example, if a data user obtained information from a data subject for one agreed purpose and then later deliberately processed the personal data derived from the information for a purpose he knew would not be agreed it would in most circumstances be likely to amount to unfair processing and a breach of the first data protection principle.

7.27 Turning to the acceptability of the marketing proposed, the Tribunal made reference to codes of practices drawn up by the Direct Marketing Association and the British Code of Advertising and Sales Promotion. Both indicated that where information supplied to a company for one marketing purpose was intended to be used for a significantly different purpose, the subjects should be informed and given a period of 30 days in which to intimate objection. Much weight, however, was placed on the somewhat special position of a former monopoly supplier of energy. Whilst it was considered, in line with the decision in *Innovations*,[1] that gas customers must be deemed to have accepted the likelihood that their data would be used for the marketing of gas and related products, the Tribunal concluded that:

> We conclude that disclosing their personal data to third parties would not be expected, nor for example, processing their personal data to promote items as far removed from gas as banking, mortgages, or health, household or endowment insurance.

[1]   *Innovations (Mail Order) Ltd v Data Protection Registrar* Case DA/92 31/49/1.

7.28 In order for such processing to be rendered fair, subject consent would be required. In respect of new customers, the Tribunal considered that there would be no difficulty in BGTL obtaining this at the time the agreement for supply was made. If customers were informed of the forms of processing envisaged:

> If no objection is then made either orally, or in an electronic or other communication from the customer or in a document returned by the customer to confirm the arrangements for the supply of gas (such as either an opt-in box ticked, or an opt-out box left blank), processing of personal data for the purposes made clear, would we consider not be unfair.

7.29 Different factors would apply in respect of existing customers. Merely sending a leaflet of the kind at issue and inviting notice of objection to be given would not suffice. Two alternative approaches were, however, identified:

> It would we consider be sufficient to prevent processing being unfair if individual customers are informed of the type or types of marketing or promotions BGTL would wish to carry out by processing their personal data, provided that they are given the choice to agree or not and either consent then and there, or do not object, to such use. Alternatively thereafter, and before such processing takes place, the customer returns a document to BGTL, or by other means of communication received by BGTL indicates consent to, or by not filling in an opt-out box, or other means, indicates no objection to, processing for such type or types of marketing or promotion. One such returned document could be, for example, a direct debit mandate form; others could be a part of a bill, or purpose designed leaflet.

7.30 Accepting that BGTL was in a different relationship with its customers than most data controllers, in that it had 'inherited' customer details from a former monopoly supplier, the case provides a warning sign to controllers that they should take care to inform data subjects at the earliest stage of all forms of processing which they might wish to use in respect of personal data. The Tribunal decision indicates clearly that it is much easier to seek consent at this stage than subsequently. A company such as BGTL, which requires to make regular contact with customers, not least to send bills, may not find the requirements unduly burdensome. The task may be more complex and expensive for other controllers. Matters will, of course, be even more difficult where sensitive data is involved and where positive consent is required.

Other factors legitimising processing

7.31 Although the concept of consent has been a high-profile aspect of the new regime, it must be noted that it constitutes only one of a number of grounds, capable of legitimising processing. Many data controllers will be able to bring their activities within one of the remaining grounds, although it should be borne in mind that the data must, save in the cases described above, be obtained in a fair and lawful manner. In respect of general data, the grounds legitimising processing are contained in the Data Protection Act 1998, Sch 2; for sensitive data, the relevant provisions are found in Sch 3.

General data

NECESSITY FOR CONCLUDING OR PERFORMING A CONTRACT WITH THE DATA SUBJECT

7.32 Processing may lawfully take place when this is necessary either for entering into or performing a contract with the subject. Some stress should be placed on the adjective 'necessary'. This appears frequently in instruments such as the European Convention on Human Rights, and the jurisprudence of the European Court of Human Rights, which has been approved by the European Court of Justice, has adopted an interpretation requiring that the practice in question be close to essential for the specified purpose.[1] Clearly, information about a data subject's income may be necessary for a lender to determine whether to grant a loan and information as to address will be vital for a mail order sale, but controllers should take care not to require more information than is strictly necessary for the purpose.

[1]   See, for example, the case of *Barthold v Germany* (1985) 7 EHRR 383.

NECESSARY FOR THE CONTROLLER TO COMPLY WITH A LEGAL OBLIGATION

7.33   Similar comments apply to this requirement. A controller may, for example, require information to ensure that credit facilities are not extended to those under 18. It would be reasonable for such a controller to require applicants to give an indication that they are over 18.

NECESSARY TO PROTECT THE VITAL INTERESTS OF THE DATA SUBJECT

7.34   It is easy to envisage situations where the interests of the data subject may require that data be processed in situations where it is not practicable to obtain consent. The limitation to the subject's 'vital interests' might mean in practice that the data is likely to be of a kind considered sensitive and so its processing will be governed by the provisions of the Data Protection Act 1998, Sch 3 discussed in Chapter 6.

NECESSARY FOR THE ADMINISTRATION OF JUSTICE ETC

7.35   Data may be processed lawfully when this is necessary for a range of specified public sector purposes. In addition to the administration of justice, processing may be carried out when necessary for the exercise of statutory functions, for example, compiling registers of data controllers, in the exercise of governmental functions or any other functions of a public nature exercised in the public interest. This might include, for example, the operation of systems of educational scholarships.

LEGITIMATE INTERESTS OF THE CONTROLLER

7.36   This final justification for processing is perhaps the most controversial. It requires that the processing be:

> ... necessary for the purposes of legitimate interests pursued by the data controller or by the third party or parties to whom the data are disclosed, except where the processing is unwarranted in any particular case by reason of prejudice to the rights and freedoms or legitimate interests of data subjects.

Regulations may be made to specify the circumstances in which this provision may or may not be applied[1].

1   Schedule 2, para 6.

7.37   On this occasion, the Data Protection Act 1998 diverges from the wording of the Data Protection Directive,[1] which requires in art 7(f) that the processing be necessary for the legitimate purpose of the controller or third parties:

> ... except where such interests are overridden by the interests for fundamental rights and freedoms of the data subject.

In Parliament, it was suggested that the Directive's wording would be more favourable to data controllers in the situation where financial and other institutions were sharing personal data with the view to prevent or detect fraud. The government resisted an attempt to bring the Act's wording into line on the basis that the Directive's phraseology was insufficiently precise. It was recognised that a balancing act will require to be drawn in such situations and it was indicated that representatives of the CBI had indicated satisfaction with the provision as drafted in the Act.

1   Directive 95/46/EC.

7.38   Although many situations might be identified in which it will be useful for a data controller to hold information, the restrictions associated with the adjective 'necessary' must be borne constantly in mind. It would, for example, be useful for an employer to record details of employees' next of kin in the event of accident or illness at work. This would not, however, be essential for the normal purposes of employment and subject consent would be required. In general, data controllers might be well advised not to place too much reliance upon this ground. In the example cited, it might be assumed that it would be a reasonably straightforward matter to obtain the details from an employee at the stage employment commences under the consent heading (although it might well be the next of kin who should be consenting). Even if consent is not forthcoming, the matter can be handled in a relatively simple manner by, for example, inserting a note to the effect that contact details have been refused. Matters become more complicated when a controller has to overcome an initial failure to seek consent by subsequent actions. The likelihood is that only a small percentage of subjects will respond to a request for retrospective consent, with the low response rate being due as much to indifference as to opposition.

SENSITIVE DATA

7.39   Although the principles proclaim the notion that sensitive data is not to be processed without the explicit consent of the data subject, this is watered down to a considerable extent by the provision of a substantial number of exceptions. The Data Protection Act 1998, Sch 3 provides a list of eight situations in which processing may take place without consent.

Employment-related processing

7.40

> The processing is necessary for the purposes of exercising or performing
> any right or obligation which is conferred or imposed by law on the
> data controller in connection with employment.[1]

It is further provided that the Secretary of State may either exclude the
application of this provision in certain cases or impose additional conditions.
It may be noted that, in respect of the processing of employment related data,
the Data Protection Directive requires the provision of 'adequate safeguards'.[2]
Unless it can be assumed that existing employment law provides adequate
safeguards for the data subject, UK law will not comply with the Directive
unless and until the regulations are made.

[1]   Data Protection Act 1998, Sch 3, para 2.
[2]   Directive 95/46/EC, art 8(2)(b).

Vital interests

7.41

> Processing is necessary to protect the vital interests of the data subject
> or of another person where the data subject is incapable of giving consent
> or where the controller cannot reasonably be expected to obtain consent.[1]

Examples of such situations might be where medical data relating to the subject
requires to be processed in order to treat the subject who is unconscious in
hospital. Again, processing may be justified where the subject is a carrier of
an infectious disease and where the data is needed to provide treatment to a
third party. It is further provided that processing may take place when this is:

> necessary to protect the vital interests of a third party and the subject
> unreasonably withholds consent.[2]

This situation may well be similar to that discussed above, but with the
distinction that the subject has been identified by the controller. An example
might be where the subject suffers from an infectious disease but refuses to
consent to the disclosure of a list of persons who might have come into contact
with the subject and who might require to be contacted to receive treatment.

[1]   Data Protection Act 1998, Sch 3, para 3(a).
[2]   Schedule 3, para 3(b).

Processing by specified bodies

7.42

> The processing is carried out in the course of legitimate activities by a non-profit making body or association existing for political, philosophical, religious or trade union purposes. In such cases, appropriate safeguards must be provided for the rights and freedoms of data subjects, the data must relate only to members of the association or those in regular contact with it and does not involve disclosure of the data to third parties without the consent of the data subject.[1]

Given the extension of the definition of processing to include the collection of data, this definition may have some unanticipated consequences. It was conceded in Parliament that political canvassing would be covered if the intention were to transfer returns onto a computer system. A similar situation would apply where religious organisations sought to obtain converts through door-to-door visits. For political data, it was indicated that special regulations might be made.[2]

[1] Data Protection Act 1998, Sch 3, para 4.
[2] 315 HC Official Report (6th series) col 613, 2 July 1998.

Information in the public domain

7.43

> The information contained in the personal data has been made public as a result of steps deliberately taken by the data subject.[1]

It is significant to note in this context that it will not suffice that the information has come into the public domain; this must have occurred through the deliberate actions of the subject. There is clearly a relationship between this provision and the statutory provisions discussed below relating to the activities of the media.

[1] Data Protection Act 1998, Sch 3, para 5.

Legal proceedings and the administration of justice

7.44

> The processing is necessary for the purpose of or in connection with legal proceedings (including prospective proceedings), for obtaining legal advice or to establish, exercise or defend legal rights.[1]

This provision was criticised in Parliament as being excessively broad. Certainly, the provision relating to 'prospective proceedings' appears somewhat opaque.

[1] Data Protection Act 1998, Sch 3, para 6.

7.45

> The processing is necessary for the administration of justice, for the exercise
> of statutory or governmental functions. Once again, the Secretary of State
> may exclude the application of this provision in certain situations or
> require that additional conditions be satisfied.[1]

An obvious example of such a situation would be the maintenance of criminal
records. It may be noted that the Data Protection Directive provides that 'a
complete register of criminal convictions may be kept only under the control of
official authority'.[2]

[1]   Data Protection Act 1998, Sch 3, para 7.
[2]   Directive 95/46/EC, art 8(5).

Processing for medical purposes

7.46

> The processing is necessary for medical purposes and is undertaken by a
> health professional or by a person owing an equivalent duty of
> confidentiality.[1]

The term 'medical purposes' is defined broadly to include 'preventative medicine,
medical diagnosis, medical research, the provision of care and treatment and
the management of healthcare services'.[2] It should be stressed that in this case,
as with all the exceptions described in the present section, the effect is essentially
to free the controller from the requirement to seek explicit consent to processing.
The processing must be carried out in accordance with the data protection
principles and other requirements of the Act.

[1]   Data Protection Act 1998, Sch 3, para 8.
[2]   Directive 95/46/EC, art 8(5).

Ethnic monitoring

7.47

> The processing relates to data indicating racial or ethnic origin but is
> carried out in order to monitor compliance with equal opportunities
> legislation. Appropriate safeguards must also be taken for the rights and
> freedoms of data subjects.[1]

Once again, it is provided that the Secretary of State may define more precisely
the activities coming within the scope of this provision. Care will certainly
require to be taken to ensure that information supplied for this purpose, for
example by an applicant for employment, is used only for monitoring purposes

and retained, at least in a form which can identify the subject, for no longer than is necessary.

[1]   Data Protection Act 1998, Sch 3, para 9.

Order of the Secretary of State

7.48

> The processing occurs in circumstances specified by the Secretary of State.[1]

This provision confers a wide-ranging power on the Secretary of State to extend the range of exemptions. As indicated above, the power will be invoked has been invoked for the benefit of canvassing by political parties. The Data Protection Directive requires that additional exemptions must be justified by 'reasons of substantial public interest'[2] and must be notified to the Commission.[3]

[1]   Data Protection Act 1998, Sch 3, para 10.
[1]   Directive 95/46/EC, art 8(4).
[2]   Directive 95/46/EC, art 8(6).

7.49   The regulatory power has been exercised with the making of the Data Protection (Processing of Sensitive Personal Data) Order 2000.[1] This provides no fewer than ten additional grounds justifying the processing of sensitive personal data.

[1]   SI 2000/417.

7.50   The first two grounds relate to processing for the purposes 'of the prevention or detection of any unlawful act' and the discharge of any functions intended to secure the public against:

(i)   dishonesty, malpractice or other seriously improper conduct by, or the unfitness or incompetence of, any person; or
(ii)   mismanagement in the administration of, or failures in services provided by any body or association.

In all cases, it is a requirement that the processing must necessarily be carried out without the explicit consent of the data subject.

7.51   A third ground might be seen as a form of whistle-blower's charter. It legitimises the disclosure of data relating to crime, dishonesty or seriously improper conduct or mismanagement when this is with a view to the publication of the information and where the party making the disclosure reasonably believes that the publication will be in the public interest.

7.52   Processing may be carried out without explicit subject consent when this is in the public interest in connection with the provision of counselling, support or other services. The exemption here is not an open-ended one, with the controller being required to demonstrate that it is impracticable, unreasonable or undesirable to seek to obtain subject consent.

7.53   With developments in DNA research and increased awareness of the role of genetic factors in influencing life expectancy, data of this kind is of potential value to insurance companies. A person applying for insurance cover might be required to supply details relating to the health of parents, grandparents or siblings. In the event that these persons remain alive, the processing of this data might contravene the requirements of the Data Protection Act 1998. The regulations legitimise this form of processing subject to three conditions: that it is not reasonable to obtain explicit consent; that the controller does not have actual knowledge that consent has been withheld; and that the processing is not used as the basis for decisions which will affect the data subjects concerned.

7.54   Processing for insurance purposes also benefits from a further transitional exemption covering activities which were under way prior to the commencement of the Data Protection Act 1998. Under the previous regime, the need for consent was less strict and it is provided that, save where there is actual knowledge that the data subject does not consent to processing, this may continue when it is necessary for the purpose and where it is not reasonable to expect the controller to seek explicit consent (or where the processing must necessarily be conducted without consent).

7.55   Two further exemptions serve to permit the continuance of activities which are generally considered desirable but which might otherwise contravene the data protection principles. Many employers may, whether required by law or otherwise, seek to process information to monitor the operation of policies relating to equal opportunities with the view to promoting such equality. It is provided that processing may take place where this is not used to support decisions affecting a particular subject and where the processing is not likely to cause substantial damage or distress to the data subject or to any other person.

7.56   One matter which attracted considerable discussion when the Data Protection Act 1998 was before Parliament was the realisation that the restrictions on the processing of sensitive data would serve to restrict the ability of political parties to conduct activities such as the canvassing of voters where this would involve maintaining a record of likely voting intentions. The regulations seek to avoid this prospect by providing that information relating to political opinions may be processed by persons or organisations registered under the Registration of Political Parties Act 1998 to the extent that this is not likely to cause substantial damage or distress. It is provided further that data subjects may give written notice that their personal data is not to be processed for such purpose. The Data Protection (Processing of Sensitive Personal Data) (Elected Representatives) Order 2002[1] makes further provisions regarding the use of such data by elected representatives.

[1]   SI 2002/2905.

7.57 A further exemption applies where data is processed for research purposes. This will apply where the processing is in the substantial public interest, for example, as part of a medical research project, will not result in action being taken with regard to the particular data subject without explicit consent and is not likely to cause substantial damage or distress.

7.58 The final exemption is the shortest of all, but carries significant implications. Sensitive data may be processed where this is:

> ... necessary for the exercise of any functions conferred on a constable by any rule of law.[1]

Given the extensive powers conferred on constables under the common law, this provision might serve to justify many forms of processing.

[1] Data Protection Act 1998, Sch 3, para 10.

Exceptions to the fair obtaining requirements

7.59 It is a feature of the data protection regime that virtually every rule is subject to exceptions. In respect of the requirements that data be obtained fairly, it is provided that, regardless of other circumstances, data will be considered to have been obtained fairly in a range of specified situations.

Parties authorised to supply

7.60 In certain situations, parties may be authorised, or even required, to make information publicly available. The Data Protection Act 1998 provides that information is to be regarded as having been obtained fairly if the source is a person who:

- is authorised by or under any enactment to supply it; or
- is required to supply it by or under any enactment or by any convention or other instrument imposing an international obligation on the UK.[1]

[1] Schedule 1, Pt II, para 1(2).

7.61 The provision that information will always be regarded as having been obtained fairly when it is obtained from a person statutorily authorised to supply it assumes considerable significance in the case of electoral registers. These constitute perhaps the most comprehensive listing of names and addresses available to data users. Under the terms of the Representation of the People (Amendment) Regulations 1990,[1] Electoral Registration Officers are obliged to supply copies of the register for their area upon request. Prior to the introduction of these regulations, the officers were required to supply copies of the Register only where these were readily available. The Data Protection Registrar commented that a number of officers 'had effectively ceased to supply their registers for use for other purposes'.[2] Following representations from the Data Protection Registrar, the Home Office introduced a scheme whereby a list of those purchasing copies of the Register is maintained by each officer and made available for public inspection.

[1]   SI 1990/520.
[2]   Sixth Report of the Data Protection Registrar (1990) p 7.

7.62   Further reform was introduced under the terms of the Representation of the People Act 2000. Following the report of a working group, the Home Secretary reported to Parliament concerns that:

> As the law stands, anyone may buy a copy of the electoral register for any purpose. The Home Office and electoral administrators receive more complaints about that than any other subject. People are unhappy about the large amount of unsolicited mail – junk mail – from companies that have obtained their details from the electoral register.
>
> Perhaps more worryingly, the advent of powerful CD-Roms compiled from the electoral register, which allow for searching by name, means for example that abusive spouses can trace their former partners with considerable ease using a single CD-Rom. People who feel threatened in that way may simply not dare to register.
>
> All of that, together with the requirements of the European Union data protection directive,[1] which was signed and agreed by the previous Administration and, generally, of the right to privacy, led the working party to conclude that it was wrong that people should be under a statutory obligation to provide their details for electoral registration purposes and then have no say about whether that information could be used for other unrelated purposes.[2]

[1]   Directive 95/46/EC.
[2]   357 HC Official Report (6th series) col 168, 30 November 1999.

7.63   Section 9 of the Data Protection Act 1998 now makes provision for regulations to be made to establish what will effectively be two versions of the electoral register. When registering, voters will be given information regarding the purposes for which data contained in the register might be used and given the opportunity to opt out of having their data disclosed. Registration officers will then be charged with producing what will effectively be two versions of the register. A complete copy, the use of which will be restricted to electoral purposes (and law enforcement), and an edited copy excluding the details of those who have opted out, which may be used for commercial purposes.[1] Delay in making the regulations led to an action being brought before the courts. In the case of *R (on the application of Robertson) v Wakefield Metropolitan Council*,[2] the High Court declared that the unavailability of any mechanism permitting an elector to object to the disclosure of his details for commercial purposes contravened the requirements both of the Data Protection Directive[3] and of the Human Rights Act 1998. The Representation of the People (England and Wales) (Amendment) Regulations 2002[4] now make such an option available.

[1]   Section 9.

2   [2001] EWHC Admin 915, [2002] QB 1052.
3   Directive 95/46/EC.
4   SI 2002/1871.

7.64 Although electoral registers may represent the most extensive record of their kind, similar issues arise with other forms of record which are required to be made available to the public. Concern has been expressed on a number of occasions at the use made of lists of company shareholders, particularly in the case of privatised undertakings which might have several hundred thousand shareholders. It may be argued that the purpose of making details of shareholders publicly available is to allow identification of the owners of a limited liability company. Use of this information for the purposes of compiling mailing lists for direct marketing purposes raises different issues, although it is difficult to see how prohibitions might be enforced against the use of publicly available information for such purposes.[1]

1   In the recent conversion process of the Halifax Building Society, members were encouraged to place their new shareholding in a nominee account administered by the Society. One advantage claimed for this was that the shareholder's name and address would not appear on publicly available registers.

Law enforcement and revenue gathering purposes

7.65 A significant exception to the operation of the first principle applies where data is acquired for the purposes of the prevention or detection of crime, the apprehension or prosecution of offenders or the assessment or collection of any tax or duty. These provisions are carried over from the Data Protection Act 1984 into the Data Protection Act 1998. In such cases, the Commissioner may not take any action against the data user involved, alleging a breach of the principle where its application would be likely to prejudice the activity in question (s 29(1)). The rationale behind the exception lies in the recognition that law enforcement agencies might reasonably acquire information in ways which might normally be regarded as unfair, for example, as the result of overhearing, or even eavesdropping on, a conversation. It might, however, be considered unfortunate that the Commissioner should not be given power to define the concept of fairness in the light of the particular situation of the user involved rather than by providing a near complete exception from the requirement to act fairly. It may also be noted that the restriction upon the Commissioner's ability to act exists even where the data has been acquired unlawfully, although here it may be difficult to sustain the argument that observance of the law would prejudice the prevention or detection of crime, the apprehension or prosecution of offenders or the assessment or collection of any tax or duty.

Relevancy and scale of the information obtained

7.66 The other principle which is pertinent to the acquisition of data is the fourth, requiring that data shall be 'adequate, relevant and not excessive'. The

Data Protection Directive[1] uses the same term. No further guidance is available in either instrument concerning the application of these requirements. The principle is, however, identically worded to that in the Data Protection Act 1984. This has been at issue before the Data Protection Tribunal in the course of proceedings brought against a number of Community Charge Registration Officers.[2]

[1]   Directive 95/46/EC.
[2]   The officers involved represented Runnymede Borough Council, South Northamptonshire District Council, Harrow Borough Council and Rhondda Borough Council.

The Community Charge

7.67   The Community Charge or 'poll tax' proved one of the most controversial forms of taxation introduced in recent times. Although much of the publicity generated concerned its financial aspects, the implementation of the requirement that registers be established of those liable to pay the tax attracted the attention of the Data Protection Registrar.

7.68   Compilation of the Community Charge Registers was the responsibility of Community Charge Registration Officers in each local authority area. Where the intention was that the register should be maintained on computer, an application would require to be submitted for registration under the Data Protection Act 1984. In the case of four applications, submitted by the Registration Officers for Harrow Borough Council,[1] Runnymede Borough Council,[2] Rhondda Borough Council[3] and South Northamptonshire District Council,[4] registration was refused on the basis that the Registrar was satisfied that the applicants were likely to contravene the fourth data protection principle. Appeals against these decisions were brought before the Data Protection Tribunal. The appeal of the Officer of Rhondda Borough Council was heard separately, the other appeals being disposed of at a combined hearing.

[1]   Case DA/90 24/49/5.
[2]   Case DA/90 24/49/3.
[3]   Case DA/90 24/49/2.
[4]   Case DA/90 24/49/4.

RHONDDA BOROUGH COUNCIL

7.69   Under the terms of the Local Government Finance Act 1988, charging authorities were required to compile and maintain a Community Charge Register (s 6). It was specifically provided that the register should include details of the name and address of every person liable to pay the Community Charge. The Community Charge was payable by everyone over the age of 18 years. To this extent, a note of the date of birth of individuals who were about to reach their eighteenth birthday would be required in order for the Registration Officers to fulfil their duty of maintaining the register. In many cases, local authorities, including Rhondda Borough Council, requested the date of birth of every member of the household, regardless of whether they were over 18 or not. Dates of birth are clearly items of personal data.

7.70   The appellant applied for registration under the Data Protection Act 1984. This application was rejected by the Registrar, who expressed the view that the inclusion of information relating to date of birth would, subject to very limited exceptions as described above, be irrelevant to the determination whether individuals were liable for payment of the Community Charge. The appellant argued that many inhabitants of the Rhondda shared surnames and forenames. The addition of a note of date of birth would limit the possibility that an individual might escape inclusion on the register because his or her identity was confused with some other person of the same name. It was also argued that the inclusion of the information would assist the Registration Officer in the efficient performance of his or her duties.

7.71   These arguments were rejected by the Tribunal. It heard evidence that, nationally, fewer than 1% of households contained persons who shared the same surname and forename. Although it accepted that the figure might be higher in the Rhondda it did not consider that this justified the appellant's actions. The Tribunal concluded:

> We find that the information the appellant wishes to hold on database concerning individuals exceeds substantially the minimum amount of information which is required in order for him to fulfil the purpose for which he has sought registration ... to fulfil his duty to compile and maintain the Community Charges Register.

RUNNYMEDE BOROUGH COUNCIL, HARROW BOROUGH COUNCIL AND SOUTH NORTHAMPTONSHIRE DISTRICT COUNCIL

7.72   Similar issues were involved in the second case before the Tribunal. Each of the appellants held, or proposed to hold, on the Community Charge Register details of the type of property occupied by each subject. Again, information of this type would be classed as personal data and the Registrar raised objection on the ground that its inclusion was, or would be likely to constitute, a breach of the fourth data protection principle. In the case of Harrow and Runnymede Borough Councils, action took the form of a refusal to accept an application for registration. In the case of South Northamptonshire District Council, whose application for registration had previously been accepted, an enforcement notice was served.

7.73   In terms of the status of the information relating to type of property, the Tribunal held that whilst there might be justification for holding some information additional to that required under the Local Government Finance Act 1988, the wish to record details of type of property in every case was excessive. The Tribunal endorsed the advice given to data users by the Registrar[1] to the effect that they should seek to identify the minimum amount of personal data which is required in order to enable them to fulfil their purpose. Where additional data might be required in certain cases, these should again be identified and the further information sought or held only in those cases.

1   Guideline Booklet No 4 *The Data Protection Principles* (1998).

Storage of data

7.74   The second data protection principle requires that data be held only for one or more specified and lawful purposes. The question whether data is held for a lawful purpose might be determined only retrospectively. Holding a list of names and addresses might normally be a non-controversial matter, but if the holder is a burglar and the addresses are of houses which are to be burgled, matters will appear in a different light. For the vast majority of users, the requirement that data be held for a specified purpose is of much greater significance. This is to be determined by reference to the controller's entry on the Register. If the purpose is not specified therein, there will be a breach of the second principle.

7.75   Both the Data Protection Act 1998 and Data Protection Directive[1] contain provisions relating to the periods of time during which data may be retained. The fourth data protection principle requires that personal data 'shall be accurate and, where necessary, kept up to date', whilst the fifth principle requires that data 'shall not be kept for longer than is necessary for that purpose or those purposes'. The Directive contains similar provisions relating to the currency of data but adopts a slightly different formulation relating to retention providing that data is to be:

> ... kept in a form which permits identification of data subjects for no longer than is necessary for the purpose for which the data were collected or for which they are further processed.[2]

This formulation appears to allow greater discretion to the data controller than is presently the case under the Act. Given the increasing processing capabilities of computers, it may be difficult to determine what steps will require to be taken in order to secure the anonymity of particular data subjects.

1   Directive 95/46/EC.
2   Article 6(1)(e).

Processing of data

7.76   Both the Data Protection Act 1998 and Data Protection Directive[1] require that personal data must be processed 'fairly and lawfully'. Under the Data Protection Act 1984, the first data protection principle referred separately to the activities of obtaining and processing. The interpretative paragraph applying to the first principle refers only to the act of obtaining data and the Data Protection Tribunal ruled that a distinction has to be drawn between the two acts and that different factors may be applied in determining whether conduct is fair. None the less, a series of linked decisions of the Data Protection Tribunal relating to the operation of credit reference agencies is of considerable significance in describing the requirements that processing must be carried out fairly by reference to a particular data subject.

[1]   Directive 95/46/EC.

Processing by reference to the data subject

7.77   Credit reference agencies constitute one of the highest-profile sectors of data processors in the private sector. Study of the Registrar's annual reports reveals that a high proportion of complaints from data subjects concern the activities of these organisations.

7.78   The operation of credit reference agencies has been subject to legal controls since the passage of the Consumer Credit Act in 1974. By s 158, this Act requires credit reference agencies to supply a copy of any information held concerning an individual upon receipt of a written request from that person.[1] Provision is made for the correction of any inaccurate information (s 159) and for details of the change to be transmitted to any third party who had received the inaccurate information within the six-month period preceding the amendment.[2]

[1]   The subject access provisions of the Consumer Credit Act 1974 have now been incorporated into the access provisions of the Data Protection Act 1998. The effect of this is discussed at para 8.10 below.
[2]   Consumer Credit (Conduct of Business) (Credit References) Regulations 1977, SI 1977/330, reg 5.

7.79   The compatibility of certain aspects of the operations of credit reference agencies was at issue in a number of cases brought before the Tribunal. Several hundred undertakings have been granted licences under the Consumer Credit Act 1974. Four agencies dominate the UK market: CCN, Credit and Data Marketing Services, Equifax and Infolink, each of which was the recipient of an enforcement notice served by the Registrar.

The nature of credit reference agency operations

7.80   Although the details of their operations vary, each of the credit reference agencies referred to above holds a core of data culled from public sources. Infolink, for example, is reported as holding:

- Electoral registration information in the form of the collected electoral rolls for the UK.
- The Scottish Valuation Roll.
- County Court Judgments from courts in England and Wales, Northern Ireland and the Channel Islands.

- Scottish Court Decrees.
- Bankruptcy information obtained from court records and other public sources such as the London, Belfast and Edinburgh *Gazette*.
- Bills of Sale.
- Postal address information. This is taken from a listing of all addresses and postcodes produced and made available by the Post Office.

7.81 In addition to this publicly available information, each agency holds information supplied by its subscribers reporting instances of bad debts and maintains records of searches made. An indication of the scale of the agencies' operations can be taken from the report of the Tribunal in the *Credit and Data Marketing* appeal, which indicated that this agency conducted in excess of 5 million searches per year, whilst Infolink conducted some 30 million searches.

7.82 The information held by the credit reference agencies and extracted in connection with a particular application for credit might be used in a variety of ways. The established method of operation would be for the agency to supply the information generated to its client, the potential creditor, leaving the determination whether to extend credit facilities entirely to the recipient. All of the credit reference agencies involved in the Tribunal actions operated on this basis. In a number of cases, the agencies also offered more extensive facilities. Instead of supplying a client with raw data, the client's own acceptance criteria might be applied. These might operate at a fairly simple level so as, for example, to reject all applicants who were not home owners. If searches revealed this fact, a recommendation that the application be rejected would be transmitted to the client.

7.83 The critical point concerning the agencies' operations, and the aspect to which exception was taken by the Registrar, is that in all cases searches were conducted by reference to an address rather than a name. Although at first sight the practice might seem illogical, it was based upon a number of factors. Names constitute a rather inefficient means of identification. A glance at any telephone directory will show that most surnames appear more than once. Even full names are unlikely to be unique and most recipients of 'junk mail' will be aware of the many and various permutations of names and initials that may appear on envelopes. By contrast, addresses tend to be represented in a reasonably static format and, especially with the use of postcodes, the possibility of duplication is limited. The consequence of processing by reference to address would inevitably be, however, that a search resulting from an application for credit by one individual would retrieve information about previous residents at the address given and as to members of family or others who shared the address with the applicant.

7.84 The extraction of third-party data in making decisions about an individual applicant was considered by the Registrar to constitute unfair processing of personal data and, as such, contravened the first data protection principle. After discussions with the credit industry failed to provide an acceptable solution, enforcement notices were served on the four major agencies in August 1990. The terms of these notices were virtually identical, requiring the recipients to ensure that:

> ... from the 31st day of July 1991 personal data relating to the financial status of individuals ceases to be processed by reference to the current or previous address or addresses of the subject of the search whereby there is extracted in addition to information about the subject of the search any information about any other individual who has been recorded as residing at any time at the same or similar current or previous address as the subject of the search.

7.85 A considerable number of issues were raised in separate Tribunal proceedings hearing appeals by each agency. The first question considered concerned the nature of the processing carried out by CCN. As defined in the Data Protection Act 1984 this involves:

> ... amending, augmenting, deleting or re-arranging the data or extracting the information constituting the data and, in the case of personal data, means performing any of these operations by reference to the data subject.[1]

This definition encompasses a considerable range of operations. In the case of credit reference agencies, it was the act of extraction that was critical to the decisions. Relating the definition to the first data protection principle, the question to be answered by the Tribunal was whether the extraction of data by the credit reference agencies was to be considered unfair.

[1]   Section 1(7).

7.86 An initial argument put forward on behalf of CCN sought to draw a distinction between the extraction and the use of the personal data. The extraction of information, typically by causing the information to be displayed on a monitor, was, it was argued, a value-free operation and not susceptible to judgment by reference to criteria of fairness. What the Registrar was objecting to, it was argued, was the use to which the data was subsequently put – perhaps to refuse an application for credit. Nowhere in the first data protection principle is there any reference to the use to which personal data might be put, mention being made only of the acts of obtaining and processing data.

7.87 This line of argument was rejected by the Tribunal. Such an approach, it was held, would rob the first data protection principle of almost all meaning. Reference was made to the long title of the Data Protection Act 1984 which described it as an 'Act to regulate the use of automatically processed information relating to individuals and the provision of services in respect of the use of such information'. This made it clear that it sought to control not the technology but its human controllers. Although the data supplied by CCN's computers would be used subsequent to the actual processing, the computers could operate only in accordance with their programs. These specified the criteria by which information was to be extracted. The extraction was not, therefore, 'value-free' and the activity had to be judged by reference to the statutory criteria of fairness.

7.88   The second element of Equifax's appeal concerned the requirement that processing be conducted by reference to the data subject. Equifax, it was argued, in common with the other agencies, extracted information by reference to address rather than name. This argument was rejected by the Tribunal. Account, it was held, had to be taken of the intended purpose of the processing. If this was to obtain information concerning a living, identifiable individual, the Data Protection Act 1984 would apply. It was noted that one of Equifax's registered purposes is to provide 'information relating to the financial status of individuals'. The company was well aware that its customers sought the information in connection with their transactions with individuals and that the results of its processing would affect these persons.

7.89   Applying these criteria, the Tribunal considered evidence submitted on behalf of the appellant arguing that depriving them of third-party information would render their operations less effective. The consequence would be either an increase in bad debts or the denial of credit to persons who might otherwise have been accepted. It might even be that certain creditors would cease to operate in the consumer field.

7.90   The Tribunal accepted that the operation of credit reference agencies provided benefits. It noted that the Data Protection Act 1984 essayed no definition of the word 'fairly' but held that the prime purpose of the legislation was to protect the rights of the individual. Whilst the interests of the credit industry should not be ignored, primacy must be given to the interests of the individual applicant. On this basis it was considered:

> ... unfair for a credit reference agency, requested by its customers to supply information by reference to a named individual, so to program the extraction of information as to search for information about all persons associated with a given address or addresses notwithstanding that they may have no links with the individual the subject of the inquiry or may have no financial relationship with that individual.

7.91   It was also argued that much of the information held in and extracted from Infolink's computers, for example, judgments from county courts, was public information. It was in the public interest that such data should be readily available. Whilst not disputing this argument, the Tribunal pointed out that they were concerned with a much narrower issue: whether the extraction of this information in connection with a search relating to an unconnected individual could be considered fair. The answer to this must be in the negative.

The form of the enforcement notice

7.92   In all of the credit reference agency decisions, the Tribunal accepted that a breach of the first data protection principle had occurred sufficient to justify the Registrar in serving an enforcement notice. In all the cases, however, the Tribunal considered that the terms of the notice were excessively broad. The value of reliable credit reference and credit scoring systems was accepted, the Tribunal commenting that it was:

> ... very conscious of the benefits of reliable credit reference and credit scoring systems in preventing over-commitment by debtors, a measure very much for their benefit and that of the community, and in ensuring a well-managed credit system for the benefit of potentially sound debtors and of the credit and supply industries.

7.93 Although the unrestricted use of third-party information was considered objectionable, the Tribunal did accept that information relating to members of the applicant's immediate family or to persons with whom the applicant shared property might be relevant to a decision concerning the grant of credit. To this extent, the terms of the Registrar's enforcement notice would be varied to permit the extraction of third-party information in a restricted set of circumstances.

> Where the third-party is recorded as residing at any address concurrently with the applicant and where the third-party shares the same surname and any recorded forenames or initials as the applicant.

7.94 An example of this situation might see a parent and sibling sharing the same name and living at the same address. In such a case it might be difficult, if not impossible, for the credit reference agency to be able to avoid extracting information about the non-applicant. Extraction of third-party data will not be considered unfair in this situation, except where the agency possesses information from which it should reasonably be aware that there are two parties involved. This might be the case when parents, perhaps acting in response to previous incidents, have informed the agency that they were not willing to accept responsibility for the actions of their child – or vice versa.

> Where the third-party is recorded as residing at any address concurrently with the applicant and where the third-party has a name 'sufficiently similar' to that of the applicant to make it reasonable for the agency to believe that the parties are one and the same.

7.95 The application of this exception is subject to the same proviso as that described above regarding the existence of information contradicting the presumption of commonality. The application of this exception must be less certain than its predecessor. It would seem reasonable for it to apply in the case of minor variations in initials and perhaps even of spelling of surnames.

> Where the third-party shares the same or a sufficiently similar surname as the applicant and it is reasonable for the agency to believe that they have 'been living as a member of the same family as the subject in a single household'.

7.96 This exception will allow extraction of information relating to members of the applicant's family. It would appear that this would apply even where the third party is residing at a different address. Extraction will not be permitted where the agency possesses information which makes it reasonable for it to believe that there is no financial connection between the applicant and the third party.

> Where the third-party does not share the same surname as the applicant but, from information possessed by the agency prior to extraction, it is reasonable to believe the third-party and the applicant are one and the same person.

7.97 This exception will apply in the situation where the applicant is suspected of using a variety of names – perhaps in order to obtain credit by means of fraud. It is subject to the same proviso as operates in the previous exception although the scope for its application must be limited.

> Where the third-party does not share the same surname as the applicant but, from information possessed by the agency prior to extraction, it is reasonable to believe has been living as a member of the same family in a single household.

7.98 A typical situation here would occur where unmarried persons share the same address, but will not apply where the agency possesses information from which they should reasonably conclude that there is no financial connection between the third party and the applicant.

7.99 The scope of these exceptions is potentially broad. An agency will not be able to extract information about third parties previously resident at the same address as that pertaining to an applicant. In cases where there appears to be some link, the agency will be able to extract third-party data in the absence of specific information. The onus will lie with data subjects to supply any information disclaiming links with other persons, and it may be doubted how effectively this might be accomplished in anticipation of the extraction of data. Most likely, information may be supplied only in response to the unfavourable use of the information extracted.

7.100 Discussions continued between the Commissioner and the credit reference industry concerning the use of third-party data. In a press release published in April 2004, the Commissioner announced that following four years of negotiations, it had been agreed that the only third-party information which might be used would concern individuals who had a financial link with a credit applicant. This change is scheduled to take effect from October 2004.

Accuracy and timeousness of data

7.101 The fourth data protection principle requires that: 'personal data shall be accurate and, where necessary, kept up to date. Data is regarded as being inaccurate when it is 'incorrect or misleading as to any matter of fact'.[1] In the event that personal data is inaccurate, a data subject may be entitled to seek its rectification and, in certain cases, compensation for any resultant damage or distress.[2]

[1]   Data Protection Act 1998, s 70(2).
[2]   Data Protection Act 1998, ss 13–14. See para 8.21 below.

7.102 Although many instances are reported of inaccurate data (for example, a recent report suggested that data on the Police National Computer was subject to an 86% error rate),[1] the question whether data is accurate will not always be susceptible of a straightforward answer. A statement may be in the format: 'Fred Smith informs us that Joe Bloggs has defaulted on three loan agreements.' If it is assumed that Joe Bloggs is in reality a person of the utmost financial probity, can it be said that the statement is false? In determining this issue the fourth data protection principle is interpreted:

> The fourth principle is not to be regarded as being contravened by reason of any inaccuracy in personal data which accurately record information obtained by the data controller from the data subject or a third party in a case where—
> (a) having regard to the purpose or purposes for which the data were obtained and further processed, the data controller has taken reasonable steps to ensure the accuracy of the data; and
> (b) if the data subject has notified the data controller of the data subject's view that the data are inaccurate, the data indicate that fact.[2]

[1] *Computer Weekly*, 27 April 2000.
[2] Data Protection Act 1998, Sch 1, Pt II, para 7. These provisions are substantially similar to those applying to the data subject's claim to compensation for or rectification of inaccurate data. See also para 8.19 below.

7.103 These requirements are cumulative and mark an extension from similar provisions in the Data Protection Act 1984, which required only that the data user mark data which had been challenged by a subject with an appropriate indication. The requirement of the Data Protection Act 1998 should oblige a controller to accept data only from sources which there is reason to believe are reliable and also to take such steps as are practicable to verify information prior to subjecting it to processing.

7.104 The second element of this principle requires that necessary updating of information shall be carried out. The Data Protection Act 1998 does not expand on this requirement, but it would appear that the question whether updating is required will be dependent upon the nature of the data and the purpose to which it will be put. If the data is merely a record of a transaction between the data user and the data subject, no updating would be either necessary or justified. Where the information is being used as the basis for continuing decisions and actions, regular updating may be essential. Thus, where information is to be used for assessing an employee's suitability for promotion, an indication of periods of absence would require to be supplemented by any explanations which might subsequently have been provided.

Duration of record keeping

7.105 Linked to the issue of the topicality of data are the provisions of the fifth principle, which require that data should be retained for no longer than is necessary for the attainment of the purpose for which it is held. The Data Protection Directive contains an equivalent provision.[1] Neither instrument expands on this provision. In many cases, data users will be under an obligation to maintain data for a specified period of time, for example, solicitor-client data. In more general terms, there would appear justification for retaining data until the expiry of any limitation period for possible legal action. Save in the situation where data is maintained as a matter of historical record (Data Protection Act 1998, Sch 8, Pt IV), the fifth data protection principle would appear to require that users operate some form of policy for monitoring their data holdings and removing items which are no longer of value or relevance to their activities.

[1]   Directive 95/46/EC, art 6(1)(e).

Use of data

7.106   The Data Protection Act 1984 made specific provision for the extent to which data might be used or disclosed. The third data protection principle, frequently referred to as the 'non-disclosure principle', stated:

> Personal data held for any purpose or purposes shall not be used or disclosed in any manner incompatible with that purpose or those purposes.

7.107   The determination whether use by a data user was lawful would be determined by reference to the relevant entry on the Register. Likewise, the range of potential dissemination of data would be specified therein. Specific reference to use and disclosure of data is not found in the 1998 principles, but the equivalent provision is now in the second principle, which states that:

> Personal data shall be obtained only for one or more specified and lawful purposes, and shall not be further processed in any manner incompatible with that purpose or those purposes.

7.108   In interpreting this principle, it is provided that the determination whether use is lawful will make reference to any entry on the Register. In the case of controllers who are exempted from the notification requirement, use will be limited to the purposes for which exemption was granted. The question of non-disclosure it is provided that:

> In determining whether any disclosure of personal data is compatible with the purpose or purposes for which the data were obtained, regard is to be had to the purpose or purposes for which the personal data are intended to be processed by any person to whom they are disclosed.[1]

[1]   Data Protection Act 1998, Sch 1, Pt II, para 5.

7.109   This is very much in line with the 1984 provisions and will require that the disclosure must be made in circumstances compatible with the purpose for which the data were originally obtained and processed. As with the Data Protection Act 1984, the Data Protection Act 1998 provides for a significant number of exceptions enabling disclosures to be made in situations which might not have been envisaged and are not connected with the original purpose of the processing.

Data security

7.110   Under the terms of the seventh data protection principle data, controllers and the operators of computer bureaux are obliged to ensure that:

> Appropriate technical and organisational measures shall be taken against unauthorised or unlawful processing of personal data and against accidental loss or destruction of, or damage to, personal data.

Additionally, controllers will be responsible for ensuring that any data processors contracted by them comply with the requirements of the principle.

7.111   The comparable requirement in the Data Protection Directive is that, taking account of the state of the art and making an assessment of costs and risks involved:

> ... the controller must implement appropriate technical and organizational measures to protect personal data against accidental or unlawful destruction or accidental loss, alteration, unauthorized disclosure or access, in particular where the processing involves the transmission of data over a network.[1]

[1]   Directive 95/46/EC, art 17(1).

7.112   The Registrar has identified a considerable number of matters which are relevant to data security. Account might be taken of the physical security of premises, of any security measures incorporated into computer systems, for example, password requirements, of the level of training and supervision of employees. Account can also be taken of the manner in which data and equipment are disposed of. A number of instances have been reported of the purchasers of second-hand computers discovering that data belonging to the original owner remained in the machine's memory. Such lapses might constitute a breach of the principle, as might any deficiency in respect of the disposal of print outs of computer-generated data.[1] In 1992, the EC adopted a 'Decision in the field of the security of information systems'.[2] This is concerned, essentially, to establish the basis for Community action and in its Action Line IV calls, inter alia, for the '(d)evelopment of specifications, standardization, evaluation and certification in respect of the security of information systems'. Such measures might be of significant value in the field of data protection, although the diversity of processing activities might defeat any simple form of classification.

[1]   Guideline No 4.
[2]   OJ 1992 L 123/19.

7.113   In November 1997, the Registrar published a Consultation Paper on information security in the context of the need to comply with the relevant provisions of the Data Protection Directive.[1] This suggested that data controllers would be required to undertake a risk-based approach in determining the relevant standard of security. Specific reference was made to BS 7799, which contains both a Code of Practice and a Specification for Information Security Management. In Parliament, however, the government rejected an amendment which would have recast the interpretative provisions attached to the principle to make specific reference to 'the risks associated with processing'[2] on the basis that as a:

> [g]eneral principle of law ... it is usually necessary to prove a degree of damage. The words 'damage' and 'harm' can be taken together. There are not many actions before the courts that are based simply on the prospect of their being a problem.[3]

It might be considered, however, that such an approach smacks of closing the stable door after the horse has bolted.

[1]   Directive 95/46/EC.
[2]   HC Official Report, SC D (Data Protection Bill), col 304, 4 June 1998.
[3]   HC Official Report, SC D (Data Protection Bill), col 305, 4 June 1998.

Unlawful obtaining of data

7.114   The seventh principle makes it clear that the data controller is responsible for maintaining data security. A successful attempt, whether by means of computer hacking or other techniques, to obtain access to the data may lead to the controller incurring the Commissioner's wrath, perhaps in the form of service of an enforcement notice, and possible claims for compensation brought by aggrieved data subjects. During the 1980s and 1990s, considerable publicity attached to the activities of private investigators and investigative journalists, who, through various forms of subterfuge or bribery, were able to secure access to personal information held by a data user. Stella Rimington, the former head of MI5, for example, has been quoted as saying:

> When I was first appointed DG, the Sunday Times employed a private investigator to find out everything it could about me. Without much difficulty through getting access to ... [various databases] ... it found where I lived, where I banked, how much I had in my account, where I regularly bought my food and on what days, my telephone number (even though I was ex-Directory) and who I regularly telephoned.[1]

[1]   *Herald*, 17 October 1996.

7.115   In the situation where the investigator obtained direct access to data held on a computer, it would be likely that an offence would be committed under the Computer Misuse Act 1990. In many instances, however, the information would be obtained either through bribing an employee of the data user or by misleading the user as to identity and entitlement to access the data. In these situations, the investigator would normally commit no offence. To remedy this situation, the Criminal Justice and Public Order Act 1994 amended the Data Protection Act 1998 to provide that:

A person who procures the disclosure to him of personal data the disclosure of which to him is in contravention of subsection (2) or (3) above, knowing or having reason to believe that the disclosure constitutes such a contravention, shall be guilty of an offence.[1]

Offences would also be committed by a person selling or offering for sale any information obtained in breach of the above provision.

[1]   Section 161, adding new sub-ss (6), (7) and (8) to s 5 of the Data Protection Act 1984.

7.116   The first prosecutions under the new provision were brought in 1996. In one case, a private investigator secured details of the keeper of a motor vehicle from the Driver and Vehicle Licensing Agency by means of a deception.[1] In the second, the employee of a credit reference agency used online search facilities made available to him in the course of employment to conduct a credit search for non-work related purposes. This conduct resulted in a successful prosecution on the basis of procuring the disclosure of data.

[1]   Thirteenth Annual Report of the Data Protection Registrar (1997) p 16. The Registrar's Fourteenth Report (1998) discloses 12 prosecutions for obtaining or selling data (p 52).

7.117   As formulated in the Criminal Justice and Public Order Act 1994, the basis for the offence was the intent to cause the user to disclose outwith the terms of an entry on the Register. With the switch to selective notification, this approach could not be continued. Section 55 of the Data Protection Act 1998 seeks to effect the same result, however, providing that an offence will be committed by a person who 'knowingly or recklessly, without the consent of the data controller' seeks to obtain or disclose personal data or procure its disclosure to a third party. An exception is provided where the data is obtained in connection with the prevention or detection of crime or in pursuance of a court order. A further offence is committed by a person who sells or offers to sell data obtained in contravention of this provision.

Codes of practice

7.118   One of the most notable features of the data protection principles is their generality. Given the range of applications across which they have to be applied and the multitude of users subjected to regulation, it is difficult to envisage any other approach. In its report, the Lindop Committee advocated that statements of general principle should be supplemented by around 50 statutory codes of practice.[1]

[1]   Cmnd 7341 (1978) para 13.26.

7.119   As originally introduced, the Data Protection Bill contained no reference to codes of practice. At a late stage in its parliamentary passage, an amendment was accepted which imposes a duty upon the Registrar:

... where he considers it appropriate to do so, to encourage trade associations or other bodies representing data users to prepare and to disseminate to their members, codes of practice for guidance in complying with the data protection principles.[1]

In common with many of the duties imposed upon the Registrar, this requirement is formulated in such a manner as to afford considerable discretion to the Registrar. In the years subsequent to the passage of the Data Protection Act 1998, a considerable number of codes have been produced giving guidance as to the interpretation of the principles within specific areas of activity.

[1]   Section 36(4).

7.120   In law, such codes possess only evidentiary value. Many of the codes contain a statement from the Registrar to the effect that:

Observance of this code does not constitute an assurance that I will accept in all cases and without qualification that data users have complied with the Act [Data Protection Act 1998]. However, in considering relevant complaints it is my intention to give careful regard to whether the data user concerned has been complying with his code of practice and will take such compliance as a positive factor in his favour.

Not all the codes have received the Registrar's unqualified blessing. That produced by the Committee of Vice-Chancellors and Principles contained advice as to a method by which students might legally be prevented from obtaining access to their examination marks. This prompted the comment that:

I note the comments made ... about examination marks. Whilst the procedure envisaged in this section is not wrong in law, it is likely to give rise to difficulties and I find it disappointing that it should appear in an otherwise positive document.

7.121   The issue of the status of codes of practice was discussed in the Tribunal decision of *Innovations v Data Protection Registrar*.[1] The substantive issues concerned with the question whether the appellant's information-gathering practices conformed with the requirement of the first data protection principle that data be obtained fairly has been considered earlier. It was also argued on behalf of the appellant that its practices conformed with a code of practice adopted by a relevant trade association, the Advertising Association. The strength of this argument was undoubtedly weakened by the fact that in a foreword to the code, the Registrar had intimated that the Association's view of what was necessary to ensure fair obtaining of data 'differs from my own', and also by the fact that the Council of the Advertising Standards Association and another trade association, the Direct Marketing Association, had adopted rules requiring prior notification to data subjects as part of their codes of conduct.

[1]   Case DA/92 31/49/1.

Codes under the Data Protection Directive

7.122   The Data Protection Directive envisages a substantial role for codes of practice to operate at both a national and a Community level. The Preamble recognises that:

> Member States and the Commission in their respective spheres of competence, must encourage the trade associations and other representative organizations concerned to draw up codes of conduct so as to facilitate the operation of this Directive, taking account of the specific circumstances of the processing carried out in certain sectors, and respecting the national provisions adopted for its implementation.[1]

[1]   Directive 95/46/EC, recital 61.

7.123   This much merely restates present practice under the Data Protection Act 1998. In implementing the provision, however, art 27 of the Data Protection Directive[1] provides that draft codes are to be submitted to the national supervisory authority, which is to ascertain 'whether the drafts submitted to it are in accordance with the national provisions adopted pursuant to this Directive'. In making this determination, the authority may seek the views of data users or their representatives. This would appear to mark a significant advance on the present situation, where although, as cited above, the Registrar may express the view that the terms of a code do not comply with the requirements of the legislation, there is no precedent for a positive assertion that the code does comply. Such a development would also go at least part of the way to meeting the suggestion of the Registrar in his 1989 review of the working of the legislation that upon receipt of the Registrar's endorsement, the provisions of a code should have a status equivalent to the Highway Code, ie that although breach of its provisions would not itself constitute an offence, this could be taken into account in determining whether any provision of the legislation had been violated.

[1]   Directive 95/46/EC.

7.124   Provision is also made for the establishment of Community codes. These may be referred to a Working Party established under the directive with the remit to examine the conformity of national implementing measures with the directive's requirements, to advise on the level of data protection applying in third countries, to advise the Commission on any amendments to the Data Protection Directive and 'to give an opinion on codes at Community level'.[1] The Working Party may also seek out the views of data subjects or their representatives before determining whether the draft is in accordance with national implementing provisions. In this event, the 'Commission may ensure appropriate publicity for the code'. Given the requirement that the directive be implemented in all of the member states, it is not clear what will be the role of Community codes.

[1]   Directive 95/46/EC, art 29.

Conclusions

7.125 The data protection principles remain pivotal to the operation of the Data Protection Act 1998. As has been discussed, it is perhaps doubtful whether any changes of substance have been made from the situation existing under the Data Protection Act 1984. It appears that there is to be an enhanced role for codes of practice and, given the nebulous nature of the principles themselves, this is to be welcomed. Given the extent to which all aspects of our lives are affected by the processing of personal information, there is vital need that effective and transparent control regimes should be established. The decisions of the Data Protection Tribunal in cases brought under the 1984 Act demonstrated a desire to interpret the provisions in a liberal and subject-friendly fashion. It is to be hoped that this will continue to be the case under the new regime.

Chapter 8

Individual rights and remedies

Introduction

Towards informational self-determination

8.1 In 1983, the West German legislature made provision for a national census. The Census Act identified items of information which would be required from citizens and also provided that elements of the data gathered might be transferred from the census authorities to other public authorities in connection with the performance of their prescribed functions. The transfer possibilities envisaged in the legislation led to the statute being struck down as unconstitutional by the Constitutional Court.[1] In what has come to be regarded as a landmark decision in the field of data protection, the court held that the proposal breached arts 1 and 2 of the Basic Law requiring the state to respect and promote the 'dignity of man' and guaranteeing the 'free development' of the individual's personality. Whilst recognising the need of the state to gather information, the court held that the processing power contained in computer systems posed substantial threats to individual liberties. It held that:

> The possibilities of inspection and of gaining influence have increased to a degree hitherto unknown and may influence the individual's behaviour by the psychological pressure exerted by public interest ... if someone cannot predict with sufficient certainty which information about himself in certain areas is known to his social milieu, and cannot estimate sufficiently the knowledge of parties to whom communication may possibly be made, he is crucially inhibited in his freedom to plan or to decide freely and without being subject to any pressure/influence.[2]

[1] 'The Census Decision' (1984) 5 HRLJ 94.
[2] (1984) 5 HRLJ 94 at 100.

8.2 Particular dangers identified were that individuals might be reluctant to participate in an 'assembly or citizens' initiative' if they were uncertain whether details of their actions might be recorded and used for other purposes. In striking down the proposed census, the court elucidated a novel doctrine, that of informational self-determination, affording this the status of a basic human right. This concept, whereby the individual's wishes and expectations are afforded a considerable degree of primacy in the legal regulation of data processing, has formed the basis for all subsequent German legislation in the field.

8.3 At a basic level, the doctrine can be seen as requiring that individuals should have the ability to discover what information is held about them, by whom and for what purposes. As was stated in the report of the UK's Committee on Privacy, 'there should be no information system whose very existence is a secret'.[1] One of the major roles of the Data Protection Register is to make it possible for data subjects to discover what forms of data are held by particular controllers and for what purposes.

[1]   Cmnd 5012.

8.4 The concept of subject access, introduced in the Data Protection 1984, is the aspect of the legislation which may impact most directly on individuals. As described in the seventh data protection principle, it required that:

> An individual shall be entitled—
>
> (a)   at reasonable intervals and without undue delay or expense—
>   (i)   to be informed by any data user whether he holds personal data of which that individual is the subject; and
>   (ii)   to access to any such data held by a data user; and
> (b)   where appropriate, to have such data corrected or erased.

[1]   Schedule 1.

8.5 The operation of the principle has proved to be somewhat problematic. Whilst most European states require that access is to be provided either free of charge or upon payment of a nominal fee, the UK system has provided for a fee of up to £10 to be levied.[1] The right of access is also subject to a number of exclusions whilst, finally, such limited evidence as exists concerning the use of the access procedures suggests that a large number of requests are made not at the behest of the data subject but as a result of the requirements of a third party, a practice referred to as enforced subject access. A perhaps apocryphal tale suggests that most requests for access to criminal records are made by individuals wishing to emigrate to Australia and who are required, in contrast to practice of several centuries ago, to demonstrate the absence of a criminal record.

[1]   The Data Protection (Subject Access) (Fees) Regulations 1987, SI 1987/1507.

8.6 Under the Data Protection Directive[1] and the Data Protection Act 1998 the concept of subject access is retained and indeed developed. The Directive provides in art 12 that:

> Member States shall guarantee every data subject the right to obtain from the controller:

(a) without constraint at reasonable intervals and without excessive delay or expense:
- confirmation as to whether or not data relating to him are being processed and information at least as to the purposes of the processing, the categories of data concerned, and the recipients or categories of recipients to whom the data are disclosed;
- communication to him in an intelligible form of the data undergoing processing and of available information as to their source; and
- knowledge of the logic involved in any automatic processing of data concerning him at least in the case of the automated decisions referred to in Article 15(1).

(b) as appropriate the rectification, erasure or blocking of data the processing of which does not comply with the provisions of this Directive, in particular because of the incomplete or inaccurate nature of the data; and

(c) notification to third parties to whom the data have been disclosed of any rectification, erasure or blocking carried out in compliance with (b), unless this proves impossible or involves a disproportionate effort.

It will be seen that the scope of this provision is significantly broader than that of the Data Protection Act 1984, a fact reflected in a change in terminology in the 1998 Act, which refers to 'subject information' provisions rather than to subject access. The reference to subject access disappears from the data protection principles, although the sixth principle requires that:

> Personal data shall be processed in accordance with the rights of data subjects under this Act.

[1] Directive 95/46/EC.

8.7 The basis for subject access is now to be found primarily in the text of the Data Protection Act 1998 itself. The main features of the system are little changed from the 1984 regime. A data controller is required to respond only to requests which are made in writing,[1] which contain sufficient information to allow for identification of the data subject and which enclose any fee required by the controller.[2] The maximum fee remains at £10.[3] In terms of the information which is to be provided, it is now stated that:

> Subject to the following provisions of this section and to sections 8 and 9, an individual is entitled—
>
> (a) to be informed by any data controller whether personal data of which that individual is the data subject are being processed by or on behalf of that data controller;
>
> (b) if that is the case, to be given by the data controller a description of—
> (i) the personal data of which that individual is the data subject;
> (ii) the purposes for which they are being or are to be processed; and
> (iii) the recipients or classes of recipients to whom they are or may be disclosed.
>
> (c) to have communicated to him in an intelligible form—
> (i) the information constituting any personal data of which that individual is the data subject; and
> (ii) any information available to the data controller as to the source of those data.

(d) where the processing by automatic means of personal data of which that individual is the data subject for the purpose of evaluating matters relating to him such as, for example, his performance at work, his creditworthiness, his reliability or his conduct, has constituted or is likely to constitute the sole basis for any decision significantly affecting him, to be informed by the data controller of the logic involved in that decision-taking.[4]

[1] Section 64 of the Act provides in respect of the access procedures and a variety of other procedures under the Act the requirement for writing may be satisfied where a notice is transmitted by electronic means, received in legible form and is capable of being used for subsequent reference. An email message would seem to satisfy these requirements, although it may be difficult for such a message to supply payment of the access fee.

[2] Section 7.

[3] The Data Protection (Subject Access) (Fees and Miscellaneous Provisions) Regulations 2000, SI 2000/191, reg 3.

[4] Section 7(2).

8.8 A single request in respect of the information referred to in the Data Protection Act 1998, s 7(2)(a)–(c) is automatically to be taken as extending to the other items. A request to be informed, therefore, whether personal data is held is to be taken as extending to a request for the information itself and for the further information specified relating to purposes etc. The provision relating to information regarding the logic of processing is treated somewhat differently. The extent of the information to be supplied under this heading was the subject of considerable debate in the House of Lords, where concerns were expressed that the controller might be required to supply information which constituted valuable intellectual property.[1] It is provided that the obligation is not to extend to any information which 'constitutes a trade secret' (s 8(5)), but, as was pointed out in Parliament, this concept is an ill-defined one. The Data Protection (Subject Access) (Fees and Miscellaneous Provisions) Regulations 2000 provide that specific request must be made for receipt of this information.[2]

[1] 586 HL Official Report (5th series) cols CWH 43–45, 23 February 1998.

[2] SI 2000/191, reg 2. Rather strangely, it is also provided that a request for information about the logic employed in processing will not automatically be taken as extending to the other items of information in s 7.

8.9 The previous obligation that a written copy of data be supplied has been replaced by the requirement that the copy be supplied in 'intelligible form'.[1] With developments in processing technology, it is possible that data may take the form of audio or video clips, and although the provision of written copies may be expected to remain the norm, expansion of the definition is clearly desirable. In terms of the material to be provided, it was stated by the Court of Appeal in *Durant v Financial Services Authority* that:

> The intention of the Directive, faithfully reproduced in the Act [Data Protection Act 1998], is to enable an individual to obtain from a data controller's filing system, whether computerised or manual, his personal data, that is, information about himself. It is not an entitlement to be provided with original or copy documents as such, but, as section 7(1)(c)(i) and 8(2) provide, with information constituting personal data in intelligible and permanent form. This may be in documentary form prepared for the purpose and/or where it is convenient in the form of copies of original documents.[2]

It is further provided that although the copy of the information is normally to be provided in permanent form, this requirement may be waived with the consent of the subject or in a case where the supply of such a copy would be either impossible or involve a disproportionate effort.[3] The information supplied must be that which was held at the time the access request was received, except where any subsequent changes 'would have been made regardless of the receipt of the request'.[4]

[1] Section 7(1)(c).
[2] [2003] EWCA Civ 1746 at [26].
[3] Section 8(2).
[4] Section 8(6).

8.10 The concept of subject access was pioneered in the Consumer Credit Act 1974, which provided that individuals should be entitled to obtain a copy of information held by a credit reference agency.[1] The 1974 Act's procedures were unaffected by the Data Protection Act 1984. Given that the majority of the complaints received by the Data Protection Registrar over the years have related to the credit sector, the retention of two separate regimes might be considered illogical. The Data Protection Act 1998 merges the provisions for access to data held by credit reference agencies, which had previously been regulated under the Consumer Credit Act 1974. Provision is made for different fee levels to be fixed by the Secretary of State and it is intended that requests which would previously have been brought under the 1974 Act's provisions will remain subject to the lower fees (currently £1) payable under that regime. One issue concerning the change did cause discussion in Parliament.[2] Under the 1974 Act, a modified access procedure applies where the subject is a business person.[3] Effectively, this limits the amount of information supplied so that, for example, the applicant would not receive information about adverse credit reports which had been provided by bankers or suppliers. Where the business constitutes a sole trader or partnership, the general access provisions of the Data Protection Act 1998 will replace the specialised provisions. Concern was expressed that the consequence might be that third parties would be reluctant to supply such information in the knowledge that it could be obtained with the consequence being that small businesses might find it more difficult to obtain credit. Whilst giving an undertaking to keep the matter under review, the government indicated that it was not convinced that the concerns were justified, and a proposal to amend the Bill to retain the current procedures was rejected.[4]

[1] Section 158.
[2] Section 9.
[3] Section 160.
[4] 316 HC Official Report (6th series) cols 578–579, 2 July 1998.

Access timetable

8.11 Valid requests for access must be satisfied within 40 days.[1] Where data is held by a credit reference agency, the current shorter time limit of seven days is to apply.[2] The information supplied must generally be that held at the date of receipt of the access request. Account may be taken, however, of any amendments or deletions made subsequently where these would been made 'regardless of the receipt of the request'.[3] Having satisfied an access request from a data subject, a controller is not obliged to comply with a subsequent identical or similar request until a reasonable interval has elapsed.[4] In making his or her determination, account is to be taken of the nature of the data, the purpose of the processing and the frequency with which amendments are made.

[1] Data Protection Act 1998, s 7(10).
[2] Data Protection (Subject Access) (Fees and Miscellaneous Provisions) Regulations 2000, SI 2000/191, reg 4.
[3] Data Protection Act 1998, s 8(6).
[4] Section 8(3).

Third-party data

8.12 In very many cases records will include data relating to more than one data subject. This can create a conflict between one data subject's wish to obtain access to information which is relevant to him or herself and the expectation of another subject that his or her personal data will not be disseminated. The conflict may arise in a number of ways. It may be that data relates to some form of joint activity; transactions, for example, in connection with the operation of a joint bank account or a social work report describing the relationships between various members of a family unit. In this situation where one subject submits an access request there is unlikely to be a serious issue concerning the identity of the other subject or subjects but there may be a case for deleting items of data such as cheque or cash machine withdrawals made under the signature or against the PIN of the other account holder. In a second situation the data may relate to the inquiring subject but emanate from a third party. An example might see a social work record recounting an allegation from a named third party that a subject is behaving in a violent manner to other family members. The record could state that 'Fred Smith has reported that Joe Bloggs is mistreating his wife and children'. There clearly is personal data about Joe Bloggs here and it may be desirable to allow the subject to see and possibly refute the allegation of violence. The record also contains personal data relating to Fred Smith as the source of the data. It is likely to be extremely unwelcome to this person if the fact of his report is disclosed to Joe Bloggs. How the balance is to be struck has been a continuing cause of difficulty.

8.13 Under the Data Protection Act 1984, a data user was under no obligation to supply information relating to a third party – including the fact that the third party had been the source of information relating to the data subject. No obligation, however, was imposed on the data user to inquire whether the third party would be willing for the information to be transmitted to the subject.[1] A significant change to the extent of access rights was introduced as a consequence of the decision of the European Court of Human Rights in the case of *Gaskin v United Kingdom*.[2] The applicant in this case had spent much of his childhood in local authority care. In adulthood, he claimed that he had been the subject of ill-treatment and instituted legal proceedings against the local authority. As part of these proceedings, he sought discovery of all documents held by the authority relating to his case. Many of the documents had been compiled by third parties, such as doctors. Acting in excess of the statutory obligations imposed upon them, the authority contacted the third parties seeking their approval to disclosure. Whilst the majority agreed to disclosure of the data, a number of parties refused consent and the authority took the view that this was determinative of the issue. Under UK law as it stood this was determinative of the issue but proceedings were raised before the European Court of Human Rights alleging that the failure of the UK legislation to provide the applicant with a right of access to the data constituted breach of its obligations under art 8 of the European Convention on Human Rights requiring respect for private and family life. The European Court of Human Rights held that whilst the applicant did not have an unqualified right of access to data, the failure to provide an independent review in the event that a third party refused consent constituted a breach of his rights.

> The Court considers ... that under such a system the interests of the individual seeking access to records relating to his private and family life must be secured when a contributor to the records either is not available or improperly refuses consent. Such a system is only in conformity with the principle of proportionality if it provides that an independent authority finally decides whether access has to be granted in cases where a contributor fails to answer or withholds consent. No such procedure was available to the applicant in the present case.[3]

[1]   Section 21(4)(a).
[2]   (1990) 12 EHRR 36.
[3]   (1990) 12 EHRR 36 at 50.

8.14   In seeking to bring UK law into conformity with the European Convention on Human Rights the Data Protection Act 1998 now provides that:

> Where a data controller cannot comply with the request (for information) without disclosing information relating to another individual who can be identified from that information, he is not obliged to comply with the request unless—
>
> (a)   the other individual has consented to the disclosure of the information to the person making the request, or
> (b)   it is reasonable in all the circumstances to comply with the request without the consent of the other individual,[1]

In determining whether it is reasonable for a controller to provide access without the third party's consent the Act provides that account is to be taken of:
  (a)   any duty of confidentiality owed to the other individual,
  (b)   any steps taken by the data controller with a view to seeking the consent of the other individual,
  (c)   whether the other individual is capable of giving consent, and
  (d)   any express refusal of consent by the other individual.[2]

[1]   Section 7(4).
[1]   Section 7(6).

8.15 It is further provided that 'reference to information relating to another individual includes a reference to information identifying that individual as the source of the information sought by the request'. The Data Protection Act 1998 continues to state that the provision 'is not to be construed as excusing a data controller from communicating so much of the information sought by the request as can be communicated without disclosing the identity of the other individual concerned, whether by the omission of names or other identifying particulars or otherwise'.

8.16 The new provisions make it clear that a data controller is empowered to override the objections of a third party to disclosure of data. It does not appear, however, that any obligation is imposed on data controllers to contact third parties with the request that they consider whether access should be granted. Given the desire to comply with the decision of the European Court of Human Rights this seems a significant omission. Whilst a failure to make an inquiry might be considered to render processing of the data unfair, it might have been preferable to have required the controller to consult with the third party before making a decision to refuse access to data.

8.17 The application of the provisions relating to third-party data was at issue in the case of *Durant v Financial Services Authority*.[1] The background to this case has been described at para 5.8 above. Although some information was supplied access to other records was provided only in partial form through the concealment or redaction of information which it was considered related to third parties. Holding that the information need not be disclosed to the appellant the court indicated first the nature of the consideration that the statute required to be given by a data controller. The criterion, it was stated was 'whether it is reasonable to *comply* with the request for information notwithstanding that it may disclose information about another, not whether it is reasonable to *refuse* to comply'. The distinction it was stated:

> may be of importance, depending on who is challenging the data controller's decision, to the meaning of "reasonable" in this context and to the court's role in examining it. The circumstances going to the reasonableness of such a decision, as I have just noted, include, but are not confined to, those set out in section 7(6) [of the Data Protection Act 1998], and none of them is determinative. It is important to note that section 7(4) leaves the data controller with a choice whether to seek consent; it does not oblige him to do so before deciding whether to disclose the personal data sought or, by redaction, to disclose only part of it. However, whether he has sought such consent and, if he has done so, it has been refused, are among the circumstances mentioned in the non-exhaustive list in section 7(6) going to the reasonableness of any decision under section 7(4)(b) to disclose, without consent.

[1]   [2003] EWCA Civ 1746.

8.18 Once a data controller had made a decision to what extent third-party data should be disclosed in the absence of that person's consent, the courts, it was held, should be reluctant to routinely:

'second-guess' decisions of data controllers, who may be employees of bodies large or small, public or private or be self-employed. To so interpret the legislation would encourage litigation and appellate challenge by way of full rehearing on the merits and, in that manner, impose disproportionate burdens on them and their employers in their discharge of their many responsibilities under the Act [Data Protection Act 1998].

It continued:

the right to privacy and other legitimate interests of individuals identified in or identifiable from a data subject's personal data are highly relevant to, but not determinative of, the issue of reasonableness of a decision whether to disclose personal data containing information about someone else where that person's consent has not been sought. The data controller and, if necessary, a court on an application under section 7(9), should also be entitled to ask what, if any, legitimate interest the data subject has in disclosure of the identity of another individual named in or identifiable from personal data to which he is otherwise entitled, subject to the discretion of the court under section 7(9). The Court of Appeal, in its turn, should have firmly in its mind its duty of 'anxious scrutiny' in such matters, but should not be expected to conduct an exercise of detailed or other inspection of documents under section 15(2) of the 1998 Act unless the Judge's reasoning or lack of it on the issue *and* the factual issues raised on the appeal demand it

...

Much will depend, on the one hand, on the criticality of the third party information forming part of the data subject's personal data to the legitimate protection of his privacy, and, on the other, to the existence or otherwise of any obligation of confidence to the third party or any other sensitivity of the third party disclosure sought. Where the third party is a recipient or one of a class of recipients who might act on the data to the data subject's disadvantage ... his right to protect his privacy may weigh heavily and obligations of confidence to the third party(ies) may be non-existent or of less weight. Equally, where the third party is the source of the information, the data subject may have a strong case for his identification if he needs to take action to correct some damaging inaccuracy, though here countervailing considerations of an obligation of confidentiality to the source or some other sensitivity may have to be weighed in the balance. It should be remembered that the task of the court in this context is likely to be much the same as that under section 7(9) in the exercise of its general discretion whether to order a data controller to comply with the data subject's request (see para. 74 below). In short, it all depends on the circumstances whether it would be reasonable to disclose to a data subject the name of another person figuring in his personal data, whether that person is a source, or a recipient or likely recipient of that information, or has a part in the matter the subject of the personal data. Beyond the basic presumption or starting point to which I referred in paragraph 55 above, I believe that the courts should be wary of attempting to devise any principles of general application one way or the other.[1]

[1] *Durant v Financial Services Authority* [2003] EWCA Civ 1746 at [60]–[66].

8.19 A further issue concerns the question of when a third party is to be considered identifiable. A controller is obliged to supply as much information as is possible without disclosing the third party's identity. In particular, it is stated, this might involve the omission of names or other identifying particulars. Account is to be taken of:

> ... any information which in the reasonable belief of the data controller, is likely to be in, or to come into, the possession of the data subject making the request.[1]

This requirement may cause some difficulties for data controllers. In a case such as *Gaskin*,[2] for example, it may be a very difficult task for a data controller to assess whether the inquiring data subject would have, after the passage of many years, any recollection of the identity of particular doctors or social workers who had been responsible for submitting reports.

[1] Data Protection Act 1998, s 7(5).
[2] *Gaskin v United Kingdom* (1990) 12 EHRR 36.

8.20 If the subject's request is not satisfied, an action seeking access may be raised before the court. Here, it is provided that the court may order the grant of access, except where it considers that it would be unreasonable to do so 'because of the frequency with which the applicant has made requests to the data user ... or for any other reason'.[1] Assuming that a £10 access fee would cover the costs incurred by most users in satisfying access requests, it may be doubted whether this provision will be utilised to any extent. It has also been suggested, however, that a campaign of mass access requests might be used as a part of an industrial or other campaign directed against a data user. In the field of local government, for example, a spokesman for one authority has commented:

> If there were a concerted campaign by some group and we suddenly had 5,000 applications arriving on the same day, we would obviously have a problem in providing the individual within the 40 day period provided by law.[2]

Short of such unusual circumstances, it is difficult to envisage that a user will be able to rely upon this provision to refuse a request for access. It may also be the case that the vast majority of disputes between data users and subjects concerning entitlement to access will be resolved before the Commissioner rather than the courts.

[1] Data Protection Act 1998, s 21(8).
[2] *Glasgow Herald*, 28 December 1987.

Matters arising subsequent to access

Rectification of inaccurate data

8.21 Data will be considered inaccurate if they are false or misleading as to any matter of fact. In such an event, the data subject may request the court to order the controller to 'rectify, block, erase or destroy'[1] the data in question.[2] These remedies may also be invoked when the data controller has acted in such a fashion as would give the subject an entitlement to claim compensation under the Data Protection Act 1998. Additionally, the controller may be ordered to amend any statement of opinion which appears to be based on the inaccurate data. Where data constitutes an accurate transcription of information received from a third party, the court may make one of the above orders. Alternatively, it may permit the data to be retained but be supplemented by a further statement of the true facts as determined by the court.[3]

[1] The distinction between erasure and destruction of the data may relate to the nature of the storage medium involved. Manual files may well be destroyed through burning or shredding. With computer records, the concept of erasure is more relevant, given that data may only be completely destroyed following complete reformatting of the storage device.
[2] Section 14(1).
[3] Section 14(2).

8.22 The above remedies are effectively identical to those operating under the Data Protection Act 1984. The Data Protection Act 1998 introduces one potentially significant extension. Where the court determines that data is inaccurate and requires that it be rectified, blocked, erased or destroyed, it may, where this is considered reasonably practical, order that the controller notify details of the changes to any third party to whom the data has previously been disclosed.[1] Such a remedy may provide a valuable audit trail allowing the detrimental consequences of inaccurate data to be minimised.

[1] Section 14(3).

Compensation

8.23 Under the Data Protection Act 1984, data subjects were entitled to claim compensation for damage and distress resulting from inaccuracy in data or from their unauthorised destruction or disclosure. These rights were seldom utilised,[1] the requirement in particular to demonstrate both damage and distress proving a substantial hurdle.

[1] The Fourteenth Report of the Data Protection Registrar (1998) cites one case where a credit reference agency wrongly registered adverse data against the complainant. The mistake continued for some considerable time and the report indicates that, following the Registrar's intervention, 'a substantial ex gratia payment was made' (p 88).

8.24 The Data Protection Act 1998 adopts a more extensive approach in terms of the basis for liability. Compensation may be claimed in respect of losses caused through any breach of the legislation. Except, however, in the situation where a claim arises as a result of the processing of data for media purposes (the 'special purposes'), the 1998 Act retains the requirement that damage be demonstrated as a prerequisite to any claim alleging distress. In all cases, the controller will have a defence if it can be shown that reasonable care was taken to avoid the breach.

Exceptions to the subject information provisions

8.25 In certain situations, the individual's interest in obtaining access to personal data has to be restricted, either in the subject's own interests or as a result of giving priority to other competing claims. Access to medical data provides an example of the first situation, whilst restrictions on access to data held for the purpose of crime prevention or detection illustrate how the subject's desire to know what information is held might reasonably be subjugated to the requirements of the data controller or those of society at large. The Data Protection Directive provides that member states may provide for exemptions from subject access when this constitutes a necessary measure to safeguard:

(a) national security;
(b) defence;
(c) public security;
(d) the prevention, investigation, detection and prosecution of criminal offences, or of breaches of ethics for regulated professions;
(e) an important economic or financial interest of a member state or of the EU, including monetary, budgetary and taxation matters;
(f) a monitoring, inspection or regulatory function connected, even occasionally, with the exercise of official authority in cases referred to in (c), (d) and (e); or
(g) the protection of the data subject or of the rights and freedoms of others.[1]

[1] Directive 95/46/EC, art 13(1).

8.26 In common with the Data Protection Act 1984, the Data Protection Act 1998 provides for a wide range of situations in which the data subject's right of access will be restricted or excluded. Prior to considering these specific situations, reference should be made to an aspect of the new system which has prompted critical comment from the Data Protection Registrar. In many instances where the controller is exempted from the requirement to provide access, there is also exemption from the first data protection principle requiring that data be processed fairly and lawfully. Under the 1984 Act, this latter exemption was defined separately from the provisions relating to subject access. In comments on the Bill, it was argued that:

> In many cases it is extremely difficult to understand the justification for this. In particular the miscellaneous exemptions in Schedule 7, Paragraph 2, Armed Forces; Paragraph 3, Judicial Appointments and Honours; Paragraph 4, Crown Employment and Crown or Ministerial Appointments; Paragraph 5, Management Forecasts; Paragraph 6, Negotiations; Paragraph 9 Information about Human Embryos; Paragraph 10, Legal Professional Privilege; are all exempt from the subject information provisions. This is a major extension of the existing exemptions.
>
> The same applies to Health and Social Work Orders in clause 29, Regulatory Activities in clause 30 and Information Available to the Public by or Under Any Enactment in clause 33. The Registrar questions whether the exemption from the fair obtaining requirements is necessary in all of these cases. For example there would be no requirement under the new legislation to inform

donors, in relation to in vitro fertilisation, how their information was to be processed. In many cases it represents a substantial extension of exemptions from control.[1]

[1] Comments of the Data Protection Registrar on the Data Protection Bill, 5 May 1998.

8.27 In respect of the various provisions to be discussed below, a variety of approaches exist. Where data is held for national security purposes, total exemption is offered from all aspects of the legislation. In the case of data held for historical, research or statistical purposes, the exemption relates only to subject access and the related supply of information relating to source, processing purpose and intended disclosures as defined in the s 7 of the Data Protection Act 1998. In other cases, however, the exemption is stated as applying also in respect of the requirements of the first data protection principle relating to the fair and lawful processing of personal data. Although in many cases, the application of the exemption is limited to instances where it is necessary to avoid prejudicing the purpose for which the data is being processed, its linkage with subject access does mean that provisions which purport to protect data subjects may, in reality, work to their disadvantage.

8.28 Prior to considering the circumstances under which a user may legally deny a subject's access request, mention should be made of a problem that may arise whenever the user determines that all or part of a request for access falls within the scope of an exception. Under the Data Protection Act 1998's definitions, personal data is classed as data to which the subject is entitled to have access. Where an exception is properly relied upon, it may be accepted that it is as undesirable from the user's standpoint to inform the subject that they hold data which they are not willing to disclose as it would be to divulge the information. In the event that a subject suspects that personal data has not been supplied pursuant to a request for access, action may be raised before the courts.[1] An alternative course of action will be to make a complaint to the Commissioner. In the event the Commissioner takes action,[2] the onus will be on the user to justify their action. Dependent, however, upon the circumstances and the nature of the data, it may be that a subject who receives the reply that no relevant personal data is held may accept this at face value and will make no attempt to pursue the matter before the courts or with the Commissioner.

[1] Section 21(8).
[2] See para 7.3ff above.

National security

8.29 Under the Data Protection Act 1984, information held for the purpose of national security was totally exempted from the legislation.[1] Given the increasing involvement of national security agencies such as MI5 in crime-related functions, such as operations against suspected drug dealers, the division between national security and criminal functions is frequently blurred. This has led the Registrar to express concern that exemptions have been claimed on an organisational rather than a task-related basis.[2] Although no changes were required to the 1984 Act in this regard, national security falling outwith the ambit of Community law making competence, the Data Protection Act 1998 does contain significant new provisions. As under the 1984 Act, a certificate may be issued by a minister of the Crown indicating that personal data is held for the purpose of national security.[3] Under the 1984 Act, such a certificate was not open to challenge. It is now provided, however, that it may, however, be challenged before the Data Protection Tribunal by any person 'directly affected'. This may include a data subject who for the first and only time is given a right to initiate proceedings before the Tribunal. Applying 'the principles applied by the court on an application for judicial review', the Tribunal may quash the certificate if it considers that the minister did not have 'reasonable grounds' for issuing it.[4] Detailed provision for the procedures to be followed in the Tribunal are now found in the Data Protection Tribunal (National Security Appeals) Rules 2000.[5]

1   Section 27.
2   See, for example, *The Sunday Times*, 1 February 1998.
3   Section 28(2).
4   Section 28(5).
5   SI 2000/206.

NORMAN BAKER V SECRETARY OF STATE FOR THE HOME DEPARTMENT

8.30   The appellant in this case,[1] a Liberal Democrat MP, had sought access in July 2000 to records which he believed were held about him by the security services. This prompted a response:

> Under the Data Protection Act 1998 the Security Service intends to notify the Data Protection Commissioner that it processes data for three purposes. These are: staff administration, building security CCTV and commercial agreements. The Security Service has checked its records and holds no data about you in any of these categories.
>
>   Any other personal data held by the Security Service is exempt from the notification and subject access provisions of the Data Protection Act 1998 on the ground that such exemption is required for the purpose of safeguarding national security, as provided for in Section 28(1) of the Act. Thus, if it were to be the case that the Service held any data regarding you other than for the purposes set out in paragraph 2 above, the Data Protection Act would not confer a right of access. There is therefore no data to which you are entitled to have access under the Act, but you should not assume from this letter that any such data is held about you.
>
>   I would point out that a right of appeal exists under section 28 of the Act. The section provides that the exemption described above can be confirmed by a certificate signed by a Minister of the Crown who is a member of the Cabinet, or by the Attorney General. A certificate relating to the work of the Security Service was signed by the Home Secretary on 22 July. Any person directly affected by the issuing of the certificate may appeal against the certificate to the Data Protection Tribunal ...[2]

1   *Norman Baker v Secretary of State for the Home Department* [2001] UKHRR 1275.
2   [2001] UKHRR 1275 at [14].

8.31 Such an appeal was brought and provided the opportunity for the first sitting of the National Security Appeals Panel of the Information Tribunal. The appellant argued before the Tribunal that he had been given information that the security services had collected information in connection with his past activities in support of an ecological group. Although his involvement with the organisation had now ceased, he indicated that he had been informed that the file remained in existence.

8.32 The Tribunal reviewed the certificate which had been issued by the Secretary of State. This it was stated, 'can fairly be described as a blanket exemption for "any personal data that is processed by the Security Service" in the performance of its statutory functions'.[1]

> By exempting the Security Service from the duty under section 7(1)(a) of the Act [Data Protection Act 1998] to inform the individual making the request whether or not his personal data are being processed, the Certificate authorises the non-committal reply which was given to Mr. Baker. This means that both the Certificate and the response gave effect to the policy which is known colloquially as 'neither confirm nor deny' and by the acronym 'NCND'. We have no doubt that they were intended to do so.[2]

The certificate at issue in the present case was typical of all certificates issued in response to requests for access under the Data Protection Act 1998. The case for applying this policy was that a reply indicating that information was held but was not being made available to an applicant could of itself compromise the national security interests for which the information had been collected.

[1]   *Norman Baker v Secretary of State for the Home Department* [2001] UKHRR 1275 at [25].
[2]   [2001] UKHRR 1275 at [30].

8.33 Although such a policy raises major issues relating to access to national security data, the issue before the Tribunal was a more limited one, namely to determine whether the Secretary of State had acted reasonably in formulating a certificate which left the decision whether and to what extent a request for access should be granted entirely to the security services. As was stated:

> if the NCND response is permitted in all cases then the practical result is that the Service is not obliged to consider each request on its individual merits. That follows if the NCND reply is invariably justified, and we were furnished with no evidence that individual consideration is given to the possible consequences of making a positive response to every request.[1]

The question for the Tribunal was whether such a blanket policy was acceptable or whether the legislation imposed an obligation to give consideration to the individual circumstances of each application.

[1]   *Norman Baker v Secretary of State for the Home Department* [2001] UKHRR 1275 at [32].

8.34 Discussion of whether the Secretary of State had reasonable grounds for issuing the certificate focused on the question whether his action constituted a proportionate response to the need to balance the interests of individual rights and state security. After reviewing the principles appropriate to an action for judicial review, the Tribunal recognised that different situations called for different approaches:

> Where the context is national security judges and tribunals should supervise with the lightest touch appropriate; there is no area (foreign affairs apart) where judges have traditionally deferred more to the executive view than that of national security; and for good and sufficient reason. They have no special expertise; and the material upon which they can make decisions is perforce limited. That the touch should be the lightest in comparative terms does not, of course, assist in weighing up how light that should be in absolute terms.[1]

Even on this basis, however, the Tribunal was of the view that the certificate should be quashed. A blanket exemption, as provided for by the certificate, was wider than was necessary to preserve national security. It was clear from the evidence that there were cases where information held by the security services could be disclosed without prejudicing national security and no evidence that the task of sifting these cases from others where the established 'neither confirm nor deny' response would impose unreasonable burdens upon the security service.

[1] *Norman Baker v Secretary of State for the Home Department* [2001] UKHRR 1275 at [76].

8.35 The decision in the *Baker* case[1] was not concerned in any respect with the merits of a decision that access should not be granted. It provides authority for the proposition that each request must be considered on its merits. In two further cases brought before the National security Appeals Panel, *Hitchens v Secretary of State for the Home Department* and *Gosling v Secretary of State for the Home Department*[2] the attempt was made to challenge the merits of decisions to refuse to supply information which the appellants believed was held by the security services concerning their past activities. In the former case the period covered was some 30 years previously when the applicant, who is now a somewhat right-wing newspaper columnist, was a member of an extreme Marxist group at York University. As was argued by the appellant:

> My request was for files held on my activities as an extreme left-wing student in the early 1970s, mainly while I was at the University of York between 1970 and 1973. As it happens I think it would have been quite legitimate for the Security Service to keep an eye on the organisation to which I then belonged, a Marxist grouplet called the International Socialists. I already have a fair idea who its informants were in our organisation, and have no intention of disclosing their identity or publicising it. My aim is purely to know what, if anything, is in these records, mainly because I feel I am entitled to know the details of such records as a matter of natural justice. Since I am no longer a revolutionary Marxist, and the politics of this country have been utterly transformed in the intervening period, and it is most unlikely that any individual mentioned in these files still holds a sensitive position of any kind, I can see no argument for withholding these files from me. I would, if asked, be quite happy to co-operate with the Security Service to ensure that no sensitive information was accidentally disclosed. Their response, however, is simple blank refusal ...

covered by the meaningless and hard-to-justify claim that this is 'safeguarding national security'. I think the Security Service needs to do better than this to justify secrecy over files almost 30 years old concerning my own youthful follies and their attempts to monitor them.

1   *Norman Baker v Secretary of State for the Home Department* [2001] UKHRR 1275.
2   The transcript of these decisions can be obtained from the Department of Constitutional Affairs website at http://www.dca.gov.uk/foi/inftrib.htm.

8.36   Following the panel's decision in *Baker*,[1] the format of the ministerial certificate had been amended to make it incumbent upon the security service to give individual consideration to each request for access. The focus of argument in this case, and in the related appeal by Gosling, was on the merits of the individual decision. Here the Panel was referred to the Investigatory Powers Tribunal which was established under s 65 of the Regulation of Investigatory Powers Act 2000 to deal a wide range of complaints that may be made about the exercise of powers under the Act. This tribunal, it was held, had jurisdiction to deal with complaints of the kind brought by the appellant. Further:

> we believe that the Investigatory Powers Tribunal is the body best placed to determine any specific complaint that the Service has applied the provisos to the certificate in a manner that is manifestly unjustified. That Tribunal is presided over by a distinguished senior judge and has the appropriate expertise to investigate a complaint of this nature.[2]

On this basis, both appeals were rejected.

1   *Norman Baker v Secretary of State for the Home Department* [2001] UKHRR 1275.
2   [2001] UKHRR 1275 at [56].

8.37   Whilst it is encouraging that another method of appeal should be available to individuals, the result appears indicative of a somewhat confused and confusing approach towards information policy. Whilst it may well be the case that the structure of the Investigatory Powers Tribunal makes it better equipped to deal with arguments on the merits of a particular access request, the question arises what is the continuing function of the National Security Appeals Panel. Having quashed the first version of the ministerial certificate in *Baker* the terms of the revised version were accepted in *Gosling* and *Hitchens*. Short of further changes in format, it is difficult to identify any circumstances in which an appeal to the panel would serve any useful purpose.

Data held for policing and revenue gathering purposes

8.38   The Data Protection Act 1984 excluded data held for the purpose of:

(a)   the prevention or detection of crime;
(b)   the apprehension or prosecution of offenders; or
(c)   the collection or assessment of any tax or duty

from the subject access provisions where this would be prejudicial to the attainment of the purpose in question.[1] The determination whether access would be prejudicial requires to be made in the context of an individual request for access.

[1]   Section 28(1).

8.39   The operation of this exception raises a number of significant issues. It is difficult to conceive of any item of personal data that could not be regarded as potentially relevant to the purpose of crime prevention. The exemption will apply only where the grant of access would prejudice this purpose. In the event a denial of access is challenged before the Registrar, the onus will be on the data user to demonstrate a likelihood of prejudice in the circumstances of the particular case. Whilst these issues may be susceptible of ready resolution in the context of criminal detection and the apprehension or prosecution of offenders, some problems may be anticipated in relation to the nebulous concept of crime prevention. To give an extreme and unlikely example, a police force may receive information that a person is planning to rob a bank. At this stage the information is held for crime prevention purposes. If the individual concerned should make a request for access it might be argued that the purpose of crime prevention would best be served by disclosing the information. Faced with this knowledge, it would be a foolhardy robber who continued with the particular scheme. It appears both unlikely and undesirable that potential criminals should receive such a helpful warning. It may be that the phrase 'crime prevention' could be interpreted in the sense of preventing the successful perpetration of the crime.

8.40   As originally submitted to Parliament, the Data Protection Act 1998 supplemented this list with provision that the Secretary of State might exempt personal data 'of a specified description' from the subject information provisions where the exemption was required for any of the above purposes. In such cases, there would be no requirement that granting access to a particular subject should prejudice the attainment of the purpose. It was explained on behalf of the government that the provision was intended primarily to benefit the Inland Revenue. An example might be that:

> ... the Inland Revenue's recently introduced self-assessment system uses a range of indicators to identify individual tax returns which justify further inquiries. Subsection 4 will allow an exemption to be made for withholding this critical risk assessment information from data subjects. If it was not withheld, tax experts, if not the individuals concerned, could soon start to compare cases and deduce the revenue's criteria for further inquiry.[1]

[1]   586 HL Official Report (5th series) col 505, 16 March 1998.

8.41   The clause, however, could potentially be applied to a wide range of public sector processing activities. Following a lengthy debate, the House of Lords voted to remove this provision from the Bill and a more closely defined provision was introduced at the Committee stage in the Commons. This provides that subject access will not be permitted where personal data is processed by a government department, local authority or other authority administering housing benefit or council tax benefit as part of a system of risk assessment relating to the assessment of collection of tax or duty, the prevention or detection of crime or the apprehension or prosecution of offenders and:

> ... where the offence concerned involves any unlawful claim for payment out of, or any unlawful application of, public funds

and where exemption is required in the interests of the operation of the system.[1]

Essentially, this provision will be applicable to systems of data matching, a practice which has in itself been the cause of some controversy. It is to be noted that the exemption relates only to the subject access provision and not to the requirements of the first data protection principle that data be obtained and processed fairly and lawfully.

[1] Data Protection Act 1998, s 29(4).

Health data

8.42 The Data Protection Act 1984 established the general principle that access should be provided to medical and social work data. The Access to Personal Files Act 1987 and Access to Health Records Act 1990 extended these rights to manual files with procedures which are now gathered under the umbrella of the Data Protection Act 1998. The 1998 Act confers power on the Secretary of State to make regulations exempting or modifying the subject information provisions in respect of health data.[1] The Data Protection (Subject Access Modification) (Health) Order 2000[2] now provides for exemption when, in the opinion of a relevant health professional, the grant of access would 'cause serious harm to the physical or mental health or condition of the data subject or any other person'. This provision is in large part identical to the position adopted under the 1984 Act, but it may be significant to note that the ground for refusal now extends to the fact that the grant of access would cause serious harm to 'any other person'.

[1] Section 30(1).
[2] SI 2000/413.

8.43 In cases where the data controller concerned is not a health professional, any decision to grant or refuse access may be made only after consultation with an 'appropriate health professional'. This term is defined as:

(a) the health professional who is currently or was most recently responsible for the clinical care of the data subject in connection with the matters to which the information which is the subject of the request relates; or

(b) where there is more than one such health professional, the health professional who is the most suitable to advise on the matters to which the information which is the subject of the request relates.[1]

[1] SI 2000/413, reg 2.

8.44 A request for access may not be denied on the ground that disclosure would identify a health professional as being responsible for the compilation of a record, except where it can be shown that serious harm is likely to be caused to the physical or mental health or condition of the health professional. This is perhaps likely to apply only in the situation where there are grounds for suspecting that the data subject might be liable to attack or harass the health professional identified.

8.45 Special provision is made for the situation where access is sought, typically by a parent or guardian, on behalf of a child or a person suffering mental incapacity. In such a case, it is provided that data are exempted from the access rights where it has been:

(a) provided by the data subject in the expectation that it would not be disclosed to the person making the request;

(b) obtained as a result of any examination or investigation to which the data subject consented in the expectation that the information would not be disclosed; or

(c) which the data subject has expressly indicated should not be so disclosed.[1]

---

[1] SI 2000/413, reg 5(3).

8.46 By providing that access may be denied only to the extent that this would cause 'serious harm' to the health of the data subject, the Order[1] must be seen as establishing a strong presumption in favour of access. Whilst recognising that circumstances, particularly those connected with psychiatric illness, may exist in which the supply of a copy of a medical record may not be in the best interests of the patient, it may be doubted whether the procedures adopted under the Order are, in themselves, likely to prove any less harmful. In common with the situations arising under other exemptions, a health professional may respond to a request for access with the statement that no relevant personal data is held. To an extent perhaps greater than with the other exceptions, the data subject is likely to be aware of the fact that data is held. The failure to supply data may well be a source of distress in itself, whilst discovery of the fact that the data has been withheld for fear that access would cause serious harm to the patient's health would, in itself, appear inimical to his or her health interests.

---

[1] SI 2000/413.

Education and social work data

8.47 The basic format of the exemptions in respect of these categories of data is similar to that applying to health records. The relevant statutory instruments are the Data Protection (Subject Access Modification) (Education) Order 2000[1] and the Data Protection (Subject Access Modification) (Social Work) Order 2000.[2] In both cases, access may be denied in situations where its grant 'would be likely to cause serious harm to the physical or mental health or condition of the data subject or any other person'. Unlike the situation with health records, however, there is no requirement that the decision whether to grant or refuse access should be made by a person possessing appropriate qualifications.

---

[1] SI 2000/414.
[2] SI 2000/415.

8.48 In both sectors, it is provided that a request for access may not be refused on the basis that the data would identify a third party where this would refer to an employee of the data controller responsible for producing a record in the course of employment, again subject to an exception where it can be shown that the grant of access would be likely to result in serious harm to the individuals concerned.

8.49 In the case of both categories of records – but especially in the case of educational records – there is a possibility that access may be sought by a third party acting on behalf of a data subject. In addition to the general ground for refusing access, it is provided in the case of educational records that access may be denied in respect of information indicating that the child is or may be at risk of child abuse, where the grant of access would not be in the best interests of the child. In respect of social work records, the criteria are identical to those described above concerning health data.

Regulatory activity

8.50 A broad range of statutory agencies engaged in regulatory tasks are provided with exemptions from the subject information provisions to the extent that compliance with these would prejudice the attainment of their purpose.[1] A number of agencies are specifically identified in the Data Protection Act 1998, namely, the Parliamentary, Health Service, Local Government and Northern Irish Assembly and Complaints Ombudsmen. Exemption is also offered to the Director General of Fair Trading in respect of the discharge of functions in the fields of consumer protection and competition policy. In addition to named agencies, exemption is also offered to those performing 'relevant functions' which are designed to protect against specified risks. The term 'relevant functions' is defined to encompass functions conferred by statute, performed by the Crown, ministers or government departments or 'any other function' which is of a 'public nature and is exercised in the public interest'. The activities involved relate to protection against loss due to 'dishonesty, malpractice or other seriously improper conduct' within the financial services, corporate and professional sectors or through the conduct of discharged or undischarged bankrupts. Also exempted are functions concerned with the supervision of charities and the protection of health and safety, both for workers and for third parties who might be affected by particular activities.

[1] Section 31.

Research history and statistics

8.51 Exemption for data of this description continues the approach adopted in the Data Protection Act 1998. Where data are 'not processed to support measures or decisions with regard to particular individuals' and where the processing is not likely to cause substantial damage or distress to any data subject, exemption is offered from the subject access provisions subject to the further condition that the results of processing are not made available in a form permitting identification of data subjects.[1]

[1]   Section 33.

Information required to be made available to the public

8.52   In many instances, personal data will be contained in some document which is made available to the public. An example would be the electoral roll, copies of which may be supplied in electronic format. In the situation where the data made available is the only data held concerning the data subject, there would be little value for the subject in exercising a right of access. Such an exemption previously applied under the Data Protection Act 1984 and continues under the Data Protection Act 1998 but, again, with the additional benefit to the data controller that there will be exemption from the first data protection principle.[1]

[1]   Section 34.

Miscellaneous exceptions

8.53   Schedule 7 to the Data Protection Act 1998 contains a substantial list of additional exceptions, which list may be supplemented by regulations made by the Secretary of State.[1] As described in the following paragraphs, the extent of the individual exemptions varies, ranging from the application of modified access procedures, through exemption from access, to exemption from the fair processing requirement.

[1]   Section 38(1).

Confidential references

8.54   In many cases under the Data Protection Act 1984, such references would have been excluded from scrutiny under provisions referring to the processing of data purely in order to create the text of a document (the word processing exemption).[1] This exemption is not retained in the Data Protection Act 1998 and the expanded definition of processing in the 1998 Act will bring such documents within its scope. It is provided that the subject access provisions will not apply to references given in connection with the data subject's education, employment or appointment to any office as well as to the provision of any services by the data subject.[2]

[1]   Section 1(8).
[2]   Schedule 7, para 1.

Armed forces

8.55   The subject information provisions will not apply where their application would be likely to prejudice the combat effectiveness of the armed forces.[1] This is a new provision and it is difficult to identify situations in which it is likely to apply.

1   Data Protection Act 1998, Sch 7, para 2.

Judicial appointments and honours

8.56   Under the Data Protection Act 1984, information held for the first of these purposes was exempted from the subject access provisions.[1] The Data Protection Act 1998 extends the scope of the exemption to data processed in connection with the 'conferring by the Crown of any honour'. Such data are exempt from the subject information provisions regardless of any issue of prejudice.[2]

1   Section 31.
2   Schedule 7, para 3.

Crown employment and Crown and ministerial appointments

8.57   Regulatory power is conferred on the Secretary of State to exempt data processed for the purpose of assessing a persons suitability for specified appointments. The Data Protection (Crown Appointments) Order 2000[1] provides that this is to apply in respect of the appointment of senior religious figures in the Church of England and a range of other dignitaries, including the Poet Laureate and the Astronomer Royal.

1   SI 2000/416.

Management forecasts

8.58   Personal data processed for this (undefined) purpose benefit from an exemption to the subject information provisions where compliance would prejudice the attainment of the purpose.[1] Under the Data Protection Act 1984, a data user was not required to give access to information indicating intentions held towards the data subject. Such information might frequently be held in records maintained for career planning purposes and these may benefit from this provision.

1   Data Protection Act 1998, Sch 7, para 4.

Corporate finance

8.59   Extensive provisions are made for exemptions under this heading. The exemption will apply to data processed by 'relevant persons' concerned with the underwriting of share issues or the provision of advice on capital structure, industrial strategy and acquisitions and mergers and will apply when the application of the subject information provisions could affect the price of any shares or other instruments. In the situation this criterion is not satisfied, it is further provided that exemption may be granted 'for the purpose of safeguarding an important economic or financial interest of the United Kingdom'. It is provided that the Secretary of State may specify in more detail the circumstances and situations in which this latter exemption is to apply and this power is exercised in the Data Protection (Corporate Finance Exception) Order 2000.[1] This specifies that account is to be taken of the 'inevitable prejudicial effect' on:

(a) the orderly functioning of financial markets; or
(b) the efficient allocation of capital within the economy,

through granting access to data which might affect the decision of any person whether or how to act within the financial markets or in respect of the conduct of any business activity.

[1] SI 2000/184.

Negotiations

8.60 Data processed in relation to negotiations between the controller and subject which record the intentions of the controller are exempt from the subject information provisions where compliance with these would be likely to prejudice those negotiations.[1] An example of such a situation might concern data relating to an employer's business strategy in a situation where an employee who has been identified as critical to the success of the business is seeking to negotiate a pay rise.

[1] Data Protection Act 1998, Sch 7, para 7.

Examination marks and examination scripts

8.61 The Data Protection Act 1984 made special provision allowing examination authorities to delay responding to requests for access beyond the normal 40-day period.[1] This was considered necessary for large-scale examinations, such as the GCSE, where a period of months might elapse between examination and publication of the results. This approach continues in the Data Protection Act 1998.[2] One point which should be noted is that where an examination authority relies upon the extended time limits upon receipt of an access request, its response must provide information as to the data held at the time of receipt of the request, at the time the request is complied with and any further data which was held at any intervening stage. An inquiring subject will, therefore, receive details of any changes made to exam marks during the various stages of the assessment process.

[1] Section 35.
[2] Schedule 7, para 8.

8.62 A novel exemption from the subject access provision relates to the materials produced by students during the examination process.[1] Under the Data Protection Act 1984, it is unlikely that these would have been covered by the legislation. With the extension to some forms of manual records and the deletion of the text processing exemption, the Data Protection Act 1998 may well govern such materials.

[1] Schedule 7, para 9.

Information about human embryos

8.63   The Data Protection Act 1998 provides an exemption from the subject information provisions in respect of information indicating that an individual was born following IVF treatment. The Data Protection Act 1984 made a similar provision with regard to the subject access right.[1] An alternative access procedure involving prior counselling is, however, provided under the Human Fertilisation and Embryology Act 1990.[2] These provisions are continued by the Data Protection (Miscellaneous Subject Access Exemptions) Order 2000.[3]

[1]   Section 35A.
[2]   Section 31.
[3]   SI 2000/419.

Legal professional privilege

8.64   Data are exempt from the subject information provisions where they consist of information in respect of which a claim to legal professional privilege (or client-lawyer confidentiality in Scotland) could be maintained in legal proceedings.[1] This provision replaces an equivalent exemption under the Data Protection Act 1984,[2] but once again with an extension from subject access to the subject information provisions.

[1]   Data Protection Act 1998, Sch 7, para 10.
[2]   Section 31(2).

Self-incrimination

8.65   Data controllers need not supply information in response to a request for access when the provision of the information would indicate that an offence might have been committed (other than under the Data Protection Act 1998), thereby exposing them to the risk of criminal prosecution. Any information supplied pursuant to a request for access is not admissible in any proceedings for an offence under the 1998 Act.[1]

[1]   Schedule 7, para 11.

Enforced subject access

8.66   The situation where access rights imprison rather than empower the data subject has long been the subject of criticism, not least by the Data Protection Registrar. Devising an appropriate method of control has proved more difficult. The major difficulty facing any attempt to control the practice is the imbalance of power typically existing in such situations. If the subject is seeking employment, for example, a request that the information be supplied may carry as much weight as a demand. The initial drafts of the Data Protection Directive provided that data subjects should be entitled:

... to refuse any demand by a third party that he should exercise his right of access in order to communicate the data in question to that third party.

In the final text, the Directive contained the somewhat enigmatic provision that data subjects should be guaranteed the right to exercise access 'without constraint'.[1] Other language versions of the Directive make it clearer that the provision is intended to apply to enforced access, the German text, for example, requiring that access be provided *frei und ungehindert*.

[1]   Directive 95/46/EC, art 11(a).

8.67   Although the government indicated the intention to act against enforced subject access from the earliest stages of the Data Protection Act 1998's parliamentary passage, finding an appropriate form of prohibition proved a difficult task. A variety of possibilities were considered. Subject access might, for example, be provided only in person rather than in writing. This would, of course, have made a dramatic change to the whole system of subject access and would have caused great inconvenience in the event, for example, a data subject was located in Glasgow and the data controller in London. An alternative suggestion canvassed was that all access requests should be filtered through the Commissioner. Again, practical constraints might make this solution unworkable. Ultimately, however, it was determined that the only feasible approach was to make the practice criminal. The prohibitions apply, however, only in respect of certain forms of records – criminal records, prison records and DSS records – and in respect of a limited range of situations. A person must not require the provision of information obtained following a request for access (a relevant record) in connection with the recruitment or continued employment of the data subject or with any contract under which the subject is to provide services. Similarly, when the person is concerned with the provision of goods, facilities or services to members of the public, it is prohibited to require the production of any relevant records as a condition for the provision of such goods, facilities or services.[1] It is further provided that any contractual terms will be void in so far as they purport to require the production of any medical information obtained pursuant to an access request.[2] Although it is provided that these categories may be extended by statutory instrument,[3] it may be queried whether the provisions comply fully with the Data Protection Directive's requirements.[4]

[1]   Section 56.
[2]   Section 57.
[3]   Section 56(8).
[4]   Directive 95/46/EC, art 11(a).

8.68   In this, as in other areas, the provisions of the Data Protection Act 1998 will not operate in isolation. Under the provisions of the Police Act 1997, new arrangements have been made for providing access to criminal records. Three categories of access are created. A basic certificate may be sought by any applicant and will reveal details of any convictions which are not spent under the Rehabilitation of Offenders Act 1974. A more extensive 'criminal record certificate', adding details of spent convictions, will be issued upon the joint application of the individual and an organisation which is exempted from the provisions of the 1974 Act. This will include professional organisations, such as the Law Society, in respect of their roles in determining whether individuals might be considered suitable for admission to the profession. The most extensive certificate, the 'enhanced criminal record certificate', will include police intelligence data and details of acquittals, will be reserved for situations where an individual is seeking to work with children or vulnerable adults (or other sensitive positions such as those related to gambling or judicial appointments).

8.69 Given the large numbers of requests for access relating to criminal records, there will clearly be a close relationship between the access provisions of the Police Act 1997 and those of the Data Protection Act 1998. It was stated in Parliament that the Data Protection Act 1998's provisions will not be implemented before those of the Police Act 1997. Again, whilst a public interest defence will be available to parties charged with an offence under the 1998 Act's provisions, this will not be available in respect of data relating to the prevention or detection of crime.

Rights to object to data processing

Direct marketing

8.70 It is a little-known fact that those persons who purchase black ash furniture are 20 times more likely to respond to a fashion promotion than those whose tastes are less exotic. Such nuggets of information may constitute interesting trivia to most people, but to those engaged in the retail industry they can represent the path to fortune. Direct marketing is one of the fastest-growing sectors of the economy. Although it tends to be referred to under the epithet 'junk mail', each item delivered represents a not inconsiderable investment on the part of the sender. In many instances, retailers will possess information linking an individual to a purchase and may use this in order to attempt to stimulate further sales. The purchaser of a motor vehicle, for example, is likely to receive a communication from the seller around the anniversary of the purchase in the hope that the buyer might be considering buying a new model. The increasing use of store-based credit cards coupled with the utilisation of laser scanning cash points provides retailers with detailed information about their customers and their purchases. There are few technical barriers in the way of processing data so as to be able to 'talk to every customer in his or her own life style terms'.[1] It has even been suggested that 'intelligent shopping trolleys' might guide customers towards promotions which analysis of their previous purchases suggests might prove alluring.[2] Assuming that the data users involved have registered the fact that they intend to process personal data for sales and marketing purposes, the only legal barrier to such techniques might come from a determination that such processing is unfair.

[1]   Roger Hymas, GE Capital executive director, quoted in *Financial Times*, 4 April 1991.
[2]   *Financial Times*, 4 April 1991.

8.71 The use of personal data for purposes of direct marketing has been the cause of some recent controversy. Reference has previously been made to the *Innovations* case[1] and the data protection implications of list broking. Additionally, however, organisations are seeking to exploit their customer databases by entering into agreements to provide mailings on behalf of other companies. This may take a variety of forms. Analysis of, for example, purchases made with a credit card may indicate that an individual frequently stays in hotels. The credit card company may then enter into an agreement with a hotel chain to include a promotional leaflet with its statement of account. In this example, no personal data will be transferred between the companies. In a Guidance Note relating to Direct Marketing,[2] the Registrar has indicated that in certain circumstances use of financial data for such purposes might constitute a breach of confidence.[3] More recently, action has been taken against a number of utilities engaging in the practice of cross-selling, with enforcement notices being served against a number of utilities which sent offers of other products and services to their customers. Significantly, the fact that the utilities offered customers the opportunity to opt out of these offers was not considered sufficient, the Registrar arguing that an opt-in system should apply.[4]

[1] *Innovations (Mail Order) Ltd v Data Protection Registrar* Case DA/92 31/49/1 (see Chapter 7).
[2] October 1995, available from the Registrar's website at http://www.open.gov.uk/dpr/dprhome.htm.
[3] Paragraphs 81–88.
[4] Thirteenth Report of the Data Protection Registrar (1997) pp 26–28.

8.72 Treatment of data obtained and used for the purposes of direct marketing constituted one of the most controversial aspects of the Data Protection Directive.[1] As originally drafted, the legislation would have imposed strict obligations on data controllers to inform subjects whenever data was to be used for such a purpose. The proposals were weakened in subsequent drafts and as enacted, the Directive offers member states a choice of control regimes. It may be provided that data subjects be given the right to object to a controller's intention to process or to disclose data for the purposes of direct marketing. No fees are to be charged in this event.[2] It is arguable that this reflects current UK practice, especially after the decisions of the Data Protection Tribunal in the *Innovations* and *Linguaphone* cases.[3] As an alternative, the Directive provides that controllers might be required to give specific notice to data subjects before data is used by or on behalf of third parties for direct marketing purposes.[4] This is coupled with the requirement that steps be taken to inform data subjects of their rights.

[1] Directive 95/46/EC.
[2] Article 14(b).
[3] *Innovations (Mail Order) Ltd v Data Protection Registrar* Case DA/92 31/49/1; *Linguaphone Institute v Data Protection Registrar* Case DA/94 31/49/1.
[4] Article 14(b).

8.73 The Data Protection Act 1998 adopts the second of these options providing that:

> An individual is entitled at any time by notice in writing to a data controller to require the data controller at the end of such period as is reasonable in the

circumstances to cease, or not to begin, processing for the purposes of direct marketing personal data of which he is the data subject.[1]

[1] Section 11(1).

Other forms of processing

8.74 In the case of direct marketing data, the subject's wishes are absolute. With other forms of processing, the subject may serve notice requiring the cessation of processing on the basis that this is likely to cause substantial and unwarranted damage or distress. This right will not apply:

* where the subject has previously consented to the processing;
* where the processing is necessary to conclude or perform a contract with the data subject;
* where it is necessary to comply with any legal obligation on the data controller; or
* where the processing is necessary to protect the vital interests of the data subject.[1]

[1] Data Protection Act 1998, s 10(1).

8.75 The Secretary of State may specify other situations in which the right to object is to be withdrawn.[1] Upon receipt of such a notice, the controller must respond in writing within 21 days, indicating either that the subject's request will be granted or giving reasons why or to what extent this should not be the case.[2] A negative response may be appealed to the courts, which may make such order for ensuring compliance as it thinks fit.[3]

[1] Data Protection Act 1998, s 10(2).
[2] Section 10(3).
[3] Section 10(4).

8.76 Whilst the principle that the data subject should be entitled to exercise control over the situations in which personal data is processed must be welcomed, the requirement that 'substantial and unwarranted damage or distress' be demonstrated, coupled with the exceptions described above, may remove much of the value from the provision. It may be noted that the Data Protection Directive, in providing for the right to object, states that this is to be based on 'compelling legitimate grounds'.[1] Whilst this term is not defined in the legislation, it does seem rather less demanding criteria than those adopted in the Data Protection Act 1998.

[1] Directive 95/46/EC, art 14.

Automated decision making

8.77 Increasingly, the results of data processing may trigger further actions affecting the data subject with minimal intervention from any human agency. A trivial example may be taken from the operation of automated cash dispensing machines. A customer may approach a machine at midnight, insert a bank card, enter a personal identifier number (PIN) and request a sum of money. Details of the customer's account will be checked with the bank's computer system and if the customer is sufficiently in funds, cash will be dispensed. If the customer is not in funds, no money will be issued. There will be no human involvement at any stage of the transaction. In other instances, it is possible that human agents may be reduced to little more than a cipher. An example might be seen in the operation of systems of credit scoring. Here an applicant for credit is required to fill in a form giving information about matters such as marital status, employment and housing status etc. Points are allocated depending on the answers. A married person, for example, may be awarded one point, a single person two and a divorced person three. The pointage values are based upon an assessment of the risk of default. Each creditor may establish a predetermined acceptance level. If a customer's total falls below this, the application will be rejected.

8.78   The operation of credit scoring has been criticised by the Director General of Fair Trading on the basis of perceived unfairness to persons whose profile may not fit the automated model, yet whose credit history may be flawless, and the recommendation has been made that those operating the technique should build in an appeals procedure. A similar approach is adopted in the Data Protection Directive which, drawing on provisions in the French Data Protection Act, provides that individuals must be granted the right:

> ... not to be subject to a decision which produces legal effects concerning him or significantly affects him and which is based solely on automated processing of data intended to evaluate certain personal aspects relating to him, such as his performance at work, creditworthiness, reliability, conduct, etc.[1]

Inevitably, this general statement is subject to exceptions, the Directive continuing to provide that automated decisions are permissible in the course of entering into or performing a contract, so long as the outcome is favourable to the subject or provision is made to safeguard 'legitimate interests'. An appeals procedure such as that referred to above, allowing the subject to present additional information, would appear to meet this requirement. It is further provided that other automated decisions may be sanctioned by law so long as this also contains safeguards for the subject's legitimate interests.

[1]   Directive 95/46/EC, art 15.

8.79   Although there might be debate about how significant any element of human intervention in a decision-making process is required to be, most applications should pose few intractable problems in that a delay in implementing a decision will not cause significant problems for either data controller or subject. The cash dispensing example cited above may be a more difficult issue. In the event a customer is denied funds late at night, there seems little doubt that the statutory criteria will be satisfied. It may be doubted whether there is any realistic prospect of providing an immediate right of appeal. In Lord Denning's memorable phrase from *Thornton v Shoe Lane Parking*[1] the customer 'may protest to the machine, even swear at it; but it will remain unmoved'.

[1]   [1971] 1 All ER 686.

Conclusions

8.80   Under the Data Protection Act 1984, the right of access to data, coupled with rights to require the correction of inaccurate data and very restricted rights to compensation, constituted the major innovation from the standpoint of data subjects. By moving to what are described as 'subject information rights', the Data Protection Act 1998 does confer new entitlements on data subjects. The right to object to data processing and to resist attempts to compel the exercise of access rights also constitute significant advances. That said, what the opening paragraphs of a section confer is often removed by the exceptions and qualifications which tend to litter subsequent paragraphs. It would not be practicable or desirable to permit a data subject an absolute right to require that data not be processed, otherwise an individual with a long history of bad debts could require that a credit reference agency expunge all records from its files. Nevertheless, the statutory provision appears somewhat mean-spirited. Much the same can be said of the provisions relating to enforced subject access. Certainly, it must be admitted that it will be very difficult to stamp out such practices. In many cases, such as the making of an application for employment, the imbalance in power between an employing data controller and applicant data subject will be such that a mere expression of desire might be sufficient to make the subject feel compelled to comply. Undoubtedly, the data subject is in a stronger position under the Data Protection Act 1998 than has hitherto been the case. The criticism may be that the level of improvement is not more pronounced.

Chapter 9

Sectoral aspects of data protection

Introduction

9.1 A feature of the new data protection system is the provision of specialised regimes for particular sectors of activity. This chapter will consider two topics concerned with the application of data protection principles within the media and telecommunications sectors. In the case of the media, the issue is principally concerned with the application of what might be regarded as 'traditional' data protection principles in the context of activities where different priorities might legitimately be identified. With the increasing importance of the telecommunications sector – as epitomised by the value placed on spectrum frequencies in the UK's recent third generation mobile licence auction – more and more data processing activities are being conducted over some communications network. Increasingly, as will be discussed also in the following chapter, the need is to ensure that data protection principles are formulated in such a way that they can realistically be enforced within a network environment.

Data protection and the media

9.2 The application of data protection provisions in respect of media activities raises a number of complex issues. At the stage of gathering information with a view to publication, investigative journalism in particular may involve the use of tactics and techniques which would normally be stigmatised as unfair (if not unlawful). At almost the other end of the publication spectrum, many newspapers and journals now maintain copies of issues in electronic format. These will certainly come within the scope of the Data Protection Act 1998, under whose general provisions a subject would be entitled to require the rectification of any errors coupled with a reformulation of any resultant statements of opinion. Whilst generally desirable, the rewriting of documents

204

which claim to represent data as published on a certain date calls to mind the operation of George Orwell's Ministry of Truth.

9.3   The Data Protection Act 1984 made no special provision for the media. In large measure, this approach was justified by the limited use of computer equipment for journalistic purposes, the existence of the text processing exemption and the limited nature of the definition of processing. Time and technology have moved on. A 1992 study produced for the Council of Europe[1] identified a range of practices within member states regarding the treatment of media activities within data protection legislation. Some countries, such as the Netherlands and Sweden, provided a total exemption from data protection laws, others provided partial exemption, in the case of Germany, for example, requiring only that media users comply with requirements relating to data security. Other regimes, including that of the UK, provided no form of special treatment. The study identified a potential conflict between the provisions of the European Convention on Human Rights relating to freedom of expression and the right to seek out and impart information and those concerned with the right to privacy. Providing solutions is a difficult task and the Council of Europe contented itself with a recommendation that the potential conflict should be borne in mind in framing legislation.

[1]   'Data Protection and the Media', a study prepared by the Committee of Experts on Data Protection.

9.4   A similar view was taken by the European Commission in framing the Data Protection Directive,[1] which provides in its Preamble that:

> Whereas the processing of personal data for purposes of journalism or for purposes of literary or artistic expression, in particular in the audiovisual field, should qualify for exemption from the requirements of certain provisions of this Directive in so far as this is necessary to reconcile the fundamental rights of individuals with freedom of information and notably the right to receive and impart information, as guaranteed in particular in Article 10 of the European Convention for the Protection of Human Rights and Fundamental Freedoms.[2]

The Preamble continues to suggest that national laws should provide for alternative measures – such as the submission of reports to the supervisory agency, to ensure that data subjects' rights are not abused. Article 9 states that:

> Member States shall provide for exemptions or derogations from the provisions of this Chapter, Chapter IV and Chapter VI for the processing of personal data carried out solely for journalistic purposes or the purpose of artistic or literary expression only if they are necessary to reconcile the right to privacy with the rules governing freedom of expression.

[1]   Directive 95/46/EC.
[2]   Recital 37.

9.5   This formula empowers rather than requires member states to act, but for the UK, the decision was taken to include special provisions for these activities, described as the 'special purposes' in the Data Protection Act 1998.

Scope of the provisions

9.6 Section 3 of the Data Protection Act 1998 defines the concept of 'special purposes'. These relate to the processing of personal data:

(a) for the purposes of journalism;
(b) artistic purposes; and
(c) literary purposes.

It was stressed in Parliament that no qualitative criteria would be applied to determine whether a work could be classed as artistic, journalistic or literary. Although much of the debate in Parliament focused on the activities of the media, this definition recognises that literary and artistic works also raise issues of freedom of expression. The prime purpose of the Act's exceptional provisions is to place limits on the ability of data subjects to invoke statutory rights to impede publication of a work. Similar restrictions are placed upon the powers of the Data Protection Commissioner, with modified provisions for the service of information and enforcement notices. Once the work is in the public domain, the provisions of the general law will apply, including the law of defamation although, as indicated in Chapter 8, the 1998 Act does provide new rights of compensation for distress caused as a result of processing carried out in connection with one of the special purposes.

Activities covered

9.7 The Data Protection Act 1998 applies a three-stage test to determine whether processing for a special purpose should benefit from exemption. Personal data must be subject to processing:

(a) ... with a view to the publication by any person of any journalistic, literary or artistic material;
(b) the data controller reasonably believes that, having regard in particular to the special importance of the public interest in freedom of expression, publication would be in the public interest; and
(c) the data controller reasonably believes that, in all the circumstances, compliance with (statutory provisions) is incompatible with the special purposes.[1]

It was suggested in Parliament that:

> We have deliberately placed on the face of the Bill, I believe for the first time in an Act of Parliament in this country, that the public interest is not the narrow question of whether this is a public interest story in itself but that it relates to the wider public interest, which is an infinitely subtle and more complicated concept.[2]

[1] Section 32(1).
[2] 585 HL Official Report (5th series) col 442, 2 February 1998.

9.8 In determining whether belief that publication is in the public interest might be considered reasonable, it is provided that account is to be taken of any relevant code of practice. Power is conferred on the Secretary of State to designate codes which are to be taken into account in this way. The Data Protection (Designated Codes of Practice) Order 2000[1] lists five codes:

• The Code on Fairness and Privacy issues by the Broadcasting Standards Commission in 1998 under the terms of the Broadcasting Act 1996.
• The ITC Programme Code issued by the Independent Television Commission in 1998 under the terms of the Broadcasting Act 1990.
• The Press Complaints Commission's Code of Practice published in 1997.
• The Producers' Guidelines issued by the British Broadcasting Corporation in 1996.
• The Programme Code issued by the Radio Authority in 1998 under the terms of the Broadcasting Act 1990.

[1]   SI 2000/418.

9.9 Citation of codes in this manner is a novel feature of the Data Protection Act 1998. It may be noted additionally that whilst three of the codes have some form of statutory basis, the remaining two have no such backing.

Scope of the exemption

9.10 Section 31 of the Data Protection Act 1998 defines a range of provisions which will not apply where processing is carried out for the special purposes. With the exception of the seventh principle relating to data security, the data protection principles will not operate, neither will the subject access provisions nor those enabling a data subject to object to data being processed. Also excluded are the provisions of s 12, relating to subject rights in respect of automated decision making, and the general provisions of s 14, relating to the subject's rights to compensation. These latter provisions are substituted, however, by special and more extensive rights.

9.11 These exceptions are wide ranging. One consequence will be that even the unlawful obtaining of personal data will not expose the controller to action under the Data Protection Act 1988 – although other criminal sanctions such as, for example, a charge of theft may be imposed in respect of the offending conduct. It should be stressed that these exceptions apply only to the period of time prior to publication of material. A data subject, for example, will not be able to exercise access rights to discover material which a newspaper has obtained about, for example, financial dealings and which will form the core of a report on the subject's activities. Once the story has appeared the subject access provisions will apply subject only to the normal exceptions.

Procedural aspects

9.12 The question whether processing is covered by one of the special purpose exemptions is likely to arise in the course of legal proceedings. In this regard, it is provided that proceedings must be stayed when the data controller claims, or it appears to the court, that the data are being processed for a special purpose and:

> With a view to publication by any person of any journalistic, literary or artistic material which, at the time twenty four hours immediately before the relevant time, had not previously been published by the data controller.[1]

The relevant time will be the moment at which the controller makes the claim for protection or the court determines that the processing is for a special purpose.

[1]   Data Protection Act 1998, s 32(4).

9.13 It will be recognised that there is no requirement that the controller's claim that processing is covered by the special purpose should have any merit. As discussed below, procedures for the lifting of such a stay are complex, and the Registrar has criticised the situation whereby an unscrupulous party could delay proceedings for a period of months, if not years, with little justification.[1]

[1]   Briefing Note, 'Media Exceptions', 16 February 1998.

9.14 Once a court has determined that procedures should be stayed, the focus of attention switches to the Commissioner, who will be required to make a written determination as to whether the processing is being conducted only in connection with one of the special purposes or with a view to the publication of material not previously published by the data controller.[1] In obtaining evidence necessary to reach such a view, the Registrar may require to exercise powers conferred under the legislation to serve a special information notice. Service of such notice may itself be the subject of an appeal to the Data Protection Tribunal. If the Registrar determines that the processing is not exempt, this finding may itself be appealed to the Tribunal. It will only be when appeal procedures have been exhausted that the determination will come into effect and the court will be in a position to lift the stay. Although reference was made to the possibility of a 'fast track' procedure for resolving appeals to the Tribunal, the Registrar has been markedly less optimistic than the government as to the possibility that disputes can be resolved speedily.

[1]   Data Protection Act 1998, s 45.

9.15 The application of the Data Protection Act 1998's provisions relating to media processing was at issue in the case of *Campbell v Mirror Group Newspapers Ltd*. Finding in favour of the claimant in the High Court,[1] Moreland J held that information relating to her drug addiction was sensitive personal data, that the defendant had failed to show that its processing of the data conformed with any of the provisions of Sch 3 setting out conditions for the lawful processing of personal data or with the Press Complaints Commission code of practice, an instrument which had been designated by the Secretary of State under s 32. In respect of the defence provided by s 32 it was held that whilst this would operate in order to prevent a claimant stopping publication, its benefit ceased at this point and did not confer any form of immunity in respect of a subsequent action for damages on the basis that the unfair or unlawful processing had caused distress to the data subject. Damages of £3,500 were awarded in respect both of the contravention of the Data Protection Act 1998 and in respect of the claimant's claim that the publication constituted breach of confidence.

¹   [2002] EWHC 499 (QB), [2002] All ER (D) 448 (Mar).

9.16   The judge's findings in respect of the Data Protection Act 1998 were overturned by the Court of Appeal.¹ Delivering the judgment of the court, Lord Phillips MR was critical of the structure of the Data Protection Act 1998. Echoing the views of Moreland J, who described the interpretative task as akin to 'weaving his way through a thicket', the Act was described as 'a cumbersome and inelegant piece of legislation'.²

¹   *Campbell v Mirror Group Newspapers Ltd* [2002] EWCA Civ 1373, [2003] QB 633.
²   [2002] EWCA Civ 1373, [2003] QB 633 at [72].

9.17   Before the Court of Appeal, the appellant did not seek to argue that their processing of Ms Campbell's personal data complied with the requirements of Sch 3 to the Data Protection Act 1998 – as was stated, 'much of their argument was founded on the submission that it was virtually impossible for journalists to comply with the requirements of the Act'¹ – but argued that the effect of the s 32 defence was to confer immunity in respect of any action for damages made subsequent to publication. The result of the High Court's ruling, it was argued for the appellants would be that:

> Without the consent of the data subject, a newspaper would hardly ever be entitled to publish any of the information categorised as sensitive without running the risk of having to pay compensation. Indeed, it would be difficult to establish that the conditions for processing any personal information were satisfied. If this were correct, it would follow that the Data Protection Act had created a law of privacy and achieved a fundamental enhancement of Article 8 rights, at the expense of Article 10 rights, extending into all areas of media activity, to the extent that the Act was incompatible with the Human Rights Convention.²

¹   *Campbell v Mirror Group Newspapers Ltd* [2002] EWCA Civ 1373, [2003] QB 633 at [74].
²   [2002] EWCA Civ 1373 at [92].

9.18   Analysing the provisions of the Data Protection Act 1998, s 32 defence, the Court of Appeal first focused on sub-ss (4) and (5). These were described as procedural measures designed to provide for the stay of proceedings brought against a publisher until after publication and there was no dispute that 'the purpose of these provisions is to prevent the restriction of freedom of expression that might otherwise result from gagging injunctions'.¹

¹   *Campbell v Mirror Group Newspapers Ltd* [2002] EWCA Civ 1373, [2003] QB 633 at [117].

9.19 The court continued to examine the provisions of Data Protection Act 1998, s 32(1)–(3) which, it was stated:

> ... on their face, provide widespread exemption from the duty to comply with the provisions that impose substantive obligations upon the data controller, subject only to the simple conditions that the data controller reasonably believes (i) that publication would be in the public interest and (ii) that compliance with each of the provisions is incompatible with the special purpose – in this case journalism.[1]

It was concluded that:

> If these provisions apply only up to the moment of publication it is impossible to see what purpose they serve, for the data controller will be able to obtain a stay of any proceedings under the provisions of sub-sections (4) and (5) without the need to demonstrate compliance with the conditions to which the exemption in subsections (1) to (3) is subject.[2]
>
> ...
>
> For these reasons we have reached the conclusion that, giving the ... provisions of the sub-sections their natural meaning and the only meaning that makes sense of them, they apply both before and after publication.[3]

[1] *Campbell v Mirror Group Newspapers Ltd* [2002] EWCA Civ 1373, [2003] QB 633 at [118].
[2] [2002] EWCA Civ 1373 at [118].
[3] [2002] EWCA Civ 1373 at [121].

9.20 Support for this approach was taken from the comments of the responsible government minister as recorded in the *Hansard* report of the Bill's second reading debate. Here it was indicated that:

> Following the meetings to which I referred, we have included in the Bill an exemption which I believe meets the legitimate expectations and requirements of those engaged in journalism, artistic and literacy activity. The key provision is Clause 31. This ensures that provided that certain criteria are met, before publication – I stress 'before' – there can be no challenge on data protection grounds to the processing of personal data for the special purposes. The criteria are broadly that the processing is done solely for the special purposes; and that it is done with a view to the publication of unpublished material. Thereafter, there is provision for exemption from the key provisions where the media can show that publication was intended; and that they reasonably believe both that publication would be in the public interest and that compliance with the bill would have been incompatible with the special purposes.[1]

[1] 585 HL Official Report (5th series) col 442, 2 February 1998.

9.21 Although it was indicated that the court, mindful of the dicta of Lord Hoffmann in *Robinson v Secretary of State for Northern Ireland* that reference to *Hansard* should be a matter of 'last resort',[1] did not base its decision on this passage, it may be queried whether the comments do fully support the interpretation that the s 32 defence applies totally pre- and post-publication. As indicated by the court, the Data Protection Act 1998, s 32 is indeed a measure in two parts. Subsections (4) and (5) provide a very straightforward method of protection against gagging orders. Subsections (1)–(3), it is submitted, should swing into action only after publication. In conformity with the Data Protection Directive's strictures that:

> Member States shall provide for exemptions or derogations from the provisions of this chapter, chapter IV and chapter VI for the processing of personal data carried out solely for journalistic purposes or the purpose of artistic or literary expression only if they are necessary to reconcile the right to privacy with the rules governing freedom of expression.[2]

1   [2002] UKHL 32, [2002] All ER (D) 364 (Jul) at [40].
2   Directive 95/46/EC, art 9.

9.22   The use of the words 'only' and necessary' must indicate both that exemptions may be provided only when and to the extent strictly necessary to reconcile the competing rights. This may involve allowing publication to take place but cannot, it is submitted, justify a removal of rights to compensation (and rectification) after the event. As was stated by the Article 29 Working Party:

> The directive[1] requires a balance to be struck between two fundamental freedoms. In order to evaluate whether limitations of the rights and obligations flowing from the directive are proportionate to the aim of protecting freedom of expression particular attention should be paid to the specific guarantees enjoyed by the individuals in relation to the Media. Limits to the right of access and rectification prior to publication could be proportionate only in so far as individuals enjoy the right to reply or obtain rectification of false information after publication.
>
> Individuals are in any case entitled to adequate forms of redress in case of violation of their rights.[2]

1   Directive 95/46/EC.
2   Recommendation 1/97 'Data Protection Law and the Media'.

9.23   The provisions of the Data Protection Act 1998, s 32(1)–(3) provide a defence to any action seeking damages for distress caused by the fact of publication which is capable of applying even where the strict conditions imposed under Sch 3 cannot be satisfied. Such an approach will neither prevent serious investigative journalism being published nor impose any form of financial burden in the form of a subsequent award damages. It would be compatible with the operation of the law of defamation which generally will not serve to prevent publication but will give remedies in the event material can be shown to be defamatory.

9.24   It was accepted by all parties in the proceedings that the Data Protection Act 1998 in general was poorly drafted and the provisions of s 32 particularly ambiguous. Whilst this is certainly fair comment, it is reflective of the confusion which continues to exist in the UK concerning the law of privacy. Given the breadth of the definition of processing included in the data protection legislation there is no doubt that it does apply to media activities. There is no doubt also that the legislation is concerned with the protection of privacy. This, however, is only part of its remit and in many respects the comments of Lord Chief Justice Lane in *R v Gold* appear apposite. In that case, concerned with the application of the Forgery and Counterfeiting Act 1981 to a case of computer hacking, he concluded:

> We have accordingly come to the conclusion that the language of the Act was not intended to apply to the situation which was shown to exist in this case ... It is a conclusion which we reach without regret. The Procrustean attempt to force these facts into the language of an Act not designed to fit them produced grave difficulties for both judge and jury which we would not wish to see repeated. The appellants' conduct amounted in essence ... to dishonestly obtaining access to the relevant Prestel data bank by a trick. That is not a criminal offence. If it is thought desirable to do so that is a matter for the legislature rather than the courts.[1]

1   [1987] 3 WLR 803 at 809–810.

Special information notices

9.25   A modified form of information notice applies where data is being processed for a special purpose. Acting either in response to a request from a data subject for an assessment whether data is being processed in accordance with the principles,[1] or where there are reasonable grounds for suspecting that a data controller has wrongfully claimed the benefit of the special purpose to, for example, refuse a request for access, the Commissioner may serve a 'special information notice'.[2] The notice will require that the controller supply the Commissioner with specified information to enable the Commissioner to determine whether the processing is being conducted for a special purpose or with a view to publication of new information. The notice must indicate the ground upon which the Commissioner is making the request and give notice of the controller's rights of appeal. The notice will not come into effect until the expiry of the period allowed for the lodging of appeals. Under the Data Protection Act 1984, this period is 28 days.[3] The period under the Data Protection Act 1998 will be fixed by Order.[4] In cases of urgency it is provided that the notice may require that information be supplied within seven days.[5]

1   Section 42.
2   Section 44.
3   Data Protection Tribunal Rules 1985, SI 1985/1568, art 4.
4   Schedule 6.
5   Section 44(6).

9.26   Having received the information required, the Commissioner will make the determination referred to above as to whether processing is being conducted only for the special purposes. If the determination is that this is not the case, the Commissioner may serve the normal form of information notice seeking information to be supplied allowing a determination whether processing is lawful.[1]

1   Data Protection Act 1998, s 46(3).

Enforcement notices

9.27 Whether following service of an enforcement notice or otherwise, a determination by the Commissioner that processing is unlawful may be followed by service of an enforcement notice. Once again, different procedures apply in relation to the special purposes. An enforcement notice may only be served with the leave of the court.[1] Leave will only be granted if the court is satisfied that 'the Commissioner has reason to suspect a contravention of the data protection principles which is of substantial public importance', and that 'except where the case is one of urgency' notice has been given to the controller of the Commissioner's intention to apply for leave.[2]

[1]   Data Protection Act 1998, s 46(1).
[2]   Section 46(2).

Individual rights and remedies

9.28   As discussed above, the Data Protection Act 1998 gives extended rights to data subjects to institute proceedings before the courts seeking compensation for damage and distress resulting from a breach of any of the Act's requirements.[1] In the case of processing for the special purposes, damages may be awarded for distress without the need for any related damage. The data subject may also bring action in the normal manner seeking rectification, blocking or erasure of inaccurate data.[2] The question whether and to what extent such remedies are provided is at the discretion of the court, and it may be assumed that account will be taken of the requirements of the special purposes so that, for example, the court will not order the alteration of the contents of a database containing the contents of stories which have been published in a newspaper. Even where a story contains errors, a notice of correction appended to the file would appear a more appropriate course of action.

[1]   Section 13(1).
[2]   Section 14.

Granting of assistance by the Commissioner

9.29   Section 53 of the Data Protection Act 1998 confers a new power on the Commissioner to provide assistance following an application from a party to proceedings relating to the special purposes.[1] This will include all the forms of proceeding described above, with the assistance taking the form of a contribution towards the costs of legal advice and representation and with indemnification against any award of costs to the other party.[2] The criterion for the award of such assistance is that the Commissioner is of the opinion that 'the case involves a matter of substantial public importance'.[3] The Commissioner's decision whether or not to grant support must be transmitted to the applicant as soon as practicable. If the Commissioner decides not to grant assistance, reasoned notification to this effect must be given.[4]

1   Section 53(1).
2   Schedule 10.
3   Section 53(2).
4   Section 53(3)–(4).

Data protection in the communications sector

9.30   In the early days of telecommunications, all calls required to be connected by human operators. In order to bill customers accurately, the operator would monitor the communication, making a record when the call was connected, the number to which it was made and when it terminated. It was not unknown for operators to eavesdrop on the conversation itself; indeed the motivation for Joseph Strowger to invent the world's first automatic telephone exchange is reported to have lain in the discovery that the wife of a competitor who was employed as a telephone operator was intercepting his calls in order to redirect business to her husband.

9.31   With the introduction of automated exchanges, first in respect of local, and then from 1979 when the UK's system of subscriber trunk dialling (STD) was completed for long-distance calls, what might be regarded as a 'golden age' of communications privacy dawned. Calls were connected without human intervention and whilst each telephone line had its own meter located in the telephone exchange, the operation of these was analogous to electricity and gas meters in that they merely recorded the number of units of connection time consumed. If for whatever reason the authorities wished to be able to identify the destination of calls, a special device referred to as a 'call logger' required to be attached to an individual line.[1] Following the passage of the Interception of Communications Act 1987, a reasonably strict regime was introduced whereby any attempt to monitor telephone conversations required the issuance of a warrant by a High Court judge.[2]

1   The use of a call logger was central to the prosecution's case in *R v Gold* [1987] 3 WLR 803, one of the first and most high-profile cases brought against alleged computer hackers.
2   Call logging was not regarded as involving interception and did not require the grant of a warrant.

9.32   From the 1980s the telephone network began a change-over to the use of digital technology with the UK becoming 'totally digital' with the closure of the last analogue exchanges on 11 March 1998.[1] Whilst the use of digital technology has brought considerable benefits both in terms of reliability and the range of services offered, an inevitable by-product is that increasing amounts of data were collected about customers. Perhaps the best example can be seen with the introduction of itemised billing. Customers now take for granted the fact that they will be presented with a bill describing, at least for long-distance calls, details of time, duration and cost of individual calls. Whilst useful for monitoring usage of the telephone, the retention and processing of the data has implications for individual privacy.

1   *UK Telephone History*, available from http://web.online.co.uk/freshwater/histuk.htm.

9.33   With the emergence of mobile networks, even more data concerning user behaviour is generated and retained. When switched on, each mobile phone transmits a signal ... every few minutes. All base stations of that network within range respond, and the firm allocates the phone to one station. At present phones can normally be tracked to within several hundred metres although with the use of appropriate software by the network operator this might be reduced to perhaps 50 metres. Third generation (3G) mobile phones will offer almost automatic location tracking, capable of locating a handset to within a range of 15 metres. This data can be retained almost indefinitely and, as will be discussed below, governments are increasingly taking powers to require that it be retained for periods of years against the eventuality that access may be sought in connection with criminal or national security investigations.

9.34   Beyond use for law enforcement purposes, operators are also beginning to develop plans to allow access to location data to commercial parties for use for marketing purposes. Cinemas and restaurants, for example, might want to send text messages promoting their services, perhaps making special offers to persons passing close to their premises. Others, it is reported, have rather more ambitious plans in seeking to combine location data with other forms of personal information to target people with adverts customised to match their preferences.[1]

[1]   http://news.bbc.co.uk/1/hi/sci/tech/874419.stm.

9.35   A further, and perhaps in quantitative and qualitative terms the most extensive source of communications data, is the Internet. As discussed previously,[1] every transmission whether in the form of sending an email or the accessing and browsing of websites gives out information about the user. Every web page viewed will be recorded by the site owner. In the context, for example, of an ecommerce site, the data recorded is analogous to that which might be obtained by a physical retailer who follows a customer around the store noting not only what goods are purchased but any others that are looked at during the course of the visit. The use of cookies[2] allows this data to be processed by reference to particular individuals and in respect of what may be multiple visits to the site. With regard to email, and perhaps even more to text messaging, although these is often regarded by users as akin to voice communications in terms of speed and informality, unlike telephone communications, electronic communications of this kind do not exist only in real time. Whereas anyone wishing to monitor a telephone conversation must do so whilst the messages are being transmitted, copies of emails will be made at various stages of the transmission process and may be recovered with relative ease days, months or even years after their transmission

[1]   See para 3.22.
[2]   See para 9.53 below.

9.36   All of these activities raise data protection-related issues whilst other forms of behaviour relating to the use of communication networks fall more naturally into the wider topic of personal privacy. The increasing number of unsolicited calls received by many consumers is frequently seen as an infringement of domestic privacy. Similar considerations apply with faxes and emails and proposals to regulate the use of these have been highly controversial.

9.37 Although many aspects of communications networks are regulated under the general provisions of data protection law, at the time the Data Protection Directive[1] was being formulated the EU identified a need for a more specialised form of regulation – to 'particularise and complement'[2] the general data protection regime. A major factor is the combination of data processing on the network combined with that by customers who will determine the use to which data is put. Systems such as 'caller id', for example, present users with information regarding the source of an incoming call. This data may be processed and used by an individual to avoid being disturbed by unwanted calls or by a commercial organisation to 'capture' telephone numbers for later use for marketing purposes. The provisions of the general Directive were therefore supplemented by more specific provisions in the form of the Directive of 15 December 1997 'concerning the processing of personal data and the protection of privacy in the telecommunications sector'.[3] This Directive was implemented in the UK by the Telecommunications (Data Protection and Privacy) (Direct Marketing) Regulations 1998[4] and the Telecommunications (Data Protection and Privacy) Regulations 1999.[4]

[1]   Directive 95/46/EC.
[2]   Directive 97/66, art 1(2).
[3]   Directive 97/66/EC, OJ 1998 L 24/01 (the Telecoms Data Protection Directive).
[4]   SI 1998/3170.
[5]   SI 1999/2093.

9.38   It is testimony to the pace of developments in the sector (and perhaps also of the slow pace of the legislative process) that less than two years after the Telecoms Data Protection Directive's[1] adoption the 1999 Communications Review commented that:

> The terminology used in the Telecoms Data Protection Directive, which was proposed in 1990, is appropriate for traditional fixed telephony services but less so for new services which have now become available and affordable for a wide public. This creates ambiguities and has led in practice to divergence in national transposition of the Directive. To ensure a consistent application of data protection principles to public telecommunications services and network throughout the EU, the Commission proposes to update and clarify the Directive taking account of technological developments converging markets.

[1]   Directive 97/66/EC.

9.39   In April 2000, a Working Document was produced describing these issues in greater detail.[1] In some instances the 1997 Directive[2] was seen as unduly restrictive. It contained, for example, an outright prohibition against the use of traffic data for purposes other than those of the network operator. The Commission now proposed to permit:

processing of traffic data ... for the purpose of value added services with the consent of the subscriber or user. With the extension of the data protection safeguards to traffic data generated by any transmission network for electronic communications, the existing possibility for further processing of traffic data, has become too narrow. Today, value added services have been developed and can be offered based on particular traffic data and there is no reason to prohibit such services in cases where the subscriber has consented with the use of traffic data for the purpose of these services.

[1]   Available from http://www.ispo.cec.be/infosoc/telecompolicy/review99/wdprot.pdf.
[2]   Directive 97/66/EC.

9.40   In other instances, the nature of communications was seen to be changing user perceptions and wishes. With directory information, for example, the assumption underpinning the Telecoms Data Protection Directive[1] had been that most subscribers would wish details of their fixed telephone number to be included in a directory. The Directive provided that details could be recorded in directories unless the customer chose to opt out. In the age of mobile phones and email addresses, it was suggested a majority of customers might not want these details to appear in a public document and so the system should move to one whereby publication would require the customer's positive assent.

[1]   Directive 97/66/EC.

9.41   A point which comes out strongly throughout the document is that data relating to communications is becoming both more extensive and more valuable. It is in the interests of the emerging information society that the maximum use should be made of valuable resources. As the volume of data traffic takes up a greater and greater percentage of telecommunications traffic, so there is clear need to reformulate provisions drawn up even a few years ago when voice telephony was still dominant. It is equally clear, however, that with systems such as the Internet, vast amounts of data may be collected concerning the actions of individuals and processed and used in ways which may not be considered desirable. The establishment of effective legal controls and safeguards is a matter of great importance.

9.42   It is indicative of the controversial nature of many of the issues involved that whilst the remainder of the Directives making up the new communications regulatory Framework were adopted in February 2002, agreement could not be reached between the European institutions regarding the proposed data protection measure and its adoption was delayed until July 2002. Particular points of controversy concerned the nature of the legal response to unsolicited commercial emails (spam) and the imposition of requirements on communications providers to retain traffic and billing data for possible access by law enforcement and national security agencies. One timetabling consequence is that whilst the bulk of the Directives required to be implemented in the member states by July 2002, the Directive 'concerning the processing of personal data and the [protection of privacy in the electronic communications sector (Directive on Privacy and electronic communications)'[1] (hereafter the Communications Privacy Directive) did not require be implemented until 31 October. Once again, the UK was dilatory in acting with implementation taking the form of the Privacy and Electronic Communications (EC Directive) Regulations 2003[2] which came into force on 11 December 2003.

[1] Directive 2002/58.OJ 2002 L201/37.
[2] SI 2003/2426.

Aim and scope of the Communications Privacy Directive

9.43 The Communications Privacy Directive's proclaimed aim is to harmonise:

> the provisions of the Member States required to ensure an equivalent level of protection of fundamental rights and freedoms, and in particular the right to privacy, with respect to the processing of personal data in the electronic communication sector and to ensure the free movement of such data and of electronic communication equipment and services in the Community. [1]

As was also the case in respect of the earlier telecommunications data protection Directive, the 2002 measure's stated aim is to 'particularise and complement' the provisions of the general Data Protection Directive.[2] It also expands the scope of this measure in one important respect by providing at least some rights for legal as well as private persons.[3]

[1] Directive 2002/58/EC, art 1.
[2] Article 1(2).
[3] Article 1(2).

9.44 Whilst this chapter will concentrate on the specific elements of the communications sector it is important to bear in mind throughout that activities will also need to comply with the requirements of the general measure in respect of topics such as fair processing, accuracy of data and subject access. Also important will be the activities of the supervisory agencies, in the case of the UK the Information Commissioner.

9.45 The scope of the Communications Data Privacy Directive[1] is defined in art 3 as extending to:

> the processing of personal data in connection with the provision of publicly available electronic communications services in public communications networks in the Community.

Personal data is defined in the Data Protection Act 1998[2] and Data Protection Directive[3] as any information which relates to a living identifiable individual. In the context of communications related activities it may be assumed that individuals will often by identifiable by reference to telephone numbers or email addresses, matched to lists of subscribers maintained by network providers or ISPs.

1   Directive 2002/58/EC.
2   Section 1.
3   Directive 95/46/EC, art 2.

9.46   The definition of processing is also found in the general data protection law, the Data Protection Act 1998 providing that the concept encompasses the:

> obtaining, recording or holding the information or data or carrying out any operation or set of operations on the information or data, including—
> (a)   organisation, adaptation or alteration of the information or data,
> (b)   retrieval, consultation or use of the information or data,
> (c)   disclosure of the information or data by transmission, dissemination or otherwise making available, or
> (d)   alignment, combination, blocking, erasure or destruction of the information or data.[1]

Given the breadth of this definition it is difficult to conceive of any communications related activity which will not involve processing and, save perhaps in the situation where a pay phone is used, will be carried out by reference to an identifiable individual.

1   Section 1.

Security and confidentiality

9.47   The first substantive obligation imposed under the Communications Data Privacy Directive[1] is that the provider of a public communication network or service must 'take appropriate technical and organisational measures' to ensure the security of the network and any messages transmitted over it.

1   Directive 2002/58/EC, art 4.

9.48   The most obvious security risk undoubtedly will be that of an unauthorised person obtaining access to data being transmitted. Beyond interception of voice traffic perhaps the most significant and certainly the most high-profile risks associated with modern communications are those associated with the Internet, with concerns frequently raised about the security of personal and financial data transmitted in the course of an ecommerce transaction. The obligations imposed upon service providers are twofold. First, appropriate security measures must be put in place to protect data and, secondly, customers must be warned of the risks involved and advised regarding self-help measures such as encryption which may be used and of the likely costs of such measures.

9.49   Whilst the provisions regarding data security are addressed to network and service operators, obligations are imposed upon governments to ensure that legal sanctions may be imposed against those who breach the confidentiality of communications. Legal prohibitions are to be imposed against 'listening, tapping, storage or other kinds of interception or surveillance of communications' other than any measures which are necessary in connection with the transmission of data. Exceptions are sanctioned in cases where interception is necessary in the interests of national security, law enforcement and 'the unauthorised use of electronic communications systems'.[1] It is also permissible to record commercial communications where this is 'carried out in the course of lawful business practice for the purpose of providing evidence of a commercial transaction'.

[1]   Directive 2002/58/EC, art 15.

9.50   For the UK, the provisions of the Telecommunications (Lawful Business Practice) (Interception of Communications) Regulations[1] will be relevant in this situation. Made under the auspices of the Regulation of Investigatory Powers Act 2000, these provide legal authority for the monitoring or recording of a wide range of electronic and voice communications. Examples would include recording of telephone calls received by businesses and the monitoring of employees' telephone and email communications by employers to determine compliance with policies regarding usage of these facilities.

[1]   SI 2000/2699.

9.51   Although the Regulations[1] and Directive[2] do provide legal authority for substantial forms of monitoring it should be recalled that the Data Protection Act 1998's requirement is that processing should be both fair and lawful. Whilst employer-directed monitoring of the kind described above may well satisfy the second requirement, the Information Commissioner has suggested that processing carried out without giving proper notice to the individuals affected might well be considered unfair.

[1]   SI 2000/2699.
[2]   Directive 2002/58/EC.

9.52   A further requirement relating to confidentiality illustrates both the breadth of the Communications Data Privacy Directive's[1] provisions but also, perhaps, the problems which may be encountered in attempting to enforce these. Article 5(3) provides that:

> Member States shall ensure that the use of electronic communications networks to store information or to gain access to information stored in the terminal equipment of a subscriber or user is only allowed on condition that the subscriber or user concerned is provided with clear and comprehensive information in accordance with Directive 95/46/EC, *inter alia* about the purposes of the processing, and is offered the right to refuse such processing by the data controller.

[1]   Directive 2002/58/EC.

9.53   The recitals to the Communications Data Privacy Directive make it clear that this applies to prohibit the use of:

> spyware, web bugs, hidden identifiers and other similar devices can enter the user's terminal without their knowledge in order to gain access to information,

to store hidden information or to trace the activities of the user and may seriously intrude upon the privacy of these users.[1]

Beyond the rather sinister sounding technologies specifically identified, it would appear that the placing of cookies[2] may well violate the prohibition. The test will be whether the user is offered the opportunity to object to the placing of such devices. The major difficulty may well be that the default setting of Internet browsers such as Microsoft Explorer is set to accept cookies. In many cases even if the user changes the setting either to require notice of and approval for the placing of a cookie or to refuse to accept any cookies, the effect will be to render access to many websites difficult or even impossible. For users the choice may be between accepting cookies or doing without access to a site. In such cases consent might not be considered either informed or freely given.

[1] Directive 2002/58/EC, recital 24.

[2] The use of cookies is fundamental to many websites. The device has been described by Viktor Mayer-Schönberger as follows:

> Cookies are pieces of information generated by a Web server and stored in the user's computer, ready for future access. Cookies are embedded in the HTML information flowing back and forth between the user's computer and the servers. Cookies were implemented to allow user-side customization of Web information. For example, cookies are used to personalize Web search engines, to allow users to participate in WWW-wide contests (but only once!), and to store shopping lists of items a user has selected while browsing through a virtual shopping mall.
>
> Essentially, cookies make use of user-specific information transmitted by the Web server onto the user's computer so that the information might be available for later access by itself or other servers. In most cases, not only does the storage of personal information into a cookie go unnoticed, so does access to it. Web servers automatically gain access to relevant cookies whenever the user establishes a connection to them, usually in the form of Web requests
>
> *The Cookie Concept*, available from http://www.cookiecentral.com/content.phtml.

9.54 Beyond issues of consent, a final question concerns the feasibility of enforcing prohibitions. A high percentage of websites are located in the US or indeed other countries outwith the jurisdiction of the EU. It is difficult to conceive of any feasible manner in which the prohibition may be enforced.

Traffic data

9.55 The term 'traffic data' encompasses any data processed in connection with the transmission of signals over a communication network. It will include data relating to the point of origin of a communication, its destination and the duration of the communication. In the case of a fixed-line telephone, the point of origin will be obvious. With mobile communications, as has been referred to previously, the location of the user may constantly be changing. Data transmitted periodically from the telephone will allow the network to remain aware of the phone's location. This is clearly necessary in order to be able to make and receive calls but the retention and processing of location data raises series issues for the individual's right to privacy.

9.56 Reflecting undoubtedly its origins in the pre-mobile era, the Telecoms Data Protection Directive[1] referred only to traffic data and provided that it might be processed subsequent to a communication only for billing purposes or, with the consent of the customer, limited items of data might be processed by the telecommunications service provider for marketing purposes.[2]

[1]   Directive 97/66/EC.
[2]   The Annex to the Directive contained a list of the types of data which might be processed. This included data relating to the volume of calls but not the destination or duration of individual calls.

9.57 The term traffic data was not defined in the Telecoms Data Protection Directive.[1] The Communications Data Privacy Directive, however, provides that it is to consist of:

> any data processed for the purpose of the conveyance of a communication on an electronic communications network or for the billing thereof;[2]

This will encompass both data relating to use of a telephone and also any data which might be processed by an ISP concerned with Internet usage.

[1]   Directive 97/66/EC.
[1]   Directive 2002/58/EC, art 2(b).

9.58 The Directive retains the basic prohibition against processing but extends the range of permissible uses. Article 6 provides that:

> For the purpose of marketing electronic communications services or for the provision of value added services, the provider of a publicly available electronic communications service may process the data referred to in paragraph 1 to the extent and for the duration necessary for such services or marketing, if the subscriber or user to whom the data relate has given his/her consent. Users or subscribers shall be given the possibility to withdraw their consent for the processing of traffic data at any time.

'Value added services' are defined as communication services requiring the processing of data 'beyond what is necessary for the transmission of a communication or the billing thereof'.[1] This would include services such as the downloading of ring tomes for mobile phones or the provision of information services. User consent is required and must be given on the same basis as that required in the Data Protection Directive which requires a 'freely given, specific and informed indication of his wishes by which the data subject signifies his agreement to personal data relating to him being processed'.[2] The key requirement is that the subject be informed of the uses proposed. In this eventuality, it is acceptable for the processing to take place unless the subject actively indicates objection (opting out). Consent can be withdrawn at any time.

[1]   Directive 2002/58/EC, art 2.
[2]   Directive 2002/58/EC, art 2.

9.59   Additionally, the Communications Data Privacy Directive makes provision for the handling of location data, defined as:

> any data processed in an electronic communications network, indicating the geographic position of the terminal equipment of a user of a publicly available electronic communications service.[1]

Beyond use for the purpose of network operation, location data may be processed only when it is rendered anonymous or, with user consent, for the provision of a value added service. Information must be provided to the user of the type of data which will be processed, the purposes for which it will be used, the duration of any further use and whether this will involve a transfer to third parties.

[1]   Directive 2002/58/EC, art 2.

9.60   Although this provision may seem at first glance to provide considerable assistance to users, it is likely that the information may be provided in a relatively lengthy and complex list of standard conditions associated with provision of the overall communications service. Albeit prior to the implementation of the Communications Data Privacy Directive, one of the major mobile networks used a clause empowering them to:

> Contact you or allow carefully selected third parties to contact you with information about products and services by post, telephone, mobile text message or email (subject to any preferences expressed by you).

9.61   Given that the processing of data will take place in real time and be associated with the movements and location of the user, the processing might be considered rather more sensitive than is the case where traffic data is used for marketing purposes. It is perhaps unfortunate that the requirement is not that the provider seek a positive indication of consent (opt in).

9.62   In addition to providing users with the right to opt out of such uses of their data, the Communications Data Privacy Directive requires that users must be given the possibility 'of temporarily refusing the processing of such data for each connection to the network or for each transmission of a communication'.[1] It is likely that this right could be exercised in a manner similar to that currently applying in relation to the use of systems of 'caller id' where prefixing a number with 141 will prevent details of the caller's number being made available to the recipient.

[1]   Directive 2002/58/EC, art 9(2).

9.63   Significant inroads upon the level of protection conferred by the Communications Data Privacy Directive came with the inclusion at a late state in the legislative process came with the acceptance by the European Parliament of an amendment permitting member states to 'adopt legislative measures providing for the retention of data for a limited period justified on the grounds laid down in this paragraph'.[1] The grounds referred to include the safeguarding of 'national security, defence, public security, and the prevention, investigation, detection and prosecution of criminal offences or of unauthorised use of the electronic communication system'.

¹ Directive 2002/58/EC, art 15.

9.64 In the UK, the provisions of the Regulation of Investigatory Powers Act 2000 empower a senior police office to require a communications provider to disclose any communications data in its possession where this is considered necessary in the interests of national security, the prevention or detection of crime or a number of other situations.¹ The term 'communications data' is defined broadly to include traffic and location data although as has been stated by the Home Office:

> It is important to identify what communications data does include but equally important to be clear about what it does *not* include. The term communications data in the Act does not include the content of any communication.²

¹ Section 22.
² Consultation Paper on a Code of Practice for Voluntary Retention of Communications Data, March 2003.

9.65 The Regulation of Investigatory Powers Act 2000 did not require that providers retain although concerns had been expressed that mobile phone operators were retaining data for a period of months and in some cases years. The conformity of this practice with the requirements of the Data Protection Act 1998 that:

> Personal data processed for any purpose or purposes shall not be kept for longer than is necessary for that purpose or those purposes¹

had been doubted. The passage of the Anti-terrorism, Crime and Security Act 2001 provided a legal basis for the retention of data. The Act conferred power on the Secretary of State to draw up a code of practice specifying periods of time during which communications providers would be required to retain communications data.² Although the Secretary of State is granted legislative power, it was envisaged that a voluntary code would be agreed between government and the communications industry. To date, however, negotiations have not produced agreement with industry concerns centering in large part on the cost implications of retaining large amounts of data. The leading service provider AOL, for example, has estimated that it would require 36,000 CDs in order to store one year's supply of communications data relating to its customers with set-up costs of £30m and annual running costs of the same amount.

¹ Schedule 1, fifth data protection principle.
² Section 102.

9.66 Initial proposals by the government for the establishment of a code of practice received heavy criticism both in terms of the period of time within which data might require to be retained and also the range of government agencies who might be granted access to this data. An initial draft code was withdrawn in July 2002 and a further draft was published in March 2003. This restricted the range of agencies which might seek access to data but retains the requirement that data be retained for a period of 12 months.

Itemised billing

9.67 The issue of itemised billing is rather less contentious than that of data retention but does serve to illustrate some of the changes which have occurred in the communications sector over the past decade and also some potential conflicts between rights to privacy and to information.

9.68 The initial provision of the Communications Data Privacy Directive may appear somewhat strange. Subscribers, it is provided, 'will have the right to receive non-itemised bills'.[1] Whilst few people may want to exercise the option the rationale lies perhaps in the fact that it has become very much the norm for individuals to receive itemised bills. In this situation, given that the Directive is seeking to provide for exceptions, the logical approach is to assume the provision of itemised bills and confer a right to refuse these.

[1] Directive 2002/58/EC, art 7.

9.69 Whilst it is almost inevitably the case that the person responsible for a communications bill would be interested in information regarding the calls made, other persons may have different preferences. The Communications Data Privacy Directive uses two terms, 'subscriber' and 'user'. The term subscriber is not defined in the Directive,[1] although it appears clear that it must refer to the party who has contracted for the provision of services. Perhaps rather inconsistently, the Directive does provide a definition of the term 'user' as 'any natural person using a publicly available electronic communications service, for private or business purposes, without necessarily having subscribed to this service'.[2]

[1] The Telecoms Data Protection Directive (Directive 97/66/EC) did define the term as 'any natural or legal person who or which is party to a contract with the provider of publicly available telecommunications services for the supply of such services' (art 2).
[2] Directive 2002/58/EC, art 2.

9.70 In a household it will be common for one member to be classed as the subscriber but for other family members to use the equipment. Whilst the former may wish to be able to analyse what calls have been made, the latter may have an interest in maintaining the privacy of their communications. Whilst in many cases it may be accepted that the wishes and interests of the subscriber should prevail, there may be instances, for example, where calls have been made to counselling or support agencies perhaps arising from the behaviour of the subscriber towards the user. The Communications Data Privacy Directive requires that national implementing measures should seek to reconcile the interests of the parties involved 'by ensuring that sufficient alternative privacy enhancing methods of communications or payments are available to such users and subscribers'.[1]

[1]   Directive 2002/58/EC, art 7(2).

9.71   Even by the general standards of EU Directives, this formulation is opaque. In the UK there are some 750,000 pay telephones and it might be argued that this provides sufficient access to telecommunications for users who do not want details of their calls made available to third-party subscribers. The recitals to the Communications Data Privacy Directive refer also recommend that member states:

> encourage the development of electronic communication service options such as alternative payment facilities which allow anonymous or strictly private access to publicly available electronic communications services, for example calling cards and facilities for payment by credit card.[1]

A further possibility canvassed is that itemised bills may delete 'a certain number of digits' from the lists of called numbers. This might well prove useful in the situation, for example, that calls are made to a medical or emotional support helpline. Again, however, it is difficult to see why such an option would be attractive to subscribers and in the event that only certain numbers were censored, the presence of these might in itself be a cause for suspicion. One reasonable option would, however, appear to be to provide that calls made to freephone (0800) numbers should not appear on bills. These are frequently provided by support agencies. Given that such calls do not involve any cost implications for the subscriber the balance of interests may be seen as lying with potential users.

[1]   Directive 2002/58/EC, recital 33.

Directory information

9.72   When the 1997 directory was adopted virtually the only form of communications directories were telephone directories published by major telecommunications operators. In the past six years there has been a massive increase in the number of telephones in use due to the continuing growth in the mobile market. Tens of millions of individuals have also acquired email addresses as this form of electronic communication has expanded to the extent that the volume of email communications dwarves that carried by the postal networks. Beyond an increase in the range of materials which might be contained in communications directories there has been a similar growth in the level of sophistication of directory services. Increasingly provided in electronic form, directories may include facilities such as reverse searching. Whilst a traditional directory can be searched only in the manner structured by the compiler, typically by alphabetical order, an electronic directory might, for example, allow a user to enter a telephone number and be presented with the name and address of the person to whom it has been allocated.

9.73   Traditionally certain individuals – Oftel have estimated the figure to be as high as 37% of residential customers[1] – have sought to keep their contact details out of the public domain. There may be a variety of reasons for this. Members of certain professions such as law and medicine may not wish to be contactable at home by their clients. In other instances individuals may hear being harassed by ex-partners.

[1]   Directory Information, http://www.oftel.gov.uk/publications/1995_98/consumer/dqchap.htm.

9.74   The Telecoms Data Protection Directive provided that the information contained in public directories should be limited to that necessary to identify particular customers, that there should be a right to require that details be withheld from the directory and also that customers should be able to indicate:

> that his or her personal data may not be used for the purpose of direct marketing, to have his or her address omitted in part and not to have a reference revealing his or her sex, where this is applicable linguistically.[1]

The first element of this requirement was met through the establishment of the telephone preference service which enabled customers to indicate their wish not to receive calls for marketing purposes.[2] Under the Telecommunications (Data Protection and Privacy) Regulations 1999[3] it is provided that marketing related communications must not be made to a telephone number which appears on a list maintained by the Director General of Communications of subscribers who have indicated objection to this practice.[4] Breach of this requirement will constitute a contravention of the Data Protection Act 1998 and may entitle the subscriber to compensation for any damage caused. It does not appear that any party has to date obtained compensation for burnt meals caused by unwarranted interruptions by telephone marketers. In 1999 the Director entered into a contract with the Telephone Preference Service for the compilation and maintenance of the list. Effect was given to the remaining requirements of the Directive by the Telecommunications (Data Protection and Privacy) Regulations 1999.[5] Over one million subscribers have now registered with the service.

[1]   Directive 97/66/EC, art 11.
[2]   http://www.tpsonline.org.uk/tpsr/html/default.asp.
[3]   SI 1999/3170.
[4]   Regulation 9.
[5]   SI 1999/2093.

9.75   The Communications Data Privacy Directive adopts a somewhat different approach. Subscribers are to be informed of the nature and purposes of the information which will be made available in a public directory or directory information service and 'of any further usage possibilities based on search functions embedded in electronic versions of the directory'. This information must be supplied prior to publication of the directory.[1]

[1]   Directive 2002/58/EC, art 12.

9.76   Having been informed of the purposes envisaged, subscribers are to have the right to require that their details be removed in whole or in part. No charge is to be made for this or for compliance with the subscriber's request that errors be corrected.

9.77 Especially with electronic directories it is possible that third parties may seek to copy significant amounts of information and use these for their own purposes. The body of the Communications Data Privacy Directive makes no provision in this respect although the recitals indicate that:

> Where the data may be transmitted to one or more third parties, the subscriber should be informed of this possibility and of the recipient or the categories of possible recipients. Any transmission should be subject to the condition that the data may not be used for other purposes than those for which they were collected. If the party collecting the data from the subscriber or any third party to whom the data have been transmitted wishes to use the data for an additional purpose, the renewed consent of the subscriber is to be obtained either by the initial party collecting the data or by the third party to whom the data have been transmitted.[1]

1   Directive 2002/58/EC, recital 39.

9.78 Although not a direct legal requirement, the Telecommunications Directory Information Fair Processing Code, drawn up by the then Data Protection Registrar in 1998, is likely to be very relevant. This provides, inter alia, that controllers should take steps to prevent information being misused. Bulk copying might be inhibited by technical measures designed to limit the number of records which can be accessed and copied by a single search. It is also suggested that encryption techniques might be used and, perhaps now outdated, that there should be no online interface to directories. Encryption of data might also be used to prevent reverse searching.

9.79 Although not legally binding, a failure to comply with the Code may be regarded as constituting unfair processing under the Data Protection Act 1998 and result in the service of an enforcement notice by the Information Commissioner. Under the Telecommunications (Open Network Provision) (Voice Telephony) Regulations,[1] an undertaking required (effectively BT) on directory information to a third party was required to obtain an undertaking that the recipient would comply with the Code. Any breach of the undertaking would render the third party's processing unfair. A similar effect is now provided by condition 22 of the General Conditions of Entitlement. This provides that every communications provider is obliged to supply details of its subscribers to any other provider upon reasonable request. This obligation is expressly stated to be 'subject to the requirements of relevant data protection legislation'.

1   SI 1998/1580.

Calling and connected line identification

9.80 Systems of calling line identification, often referred to as 'caller id', allow a user to identify the number from which a call originates prior to answering the call. A related system allows a user to discover details of the last call made to the telephone by dialling 1471. As with itemised billing the systems offer major benefits to individuals, not least as a means of deterring the making of hoax or malicious calls, but there may also be good reason why a party making a call may not wish details to be available to a called party. At a trivial level, a husband may not wish his wife to be aware that rather than a call originating from the office where work demands are requiring a late departure, it is coming from a local pub. Following the break-up of a relationship, one party may wish to contact the other but not to allow the possibility of the call being returned or, especially in an era of reverse searchable directories, to allow their physical location to be discovered. Caller id is also used extensively for commercial purposes. Some companies use systems linked to a database of customers so that the caller's identity is known at the time the call is answered. Many taxi companies use such systems to simplify the task of despatching vehicles and also to provide some check against the making of hoax calls. Less desirable perhaps is the situation where a company 'captures' phone numbers from persons calling to inquire about goods or services and uses these for subsequent marketing activities.[1] The situation may therefore arise where subscribers may wish to know who is calling them but, at least in certain situations, may not want their telephone number to be made available to the party they are calling.

[1]   Such processing may, of course, be considered unfair under the provisions of the Data Protection Act 1998.

9.81   As well as presenting the called party with information about the origin of a call, the same technology, referred to in this case as connected line information, allows the caller to see the actual number at which the call is answered. Although in the majority of cases this will be the number which was dialled, it may also be the case that calls are forwarded to another number. Whilst in the vast majority of cases the practice will be unobjectionable there may situations where the called party is reluctant for this to happen. Out of hours calls to a doctor's surgery may be forwarded to the physician's home number. There may be reluctance to allow patients to know this number.

9.82   In respect of caller id the Communications Data Privacy Directive requires that subscribers and users be presented with a range of options. Users are to be offered the option, free of charge of blocking the presentation of the number from which they are making a call. In the UK this is normally accomplished by prefixing the telephone number called with '141'. Users should also be offered the option of blocking the display of information on a permanent basis although a charge may be levied for this.[1]

[1]   Directive 2002/58/EC, art 8(1).

9.83   Whilst callers will be entitled to block presentation of their identity, the Communications Data Privacy Directive sets the scene for what might almost be regarded as a battle of the systems by providing that subscribers are to be offered the option to reject incoming calls where the caller has chosen to prevent display of his or her number.[1] One limitation of this approach is that identification details may be withheld either by the deliberate act of the caller or because, as typically happens in a work environment, because outgoing calls will be routed through a central switchboard. Even though each instrument may have its own number which can be dialled directly by callers from outside the premises, the identification details will be stripped out in respect of outgoing calls.

¹ Directive 2002/58/EC, art 8(2). BT currently charges £3.33 per month for use of this facility.

9.84 In exceptional cases it may be provided that attempts by callers to conceal details of the number from which a communication originates can be overridden. This may take place on a temporary basis in the event a subscriber requests the assistance of the service provider in tracing the origin of malicious or nuisance calls and permanently in respect of lines used by the emergency services.¹

¹ Directive 2002/58/EC, art 10.

9.85 Broadly similar provisions apply in respect of connected line identification. Here subscribers must be offered the possibility, 'using a simple means and free of charge of preventing the presentation of the connected line information'.¹

¹ Directive 2002/58/EC, art 8(4).

Unsolicited communications

9.86 For many persons, receipt of unsolicited commercial communications, whether by post, telephone, fax or email, is a major cause of aggravation. Oftel research has indicated that up to 20% of customers choosing to remove their details from telephone directories do so in order to minimise the numbers of unsolicited marketing calls.¹ As indicated above, very considerable numbers of persons have signed up to the telephone and fax preference service. Currently much publicity has attached to the use of the Internet for unsolicited or junk emails, generally referred to as spam. The amount of spam was estimated to have increased by 80% in 2002² with current estimates suggesting that 30% of all Internet-based emails are spam.³ Some commentators have predicted that continued growth in the volume of email would 'render the Internet unusable by 2008'.⁴ According to a recent Harris poll, 80% of Internet users claimed to be 'very annoyed' about spam with 74% of those surveyed favouring a legal ban.⁵

¹ Directory Information, http://www.oftel.gov.uk/publications/1995_98/consumer/dqchap. htm.
² http://news.bbc.co.uk/1/hi/technology/2409855.stm.
³ http://news.bbc.co.uk/1/hi/technology/2688619.stm.
⁴ http://www.theregister.co.uk/content/archive/21846.html.
⁵ http://news.zdnet.co.uk/story/0,,t269-s2128193,00.html.

9.87 A further tactic, which has not been widely used in the UK concerns the use of automated calling systems. With these, numbers are dialled automatically and when the call is answered a recorded message is played to the recipient. Beyond any nuisance value, these systems have been implicated in at least one fatality in Canada where a fire broke out in property just at the moment an automated call was received. Although the householder attempted to terminate the call so that the emergency services might be summoned, the message continued to be transmitted with the result that the user was unable to make an outgoing call.

9.88 Controls over the use of electronic communications services for marketing purposes were introduced in the Telecoms Data Protection Directive.[1] As indicated above, prohibitions were imposed against the use of the telephone to contact to individuals who had expressed a preference not to receive marketing calls. The use of automated calling machines was also prohibited except in situations where consumers had specifically requested such communications.

[1]   Directive 97/66/EC.

9.89 A similar 'opt in' approach was adopted in respect of the use of fax machines for the purposes of unsolicited marketing. The rationale for treating fax transmissions more restrictively than voice communications was an economic one. Whilst receipt of a telephone call does not have any cost implications for the subscriber, paper and ink will require to be used to print out the contents of a fax. This was undoubtedly a more significant consideration in 1990 when the Telecoms Data Protection Directive was initially drafted as at that time fax machines required to use special and very expensive paper.

9.90 Perhaps unsurprisingly, the Telecoms Data Protection Directive[1] made no reference to email. Both with the growth in Internet usage and also with the expansion in the scope of the legislation, inclusion of provisions concerning email has been a major and contentious feature of the new legislation. As originally introduced, the explanatory memorandum accompanying the draft Communications Data Privacy Directive indicated that:

> Four Member States already have bans on unsolicited commercial e-mail and another is about to adopt one. In most of the other Member States opt-out systems exist. From an internal market perspective, this is not satisfactory. Direct marketers in opt-in countries may not target e-mail addresses within their own country but they can still continue to send unsolicited commercial e-mail to countries with an opt-out system. Moreover, since e-mail addresses very often give no indication of the country of residence of the recipients, a system of divergent regimes within the internal market is unworkable in practice. A harmonised opt-in approach solves this problem.

Accordingly a prohibition was proposed except in respect of individuals who had indicated the wish to receive commercial emails. This approach was highly controversial and in October 2001 the European Parliament voted in favour of an 'opt out system'. In December 2001, however the Council voted to reinstate the 'opt in' approach and the Communications Data Privacy Directive was finally adopted with this format, the Directive providing that the sending of:

electronic mail for the purposes of direct marketing may only be allowed in respect of subscribers who have given their prior consent.[2]

¹   Directive 97/66/EC.
²   Directive 2002/58/EC, art 13(1).

9.91   Although the term 'prior consent' might appear compatible with the use of an 'opt out' approach where failure on the part of a user to indicate a preference would equate to consent, the recitals make reference to the need to ensure that the 'prior explicit consent of the recipients is obtained before such communications are addressed to them'.[1] Use of the adjective 'explicit' clearly imposes a heavier burden upon persons wishing to send emails.

¹   Directive 2002/58/EC, recital 40.

9.92   The Communications Data Privacy Directive does provide for one situation where commercial emails can be sent without prior consent. This applies where there has been a previous commercial relationship between the parties and:

> a natural or legal person obtains from its customers their electronic contact details for electronic mail, in the context of the sale of a product or a service … the same natural or legal person may use these electronic contact details for direct marketing of its own similar products or services provided that customers clearly and distinctly are given the opportunity to object, free of charge and in an easy manner, to such use of electronic contact details when they are collected and on the occasion of each message in case the customer has not initially refused such use.[1]

Use of a hypertext link in the emails allowing recipients to 'click here to unsubscribe from mailings' would suffice to meet with this requirement.

¹   Directive 2002/58/EC, art 13(2).

9.93   Even where consent has been given to the transmission of commercial emails or where the email is sent to a previous customer the Directive imposes a final requirement that commercial emails should be clearly identifiable as such and that they should always use a valid return address.[1] In many cases it may be obvious from the heading of the email that its subject is commercial. A trawl through the author's mailbox reveals subjects such as:

> Need a NEW Computer? No Credit – No Problem

> Earn $75/hr with Your Own Home Based Business Processing

> sample the weight loss patch … on us!

Nothing more need to be done in these situations. Other spammers, perhaps aware that messages with obviously commercial headings may be deleted unread make use of headings such as:

Please get back to me

re your enquiry

Hello

Headers such as this are now unlawful under the Communications Data Privacy Directive.

¹ Directive 2002/58/EC, art 13(4). Many spammers attempt to conceal the genuine address from which the message is sent to avoid possible action by the ISP involved who may well have an anti-spam condition in its contract of supply.

9.94 Whilst well meaning it is uncertain how effective the Directive's approach will be. A very considerable percentage of commercial email originates from the US or from other countries outwith the EU. Unless and until these legal systems adopt a similar approach there will be little that can practically be done to bring proceedings against spammers. Even within the EU, given the ease with which persons can set up email accounts , the task of tracking down offenders will be a difficult one.

Conclusions

9.95 Those using communications services justifiably have an expectancy that the privacy of their communications will be respected. There are, of course, significant issues concerned with the intrinsic security of certain forms of communication. Transmitting an email has been analogised, for example, with using a postcard to send a communication by post. Although the Communications Data Privacy Directive¹ is relevant in respect of these issues perhaps its most important role relates to the use of traffic data generated as a consequence of the use of networks. Although subject to the inevitable exceptions in the interests of national security and law enforcement, these will provide a reasonable degree of protection.

¹ Directive 2002/58/EC.

9.96 Undoubtedly the most publicised provisions in the Communications Data Privacy Directive¹ are those dealing with the processing of junk mail and other forms of unsolicited commercial communications. Whilst likely to be welcomed by the majority of users, it may be queried how effective the prohibition against unsolicited email communications is likely to be. Although estimates as to the costs incurred by industry in dealing with email spam are legion,² it is doubtful whether these stand serious comparison with losses due to improper or wasteful use of other resources such as telephones, stationery or even heating and lighting. It is difficult to justify the adoption of an opt-in approach for this specific sector whilst other forms of unsolicited communication using media such as such as the mail or telephone can continue to operate on an 'opt-out' basis.

1   Directive 2002/58/EC.
2   One estimate puts the global cost at $9bn per year: see http://news.bbc.co.uk/1/hi/
    technology/2983157.stm.

Chapter 10

Transborder data flows

Introduction

10.1 During the nineteenth century, the development of telegraph networks provided a medium for the speedy transfer of data both nationally and internationally. The possibility that messages might be sent into or out of the jurisdiction without possibility of control caused concern to many governments. A response was to require a physical break in the telegraph network at the national border and to require that messages be:

> ... sent to the terminal at the border, decoded and walked across to the next country where the message was again encoded and sent on to the terminal at the next border and so on.[1]

The International Telegraph Union (ITU) (now the International Telecommunications Union) was established in 1865 in large measure to promote governmental confidence in the integrity of the system and to avoid such artificial barriers to the use of communications technology.

[1]   J Pelton *Global Talk* (1981, Harvester Press) p 233.

10.2 In keeping with history's tendency to repeat itself, concerns at the implications of transborder data flows have evolved paralleling the development of national data protection statutes. Typically, the fear is expressed that an absence of control may result in evasion of national controls. As has been stated:

> ... protective provisions will be undermined if there are no restrictions on the removal of data to other jurisdictions for processing or storage. Just as money tends to gravitate towards tax havens, so sensitive personal data will be transferred to countries with the most lax, or no data protection standards. There is thus a possibility that some jurisdictions will become 'data havens' or 'data sanctuaries' for the processing or 'data vaults' for the storage of sensitive information.[1]

Controls over transborder data flows have been a feature of almost all national data protection statutes, with restrictions being justified on the basis of safeguarding the position of individuals. Whilst there may be concerns at the implications of transfers, however, transborder data flows are essential for commercial activities. Many thousands of messages must be transmitted prior to an aircraft flying from London to New York. This will include passenger details. In this context, transborder data flows constitute no mere esoteric topic. If the data cannot flow, planes cannot fly.

1   C Millard *Legal Protection of Computer Programs and Data* (1985, Sweet and Maxwell) p 211.

International initiatives

10.3   As concern at the impact of national controls over telegraphic and then voice traffic led to the establishment of the ITU, so international initiatives have sought to establish what are effectively free trade zones in respect of personal data. In 1980, the OECD adopted 'Guidelines on the Protection of Privacy and Transborder Flows of Personal Data'. These Guidelines, which have no legal effect, were supplemented by a Declaration on Transborder Data Flows adopted in 1995. This declared its signatories' intention to 'avoid the creation of unjustified barriers to the international exchange of data and information'. The United Nations has also adopted 'Guidelines Concerning Computerised Personal Data Files', whilst the most extensive and effective form of international action has been taken by the Council of Europe. Beginning with sets of recommendations directed at public and private sector data processing adopted in 1973, the Convention for the Protection of Individuals with regard to the Automatic Processing of Personal Data (the Council of Europe Convention) was adopted in 1981 and ratified by the UK following the enactment of the Data Protection Act 1984. As has been stated previously, commercial pressure to put the UK in a position to ratify the Convention was the main factor behind the enactment of the 1984 Act. The Convention prescribed minimum standards which were to be provided in national data protection statutes, and provided that no barriers were to be imposed on grounds of protection of privacy in respect of data flows between those states which had signed and ratified the Convention. Although the Convention makes provision for signature by states which are not members of the Council of Europe, to date this has not occurred.

10.4   The Council of Europe Convention has been shaped by the experiences and practices of the western European states which have adopted data protection legislation. Such legislation has three major features: first, it applies to all sectors of automated data processing; secondly, it contains substantive provisions regulating the forms of processing which can take place and the rights and remedies available to individuals; and, finally, it provides for the establishment of some form of supervisory agency. As indicated above, a different approach has prevailed in other countries, notably the US.

10.5 To date, the discrepancies in approach between Europe and the rest of the world have been of limited practical significance. With the implementation of the European Data Protection Directive[1] containing stringent provisions regulating transborder data flows, this may change, the Directive's provisions in this respect being the cause of considerable and continuing trans-Atlantic controversy. The provisions will be of particular significance to the operation of multinational companies, as well as to undertakings such as airlines, which operate on a worldwide basis.

[1] Directive 95/46/EC.

Transborder data flows under the Council of Europe Convention and the Data Protection Act 1984

10.6 The approach which has generally been adopted by states implementing data protection statutes has been to impose some form of control over the transfer of personal data, unless there can be a degree of assurance that data protection standards will be observed in the recipient country. The extent of national controls varies. In Sweden and Austria, for example, transborder data flows to countries that are not signatory to the Council of Europe Convention require to be licensed by the data protection authorities. In other countries, such as the UK, data users will be required to register their intent to make transfers. These may subsequently be carried out unless specifically prohibited. Experience suggests that this is an unlikely prospect. Although the Data Protection Act 1984 provides that the Registrar may serve a transfer prohibition notice where he or she is satisfied that 'the transfer is likely to contravene or lead to a contravention of any of the data protection principles',[1] to date, only one such notice has been served by the Registrar. This prohibited the transfer of personal data in the form of names and addresses to a variety of US organisations bearing such titles as the 'Astrology Society of America', 'Lourdes Water Cross Incorporated' and 'Win With Palmer Incorporated'. These companies, which had been involved in the promotion of horoscopes, religious trinkets and other products in the UK, were the subject of investigations by the US postal authorities alleging wire fraud and a variety of other unsavoury trading practices.[2]

[1] Section 12(2).
[2] Details of this incident are to be found in the Seventh Report of the Data Protection Registrar (1991) pp 33–34.

Transborder data flows under the Data Protection Directive and the Data Protection Act 1998

Requirement for an adequate level of protection

10.7 Whilst the Council of Europe Convention is silent concerning control of transborder data flows, this topic receives extensive consideration in the Data

Protection Directive.[1] Major decisions concerning the operation of the new system will be made at a Community level. To this extent, the provisions of the Directive are more important in the field than those of the Data Protection Act 1998. The topic has been, and promises to remain, one of the most controversial aspects of the legislation. The Directive's Preamble recognises the dilemmas arising in this area:

> Whereas cross-border flows of personal data are necessary to the expansion of international trade; whereas the protection of individuals, guaranteed in the Community by this Directive does not stand in the way of transfers of personal data to third countries which ensure an adequate level of protection.[2]

The critical questions are, of course, what might be considered an adequate lack of protection and whether any perceived inadequacies in general legal provisions might be overcome by other sources of rights and remedies.

[1]   Directive 95/46/EC.
[2]   Recital 56.

10.8   In implementing this principle, the Data Protection Directive requires member states to ensure that:

> ... the transfer to a third country of data which are undergoing processing or which are intended for processing take place only if ... the third country ensures an adequate level of protection.[1]

Effect is given to this provision by the Data Protection Act 1998's eighth data protection principle which provides that:

> Personal data shall not be transferred to a country or territory outside the European Economic Area unless that country or territory ensures an adequate level of protection for the rights and freedoms of data subjects in relation to the processing of personal data.

[1]   Directive 95/46/EC, art 25(1).

10.9   By including the matter in the principles, it follows that any breach, or anticipated breach, can be answered by service of an enforcement notice. The need, therefore, for an additional transfer prohibition notice disappears. This formulation does mark a significant change to the existing UK system, whereby a data user can register an intent to transfer data on a worldwide basis and proceed with such transfers unless served with a transfer prohibition notice. The Registrar has indeed supplied guidance to data users conducting business on the Internet that they should register in this way.

Determining adequacy

10.10   The determination of what might be considered an adequate level of protection has been the cause of considerable and continuing controversy and uncertainty. It would appear that the determination is to be made by reference to both substantive and structural provisions in the third country. Given that the notion of having omnibus data protection statutes is largely limited to Europe, the effect might have been to cut the continent off from data links with the rest of the world. Even where a third country accepted a right of privacy and the notion of subject access, its regime might be stigmatised for lack of any supervisory agency along the lines of the UK Data Protection Commissioner.

10.11   Mirroring provisions in the Data Protection Directive,[1] the interpretative provisions attached to the principle provide that the issue of adequacy is to be assessed by reference to a range of factors, including the nature of the data and of the proposed transfer, the legal position in the recipient country, including any international obligations, together with any relevant codes of practice and any provisions relating to data security.[2]

[1]   Directive 95/46/EC.
[2]   Data Protection Act 1998, Sch 1, Pt II, para 13.

10.12   Use of the phrase 'adequate level of protection' clearly does not carry the requirement that the laws of the recipient state conform in every respect with the provisions of the Data Protection Directive.[1] It would appear unlikely, however, that a total absence of data protection legislation could be regarded as providing adequate protection. As has been discussed earlier, the US has followed a very different model of privacy protection from that adopted in Europe. Although proposals have been brought forward for the introduction of a data protection statute, there appears little prospect that this situation will change in the near future.

[1]   Directive 95/46/EC.

The Commission Working Party

10.13   The uniform application of the Data Protection Directive[1] would clearly be threatened if the decision whether third countries offered an adequate level of protection was to be made by each member state. It is provided, therefore, that the member states and the Commission are to inform each other of any cases where they feel that a third country does not provide an adequate level of protection.[2] In practice, general decisions regarding adequacy will be made at a Community level. Article 29 of the Directive establishes a Working Party on the Protection of Individuals with regard to the Processing of Personal Data. This Working Party is to be:

> ... composed of a representative of the supervisory authority or authorities designated by each Member State and of a representative of the authority or authorities established for the Community institutions and bodies, and of a representative of the Commission.

and will:

(a)   examine any question covering the application of the national measures adopted under this Directive in order to contribute to the uniform application of such measures;

(b) give the Commission an opinion on the level of protection in the Community and in third countries;

(c) advise the Commission on any proposed amendment of this Directive, on any additional or specific measures to safeguard the rights and freedoms of natural persons with regard to the processing of personal data and on any other proposed Community measures affecting such rights and freedoms; and

(d) give an opinion on codes Community level.[3]

[1] Directive 95/46/EC.
[2] Article 25(3).
[3] Article 30.

10.14 If the Working Party determines that a third country does not provide an adequate level of protection, a report is to be made to a committee established under art 31 of the Data Protection Directive.[1] Consisting of representatives of the member states and chaired by the Commission, the Committee will consider a proposal from the Commission for action on the basis of the Working Party's findings and deliver an opinion. The Commission may then adopt legal measures. If these are in accord with the Committee's opinion, the measures will take immediate effect. If there is any variation, application will be deferred for three months, within which time the Council of Ministers may adopt a different decision. Member states are obliged to take any measures necessary to prevent data transfers to the country involved.[2] Utilisation of this procedure may have the result of establishing a 'black list' of countries to which data transfers will be prohibited. Given the reference in the Directive to the role of 'sectoral rules' and 'professional rules and security measures', it is perhaps unlikely that there will be many 'black listings' affecting all data processing activities in a particular jurisdiction. Indeed, to date no such 'black listings' have been made.[3]

[1] Directive 95/46/EC.
[2] Article 25(4).
[3] For an indication of possible techniques for determining adequacy, see the Report of the Working Party *First Orientations on Transfers of Personal Data to Third Countries* XV D/ 5020/97-EN final WP4. This document is reproduced in the Fourteenth Report of the Data Protection Registrar (1998).

10.15 The Data Protection Directive[1] (art 25(6)) also provides for the procedures described in art 31(2) to be used to identify countries which the Commission considers does provide an adequate level of protection. In addition to a number of opinions provided as part of the US safe harbour negotiations (see para 10.29 below), the Article 29 Working Party has issued opinions on the adequacy of protection provided by the following third countries: Hungary, Switzerland, Australia, Canada, Argentina and Guernsey. The Commission has approved the protection provided under the laws of Hungary (July 2000), Switzerland (July 2000), Canada (December 2001) and Argentina (June 2003), as well as approving the safe harbor rules for US transfers (see para 10.29 below).

[1] Directive 95/46/EC.

10.16 Within the UK, the Data Protection Act 1998 provides that where:

(a)   in any proceedings under this Act any question arises as to whether the requirements of the eighth principle as to an adequate level of protection is met in relation to the transfer of data to a country or territory outside the European Economic Area, and

(b)   a Community finding has been made in relation to transfers of the kind in question,

that question is to be determined in accordance with that finding.[1]

It is further provided that the Commissioner shall be obliged to comply with any decision made by the Commission under the above procedures.[2]

[1]   Schedule 1, Pt II, para 15(1).
[2]   Section 54(6).

10.17   Utilisation of this procedure may have the result of establishing a 'black list' of countries to which data transfers will be prohibited. The Data Protection Directive[1] also provides for the procedures described to be used to identify countries which the Commission considers do provide an adequate level of protection. Given the reference in the Directive to the role of 'sectoral rules', 'professional rules and security measures', it is perhaps unlikely that there will be many 'black listings' affecting all data processing activities in a particular jurisdiction.

[1]   Directive 95/46/EC.

Transfers where an adequate level of protection is not provided

10.18   As originally drafted, the Data Protection Directive's prohibition of data transfers to a country where an adequate level of protection was not offered admitted no exceptions. Even allowing for the provisions relating to acceptance of sectoral and professional rules, such an approach would have posed major problems for transborder data flows. As adopted, the Directive modifies this provision to a considerable extent, it now being provided that national implementing statutes may authorise transfers, notwithstanding the absence of adequate protection in the recipient state where:

(a)   the data subject has given his consent unambiguously to the proposed transfer; or

(b)   the transfer is necessary for the performance of a contract between the data subject and the controller or the implementation of pre-contractual measures taken in response to the data subject's request; or

(c)   the transfer is necessary for the conclusion or performance of a contract concluded in the interest of the data subject between the controller and a third party; or

(d)   the transfer is necessary or legally required on important public interest grounds, or for the establishment, exercise or defence of legal claims; or

(e)   the transfer is necessary in order to protect the vital interests of the data subject; or

(f)   the transfer is made from a register which according to laws or regulations is intended to provide information to the public and which is open to consultation either by the public in general or by any person who can demonstrate legitimate interest to the extent that the conditions laid down in law for consultation are fulfilled in the particular case.[1]

¹ Directive 95/46/EC, art 26(1).

10.19   The Data Protection Act 1998 makes full use of these provisions. In the main, the Act's wording follows that of the Data Protection Directive,[1] but there is a divergence in respect of the exception relating to subject consent. Whilst the Directive requires unambiguous consent, the Act refers merely to the fact that 'the data subject has given his consent to the transfer'. The Act also confers regulatory power on the Secretary of State to define more closely the circumstances under which transfers may, or may not, take place 'for reasons of substantial public interest'.[2]

¹ Directive 95/46/EC.
² Schedule 4, para 4(2).

10.20   Transfers coming under these headings may take place, subject to their being in conformity with any entry on the Data Protection Register, without the need for any further permissions. The Data Protection Directive provides additionally that:

> ... a Member State may authorize a transfer or a set of transfers or personal data to a third country which does not ensure an adequate level of protection ... where the controller adduces adequate safeguards with respect to the protection of the privacy and fundamental rights and freedoms of individuals and as regards the exercise of the corresponding rights; such safeguards may in particular result from appropriate contractual clauses.[1]

Any exercise of this power must be reported to the Commission and the other member states. If any party so informed objects 'on justified measures involving the protection of the privacy and the fundamental rights and freedoms of individuals', a proposal for action may be tabled before the Committee by the Commission and, if approved, will require the member state involved to take necessary measures to conform.[2]

¹ Directive 95/46/EC, art 26(2).
² Article 26(3).

Transfers sanctioned by the Commissioner

10.21   In addition to the general exemptions, the Data Protection Act 1998 provides that transfers will be acceptable when:

- Made on terms which are of a kind approved by the Commissioner as ensuring adequate safeguards for the rights and freedoms of data subjects.[1]
- Authorised by the Commissioner as being made in such a manner as to ensure adequate safeguards for the rights and freedoms of data subjects.[2]

Any approvals granted under these provisions is to be notified to the Commission and the supervisory authorities of the other European Economic Area states.[3]

[1]   Schedule 4, para 8.
[2]   Schedule 4, para 9.
[3]   Section 54(7).

10.22   Authorisation may be given under the above provisions on an individual basis, but may also make reference to the controller's adherence to model contractual terms and conditions. There appears to be a general acceptance that the volume of transborder data flows is such that it is undesirable for decisions as to acceptability to require to be made in the context of individual transfers, and that more general provisions should be laid down. The nature of the procedures adopted by the Data Protection Directive,[1] and the open-ended prospect that national measures might be challenged at the instance of any other member state, does not seem conducive to speedy resolution of the issues involved.

[1]   Directive 95/46/EC.

Contractual solutions

10.23   In recent years, some attention has been paid to the possible role of contract in ensuring equivalency of protection in respect of transborder data flows. The Council of Europe, in co-operation with the Commission of the European Communities and the International Chamber of Commerce, has produced a model contract which might be used by data users for this purpose.[1]

[1]   Adopted by the Consultative Committee of the Convention for the Protection of Individuals with Regard to Automatic Processing of Personal Data, Strasbourg, 14–16 October 1992.

10.24   The objectives of the model contract are stated as being:

   a.   to provide an example of one way of resolving the complex problems which arise following the transfer of personal data subjected to different data protection regimes;
   b.   to facilitate the free circulation of personal data in the respect of privacy;
   c.   to allow the transfer of data in the interest of international commerce; and
   d.   to promote a climate of security and certainty of international transactions involving the transfer of personal data.[1]

The contract terms are divided into five sections. The first two concern the obligations of the party initiating the transfer, the licensor and those of the recipient, the licensee. The licensor is obliged to ensure that all domestic data protection requirements have been satisfied, whilst the licensee undertakes to ensure that these are complied with in the course of his or her activities. The contract also proposes a number of more detailed obligations which should be accepted by the licensee. Thus, the purpose for which the data will be used should be specified, there should generally be a prohibition on processing of sensitive data, the data shall be used only for the licensee's own purposes and any errors subsequently notified by the licensor will be rectified immediately upon receipt.

[1]   Explanatory Memorandum, para 23.

10.25 Further provisions would hold the licensee liable for any use which may be made of the data, and require that the licensor be indemnified in the event of liability arising through the licensee's breach of contract or negligent act. In the event of any dispute between the parties, the model contract contains provisions for dispute resolution. Reference is made to the possibility that disputes may be submitted to arbitration under the rules established by the ICC or UNCITRAL. Finally, provision is suggested for the termination of the contract in the event of a failure by the licensee to demonstrate good faith or to observe the terms of the agreement. Any personal data held by the licensee must be destroyed in such an eventuality.

10.26 Traditionally, the problem for such an approach in England was that the doctrine of privity of contract made it difficult for data subjects to enforce the terms of a contract which has been made between the data controller and the third country processor. This doctrine is not a part of Scots law (cf ius quaesitum tertio) and its application in England was undermined with the enactment of the Contracts (Rights of Third Parties) Act 1999. This provides in s 1 that:

(1)   Subject to the provisions of this Act, a person who is not a party to a contract (a 'third party') may in his own right enforce a term of the contract if—
   (a)   the contract expressly provides that he may, or
   (b)   subject to subsection (2), the term purports to confer a benefit on him.
(2)   Subsection (1)(b) does not apply if on a proper construction of the contract it appears that the parties did not intend the term to be enforceable by the third party.
(3)   The third party must be expressly identified in the contract by name, as a member of a class or as answering a particular description but need not be in existence when the contract is entered into.

Although hedged with caveats, the statute provides an appropriate basis to allow data subjects to take action to enforce contracts imposing safeguards upon the transfer of personal data. How feasible such an approach will be in practical terms is perhaps more debatable.

The Commission Working Party

10.27 The Working Party produced a report in April 1998 outlining its 'preliminary views on the use of contractual terms in the context of transfers of personal data to third countries'.[1] This document identified a number of elements that must be found in any relevant contract. The contract must provide for observance of the data protection principles. Whilst it was recognised that no system could provide a total assurance of compliance, it would be required that the provisions should provide a reasonable level of assurance, should provide support and assistance for data subjects and appropriate forms of redress.

[1]   XVD/5009/98 final WP10. This document is reproduced in the Fourteenth Report of the Data Protection Registrar (1998) p 133.

10.28 Extensive work has been carried out on the development of a satisfactory contractual model under the EU Data Protection Directive.[1] Decision 2001/497/EC on Standard Contractual Clauses for the transfer of personal data to third countries was adopted in June 2001.[2] This required member states to accept transfers conducted under its terms (ie using the standard form contract within the Decision) as satisfying the requirements of adequacy.[3] This Decision did not apply to transfers of data to a processor in a third country, only to controller to controller transfers. The Article 29 Working Party expressed its Opinion on the proposals which led to this Decision in a document published in January 2001.[4] A further Decision[5] contained standard contract terms relevant to the situation where an EU-based data controller wishes to transfer data to a processor established in a third country. Finally, the Article 29 Working Party has issued its Opinion as part of a Working Document (adopted in June 2003) on transfers of personal data to third countries subject to Binding Corporate Rules.[6] In the working document, the Working Party considers the merits of accepting binding (not voluntary) corporate rules as providing sufficient guarantees that personal data is adequately protected in a third country. It concluded that the guidance provided in that document would: 'lead to a certain degree of simplification for multinational corporate groups routinely exchanging personal data on a world-wide basis.'

[1] Directive 95/46/EC.
[2] OJ 2001 L 181/19.
[3] Article 1.
[4] Opinion 7/2001
[5] Decision 2002/16/EC of 27 December 2001.
[6] WP 74.

The 'safe harbor' principles

10.29 As has been discussed throughout this section, significant differences exist between the US and European systems. Following the adoption of the Data Protection Directive,[1] extensive discussions took place between the Commission and the US Department of Commerce with a view to devising mechanisms to avoid the prospect of a transatlantic data war. The discussions centred on the quest to agree a set of conditions, generally referred to as the 'safe harbor' principles, observance of which by US-based companies would be accepted by the Commission as ensuring conformity with European requirements.

[1] Directive 95/46/EC.

10.30 Negotiations between the Commission and the US Department of Commerce proved somewhat protracted, leading to the finalisation of the safe harbor arrangements in the summer of 2000. In April 2000, the Commission indicated its intention to seek the support of the member states for the adoption of the safe harbor principles. This view was criticised by the Article 29 Working Party which had issued a number of documents concerned with the negotiations.[1] These demonstrated a significantly greater degree of scepticism concerning the effectiveness of enforcement mechanisms than was exhibited by the Commission. In Opinion 7/99, published in December 1999, the Working Party indicated the view that the then version of the principles did not constitute a satisfactory basis for action. Referring to its previous reports it stated that:

> The Working Party notes that some progress has been made but deplores that most of the comments made in its previous position papers do not seem to be addressed in the latest version of the US documents. The Working Party therefore confirms its general concerns.

[1]   See Documents WP15, WP19, WP21 and WP23.

10.31   The Working Party's major concerns have centred on the limitations of a system of self-certification and also concerns that the jurisdiction of the Federal Trade Commission is restricted to actions to 'in or affecting commerce' with the consequence that:

> This seems to exclude most of the data processed in connection with an employment relationship (FAQ 9) as well as the data processed without any commercial purpose (e.g.: non-profit, research).

The nebulous nature of the assertion that other Federal and state laws might be applicable in certain situations was also criticised.

10.32   In a further Opinion[1] on the topic delivered in May 2000, the Working Party stated:

> Before the final version of the arrangement is submitted to the Article 31 Committee, the Working Party expects to be given the opportunity to examine the complete set of documents and express its views on the adequacy of the US system, in accordance with Article 30.1(b) of the [Data Protection] Directive.[2]
>
> The Working Party thus invites the Article 31 Committee and the Commission to ensure that the final steps of this important process are taken only in the light of the final opinion of the Working Party, not least because the outcome will have important consequences for the national authorities represented in the Working Party.
>
> The Working Party recalls that Members of the European Parliament have asked to see the final opinion of the Working Party before the Parliament expresses its views.

[1]   Opinion 4/2000.
[2]   Directive 95/46/EC.

10.33   The Commission indicated also in 2000 that provisional agreement had been reached on the contents of the principles. The draft was approved by the Article 31 Committee. In July, however, the Parliament passed a resolution indicating that it felt that the principles required to be strengthened before they could be considered acceptable. In spite of this view, the Commission issued a Decision on July 27[1] requiring the member states to give effect to the principles in respect of transfers with the US.

[1]   Decision 2000/520/EC OJ 2000 L 215/7.

10.34   The result of the negotiations was the establishment of a set of rules, basically encapsulating the contents of the Data Protection Directive's[1] principles relating to data quality. The rules themselves are accompanied by a set of Frequently Asked Questions (FAQ) and answers.[2] They require that notice must be given of the fact that data is held and the purposes for which it will be processed, and relevant 'opt out' opportunities must be given where it is intended that data will be used or disclosed for purposes other than envisaged or notified at the time of collection. Requirements relating to data security and integrity must also be accepted as must the principle of subject access.[3]

[1]   Directive 95/46/EC.
[2]   Available from http://www.export.gov/safeharbor/sh_documents.html.
[3]   Copies of the safe harbor documents together with much useful background material can be found on the US Department of Commerce web site at http://www.export.gov/safeharbor/.

10.35   The principles are very much compatible with the contents of the OECD Guidelines. Given the extensive involvement of the US in the work of this organisation, it is not surprising that discussions with the EU on the principles themselves have not proved particularly contentious. Most difficulty has centred on the issue of enforcement. As has been discussed, the US has tended to reject the concept of specialised supervisory agencies which is integral to the European data protection model. In respect of enforcement, the principles state that:

> Effective privacy protection must include mechanisms for assuring compliance with the principles, recourse for individuals to whom the data relate affected by non-compliance with the principles, and consequences for the organization when the principles are not followed. At a minimum, such mechanisms must include (a) readily available and affordable independent recourse mechanisms by which each individual's complaints and disputes are investigated and resolved by reference to the principles and damages awarded where the applicable law or private sector initiatives so provide; (b) follow up procedures for verifying that the attestations and assertions businesses make about their privacy practices are true and that privacy practices have been implemented as presented; and (c) obligations to remedy problems arising out of failure to comply with the principles by organizations announcing their adherence to them and consequences for such organizations. Sanctions must be sufficiently rigorous to ensure compliance by organizations.

10.36   The FAQ indicate that points (a) and (c) in this paragraph may be satisfied by the organisation indicating a willingness to co-operate with European Data Protection Authorities. US based organisations self-certify their intention to observe the safe harbor principles. This is done by means of a letter to the Department of Commerce indicating as a minimum the:

1.   name of organization, mailing address, email address, telephone and fax numbers;
2.   description of the activities of the organization with respect to personal information received from the EU;
3.   description of the organization's privacy policy for such personal information, including:
     a.   where it is available for viewing by the public,

b.   its effective date of implementation

c.   a contact person for the handling of complaints, access requests, and any other issues arising under the safe harbor,

d.   the specific statutory body that has jurisdiction to hear any claims against the organization regarding possible unfair or deceptive practices and violations of laws or regulations governing privacy;

e.   name of any privacy programs in which the organization is a member,

f.   method of verification (e.g. in-house, third party)(footnote omitted), and

g.   the independent recourse mechanism that is available to investigate unresolved complaints.

Breach of the terms of such a letter may expose the organisation either to action by the Federal Trade Commission under s 5 of the Federal Trade Commission Act which prohibits unfair or deceptive actions or to other (unspecified) action by other (unspecified) statutory bodies.

10.37 In accordance with the establishing Commission Decision 520/2000/EC of 26 July 2000, the development of the safe harbor arrangements were to be closely monitored by the Commission. In the first report in 2002 on the operation of the safe harbour arrangements, it was reported that:

> All the elements of the Safe Harbour arrangement are in place.
>
> Compared with the situation before it was available, the framework is providing a simplifying effect for those exporting personal data to organisations in the Safe Harbour and reduces uncertainty for US organisations interested in importing data from the EU by identifying a standard that corresponds to the adequate protection required by the [Data Protection] Directive.[1]
>
> Individuals are able to lodge complaints if they believe their rights are been denied, but few have done so and to the Commission's knowledge, no complaint so far remains unresolved.
>
> A substantial number of organisations that have adhered to the Safe Harbour are not observing the expected degree of transparency as regards their overall commitment or the contents of their privacy policies. Transparency is a vital feature in self-regulatory systems and it is necessary that organisations improve their practices in this regard, failing which the credibility of the arrangement as a whole risks being weakened.
>
> Dispute resolution mechanisms have in place an array of sanctions to enforce Safe Harbour rules. These mechanisms have not yet been tested in the Safe Harbour context. Not all of them have indicated publicly their intention to enforce Safe Harbour rules and not all have put in place privacy practices applicable to themselves that are in conformity with the Principles, as required by Safe Harbour rules. Given the importance of enforcement and the role of these bodies in it, it is necessary that Safe Harbour organisations use only dispute resolution mechanisms that fully conform to Safe Harbour requirements.

[1]   Directive 95/46/EC.

10.38 Following this report, in July 2002, the Working Party produced a working document on the functioning of the safe harbor arrangements. This brief document hinted that more information about the practice of safe harborites was needed to determine whether the safe harbour was functioning as anticipated, despite the acknowledgement from the Commission report that the necessary arrangements were in place.

10.39   Initially take up of the safe harbor scheme was limited. At the time of writing, 528 US companies had signed up to the safe harbor principles. After a rather slow start, there does seem to be increased awareness of the concept following the accession to the principles by Microsoft, Intel, Hewlett-Packard and Procter & Gamble.

Data protection in the age of the Internet

10.40   The EU-US safe harbor negotiations can be seen as a significant attempt to control uses of information technology on an international scale. Given estimates that North America and Europe account for almost 90% of websites, the significance of the initiative is undoubted. Especially given the US dominance in the field of electronic commerce and less welcome accompaniments such as email spamming, the principles might offer a measure of protection to European computer users. The WTO accepted an EU request that the topic of data protection should be included in the context of its work on the topic of ecommerce.

10.41   Perhaps more fundamental is the question in what manner the law should attempt to regulate activities conducted over the Internet. The OECD conducted a study in 1998 on 'Implementing the OECD "Privacy Guidelines" in The Electronic Environment: Focus on the Internet'. Referring to the 1980 OECD Guidelines, the report highlighted the view of the OECD that despite changes in technology over the years:

> these changes in technology do not diminish the relevance of the consensus achieved in 1980: despite technological advances and the evolution of an electronic environment based on world-wide information and communications networks, the Guidelines are still applicable today.

This was followed by a Ministerial Declaration on the Protection Of Privacy On Global Networks. In this, the ministers reaffirmed:

> their commitment to the protection of privacy on global networks in order to ensure the respect of important rights, build confidence in global networks, and to prevent unnecessary restrictions on transborder flows of personal data;
> They will work to build bridges between the different approaches adopted by Member countries to ensure privacy protection on global networks based on the OECD Guidelines;
> They will take the necessary steps, within the framework of their respective laws and practices, to ensure that the OECD Privacy Guidelines are effectively implemented in relation to global networks, and in particular:

>encourage the adoption of privacy policies, whether implemented by legal, self-regulatory, administrative or technological means;
>encourage the online notification of privacy policies to users;
>ensure that effective enforcement mechanisms are available both to address non-compliance with privacy principles and policies and to ensure access to redress;
>promote user education and awareness about online privacy issues and the means at their disposal for protecting privacy on global networks;
>encourage the use of privacy-enhancing technologies; ...

The reference to the desire to make use of privacy enhancing technologies is significant. Increasingly it has to be recognised that legal provisions alone cannot provide satisfactory safeguards for individuals.

10.42 As technology poses threats, so it may also provide solutions. This theme has been picked up by the Article 29 Working Party on Data Protection which has produced a number of documents on the topic. Of particular relevance are:

>Working Document on Processing of Personal Data on the Internet of 23 February 1999
>Recommendation 3/97: Anonymity on the Internet
>Recommendation 2/97: Report and Guidance by the International Working Group on Data Protection in Telecommunications ('Budapest/Berlin Memorandum on Data Protection and Privacy on the Internet')
>Opinion 1/98: Platform for Privacy Preferences (P3P) and the Open Profiling Standard (OPS)
>Recommendation 1/99 on Invisible and automatic processing of personal data on the Internet performed by software and hardware, adopted on 23 February 1999
>Working Document on Privacy on the Internet of 21 November 2000
>Opinion 1/2000 on certain data protection aspects of electronic commerce
>Opinion 7/2000 on the processing of personal data and the protection of privacy in the electronic communications sector
>Recommendation 2/2001 on minimum requirements for collecting personal data on-line in the European Union
>Working Document on online authentication services
>Opinion 2/2002 on the use of unique identifiers in telecommunication terminal equipments: the example of IPV6
>Working document on determining the international application of EU data protection law to personal data processing on the Internet by non-EU based web sites
>Opinion 2/2003 on the application of the data protection principles to the Whois directories[1]

---

[1] The texts of the documents are available from http://europa.eu.int/comm/internal_market/privacy/workinggroup_en.htm.

10.43 As can be seen from the titles of these documents, there has also been a growing requirement for further guidance in the application of the general rules on data processing to specific challenges posed by the Internet environment. In the UK, the Information Commissioner has issued some guidance on these matters, covering aspects of interpretation of the Data Protection Act 1998 in relation to the Internet, but many questions remain unanswered.

10.44 Unfortunately, as has been indicated above, there appears little evidence that the public in general is willing to pay any form of economic price in order to safeguard privacy. If the 'cost' of systems such as those referred to above is a slow-down of Internet access or the introduction of more complex procedures, it is unlikely that they will be used widely. Support for this view may be found with reference to the use of technical devices to render difficult the task of copying software in infringement of the producer's copyright. Market resistance ensured that the use of such devices had a short lifespan. It appears that a similar trend is now being followed with respect to the incorporation of copy protection devices in DVD players. Nevertheless, despite the apparent consumer reluctance to trade efficiency for privacy, the EU has taken some (albeit token) steps to improve individual safeguards by introducing measures in relation to cookies etc. A look at the some of the recitals from Directive 2002/58/EC which establishes a special regime for the communications sector encapsulates the current status of the debate:

> … The Internet is overturning traditional market structures by providing a common, global infrastructure for the delivery of a wide range of electronic communications services. Publicly available electronic communications services over the Internet open new possibilities for users but also new risks for their personal data and privacy …
>
> Terminal equipment of users of electronic communications networks and any information stored on such equipment are part of the private sphere of the users requiring protection under the European Convention for the Protection of Human Rights and Fundamental Freedoms. So called spyware, web bugs, hidden identifiers and other similar devices can enter the user's terminal without their knowledge in order to gain access to information, to store hidden information or to trace the activities of the user and may seriously intrude upon the privacy of these users. The use of such devices should be allowed only for legitimate purposes, with the knowledge of the users concerned …
>
> However, such devices, for instance so-called 'cookies', can be a legitimate and useful tool, for example, in analysing the effectiveness of website design and advertising, and in verifying the identity of users engaged in on-line transactions. Where such devices, for instance cookies, are intended for a legitimate purpose, such as to facilitate the provision of information society services, their use should be allowed on condition that users are provided with clear and precise information in accordance with Directive 95/46/EC about the purposes of cookies or similar devices so as to ensure that users are made aware of information being placed on the terminal equipment they are using. Users should have the opportunity to refuse to have a cookie or similar device stored on their terminal equipment. This is particularly important where users other than the original user have access to the terminal equipment and thereby to any data containing privacy-sensitive information stored on such equipment. Information and the right to refuse may be offered once for the use of various devices to be installed on the user's terminal equipment during the same connection and also covering any further use that may be made of those devices during subsequent connections. The methods for giving information, offering a right to refuse or requesting consent should be made as user-friendly as possible. Access to specific website content may still be made conditional on the

well-informed acceptance of a cookie or similar device, if it is used for a legitimate purpose …

The key questions for the data protection debate and the Internet is how far this approach should go to defend privacy interests and where should this approach stop?

Chapter 11

Emerging legal responses to computer crime

Introduction

11.1 It appears an inevitable feature of technological developments that criminal applications follow legitimate uses with only a very short time lag. The computer has proved no exception to the rule. The first instances of computer-related crime date back to the 1960s, with the topic beginning to attract the attention of academic and industrial commentators from the early 1970s. Today just as legitimate computer-based activities penetrate most aspects of life, if credence is given to many media reports, the Internet and financial institutions are the constant target of fraudsters, the WWW is a haven for paedophiles and pornographers, computer viruses endlessly threaten the survival of computer networks, whilst the most secret information held on computer systems is at the mercy of the computer hacker.

11.2 It is typical to regard computer criminals as sophisticated and expert practitioners. This is not always borne out in reality. The UK's National Criminal Intelligence Service (NCIS) published a report in 2003 'UK Threat Assessment of Serious and Organised Crime'.[1] Although identifying a number of potential risks including fraud and extortion, these are referred to as constituting the 'new tools, old crimes' element of high-technology crime. Even where crimes appears more directly linked to computer technology as is the case with hacking and the creation and dissemination of computer viruses, the element of skill involved is often limited. One of the first significant UK cases in the field is that of *R v Gold*.[2] Here a hacker accessed the contents of an electronic information service after visiting a computer exhibition where the system was being demonstrated by an engineer. A spell of what is referred to as 'shoulder surfing' enabled the password details to be memorised, a task made easier by the fact that it consisted of the letter 'A' repeated several times. With computer viruses, also, the NCIS report identifies the emergence of websites which:

> contain downloadable prepared viruses, worms and Trojans. These 'point and click' attack tools have removed the need for detailed knowledge of computer

code programming, and have allowed a new breed of much younger hackers, nicknamed Script Kiddies to develop.

The phenomenon of deskilling is clearly not limited to more legitimate forms of employment!

1   Copies of the report are available from http://www.ncis.co.uk/ukta/2003/default.asp
2   [1988] 1 AC 1063.

Forms of computer-related crime

11.3   The NCIS report seeks to define the environment within which high-technology crime may take place. This is defined as involving 'networked computers and internet technology'. Tools and techniques, it is suggested, can either be 'misused criminally or used legitimately in support of criminal activity'. The former scenario might see the creation of a computer virus, whilst the use of email as a communication channel to plot the commission of a bank robbery would be an example of the latter. With such a broad-ranging approach it is not surprising that the report suggests that:

> The range of crimes that can be committed, either through or with the support of hi-tech tools and techniques is limited only by the imagination and capability of the criminals.[1]

1   http://www.ncis.co.uk/ukta/2003/default.asp, para 8.1.

11.4   As in real life, one of the major categories of computer-related crime involves the attempt to secure some form of unauthorised and unwarranted financial benefit. Given that banks and other financial institutions were amongst the first large-scale computer users in the private sector it is not surprising that much early attention was paid to this aspect of the topic. One of the first cases cited as an instance of computer fraud involved the Equity Funding Corporation in the US. In its essentials, the fraud was comparatively simple, with the directors of an insurance company engaging in a sustained and substantial scheme of embezzlement. In the effort to conceal the conduct from the auditors, the company's computers were used to generate records of fictitious life insurance policies. The fraud was assisted by the fact that auditors and regulators accepted computer printouts as definitive evidence of policies and did not ask to see original documentation. By the time the fraud was discovered, some 64,000 out of 97,000 policies allegedly issued by the company were false. Total losses were estimated at some £1bn.[1]

1   The case has been widely reported. A useful account is to be found in A Norman, *Computer Insecurity* (1983, Chapman and Hall) p 119.

11.5   As has been discussed in previous chapters, first-generation computers were massive devices which could only be operated by persons in direct physical proximity to the machine. Beginning in the 1970s, communications capabilities began to be installed allowing computers to be accessed and operate remotely. With the development of global communications networks, computer fraud – as with other forms of computer-related crime – is increasingly adopting an international dimension. In one recent case,[1] banking computers located in the US were penetrated by hackers in St Petersburg, accounts belonging to a company from Indonesia were fraudulently debited and the proceeds diverted to accounts in Finland, Germany, Israel, the Netherlands and the US. One of the individuals suspected of involvement in the scheme was subsequently arrested at Stansted Airport in England and extradition proceedings were initiated by the US. Not surprisingly, extradition proceedings proved prolonged and protracted, with the key questions being concerned with the issue when and where offences were committed.

[1]   *Re Levin* (1997) Times, 21 June, HL. The first hearing was in March 1996 and is reported at 140 SJ LB 94. The case is discussed in more detail at para 13.38 below.

11.6   Beyond the financial sector, telephone companies were other early users of computer systems and the practice referred to as 'phone phreaking' revolved around attempts by users to manipulate telephone networks and their controlling computers in such a way as to obtain free telephone calls. Developing from extremely basic origins, when it was discovered that a toy whistle supplied as a free gift with packets of breakfast cereal mimicked exactly the frequency used by telephone network codes, practitioners developed more elaborate electronic techniques to bypass charging mechanisms.

11.7   Once again, the activities involved could be characterised as a species of fraud and a number of individuals were prosecuted and convicted on this basis. As the number of computer systems increased, new forms of conduct became possible. By the early 1980s, communication between geographically separate computer systems was possible, and with it the possibility of external access to computer systems. Although the terms 'hacking' and 'hacker' have a lengthy and indeed respectable pedigree in computer technology, they have now become largely synonymous with the act of obtaining unauthorised access to a computer system and, more specifically, obtaining this access by means of a telecommunications connection from another computer.

11.8   In some cases, the obtaining of unauthorised access to a computer system is seen as an end in itself, with hacking being considered a form of intellectual pursuit. In other instances, the motives of hackers are considerably less benign. Obtaining access may well be used as the precursor to some fraudulent scheme, or may be followed by conduct intended to corrupt or destroy data held on the computer. This latter effect may not require direct human access to a computer system. Often linked in the public mind with the activity of hacking is the promulgation of computer viruses. The dictionary defines the word virus as:

> ... the transmitted cause of infection: a pathogenic agent, usually a protein-coated particle of RNA or DNA, capable of increasing rapidly inside a living cell.

11.9 For the computer equivalent, a simple definition refers to 'malicious software which replicates itself'. Although some viruses can be relatively harmless (and, indeed, it has been suggested that the programming techniques incorporated in some forms of virus could usefully be used for purposes such as copying documents), there is no doubt that the concept has entered into popular demonology. Like their human equivalent, computer viruses can readily be transmitted from one computer to another. Initially, the act of dissemination would typically occur as the result of the exchange of infected disks, but, increasingly, the Internet has become the chosen method of transmission. A virus may be transmitted when an unsuspecting individual visits a website, but most recent incidents of viral infections have been spread by means of attachments to email messages. In Spring 2000, for example, the 'Melissa' virus infected around 100,000 computer systems. In common with a number of recent viruses, it relied for its effect on the integration between various aspects of the Microsoft operating system and applications programs. Once infected with the virus, a computer would automatically send copies of a Word document to the first 50 names in the user's Microsoft Outlook email address book. Once opened by the recipients, the process would be repeated. Although most virus attacks have followed a similar technical pattern, the more recent 'Sasser' virus adopted a new approach. Although, as has been the case with most viruses, it achieved its effects through exploiting a weakness in the Windows operating system, it was capable of infecting any computer which connected to the Internet without the owner needing to take any further action such as opening an email attachment.

11.10 In the case of some viruses such as 'Melissa' and the 'I Love You' attachment, the main consequence has been to create such a surge in the volume of email traffic that network performance has been significantly degraded. A closely related form of activity consists of what is generally referred to as a 'denial of service' attack. Often aimed at businesses engaging in ecommerce or at hacker 'bogey figures' such as Microsoft, the aim is to generate such a volume of spurious messages that the victim site becomes clogged up and is unable to accept messages from genuine users wishing to place orders for goods or services. The website Watis.com defines this concept as:

> a denial of service (DoS) attack is an incident in which a user or organization is deprived of the services of a resource they would normally expect to have. Typically, the loss of service is the inability of a particular network service, such as e-mail, to be available or the temporary loss of all network connectivity and services. In the worst cases, for example, a Web site accessed by millions of people can occasionally be forced to temporarily cease operation. A denial of service attack can also destroy programming and files in a computer system. Although usually intentional and malicious, a denial of service attack can sometimes happen accidentally. A denial of service attack is a type of security breach to a computer system that does not usually result in the theft of information or other security loss. However, these attacks can cost the target person or company a great deal of time and money.[1]

---

[1]   http://whatis.techtarget.com/.

11.11 The most common kind of DoS attack is simply to send more traffic to a network address than the programmers who planned it anticipated someone might send. The attacker may be aware that the target system has a weakness that can be exploited or the attacker may simply try the attack in case it might work. As will be discussed, there may be some uncertainty whether such conduct can be considered illegal under existing UK formulations of criminal law. Other viruses may be considerably more damaging, causing corruption or erasure of programs and data stored on a victim computer. The NCIS report estimates that 'the next major virus attack on the UK will cost business in the region of £2.1 billion and that 2.2 million office days will be lost in downtime'.[1]

[1]   http://www.ncis.co.uk/ukta/2003/default.asp para 8.10.

11.12 The dissemination of viruses is, of course, merely an (undesired) adjunct to the Internet's main purpose of permitting the exchange of information. A huge range of textual and audio-visual material can be transmitted over the Internet. At a basic level, a vast number of websites provide information on virtually every conceivable topic. As capacity constraints diminish, more and more sophisticated audio-visual materials are being transmitted. Many radio programmes, for example, can be listened to in real time over the Internet, a facility which permits worldwide broadcasting. Television broadcasts are likely to follow in the near future, and it is feasible that the Internet will become a viable delivery mechanism alternative to systems of satellite and cable broadcasting. Today, much of the concern is centred on what the European Commission have referred to as 'illegal and harmful content on the Internet'.[1] Particular concerns are expressed at the use of the Internet to disseminate material which is pornographic in nature or which is calculated to inflame racial hatred. Whilst the fact that material is transmitted over the Internet does not in any way mean that it is immune from legal control, questions have arisen concerning categorisation: to determine, for example, whether rules relating to content of television or cinema programmes should be applied where material is made available over the Internet. In common with most other aspects of Internet regulation, questions also arise whether national laws can realistically be applied in the context of a global network.

[1]   Commission Communication COM (96) 487, available from http://www2.echo.lu/legal/en/internet/communic.html.

The legal response

11.13 In considering the application of the criminal law to instances of computer-related conduct, a variety of issues arise. One of the most critical is whether computer-related conduct should be regarded as requiring technology-specific legislation or whether it might satisfactorily be regulated through the application of more general criminal law provisions. Although a trend can be identified throughout Europe and the US to enact computer crime statutes, experience in the UK with the Computer Misuse Act 1990 suggests that such an approach is not without its pitfalls. Not least, perhaps, developments in technology may challenge the continuing relevance of technologically based approaches. It has been indicated, for example, that amendments will be introduced to the Computer Misuse Act 1990 in the parliamentary session 2004–05 in order, inter alia, to clarify whether denial of service attacks constitute a form of unauthorised access or modification. The problem which has been identified is that many of the victims of such attacks explicitly authorise parties to access their website for the purpose of ecommerce. Having sanctioned access, it is uncertain whether an offence is committed when access is sought for other purposes. The debate preceding the enactment of this statute was notable for a difference of opinion between the Law Commissions for Scotland and England concerning the proper role and scope of computer-specific legislation, the Scottish Law Commission being considerably more sanguine about the effectiveness of general provisions of the criminal law. It is to be noted that the Council of Europe Convention on Cybercrime adopted in 2001 requires that certain forms of computer-related conduct should be criminalised but leaves it to states to determine how this should be achieved.

11.14   Another issue which is sometimes neglected in the debate on the role of the criminal law concerns the availability of other legal remedies. In the case of *Denco v Joinson*,[1] for example, the Employment Appeals Tribunal ruled that the act of an employee in seeking to obtain unauthorised access to information held on the employer's computer constituted serious industrial misconduct, justifying summary dismissal. Although the case of *Rodrigues v British Telecom*[2] indicates that an employer must take steps to bring such a prospect unequivocally to the notice of employees, it may be considered that the threat of dismissal is a more real sanction in the employment relationship (or indeed the threat of disciplinary action against students in educational establishments) than that of criminal prosecution.

[1]   [1992] 1 All ER 463.
[2]   20 February 1995, reported at [1995] 5 Masons Computer Law Reports 9.

11.15   The relevance of alternative sanctions in considering whether an extension of criminal law is warranted was accepted in Home Office Guidelines, published in 1982, outlining principles to be taken into account in determining whether new criminal provisions should be introduced. First, it was stated, the behaviour must be so serious that it cannot satisfactorily be dealt with on the basis of civil law remedies, for example, damages. Secondly, criminal sanctions should only be created where other less drastic means of control would be ineffective, impractical or insufficient. A final principle required that any new offence should be susceptible to enforcement.

11.16   Regardless of the form of the legal response, two propositions may be put forward for consideration:

•   In the event conduct is criminal when it is conducted other than on or by means of a computer, the same result should apply when the technology is utilised.

- In the event that conduct is not generally regarded as criminal, it should not become so when it occurs in a computer context.

11.17 The topics of computer fraud and of damage to data provide the main examples of conduct which will generally attract criminal sanctions in a non-computer context. The relatively uncontroversial element of recent law reform has concerned the attempt to remove lacunae created by the inappropriateness of traditional formulations and concepts within the context of information technology applications. As will be discussed below, these efforts have not always been successful and it appears a feature of case law that modern statutes, drafted to take account of the features of computer technology, have not fared notably better before the courts than more venerable enactments.

11.18 The second proposition is more contentious, and debate has been especially heated on the issue of whether the act of obtaining unauthorised access to information held on a computer (commonly referred to as hacking) should be criminalised in the situation where the act of obtaining access does not serve as the precursor to further aggravating conduct, such as the deletion of data or the evasion of access charges. Apologists for hackers would argue that activities are driven by the challenge of identifying weaknesses in security measures. On this analysis, hacking becomes a intellectual pursuit similar in concept, perhaps, to solving crossword puzzles. In terms of the legal response, the act of obtaining unauthorised access to information might be analogised with conduct which is invasive of individual privacy. As has been discussed previously, neither English nor Scots law currently recognises any specific right to privacy although remedies may be given in the event private information is used in an unreasonable manner and it may be queried whether the notion of informational privacy should be defined in the sense of conferring rights of privacy on information (and information holders).

11.19 In many respects, the essential components of the activities involved will be the same regardless of the legal category in which the conduct may be located. In their work, the Scottish Law Commission[1] identified eight forms of computer-related behaviour and considered their possible criminal implications. These were:

- Erasure or falsification of data or programs so as to obtain a pecuniary or other advantage.
- Obtaining unauthorised access to a computer.
- Eavesdropping on a computer.
- Taking of information without physical removal.
- Unauthorised borrowing of computer disks or tapes.
- Making unauthorised use of computer time or facilities.
- Malicious or reckless corruption or erasure of data or programs.
- Denial of access to authorised users.

[1] Sc Law Com Consultative Memorandum no 68, Sc Law Com no 106.

11.20 In much the same manner as the number of data protection principles fluctuated from report to report whilst retaining the same basic content, the Law Commission[1] investigated five forms of behaviour:

- Computer fraud.
- Unauthorised obtaining of information from a computer.
- Unauthorised alteration or destruction of information stored on a computer.
- Denying access to an authorised user.
- Unauthorised removal of information stored on a computer.

These categories subsume all of the topics included in the Scottish Law Commission's list. It is noteworthy that the Law Commission's work, conducted during the 1980s, made virtually no reference to the Internet nor to the issue of liability for content.

[1] Law Com Working Paper no 104, Law Com no 186.

11.21 For the UK, the major computer-specific criminal statute is currently the Computer Misuse Act 1990. Its background and provisions will be considered in detail in Chapter 12. At this stage it may be noted, however, that whilst the enactment of the Act followed the deliberations of the Law Commissions, no attempt was made to develop a comprehensive computer crime statute. To this extent, the provisions of the Computer Misuse Act 1990, albeit of considerable significance, should not distract attention from the role played by other aspects of the criminal law. In most respects, the provisions of this statute supplement rather than substitute for the provisions of the general criminal law.

The international dimensions of computer crime

11.22 Traditionally, the criminal law has been seen as the province of national authorities. Although the common nature of the threat posed by computer misuse has tended to produce similar responses, there has been limited international harmonisation. Within Europe, the EU has very limited legislative competence in the criminal field and although, as indicated above, it has been active in respect of Internet content, this has primarily taken the form of encouraging the development of schemes to categorise the contents of websites and of filtering mechanisms which can be used to restrict the range of sites which may be accessed from a particular computer. Typically, parents would be able to restrict their children's access to sites which displayed sexual or violent material.

11.23 A more substantive EU development takes the form of a proposal for a Framework Decision on attacks against information systems.[1] The genesis of this proposal rests in the conclusions of the Lisbon European Council of March 2000, which:

> stressed the importance of the transition to a competitive, dynamic and knowledge-based economy, and invited the Council and the Commission to

draw up an eEurope Action plan to make the most of this opportunity This Action Plan, prepared by the Commission and the Council, adopted by the Feira Summit of the European Council in June 2000, includes actions to enhance network security and the establishment of a co-ordinated and coherent approach to cybercrime by the end of 2002.

1   COM (2002) 173 final.

11.24   Acting on this manifesto, the Commission published a Communication entitled 'Creating a Safer Information Society by Improving the Security of Information Infrastructures and Combating Computer-related Crime'.[1] This proposed a number of legislative and non-legislative measures. In the latter respect the Commission has published a Communication on 'Network and Information Security: A European Policy approach'.[2] This analysed the current problems in network security, and provided a strategic outline for action. A Council Resolution of 6 December 2001[3] advocated a common approach to and specific actions in the area of network and information security. More significantly, and perhaps more contentiously in terms of its legislative competence, the Commission advocated also the necessity for the harmonisation of substantive criminal law provisions across the EU. The explanatory memorandum attached to the draft Decision states that it seeks:

> to approximate criminal law in the area of attacks against information systems and to ensure the greatest possible police and judicial co-operation in the area of criminal offences related to attacks against information systems. Moreover, this proposal contributes to the efforts of the European Union in the fight against organised crime and terrorism.[4]

1   COM(2000) 890 final
2   Available from http://europa.eu.int/information_society/eeurope/2002/news_library/new_documents/text_en.htm
3   OJ 2002 C 43/02
4   COM (2002) 173 final, para 1.6.

11.25   In terms of substantive offences, the Decision proposes that member states criminalise the acts of attempting or obtaining illegal access to or perpetrating illegal interference with, information systems together with acts intended to instigate aid or abet the practice.[1] The Decision proposes also extensive measures to ensure co-operation between national law enforcement agencies including the establishment of 24-hour operational points of contact available 24 hours a day and seven days a week.[2]

1   Articles 3-5.
2   Article 12.

11.26   The fate of the draft Decision remains unclear. Paralleling developments in the data protection field, the contents of the measure relate closely to the provisions of the only current international legal instrument in the form of the Council of Europe Convention on Cybercrime. Again in a manner similar to that followed in the data protection field, the Convention followed the adoption by the Council of recommendations in 1989 and 1995 dealing respectively with substantive and procedural aspects of criminal law.[1] The former identifies 12 topics as suitable for the attention of the criminal law:

- Computer-related fraud.
- Computer forgery.
- Damage to computer data or programs.
- Computer sabotage.
- Unauthorised access.
- Unauthorised interception.
- Unauthorised reproduction of a protected computer program.
- Unauthorised reproduction of a topography.
- Alteration of computer data or computer program.
- Computer espionage.
- Unauthorised use of a computer.
- Unauthorised use of a protected computer program.

[1] 'Computer Related Crime' Recommendation No R(89)9.

11.27   Perhaps the major value of this list is that it draws attention to the fact that criminal provisions may be incorporated in what are normally considered to be areas of the civil law, notably those regulating intellectual property rights. Although influential, these recommendations had no binding effect. More recently, in an initiative which echoes its approach to the topic of data protection, the Council of Europe adopted a 'Convention on Cybercrime'.[1] A draft text was published in February 2000, with an accompanying press release stating that:

> ... this Council of Europe text will be the first international treaty to address criminal law and procedural aspects of various types of offending behaviour directed against computer systems, networks or data, as well as other similar abuses.
>
> This legally-binding text aims to harmonise national legislation in this field, facilitate investigations and allow efficient levels of co-operation between the authorities of different States.

[1] Available from http://conventions.coe.int/Treaty/en/Treaties/Html/185.htm.

11.28   The Convention on Cybercrime was opened for signature on 23 November 2001. Although concluded under the auspices of the Council of Europe, the Convention (as was the case with the data protection convention) is open for signature and ratification by non-member states. To date, 36 countries have signed the Convention, including the non-member states of Canada, Japan South Africa and the US and Albania, Bulgaria Croatia, Estonia, Lithuania and Romania have ratified it. Ratification by Lithuania on 18 March 2004 was of particular significance in that the Convention required five ratifications before it entered into force. This has now occurred with effect from 1 July 2004. The Convention is a substantial document. Its drafting was a lengthy process occupying some four years and more than 50 meetings of the 'Committee of experts on Crime in Cyberspace'. The Convention contains a mix of substantive and procedural aspects. In a manner similar to that adopted in the Data Protection

Convention, the instrument specifies attributes which must be found in the national laws of its signatory states. It will then be a matter for each state to implement the provisions in domestic law. Although many aspects of the Convention are rather technical and non-contentions, procedural provisions relating to interception and retention of communications data have caused more controversy. The Civil Rights organisation, 'Treatywatch', for example, has commented that:

> The Cybercrime Treaty is an international agreement created for the ostensible purpose of helping police cooperate on crimes that take place on the Internet. Unfortunately, the treaty, which was drafted with very little public input, requires signatory nations to cooperate with foreign dictatorships and give invasive new surveillance powers to law enforcement. It also lacks protections for privacy or other civil liberties, and applies far more broadly than to just the Internet.[1]

[1] http://www.treatywatch.org/.

Structure of the Convention on Cybercrime

Substantive provisions

11.29 The Convention on Cybercrime divides offences into four categories

- Offences against the confidentiality, integrity and availability of computer data and systems (Title One)
- Computer-related offences (Title Two)
- Content-related offences (Title Three)
- Offences related to infringements of copyright and related rights (Title Four)

Title One offences

11.30 In many respects these provisions of the Convention on Cybercrime replicate features which have been found in computer crime statutes since their earliest appearance and which will be discussed in more detail in the following chapters. Article 2 is fairly typical, providing for the criminalisation of some forms of unauthorised access:

> Each Party shall adopt such legislative and other measures as may be necessary to establish as criminal offences under its domestic law, when committed intentionally, the access to the whole or any part of a computer system without right. A Party may require that the offence be committed by infringing security measures, with the intent of obtaining computer data or other dishonest intent, or in relation to a computer system that is connected to another computer system.

Section 1 of the UK's Computer Misuse Act 1990 already complies with this provision although as has been noted, there is no requirement for the additional elements identified in the Convention article.

11.31 Article 3 of the Convention on Cybercrime provides that the interception of communications between or within computer systems is to be made a criminal offence. The purpose of the article is stated in the explanatory report:

> The right to privacy of correspondence is enshrined in Article 8 of the European Convention on Human Rights. The offence established under Article 3 applies this principle to all forms of electronic data transfer, whether by telephone, fax, e-mail or file transfer.

The established form of interception has involved a party seeking access to information in the course of transmission, normally whilst in transit over a telecommunications or postal network. With computers and electronic messages, alternative techniques are viable. Given the use of packet switched systems, separate packets of data may be transmitted over different circuits. Eavesdropping in 'real time' may not therefore be viable. Messages will be pieced together at various stages, typically by an ISP and the article extends to interception at this stage. Another technique may make use of the fact that all computers emit electromagnetic radiation. These signals can be detected by unauthorised persons and with use of suitable equipment it is possible to replicate the information being processed at any particular time.

11.32 Article 4 of the Convention on Cybercrime requires that the unauthorised deletion or amendment of data requires to be criminalised. This, of course, has been a feature of most computer crime statutes. Article 5 of the Convention, however, moves a stage further providing that:

> Each Party shall adopt such legislative and other measures as may be necessary to establish as criminal offences under its domestic law, when committed intentionally, the serious hindering without right of the functioning of a computer system by inputting, transmitting, damaging, deleting, deteriorating, altering or suppressing computer data.

This provision is aimed primarily at denial of service attacks.

11.33 The final offence in this section of the Convention on Cybercrime concerns the:

> production, sale, procurement for use, import, distribution or otherwise making available of:
>
> 1. a device, including a computer program, designed or adapted primarily for the purpose of committing any of the offences established in accordance with Article 2
> 2. a computer password, access code, or similar data by which the whole or any part of a computer system is capable of being accessed
>
> with intent that it be used for the purpose of committing any of the offences described above.[1]

This provision is aimed at persons producing or supplying devices which may be used to facilitate hacking. Provisions of this nature have been applied in the past in the field of copyright law. The difficulty which has frequently been encountered in this context has been to establish that an object is 'primarily' designed to be used for illegal purposes. It will also be necessary to show that conduct is intended to result in the commission of an offence of the kind covered in the previously described Convention articles. Many, perhaps most items can be used for legitimate as well as illegitimate purposes.[2] It would appear, however, that programs such as 'password snuffers' would be covered. The offence would also be committed by a person who disclosed password or access details with the intent that they be used for unlawful purposes.

[1]   Article 6.
[2]   See discussion of the case of *CBS Songs Ltd v Amstrad Consumer Electronics* [1988] AC 1013 at para 21.25 below for an example how equipment may be used for both legitimate and illegitimate purposes.

11.34   Signatory states are given discretion whether to apply the prohibition in respect of devices primarily designed for facilitating offences. The provisions regarding the use of passwords is, however, mandatory.[1]

[1]   Convention on Cybercrime, art 6(3).

Title Two offences

11.35   This part of the Convention on Cybercrime refers to the offences of computer forgery and computer fraud. It provides in Article 7 that:

> Each Party shall adopt such legislative and other measures as may be necessary to establish as criminal offences under its domestic law, when committed intentionally and without right, the input, alteration, deletion, or suppression of computer data, resulting in inauthentic data with the intent that it be considered or acted upon for legal purposes as if it were authentic, regardless whether or not the data is directly readable and intelligible. A Party may require an intent to defraud, or similar dishonest intent, before criminal liability attaches.

Whilst Article 8 continues:

> Each Party shall adopt such legislative and other measures as may be necessary to establish as criminal offences under its domestic law, when committed intentionally and without right, the causing of a loss of property to another person by:
>
> –   any input, alteration, deletion or suppression of computer data;
> –   any interference with the functioning of a computer system,
> with fraudulent or dishonest intent of procuring, without right, an economic benefit for oneself or for another person.

11.36   Such conduct will normally be unlawful either under provisions of the general criminal law or under computer crime statutes. The major potential lacunae addressed by these provisions is the possibility that the data modified is not 'directly readable and intelligible'. The explanatory report comments that Article 7 of the Convention on Cybercrime:

... aims at filling gaps in criminal law related to traditional forgery, which requires visual readability of statements, or declarations embodied in a document and which does not apply to electronically stored data. Manipulations of such data with evidentiary value may have the same serious consequences as traditional acts of forgery if a third party is thereby misled. Computer-related forgery involves unauthorised creating or altering stored data so that they acquire a different evidentiary value in the course of legal transactions, which relies on the authenticity of information contained in the data, is subject to a deception. The protected legal interest is the security and reliability of electronic data which may have consequences for legal relations.

Title Three offences

11.37 The sole topic covered here is that of child pornography with the requirement being that states criminalise the production or distribution of materials depicting a minor, or person appearing to be a minor, 'engaged in sexually explicit conduct' with the intent that they be transmitted over a computer system or the possession of material either on a computer system or on a computer storage device such as a disk or CD. Also prohibited are what are sometimes referred to as 'pseudo-photographs', defined in the Convention on Cybercrime as 'realistic images' which convey the impression of relating to children. In terms of age, the Convention defines a minor as a person under 18 years but leaves it open to states to apply a lower age level of 16 years.[1]

[1] Article 9.

Title Four offences

11.38 As is frequently reported in the media, the Internet provides a superb copying facility. Many acts of copying will involve breach of copyright. There has been a trend in recent years for states to introduce criminal sanctions for copyright infringement in addition to the civil actions which might be pursued by the right holder. These topics will be discussed in more detail in the intellectual property module. It may be noted here that the Convention on Cybercrime requires that:

Each Party shall adopt such legislative and other measures as may be necessary to establish as criminal offences under its domestic law the infringement of copyright, as defined under the law of that Party ... where such acts are committed wilfully, on a commercial scale and by means of a computer system.[1]

[1] Article 10.

Procedural law

11.39 Matters of procedural law are mainly outside the scope of this book. Brief reference to some key provisions of the Convention on Cybercrime may serve however to provide linkage with the discussion regarding privacy and technology and also with the provisions regarding data protection in the communications sector.

11.40 Measures relating to the acquisition of evidence of Internet related crime have proved highly controversial involving as it frequently does the interception of communications. The Convention's provisions regarding these matters have provoked significant comment and criticism. The main provisions of the Convention on Cybercrime relate to the establishment of procedures whereby law enforcement agencies can:

- Obtain orders requiring the preservation of data, perhaps held by an ISP, which it is considered may indicate criminality and which it is considered might be vulnerable to destruction.[1]
- Require the retention of traffic data.[2]
- Require the production of data held on a computer system.[3]
- Require ISPs to supply subscriber information.[4]
- Provide for search and seizure of computer data in the context of a criminal investigation.[5]
- Empower the interception of electronic communications.[6]
- Collect or require an ISP to collect real-time data and pass this on to a law enforcement agency.[7]

[1] Article 16
[2] Article 17.
[3] Article 18.
[4] Article 18.
[5] Article 19
[6] Article 21
[7] Article 20

Jurisdictional issues and international co-operation

11.41 As incidents involving the dissemination of computer viruses frequently illustrate, the effects of computer-related conduct may be felt around the world. International consensus regarding the need for, and content of, criminal provisions is important for two reasons. First, to bring about the prosecution of an offender in any particular jurisdiction. Secondly, in the situation where the acts of a party resident in one jurisdiction impact adversely on computer owners in other jurisdictions, the attempt may be made to extradite the party responsible to face prosecution in the jurisdiction where damage has been caused. It is generally a prerequisite for a successful application that the conduct complained of should be unlawful in the country where the suspect is located as well as in the jurisdiction where the effects are felt.

11.42 The Convention provides in art 22 that contracting states will have jurisdiction in respect of offences committed on its territory (including ships and planes registered in that state) or by any of its nationals outside the state if the conduct is criminal in the place where it is committed or in the event that the offence is committed outside the jurisdiction of any state.

11.43   The Convention provides in art 24 that extradition is to be possible for any of the offences established under the Convention's requirements provided that a term of imprisonment of one year or more may be imposed in both states involved.

11.44   In addition to formal procedures, the Convention provides also 'general principles relating to international cooperation'. These require signatory states to co-operate with each other in the investigation of any suspected crimes. In particular, the investigatory provisions and powers described above are to be implemented at the request of the authorities in another contracting state on the same basis as applies to national authorities. A point of contact is to be nominated by each state which is to provide assistance and cooperation on a 24-hour, seven day a week basis.[1]

[1]   Article 23.

Chapter 12

Computer fraud and the move to computer specific legislation

Introduction

12.1   As was indicated in Chapter 11, computers have been used for fraudulent purposes since their application began to spread into the commercial and industrial sectors in the 1960s. Given that the banking sector was an early user of computer technology, and that the use of computers for payroll and accounting purposes marked many organisations' introduction to the technology, the potential for fraud is apparent.

12.2   Although a great deal has been and continues to be written on the topic of computer fraud, determination of its key characteristics remains uncertain, at least from a legal perspective. One early commentator suggested that distinctions could be drawn depending upon the nature of the role played by the computer.[1] In the context of fraud, the computer could be seen as proving either the means by which, or environment within which, crime might be perpetrated. The computer might also be used symbolically to intimidate or deceive victims. In reality, as epitomised by the Equity Funding case referred to at para 11.4 above, many schemes of fraud involve the computer in all of these roles. It might fairly be said that but for the involvement of the computer, the fraud could not have been conducted on such a scale or avoided detection for so long.

[1]   D Parker *Crime by Computer* (1976, Scribner).

12.3   In the UK, much useful empirical work concerning the scale of computer fraud has been carried out by the Audit Commission. Six surveys have been published to date: in 1981, 1984, 1987, 1990, 1994 and 1998. The last three surveys include losses incurred by computer users through damage to their data or computer hacking as well as those resulting from fraud. The Audit Commission's definition, which was subsequently adopted by the Law Commission in its studies in the area, states that the term computer fraud encompasses:

... any fraudulent behaviour connected with computerisation by which someone intends to gain financial advantage.[1]

The scope of this definition is extremely broad. It would, for example, encompass the situation where possession of a cash dispensing card was obtained through a trick and used to withdraw money although it may be argued that the involvement of computer technology was peripheral rather than integral to the conduct.

---

[1] This definition has been utilised throughout the Audit Commission's surveys. See, for example, the 1987–90 study,, para 7.

12.4 The prosecution of even such low-technology conduct as the misuse of a cash dispensing card has posed problems in certain jurisdictions, where the basis of theft-type offences is the removal of property without the consent of the owner.[1] In both England and Scotland, such instances have been successfully prosecuted under the law of theft, where the determining factor is the perpetrator's intention to deprive the owner of his or her property.[2]

---

[1] Council of Europe Computer-related crime, Report by the European Committee on Crime Problem (1989) p 28.
[2] See Sc Law Com Consultative Memorandum no 68 (1986) para 3.5.

Forms of computer fraud

12.5 For present purposes, attention must be restricted to the situation where manipulation of the operation of a computer system is integral to a fraudulent scheme. The Audit Commission, in common with other writers on the topic, identifies three stages at which fraud may occur, referring to input fraud, output fraud and program fraud.

Input fraud

12.6 Input fraud involves the falsification of data prior to, or at the moment of, its entry into a computer. The instance of the misuse of a cash dispensing card might be taken as an example of this form of behaviour, although the falsification might be considered to relate to the entitlement of the party to use the card rather than to the validity of the data inserted. Other examples culled from the reports of the Audit Commission include the creation of a 'ghost' employee by a dishonest wages clerk. Documentation relating to this fictitious individual was entered into the computer. Ultimately, a payment was raised and was collected by an accomplice of the clerk. In many respects, this was a comparatively minor fraud. The scheme lasted for no more than three weeks and the loss to the employer was put at £407.[1] A similar, though more extensive, scheme reported involved a conspiracy between a local government wages clerk and about 20 manual employees. Here, the wages clerk made false entries on time sheets, resulting in the workers receiving additional payments. The proceeds were then shared with the clerk. This scheme lasted for three years and netted the parties involved a sum of £54,500.[2] The Audit Commission's surveys indicate that input fraud is the most extensive form of computer fraud, although it is also the form of activity which is least significant in legal terms. In neither of the cases cited above, and in very few of those reported by the Audit Commission, was there any room to doubt that the conduct involved was illegal.

[1] Case 3 cited in the 1984–87 survey.
[2] Case 2 cited in the 1984–87 survey.

Output fraud

12.7   Output fraud is a less frequent occurrence, and again raises few significant issues concerning the applicability of provisions of the criminal law. As the name would suggest, it consists of the fraudulent manipulation of data at the point it is outputted from a computer. One example cited by the Audit Commission concerned an incident at a computer centre which was responsible for printing cheques. On a Friday evening prior to a bank holiday weekend, the staff, it was reported, 'left the computer suite without any authority and in breach of regulations to go to the pub'. Whilst they were away, a theft occurred and pre-signed cheques with a value of £931,000 were stolen. The losses resulting were estimated at almost £230,000.[1] The theft falls within the Audit Commission's definition, as the cheques were printed by the computer equipment. They were also output from the computer. Beyond this, again, it is difficult to identify any significant legal issues in instances of output fraud. In many instances, although data may be inputted by a relatively junior employee, the capacity to receive and to modify the output of the computer may be restricted to higher levels of management. In one case reported by the Audit Commission, a bank manager falsified accounts (input fraud) to conceal the fact that he was embezzling funds. The bank's computer system generated records which would have revealed his activity, but he misused his position in order to suppress these records. The amount of the fraud was some £44,000.[2] Once again, the fact that the conduct at issue was criminal could not be doubted, but with this instance we see the first signs of what is one of the major difficulties arising from the involvement of computers, that of securing evidence relating to the conduct involved.

[1] Case 40 cited in the 1981–87 survey.
[2] Case 39 cited in the 1981–87 survey.

Program fraud

12.8   In very many cases of input and output fraud, the degree of computer literacy required of the perpetrators is minimal. Indeed, it may not even be necessary for them to use a computer themselves. The concept of program fraud involves a greater level of sophistication. The Audit Commission have commented that:

The alteration of a computer program is often regarded as the 'true' computer fraud but evidence from all other surveys, including those in North America and overseas generally, suggests that relatively few actually occur. There is a degree of misunderstanding by some that the computer user sitting at a keyboard entering data and responding to questions asked by the system is 'programming' the computer. In reality, the program has already been written and merely provides well-defined options to the user to process data according to different criteria.[1]

[1]   1984–87 survey, p 16.

12.9   Program fraud involves either the creation of a program with a view to fraud or the alteration or amendment of a program to such ends. A wide variety of species of program fraud have been identified. One of the most notorious is the so called 'salami fraud'. This involves the perpetrator taking a small sum from many accounts and transferring this to an account which he or she controls. Few customers might notice or query a withdrawal of 10p from their bank account. In the event that thousands of accounts were involved and the process repeated over a period of months, the total involved could be very extensive. As the Audit Commission comment, such 'stories are often told, but evidence of such frauds is less forthcoming'.[1] One case which was reported in their survey concerned the insertion of a routine into an accounting program. This program was designed to be used by video rental stores and provided facilities for stock-keeping, recording hires and rental income. The storekeepers' liability to tax would obviously be affected by their income. For the benefit of dishonest persons, this program contained an additional feature. When a special password was entered, the program would generate false data which would have the effect of reducing the perpetrator's apparent liability for VAT. The program was sold to 120 retailers, although it would appear that only 12 of these were informed of the existence of this special feature. It was estimated that the losses to the tax authorities might have amounted to £100,000.[2]

[1]   1984–87 survey, p 17.
[2]   Case 59 cited in the 1984–87 survey.

Internet fraud

12.10   Perhaps the most publicised form of fraud today involves activities conducted over the Internet. As in the general field, many of the techniques applied are rather basic. Project Trawler, a report published by the National Criminal Investigation Service[1] in 1999, suggested that in the majority of cases, traditional methods of fraud such as misuse of credit cards, failure to deliver goods ordered and paid for, pyramid selling, 'pump and dump' share pushing and get-rich quick schemes 'have been given a new lease of life on the Internet'. Although the fear is often expressed that credit card numbers might be intercepted by hackers in the course of transmission over the Internet, there does not appear to have been a documented case of this occurring. The risk of credit card misuse is, however, significant. Instances have been reported where credit card details held on a retailer's computer system have been accessed by hackers with, on occasion, the numbers being posted on websites for use by anyone intent on a career in crime. Computer programs exist, and can be accessed over the Internet, which mimic the algorithms employed by credit card companies and so allow for the creation of genuine credit card numbers. It is reported that:

> Visa, the international payments card group, claimed in April 1999 that 47% of disputes and frauds arising from use of its cards in the European Union (EU) were Internet-related. Some 22% involved people denying that they had carried out the transaction, and 25% involved miscellaneous complaints such as wrong or late delivery. The 47% figure is extraordinarily high given that only 1% of Visa's EU turnover is Internet-related.[2]

Whilst not all of the complaints described above will involve criminal conduct, in cases where fraud is at issue there will generally be no doubt that an offence has been committed. In common with the other forms of activity described above, the most important question will be to decide when and where the offence has been committed.

[1] http://www.ncis.co.uk/contact.html.
[2] Project Trawler, para 49.

Assessing the scale of computer fraud

12.11 Prior to essaying detailed consideration of the legal response to the forms of conduct discussed above, some attempt should be made to assess the scale of the problem. Here, it would appear that as many estimates can be identified as there are commentators on the topic. In the specific context of Internet fraud, the Fraud Advisory Panel, established by the Institute of Chartered Accountants for England and Wales, estimated in 1999 that losses in the UK might range from £400m to £5bn. In the US, the Internet Fraud Complaint Center (IFCC) Report for 2002, prepared by the National White Collar Crime Center and the FBI, reported more than 48,000 cases of Internet fraud resulting a total loss of $54 million.[1] This was more than three times the amount of fraud identified in the previous years, an increase which may reflect greater awareness of the existence of the Center, which bases its work on reports from injured parties, than an absolute increase in the amount of fraud.

[1] http://www.fraud.org/internet/intstat.htm.

12.12 Beyond the headlines the reality of Internet fraud is rather prosaic. The 'top ten' list of crimes is depicted below along with the proportion of complaints relating to the particular forms of conduct.

Crime	Complaints (%)
Auction Fraud	46.1
Non-Delivery of goods or services	31.3
Credit card fraud	11.6
Investment Fraud	1.5
Confidence Fraud	1.1
Identity Theft	1.0
Check Fraud	0.5
Nigerian letter fraud	0.4
Communications Fraud	0.1

Although the Nigerian letter (or email) fraud[1] comes relatively low on the list it is responsible for the largest average loss per affected individual. Seventy-four victims lost a total of $1.6m, an average of almost $4,000 each. It is noteworthy that, at least in the context of the Internet, schemes of identity theft, which feature prominently in the ongoing UK debate concerning the introduction of identity cards, are not a major problem. Most of the conduct identified is depressingly banal and familiar. Electronic auctions such as Ebay emulate their real life equivalents in the form of car boot sales and street markets in attracting 'fly by night' merchants who take money and either disappear or supply goods of extremely dubious quality or, in the case of material subject to intellectual property rights, legality.

[1] This form of fraud involves contacting individuals with the request that they assist in transferring large amounts of money from a country. The money invariably represents the fruit of some dubious conduct, perhaps bribes paid to a relative of the letter author in return for the award of a contract, and the assistance of the victim will, it is claimed be rewarded by the payment of a generous commission. Some up-front costs will have to be met. The victim may send this money but will certainly never receive the promised commission.

12.13   Although many surveys offer estimates of the scale of computer fraud, the extent of losses is often virtually impossible to calculate precisely. A particular problem occurs when the conduct relates to data which has value but is not made available on a commercial basis. In one case in the US, a number of individuals were charged with the theft of data from a telephone company. The prosecution alleged that the value of the information taken was $79,499. This represented the costs in staff time and computer usage required to generate the information. Clearly, this would render it a major incident. At trial, the defence were able to produce copies of publications sold by the telephone company containing a more extensive version of the information and retailing at $13. At this point, the prosecution collapsed.[1] The circumstances of the particular case may have been unusual, and a number of the issues raised will be considered more fully in the context of the topic of theft of information, but if the essence of fraud is accepted as being that the perpetrator makes a gain at the expense of the victim, the question 'how much?' is not always susceptible of a ready answer.

[1] For a description of this and other US prosecutions, see B Sterling *The Hacker Crackdown* (1993, Viking Press).

12.14 Although the evidence of large-scale computer fraud might be limited and contradictory, there can be little doubt concerning the extent of reliance upon information technology within the financial sector. Literally billions of pounds are transferred every day between banks making use of computerised payment and electronic funds transfer (EFT) systems. Some 85% by value of all money transactions in the UK are handled by some form of EFT. Not only do the transactions represent vast amounts of money, their speed is also significant. It has, for example, been estimated that all of the UK's foreign currency reserves could be transferred abroad within 15 minutes. Under international protocols agreed between the participating banks, such transfers are regarded as irrevocable. To this extent, therefore, an electronic signal transferring funds from one account to another represents more than just evidence of the payee's entitlement to the specified assets. The ex-head of Scotland Yard's Computer Crime Unit has commented:

> The prevention of crime here is important. No, it's not important, it's vital.
> These days money is not the pound in your pocket; it's the $234 billion worth of transactions which go out from the City of London and back every day. All that money really amounts to is electronic digits travelling down wires. That's real money.[1]

[1] *Guardian*, 8 January 1987.

Legal responses to computer fraud

12.15 In considering this aspect of the criminal law, two forms of conduct may be identified. The first occurs where a fraudulent scheme is devised with the aim of securing some direct pecuniary benefit, for example, to cause £500,000 to be transferred to the perpetrator's bank account. The alternative form of advantage occurs when the perpetrator is relieved of payments that he or she would otherwise be obliged to make. An example might see the perpetrator using a third party's password to secure free use of a database, with any bills being sent to the third party. In this situation, the perpetrator benefits in a more indirect manner.

Direct benefit

12.16 In respect of the first form of conduct, there will be little doubt concerning the criminality of conduct. Both Law Commissions expressed the view that 'when a computer is manipulated in order dishonestly to obtain money or other property, a charge of theft or attempted theft will generally lie'.[1]

[1]   Law Com Working Paper no 110 (1988) para 3.4.

12.17   An alternative offence which might be relevant is that of obtaining property by deception. Difficulties occurring in respect of this offence where the deception is perpetrated upon a machine will be considered in more detail below. In the event, however, that a cash dispensing card is obtained by means of a trick perpetrated on its owner, the charge of obtaining property by deception might be an appropriate riposte.

12.18   If there is little doubt concerning the fact that an offence will be committed, a matter which assumes some significance is the question when the offence is committed. In this respect, the case of *R v Thompson*[1] furnishes a helpful illustration.

[1]   [1984] 3 All ER 565.

12.19   Thompson was employed as a computer programmer by a bank in Kuwait. Whilst so employed, he devised a plan to defraud the bank. Details of customers' accounts were maintained on the bank's computer system and, in the course of his work, Thompson was able to obtain information about these. A particular goal was to identify what are referred to as 'dormant accounts'. These possessed substantial credit balances, but had not been the subject of any debits or credits over a considerable period of time. This might well have been caused by the fact that the account holder had forgotten about the account's existence or had died. The chances of fraud being identified by the account holder would thus be minimised.

12.20   Having identified five target accounts, Thompson opened an equal number of accounts in his own name at various branches of the bank. In what might be regarded as a classic form of program fraud, he compiled a program which instructed the computer to transfer sums from these accounts to accounts which he had opened with the bank. In an effort to reduce further the risks of detection, the program did not come into effect until Thompson had left the bank's employ to return to England. The program was also intended to erase itself and all records of the transactions once this task had been accomplished. Although the law report does not go into detail on this matter, the fact that Thompson stood trial for his actions might indicate that this part of the scheme was not completely successful.

12.21   On his arrival in England, Thompson opened a number of accounts with English banks and wrote to the manager of the Kuwaiti bank instructing him to arrange for the transfer of the balances from Kuwait to his new English accounts. This was done. Subsequently, his conduct was discovered and Thompson was detained by the police. Charges of obtaining property by deception were brought against him and a conviction secured. An appeal was lodged on the basis that the English courts had no jurisdiction in the matter as any offence would have been committed in Kuwait.

12.22 This plea did not commend itself to the Court of Appeal, which held that the offence was committed at the moment when the Kuwaiti manager read and acted upon Thompson's letter. At this stage, Thompson was subject to the jurisdiction of the English courts. Delivering the judgment of the court, May LJ stated:

> Discard for the moment the modern sophistication of computers and programmes [sic] and consider the old days when bank books were kept in manuscript in large ledgers. In effect all that was done by the appellant through the modern computer in the present case was to take a pen and debit each of the five accounts in the ledger with the relevant sums and then credit each of his own five savings accounts in the ledger with corresponding amounts. On the face of it his savings accounts would then have appeared to have in them substantially more than in truth they did have, as the result of his forgeries; but we do not think that by those forgeries any bank clerk in the days before computers would in law have thus brought into being a chose in action capable of being stolen or of being obtained by deception.[1]

---

[1]   *R v Thompson* [1984] 3 All ER 565 at 569. The decision in *Thompson* has been strongly criticised by Smith in *Property Offences* (1994, Sweet and Maxwell) paras 325–326, on the basis that if the transaction in Kuwait had been a nullity, its transfer to the UK could not become the theft of a 'chose in action'.

12.23 The conclusion that no offence involving theft or the fraudulent obtaining of property had been committed at the stage of making the false entry on the computer does not entail that no offence would have been involved. Thompson's conduct might have constituted forgery and, in Scotland, the offence of 'uttering'. Recalling, however, the speed with which large sums of money may be transmitted, the effect of the decision is to deny the protection of a substantial part of the criminal law to those financial institutions which rely on computers in the course of their operations. As will be discussed, the provisions of s 2 of the Computer Misuse Act 1990, which establish what is referred to as the 'ulterior intent' offence, are designed to bring forward in time the moment at which a criminal offence is committed. Whilst this offence might be applicable in respect of the actions of an external hacker, the basis for its commission is an act of unauthorised access. A distinction is drawn between unauthorised access and the use of authorised access for an unauthorised purpose. It would appear that Thompson's conduct would fall into the latter category and, as such, could not be prosecuted under this provision.

Indirect benefit

12.24 A vast market exists for the provision of electronic information services. It has been estimated that Western Europe's online information market is valued at around US$3.24bn.[1] In the legal field, information services such as 'Lexis' and 'Justis' offer their wares to the legal world – at a price. In a typical scenario, a person wishing to make use of an information service will enter into an agreement with the service provider, and be provided with a password or other identifier allowing access to all or part of the contents of the database in return for an agreement to make specified payments.

¹ Information Market Observatory 'The main events and developments in the Information Market' (1994).

12.25 In the event a party manages to secure unauthorised access to such a database, either by dishonestly obtaining password details or by finding a way to bypass the security system, information will be obtained without proper payment being made. As will be discussed in more detail in Chapter 13, information is not regarded as a form of property capable of being stolen. A charge of theft will not, therefore, be an appropriate legal response. Attention might therefore focus on the offence of obtaining services by means of a deception. Although it might appear that this is what has occurred, the legal difficulty is that the perpetrator's only contact has been with a computer system. The question arises whether a computer can be deceived.

12.26 In part, the issue can be seen as having arisen through a well-meaning, though perhaps short-sighted, incident of law reform. Under the provisions of the Larceny Act 1916,¹ conduct of the kind at issue might have been prosecuted on the ground of obtaining services by means of a false pretence. This remains the basis of liability in Scots law and, in its Consultative Memorandum,² the Scottish Law Commission expressed the view that in determining whether this offence has been committed, attention should be paid to the conduct of the perpetrator. If the intention is to obtain services dishonestly, the offence will be committed and the fact of whether the conduct operates upon a human or a machine is irrelevant.

¹ Section 32(1).
² Sc Law Com Consultative Memorandum no 68 (1986) para 3.9.

12.27 In England, the Eighth Report of the Criminal Law Revision Committee recommended a shift from false pretence to deception, on the basis that the word deception:

> ... has the advantage of directing attention to the effect that the offender deliberately produced on the mind of the person deceived, whereas 'false pretence' makes one think of what exactly the offender did in order to deceive.¹

This report was published in 1966, before the problems of the computer had fully penetrated general legal consciousness. Its recommendations were adopted in the Theft Act 1968, which defines the concept of 'deception' as involving:

> ... any deception (whether deliberate or reckless) by words or conduct as to fact or as to law, including a deception as to the present intentions of the person using the deception or any other person.²

1   *Theft and Related Offences* (Cmnd 2977, 1966) para 87.
2   Section 15(4).

12.28   Although the point has not been definitively settled, the assumption has been that only a human being can be the victim of deception. In the case of *Davies v Flackett*,[1] a motorist was charged with obtaining car-parking services by deception. The car park in question had an automatic barrier control at its exit. Upon a motorist inserting payment of 5p into a machine, the barrier would be raised allowing egress. The appellant approached the exit barrier only to discover passengers from the preceding car forcibly lifting the barrier to allow that car to exit. Considerately, they remained holding the barrier and invited the appellant to leave. This conduct was observed by the police, who proved less charitably disposed, charging the appellant (and presumably the other actors in the drama) with dishonestly obtaining a pecuniary advantage by deception contrary to s 16 of the Theft Act 1968. The charge against the appellant was dismissed by the justices on the basis that a machine had no mind and therefore could not constitute the victim of a deception. The prosecution appealed, seeking the opinion of the Divisional Court on the question whether 'an act of deception directed towards a machine in the absence of any human agent is sufficient to support a prima facie case in the preferred information'.[2]

1   [1973] RTR 8.
2   [1973] RTR 8 at 10.

12.29   The Divisional Court agreed with the justices that the defendant should be acquitted, but expressed the view that the major flaw in the charge lay in the absence of any evidence that the defendant intended to evade payment. The evidence, it was held, indicated that the defendant had intended to pay when he entered the car park and remained of this intention until the very last moment, when the opportunity to avoid payment was presented to him. The question whether a machine could be deceived was treated very much as a subsidiary question, and differing views were expressed by the judges. Bridge J indicated doubt that this might be the case, commenting 'even if it is possible for a deception to be practised so as to establish that ingredient of the offence under section 16 [of the Theft Act 1968] without there being a human mind to deceive (though for myself I doubt it)',[1] whilst Acker J, after holding that the case was not properly to be regarded as one involving deception of a machine, stated:

> Nothing which I say expressing my agreement that this appeal should be dismissed in any way suggests that an offence cannot be committed where there is any mishandling of a machine, and thereby an advantage is incurred.[2]

Although the Law Commission, in their Working Paper on Conspiracy to Defraud,[3] advocated that the law should be amended to bring conduct of this nature within the scope of the offence, no action has been taken, the issue perhaps being subsumed in the rush to enact the Computer Misuse Act 1990.[4] In this process, the decision of the House of Lords in the case of *R v Gold*[5] was to assume massive importance. Although the particular conduct involved will now be caught by the Computer Misuse Act 1990, the decision continues to represent a compelling case study illustrating the problems which the law faces in regulating and controlling new forms of computer related conduct.

1   *Davies v Flackett* [1973] RTR 8 at 11.
2   [1973] RTR 8 at 11.
3   Working Paper 104, 1987.
4   See also discussion of the Law Commission Consultation Paper no 155 on Fraud and Deception at para 14.54 below.
5   [1988] 1 AC 1063. The decision of the Court of Appeal is also reported at [1987] 3 WLR 803.

The Prestel hack

12.30   The 'Prestel' system offers subscribers access to a variety of database services. Upon agreeing to pay rental charges, plus further charges dependent upon the nature and extent of usage, users would be allocated a password and user identification number. This would entitle them to access a variety of news and information services. In addition to the publicly available facilities, Prestel also serves as a host computer for a variety of services made available to a more restricted class of user. Many tour operators, for example, make use of online booking facilities available to travel agents using the Prestel service. The service also provides email facilities for its subscribers. By means of what the Law Report refers to as a 'dishonest trick', Gold, together with his co-accused, Schifreen, obtained knowledge of a password allowing use of the Prestel system operated by British Telecom.[1]

1   It would appear that the dishonest trick consisted of nothing more than looking over the user's shoulder as he typed the password whilst demonstrating the system at a computer exhibition. The password details themselves are indicative of a worrying lack of security on the part of the system owners. The password itself consisted of the number 2 repeated eight times, whilst the user identification number was the sequence 1234.

12.31   The password that Schifreen and Gold had obtained was no ordinary password. It was one issued to a British Telecom engineer, who would require widespread access to the system in order to maintain it and repair any faults which might occur. Whilst entry of a 'normal' password would cause records of usage to be made for billing purposes, it would appear that this did not occur with an engineer's password, a factor which is significant in any assessment of the case.

12.32   Extensive use was made of the password by Schifreen and Gold. After some time, British Telecom became suspicious about the activities, and details were recorded of the telephone numbers called from Gold's own phone. Scrutiny of these records coupled with the information retained on the Prestel computer revealed the nature and extent of Schifreen and Gold's predatory activities. The question then arose what, if any, offence had been committed. Although academic lawyers might have applauded the decision to obtain a definitive ruling on the applicability of the offence of obtaining services by deception, the doubts described above resulted in the decision being taken that a prosecution should be brought under the auspices of the Forgery and Counterfeiting Act 1981. This provides that:

> A person is guilty of forgery if he makes a false instrument, with the intention that he or another shall use it to induce somebody to accept it as genuine, and by reason of so accepting it to do or not do some act to his own or any other person's prejudice.[1]

The problems identified above relating to the possibility, or impossibility, of deceiving a machine are overcome in this statute, with s 10 providing that attempts to induce a machine to accept the instrument are to be equated with attempts so to induce a person. Schifreen and Gold were tried at Southwark Crown Court, convicted and fined.[2] Appeals were lodged against these convictions.

[1]   Section 1.
[2]   *R v Gold* [1988] 1 AC 1063.

12.33   The critical issue before the appellate courts was whether any false instrument had been made. One reason why the Forgery and Counterfeiting Act 1981 had proved attractive to the prosecution was that it had been reduced following a report by the Law Commission, which had sought to update the law to, inter alia, take account of technical developments.[1] To this extent, the Act's definition of 'instrument' sought to move away from the traditional concentration on paper-based documents, providing that the word's definition should include 'any disc, tape, sound track or other device on or in which information is recorded or stored by mechanical, electronic or other means'.[2]

[1]   Law Com no 55 'Criminal Law Report on Forgery and Counterfeit Currency' (1973).
[2]   Section 8(1).

The search for an instrument

12.34   An offence can be committed under the Forgery and Counterfeiting Act 1981 only when a false instrument is used. The obvious question in the present case was 'where is the instrument?' Discussion of this issue requires consideration of the nature of the Prestel system's operations. A Prestel user would need to be equipped with equipment such as a monitor, keyboard and telephone modem. These would permit data to be transmitted and received via the telephone system. By dialling the Prestel telephone number, the user would initiate communications with the system. From the user's viewpoint, this initial stage would involve the display of a message informing them that they were in contact with Prestel and asking them to enter their password details. From a more technical perspective, the initial contact would be made with a device called a 'port', which would channel the call to an area of the computer called the 'user segment'. Each port had its own user segment allocated to it. The user segment consisted of three parts: an *input buffer* in which messages from the user would be received and held until they could be processed further, a *control area* which would hold data and direct it onwards to the relevant sectors of the computer via an *output buffer*.

12.35 The procedure for accessing the system was as follows. Upon contact being made with the system, a user would be asked to transmit the appropriate password details. These would be held in the *control area*, which would cause the details to be transmitted to the portion of the computer which held details of authorised users. If the password details corresponded with such a user, the *control area* would be instructed to allow access. At this stage, the password information would be deleted from the *control area's* memory. The entire log-in procedure would occupy a very short period of time, normally less than one second. For normal users, details of their usage would be recorded and retained for billing purposes. In the present case, once the password details were identified as belonging to a British Telecom engineer, no further records were made.

12.36 An initial candidate for the role of false instrument might appear to be the password details as generated and transmitted by the user in the form of electronic impulses. This suggestion was rejected by the courts, which held that an instrument had to be eiusdem generis with those devices listed in the statute. These all required that the instrument be a physical object. Obviously, signals being transmitted along a telephone line have no physical existence.

12.37 Given that the electronic signals could not themselves be classed as an instrument, attention turned to the Prestel computer itself. When asked by the Court of Appeal to define precisely what constituted the instrument, the prosecution argued that the user segment as holding the password details constituted the false instrument. This submission was clearly accepted by the trial jury, as Gold and Schifreen were convicted. The Court of Appeal and the House of Lords disagreed. A variety of reasons were advanced by the various appellate judges as underpinning this conclusion. Two are of particular significance. First it was held in the Court of Appeal by the Lord Chief Justice (Lane) that:

> ... neither the Law Commission ... nor the Forgery and Counterfeiting Act 1981, so it seems to us, seeks to deal with information that is held for a moment whilst automatic checking takes place and is then expunged. That process is not one to which the words 'recorded or stored' can properly be applied, suggesting as they do a degree of continuance.[1]

[1] *R v Gold* [1987] 3 WLR 803 at 809.

12.38 We are told in the Bible that 'one day is with the Lord as a thousand years, and a thousand years is as one day'.[1] Much modern mathematical and scientific research supports the view that time is a more flexible commodity than has been generally accepted. It might be argued that human standards of time should not be applied to the operations of computer technology. Holding data for a period of time which is insignificant in human terms may permit extensive computer operations to be conducted upon it.

[1] Second Letter of St Peter.

12.39 A second reason advanced for the inapplicability of the charge resulted from the nature of the offence of forgery. This requires that an instrument should convey a message about itself, that message being false. An example might be of a forged signature, where the writing falsely purports to be that of the apparent signatory. Although the point was not discussed at length, it would appear that the password details were not false. The password was genuine; any falsity lay in the appellants' implicit assertion that they were entitled to use it. The case is perhaps analogous with that of a person presenting a stolen cheque and claiming to be the authorised payee. Regardless of any other charges which might be relevant, it seems unlikely that the offence of forgery will have been committed. This is a point which may assume considerable significance in the case of digital or electronic signatures. Given the feasibility of producing an exact reproduction of such a identifier, it may be difficult to argue that the element of deception lies in the nature of the instrument rather than in terms of the perpetrator's entitlement to use it. The view might be taken, however, as was expressed by Bowen LJ in *Wenham Gas Ltd v Champion Gas Lamp Co* that 'the superadding of ingenuity to a robbery does not make the operation justifiable'.[1]

[1]   (1891) RPC 49 at 56.

12.40   A final reason advanced for the court's decision related to the nature of the Prestel system's operations. The user segment both received the data and transmitted it onwards to the computer's subscriber database. To this extent, the user segment was both victim and deceiver, undoubtedly a somewhat schizophrenic state of affairs and one which their Lordships were not prepared to tolerate.

12.41   Although the court's reasoning on this point has been criticised,[1] both tribunals were critical of the attempt to invoke the Forgery and Counterfeiting Act 1981. The Lord Chief Justice concluded:

> We have accordingly come to the conclusion that the language of the Act was not intended to apply to the situation which was shown to exist in this case ... It is a conclusion which we reach without regret. The Procrustean attempt to force these facts into the language of an Act not designed to fit them produced grave difficulties for both judge and jury which we would not wish to see repeated. The appellants' conduct amounted in essence ... to dishonestly obtaining access to the relevant Prestel data bank by a trick. That is not a criminal offence. If it is thought desirable to do so that is a matter for the legislature rather than the courts. We express no view on the matter.[2]

[1]   See [1988] LQR 202.
[2]   [1987] 3 WLR 803 at 809–810.

The impact of the decision

12.42   The unequivocal rejection of the prosecution's case in *R v Gold*[1] had a significant effect upon the ongoing debate concerning the legal response to aspects of computer misuse. Although the case has been discussed in the context of fraud, the financial losses caused to British Telecom were relatively minor. The case might be seen as the first occasion on which instances of computer hacking reached the attention of the appellate courts. The failure of the prosecution received considerable publicity and was seen, perhaps erroneously,[2] as indicating that computer hacking and fraud were immune from criminal sanctions.

1   [1988] 1 AC 1063.
2   It would appear that a prosecution might have been brought successfully under the provisions of the Telecommunications Act 1984. This provides in s 42 that: 'A person who dishonestly obtains a service provided by means of a licensed telecommunications system with intent to avoid payment of any charge applicable to the provision of that service shall be guilty of an offence.'

12.43   The work of the Scottish Law Commission was concluded prior to the decision of the House of Lords in *R v Gold*,[1] taking the form of a Consultative Memorandum, published in 1986,[2] and a Report in 1987.[3] In many respects, the Scottish Law Commission took the view either that existing criminal provisions could satisfactorily be applied, or were not persuaded that the mere fact of the involvement of a computer justified making criminal conduct that would not otherwise be so regarded. On this basis, the recommendation was for a very limited measure of reform, with the Commission suggesting the enactment of a Computer Crime (Scotland) Act.

1   [1988] 1 AC 1063.
2   Sc Law Com Consultative Memorandum no 68.
3   Sc Law Com no 106.

12.44   A draft Bill was appended to the 1987 Report. This was a short document containing five clauses, creating a criminal offence capable of being committed by a person who obtained unauthorised access to a program or data stored in a computer. This access would require to be sought either with the view to acquiring knowledge of the program or the data or with the intention of adding to, erasing or otherwise altering the data so as to procure some advantage for themselves or another person or to damage the interests of the computer owner or any other person. It was further provided that the offence could be committed where the addition, alteration or erasure of data resulted from the reckless act of an unauthorised user.[1] Penalties for the offence would have been dependent upon whether proceedings were summary or solemn. In the former case, a sentence of up to six months' imprisonment might be imposed; in the latter, a term of up to five years' would be sanctioned.[2]

1   Clause 1.
2   Clause 3.

12.45   Adoption of the Scottish Law Commission proposals would have entailed that the limited act of obtaining unauthorised access would not constitute a criminal offence. This approach was justified by the Commission on the ground that, whilst much hacking was conducted with some ulterior end in view, many hackers, who:

... are often quite young and possibly still at school, attempt to gain access to other people's computers simply because of the intellectual and technical challenge which that activity presents ... Although we are not sympathetic to the view that unauthorised hacking should be encouraged so long as it is only a kind of intellectual game, we recognise that as a matter of public policy it is probably preferable to express any new offence or offences in terms which actually draw attention to the real mischief at which they are aimed.[1]

A related point concerned the difficulty which might be encountered in sentencing an offence expressed in terms of unauthorised access of any kind. The analogy was drawn to the situation existing in the area of road traffic law, where it has been held in both Scotland and England that a court should not, in passing sentence for an offence of careless driving, take any account of the consequences of the act. It was suggested that similar constraints would apply to an unauthorised access offence.[2]

[1]   Sc Law Com no 106 (1987) paras 4.4–4.8.
[2]   Sc Law Com no 106 (1987) para 4.6.

12.46   Other commentators also expressed the view that the mere act of obtaining unauthorised access should not be criminalised. The Data Protection Registrar posited the possibility of a hacker gaining access to a system 'with no intent of abusing its contents and who causes no damage'. Such conduct, he argued, was generally regarded as:

> ... juvenile 'hobby' behaviour. The Registrar recognises the undesirability of 'criminalising' juveniles and the concern that young people should not be introduced to the criminal justice system unless necessary.[1]

[1]   Fifth Report of the Data Protection Registrar (1989) p 31.

12.47   Others have been much less sanguine in respect of the activity, and it is fair to suggest that even a number of those initially in favour of a 'kid glove' legal response have become more concerned at the implications of the behaviour as societal dependence on the technology becomes more and more extensive.[1] A more stringent approach was advocated by the Law Commission and subsequently adopted in the Computer Misuse Act 1990. The Commissioners rejected the argument that the attempt to access a computer system out of curiosity or as a form of intellectual challenge posed no serious threat to the owners of the systems involved. The Commission reported a number of cases[2] where knowledge of the fact that unauthorised access had occurred led computer owners to expend significant amounts of time and labour in checking, or even rebuilding, a system in order to be certain that no damage had occurred. A not untypical example of such a situation has recently been reported from the University of Cambridge, and concerned the application of a practice referred to as 'packet sniffing':

> 10,000 academics and students were now changing their passwords. 'Someone gained access to our system via the Internet and could have got to around 10,000 users' files. The potential damage to Cambridge University and beyond is enormous' ... The hacker used a so-called sniffer program, which sat silently

within the computer system for four weeks, monitoring its activities. This could allow the hacker to compile a list of all passwords to give him unhindered access to every computer on the university's network.[3]

1   See, for example, D Denning 'Concerning Hackers Who Break Into Computer Systems. Postscript' in P Ludlow (ed) *High Noon on the Electronic Frontier* (1996, MIT Press).
2   Law Com no 186 (1989) paras 1.33–1.35.
3   *Daily Telegraph*, 27 April 1996.

12.48   The cost and inconvenience involved in an incident such as this is substantial. It may be queried, however, whether the degree of solicitude expressed for the peace of mind of computer owners is replicated in other areas of the criminal law. If, for example, a house owner suspects that an unknown person has had possession of their keys and the opportunity to copy them, they may feel obliged to install new locks. It would appear unlikely that, in the absence of any attempt to secure entry to the premises involved, a criminal offence would have been committed by the other party. Again, if the operator of an aeroplane discovers that an engine casing has been opened by an unauthorised person, they may well conduct extensive checks of the engine looking for evidence of damage. It may even be that they would be considered negligent if they allowed the plane to fly without conducting an extensive examination. If caught, however, the perpetrator's liability will be limited to the act of opening the casing. In many cases, it may be doubted whether this will constitute a criminal offence.

12.49   A related issue concerns the question whether there should be a requirement that the computer user maintain adequate security measures (a requirement imposed under the Data Protection Act 1998) in order to qualify for the protection of the criminal law against instances of unauthorised access. In their recommendations as to the form of computer crime legislation, the Council of Europe advocated the creation of an offence involving 'the access without right to a computer system or network by infringing security measures'. Such an approach, it was suggested, would analogise computer hacking with burglary-style offences.[1] Although the Law Commission report lays considerable stress on the security implications of hacking, stating:

> In our view ... the most compelling arguments for the criminalisation of hacking are those stemming from first, the actual losses and costs incurred by computer system owners whose security systems are or might have been breached; secondly that unauthorised entry may be the preliminary to general criminal offences; and thirdly, that general willingness to invest in computer systems may be reduced, and effective use of such systems substantially impeded, by repeated attacks and the resulting feeling of insecurity on the part of computer operators[2]

the Computer Misuse Act 1990 does not require that any security measures be overcome. Certainly, access must be unauthorised, a point which will be discussed below, but the analogy may be with a person who ignores 'No Trespassing' notices and enters private property. Save in the situation that their conduct is aggravated by other acts such as the removal of property, no criminal offence will be committed.

1   Report on Computer Related Crime (1997) p 38.
2   Law Com no 186 (1989) para 2.14.

12.50   In Committee, an attempt was made to amend the Bill to provide a defence for a person charged under its provisions that 'such care as in all the circumstances was reasonably required to prevent the access in question was not taken'. In advocating this approach, reference was made to a press release issued by the Data Protection Registrar arguing:

> We should not lose sight of the fact that computer users ought to protect their own systems and, as regards personal data there is a duty clearly established in the Data Protection Principles. You've only yourself to blame if your neighbour's cattle get into your unfenced field.[1]

1   Cited in HC Official Report, SC B (Computer Misuse Bill), col 15, 14 March 1990.

12.51   The amendment, however, was rejected, one of the most telling objections being that it would be extremely difficult to make any assessment of what was to constitute reasonable care. The point was also made that English law has not recognised the concept of contributory negligence as a defence in criminal cases. A burglar, it was commented, could not demand an acquittal because his victim had left a window open.

12.52   The Law Commission's investigation of the topic of computer crime began somewhat later in time, and was prompted by its review of the law of conspiracy to defraud.[1] It was not until 1988 that a Working Paper was published,[2] just before the decision of the House of Lords in *R v Gold*.[3] The tone of this document was similar to that of the Scottish Report. Although it did not come to any definite conclusions, it also proposed that a new offence of unauthorised access should be created and sought views on the particular form which the offence should take. The Law Commission's final report was published in 1989,[4] and displayed significant differences from the working paper. Whilst the former had been almost dismissive of the problems of computer abuse, the final Report, based in part on confidential consultations with computer users, took a much more serious view of the problem and of the need for reform. Once again, the issue of unauthorised access was at the core of the recommendations. Whereas the Scottish Law Commission had proposed to make such access illegal only when it served as a precursor to further acts, the Law Commission were influenced by commentators who argued that a computer owner who became aware that a party had secured unauthorised access would have to proceed on the assumption that further damage had been caused, and would be put to considerable expense in checking data and, perhaps, replacing programs or data with back-up copies. Accordingly, the Law Commission proposed that the mere act of obtaining unauthorised access should be made unlawful, albeit subject to lesser penalties than those applicable to more destructive forms of computer-related behaviour.

1   Law Com Working Paper no 104 (1987).
2   Law Com Working Paper no 110 (1988).
3   [1988] 1 AC 1063.
4   Law Com no 186 (1989).

12.53 The Law Commission's final report was published in Autumn 1989[1] and recommended the enactment of a Computer Misuse Act 1990. Unusually, the report did not include a draft Bill, an omission explicable by the fact that it was believed at the time proposals for computer crime legislation were to be included in the government's legislative programme for 1989–90 and, therefore, that the report needed to be completed and published without delay. In the event, the Queen's Speech was silent on this point and, in the absence of a government-sponsored measure, a Bill seeking to give effect to the Law Commission's recommendations was introduced by Michael Colvin MP, who had secured a high placing in the ballot for introducing private members' legislation. The drafting of the measure received a measure of support from the parliamentary draftsmen, but a number of cases brought under the legislation have highlighted definitional weaknesses which might have been overcome had the measure been introduced on behalf of the government.

[1] Law Com no 186.

12.54 In line with the Law Commission's recommendations, the Computer Misuse Act 1990 creates three new offences. Section 1 provides that the act of obtaining unauthorised access to programs or data held on a computer will constitute an offence punishable by a term of imprisonment of up to six months. Sections 2 and 3 create additional and more serious offences relating, respectively, to securing unauthorised access with a view to facilitating the commission of a further serious offence and of causing an unauthorised modification to the contents of a computer system. The maximum penalty in respect of these offences is a term of imprisonment of up to five years.

Conclusions

12.55 It is difficult to overstate the impact of the decision in *R v Gold*.[1] It was largely responsible for transforming what was a relatively relaxed and measured examination of the need for computer-specific legislation into something of a sprint to reach the statute book. The following chapters will consider the application of the Computer Misuse Act 1990 and attempt to analyse both how successful the measure has been and how appropriate the underlying concepts remain in the age of the Internet and with the dissemination of viruses on a global scale.

[1] [1988] 1 AC 1063.

Chapter 13

The Computer Misuse Act 1990

Introduction

13.1   As indicated in Chapter 12, although the prospect of introducing computer-specific legislation had been considered by the Law Commissions for around six years, the introduction of legislation occurred in circumstances of considerable haste. With laws, as with most aspects of life, the maxim 'act in haste, repent at leisure' is frequently proved true. Although it has now been in force for more than a decade, the impact of the Computer Misuse Act 1990 has been limited and with the adoption of the Council of Europe adopts its Convention on Cyber-Crime, it has been indicated that amending legislation will be introduced in parliamentary session 2004–05 in order to rectify possible gaps in its coverage.

13.2   The major lacunae identified by both Law Commissions in their work during the 1980s was the fact that the act of obtaining unauthorised access to data held on a computer did not, in the absence of further aggravating conduct, constitute a criminal offence. This conclusion, coupled with the decision in *R v Gold*,[1] created what was perhaps a misguided perception that computer hackers could seek to penetrate any computer system without fear of incurring the attention of the criminal law. In order to resolve this problem, s 1 of the Computer Misuse Act 1990 establishes an offence of obtaining unauthorised access to programs or data held on a computer – generally referred to as the 'basic offence'. Although well intended, the consequence has perhaps been to frame legislation by reference to particular and now outdated forms of technology. In some respects the coverage of the provisions is too broad whilst, in common with the data protection regimes discussed previously, the emergence of the Internet and systems of networked challenge the effectiveness and relevance of the regulatory schema.

[1]   [1988] AC 1063.

The scope of the unauthorised access offence

13.3 Although in terms of its penalties, the unauthorised access offence is the least significant of the new provisions, its linkage with other provisions makes it the most critical element of the legislation. The offence is defined in s 1 of the Computer Misuse Act 1990, which provides that:

> (1) A person is guilty of an offence if—
> (a) he causes a computer to perform any function with intent to secure access to any program or data held in any computer;
> (b) the access he intends to secure is unauthorised; and
> (c) he knows at the time when he causes the computer to perform the function that that is the case.

13.4 In common with other statutory interventions in the computer field, no attempt is made to define any of the more technical terms referred to above. It will be seen that in order for the unauthorised access offence to be committed, a variety of conditions have to be satisfied. Three elements call for detailed consideration. The concept of access raises a number of issues and the scope of the definitions may be extremely broad. Next comes the question of whether access is authorised. Finally, and significantly in view of recent developments, is the degree of intent that must be ascribed to a person charged with this offence.

The concept of access

13.5 Merely sitting at a computer keyboard will not constitute unauthorised access. The first stage in the commission of the offence will consist of causing a computer 'to perform any function with intent to secure access to any program or data held in any computer'. A variety of elements from this definition call for further discussion and comment.

Performing a function to secure access

13.6 This term is defined in such a manner that virtually any act involving use of the computer will suffice. Thus access will be secured to a program or data when the user, by causing the computer to operate in any manner:

(a) alters or erases the program or data;
(b) copies or moves it to any storage medium other than that in which it is held or to a different location in the storage medium in which it is held;
(c) uses it; or
(d) has it output from the computer in which it is held (whether by having it displayed or in any other manner).[1]

Although the above provisions are somewhat tortuous (and are themselves subject to further definition in the Computer Misuse Act 1990), it seems clear that most actions whereby a user makes contact with a computer system and causes that system to display or to transmit information will come within its ambit. Thus, the simple act of switching on a computer will cause various messages to be displayed on the screen, whilst the act of making contact with some external system will cause some form of 'log on' screen to be displayed.

1   Section 17(1).

To a program or data held in any computer

13.7   The basic offence requires that access be sought to any program or data held in any computer. In order to commit the offence, it is not necessary that the unauthorised user should direct their attention at any particular computer system or seek to inspect any specific programs or data held in the system.[1] The effect of this provision is to render liable to prosecution those hackers who, perhaps by dialling telephone numbers at random, seek to discover those which serve as the gateway to a computer system.

1   Computer Misuse Act 1990, s 1(2).

The location of access

13.8   The popular image of a computer hacker is of someone who accesses computer systems by making a telephone connection from their own computer. This perception caused considerable problems in the first prosecution brought under the Computer Misuse Act 1990. The case resulted in the accused being acquitted of charges under the Act on the direction of the judge. This was based upon an extremely restrictive interpretation of the scope of the unauthorised access offence. The case was referred to the Court of Appeal by the Attorney-General, where it is reported as *A-G's Reference (No 1 of 1991)*.[1] The defendant in this case had been employed as a sales assistant by a wholesale locksmith. He left their employ, but subsequently returned to the premises indicating the intention to purchase an item of equipment. Details of sales transactions were entered into a computer terminal. The defendant was familiar with the use of the system and, taking advantage of a moment when the terminal was left unattended, entered a code into the system. The effect of this was to instruct the computer to give a 70% discount on the sale. The invoice which was subsequently generated charged the sum of £204.76 instead of the normal price of £710.96. Upon these facts coming to light, the defendant was arrested and charged with an offence under the Computer Misuse Act 1990. At trial, the judge dismissed the charge, holding that the phrase in s 1(1)(a) referring to obtaining access to 'any program or data held in any computer' required that one computer should be used to obtain access to a program or data held on another computer.

1   [1992] 3 WLR 432.

13.9   Given the evidence from the Audit Commission surveys to the effect that most instances of computer misuse are perpetrated by 'insiders', and the fact that most computer systems are not accessible from outside, such a restriction would severely limit the application of the statute. The Attorney-General, acting under the authority of the Criminal Justice Act 1972,[1] sought the opinion of the Court of Appeal on the question whether:

> In order for a person to commit an offence under section 1(1) of the Computer Misuse Act 1990 does the computer which the person causes to perform any function with the required intent have to be a different computer from the one into which he intends to secure unauthorised access to any program or data held therein?

Delivering the judgment of the court, the Lord Chief Justice answered this question in the negative. There were, he ruled:

> ... no grounds whatsoever for implying or importing the word 'other' between 'any' and 'computer', or excepting the computer which is actually used by the offender from the phrase 'any computer'.[2]

[1] Section 36.
[2] *A-G's Reference (No 1 of 1991)* [1992] 3 WLR 432 at 437.

13.10 Such an approach is in line with the recommendations of the Law Commission, which stated that whilst:

> ... 'hackers' are quintessentially thought of as outsiders ... [i]t is in our view important to ensure when settling the terms of an offence that it is directed at unauthorised users of a system or part of a system, whether outsiders or insiders, that one does not concentrate exclusively on outside hackers.[1]

[1] *A-G's Reference (No 1 of 1991)* [1992] 3 WLR 432 at para 3.6.

13.11 During the Committee stage of the Computer Misuse Act 1990's passage, an amendment was unsuccessfully moved which, by substituting the word 'another' for 'any', would have produced precisely the result attained through the trial judge's interpretation. This amendment provoked strenuous objection from the Bill's sponsor, Michael Colvin MP, who argued that:

> The key issue is that unauthorised access to any computer system undermines the so-called integrity or trustworthiness of that computer system. One of the Bill's principal aims is to guard against that. As I said, so much of the hacking is carried out by insiders that to remove them from the effect of the Bill's provision would render it especially defective.[1]

All available empirical evidence lends support to this argument.

[1] HC Official Report, SC C (Computer Misuse Bill), col 7, 14 March 1990.

To a program or data held on a computer

13.12 One further point deserves consideration as relevant to all of the offences established under the Computer Misuse Act 1990. No attempt is made to define the word 'computer'. This is very much in line with the approach adopted in other statutes (such as the Data Protection Act 1998) operating in the area. The offences, it will be recalled, relate to dealings in respect of programs or data and may be triggered by an act causing a program to perform its function. Many modern appliances make extensive use of simple computers, often consisting of a single semiconductor chip, to control their functioning. A washing machine may, for example, have its operation controlled by such chips, whose circuitry will contain the programs necessary for the performance of their dedicated tasks. In such a situation, it might be argued that an unauthorised person who used the washing machine might be guilty of the unauthorised access offence. Such a prospect was identified in Parliament, where the prospect was welcomed by at least one MP, who in opposing proposals to amend the offence to restrict its scope argued:

> This is a computer misuse Bill. It seeks to tackle unauthorised access to computers which may well include electronic locks ... Someone breaking into a car using an electronic key to operate the lock may not be caught under the present legislation if a policeman puts his hand on his shoulder before he gets in and tries to drive away. We are attempting to make it an offence for people to gain unauthorised access to an electronic system. The clause is properly drafted.[1]

Such a result would appear not a little bizarre and, if it were to be endorsed by the courts, would put the unauthorised access offence in conflict with the recommendations of both Law Commissions that the unauthorised use of a computer should not, per se, be made unlawful.

[1]   HC Official Report, SC C (Computer Misuse Bill), col 9, 14 March 1990.

13.13   The vast majority of computer operations, it may be assumed, will be conducted by the computer owner or with their knowledge and consent and will raise no issues under the Computer Misuse Act 1990. Liability will arise only when the access is unauthorised and where the party responsible is aware that this is the case.

Limits of authority

13.14   The question whether access is authorised can be determined only by reference to the intentions of a party entitled to determine such matters. Thus, access is held to be unauthorised when the user:

(a)   is not him or herself entitled to control access of the kind in question to the program or data; and

(b)   he or she does not have the consent to access of the kind in question to the program or data from any person who is so entitled.[1]

In many cases, the person entitled to control access will be the owner of the computer system itself. In other cases, a computer system may serve as a 'host', providing storage space and access facilities for programs or data controlled by other parties. In this situation, the question who has the right to consent to access may be more complex. Most university computer systems provide illustrations of this form of activity. Here, the fact that a student is granted rights of access does not confer any entitlement to transfer these on to a third party.

[1]   Computer Misuse Act 1990, s 17(5).

13.15   From the perspective of the controller of a computer system, the major impact of these provisions will lie in the fact that the unauthorised access offence will be committed only when a user is aware that access is unauthorised. In the situation where the controller makes no attempt to bring restrictions to the notice of users and applies no form of security, it may be difficult for a prosecution to succeed.

Knowledge that access is unauthorised

13.16   The question whether a particular use by a particular user is authorised will be determined by reference to the state of mind of the computer owner or any other person entitled to control access to programs or data held on a computer system. In order for an offence to be established, however, it must be proved that the party obtaining or seeking to obtain access to any programs or data knew that this was not authorised. The restriction of the Computer Misuse Act 1990's application to the situation where an accused acted intentionally might be contrasted with the Scottish Law Commission's recommendation that the prosecution should have to establish that an accused person acted recklessly. As has been stated previously, however, the mere act of obtaining access to programs or data would not have been sufficient to constitute the offence. Enhancement of the burden of proof might be seen as the quid pro quo for the enhancement of the scope of the offence.

Establishing intent

13.17   Establishing intent may prove a difficult task. In one case involving a prosecution under the Computer Misuse Act 1990, a jury acquitted a defendant who had admitted to obtaining unauthorised access to numerous computer systems. Although no reasons are given why any jury reaches a particular verdict, it would appear that they may have accepted the claim by the defence that the accused was addicted to hacking and therefore acted under a form of compulsion rather than with intent, notwithstanding directions from the judge that this would not constitute a proper defence to the charges.[1]

[1]   The case is described in A Charlesworth 'Addiction and Hacking' [1993] NLJ 540. The accused, Paul Bedworth, had been charged with two other individuals with various counts of conspiracy to commit offences under the Computer Misuse Act 1990. The two defendants, perhaps to their subsequent regret, pled guilty and were sentenced to terms of imprisonment.

13.18 Beyond the rather dubious point whether addiction might destroy the capacity to form an intention, a number of real difficulties may be anticipated in applying this provision. In most cases, the initial act of making contact with a computer system will not suffice. Even though a hacker dialling telephone numbers at random (or making use of a number supplied by a fellow enthusiast) may well suspect that their attentions may not be welcome, and be reckless whether this would be the case, it may be very difficult to establish that they had actual knowledge that access was unauthorised.

13.19 A further scenario might also be identified. User A has been allocated a password by the computer owner. A discloses this password to B and encourages B to use the password to obtain access to the computer. It is likely that B's access will be regarded as unauthorised as, although A is entitled to access the computer, they are not entitled to 'control' access. The question which may require to be determined by a court is whether B could possess the necessary mens rea for commission of the unauthorised access offence.

13.20 The dividing line between reckless and intentional conduct may well be crossed at the time access is obtained to a computer system. A user accessing the main computer system at the author's university is presented with the message 'Unauthorised access to this system is ILLEGAL: Computer Misuse Act 1990'. The mere presence of such a notice might be sufficient to justify the assumption that any further attempts to operate or access the contents of the system will be conducted in the knowledge that this is unauthorised. The installation of a security system, typically allocating authorised users with passwords and requiring these to be entered at the stage of initial contact, would undoubtedly reinforce this position.

13.21 More difficult situations will arise where the user has limited access rights. Typically, this may arise within an employment relationship or where computing facilities are made available to students. Here, establishing that the user was aware of the fact that their access rights had been exceeded will require that the limitations be specified unambiguously. The Law Commission refer to the distinction between conduct which constitutes 'a deliberate act of disobedience, and indeed of defiance of the law' and that which amounts to 'merely carelessness, stupidity or inattention'.[1] Only the former, it was recommended, should face prosecution under the Computer Misuse Act 1990.

[1]   Computer Misuse. Law Com no 186 (1989) para 3.36.

Unauthorised use by authorised users

13.22 A further distinction should also be made at this point. The legislation prohibits unauthorised access. It does not strike at the situation where access is authorised but the use to which it is put is unauthorised. As the Law Commission point out, the use of an office typewriter to type a private letter will not expose a typist to criminal sanctions and it would be most inequitable to alter that situation merely because a word processor was used. There may, however, be situations where such an approach may limit the effectiveness of the legislation. In the case of *R v Bignall*,[1] a police officer obtained access to data held on the police national computer in order to identify the owner of a motor vehicle. The information was sought for the owner's personal interest and was not connected with his duties as a police officer. The conduct being discovered, he was charged with an offence under s 1 of the Computer Misuse Act 1990. Although it was not contended that the use to which the data was put was unauthorised, the Divisional Court accepted submissions by counsel for the respondent to the effect that:

> ... the primary purpose of the Computer Misuse Act was to protect the integrity of computer systems rather that the integrity of information stored on the computers ... a person who causes a computer to perform a function to secure access to information held at a level to which the person was entitled to gain access does not commit an offence under S.1 even if he intends to secure access for an unauthorised purpose because it is only where the level of unauthorised access has been knowingly and intentionally exceeded that an offence is committed, provided the person knows of that unauthorised level of access

and held that no offence had been committed under the Computer Misuse Act 1990. It was suggested by the court that an offence may have been committed under the Data Protection Act 1984. An example of this possibility can be taken from a recent Scottish case. Here, the assistance of a police officer was sought by a friend who considered that his daughter had entered into an unsuitable relationship. Upon consulting the police computer, the officer discovered a reference that the man involved was a hepatitis risk. He subsequently telephoned the woman involved urging her to break off the relationship on the ground that the man was 'riddled with AIDS'.

[1]   (1997) Times, 6 June.

13.23   This conduct was held to constitute an unauthorised disclosure of data and the officer was convicted of a breach of s 5 of the Data Protection Act 1984[1] and fined £500.[2] Under the provisions of this section, any obtaining, holding, disclosure or international transfer of data by a servant or agent of a data user which contravenes the terms of the latter's entry on the Register will render the individual concerned liable under both criminal and civil law on the same basis as the data user.[3]

[1]   Section 55 of the Data Protection Act 1998 contains an equivalent provision.
[2]   The case is reported in the *Glasgow Herald*, 20 February 1993.
[3]   Section 5(3).

13.24   The decision in *Bignall*[1] was considered in the later case of *R v Bow Street Magistrates' Court, ex p Allison*.[2] This case concerned an application by the US authorities for the extradition of the applicant to face charges, inter alia, of securing unauthorised access to the American Express computer system with the intent to commit theft and forgery. It was also alleged that the applicant had caused an unauthorised modification to the contents of the computer system.

¹   *R v Bignall* (1998) 1 Cr App R 1.
²   [1999] 4 All ER 1. The decision of the Divisional Court is reported at [1999] QB 847

13.25   The applicant had allegedly conspired with another party, Jean Ojomo, who had been employed by American Express. In the course of her work, she was instructed to access specific accounts but once online could access other account information. This was passed on to Allison, who was able to use it to encode credit cards, obtain personal identification numbers and make withdrawals from automatic teller machines. Allison was arrested in England in possession of forged cards, having been photographed using such a card to make a cash withdrawal.

13.26   The conduct at issue, it was alleged would have constituted a breach of ss 1, 2 and 3 of the Computer Misuse Act 1990.[1] An initial debate concerned the question whether offences under this Act could form the basis of a request for extradition. The issue was a fairly technical one but the court was firmly of the view that extradition proceedings were competent. The question then arose whether the facts as indicated would have constituted a breach of the relevant statutory provisions. Following the decision in *Bignall*,[2] it was held by the Divisional Court that the s 1 offence had not been committed, Kennedy LJ ruling that:

> Miss Montgomery (counsel for the applicant) submits that it is clear from the evidence that Joan Ojomo was entitled to control access of the kind in question to the program or data – just like the police officers in Bignell's case – so the access was not unauthorised even though she misused the information she obtained. Mr Lewis (counsel for the DPP and US Government) submits that her access was unauthorised because it was intentional, unauthorised by a person entitled to authorise access to that particular data and carried out when she knew that the access to that data was unauthorised. I confess that I found Mr Lewis's approach to be the more attractive but at the end of the day it seems to me that it fails to do justice to the words 'of the kind in question' which qualify the word access in s 17(5) [of the Computer Misuse Act 1990]. Joan Ojomo was entitled to control access of the kind in question. She was operating in a regular way at her authorised level. As Astill J said in *Bignell*'s case at page 12B the 1990 Act was enacted to criminalise the 'hacking' of computer systems, and the Data Protection Act 1984 was enacted to criminalise improper use of data.[3]

¹   Sections 2 and 3 are considered below. Section 2 creates what is referred to as the 'ulterior intent' offence. This involves securing unauthorised access to programs of data with the intention of using the access to facilitate the commission of a further serious offence. Although extradition could only be authorised for a s 2 offence, the penalties for breach of s 1 being too low to warrant this process, it was necessary for the prosecution to establish commission of the unauthorised access offence as a prerequisite for liability under s 2.
²   *R v Bignall* [1998] 1 Cr App Rep 1.
³   *R v Bow Street Magistrates' Court, ex p Allison* [1999] QB 847 at 857.

13.27   The consequences of the Divisional Court's decisions in *Bignall*[1] and *Allison*[2] for the operation of the Computer Misuse Act 1990 were potentially significant. It would appear that most instances of computer fraud (and perhaps fraud in general) are committed by insiders. The decisions, therefore, were seen as conferring a degree of immunity upon such actors. An appeal was made in the case of *Allison* and resulted in a robust rejection by the House of Lords of the notion that the misuse of access rights could not incur criminal sanctions. Delivering the judgment of the House, Lord Hobhouse quoted from the provisions of s 17, which defines the concept of access and authorisation. This provides that access is unauthorised if a person:

(a)   is not himself entitled to control access of the kind in question to the program or data; and

(b)   he does not have consent to access by him of the kind in question to the program or data from any person who is so entitled.

1   *R v Bignall* [1998] 1 Cr App Rep 1.
2   *R v Bow Street Magistrates' Court, ex p Allison* [1999] 4 All ER 1.

13.28   In both situations, it was held, account had to be taken of the use to which access was put rather than merely to the data which was accessed. The section, it was held:

> ... makes clear that the authority must relate not simply to the data or programme but also to the actual kind of access secured. Similarly, it is plain that it is not using the word 'control' in a physical sense of the ability to operate or manipulate the computer and that it is not derogating from the requirement that for access to be authorised it must be authorised to the relevant data or relevant programme or part of a programme. It does not introduce any concept that authority to access one piece of data should be treated as authority to access other pieces of data 'of the same kind' notwithstanding that the relevant person did not in fact have authority to access that piece of data. Section 1 [of the Computer Misuse Act 1990] refers to the intent to secure unauthorised access to any programme or data. These plain words leave no room for any suggestion that the relevant person may say: 'Yes, I know that I was not authorised to access that data but I was authorised to access other data of the same kind.'[1]

1   *R v Bow Street Magistrates' Court, ex p Allison* [1999] 4 All ER 1 at 7.

13.29   In terms which are reflective of the first decision under the Computer Misuse Act 1990, *A-G's Reference (No 1 of 1991)*,[1] the Divisional Court was criticised for importing words into the statute. The Act, it was held was not concerned with access to 'kinds' of data. It looked rather at the entitlement to access particular programs or items of data. The decision of Kennedy J in the Divisional Court, it was held:

> ... treats the phrase 'entitlement to control' as if it related to the control of the computer as opposed to the entitlement to authorise operators to access to programs and data. He adopts the extraneous idea of an authorised level of access without considering whether, on the facts of the case, it corresponds to the relevant person's authority to access the data in fact accessed. He confines s.1 of the Act to the 'hacking' of computer systems as opposed to the use of a computer to secure unauthorised access to programs or data. Upon a misreading of s.17(5) [of the Computer Misuse Act 1990], he fails to give effect to the plain words of s.1. The meaning of the statute is clear and unambiguous.[2]

The decision in *Allison*[3] undoubtedly closes a significant loophole in the Computer Misuse Act 1990. It is clear that the statute is much more than an 'anti-hacking' measure and that misuse of facilities by authorised users will expose them to the risk of criminal prosecution.

[1] [1992] 3 WLR 432. See discussion at para 13.8 above.
[2] [1999] 4 All ER 1 at 9.
[3] *R v Bow Street Magistrates' Court, ex p Allison* [1999] 4 All ER 1.

The ulterior intent offence

Criminal attempts

13.30 One of the most complex areas of the law is that concerned with the concept of criminal attempts. In most cases, including the offences established under the Computer Misuse Act 1990, the attempt to commit an offence will be considered as serious a matter as its successful completion. The question arises, however, when an attempt can be considered to have been made. The Criminal Attempts Act 1981 draws a distinction between conduct which is preparatory of the commission of an offence and that which constitutes part of its perpetration.[1]

[1] Section 1.

13.31 The dividing line between preparation and perpetration is seldom clear-cut. The Law Commission, in their report, identified a number of problems which might arise in the computer field creating circumstances where conduct might not constitute an attempt under the general provisions of criminal law, but which was felt to justify special treatment within the computer context.[1]

[1] Law Com no 186 (1989) paras 3.52–3.53.

13.32 The first example concerned a hacker who secured access to a bank's computer system, the system being used for electronic fund transfers. In order to accomplish a transfer, a password would have to be transmitted. The Law Commission hypothesised that the hacker might attempt to transmit a large number of combinations in the hope of finding the correct one. In the event that the password was discovered, used and a transfer of funds accomplished, the Law Commission were in no doubt that the offence of theft would be committed. The act of transmitting combinations of numbers and letters in the attempt to discover a valid password would not, they considered, be regarded as more than conduct preparatory to the commission of a crime. As such, it would not constitute a criminal attempt, especially in the event that further steps would be required in order to complete the transfer. In such a situation, the existence of the ulterior intent offence would serve to bring forward in time the moment at which a serious criminal offence might be committed.

13.33 A second illustration utilised by the Law Commission concerned a would-be blackmailer, who obtained access to data held on a computer in order to obtain confidential personal information which might be used for the purpose of blackmail. A more detailed example of this form of behaviour was reported during the second reading debate in the House of Commons, where it was alleged that the medical records of a patient who was HIV positive were penetrated and the information used for blackmail purposes. Once again, it is unlikely that conduct of that nature could, at the stage of obtaining the data from the computer, constitute a criminal attempt.

13.34 Reference has previously been made to the speed at which vast sums of money may be transferred using the electronic fund transfer system. In terms of time, it seems clear that the gap between conduct preparatory of a crime and its perpetration may be very short where this form of conduct is at issue. Assuming the correctness of the Law Commission's expressed view that the conduct in their first example would not suffice to constitute an attempt, there would appear a case for the extension of the criminal law. It might be argued, however, that this should take the form of modifying the law of attempt rather than establishing a new offence.

13.35 The blackmail example utilised by the Law Commission appears less satisfactory. Certainly, such conduct is to be regarded as reprehensible, but there appears little difference in principle between a party who secures access to medical data held in paper files and those held on computer. The only justification for the approach adopted might be that in many instances the 'old-fashioned' blackmailer might engage in some form of unauthorised entry to property coupled with theft of documents in order to secure the information. Such conduct will be criminal in its own right and may well attract heavier penalties than those available under the basic offence in the Computer Misuse Act 1990.

The new offence

13.36 In seeking to give effect to the Law Commission's recommendations as described above, the Computer Misuse Act 1990 provides in s 2 that:

> (1) A person is guilty of an offence under this section if he commits an offence under section 1 above ('the unauthorised access offence') with intent—
> (a) to commit an offence to which this section applies; or
> (b) to facilitate the commission of such an offence (whether by himself or by any other person).[1]

The offences referred to in the above passage are defined as being those for which the sentence is prescribed by law[2] – effectively the offence of murder or those for which a person with no previous criminal record might, upon conviction, be sentenced to a term of imprisonment of five years or more.[3]

[1] Section 2.
[2] Section 2(2)(a).
[3] Section 2(2)(b).

The impossible dream

13.37 It is immaterial for the purpose of the ulterior intent offence whether the further offence is intended to be committed on the same occasion as the unauthorised access offence or at some future time.[1] It will also constitute no form of defence that the commission of the further offence would prove impossible.[2] In the banking example cited above, the basis for the ulterior intent offence will be established even though, unbeknown to the perpetrators, further security precautions would render impossible the successful completion of their scheme.

[1]   Computer Misuse Act 1990, s 2(3).
[2]   Section 2(4).

Application of the ulterior intent offence

13.38   The application of the ulterior intent offence was at issue in the case of *Re Levin*.[1] The appellant had used his computing skills to obtain access from his computer in St Petersburg to Citibank's computer system in New Jersey. He had been able to monitor the accounts of customers and to cause transfers to be made from these accounts to others controlled by himself or a number of accomplices. If successful, it was alleged, the scheme could have obtained funds in excess of $10m. In the event, the activity was discovered and traced to Levin, who was arrested when he made a trip to the UK in order to attend a computer exhibition. The US authorities sought his extradition.

[1]   [1997] QB 65.

13.39   In order for the US extradition request to be met, it was necessary to establish that the acts committed by the defendant would have constituted criminal offences under English law. There was no doubt that Levin, in hacking into the Citibank's computer system, had committed the unauthorised access offence. The court also had little hesitation in holding that he did so with intent to commit further offences of forgery and false accounting. It was held by Beldam LJ:

> Such offences are offences within sec. 2 of the Computer Misuse Act and it is clear that on the evidence he had the intent to commit or facilitate the commission of those offences. It is argued on the applicant's behalf that the charges thus framed are bad for uncertainty because they do not specify the particular offence of each kind he intended to commit and for duplicity because they encompass more than one offence in the same charge. In our view it is not necessary to do more than specify the type of offence which the accused had in mind so as to bring it within the requirements of sec. 2(2). The offence charged is the commission of an offence under sec. 1 of the Act with the required intent. A person commits the offence whether he intends to commit one or more than one such subsequent offence. The charges laid are not bad for either reason.[1]

[1]   *Re Levin* [1997] QB 65 at 78.

13.40   The case of *Allison*[1] represents the only other case in which the ulterior intent offence has been successfully invoked. The only other case in which the ulterior intent offence has been at issue was that of *A-G's Reference (No 1 of 1991)*[2] discussed at para 13.8ff above.[3] Here, it was alleged that access was sought with a view to obtaining an unwarranted discount on goods, conduct which would constitute the offence of false accounting contrary to s 17(1)(a) of the Theft Act 1968. Given the dismissal of the prosecution on the basis of the trial judge's interpretation requiring that access be obtained to 'any other computer', the ulterior intent offence also fell.

[1] *R v Bow Street Magistrates' Court, ex p Allison* [1999] 4 All ER 1.
[2] [1992] 3 WLR 432.
[3] [1992] 3 WLR 432 at para 13.8.

13.41 It may be queried how useful a role is played by the ulterior intent offence. In the *Levin* case,[1] the extradition request was upheld upon a range of grounds – including breach of the unauthorised modification offence established by s 3 of the Computer Misuse Act 1990. The finding that the ulterior intent offence had been committed was not critical to the decision.

[1] *Re Levin* [1997] QB 65.

Unauthorised modification of data

13.42 Given its intangible nature, information is not susceptible of being destroyed in any physical sense. A simple example might be a user erasing a piece of music stored on an audio tape. If the original recording was of a chart-topping song, destruction of one copy does not affect the song itself. Equally, the physical elements of the tape suffer no harm. The tape was and remains a physical item capable of recording and storing certain forms of data. Two consequences may follow from this act. First, assuming that the erasure was carried out erroneously, the owner of the tape may require to expend time and money in securing a further copy.

13.43 The second consequence may be even more serious. If the tape represented not a copy of a chart-topping song but the only recording of the work in question, a unique item would be lost to the world. If an author types out a chapter of a book on information technology law using a word processor, the contents represent a recording of the author's knowledge of the subject. If the text is erased, and assuming that the author was sufficiently negligent to fail to maintain back-up copies, the knowledge remains but it is most unlikely that the particular recording can ever be reproduced. In the illustration given, the damage may be principally to the author's peace of mind. In other situations, significant financial loss may arise. If a mail order company's list of customers should be deleted and no replacement be readily available, the ability of the company to continue in business might be imperilled to a considerable extent.

13.44 Anyone possessing a degree of familiarity with computers and their method of operation will be only too well aware how fragile is the hold on its electronic life of any piece of data. The accidental depression of a key or the placing of a computer disk in undue proximity to a magnetic field as produced by electrical motors, or even telephones, can speedily consign data to electronic oblivion. To the risks of accidental damage must be added those of deliberate sabotage.

13.45 The vulnerability of computer users to such events is not questioned. Once again, our concern must be with the legal consequences which may follow such behaviour. The basic scenario involves a party altering or deleting data held on a computer system, such action taking place without the consent of the system owner. Within this, a wide range of activities can be identified. At the most basic level, the perpetrator may use 'delete' or 'reformat' commands or even bring a magnet into close proximity to a computer storage device. Amendment of data may be made for a variety of motives. In some cases, such as that of *Levin*[1] discussed at para 13.38ff above, amendment of data may be a component of a scheme of fraud. Other actions may be driven by the intent to cause disruption to the computer owner's activities. This might involve manipulation of computer programs through, for example, the insertion of logic bombs, whilst an ever-expanding range of computer viruses present a continual threat to the well-being of computer owners.

[1]   *Re Levin* [1997] QB 65.

Logic bombs

13.46   A logic bomb may be defined as a program which is designed to come into operation at some later date or upon the occurrence of specified conditions. Two examples cited by the Audit Commission are not untypical of this form of behaviour. In the first case,[1] a departing employee inserted a program into the computer with the intention that it would cause messages to be displayed on the screen whenever his leaving date was entered into the system. The program did not operate in the manner intended but proved more harmful, resulting in the unavailability of the system for a period of about two hours. In this case, the computer breakdown would appear to have been an unintended consequence of the program, although the employee involved was successfully prosecuted on a charge of criminal damage.

[1]   Case 61 cited in the Audit Commission's 1984–87 survey 'Computer Fraud'.

13.47   The second illustration is not dissimilar. Here, prior to leaving their employment, an employee made an alteration to the language preferences of the system software so that error messages would be presented in French, Dutch or German instead of in English. The modification was structured in such a way that it would not take effect until some time after the employee's departure. On this occasion no prosecution was brought, the Audit Commission reporting that the individual was rebuked and agreed to make a contribution towards the cost of correction.[1]

[1]   Case 65 cited in the Audit Commission's 1981–84 survey 'Computer Fraud'.

13.48 Although the instances reported above might appear lacking in malicious intent, other logic bombs are specifically designed to cause the corruption or erasure of data. An example might be taken from the case of *R v Thompson*,[1] discussed above, and the appellant's attempt to cause the computer to erase records of his activities.

[1]   [1984] 3 All ER 565. See discussion at para 12.18ff above.

Computer viruses

13.49 Perhaps the most notorious form of misconduct in the computer field consists of the creation and/or dissemination of computer viruses. In many instances, the effect of a virus will be indistinguishable from that of a logic bomb. The difference between the two concepts is that whilst a logic bomb is normally created on and applied to a particular computer system, a virus will typically be transferred from one system to another. This may occur through the transfer of disks or other storage devices.

13.50 Computer viruses can take a wide variety of forms. One of the less harmful examples of the species is the 'Cookie Monster'. Inspired by a US television character, this causes the message 'I want a cookie' to appear on the computer screen. If the user types the word 'cookie', the message disappears, otherwise it returns with increasing frequency. In similar vein, the 'ping pong' virus causes the image of a bouncing ball to cross and re-cross the screen. In neither instance are any data or programs affected.

13.51 Other viruses are considerably more malign. One which is reported to have infected computers in a Maltese bank had the effect of corrupting data. Evidencing a somewhat warped sense of humour on the part of its creator, the virus gave the user the opportunity to play what was effectively a game of chance. If the user won, the data would be restored, otherwise it would be permanently erased.

13.52 In other cases, not even this degree of opportunity is given to the user to avoid permanent loss of their data. One of the most notorious examples of a computer virus was the so-called 'AIDS' virus. This was contained on a disk which was mailed to subscribers of a popular computing magazine. Purporting to be an informational program on the AIDS virus, the program would corrupt and render useless the data on any computer on which it was loaded.

13.53 The instance of the 'AIDS' virus raises a number of interesting legal questions. The disks were accompanied by an instruction leaflet which incorporated a licence agreement. This offered a licence to recipients and gave instructions as to the fees involved and the address (in Panama) to which these should tendered. The document went on:

> You are advised of the most serious consequences of your failure to abide by the terms of this license agreement: your conscience may haunt you for the rest of your life ... and your computer will stop functioning normally.

Although the circumstances of the particular case where disks were mailed on an unsolicited basis might elicit little sympathy for the supplier, it may be queried whether the use of a virus as a form of deterrence against illicit copying of software might be considered legitimate in certain situations.

13.54 In the event, a person allegedly responsible for the promulgation of the 'AIDS' computer virus was arrested in the US and extradited to stand trial on a charge of demanding money with menaces. Proceedings were dropped prior to trial in England when the prosecution accepted that the defendant's mental state was such that he was unfit to plead.[1]

[1] For a fuller description of these and many other incidents of computer virus infections, see B Clough and P Mungo *Approaching Zero* (1992, Faber).

13.55 A final illustration of the destructive power of viruses may be taken from a comment made in the House of Commons during debate on the Computer Misuse Bill. Quoting from a Hong Kong-based computer consultant, the view was expressed that: 'It's quite simple. If I wanted my competitor to go bankrupt, I would just anonymously send someone in that company an infected games disk.'[1]

[1] 166 HC Official Report (6th series) col 1161, 9 February 1990.

13.56 In other cases, the dissemination of a virus may not be a part of any scheme of extortion. In some cases, the virus may produce harmful effects beyond anything intended by its originator. In one of the major cases brought under the US Computer Fraud and Abuse Act, a student at Cornell University produced and released a virus program which had the effect of infecting some 6,000 computers in academic institutions throughout the US. The student's intention, it would appear, was to demonstrate his programming ability by causing a single copy of the program to be placed on all these computers.[1] This would have caused no damage or inconvenience, but the program replicated itself over and over again, effectively using up all of the victims' processing capacity and preventing their normal operations.[2]

[1] The program produced by Morris might more accurately be described as a 'worm'. A worm is a program which replicates itself. Although initially causing no damage, the continual doubling in size consumed vast amounts of storage space and impaired significantly the working of the computers affected.
[2] This case is described in some detail in Hafner and Markoff *Cyberpunk* (1991, Simon and Schuster). The individual involved, Robert Morris, was sentenced to three years' probation and fined $10,000 dollars. See *United States v Morris* (1991) 928 F 2d 504.

The legal response

13.57 Reference was made in a number of the instances cited by the Audit Commission to the fact that criminal sanctions had been imposed against those held responsible. The application of offences relating to damage to property represented some of the first attempts to apply general legal provisions in the context of computer-related conduct. At least in terms of reported cases, these prosecutions met with a considerable measure of success. In Scotland, where most offences remain rooted in the common law, the offence of malicious mischief was held applicable in a case where conduct prevented the profitable exploitation of property (in this case a nuclear power station) even though no physical damage was caused.[1] In England, the cases of *Cox v Riley*[2] and *R v Whiteley*[3] provided authority for the application of the Criminal Damage Act 1971 to forms of computer-related conduct. This statute provides that:

> A person who without lawful excuse destroys or damages any property belonging to another intending to destroy or damage any such property ... shall be guilty of an offence.[4]

The word 'property' is defined in s 10 as 'property of a tangible nature whether real or personal'.

[1] *HMA v Wilson* (1984) SLT 116.
[2] (1986) 83 Cr App Rep 54.
[3] (1991) 93 Cr App Rep 25.
[4] Section 1.

13.58 In *Cox v Riley*, the appellant was employed to operate a computerised saw. This consisted of a powered saw whose operations could be controlled by the insertion of a printed circuit card containing a number of computer programs. The equipment contained a program cancellation function. The appellant, deliberately and without due cause, caused the programs to be erased. Although the saw could also be used under manual control, its practical utility was impaired significantly until the owner could obtain a replacement card. This, it was stated, required the expenditure of 'time and effort of a more than minimal nature'.[1]

[1] (1986) 83 Cr App Rep 54 at 57.

13.59 The key question before the court was whether any property had been damaged or destroyed. Counsel for Cox argued that his conduct had affected only the electronic impulses making up the computer programs. These could not fall within the definition of property. This contention was rejected by the Divisional Court,[1] which held that the critical factor was that as a result of Cox's conduct, the saw's owner was required to expend time and money in restoring the saw itself to its original condition, ie as a device which could be used to cut wood in accordance with instructions transmitted from a computer program.

[1] *Cox v Riley* (1986) 83 Cr App Rep 54.

13.60 The offence of criminal damage was successfully invoked in a small number of subsequent English prosecutions. In its original Working Paper on computer misuse, the Law Commission indicated that it considered the legal position in the area of damage to data to be satisfactory.[1] By the time of the publication of their final report, this view had changed. *Cox v Riley*,[2] it was suggested, had not confronted fully the point that the dictionary definition of damage required 'some injury to a thing'. The Law Commission concluded:

> That the practical meaning of 'damage' has caused practical as well as theoretical problems following the decision in *Cox v Riley* is evidenced by the experience of the police and prosecuting authorities who have informed us that, although convictions have been obtained in serious cases of unauthorised access to data or programs, there is recurrent (and understandable) difficulty in explaining to judges, magistrates and juries how the facts fit in with the present law of criminal damage.[3]

[1]   Law Com no 110 (1987) para 3.68.
[2]   *Cox v Riley* (1986) 83 Cr App Rep 54.
[3]   Law Com no 186 (1989) para 2.31.

13.61   Supporting this view, reference was made in the House of Commons to the fact that:

> ... of 270 cases that have been verified by the Department of Trade and Industry as involving computer misuse over the past five years, only six were brought to court for prosecution and only three of these were successfully prosecuted for fraud. There must be some inadequacy in the law as it stands.[1]

Such comments sit a little uneasily with the findings of the Audit Commission. In their report covering the period 1984–87, a span encompassed within the DTI figures, they found 118 instances of computer fraud and misuse and indicated that prosecutions were initiated in 40 cases. Of these prosecutions, 35 were successful, three unsuccessful and two pending at the time of the survey's publication.[2]

[1]   166 HC Official Report (6th series) col 1134, 9 February 1990.
[2]   Audit Commission 1984–87 survey, 'Computer Fraud and Misuse' p 22.

Unauthorised modification in the Computer Misuse Act 1990

13.62   The recommendation of the Law Commission was that the Criminal Damage Act 1971 should be amended, effectively to reverse the decision in *Cox v Riley*[1] by making it clear that damage to programs or data would not constitute the offence of criminal damage. Parallel to this, a new computer-specific offence should be established. Acting on this recommendation, the Computer Misuse Act 1990 provides that an offence will be committed by a person who, acting with intent, causes an unauthorised modification of the contents of any computer.[2]

[1]   *Cox v Riley* (1986) 83 Cr App Rep 54.
[2]   Section 3(1).

13.63   The new provision is intended to overcome the uncertainty concerning the application of the Criminal Damage Act 1990. To avoid the possibility of overlap between the two statutes it is provided that:

For the purposes of the Criminal Damage Act 1971 a modification of the contents of a computer shall not be regarded as damaging any computer or computer storage medium unless its effect on that computer or computer storage medium impairs its physical condition.[1]

[1] Section 3(6).

The resurrection of criminal damage?

13.64 Ironically, no sooner was the Computer Misuse Act 1990 to reach the statute book than a further case, *R v Whiteley*,[1] involving the application of a charge of criminal damage to computer-related behaviour was decided by the Court of Appeal. In view of the interpretation of the Criminal Damage Act 1971 adopted by the court, it would appear that the attempt to exclude its application in the computer context may not be effective.

[1] (1991) 93 Cr App Rep 25.

13.65 Within the UK, computers operated by most institutions in the field of higher education are linked together in a network known as JANET (Joint Academic NETwork). Although access to the network is controlled by password, a failure in security at one institution allowed the appellant to obtain access to its computer network. From there, access could readily be obtained to all the other computers on the network.

13.66 Operating under the pseudonym 'The Mad Hacker', the appellant made extensive (and expensive) use of the system. Using his computing skills, he was able to extend his user rights steadily, eventually obtaining the status of the controller of particular computers. This allowed him to delete the files 'Accounts Journal' and 'Systems Journal', which would otherwise have recorded details of his activity.

13.67 After some time, the computer operators became aware of unusual activities on their machines. Efforts were made to detect the intruder and for some considerable time a game of 'cat and mouse' was played between the appellant and the operators. On one occasion, the appellant was reported as having been sufficiently 'astute to detect a special programme [sic] inserted by the legitimate operator to trap him and deleted it'.[1] On a further occasion, the appellant succeeded in 'locking' legitimate users out of the computer systems. On occasion, the appellant's activities caused computer systems to 'crash' and increasingly insulting messages were left in files.

[1] (1991) 93 Cr App Rep 25 at 26.

13.68 Ultimately, British Telecom instituted monitoring of telephone calls into computers favoured by the appellant. Detecting a suspicious call, this was traced back to the appellant's home. He was arrested and charges of criminal damage were subsequently brought.

13.69 As with many incidents recounted previously, no damage was caused to any physical components, but operations were seriously impaired and considerable staff time was expended in restoring the systems to full operation and in tracking down the perpetrator. The prosecution's contention, which was accepted both by the jury and the Court of Appeal, was that the changes made to the information held on the system would constitute criminal damage. Delivering the judgment of the court the Lord Chief Justice (Lane) ruled:

> What the Act requires to be proved is that tangible property has been damaged, not necessarily that the damage itself is tangible. There can be no doubt that the magnetic particles upon the metal discs were a part of the discs and if the appellant was proved to have intentionally and without lawful excuse altered the particles in such a way as to cause an impairment of the value or usefulness of the disc to the owner, there would be damage within the meaning of section 1 [of the Criminal Damage Act 1971].[1]

[1] (1991) 93 Cr App Rep 25 at 28.

13.70 Although the judge went on to refer to the provisions of the Computer Misuse Act 1990 and comment that 'no doubt it will be used as the basis of criminal prosecution in the case of computer misuse', the passage cited above would appear to suggest that damage to data held on a computer disk might still be regarded as adversely affecting its 'physical condition'. Such a result would have significant consequences, first, in that the penalties which might be imposed under the Criminal Damage Act 1971 are more substantial than those applying under the Computer Misuse Act 1990 and, secondly, that the prosecution in a case brought under the 1971 Act requires to prove only that the accused acted 'recklessly'. The standard under the Computer Misuse Act 1990 is, of course, that the accused acted intentionally. It might also be noted that the 1990 Act makes no change to Scots law, and indeed the Scottish Law Commission were of the view that existing provisions were adequate as a response to instances of computer misuse, so that existing offences of malicious mischief and vandalism might still be invoked.

13.71 The issue of the continuing applicability of existing provisions may assume particular significance in one situation. As indicated above, the Computer Misuse Act 1990 prohibits unauthorised modification of the 'contents of a computer'. The contents of computer disks or other forms of storage device are protected only when the disks are held in a computer. A scenario can be identified in which two individuals secure unauthorised access to an office containing a computer and a box of computer disks. Both individuals carry a magnet. One uses this to corrupt the contents of the computer's hard disk; the other produces a similar effect on the contents of the box of disks. We can assume further that the box of disks represents a 'back-up copy' of the material held on the computer. In this situation, one person will be guilty of an offence under the Computer Misuse Act 1990 and the other will not. Given the nature and purpose of the legislation, this may be a justifiable situation. The question will be whether the second party might be prosecuted under the Criminal Damage Act 1971. Certainly, there is no doubt that conduct of this kind could, prior to 1990. Although it might be argued that the wording of s 3(6) excludes the application of the Criminal Damage Act 1990 only where damage occurs whilst storage devices are held in a computer system, the expository problems identified by the Law Commission would pale into insignificance compared with those of distinguishing 'damage' to the contents of a disk occurring whilst it is held in a computer and the same damage occurring when it is outside.

Operation of the unauthorised modification offence

What constitutes an unauthorised modification?

13.72   The concept of modification encompasses the addition of data or its alteration or erasure. A modification will be regarded as unauthorised if the person causing it is not authorised so to act or does not possess the consent of a person who is so entitled.[1] Again, the possibility of different categories of rights and privileges attaching to different users must be borne in mind. Typically, an employee or a student may be entitled to use the facilities of a computer system but will not be entitled to delete any portions or to add any programs.

[1]   Computer Misuse Act 1990, s 17.

13.73   The effect of the modification must be:

(a)   to impair the operation of any computer;
(b)   to prevent or hinder access to any program or data held in any computer; or
(c)   to impair the operation of any such program or the reliability of any such data.

It is immaterial whether the modification or its effects are intended to be permanent or merely temporary.[1]

[1]   Computer Misuse Act 1990, s 3(5).

13.74   At the most basic level of activity, it would apply in the situation where a user intentionally causes the deletion of programs or data held on a computer. The manner in which this is accomplished will be immaterial. At the simplest level, the user may operate delete functions so as to remove programs or data.[1] In the first prosecution brought under this provision of the Computer Misuse Act 1990, the accused had installed a security package on a computer belonging to a firm which he claimed owed some £2,000 in fees. The effect of the installation was to prevent the computer being used unless a password was entered. As this was not disclosed, the computer was effectively rendered unusable for several days, with resultant losses estimated at some £36,000. The accused was convicted and fined £1,650.[2] Amendments to data may also produce adverse effects. In one reported case, a nurse altered prescription details and other records on a hospital computer. The possible consequences of such activities do not need to be described and a conviction was secured under the Act.

1   The use of such commands may well remove details of the programs or data from any directories. The program or data will not be removed at that stage, the effect of the command being to render it liable to being overwritten as further programs or data are added to the computer. Such conduct will constitute the unauthorised modification offence, even though the 'damage' may be recoverable.

2   *R v Whitaker* (1993) Scunthorpe Magistrates' Court. Details of this and a range of other prosecutions under the Computer Misuse Act 1990 are reported in Battcock 'Prosecutions Under the Computer Misuse Act' (1996) 6 Computers and Law 22.

13.75 An offence may also be committed when data is added to a computer system. One instance of this, which will be discussed below, occurs when a computer is infected with a virus. The offence will also be committed where logic bombs or other programs are added to the computer system with the intent that these will operate so as to cause inconvenience to the computer user. In one instance, an IT manager added a program to his employer's system which had the effect of encrypting incoming data. The data would automatically be decrypted when it was subsequently accessed. The manager left his employment following a disagreement and some time later the decryption function ceased to operate. Once again, the effect was to render the computer unusable. Despite claims that the encryption function was intended as a security device and that the failure of the decryption facility was an unforeseen error, the manager was convicted of an offence under the Computer Misuse Act 1990.[1]

1   R Battcock 'Prosecutions Under the Computer Misuse Act' (1996) 6 Computers and Law 22.

13.76 A more interesting case brought under the legislation concerned a contract for the supply of bespoke software. The customer was late in making payment for the software and shortly afterwards the software stopped working. It transpired that the supplier, anticipating possible problems with payment, had inserted a time-lock function. Unless removed by the supplier upon receipt of payment, the software would stop working from a specified date. This conduct resulted in prosecution and conviction under the unauthorised modification offence.[1]

1   R Battcock 'Prosecutions Under the Computer Misuse Act' (1996) 6 Computers and Law 22.

13.77 The issues raised in this case are undoubtedly less clear-cut than in a number of the other prosecutions brought under the Computer Misuse Act 1990. It was argued that the use of such time-locks was a legitimate response to the failure of the customer to meet the contractual obligation to pay for the software. A further point which does not appear to have been raised was whether the supplier would retain sufficient intellectual property rights in the software to be entitled to control its continued use. It could also be argued that the action would have been lawful had notice been given to the customer of the fact that the software would stop working if payment was not made timeously. It may also be noted that in the US, the recently developed Uniform Computer Information

Transactions Act (UCITA) makes provision allowing the owner of copyright in software products to install devices permitting them to monitor the contents of a user's computer system in order to determine whether the software is being used in conformity with the terms of a licence.[1]

[1] See s 816, which places limits on the situations in which the right may be exercised. Although adopted by the National Conference of Commissioners on Uniform State Laws, the Act has been adopted only in the states of Maryland and Virginia.

13.78 It may be that the drafting of the offence is sufficiently broad to make the mere act of unauthorised use illegal. An example might concern an employee who types a private letter using their employer's computer. As s 2(5) of the Computer Misuse Act 1990 states that the fact whether a modification is permanent or temporary is immaterial, it would not even appear that there is a necessity for the text of the letter to be stored on the computer. In the event that a portion of text is stored on a computer's hard disk, utilising only a minuscule fraction of the disk's storage capacity, any degree of impairment of the computer's capabilities will be similarly minute. The Act, however, does not require that the degree of impairment be substantial or significant. Such conditions would add further levels of complexity and uncertainty to the task of defining the scope of the legislation. It is to be recognised, however, that the act of making an unauthorised modification constitutes only one element of the offence and that the prosecution is required, additionally, to establish that the party responsible intended to impair the operation of the computer.[1] In addition to proscribing acts impairing the operation of a computer, the unauthorised modification offence may be committed when data held on a computer is modified in a fashion which may affect its reliability. A possible scenario might involve an individual giving false information with a view to causing the modification of an unfavourable entry on a credit reference agency's files. This might render unreliable the data held on the computer and, as such, may constitute an offence under s 3.

[1] Section 2(2).

Viruses and the unauthorised modification offence

13.79 Taking the concept of an unauthorised modification as a whole, it would seem clear that the offence might be committed by a person who creates a computer virus and sends it out into the world with the intention that it will infect other computers. The Computer Misuse Act 1990 provides in this respect that:

(3) The intent need not be directed at—
    (a) any particular computer;
    (b) any particular program or data or a program or data of any particular kind; or
    (c) any particular modification or a modification of any particular kind.[1]

[1] Section 3(3).

13.80 The originator will cause the modification of any computer which is infected, even though they may not be directly responsible for the infection of any particular machine, this being brought about by an unsuspecting (or even reckless) authorised user. To this extent, the phrase 'to cause' must be interpreted in two senses: in respect of the act which causes the effect and also of the act which is proximately responsible for its occurrence.

13.81 One of the most publicised cases brought under the Computer Misuse Act 1990 involved the prosecution of Christopher Pile. Using the pseudonym 'Black Baron' the accused was reported as having told detectives that 'he had wanted to create a British virus which would match the worst of those from overseas'. A number of viruses were created by Pile and concealed in seemingly innocuous programs which he published on the Internet, from there they would infect any computer onto which they were downloaded. It was estimated that the effects of the virus cost companies in the region of £500,000 and Pile secured the dubious distinction of being the first virus writer convicted under the Act, being sentenced to a term of 18 months' imprisonment.[1]

[1]   M2 Presswire, 24 March 1997.

13.82   In addition to being used against those who create a virus, the Computer Misuse Act 1990 could also be used against those who deliberately cause a computer to be infected. Once again, the requirement that the prosecution establish intent may prove difficult to satisfy. In many cases, viruses are spread through users bringing infected disks into offices or educational establishments. Many users now have policies either prohibiting the practice or requiring that disks be checked on a dedicated virus-checking machine prior to being used. If an individual ignores these requirements and causes a viral infestation the conduct might reasonably be characterised as reckless, but this would still fall some way short of the statutory standard.

Where next for computer crime?

13.83   Following, at least, the decision of the House of Lords in *Allison*,[1] there seems little doubt that the Computer Misuse Act 1990 provides an effective response to incidents of computer hacking and of damage to data. Certain forms of Internet-related conduct may prove extremely damaging to computer owners, especially those involved in ecommerce, but may not fall foul of the legislation. The most serious aspect relates to what are generally referred to as 'denial of service attacks'. These involve an individual – or group of persons – in causing massive numbers of connections to be made to a target website, with the effect that the site becomes clogged and is unable to process transmissions from more genuine users. In some cases, perpetrators may cause third-party equipment to be used to generate traffic. In this event, it may well be that a s 3 offence will be committed. If this is not the case, matters may become more problematic. Although the effect of receiving a connection over the Internet will cause a modification of the contents of the victim's computer, it can be argued that commercial users, and perhaps anyone with a presence on the Internet, invites third parties to make contact. Any modification might therefore be seen as authorised.

¹ *R v Bow Street Magistrates' Court, ex p Allison* [1999] 4 All ER 1.

13.84 The Council of Europe Convention on Cybercrime may provide an appropriate basis for the prosecution of such forms of Internet-related conduct. The Convention provides that:

> Each Party shall adopt such legislative and other measures as may be necessary to establish as criminal offences under its domestic law, when committed intentionally, the serious hindering without right of the functioning of a computer system by inputting, transmitting, damaging, deleting, deteriorating, altering or suppressing computer data.¹

¹ Article 5.

13.85 As the Convention's provisions indicate, the emergence of the Internet does pose challenges to the efficiency of 'older' computer misuse statutes such as the Computer Misuse Act 1990. As important as the development of substantive laws is, the recognition of the global nature of the Internet and the need to ensure international co-operation at the stages of detecting and prosecuting instances of computer crime. These topics will be considered in Chapter 16.

Chapter 14

Theft of information

Introduction

14.1   Chapter 13 considered the extent to which the various aspects of hacking might constitute criminal offences. In many instances, obtaining unauthorised access to the contents of a computer system will be sought as the precursor to other activities. In the Cambridge packet sniffing case, for example, it was stated that:

> The authorities had no indication that the hacker deleted or altered files, 'although there was the potential for that', he said. Files belonging to world-renowned research scientists may have been viewed or copied, giving the hacker an insight into commercially and academically sensitive material. Cambridge is well known for its scientific work, particularly drug design and genetics. A well-informed source within the university said that some of the material to which the hacker had access would be extremely valuable. 'Much of the medical research is funded by industry. Other companies would dearly like to know what research their rivals are involved with,' he said ...[1]

[1]   *Daily Telegraph*, 27 April 1996.

14.2   There may be little doubt that the victim of this form of conduct might cry 'theft'. There is frequently, however, a gulf between popular perception and legal reality. As has been commented:

> It is not too much to say that we live in a country where ... the theft of the board room table is punished far more severely than the theft of the board room secrets.[1]

Although there might be a case for the application of the ulterior intent offence, in many cases, misuse of information is considered a matter for the civil rather than the criminal courts. Whilst government information is protected extensively by the provisions of the Official Secrets Acts of 1911 and 1989 no such protection is extended to commercial information. Given the growing importance of the information sector in modern society, there may be the case for the extension of the criminal law and consideration will be given in this chapter to the question whether forms of conduct relating to information might attract criminal consequences outwith the bounds of the Computer Misuse Act 1990.

1   775 HC Official Report (5th series) col 806, 1968.

14.3   In the situation where information is held on some physical object and where the latter is unlawfully removed, there is no doubt that a charge of theft might be competent. In such a situation, the informational content of an item will be taken into account in determining the value of property which is the subject matter of theft. A computer disk, for example, may have a value of less than £1, but if it should contain a program and be offered for sale in a shop for £50, that will be the value ascribed to it in the event it is stolen. The principle that information may add value to physical objects was applied in the US case of *Hancock v Texas*,[1] where a quantity of print-outs containing copies of computer programs had been stolen. Under Texan law, theft of property valued at less than $50 constituted a misdemeanour rather than the more serious felony.[2] Although the value of the paper involved was less than $50, the court accepted evidence that several thousands of dollars had been expended in the creation of the programs and, without determining a precise value, determined that the conduct should be regarded as a felony. As has been described, however,[3] the attachment of an economic value to information can be a problematic task especially in cases where its value resides primarily in its remaining confidential to only one party.

1   402 SW 2d 906 (1966) Tex Crim App.
2   Although neither English nor Scots law recognises different categories of theft at the conceptual level, the value of the property involved may influence the decisions as to whether prosecution should proceed on a summary basis or on indictment, and also the level of court before which the case is brought. In the event that a conviction is secured, the value of the property involved may also affect the severity of any sentence which may be imposed.
3   See para 12.13 above.

14.4   The critical issue, which goes to the heart of the legal response to information technology concerns the question whether information, separated from its connection with a tangible object, may constitute the subject matter of theft. The following section will examine the nature of the offence of theft and describe the obstacles which will confront the attempt to utilise it in response to the situation where access is sought to information purely in order to acquire knowledge of material in circumstances which are unacceptable to the holder of the information.

The basis of the offence of theft

14.5   In Scotland, theft remains a common law offence. A variety of definitions can be found in the works of the institutional writers. *Hume*, for example, defines it as encompassing 'the felonious taking and carrying away of the property of another'. In England, the offence of theft has a statutory basis, with the Theft Act 1968 providing that a person will be guilty of theft where they dishonestly appropriate the property of another with the intention of permanently depriving the owner of that property.[1] 'Property' is defined as including 'money and all other property, real or personal, including things in action and other incorporeal property'.[2]

[1] Section 1.
[2] Section 1.

14.6 In the case of information, two objections lie to the relevance of a charge of theft. First, unless the information is held on some storage device which is also removed, it is difficult to see how the Scottish requirement of 'taking and carrying away' or the English requirement of depriving the owner of property can be satisfied. With recognised forms of theft, the conduct has two elements. The owner loses possession of the property and the thief acquires possession. Unlike the situation where, for example, a car is stolen, possession of the information will not be lost.

14.7 It is possible that this objection could be countered with the proposition that the holder has lost exclusive possession or knowledge of the information, but even if this argument were to be accepted[1] – and it could clearly apply only to information that was in some way confidential – a second objection relates to the question of whether information might be regarded as property for the purpose of the law of theft. During parliamentary debate on the Theft Act 1968, it was suggested that the statutory definition of 'property' would encompass the theft of a trade secret. Such an interpretation, however, does not appear compatible with the decision of the Divisional Court in the case of *Oxford v Moss*.[2]

[1] The Law Commission have expressed the view that financial loss is not to be equated with the physical deprivation involved in theft. See Law Com Working Paper no 104 'Conspiracy to defraud' (1987) para 10.46.
[2] (1978) Cr App R 183.

14.8 Moss was a student at Liverpool University. In a manner unfortunately not disclosed in the Law Report, he discovered and surreptitiously removed a proof copy of an examination paper which he was due to sit. His plan was to copy the contents of the paper and, being aware that if the paper were discovered to be missing a replacement paper would be set, to return the paper to its original location.

14.9 Upon his conduct being discovered, the question arose as to whether any criminal offence had been committed. As it was an integral part of his scheme that the original paper should be returned, it was considered that he could not be charged with the theft of the paper. A prosecution was brought, however, alleging theft of the confidential information contained in the paper.

14.10 Moss was acquitted by the Liverpool magistrates on the basis that confidential information could not be regarded as property. This conclusion was upheld by the Divisional Court, which declared that whilst the holder of information might possess limited rights in it which could be upheld at civil law, the information itself was not property and hence could not be stolen.[1] A similar approach can be seen in the case of *R v Absolon*.[2] Here, a jury was directed to acquit a defendant who had attempted to sell to a competitor data relating to an oil company's exploratory work. Although the work represented an investment of some £13m and the data was assessed as having a commercial value of up to £100,000, it was ruled that it could not constitute property.

[1]   *Oxford v Moss* (1978) Cr App R 183. In a commentary ((1979) Cr LR 120 at 122) on this decision, it was suggested that a charge might have been brought under s 6 of the Theft Act 1968. Following the decision of the Court of Appeal in the case of *R v Lloyd* [1985] 2 All ER 661, this point must now be doubted.
[2]   (1979) 68 Cr App R 183.

14.11   An example of the distinction between rights in and property rights over information can be taken from the decision of the House of Lords in the case of *Rank Film Distributors Ltd v Video Information Centre*.[1] In the course of civil proceedings involving an allegation of breach of copyright, the appellants sought discovery of a variety of documents in the possession of the respondents. In resisting this application, the latter claimed that disclosure would expose them to the risk of criminal proceedings for, inter alia, theft of the appellants' copyright interests and, therefore, would infringe their privilege against self-incrimination. This prospect was dismissed by Lord Fraser, who commented:

> The risk of prosecution under the Theft Act 1968 may, I think, be disregarded as remote, because that Act applies to theft of 'property' which is defined in a way which does not appear to include copyright but only, so far as this appeal is concerned, to the physical objects such as tapes and cassettes which are of small value by themselves.[2]

In the Copyright Designs and Patents Act 1988, it is now provided that copyright 'is a property right which subsists in accordance with this Part in the following descriptions of work ...'[3]

[1]   [1982] AC 380.
[2]   [1982] AC 380 at 387.
[3]   Section 1.

14.12   Despite this apparent grant of property status, it would appear that the rights conferred under the copyright legislation are exhaustively defined therein. In the case of *Paterson Zochonis v Merfarken Packaging*,[1] Oliver LJ, sitting in the Court of Appeal, dismissed an allegation that the respondents owed a common law duty of care to avoid actions which might result in an infringement of the appellants' copyright interests, holding that:

> ... the plaintiffs' case ultimately depends upon the existence, alongside the statutory duty not to infringe copyright, of a parallel common law duty owed to the copyright owner to take reasonable care not to infringe copyright. For my part I am wholly unable to accept the existence of such an additional or parallel duty.[2]

Such a conclusion is in conformity with the principles of intellectual property law, which constitutes an exception to the general rules against acts restricting competition. As such, the extent of copyright protection is to be found in the copyright legislation.

[1]   [1983] FSR 273.
[2]   [1983] FSR 273 at 285.

14.13   A number of cases within the US have held that information can be the subject matter of theft. In the case of *United States v Girard and Lambert*,[1] for example, the Court of Appeals for the Second Circuit interpreted a statutory prohibition against the unauthorised sale of any 'record ... or thing of value' as encompassing the unauthorised abstraction and sale of information. Given the different definitions applied to the subject matter of theft, it is doubtful whether consideration of US precedents assists significantly in the consideration of the UK situation. Of greater relevance is the recent Canadian decision in the case of *R v Stewart*,[2] where detailed consideration was given by the judges of the High Court, Court of Appeal and Supreme Court to the question of the property status of information.

[1]   601 F 2d 69.
[2]   The case is reported at the respective stages at 138 DLR (3d) 73; 149 DLR (3d) 583; 50 DLR (4th) 1.

14.14   Stewart attempted to obtain details of the names and addresses of hotel employees. This information was sought by a trade union which wished to recruit members from amongst these employees. The information was contained in personnel files held on the employer's computer. Stewart's scheme was to persuade an employee to copy the data from the computer without, however, removing any tangible objects. The scheme being discovered, Stewart was charged with the offence of counselling the offence of theft 'to wit: to steal information, the property of the ... Hotel contrary to section 283 of the Criminal Code'. This provides that:

> Everyone commits theft who fraudulently or without colour of right takes, or fraudulently and without colour of right converts to his use or the use of another person, anything whether animate or inanimate ...

Although the word 'anything' appears in the above provision, all the courts dealing with the case were agreed that the word had to be interpreted in the sense of 'any property'.

14.15   At trial, Stewart was acquitted by the judge (Krever J), who held that information, even confidential information, could not be regarded as property:

> ... confidential information is not property for the purpose of the law of theft in Canada ... If this interpretation should be thought to be inadequate to meet the needs of modern Canadian society, particularly because of its implications for the computer age, the remedy must be a change in the law by Parliament. It is not for a court to stretch the language used in a statute dealing with the

criminal law, to solve problems outside the contemplation of the statute. If an accused person's conduct does not fall within the language used by Parliament, no matter how reprehensible it might be, it ought not to be characterized as criminal.[1]

[1]   *R v Stewart* 138 DLR (3d) 73 at 85.

14.16   This view was supported by Lacourciere JA in the Court of Appeal, but the majority were in favour of conferring at least a limited property status upon confidential information, Houlden JA stating:

> While clearly not all information is property, I see no reason why confidential information which has been gathered through the expenditure of time, effort and money by a commercial enterprise for the purpose of its business should not be regarded as property and hence entitled to the protection of the criminal law.[1]

[1]   *R v Stewart* 149 DLR (3d) 583 at 595.

14.17   The Court of Appeal decision[1] was subjected to considerable criticism[2] and ultimately was overturned in the Supreme Court[3] on grounds similar to those adopted by Krever J. Thus, it was held that should it be determined that the protection of the law of theft should be extended to confidential information, this was a decision for Parliament. It was also pointed out that there were competing interests involved in the free flow of information and in the right to confidentiality.

[1]   *R v Stewart* 149 DLR (3d) 583 at 595.
[2]   See (1986) OJLS 145.
[3]   *R v Stewart* 50 DLR (4th) 1.

14.18   In their Consultative Memorandum on Computer Crime, the Scottish Law Commission concluded that information could not be the subject of theft under Scots law. It quoted with approval[1] the words of the Canadian House of Commons Standing Committee on Justice and Legal Affairs, which had argued:

> For reasons of public policy the exclusive ownership of information which, of necessity, would flow from the concept of 'property', is not favoured in our socio-legal system. Information is regarded as too valuable a commodity to have its ownership vest exclusively in any particular individual.[2]

[1]   Sc Law Com no 68 (1986) para 4.13.
[2]   Canadian House of Commons, Standing Committee on Justice and Legal Affairs *Report of the Sub-Committee on Computer Crime* (1983) p 14.

14.19   The Scottish Law Commission concluded that questions of the status of information and as to whether certain forms of dealing in it should be subject to criminal sanctions raised wide issues of policy that extended beyond the computer field. For this reason, and taking account of the problems previously identified in applying the law of theft to information, no recommendation was made for change in this area.[1]

[1]   Sc Law Com no 68 (1986) pp 94–95.

14.20   The same approach was adopted by the Law Commission, whose Working Paper makes the point that:

> ... the definition of property for the law of theft, and the argument as to whether it is possible to appropriate information belonging to another with the intention of permanently depriving the other of it are problems which have general implications outside the region of computer misuse.[1]

This view is in line with the earlier findings of the Working Paper on Conspiracy to Defraud.[2] Here, whilst affirming that '(i)nformation, particularly confidential information, will often be regarded as a valuable commodity. Information of one kind or another is frequently bought and sold',[3] the view was taken that the authorities referred to in this chapter established that it could not possess a sufficient property status to constitute the subject matter of theft.

[1]   Law Com Working Paper no 110 (1988) para 3.69.
[2]   Law Com Working Paper no 104 (1987).
[3]   Law Com Working Paper no 104 (1987) para 4.41.

Alternative approaches

14.21   Given the strength of the objections to the application of the law of theft to cases involving information per se the focus of some attention has been on the role which other doctrines might play. Much of the work has been conducted by the Law Commission whose Working Papers on Conspiracy to Defraud,[1] Misuse of Trade Secrets[2] and Fraud and Deception[3] contain much useful background materials although the studies themselves do not appear likely to lead to immediate legislative intervention.

[1]   Law Com no 104 (1987).
[2]   Law Com no 150 (1997).
[3]   Law Com no 155 (1999). The Law Commission have also published a report on Fraud (Law Com no 276 (2002)).

Dishonest acquisition of confidential information

14.22   The possibility that an offence to this effect should be introduced into English law was considered by the Law Commission in its Working Paper on Conspiracy to Defraud. The view was taken that, save in the situation where a conspiracy might be formed to deprive a person of confidential information to their financial prejudice, no offence would be committed. The Commission declined to consider in any detail whether there was justification for introducing such an offence on the basis that:

> ... the whole area of obtaining confidential information and invasion of privacy is a complex one involving many aspects of both civil and criminal law going far beyond the realms of fraud.[1]

It was additionally considered that even if the need for an extension of the criminal law were to be recognised, 'the scope and definition of any offence would require much greater consideration than we would be able to give it in this paper'.[2]

[1]   Law Com no 104 (1987) para 10.45.
[2]   Law Com no 104 (1987) para 10.46.

14.23   Although eminently justifiable, the views of the Law Commission perhaps serve also as a basis for criticism of the approach of enacting computer-specific statutes. In many areas, the fact of a computer's involvement in conduct raises issues of practice rather than principle and, short of a fundamental reform of the criminal law to take account of the enhanced value and status of information, it might be argued that computer-related activities should be left within the structure of the general criminal law.

Dishonest exploitation of confidential information

14.24   Issues similar to those described above were discussed in the Scottish case of *Grant v Allan*.[1] The case is of interest both in its own right and also in demonstrating the benefits and pitfalls encountered in attempting to apply precedents from previous centuries in the context of modern practices. The appellant, Grant, was employed by a firm of carriers. In the course of his employment, it was alleged that he did 'clandestinely take and without lawful right or authority, given by your said employers or otherwise, detain copies of a quantity of ... computer printouts'.[2]

[1]   1987 SCCR 402.
[2]   In Scots law, charges are typically drafted to meet the circumstances of a particular case rather than alleging breach of a general statutory or common law offence.

14.25   It was common ground between the parties that the word 'take' was to be interpreted in the sense of causing a computer to make the print-outs rather than in that of removing print-outs which had already been made.[1] The print-outs detailed the employer's customers and it was alleged that Grant offered to sell these to a competitor. A meeting was arranged for this purpose. The competitor subsequently reported the approach to the police and Grant was arrested when he sought to keep the appointment.

[1]   On the assumption that the paper involved belonged to the employer, it is arguable that a charge of theft might have been brought in respect of this.

14.26   Before the Sheriff, a plea was taken to the relevancy of the charge. This was rejected but an appeal was brought before the High Court.[1] The debate here centred on two issues: first whether the conduct complained of constituted a crime under the law of Scotland and, secondly, on the assumption that the conduct was not currently illegal, whether the High Court should exercise its historic declaratory power to 'punish every act which is obviously of a criminal nature'.[2]

1   *Grant v Allan* 1987 SCCR 402.
2   *Hume*, vol i, p 12.

14.27   In arguing that the complaint libelled against Grant was one recognised under Scots law, the Advocate Depute made reference to a variety of authorities, including two dating back to the seventeenth and eighteenth centuries. In the case of *Dewar*,[1] the defender was an apprentice to a printing company. The proprietors of the company made use of a variety of formulae in mixing printing ink. This information was regarded as confidential, and details were recorded in books which were normally kept under lock and key. Wishing to obtain details of the formulae, Dewar broke into the room where the books were kept, 'carried them away, got them copied, and afterwards replaced them in the situation from which they had been taken'.

1   *Re Dewar* (1777) Burnett 115.

14.28   Although no full report of the case exists, Burnett reports that the court held that Dewar had committed a punishable act. In the event, despite the Advocate Depute's argument that the taking and retaining of the books constituted the 'mechanics' rather than the 'essence' of the crime which, he contended, lay with the unlawful dealing in the information, the court rejected the argument that *Dewar*[1] was authority for the 'proposition that the law of Scotland recognises as a crime the dishonest exploitation of the confidential information of another'. Rather, it was concluded, the unlawful means by which Dewar had obtained the books constituted the basis of the conviction.

1   *Re Dewar* (1777) Burnett 115.

14.29   The authority which appeared most relevant to the present case[1] was that of *HMA v Mackenzie*.[2] The defender in this case was charged with two offences, first, stealing a book of chemical recipes belonging to his employer and, secondly, with making copies of the recipes with intent to dispose of them for profit in breach of an agreement of secrecy with his employer.

1   *Grant v Allan* 1987 SCCR 402.
2   1913 SC(J) 107.

14.30   This second charge was dismissed by the Lord Justice Clerk (Macdonald) who held that 'I am quite unable to hold that this is a relevant charge of crime, either completed crime or attempted crime'.[1] The point will again be relevant in considering the provisions of the Computer Misuse Act 1990. Essentially, it was considered that Mackenzie's scheme had not progressed sufficiently far to constitute a criminal attempt.

1   *HMA v Mackenzie* 1913 SC(J) 107 at 111.

14.31   Having found that the conduct libelled was not the subject of an existing offence, the court considered whether it should exercise its declaratory power to make it so.[1] Such a suggestion was unanimously condemned by the court. Both the Lord Justice Clerk and Lord Wylie quoted a further passage from Lord

Salvesen's judgment in *Mackenzie* to the effect that the second charge 'sets forth a breach of the accused's contract of service with his employers, but this is primarily a civil wrong'.[2]

1   *Grant v Allan* 1987 SCCR 402.
2   *HMA v Mackenzie* 1913 SC(J) 107 at 113.

14.32   Such a proposition was also held relevant in *Grant v Allen*. The conduct, it was held, was not so clearly of a criminal nature that it should be so declared. Concurring, Lord Macdonald concluded:

> To make a declaratory finding that it is a crime dishonestly to exploit confidential information belonging to another would have far reaching consequences in this technological age. If it is felt that the sanction of the criminal law is required to prohibit such a practice this should be introduced by legislation and not by the declaratory power of the High Court.[1]

Although the doctrine of the High Court's declaratory power applies only in Scots law, the case and the discussion serves to illustrate the limits of legitimate judicial creativity. Given the vital importance of information in the eponymous 'Information Society' there is need for the legislature to consider whether its legal status should be amended to reflect its increasing economic, political and societal value.

1   1987 SCCR 402 at 409.

Misuse of trade secrets

14.33   In its Working Paper on Conspiracy to Defraud,[1] the Law Commission considered whether criminal sanctions should be imposed against those guilty of 'taking confidential information by dishonest means'. It was concluded that the topic was outwith the bounds of that study, although a number of those responding to the Working Paper expressed support for reform in this area. In 1994 the Law Commission published its final report (Law Com 228) on the topic. This pointed out the anomalous situation where two people conspiring to 'steal' a trade secret would be guilty of the offence of conspiracy to defraud whilst a individual acting alone would have nothing to fear from the criminal law. It was considered, however that rather than changing the nature of the offence of fraud to make the conduct illegal when carried out by an individual further work should be conducted in respect of the relationship between dealings in trade secrets and the criminal law. A further Consultation Paper 'Legislating the Criminal Code: Misuse of Trade Secrets'[2] was the result.

1   Law Com no 155 (1999).
2   Law Com no 150 (1997)

14.34   An initial problem in this area concerns the definition to be given to the concept of trade secrets. It is relatively easy to identify individual items which might be so considered. In the case of *R v Stewart* considered at para 14.13ff above it was accepted that:

> Compilations of information are often of such importance to the business community that they are securely kept to ensure their confidentiality. The collated, confidential information may be found in many forms covering a wide variety of topics. It may include painstakingly prepared computer programs ... meticulously indexed lists of suppliers ... For many businessmen their confidential lists may well be the most valuable asset of their company. Their security will be of utmost importance.[1]

[1]   149 DLR (3d) 583.

14.35   It is normal to refer to such material as trade secrets. A legal difficulty with this approach, however, concerns the lack of a accepted exhaustive definition of the term. Some trade secrets relate to matters which are vital to the well-being of a company. An oft-cited example concerns the formula for Coca Cola. Although chemical analysis might allow competitors to discover the ingredients of the product, the actual method of manufacture remains a closely guarded secret. Other trade secrets may relate to innovations or improvements in methods of production which confer a competitive advantage on their 'owner'. The final forms of trade secret relate to information, and here there is a strong link with the more generic topic of confidential information and the civil action for breach of confidence. Details of customers, marketing strategies and business forecasts as was the case in *Grant v Allan*[1] would constitute one category. Here, as was again stated in *R v Stewart*:

> If questioned, a businessman would unhesitatingly state that the confidential lists were the 'property' of his firm. If they were surreptitiously copied by a competitor or outsider, he would consider his confidential data to have been stolen.[2]

[1]   *Grant v Allan* 1987 SCCR 402.
[2]   149 DLR (3d) 583.

14.36   A final category of trade secret would consist of collations of information where the value would lie not in the individual items of data, which might be publicly available, but through the application of techniques such as data mining to produce compilations. This category sits somewhat uneasily with the requirement that the information should not be 'generally known'. The Law Commission suggest that a definition similar to that proposed in their report on Breach of Confidence might be applied in this context so that:

> ... information which is capable of being extracted from any matter in the public domain (whether a document, product, process or anything else) is not in the public domain on that ground alone if such extraction would require a significant expenditure of labour, skill or money.[1]

[1]   Law Com no 150 (1997) para 4.33.

14.37   By definition, trade secrets have been limited to the situation where the holder is acting in the course of trade. In our more service-oriented economy, such a limitation is hard to justify. One of the issues considered by the Law Commission concerned the question whether information held by a member of a profession should also be protected. This raises the issue of the relationship between the concept of trade secrets and that of confidential information. It is clear that any trade secret will also be classed as containing information the use of which might be restricted under the law of breach of confidence, and much of the content of the Law Commission's paper relates to the law concerning confidential information. An essential feature of the notion of trade secrets as discussed above is that the information should possess some commercial value. Other data may be classed as confidential without its value residing in financial terms. Medical records might well be regarded as coming under this heading, and one might also consider the situation at issue in *Oxford v Moss*.[1] If misuse of data constituting a trade secret such as, for example, a list of customers is to be considered criminal, there seems little justification for treating misuse of a medical record or proof examination paper in a different manner. It may be that some instances of such conduct could be prosecuted under other statutes, such as the Computer Misuse Act 1990, but, as was argued by the Solicitor General in welcoming the Law Commission's initiative in respect of trade secrets:

> The modern sorts of commercial activity, and the modern methods by which dishonest activity may be effected makes one constantly worried that the un-overhauled bus may not be able to cope. Simply by way of example, one asks how is the law going to be able to cope with the increasing prevalence of commercial espionage both by computer and otherwise where the commercial rival or predator obtains information which he then covertly uses to benefit himself ... No doubt the law will be able to concoct some niche in the criminal calendar. But it depends on the ingenuity of the prosecutor, the learning and advocacy of the defence, and the judge on the day.[2]

[1]   (1978) Cr App R 183.
[2]   'Commercial Fraud or Sharp Practice – Challenge for the Law' Denning Lecture, October 1997, quoted in *Misuse of Trade Secrets* Law Commission Consultative Paper no 150 (1997).

14.38   Clearly, a less than satisfactory means of proceeding. When confidential information moves outwith the trade-related sector, however, a variety of other interests, not least those concerned with privacy and journalistic freedom of expression, require to be taken into account in proposing changes to the law, and it is noteworthy that in its extensive studies on breach of confidence, the Law Commission did not propose the enactment of any new criminal offences.

14.39   It may be noted that, albeit again under civil law, the Data Protection Act 1998 provides individuals with rights of compensation in certain situations where personal data is misused. Compensation will be normally be payable in respect of 'damage and distress'; a formulation which requires evidence of financial loss as a prerequisite to any claim.[1]

[1]   See para 8.21ff above.

The Law Commission's proposals

14.40   The Law Commission's paper contains a valuable summary of the debate concerning the legal status of information. A point which comes through strongly from English (and Scottish) decisions on the topic is that, although a range of opinions have been expressed in civil and criminal cases, the issue has not been analysed at any level of detail. After summarising a range of judicial dicta, the conclusion of the Law Commission is that although confidential information displays some of the attributes of property, not least in the perception of its holder:

> Our provisional view is that confidential information is not property in the strict sense, and that it would be a mistake for the criminal law to pretend that it is. For this reason, the extension of the criminal law that we propose is not modelled on the law of theft or other offences against property. This approach is supported by the fact that trade secret misuse typically affects only the 'monopoly value' of the secret, not its 'use value'. But the form that an offence might take is a separate issue.[1]

[1]   Law Com no 150(1997) para 3.26.

14.41   The Law Commission has now proposed that the use or misuse of a trade secret should become a criminal offence where this takes place without the consent of 'anyone entitled to the benefit of it'. The onus would be on the prosecution to establish that the defendant knew that the information involved constituted a trade secret.

14.42   No conclusion was reached on the further issue whether the act of acquiring or seeking to acquire knowledge of a trade secret should itself be rendered criminal. Considering the topic in the context primarily of industrial espionage, the Law Commission identify three options for future action.[1] The first would seek to criminalise the act of acquiring information constituting a trade secret with the intent to use it. The second option is to target wrongful methods of acquiring information. In its studies on the law of breach of confidence,[2] the Scottish Law Commission had suggested, in a consultative memorandum, the establishment of an offence to be committed by a person who entered 'upon premises without the occupier's consent, and without lawful authority, for the purpose of obtaining confidential information which is of value'. It was also proposed that the 'use of certain technical surveillance devices' should be declared unlawful. Even though the restriction in the scope of the offence to information possessing financial value would have limited its scope, the proposal was not pursued in the final report, the Commission being persuaded that the approach was:

> ... too ambitious, impinging upon wider issues of privacy and data protection quite unrelated to questions of breach of confidence.[3]

[1]   Law Com no 150 (1997) paras 7.22–7.31.
[2]   Sc Law Com memorandum No 40 (1977).
[3]   Law Com no 150 (1997) para 7.21.

14.43 Recognising these concerns, the Law Commission emphasise that its work (and any recommendations) is limited to the specific category of trade secrets. Thus:

> The effect would be that the methods of acquiring information which, in the Breach of Confidence report, we concluded were reprehensible (or those which the Calcutt Committee subsequently proposed should become criminal where personal information was involved) would be proscribed only in the commercial field.[1]

The final option identified by the Law Commission was for the retention of the status quo. It was pointed out that in many cases, those obtaining information in an improper manner might incur substantial civil liabilities, whilst those securing access to trade secrets held on a computer might face prosecution under the Computer Misuse Act 1990. The existence of such sanctions, it was suggested, might remove the need for further legislation.

[1]   Law Com no 150 (1997) para 7.29.

The Law Commission Consultation Paper on Fraud and Deception[1] and Report on Fraud[2]

14.44 The Law Commission's work in this field was conducted in response to a request from the Home Secretary that it:

> As part of their programme of work on dishonesty, to examine the law on fraud, and in particular to consider whether it: is readily comprehensible to juries; is adequate for effective prosecution; is fair to potential defendants; meets the need of developing technology including electronic means of transfer; and to make recommendations to improve the law in these respects with all due expedition. In making these recommendations to consider whether a general offence of fraud would improve the criminal law.[3]

[1]   Consultation Paper no 155 (1999).
[2]   Law Com no 276 (2001).
[3]   Paragraph 1.1.

14.45 Concern had been expressed on a number of occasions at the adequacy of English law to deal with offences involving deception. This was highlighted by the decision of the House of Lords in the case of *R v Preddy*.[1] The appellants in this case had obtained mortgage loans to purchase properties following the making of false representations. In most cases, the funds had been transferred from the lender's bank account into the appellants. Charges were brought of obtaining property by deception. The defendant was convicted at trial, but an appeal to the House of Lords was upheld on the basis that no property could be identified as having been obtained. Prior to the transaction, the lender's bank account stood in credit to a certain extent. That was then extinguished. Although a credit of an equal amount was raised in the appellant's account, the two credits were different things. To this extent there was no obtaining of property.

[1]   [1986] AC 815.

14.46   The effects of the decision in *Preddy*[1] were speedily reversed with the passage of the Theft (Amendment) Act 1996, but concern remained at the adequacy of the law, especially in situations where technological means such as electronic fund transfers were used. The Consultation Paper, published in March 1999,[2] covers a range of topics, most relevantly for the present work including the response to forms of deception involving a machine.

[1]   *R v Preddy* [1986] AC 815.
[2]   Law Com No 155 (1999).

14.47   In 1993, the Law Commission had undertaken a consultation exercise seeking the views of a range of business associations 'whether there currently existed, or were likely to be developed any systems involving the supply of false information to a machine which would warrant a new offence. No such procedure was identified'.[1] By 1999, the situation was considered to have changed, principally because of the Internet. Considering the economic and commercial significance of the network, the Commission accepted the need to ensure that the protection of the criminal law was made available to those acting in this sector. Traditionally, it was stated, a distinction had been drawn between goods and services:

> Consideration of the best approach to criminalising such conduct raises some fundamental questions about the structure of the law of dishonesty. As Archbold points out, 'The lay view [is] that theft is taking without permission, and obtaining property by deception is tricking an owner into parting with possession'. Since *Gomez* this may now be only the lay view, but it is also the historical foundation of the distinction in law between theft and deception (or false pretences). Because the paradigm of theft is taking without permission, originally the only things that could be stolen were those that could be carried away (though after 1968 this was extended to intangible property). Theft has not been defined to include the 'taking' of services, because until recently this possibility has not been a significant one. By contrast, the obtaining of services by deception clearly is covered, at least since the 1978 Act, because it clearly is possible to trick the person who has the right to bestow a service into bestowing it. The effect of the technical innovations of recent years, and particularly the development of the internet, has been to effect a fundamental change to this practical justification for the distinction between the two types of offence.[2]

[1]   Law Com 155 (1999) para 8.38.
[2]   Paragraph 8.51.

14.48   Consideration was given to the possibility that reform should take the form of providing for deception of a machine to become a criminal offence. The Law Commission argued, however, that this approach was open to a number of objections. It was considered to be a fiction to suggest that 'an inanimate object has a mental state'. Further, whilst the concept of deception might be appropriate in cases where false information was input into a computer, it would not apply to other forms of conduct. The case of *Davies v Flackett*[1] would provide an apposite example. Here, it will be recalled the motorist left the car park after others forcibly raised a barrier. A more appropriate response, it was suggested, was to consider reform of the law of theft:

If the law were extended to catch these kinds of conduct, it would effectively criminalise the 'taking' of services and that, in the terms of the distinction drawn above, is clearly a theft-like offence. It could either stand alone or be added to the definition of theft itself. The definition of theft is a question to which we intend to return in another consultation paper; in particular, the best way to deal with what is now the concept of 'appropriation' will be a key issue. For present purposes it is sufficient to suggest that extending the law of theft would be one way, and in our provisional view the most principled way, of dealing with the problem. For these purposes, the person who, in respect of a service, is in a position analogous to the owner of property in theft is the person who has the legal right to bestow (or decline to bestow) the service on a consumer – the 'service controller'. The equivalent of the defendant's appropriation of property would be his or her act in making use of the service without permission that is, without fulfilling one or more conditions as to payment which the service controller requires to be fulfilled before consenting to bestow the service.[2]

[1]   [1973 RTR 8.
[2]   Law Com No 155 (1999) para 8.54.

Conclusions

14.49   It is noteworthy how prominently aspects of computer-related conduct have featured in recent reports by the Law Commissions. There is no doubt that as information becomes a more and more valuable commodity, the availability of effective forms of legal protection will be essential to maintain consumer and business confidence in the emerging information society. It is equally noteworthy, however, that to date little of the Law Commissions' work in the field has come to statutory fruition. We remain in a state criticised by Professor Glanville Williams as far back as 1983 whereby:

> It is absurd and disgraceful that we should still be making do without any legislation specifically designed to discourage this modern form of commercial piracy. Abstracting or divulging an official secret is an offence under the Official Secrets Act 1911, sections 1 and 2; but Leviathan is not much concerned to protect the secret and immensely valuable know-how of its subjects.[1]

[1]   *Textbook on Criminal Law* (2nd edn, 1983, Stevens) p 739.

14.50   Unfortunately this is an area of law where it is much easier to identify problems than workable solutions. Whilst impressive in their own right, the various Law Commission reports are designed more to work around problems rather than to resolve the underlying issue. Although English law has moved away from the strict requirement that the offence of theft can be committed only where there is the intent permanently to deprive the owner of property, there remains a requirement for linkage with a physical object. It has been a theme throughout much of this chapter that not all information is the same, not least in terms of its economic value. The same can, of course, be said about physical objects. Such matters should go towards assessing the gravity of any offence rather than determining whether one has been committed. Overall, perhaps the major cause for criticism is that in spite of all political rhetoric concerning the vital importance of the information sector for the national and global economies we are approaching the middle of the first decade of the twenty-first century with criminal legislation that is almost 15 years old and woefully ill-prepared, which fails to address still let answer fundamental questions concerning the commodity which is fundamental to the whole concept of the information society.

Chapter 15

Internet and computer pornography

Introduction

15.1   From its earliest days the Internet has been used for the display and transfer of pornographic and other forms of unsavoury material. Its status as a communication channel largely outside existing schemes of broadcasting and publishing regulation has made it attractive to those whose activities operate on or beyond the edges of legality. In 1995, at the meeting of the British Association for the Advancement of Science, estimates were put forward to the effect that almost half of all searches made using Internet search engines were seeking pornographic material.[1] Although there is no doubt that much material on the Internet is unsavoury in nature, the view that the Internet constitutes no more than a 'heavily used red light district' appears somewhat exaggerated.[2] In most instances, it is questionable whether the involvement of the computer adds a new dimension to the question whether conduct may be classed as criminal. In early 1995, considerable publicity surrounded the arrest in the US of a university student who transmitted violent sexual fantasies over the Internet. Charges were brought under a statute prohibiting the transmission of threats across state lines.[3] Less publicity attended the dismissal of these charges in June 1995 by US District Judge Cohn. Although the messages were 'a rather savage and tasteless piece of fiction', he ruled, they remained protected by the provisions of the First Amendment.[4] The matter, it was suggested, should have been dealt with as a disciplinary matter under the university's computer use policy.

---

[1]   *Independent*, 13 September 1995.
[2]   For a comprehensive collection of materials on the topic, see the website at http://www2000.ogsm.vanderbilt.edu/cyberporn.debate.cgi.
[3]   The charges related to the contents of email messages sent by the defendant to another unidentified individual rather than to the Usenet postings.
[4]   *National Law Journal*, 3 July 1995.

15.2   A number of instances of successful prosecutions will be described below. Problems may, however, arise in two areas. First, there is the problem of defining or categorising the Internet. Different forms of regulation have tended to apply to different storage media and means of delivery. In part, this has been dictated by the accessibility of material. A television broadcast, for example, is more accessible than a film in a cinema and is subject to more stringent regulation. Likewise, a greater degree of tolerance has tended to be given to printed works than to photographic materials. As has and will be discussed, the Internet does not fall easily into existing categories of communications media. A second problem may prove even less soluble. The Internet is a global network. Material may be placed on a server anywhere in the world and accessed anywhere else. In theory, this means that the Internet is perhaps the most heavily regulated sphere of activity in existence, as any country may claim jurisdiction in respect of material accessible from its territory. Claiming jurisdiction is very different from being able to enforce it in any meaningful manner. If material is lawful in the country from which it originates, there may be little that any other jurisdiction can do to regulate it. In a report on the work of the UK's Internet Watch Foundation, it was suggested that of 453 reports made concerning the presence of pornographic material, in only 67 cases was the material held on a UK-based server. The bulk of the material was held in the US with, rather more surprisingly, Japan constituting the second largest host country.[1]

[1]   Available from http://www.dti.gov.uk/iwfreview.

15.3   Concern at the possibilities for misuse inherent in the Internet has spawned a number of international, governmental and industry based-initiatives. In January 1999, the European Commission adopted an 'Action Plan on Promoting Safe Use of the Internet'.[1] This claims as its objective:

> ... promoting safer use of the Internet and of encouraging, at European level, an environment favourable to the development of the Internet industry.[2]

In order to attain these objects, provision is made for funding to be provided to encourage work to be conducted in the member states, under the guidance of the Commission, to undertake work in specific fields. Particular reference is made to:

*   the promotion of industry self-regulation and content-monitoring schemes (for example, dealing with content such as child pornography or content which incites hatred on grounds of race, sex, religion, nationality or ethnic origin);
*   encouraging industry to provide filtering tools and rating systems, which allow parents or teachers to select content appropriate for children in their care while allowing adults to decide what legal content they wish to access, and which take account of linguistic and cultural diversity;
*   increasing awareness of services provided by industry among users, in particular parents, teachers and children, so that they can better understand and take advantage of the opportunities of the Internet;
*   support actions such as assessment of legal implications; and
*   activities fostering international co-operation in the areas enumerated above.[3]

[1]   Decision 276/1999. Available from http://158.169.50.95:10080/iap/decision/en.html.
[2]   Article 2.
[3]   Article 3.

15.4 The 'Safer Internet Programme' was originally scheduled to run for a three-year period between 1999–2000 with funding of some €38m. This was extended for a further two years and proposals for an additional four-year extension with a budget of €50m were announced by the Commission in May 2004.

15.5 Much of the EU-funded work has concerned matters such as the development of net filters and the promotion of industry self-regulation. A number of industry initiatives operate in the UK. UKERNA, which is the agency responsible for the operation of the academic network, JANET, maintains a list of newsgroups which may not be accessed over its facilities.[1] More generally, the Internet Watch Foundation was established by a number of the largest ISPs in 1996.[2] In part, this was a response by the industry to suggestions made by the Metropolitan Police that prosecutions might be brought against ISPs unless the industry took steps to regulate material accessible through its servers. As a number of recent cases have demonstrated, possession of material classed as child pornography is unlawful, whilst ISPs could also be classed as publishers and subject to prosecution under statutes such as the Obscene Publications Act 1964.

[1] Available from http://www.ja.net/operational-services/usenet/banlist.html.
[2] http://www.internetwatch.org.uk/.

15.6 The Internet Watch Foundation's activities can be divided into two categories. It seeks to encourage the use of systems of content rating. A number of systems exist, such as PICS (Platform for Internet Content Selection) and RSACi, devised by the Recreational Software Advisory Council.[1] The Foundation also acts to report instances of potentially illegal material to the appropriate ISP and law enforcement agencies. To date, its efforts in seeking to prevent prosecutions being brought against service providers appear to have been successful, although it has been stressed by law enforcement agencies that no guarantee of immunity has been given. Implementation of the EU's Directive on 'certain legal aspects of information society services, in particular electronic commerce, in the Internal Market'[2] might reduce the liabilities of ISPs as a matter of law. Discussed in more detail in Chapter 28, this provides in art 12 that service providers will not be liable (other than to an injunction regarding future behaviour) where the provider:

(a)   does not initiate the transmission;
(b)   does not select the receiver of the transmission; and
(c)   does not select or modify the information contained in the transmission.

[1] For information on rating schemes and a demonstration of their use, see http://www.icra.org/.
[2] Directive 2000/31/EC (the Electronic Commerce Directive).

The Internet and child pornography

15.7 Whilst initial concern tended to relate to pornography per se with relatively conservative countries such as the UK fearing that national controls might be overwhelmed, attention has tended to become more and more focused on the specific topic of the use of the Internet as a vehicle for disseminating paedophilic material. Incidents such as Operation Ore where the UK police forces are engaged in an ongoing investigation of several thousand UK citizens whose credit cards were used to pay for access to paedophilic sites based in the US[1] mean that the topic is seldom out of the news. It is perhaps testimony to the extent of public concerns that the Council of Europe's Convention on Cybercrime contains only one provision in its Title 3 section headed 'Content Related Offences'. This provides that:

1. Each Party shall adopt such legislative and other measures as may be necessary to establish as criminal offences under its domestic law, when committed intentionally and without right, the following conduct:

a.   producing child pornography for the purpose of its distribution through a computer system;

b.   offering or making available child pornography through a computer system;

c.   distributing or transmitting child pornography through a computer system;

d.   procuring child pornography through a computer system for oneself or for another;

e.   possessing child pornography in a computer system or on a computer-data storage medium.

2. For the purpose of paragraph 1 above 'child pornography' shall include pornographic material that visually depicts:

a.   a minor engaged in sexually explicit conduct;

b.   a person appearing to be a minor engaged in sexually explicit conduct;

c.   realistic images representing a minor engaged in sexually explicit conduct.

3. For the purpose of paragraph 2 above, the term 'minor' shall include all persons under 18 years of age. A Party may, however, require a lower age-limit, which shall be not less than 16 years.

4. Each Party may reserve the right not to apply, in whole or in part, paragraph 1(d) and 1(e), and 2(b) and 2(c).[2]

---

[1]   An indication of the global scale of pornographic activity can be taken from the fact that the US Postal Inspection Service, a federal agency charged with investigating online paedophile activity, seized records of credit card payments by some 250,000 persons, of whom around 7,000 were resident in the UK. More than two years after the details were passed to the UK authorities, although 1,230 individuals have been convicted of offences (only one prosecution having been unsuccessful) with the longest sentence being one of 12 years' imprisonment, 1,300 cases are still under investigation: http://news.bbc.co.uk/1/hi/uk/3625603.stm. The organiser of the original website was sentenced to 1,335 years imprisonment.

[2]   Article 9.

15.8   The inclusion of this provision in what is intended to be a template for computer crime legislation at a global level highlights the point that there is near-universal legislative condemnation of child pornography. The Convention on Cybercrime provides no definitions of any of the terms used in the article.

The explanatory memorandum accompanying the Convention is rather more explicit although even here elements of uncertainty persist. It is provided, for example, that:

> The term 'pornographic material' in paragraph 2 is governed by national standards pertaining to the classification of materials as obscene, inconsistent with public morals or similarly corrupt. Therefore, material having an artistic, medical, scientific or similar merit may be considered not to be pornographic. The visual depiction includes data stored on computer diskette or on other electronic means of storage, which are capable of conversion into a visual image.

15.9   It is noteworthy that although there is absolute condemnation of those involved in the production, sale, or distribution of material, the Convention on Cybercrime leaves it open to signatory states to determine whether and to what extent the acts of obtaining or possessing material should be considered unlawful. Even in this context, international consensus is limited.

15.10   For the UK, the provisions of the Convention on Cybercrime do no more than restate existing legal provisions. Under the Protection of Children Act 1978, it is provided that it will be an offence for a person:

(a)   to take, or permit to be taken or to make, any indecent photograph or pseudo-photograph of a child; or

(b)   to distribute or show such indecent photographs or pseudo-photographs; or

(c)   to have in his possession such indecent photographs or pseudo-photographs, with a view to their being distributed or shown by himself or others; or

(d)   to publish or cause to be published any advertisement likely to be understood as conveying that the advertiser distributes or shows such indecent photographs or pseudo-photographs, or intends to do so.[1]

[1]   Section 1(1).

15.11   Only limited defences are made available to a person charged with this offence. Effectively the burden of proof is partly reversed with the accused being required to show that:

(a)   that he had a legitimate reason for distributing or showing the photographs or pseudo-photographs or (as the case may be) having them in his possession; or

(b)   that he had not himself seen the photographs or pseudo-photographs and did not know, nor had any cause to suspect, them to be indecent.[1]

Given the manner in which the Internet functions with copies of pages being readily recorded in a computer's memory cache a claim that a party who had stumbled onto a pornographic website was not aware that a copy was held on his computer is not as infeasible as might initially appear and in a number of cases defendants have been acquitted on this basis.

[1]   Protection of Children Act 1978, s 1(4).

Computer pornography before the courts

15.12 In the vast majority of cases, the fact that images or text are recorded and transmitted on digital media rather than on paper or video tape will not affect the determination of whether contents are obscene or pornographic. In similar manner to the topic of computer fraud, the use of computers and computer communications networks such as the Internet to disseminate material considered to contravene criminal statutes relating to obscene or pornographic material raises comparatively few substantive legal issues. If material is considered to be illegal, this conclusion will generally not be affected by the medium in which it is displayed or disseminated. A number of issues have, however, arisen in recent years which provide useful illustrations of the problems encountered in trying to fit forms of computer-related conduct into regulatory schema devised in the light of previous forms of technology.

Pseudo photographs

15.13 In the Criminal Justice and Public Order Act 1994,[1] provisions were included to extend the ambit of the Criminal Justice Act 1988[2] and the Protection of Children Act 1978[3] to prohibit the possession or distribution what are referred to as 'pseudo-photographs', where what appears to be an indecent image of a child is made up of a collage of images, modified by the use of computer painting packages, none of the elements of which is indecent in itself. It is now provided that an offence will be committed where:

> If the impression created by a pseudo-photograph is that the person shown is a child, the pseudo-photograph shall be treated for all the purposes of this Act as showing a child and so shall a pseudo-photograph where the predominant image conveyed is that the person shown is a child notwithstanding that some of the physical characteristics shown are those of an adult.[4]

[1] Section 84.
[2] Section 160.
[3] Section 1.
[4] Protection of Children Act 1978, s 7(7).

15.14 The definition of a photograph extends to 'data stored on a computer disc or by other electronic means'.[1] Although this will certainly cover the situation where images are held on a computer disc on a permanent basis, the case of *R v Gold*[2] discussed at para 12.30 above may be relevant as suggesting that a more transitory storage will not suffice. Given the development of communications technologies, possession of data or software is becoming of less importance than the knowledge that it can be accessed whenever desired.

[1] Protection of Children Act 1978, s 7(4)(b).
[2] [1988] AC 1063.

15.15 Under the terms of the Protection of Children Act 1978, an offence is committed by a person who distributes such a photograph or who has 'in his possession such photographs or pseudo-photographs with a view to their being distributed or shown by others'.[1] The fact that possession may be a basis for conviction should give service providers cause for concern. A defence is provided that an accused 'had not himself seen the photographs or pseudo-photographs and did not know, nor had any cause to suspect, them to be indecent'.[2] In the situation where users of a service are responsible for loading images, the service provider may be able to make use of this defence. As with other areas of potential liability, it is unclear to what extent a service provider may be entitled to turn a blind eye to activities on the system. The phrase 'nor have any cause to suspect' might impose a higher standard in this area than is the case with liability for defamatory statements or conduct constituting a breach of copyright.

[1]   Section 1(1).
[2]   Section 1(4)(b).

15.16   An indication of the conduct which would now be prosecuted under the Criminal Justice and Public Order Act 1994 can be seen in the case of *R v Fellows*.[1] The appellant, who was at the time employed by Birmingham University, had, without its knowledge or consent, compiled a large database of pornographic images of children. The database was maintained on an Internet-linked computer belonging to the university. The conduct in question occurred before the entry into force of the provisions of the 1994 Act. Given these changes to the law, it is now significant in only two respects. First, it appears to have been the first case in which the word 'Internet' appears in the judgment of an English court. Secondly, it provides an indication of judicial response to the situation where new technology enables forms of behaviour which could not have been foreseen when statutory provisions were enacted.

[1]   [1997] 2 All ER 548.

15.17   Under the Protection of Children Act 1978 an offence is committed by a person possessing an indecent photograph of a child.[1] It is provided that 'references to a photograph ... include the negative as well as the positive'.[2] The question before the Court of Appeal in *R v Fellows*[3] was whether images stored on a computer disk could be classed as photographs?

[1]   Section 1(1)(c).
[2]   Section 7(4).
[3]   [1997] 2 All ER 548.

15.18   Answering this question in the affirmative, two issues addressed by the Court of Appeal call for comment. First, whether graphical files held on a computer fell within the statutory definition of a copy of a photograph for the purposes of the Protection of Children Act 1978 and, second, whether a computer hard disk containing these files could be classed as an 'article' for the purposes of the Obscene Publications Act 1959?

15.19   Although aspects of the noun 'photograph' are defined in Protection of Children Act 1978, for example, that 'references to a photograph include the positive as well as the negative version', there is no general definition. In the Copyright Act 1956, 'photograph' was defined as 'any product of photography or of any process akin to photography'.[1] The trial judge and Evans LJ both made reference to dictionary definitions of the term as 'a picture or other image obtained by the chemical action of light or other radiation on specially sensitised material such as film or glass'.[2] On this basis, the data stored on the computer's hard disk could not be classed as a photograph. The statutory prohibitions, however, extended to 'a copy of a photograph'. The computerised images had been produced by scanning 'conventional' photographs and it was held that nothing in the 1978 Act required that the copy of a photograph should itself be a photograph.[3] Given the copyright status of a photograph as an artistic work and the broad definitions of copying applying to such works, there can be little ground to challenge such a finding.

[1] Section 48.
[2] *R v Fellows* [1997] 2 All ER 548 at 556.
[3] [1997] 2 All ER 548 at 557.

15.20 Although this approach sufficed in the particular case, many cameras now record images directly onto disk rather than film. The contents of the disk may then be transferred directly to a computer and the image viewed on screen. There need never be any 'traditional' photograph to act as an original. In such a situation, it may be doubted whether even the most purposive interpretation of the Protection of Children Act 1978 could have sustained a conviction.

15.21 The Copyright, Designs and Patents Act 1988 adopted a new definition of photograph as 'a recording of light or other radiation on any medium on which an image is produced or from which an image may by any means be produced, and which is not part of a film'.[1] This marks a significant move away from the dictionary definition referred to above. In 1994, the Criminal Justice and Public Order Act 1994 adopted a different approach, providing that references to a photograph should include 'data stored on a computer disc or by other electronic means which is capable of conversion into a photograph'.[2] Juxtaposition of the two definitions can produce a sense of giddiness, but this aspect of changing technology does justify the need for reform of the Protection of Children Act 1978's provisions. Indeed, as is seen by the introduction of the new concept of a 'pseudo-photograph' in the 1994 Act, it may be queried whether the concept of a photograph remains apposite in the digital age. On this point, there is obiter comment by Evans LJ suggesting that the definition 'seems to us to be concerned with images created by computer processes rather than the storage and transmission by computers of images created originally by photography'.[3] Such a view appears unduly restrictive, and leaves open to question whether it would cover the situation where an original photograph was manipulated electronically so as to change the nature of the image.

[1] Section 4(2).
[2] Section 84(4).
[3] *R v Fellows* [1997] 2 All ER 548 at 557–558.

15.22   Both the Obscene Publications Act 1959 and the Protection of Children Act 1978 were enacted before the impact of computers had permeated the legislature's consciousness. The Court of Appeal's judgment indicates that, providing basic concepts are robust, a purposive interpretation can maintain the relevance of statutory formulations so long as electronic activities retain a connection with tangible acts or items.[1] More substantial problems occur when electronic signals constitute the original record rather than a reproduction of a physical object. Here, law reform will often be required. It is somewhat ironic, however, that in a number of cases concerned with computer-oriented statutes, the purposive interpretative techniques adopted in the present case appear to have been replaced by a much more literal and restrictive approach.

[1]   *R v Fellows* [1997] 2 All ER 548.

Multimedia products

15.23   A further case concerned with the application of obscenity law to computer-related material is that of *Meechie v Multi-Media Marketing*.[1] The defendant company established a club, 'The Interactive Girls Club', described as being an 'organisation dedicated to the production of erotic computer entertainment for broad-minded adults'. One product presented users with a short game. Successful completion of this would cause the display of a series of erotic images. A knowledgeable user would have been able to isolate the game element, moving directly to the erotic display.

[1]   (1995) 94 LGR 474.

15.24   Under the provisions of the Video Recordings Act 1984, introduced to control the distribution of so-called 'video nasties', it is an offence to supply video recordings which have not been issued with a classification certificate. No certificate had been sought or issued for the particular game and charges were brought under ss 9 and 10 of the Act, alleging respectively supply and possession with a view to the supply of infringing recordings.

15.25   These charges were dismissed before the magistrates, who held that the product in question did not come within the scope of the legislation. Section 1 of the Video Recordings Act 1984 defines a 'video work' as:

... any series of visual images (with or without sound)—

(a)   produced electronically by the use of information contained on any disc or magnetic tape; and
(b)   shown as a moving picture.

15.26   Although it was accepted that the disc in question satisfied the requirements of s 1(a) of the Video Recordings Act 1984, it was held that the images did not constitute a 'moving picture' by reason both of their brevity and of the staccato nature of the presentation, which appeared more akin to a series of still images. It was further held by the magistrates that the work in question was excluded from the legislation by the provisions of s 2, which provides that a video game is not to be subject to the classification requirements.

15.27   Both of these findings were reversed by the Divisional Court.[1] In a finding which may be contrasted with the dicta of the House of Lords in *R v Gold*[2] to the effect that the term 'recording' required storage for a more than transient period of time, it was held that the short duration of the images in no way prevented their being regarded as a 'moving picture'. A significant development arising from advent of fast and powerful personal computers has been the linkage between text, sound and graphics. In the present case, this relates to a computer game and picture sequences, but the same could be said of most multi-media products. It would appear arguable following the decision of the Divisional Court that many multi-media products could also be classed as video recordings, and hence be required to seek classification under the regulatory schema. Although there may be an argument in favour of such an approach, it would be difficult to explain to average computer users that their multi-media encyclopaedias are in reality video recordings.

1   *Meechie v Multi-Media Marketing* (1995) 94 LGR 474.
2   [1988] AC 1063.

15.28   The exemptions under the legislation apply to computer games and to works 'designed to inform, educate or instruct'. In the present case,[1] the court was able to separate the picture sequences from the game-playing element and so remove the former from the scope of the exemption. It must be likely that in the future there will be instances where video images are integrated more fully with the elements of a game, thereby making the classification more difficult. This will almost inevitably be the case with multi-media products. The court's dicta, which must be seen as affording a very restricted scope to the exemption, may make this of limited significance, and it would be arguable that many examples of multi-media products dealing with medical or artistic topics would be taken outside its scope.

1   *Meechie v Multi-Media Marketing* (1995) 94 LGR 474.

15.29   A further point which may be a cause for future difficulty concerns the definition of a moving picture. Although the finding of the court to the effect that the duration of a recording is of minimal significance in determining whether it is to be classed as a 'moving picture', there cannot have been many traditional recordings with a running time of less than 30 seconds. In the present case,[1] the images could be analogised to a more traditional cinematographic recording. In other computer-related products, the duration of individual picture sequences may be very much shorter. Even more problematically, a user may be afforded the opportunity to select particular aspects of an image for expansion or, perhaps, to manipulate the form of the still image. Such activities may present the impression of movement, but it is not clear how they should be regarded for the purpose of the legislation.

1   *Meechie v Multi-Media Marketing* (1995) 94 LGR 474.

Jurisdictional issues

15.30 A further, and perhaps more significant, issue concerns the difficulty of applying localised concepts of obscenity, which are dictated by cultural, religious and societal values in the global environment of the Internet. Attempts by Nottingham County Council to prevent publication on the Internet of a copy of a summary of a report into the handling by social work officials of a case of alleged Satanic abuse illustrate graphically the near impossibility of such an endeavour.[1] Following publication of a copy of the report on a UK-based website, the Council obtained a High Court injunction preventing publication of the report on the basis that its reproduction infringed their copyright. It was stated that the order extended to any hypertext links to other sites maintaining copies of the report. Although the order was observed within the UK, by the time it was issued, copies of the report were also to be found on a number of other websites around the world. A letter from Nottinghamshire's County Solicitor to the operator of a US website threatening legal proceedings unless its copy was removed drew a somewhat stinging response. Admitting to the presence of a copy of a report, it was pointed out that the Council:

> ... ignore the fact that I and my web site are located in Cleveland, Ohio, in the United States of America, a locus where the writs of the courts of the United Kingdom have never run.

As for the threat of legal action:

> My first reaction was simply to ignore this bit of silliness, grounded as it was on the misconception that the 'Copyright, Designs and Patents Act 1988' of the United Kingdom applies to actions taken in the United States when, as I trust you know, that Act specifically provides that copyright holders' exclusive rights apply only to 'acts in the United Kingdom' ...
>
> But I confess that I found your threats irritating enough that I began to think that I should comply with your demand – publicly. I have little difficulty in imagining the headlines that would have resulted had I taken such a course of action: 'English Prosecutor Forces U.S. Law Professor to Suppress Report on Satanic Social Workers' or 'Satanic Coverup Spreads to US'.
>
> After all, no one would have mirrored the Broxtowe report at their sites on the World Wide Web had you not sought to enjoin its original publication. One would have thought that you would have learned that lesson by now. There are at least a dozen web sites where the report is mirrored, not one of which would have existed if you had not sought to suppress its original publication on the web. And at my site alone the report has already been retrieved more than 2,500 times. For those of us who are opposed to governmental censorship of information on the World Wide Web, this reaction is gratifying. I doubt that it is so for your client.

[1] For a comprehensive collection of material on the case, see http://samsara.law.cwru.edu/comp_law/#Not.

15.31 Numerous other instances could be cited of the failure of attempts to impose national controls. In the, so called, Homulka case in Canada, a husband

and wife were accused of committing a horrendous double murder and were to be the subject of separate trials – the wife tendering a plea of 'guilty' to the charge of manslaughter. An order was made prohibiting the publication in Canada of any report of the hearings involving the wife until the husband's trial had been concluded. Once again, the ban was of some effect where traditional media were concerned, but served to prompt the establishment of a number of Usenet newsgroups, which carried full details of the case.

15.32 Other developments in the US raise a further issue which is of wider significance. The individual states retain power to determine what constitutes obscene material. This has raised questions whether the operators of online services may be subjected to the most restrictive laws of the range of jurisdictions where the service is made available. Whilst this may be the case in the situation where a service provider has a physical point of presence in a particular locality, in other instances:

> We may see a 'race to the bottom' of the type that created Delaware corporate law. Local jurisdictions may compete to provide a regulatory framework that rewards local placement of a hard disk. In a world of cheap bandwidth, users won't care where data is stored, any more than they care about where the corporate charter is filed ... Even if we don't see a rise of 'data havens', there will be a natural selection of regulatory regimes that favor the net.[1]

[1] *Legal Times*, 5 December 1994.

15.33 Against this, however, the case of *US v Thomas*[1] illustrates that parties located within one jurisdiction but offering services or facilities over the Internet may find themselves subject to the most restrictive legal regime reached by their activities. In this case, the defendants operated a computer bulletin board allowing subscribers to download pornographic images (which appear to have been placed on the system in breach of copyright in the original pictures). Subscribers, who were required to submit a written application giving details of name and address, could also order videos which would be delivered by post. Under US law, a federal statute provides that an offence is committed by a person who:

> ... knowingly transports in interstate or foreign commerce for the purpose of sale or distribution, or knowingly travels in interstate commerce, or uses a facility or means of interstate commerce for the purpose of transporting obscene material in interstate or foreign commerce, any obscene, lewd, lascivious, or filthy book, pamphlet, picture, film, paper, letter, writing, print, silhouette, drawing, figure, image, cast, photograph, recording, electrical transcription or other article capable of producing sound or any other matter of indecent or immoral character. (Title 18 USC 1465)

[1] 1997 US App LEXIS 12998.

15.34 The interpretation of this provision may vary between states, the Supreme Court having accepted that the determination of whether material is obscene is to be made having regard to 'contemporary community standards'. The material in question was considered lawful in California.

15.35 Following a number of complaints, a postal inspector in Tennessee subscribed to the board under an assumed name. In return for a fee of $55, he was able to download a number of images. The defendants were charged and convicted before the Tennessee courts of breach of the federal statute cited at para 15.33 above. Appealing against conviction, it was argued that material had not been transported by the defendants. Alternatively, it was contended that that the trial court had erred in applying Tennessee standards of morality. Both arguments are clearly significant in the context of WWW activities.

15.36 The argument against transportation is essentially a simple one. The material in question remained on the defendants' bulletin board. All that was transmitted was a series of intangible electrical impulses, whilst the terms of the statute related to tangible objects. This argument was rejected by the Court of Appeal:

> Defendants focus on the means by which the GIF files were transferred rather than the fact that the transmissions began with computer-generated images in California and ended with computer-generated images in Tennessee. The manner in which the images moved does not affect their ability to be viewed on a computer screen in Tennessee or their ability to be printed in hard copy in that distant location.[1]

[1] *US v Thomas* 1997 US App LEXIS 12998.

15.37 A similar approach would appear to apply in the UK. In July 1999, an individual pleaded guilty to several specimen charges of publishing obscene materials contrary to the provisions of the Obscene Publications Act 1959.[1] The pornographic materials in question were stored on computers in the US but could be accessed by customers in the UK (or anywhere else in the world) upon payment of a fee of around £20 per month.

[1] *R v Graham Waddon* (1999, Southwark Crown Court, unreported).

15.38 Two contentions were critical to the defendant's case. First, it was argued that publication of the material took place in the US. This argument was dismissed, with the judge ruling that publication took place whenever the images were downloaded onto a computer in the UK.[1] A further claim related to evidential requirements. As will be discussed in Chapter 16, the Police and Criminal Evidence Act 1984 requires that evidence be led indicating that a computer whose output is relied upon was operating properly at the relevant time. It was argued that this would have obliged the prosecution to lead information relating to the operation of the servers in the US. Once again, the judge ruled against the defence, holding that the requirement was limited to demonstrating the reliability of the computer used to access the materials in the UK.

[1] See also the ruling in the defamation case *Godfrey v Demon* [1999] EMLR 542, discussed at para 31.23 below.

15.39 Although of limited precedential value, the case, coupled with the US decision in *Thomas*,[1] provides useful evidence that the 'lowest common denominator' standard will not always prevail. The prosecutions, however, could only succeed because the defendants were or could be brought within the court's jurisdiction. Where service provider and user are located in different jurisdictions, enforcement will become much more problematic. Invariably, extradition will only be sanctioned by national authorities where the conduct complained of would constitute an offence if committed on its own territory. If the service providers had been resident in the US and had not made the mistake of entering the UK, it is unlikely that any prosecution could have been brought. In the Press Association report of the case, it was noted that:

> Vice Officers are increasingly finding that porn sites siphon subscription money through companies based in countries such as Costa Rica to avoid the attentions of authorities in Britain and the States. And while Internet Service Providers in Britain shut down sites after they are contacted by the police, Scotland Yard's appeals to American companies have fallen on deaf ears in a country where adult porn, however base, remains legal in some states.[2]

[1] *US v Thomas* 1997 US App LEXIS 12998.
[2] Press Association Newsfile, 30 July 1999.

15.40 With the development of Internet banking, it is a relatively simple matter for accounts to be opened and maintained in off-shore locations. Location is becoming an irrelevant consideration for ecommerce and in this, as in many other fields of activity, the prospects for effective national control are limited. As has been seen with Operation Ore, however, where the US authorities passed on details of credit card payments to their UK counterparts, there is evidence that international co-operation is increasing in this respect.

Conclusions

15.41 From media coverage, it is tempting to believe that Internet pornography poses massive challenges to the law. This is perhaps misleading. What has become clear over the past two decades is that it is difficult for nation states to enforce their own policies regarding what is or is not acceptable. There is no doubt that a computer user in the UK can readily access material which could not lawfully be purchased over (or under) the counter in a shop. There is very little that law enforcement agencies can do in this situation. Where matters take on a different aspect is where there is a commonality of approach between the jurisdiction where material is hosted and where it is accessed. In this, as in many other respects, the Council of Europe Convention on Cybercrime is a significant, albeit limited, development.

Chapter 16

Detecting and prosecuting computer crime

Introduction

16.1   The preceding chapters have considered a variety of forms of conduct which may affect adversely the interests of computer users. A number of computer-specific or general criminal offences have been identified as potentially relevant in such situations. Assuming that the fact of damage may be established, a variety of practical and legal problems may face the task of establishing the identity of the wrongdoer and obtaining sufficient evidence to support a criminal conviction. Issues of jurisdiction will also be of considerable significance in the situation where access is obtained to a computer system by means of some telecommunications link. In this situation, it is very possible that the perpetrator may be located in one jurisdiction and the victim in another.

Obtaining evidence of criminality

16.2   This may well include computers or other items of hardware upon which allegedly illegal material is held. In a memorandum submitted by the Association of Chief Police Officers of England, Wales and Northern Ireland to the Home Affairs Committee of the House of Commons in connection with its investigation into the subject of computer pornography,[1] the point was made that:

> ... it is quite possible that a computer system could be used for purposes other than the distribution of pornography. In such cases (e.g. a person using a computer at work for the publication of pornography) it would be wrong for investigators to seize the whole system. We recommend that there should be a provision that where the investigators can copy the required material from the system, this should be admissible as 'best evidence'.[2]

In the situation where the conduct occurs entirely on the premises of the victim, as in the case of *A-G's Reference (No 1 of 1991)*,[3] no particular problems may be anticipated in the acquisition of evidence. All matters will be within the control of the computer user and, assuming their willingness to co-operate, there are no legal problems facing the acquisition of evidence.

1   HC Paper 126 (1993–94). Home Affairs Committee: First report on Computer Pornography, 1994, London: HMSO.
2   HC Paper 126 (1993–94) p 33.
3   [1992] 3 WLR 432.

16.3   Greater difficulties arise where access is obtained remotely. The cases of *R v Gold*[1] and *R v Whiteley*[2] might be taken as illustrative of such situations. In both instances, the intruders obtained access to computer systems from their own homes. Certainly, in such a situation, it is open to the victim to make available to the police and prosecution authorities any evidence within their control. This might include details of the time at which access was obtained to the computer system and details of activities undertaken in respect of the system.

1   [1988] 1 AC 1063.
2   (1991) 93 Cr App Rep 25.

16.4   The problem may remain of identifying the intruder. The introduction of systems of caller identification might facilitate the task of obtaining such information, at least at the level of identifying the telephone number from which a call originated. In the absence of such systems, efforts will have to be made to trace the transmissions to their point of origin. Information as to the point of origin may have to be supplemented for the purpose of criminal prosecution by further evidence identifying a particular person or persons as being responsible for the conduct at issue. In the event, for example, that communications are traced to a telephone which is located in premises to which a number of people have access, it will be impossible to establish from this which of these is responsible for the activities in question. In this situation, the evidence obtained from identification of the point of origin of the communication will have to be supplemented. This will often require that a search be conducted of the premises in question.

The Regulation of Investigatory Powers Act 2000

16.5   This controversial statute replaces the Interception of Communications Act 1985. The provisions of the earlier statute had been designed to cover situations where voice telephony messages were intercepted in the course of their transmission over a telecommunications network. In a number of respects, the application of this statute has been overtaken by developments in technology. A particular factor has been the explosion in electronic communications. Unlike voice messages, which are transmitted and require to be intercepted in real time, email communications will be passed from one mail server to another en route to their destination. Copies of the messages will be made at each stage of the journey and may also be held on equipment belonging to an ISP, even after they have been read by the designated recipient. Such factors render easier the task of discovering the contents of email messages. Against this, however, the emergence of systems of cryptography as a tool which can be used by the average person means that interception of a message may reveal no useful or usable information.

16.6 The Regulation of Investigatory Powers Act 2000 retains the basic structure for the provision of warrants to authorise the interception of communications where this is considered by the Secretary of State to be necessary:

(a)   in the interests of national security;
(b)   for the purpose of preventing or detecting serious crime;
(c)   for the purpose of safeguarding the economic well-being of the UK; or
(d)   for giving effect to international mutual assistance agreements in connection with the prevention or detection of serious crime.[1]

[1]   Section 5.

16.7   Differences between the nature of voice and data traffic has promoted the decision to adopt a different basis for interceptory techniques in respect of the latter sector. Here, rather than seeking to intercept email and similar messages in the course of transmission, the Regulation of Investigatory Powers Act 2000 provides for this to take place at the premises of, and on the equipment of, ISP (or similar operators). The approach is justified on grounds of cost and efficiency. Individuals, it is suggested, may use a variety of methods to access services such as email. With systems such as 'hotmail', for example, it is a major selling point that users can access their accounts from anywhere in the world. It is argued that:

> These developments and others are resulting in a far more diverse range of technologies being used for access to the Internet. It may be expected that this diversity will increase further in the future.
>
> 2.4.7   The approach of intercepting Internet services in the telecommunications network, which requires a different interception solution for each service, will become less cost-effective as service diversity increases. It will also be difficult for the interception community to keep up with rapidly developing communication services.
>
> 2.4.8   It is also likely that a selected subscriber will utilise Internet services (eg a single email account) using multiple access technologies. Invocation of interception will therefore be more straightforward at the Internet Service Provider, rather than in multiple access networks.
>
> ...
>
> 2.4.11 There are a number of anonymous communication services that selected subscribers may exploit to access Internet services. Examples include pre-pay mobile phones and Internet cafés.
>
> 2.4.12 In these cases where a selected subscriber may not be identified through their access telecommunication service, interception of the selected subscriber's traffic may only be effected by intercepting the Internet service directly, eg access to a known email account or authentication with an ISP.[1]

[1]   'Technical and cost issues associated with interception of communications at certain communication service providers', report produced for the Home Office in conjunction

with the Regulation of Investigatory Powers Bill, available from http://www.homeoffice.gov.uk/oicd/techcost.pdf.

16.8   It may be argued to what extent these factors differ from those associated with voice traffic. Very many individuals will have land-based and mobile telephones and can also make use of public call boxes. The suspicion may be that the involvement of ISPs creates the potential for more effective and cost-efficient surveillance of electronic communications. In seeking to give effect to this policy, the Regulation of Investigatory Powers Act 2000 provides that:

> (1)   The Secretary of State may by order provide for the imposition by him on persons who—
>
>> (a)   are providing public postal services or public telecommunications services; or
>>
>> (b)   are proposing to do so
>
> of such obligations as it appears to him reasonable to impose for the purpose of securing that it is and remains practicable for requirements to provide assistance in relation to interception warrants to be imposed and complied with.[1]

Such obligations are only to be imposed following a system of statutory consultation[2] and subject to parliamentary approval.[3] It is provided that grants are to be given to ISPs to cover additional costs incurred in providing the interceptory capabilities required under the Act.[4]

[1]   Section 12.
[2]   Section 12(9).
[3]   Section 12(2).
[4]   Section 14.

16.9   These provisions were the subject of extensive parliamentary debate and controversy. Questions were raised concerning the practicality of intercepting messages sent using the packet switching system (PSS), given that these may be split into many different sections and routed in as many different ways. Concerns were also expressed that the requirement to maintain an interceptory capacity in systems would create a ready-made opening for hackers. Additionally, concerns were raised that the cost implications of introducing such facilities would impose a substantial burden upon UK-based ISPs and would therefore conflict with the government's oft-stated intention of making the country the world's most ecommerce-friendly environment. Against this, the argument was put by the government that obligations to provide for interception of communications have traditionally been imposed upon telecommunications companies and that ISPs are licensed under the same regime. Whilst correct, it may be noted that there are very significantly more small and medium-sized ISPs than there are telecommunications companies. It was suggested in Committee[1] that such providers would be compensated for marginal costs incurred in providing the necessary facilities. Implementing the Regulation of Investigatory Powers Act 2000's provisions, the Regulation of Investigatory Powers (Maintenance of Interception Capability) Order 2002,[2] applies to companies that provide a public telecommunications service to more than 10,000 customers. This will include mobile phone companies and ISPs. Such companies may be required by the

Secretary of State to maintain a capability to intercept communications at a level permitting the simultaneous interception and transmission to law enforcement agencies of transmissions in a ration of one for every 10,000 users. Responses are to be provided within one working day of receipt of a request for interception.

[1]   HC Official Report, SC F (Regulation of Investigatory Powers Bill), 28 March 2000 (morning).
[2]   SI 2002/1931.

16.10   More discussion surrounded the provisions of Chapter 2 of the Regulation of Investigatory Powers Act 2000, which provides for law enforcement agencies to seek access to communications data. Such access may be sought under less restrictive conditions than those required to authorise interception of communications. With modern communications systems, especially mobile networks, data of the kind at issue might be used to track movements of subscribers, whilst the detailed records of calls made and received could allow a detailed picture to be developed concerning the activities and relationships of individuals. It was indicated in Committee that a code of practice will be developed governing access to such data.

16.11   The final provision of the Regulation of Investigatory Powers Act 2000 which should be commented on in the context of information technology law concerns its provisions regarding encryption. The use of encryption is widely seen as providing a weapon to criminals to enable their plans to be communicated with minimal risk that, even if the communication is intercepted, its content could be deciphered. Various suggestions have been made by law enforcement agencies as to how the use of encryption might be regulated. One system which was proposed in the US would have seen user's depositing a copy of their encryption keys with an escrow organisation which could, in response to a warrant issued to a law enforcement agency, transmit the key to that agency. Within the UK, the development of cryptography support systems (or trusted third parties) would see such details being held by agencies. The Act provides that where encrypted material has been intercepted in accordance with its provisions and there are reasonable grounds to believe:

(a)   that a key to the protected information is in the possession of any person;
(b)   that the imposition of a disclosure requirement in respect of the protected information is—
    (i)   necessary on grounds falling within subsection (3); or
    (ii)   necessary for the purpose of securing the effective exercise or proper performance by any public authority of any statutory power or statutory duty,
(c)   that the imposition of such a requirement is proportionate to what is sought to be achieved by its imposition; and
(d)   that it is not reasonably practicable for the person with the appropriate permission to obtain possession of the protected information in an intelligible form without the giving of a notice under this section,

the person with that permission may, by notice to the person whom he believes to have possession of the key, require a disclosure requirement in respect of the protected information.[1]

Notices under this heading may be served either on the owner of the key or on any third party who holds a copy. As an alternative to disclosing the cryptographic key, a copy of the information in decrypted format may be supplied.[2] A deliberate failure to comply with such a notice will constitute an offence.[3]

[1] Section 49.
[2] Section 50(1).
[3] Section 53.

16.12 It remains uncertain how effective, or indeed how intrusive, the provisions of the Regulation of Investigatory Powers Act 2000 will be. There is no doubt that there is concern at the extent to which new communications technologies are threatening the effectiveness of traditional forms of law enforcement. As was said by the Minister of State at the Home Office in Committee:

> I should emphasise what the Home Secretary stated on Second Reading: we expect law enforcement to suffer as a result of the development of new technologies. That is a fact of life. That applies not only to encryption, which has been widely discussed, but to more fundamental developments in communications technology. We are trying to preserve as much as we can of valuable intelligence, while always focusing on the key purposes set out in clause 5 and remaining consistent with our e-commerce objectives. We should not adopt – and the hon. Gentleman is not proposing – a philosophy of despair, of saying that we can do nothing about the matter or make any progress. However, we acknowledge that law enforcement will suffer from the development of new technology. Communications will be missed. We cannot establish a system that is totally rigid.[1]

The challenge for any new legislation in this field is to provide for effective systems of crime prevention and detection without affecting adversely the rights of the vast majority of totally innocent individuals. It does seem clear that as more and more personal information is recorded in electronic format, so the balance will have to be struck between protecting personal privacy and making use of what can be a valuable intelligence resource for law enforcement agencies.

[1] HC Official Report SC F (Regulation of Investigatory Powers Bill), 28 March 2000 (morning).

Search warrants

16.13 Provisions relating to the grant of search warrants are contained in the Police and Criminal Evidence Act 1984 and, in respect of the basic offence, in the Computer Misuse Act 1990 itself. The provisions of the Copyright, Designs and Patents Act 1988[1] may also be relevant in respect of cases where software piracy is suspected. The offences under ss 2 and 3 of the Computer Misuse Act 1990 may class as serious arrestable offences for the purposes of the 1984 Act.[2] In this event, an application may be made to a justice of the peace for a search warrant, who, if satisfied that a serious arrestable offence has been committed and that evidence relevant to the case is likely to be found on specified premises, may issue a search warrant.[3] Such a warrant will, with the exception of specified material,[4] empower the seizure of any item of property which is reasonably considered to relate to the offence under investigation. In addition, it is provided that where information is contained in a computer, the constable exercising the warrant may require that a print-out be taken of that information if it is considered 'necessary to do so in order to prevent it being concealed, lost, tampered with or destroyed'.[5]

[1]   Section 9.
[2]   Section 116.
[3]   Section 8. In certain cases, as prescribed in s 17, a search may take place without a warrant.
[4]   Section 14.
[5]   Section 19(4).

16.14   In the US, seizure of computers and software was at issue in the celebrated *Steve Jackson* case, where the prolonged detention of the equipment was held by the courts to violate the constitutional guarantees of free speech.[1] Although the submission of the Association of Chief Police Officers suggests that innocent service providers should not be penalised for the actions of their users, there have been suggestions that extensive use has been made of the power of search and seizure. Under the provisions of the Police and Criminal Evidence Act 1984, it is provided that: 'Nothing may be retained ... if a photograph or copy would be sufficient for that purpose.'[2] One barrister has been quoted as saying that more extensive and prolonged seizures have been justified on the basis that the equipment itself is needed as evidence at the trial.[3]

[1]   *Steve Jackson Games Inc v United States Secret Service* 816 F Supp 432 (1993); affirmed 36 F 3d 457 (1994).
[2]   Section 22(4).
[3]   Alistair Kelman, quoted in 'Privacy: The Strong Arm of the Law' *Guardian*, 22 September 1994.

16.15   In respect of the basic offence, the Law Commission's recommendation was that there should be no provision for the issuing of a search warrant. In parliamentary debate, the case was argued that such a facility would be needed if there were to be any realistic possibility of the Computer Misuse Act 1990, s 1 offence being enforced. Particular reference was made to the situation where premises were subject to multiple entry. Although search warrants are not generally made available in respect of summary offences, the Minister of State accepted that:

> ... the basic hacking offence ... is not untypically committed in a private house, remote from public gaze and with no one else present. I am not saying that this is a unique offence, but I cannot immediately think of many others that are committed in private houses to which the police have no access and that do not involve some party other than the offender.[1]

[1]   HC Official Report, SC C (Computer Misuse Bill), col 65, 28 March 1990.

16.16   An amendment was accordingly made to the Bill, providing that a search warrant might be issued by a circuit judge where there are 'reasonable grounds for believing' that a Computer Misuse Act 1990, s 1 offence has been or is about to be committed in the premises identified in the application.[1] This provision does not extend to Scotland, it being stated in Parliament that equivalent powers already existed in Scotland, where applications for a warrant would be made to a Sheriff.

[1]   Section 14.

Jurisdictional issues

16.17   A practical problem relating to the prosecution of computer crime has previously been identified, in as much as the perpetrator of the conduct and the victim computer may be located within different jurisdictions. This is not, of course, an issue which is peculiar to instances of computer crime, but may occur in respect of many instances of fraud. A very simple example might see a person resident in Liverpool ordering goods from a mail order firm based in Edinburgh tendering in payment a cheque which is known to be worthless.

16.18   In both England and Scotland, the status of the law relating to jurisdiction is unclear. The Law Commission have called for urgent reform in the area, arguing that:

> International fraud is a serious problem ... It is essential that persons who commit frauds related to this country should not be able to avoid the jurisdiction of this country's courts simply on outdated or technical ground, or because of the form in which they cloak the substance of their fraud.[1]

[1]   Jurisdiction over Fraud Offences with a Foreign Element (1989) Law Com no 180 para 2.7.

16.19   The Scottish Law Commission indicated that the approach of the Scottish courts has been to claim jurisdiction in the event that the 'main act' of the offence occurred within Scotland.[1] Until recently, the view has been taken that the 'main act' occurs when the fraud produces its result. In the example given, this would happen in Edinburgh when the goods were posted to the customer. A somewhat different approach is evident in the recent case of *Laird v HM Advocate*.[2] This concerned a complex case of fraud in which individuals resident in Scotland fraudulently induced other parties to enter into a contract for the sale of a quantity of steel, the steel to be supplied from England. In this situation, the application of the 'main act' test would appear to dictate that the Scottish courts would not be entitled to claim jurisdiction. In the event, criminal proceedings were instituted and convictions secured in Scotland. An appeal against conviction based on the lack of jurisdiction was rejected by the High Court. Two main points can be identified in the decision of the Lord Justice Clerk (Wheatley). First, it was suggested, where a 'continuous crime' is involved there may be dual jurisdiction within both countries concerned. In terms of the circumstances under which the Scottish courts might claim jurisdiction he commented:

353

... where a crime is of such a nature that it has to originate with the forming of a fraudulent scheme, and that thereafter various steps have to be taken to bring that fraudulent plan to fruition, if some of these subsequent steps take place in one jurisdiction and some in another, then if the totality of the events in one country plays a material part in the operation and fulfilment of the fraudulent scheme as a whole there should be jurisdiction in that country.[3]

1   Sc Law Consultative Memorandum no 68 (1986) para 7.1.e.
2   1984 SCCR 469.
3   1984 SCCR 469 at 472.

16.20   The concept of joint jurisdiction is one which the Scottish Law Commission recommended should be adopted in respect of any new statutory offences which might result from their deliberations. In similar vein, the Law Commission recommended that the English courts should enjoy jurisdiction when either the perpetrator or the victim computer was located within England.[1] This approach as been adopted in the Computer Misuse Act 1990, although the enabling provisions are somewhat tortuous. Separate provision is made for Scotland, England and Wales and Northern Ireland.

1   Law Commission Report no 186 (1989) para 4.2.

16.21   The basis for any court to claim jurisdiction will be the existence of a 'significant link' with the country in question.[1] In this respect, the provisions relating to jurisdiction can be divided into two categories with the Computer Misuse Act 1990, s 1 and s 3 offences being considered together. In respect of these, a domestic court will have jurisdiction if either the accused person was located in the territory at the time the conduct complained of occurred or the computer to which access was obtained or whose data or programs were modified was so located.

1   Section 5.

16.22   The provisions relating to Computer Misuse Act 1990, s 2 offences are considerably more complicated. Under these, a domestic court may claim jurisdiction in three circumstances:[1]

1.   All aspects of the conduct take place in that country.
2.   The further offence referred to in s 2 is intended to take place in that country, regardless of whether the 'significant link' required for the establishment of the unauthorised access component of the offence can be established. Effectively, this means that the victim computer will be located in the territory.
3.   The 'significant link' requirement can be satisfied in respect of the domestic country and the further offence will be committed (either wholly or in part) in a country (or countries) which recognise such conduct as constituting an offence. In this event, it will also be necessary for the further conduct to satisfy the s 2 requirements of seriousness.

1   See s 7 (adding a new s 1(1A) to the Criminal Law Act 1977 for England and Wales, s 13 for Scotland and s 16 for Northern Ireland).

Procedural matters and extradition

16.23   Proceedings for an offence under the Computer Misuse Act 1990, s 1 must be brought within six months from the date when the prosecutor or procurator fiscal obtained sufficient evidence to warrant proceedings.[1] No proceedings may be brought more than three years after the commission of the offence.[2]

[1]   Sections 11(2), 12(3).
[2]   Sections 11(3), 12(4).

16.24   Finally, in considering issues relating to the application of the Computer Misuse Act 1990, the provisions of s 15 should be noted. This provides that a person resident in the UK may be extradited to another country where it is alleged that they have engaged in conduct which would, in the UK, constitute an offence under s 2 or s 3 of the Computer Misuse Act 1990.

The computer in court

16.25   In many cases, the major evidence indicating that a crime has been committed will be generated by a computer. In cases where a computer fraud has been perpetrated, the evidence may be found in the computer records themselves. In such instances, it will be vital for the prosecution's case that they should be permitted to produce such evidence in court. Two situations will be considered in which difficulties may arise. The first concerns the situation when the computer serves to record information supplied by some person. Here, any records which may subsequently be obtained from the computer might be regarded as falling under the prohibition against hearsay evidence. The second situation concerns the situation where the evidence is effectively generated by the computer itself. Many breath-analysing devices used to detect instances of drink-driving use microprocessors to process a sample of breath, providing a print-out of the resultant analysis. Here, the challenge to the evidence may be based more on considerations of reliability.

Hearsay evidence

16.26   One of the landmark cases in the law of evidence is that of *Myers v DPP*.[1] The case concerned an alleged conspiracy to deal in stolen motor vehicles. Evidence produced by the vehicle manufacturers at the time of the production of the vehicles was critical to the prosecution's case. As the vehicles moved along the production line, workers recorded details of the serial numbers of the various components fitted to a particular vehicle. These details were recorded on a card by the worker responsible. Eventually, the completed card was photographed and recorded on microfilm. By a 3-2 majority, the House of Lords held that this evidence would be inadmissible as hearsay. As the prosecution had failed to produce evidence demonstrating reason why the workers responsible for making the original records could not give evidence, there was no justification for admitting the microfilm.

¹   [1965] AC 1001.

The Criminal Evidence Act 1965

16.27   The decision in *Myers*[1] was effectively and speedily reversed by the enactment of the Criminal Evidence Act 1965. This short measure provided that documentary hearsay evidence could be admitted where the document was:

1.   created in the course of a trade or business;
2.   from information supplied by a person who might reasonably be supposed to have personal knowledge of the information contained therein; and
3.   where the person in question is dead, beyond the seas or could not reasonably be expected to have any recollection of the matters contained in the record.[2]

This would be the case in a situation such as *Myers*, where it would be unreasonable to expect a factory worker to have any direct recollection of the numbers entered on to one card when they may well have entered hundreds of such numbers every working day.

¹   *Myers v DPP* [1965] AC 1001.
²   Section 1.

16.28   The provisions of the Criminal Evidence Act 1965 were first tested in a computer context in the case of *R v Pettigrew*.[1] Pettigrew was convicted of theft of a quantity of money. Critical evidence was contained in a computer print-out from the Bank of England, which indicated that the banknotes found in Pettigrew's possession had been sent to a bank in Newcastle. The records had been generated by a machine in the bank which fulfilled two functions. A quantity of banknotes would be inserted by a bank employee. The machine would check the notes for validity, rejecting any defective specimens. It would then divide the notes into bundles of 100 and produce a print-out showing the serial number of the first and the last note in each bundle, together with a note of the numbers of any rejected notes. It was accepted that the notes would be numbered sequentially. Pettigrew having been convicted, an appeal was made on the issue of the admissibility of the computer evidence. This appeal succeeded, the Court of Appeal holding that the requirements of s 1 were not satisfied, as the bank employee responsible for operating the machine had no personal knowledge of the information produced.

¹   (1980) 71 Cr App Rep 120.

16.29   The decision in *Pettigrew*[1] was subjected to extensive criticism. In particular, it was argued that the evidence in question should not have been classed as hearsay evidence, but rather as evidence generated directly by the machine. This view was supported by a subsequent decision of the Court of Appeal in the case of *R v Wood*.[2] This case concerned the admissibility of computer-processed evidence concerning the composition of a quantity of metals which were alleged to have been stolen by the appellant. It was held by the Court of Appeal that the provisions of the Criminal Evidence Act 1965 were not applicable. The analysis in question had been carried out by scientists acting on behalf of the prosecution authorities. As such, they were not acting in the course of a trade or business. The evidence should rather, it was held, be considered as direct evidence. The computer was being used as a calculator and the question for the court was whether sufficient evidence had been submitted indicating that its output could be relied upon. This was held to be the case.

1 *R v Pettigrew* (1980) 71 Cr App Rep 120.
2 (1983) 76 Cr App Rep 23.

16.30 In *Wood*, the case of *Pettigrew*[1] was distinguished almost out of existence, the Lord Chief Justice indicating that it was to be considered authority only for the proposition that:

> ... where it is sought to make a document admissible under the Act, the requirements of the Act have to be satisfied and one of those requirements is a personal knowledge of the person or persons who supplied the information to the record keeper.[2]

The application of the Criminal Evidence Act 1965 was undoubtedly critical in the case of *R v Ewing*.[3] In this case, the appellant had been convicted of theft on the basis, inter alia, of computer print-outs generated by a bank's computer detailing transactions in respect of particular accounts. Before the Court of Appeal, counsel for the appellant contended on the authority of *Pettigrew* that this evidence should not have been admitted. This contention was rejected, the court holding that all the statutory conditions required for the admissibility of the evidence had been satisfied. *Pettigrew* was once again distinguished as a case decided on the basis of a particular factual situation.

1 *R v Pettigrew* (1980) 71 Cr App Rep 120.
2 *R v Wood* (1983) 76 Cr App Rep 23 at 29.
3 [1983] 2 All ER 645.

16.31 The provisions of the Criminal Evidence Act 1965 remain in force for Scotland. This was the cause of some judicial criticism in the case of the *Lord Advocate's Reference (No 1 of 1992)*,[1] although the case also demonstrates a more robust attitude towards the admissibility of computer-generated evidence. Two persons had been accused and acquitted of charges of fraud against a building society. In the course of the trial, computer-generated evidence had been held inadmissible as hearsay by the Sheriff. The Lord Advocate sought the opinion of the High Court on the question as to whether evidence of the kind at issue should be admissible.

1 1992 SLT 1010.

16.32 The computer evidence in question had been generated by computers operated by a health authority. In line with the finding in *Wood*,[1] it was held that this took it outside the scope of the Criminal Evidence Act 1965 as the records were not made in the course of a trade or business. The High Court considered the judgment of the House of Lords in *Myers*[2] and concluded that the judgments of the dissenting minority more accurately reflected Scots law on this point. The High Court, it was stated by the Lord Justice General:

> ... has shown itself willing to adapt the criminal law of this country in order to meet changes in social conditions and attitudes ... In my opinion that is a proper exercise of the judicial function and it is within the inherent power of this court.[3]

[1]   *R v Wood* (1983) 76 Cr App Rep 23 at 29.
[2]   *Myers v DPP* [1965] AC 1001.
[3]   *Lord Advocate's Reference (No 1 of 1992)* 1992 SLT 1010 at 1017.

16.33   The information in question had been generated through the activities of a number of employees. It was impossible to state which employee had been responsible for entering a particular piece of information. The procurator had sought to present the evidence of the health authority's computer operations controller regarding the contents of the information. This evidence was rejected as hearsay by the Sheriff. The High Court disagreed, with the Lord Justice General holding that the computer evidence would be admitted as the best available evidence, subject to it being established that it would be impossible to produce any other witnesses. It was not considered appropriate for the court to try to define the circumstances under which this might be the case, but the suggestion was made that:

> ... the reliability and sophistication of modern systems for the storage and retrieval of information electronically may well result in impossibility. Hard copy may be destroyed because it can be assumed that there is no need to refer to it, and checks carried out at the time of entry may make the keeping of references to its authorship unnecessary.[1]

[1]   *Lord Advocate's Reference (No 1 of 1992)* 1992 SLT 1010 at 1018.

The Police and Criminal Evidence Act 1984

16.34   If judicial activism has provided a Scottish response to the perceived limitations of the Criminal Evidence Act 1965, the English approach to reform was contained in the Police and Criminal Evidence Act 1984. Following the recommendations of the Roskill Committee on Fraud Trials,[1] the provisions of the Criminal Justice Act 1988[2] introduced more liberal rules for the admissibility of documentary evidence. Initially, the Police and Criminal Evidence Act 1984 contained provisions relating to documentary evidence in general. These provisions, as now contained in the 1988 Act, provide for its admissibility in circumstances broadly similar to those envisaged under the Criminal Evidence Act 1965, but applying in situations where the document is produced other than in the course of a trade or business. Additionally, the Police and Criminal Evidence Act 1984 provides in s 69 that:

> In any proceedings, a statement in a document produced by a computer shall not be admissible as evidence of any fact stated therein unless it is shown – (a) that there are no reasonable grounds for believing that the statement is inaccurate because of improper use of the computer; (b) that at all material times the computer was operating properly, or if not, that any respect in which it was not operating properly or was out of operation was not such as to affect the production of the document or the accuracy of its content.

It is further provided that rules of court may be made to require that a statement to this effect be given in a prescribed form. Schedule 3 to the 1984 Act provides that where a certificate is tendered as evidence of any of the matters referred to above:

> ... a certificate (a) identifying the document containing the statement and describing the manner in which it was produced; (b) giving such particulars of any device employed in the production of that document as may be appropriate for the purpose of showing that the document was produced by a computer; (c) dealing with any of the matters mentioned in section 69(1) above; and (d) purporting to be signed by a person occupying a responsible position in relation to the operation of the computer, shall be evidence of anything stated in it.[3]

[1]	HMSO, 1986.
[2]	Section 24.
[3]	Part III, para 8.

16.35 The provisions of the Police and Criminal Evidence Act 1984 were at issue before the Court of Appeal in the case of *R v Minors, R v Harper*.[1] The court considered the status of ss 68 and 69 of the Act, commenting that:

> In the courts below, it was assumed by all that section 69 constitutes a self-contained code governing the admissibility of computer records in criminal proceedings.[2]

[1]	[1989] 2 All ER 208.
[2]	[1989] 2 All ER 208 at 212.

16.36 This, it was held, was not the case, the statutory requirements being cumulative rather than alternative. In the first appeal, the appellant had been convicted of offences of attempted deception and the use of a false instrument. These offences involved the use of a passbook. The conduct had related to a building society. A computer print-out produced by the building society indicated that the last four entries in the passbook were false. Although evidence was led concerning the reliability of the computer equipment used to produce the print-out, no attempt was made to establish the requirements of s 68 of the Police and Criminal Evidence Act 1984. This, it was held by the Court of Appeal, rendered the evidence inadmissible although the conviction was sustained on the basis of other evidence.

16.37 In the second appeal, the appellant had been convicted of handling stolen goods in the form of a London Transport travel pass. Details of the pass were recorded on a computer operated by London Transport and a print-out was supplied to the court. The print-out was produced by a revenue protection official who had no knowledge of the manner in which the computer functioned and could not testify as to its reliability. The judge ruled that this evidence satisfied the requirements of s 69 of the Police and Criminal Evidence Act 1984. The Court of Appeal disagreed, holding that the witness was not suitably qualified to testify to matters coming within the ambit of s 69. Additionally, it was held that the evidence should have been declared inadmissible as no attempt had been made to satisfy the requirements of s 68.

16.38   The linkage identified by the Court of Appeal[1] between the requirements of the Police and Criminal Evidence Act 1984, ss 68 and 69 was further at issue in the case of *R v Spiby*.[2] Once again, the Court of Appeal was faced with a question of the admissibility of computer-generated evidence. In this case, the evidence took the form of an automatically produced print-out of details of telephone calls made from a hotel room. The equipment was used by the hotel to bill its customers for any telephone calls made. Upholding the findings of the Recorder in the Crown Court, it was held that given the automated nature of the equipment in question, the evidence had to be regarded as real as opposed to hearsay evidence. In this case, it was held, the provisions of s 69 of the 1984 Act were not applicable.

[1]   *R v Minors, R v Harper* [1989] 2 All ER 208.
[2]   (1990) 91 Cr App Rep 186.

16.39   More recently, the application of the Police and Criminal Evidence Act 1984 has been discussed by the House of Lords in the case of *R v Shepherd*.[1] The appellant had been convicted of theft by shoplifting. Significant evidence in the case against her had been constituted by the print-outs from computer-controlled tills. These purported to show that no goods of the kind alleged to have been stolen by the appellant had been sold on the day in question. Evidence as to the till receipts and their reliability was led by a store detective. This witness explained the manner in which the tills operated and the procedures which had been conducted in order to examine the till receipts. It was also stated that no problems had been identified with the operation of the equipment.

[1]   [1993] 1 All ER 225.

16.40   The evidence of the store detective being held admissible, the appellant was convicted. An appeal against conviction being dismissed by the Court of Appeal, a final appeal was made to the House of Lords.[1] This proved no more successful, although their Lordships expressed a measure of disagreement with the earlier decisions of the Court of Appeal in this area.

[1]   *R v Shepherd* [1993] 1 All ER 225.

16.41   The point of divergence centred upon the relationship between ss 68 and 69 of the Police and Criminal Evidence Act 1984. In *R v Minors*, the attempt to link the requirements of ss 68 and 69 led to the statement that:

... to the extent to which a computer is merely used to perform functions of calculation, no question of hearsay is involved and the requirements of ss 68 and 69 do not apply.[1]

[1]   [1988] 2 All ER 208 at 212.

16.42   Delivering the leading judgment in the House of Lords, Lord Griffith stated that no authority existed to support this proposition.[1] In so far as this dictum had been followed by the Court of Appeal in *Spiby*,[2] that decision was overruled. The application of s 69 of the Police and Criminal Evidence Act 1984, it was held, extended to all cases where the admissibility of computer-generated evidence was at issue, not merely cases when the evidence was hearsay in nature.

[1]   *R v Minors* [1988] 2 All ER 208 at 212.
[2]   *R v Spiby* (1990) 91 Cr App Rep 186.

16.43   The next issue to be determined was whether the evidence submitted in the present case satisfied the requirements of the section. Although the evidence of a revenue protection official had been declared inadmissible in the case of *R v Harper*, that of the store detective was held admissible. Making reference to the provisions of Sch 3 to the Police and Criminal Evidence Act 1984 regarding the issuance of a certificate relating to the operation of a computer, it was held that a person giving oral evidence need not possess the qualifications which would be required of such a signatory. Particular stress was laid upon the point that the evidence of such a witness might be challenged in the course of cross-examination. Lord Griffiths commented that:

> Documents produced by computers are an increasingly common feature of all business and more and more people are becoming familiar with their uses and operation. Computers vary immensely in their complexity and in the operations they perform. The nature of the evidence to discharge the burden of showing that there has been no improper use of the computer and that it was operating properly will inevitably vary from case to case. The evidence must be suited to meet the needs of the case.[1]

[1]   [1993] 1 All ER 225 at 231.

16.44   The decision of the House of Lords in *R v Shephard*[1] has been criticised as rendering too easy the task of tendering computer-generated evidence in criminal cases. Such criticism may be unfair. Almost since the enactment of the Police and Criminal Evidence Act 1984, calls have been made for the replacement of formal rules of admissibility by more general codes of practice relating to the weight properly to be attached to items of computer evidence.[2] Mechanistic formulations as to the forms of evidence deemed acceptable are always likely to run the risk of being rendered obsolete by developments in technology. Recent judicial tendencies in both Scotland and England might, at least on one analysis, demonstrate a welcome degree of flexibility in allowing the admission of evidence to the judicial forum wherein its weight might legitimately be challenged.

[1]   [1993] 1 All ER 225.

2   See the VERDICT and APPEAL studies carried out by the Central Computer and Telecommunications Agency and summarised in Castell 'The Legal Admissibility of Computer Generated Evidence' (1984) 2 CLSR 2.

Chapter 17

Intellectual property law

The nature of intellectual property law

17.1   The subject of intellectual property has had a long and varied history. Introduced during the Middle Ages, it initially aroused considerable controversy. From the eighteenth century, however, it almost faded from the popular consciousness. Even for lawyers it was often seen as a somewhat esoteric subject. Until very recently, few law degrees exposed students to more than the most cursory examination of its scope and role and few legal practitioners would have any dealings with the topic.

17.2   As this book has sought to describe, times are changing and the needs of the information society differ from those of its industrial predecessor. Information has become a commodity as valuable as coal or steel in previous eras. During the late 1980s the proportion of the GDP of countries such as the US and the UK relating to the manufacturing sector dropped below 50% for the first time since the early stages of the industrial revolution. The services sector is now responsible for most of our national income. Software (and electronic information services) makes up a significant and growing element of the sector. In its Green Paper *Copyright and Related Rights in the Information Society*,[1] the EC indicate that 'activities covered by copyright and related rights account for an estimated 3–5% of Community gross domestic product'. The European information services market itself has been valued at almost €2.2bn (approximately £1.5bn) per annum. Intellectual property has become an important element in international trade, to the extent that it is the subject of a protocol to the GATT agreement.[2] As will be discussed, the GATT and the World Trade Organization established under its auspices are playing significant roles in the development of intellectual property law.

[1]   http://www.ispo.cec.be/infosoc/legreg/com95382.doc.
[2]   *Agreement on Trade Related Aspects of Intellectual Property Rights, Including Trade in Counterfeit Goods.* This agreement obliges signatories to recognise the main forms of intellectual property rights in their domestic laws and to 'accord to the nationals of other Members treatment no less favourable than that it accords to its own nationals' (art 3).

17.3   The nature and purposes of systems of intellectual property have evolved over centuries. Copyright in particular has proved to be a very flexible concept being extended over the years to forms of recording technologies which could scarcely have been envisaged when the system originated. Even the most pliable objects, however, have a breaking point and notions which were appropriate in an analogue age when the information industry was a relatively minor player on the national and global stage may not be appropriate for the information society. In some instances, debate and controversy concerning the operation of the system reaches levels not seen since the introduction of the concepts. The emergence of the World Trade Organization is projecting issues of intellectual property onto the global stage. This is especially noticeable in the field of patent law which traditionally has been much more nationally based and geographically limited than the more ubiquitous copyright system. Although there is no doubt that intellectual property is currently of greater importance than ever before, a system which is based on the notion of exclusive rights sits uneasily with the distributive nature of increasingly networked societies.

Forms of intellectual property rights

17.4   In general terms, the phrase 'intellectual property' can be regarded as encompassing anything emanating from the working of the human brain: ideas, concepts inventions, stories, songs – the list is almost unending. A basic distinction has to be drawn between intellectual property – which, as indicated above, covers a vast range of material – and intellectual property rights, which delimits the subject to encompass those aspects of the topic which receive a measure of legal protection.

17.5   Three main forms of right have traditionally been identified as operating in this area of the law:

- Patents.
- Copyright.
- Trade marks.

In terms of terminology, a distinction is sometimes drawn between industrial and intellectual property rights. The former term refers to topics which are of practical application and importance. One of the key criteria for the award of a patent, for example, is that the subject matter should be capable of 'industrial application'. Trade marks, which seek to protect a holder's economic interests in some form of trading name or sign, can also be classed under this heading, as can the law of designs which protects aspects of the design of products, such as a motor car or a table. Although beauty is always in the eye of the beholder, the essential feature of these systems is that they protect items which serve some functional purpose. Intellectual property rights, principally the copyright system, are concerned with the protection of rights in some aesthetic or artistic work. Protection of literary, artistic, musical and dramatic works is at the core of the copyright regime. If consideration is given to the nature of computer software, it will be apparent that it exists at the interstices of the industrial and intellectual property systems. Software, especially at the level of operating systems, is concerned with function, yet concepts such as 'ease of use' are also of great importance. Recognising this situation, the term 'intellectual property law' will be used throughout this book as denoting all forms of intellectual and industrial property rights.

17.6 The patent and copyright systems both have a lengthy lineage dating back to the Middle Ages. Traditionally, patents have provided the means for protecting and rewarding the practical work of inventors, whilst copyright has operated in more aesthetic areas of human activity, such as music, art and literature. Both systems seek to protect creative or intellectual effort by conferring an exclusive right on the owner in respect of the exploitation of a protected work. The system of registered trade marks originated in the Trade Marks Act 1875 and serves to provide an indication of the origin of a product. Typically, marks might consist of brand names or logos. Until the emergence of the WWW, trade marks played a very limited role in the information technology field. Certainly brand names, such as 'Microsoft', would be protected, but no specific information technology issues arose. With the emergence of Internet domain names as described in Chapter 2, matters assumed a very different perspective and trade mark law (together with its common law relative, the doctrine of 'passing off') has come to assume considerable significance.

17.7 At the outset, it may be stated that the role of intellectual property rights is to confer rights on the person responsible for conceiving ideas and reducing these to some usable format. In some situations, most notably concerned with the patent system, the right is close to the monopoly entitlement associated with the ownership of items of real property. In the case of copyright, however, the right is much more limited. The difference between the two regimes might be illustrated by reference to the story of Alexander Graham Bell and Elisha Grey. Both men invented the telephone. Alexander Graham Bell reached the US Patent Office slightly ahead of Grey. The patent system works in large measure on the principle 'first come, first served'. Bell was awarded a patent and the exclusive right to exploit the technology described therein. Even though Grey had worked totally independently, he was unable to exploit his own work as this would have conflicted with Bell's patent. In the event that the case should have centred on a copyright claim, Bell's protection would have been limited to preventing the copying of his work. Grey would not have infringed Bell's copyright and would, indeed, have obtained his own copyright for his own work. Patents, it might be concluded, confer a monopoly whereas copyright can only be invoked to prevent copying or certain other forms of unfair exploitation of the work.

Intellectual property rights and software

17.8 Until recently, the law of copyright was seen as having the most relevance to information-related products and activities. At a time when software development was widely seen as an art or craft rather than an industrial process, it was a relatively simple step to class computer programs as a form of literary work – an approach which features in many national and international copyright instruments. The patent system has always been seen as applying to the industrial sector and, initially, was regarded as having little application in the computer field. This approach was relatively easy to support and apply in the days when computers were large, stand-alone machines used mainly for the making of mathematical calculations. With the spread of computers and the introduction of microprocessors, it is a rare industrial process which is not influenced by some form of computer program. We invariably talk in terms of 'the software industry' and the software company Microsoft is now the world's most valuable company. The exclusion of software from the patent system has become increasingly difficult to defend.

17.9 The question whether and to what extent software should be considered patentable has been the subject of considerable debate over the past two decades. During the 1970s and 1980s, when the judicial tendency appeared to favour the liberal application of provisions of copyright law, the role of the patent system seemed to have been marginalised. More recent decisions in both the US and Europe have marked a retrenchment in this line of judicial thinking. In the leading US authority of *Computer Associates v Altai*,[1] the Court of Appeals opined that:

> Generally we think that copyright registration, with its indiscriminating availability – is not ideally suited to deal with the highly dynamic technology of computer science ... patent registration, with its exacting up-front novelty and non-obviousness requirements, might be the more appropriate rubric of protection for intellectual property of this kind.[2]

Decisions by the patent authorities and courts in a range of countries have indicated increasing willingness to allow patents to be granted for what are frequently referred to as 'software-related inventions'. Whilst the criteria for the grant of a patent are considerably more demanding than those relating to the acquisition of copyright, the greater legal strength of this form of protection is making the patent route increasingly the preferred option for software developers.

[1]   982 F 2d 694 (1992).
[2]   982 F 2d 694 (1992) at 712.

17.10 If copyright and patents can be seen as overlapping to some extent, the role of trade mark law is significantly different. In the first edition of this book, written no more than seven years ago, the topic received only the most passing mention.[1] The role of a trade mark is to serve to distinguish the goods or services offered by one party from those of anyone else. The current UK law concerning trade marks is to be found in the Trade Marks Act 1994, which itself seeks to implement the EU Directive to approximate the laws of the Member States relating to trademarks.[2] Also relevant is the common law doctrine of 'passing off'. As the name suggests, this operates to prevent a party using names or other indicators which are likely to mislead third parties as to the true identity of the person with whom they are dealing. Typically, the impression will be given that a person is connected with some well known and regarded organisation.

1   To note that the names of IT companies such as Apple and Microsoft were protected by trade marks along with devices such as logos.
2   Directive 89/104/EEC (the Trade Mark Directive), OJ 1998 L 40/1,

17.11   A trade mark may consist of anything which may be recorded in graphical format. Traditionally, marks have tended to take the forms of names or logos but the scope is increasing, with sounds and even smells forming the subject matter of trade mark applications. For the present purpose, attention can be restricted to the use of names. Given the increasing commercialisation of the Internet, organisations frequently seek the registration of a domain name which creates an obvious link with their real-life activities. The software company Microsoft, for example, can be found at http://microsoft.com. In many cases indeed, firms have obtained trade mark registration for their domain name as such. Amazon.com, for example, is a registered trade mark in the US.

New forms of protection

17.12   As will be discussed in the following chapters, the task of fitting software and software-related applications into traditional forms of intellectual property law has not been a simple one. In some areas, the attempt has been made to develop new, specialised forms of protection. The two main areas in which this has been attempted have been in the fields of database and semiconductor chip design protection. In both areas, the impetus for reform in the UK has lain in EU Directives. Whilst providing specialised or sui generis forms of protection, both regimes draw heavily on the principles and policies of copyright law.

Lessons from history

17.13   In our fast-changing societies it is tempting to conclude that history has few lessons to teach us. Much depends, perhaps, on whether we see change as evolutionary or revolutionary. Prior to considering where and how intellectual property should develop it is perhaps useful to look back to consider how and why the systems developed. The first intellectual property statutes were motivated very much by economic and trade considerations. In the English patent system, for example, invention took second place to the need to overcome by force of law the obstacles placed by local tradesmen against those seeking to apply techniques and technologies, established in other countries but novel in England.

17.14   A similar trend can be mapped in respect of the copyright system. Essentially a product of the invention of the printing press, this seeks to protect a range of interests. The world's first copyright statute was the UK's Statute of Anne enacted in 1709. The date of the Act's passage is significant. Although the notion of copyright had been developed under the English common law, it had not featured significantly in Scots law. Under the Act of Union between Scotland and England in 1707, an eighteenth-century equivalent of the European Single Market was established, with Scottish producers enjoying access to the economically stronger English market. Scots law was retained under the Act of Union and Scottish publishers discovered a useful source of income by producing what today would be regarded as 'pirate' copies of leading English literary works. One of the motives of the Statute of Anne was to introduce copyright notions into Scots law and prevent what was seen as a form of unfair competition.

17.15 Matters have not changed greatly over the past three centuries. In 1707 a relatively poor country saw little benefit in systems of intellectual property law and some advantage in their absence. Its richer, more powerful neighbour used economic and political muscle to cause the introduction of laws. Today, it is not self-evidently to the benefit of the developing world to enforce intellectual property rights which primarily benefit first world owners. The price of entry to the World Trade Organization and access to first world market under the GATT and GATS treaties is, however, that they accept the World Trade Organization Protocol on Trade Related Aspects of Intellectual Property Rights (TRIPS). This obliges signatories to recognise intellectual property rights and to provide enforcement mechanisms in the event rights are nor observed. This obligation has been the cause of considerable controversy, most notably perhaps in relation to the production and distribution of anti-AIDS drugs which are invariably protected by patent rights.

17.16 Perhaps surprisingly, almost no empirical evidence exists whether the patent system is effective in either economic terms or in ensuring that information regarding technical innovations enters into the public domain. Some studies have suggested that small and medium-sized enterprises make little or no use of patent specifications as a source of information regarding developments in their field of activity. In cases such as DNA research it may be argued whether the publication of details of an end product adds anything to the sum of human knowledge and, as such, whether the award of a patent adequately advances the aims of the patent system. A recent study conducted for the Commission on 'The Economic Impact of Patentability of Computer Programs'[1] considered the literature on the economics of the patent system before concluding:

> The economics literature does not show that the balance of positive and negative effects lies with the negative. All it says is that there are grounds for supposing that the negative forces are stronger relative to the positive forces in this area than in some others and that any move to strengthen IP protection in the software industry cannot claim to rest on solid economic evidence

[1] Study Contract ETD/99/B5-3000/E/106, available from http://www.europa.eu.int/comm/internal_market/en/intprop/indprop/study.pdf

17.17 In fields such as software and with projects such as the mapping of the human genome it may be questioned how far the award of patents serves the end of encouraging further innovation. As in the example cited above involving

Elisha Grey and Alexander Graham Bell, different people may be working independently on the same idea simultaneously. It may be a matter of chance who stumbles on a practical method of implementation first. It may be questioned whether the interests of society in the development of technology are likely to be best served by the grant of a monopoly to one person or whether the existence of at least one competitor might have served as a spur to more rapid developments.

Chapter 18

Key elements of the patent system

Origins and nature of the patent system

18.1   The patent system is probably the oldest form of intellectual property right. Its development has been at times a convoluted and complex one and the concept featured in some of the major political upheavals in the late Middle Ages, testimony to the fact that the element of monopoly conferred upon the holder of a patent has at least the potential to provide very significant economic benefits.

18.2   The first recorded patent was issued in Florence in the fifteenth century. We are told that: Filippo Brunelleschi, the architect of Florence's remarkable cathedral, won the world's first patent for a technical invention in 1421. Brunelleschi was a classic man of the Renaissance: tough-minded, multi-talented and thoroughly self-confident. He claimed he had invented a new means of conveying goods up the Arno River (he was intentionally vague on details), which he refused to develop unless the state kept others from copying his design. Florence complied, and Brunelleschi walked away with the right to exclude all new means of transport on the Arno for three years.

18.3   That Florence acceded to Brunelleschi's demands is hardly surprising. The Italian Renaissance city-states, locked in a struggle for wealth and power, habitually gave monopolies to those who would build a needed bridge or mill, or who introduced some useful craft or industry. They would issue 'letter patents' public declarations that openly (patently) announced the privilege. What distinguished Brunelleschi's bargain was invention – he was awarded the exclusive use of his own creation.

18.4   Initially, the English system was to give monopolies to those bringing new or useful technology to the country. In the early Middle Ages, each town would have its guilds of craftsmen, who would guard access to the various trades jealously. Only a member of the appropriate guild could, for example, act as a butcher or carpenter. One of the major weaknesses of such an approach was that the guilds stifled innovation. Recognising that the country was lagging behind its continental rivals in terms of technology, the practice began whereby the Sovereign would encourage foreigners to come to England, bringing with them their advanced technical skills. To overcome the objections of the craft guilds, letters patent would be issued. Signed with the Royal seal, these would command any citizen to refrain from interfering with the bearer in the exercise of the technical skills referred to in the letter. The first recorded English patent of this kind was issued to a Flemish glazier who came to the country to install stained glass windows in Eton College. Unlike Brunelleschi's patent, the technology covered by the patent was new to the country rather than new in itself. In the sixteenth and seventeenth centuries the system fell increasingly into disrepute. Although some patents were granted in respect of what might be regarded as inventions (the first recorded patent of this kind being awarded to an Italian émigré, Annoni, who developed a novel system of fortification, used to safeguard the town of Berwick against the Scots invaders), the system was all too often used to boost the Royal revenues by conferring a monopoly in respect of basic commodities for a fee. A prime example was the grant of a patent in respect of playing cards. In 1602 the courts declared unlawful a Royal monopoly relating to the manufacture of playing cards and in 1623 the Statute of Monopolies rendered illegal all monopolies except those:

> ... for the term of 14 years or under hereafter to be made of the sole working or making of any manner of new manufactures within this Realm to the true and first inventor; monopolies should not be 'contrary to the law nor mischievous to the State by raising prices of commodities at home or hurt of trade'.[1]

It was almost another hundred years, however, before it was settled that in return for the award of a patent, the inventor was required to specify details of the manner in which the invention functioned, and not until the enactment of the Patent Act 1902 that even a rudimentary form of examination of patent applications was made with a view to establishing novelty.

[1]   Section 6.

18.5   In recent UK statutes, principally the Patents Acts of 1949 and 1977 it has been absolutely clear that the element of invention is critical for any award. An oft-quoted description of the modern system explains that:

> The basic theory of the patent system is simple and reasonable. It is desirable in the public interest that industrial techniques should be improved. In order to encourage improvement, and to encourage the disclosure of improvements in preference to their use in secret, any person devising an improvement in a manufactured article, or in machinery or methods for making it, may upon disclosure of the improvement at the Patent Office demand to be given a monopoly in the use for a period of years. After that period it passes into the public domain; and the temporary monopoly is not objectionable, for if it had not been for the inventor who devised and disclosed the improvement nobody would have been able to use it at that or any other time, since nobody would have known about it. Furthermore, the giving of the monopoly encourages the

putting into practice of the invention, for the only way the inventor can make a profit from it (or even recover the fees for his patent) is by putting it into practice; either by using it himself, and deriving an advantage over his competitors from its use, or by allowing others to use it in return for royalties.[1]

[1] Blanco White *Patents for Inventions* (1983, Stevens) p 1. For a good description of the history of the UK patent system, see the Patent Office website at http://www.patent.gov.uk/dpatents/fivehund.html.

18.6 It is the element of monopoly protection which gives patents their legal strength. Unlike copyright, which recognises the possibility that two parties may independently create similar works, the fact that an alleged infringer created a similar product following totally independent research will not provide a defence to an action alleging infringement.

18.7 Today, the UK's patent system is based primarily on the Patents Act 1977. This statute was enacted in part to reform and update the UK law relating to patents but also in order to bring domestic law into conformity with the provisions of the European Patent Convention, opened for signature in 1973, which, as will be discussed at para 18.14ff below, provides for a measure of harmonisation in matters of substance and procedure amongst signatory states.

18.8 Whilst there is no doubt that inventiveness is a key requirement of the patent system what has been more debatable has been the application of the system to software-related inventions – innovations where novelty resides primarily or exclusively in software components. Concern has tended to focus on two elements, first, whether software developments fit conceptually into the industrial nature of the system and, secondly, whether the library and related resources exist to allow claim to novelty to be adequately assessed. This remains the most problematic aspect of the subject and will be discussed in more detail below.

Patents in the international arena

18.9 Until recent times, patent systems tended to be found only in the developed world. The advent of the World Trade Organization has resulted in many more countries introducing systems of patent protection. Although there is some element of harmonisation this is at a lower level than provided for under the Berne Copyright Convention, first adopted in that city in 1886 and subject thereafter to periodic revisions, , which provides for almost worldwide protection to be conferred automatically on literary, dramatic and musical works. A UK patent will be valid within the UK but of no effect in Japan or the US and vice versa. A person wishing to secure widespread patent protection for an invention will have to undergo the time-consuming and expensive process of seeking to obtain a patent from each country where protection is desired.

18.10 The oldest international instrument is the Paris Convention (an instrument signed by 96 states, including all of the major industrial states).[1] This provides that the submission of an application for patent protection in one signatory state will serve to establish priority for the applicant in the event that equivalent applications are submitted in other signatory states within 12 months.[2] Although such a facility is of considerable value for inventors, the practical problems involved in obtaining patent protection on anything like a worldwide basis are immense, and a number of subsequent agreements have sought to ease the task facing applicants.

[1]   The Convention was first opened for signature on 20 March 1883, with the most recent revision occurring in Stockholm in 1968.
[2]   Article 4.

The Patent Co-operation Treaty

18.11 The Patent Co-operation Treaty, which was opened for signature in 1970, prescribes basic features which are to be found in the national laws of signatory states. As indicated above, the enactment of the Patents Act 1977 was in large measure designed to ensure the UK's conformity with the Patent Co-operation Treaty.

18.12 Under the provisions of the Patent Co-operation Treaty, an application may be directed to the patent authorities in any state and will indicate the countries within which patent protection is sought.[1] The national authority will then transmit the application to an International Searching Authority (the national patent offices of Austria, Australia, Japan, Russia, Sweden and the US, together with the European Patent Office).[2] The procedure to be adopted subsequently will depend upon the extent to which the state in question adheres to the Treaty. At the most basic level, the International Searching Authority will carry out a prior art search and submit reports to the designated national authorities.[3] Signatory states are given the option to adhere to a more significant regime which will permit the searching authority to conduct a preliminary examination.[4] Once again, reports will be sent to the designated national authorities. The Patent Co-operation Treaty does not contain any specific prohibition against the award of patents for computer programs,[5] but does state that an International Searching Authority is not to be obliged to conduct a search of the prior art in respect of a computer program 'to the extent that the International Searching Authority is not equipped to search prior art concerning such programs'.

[1]   Article 3.
[2]   Article 12.
[3]   Article 15.
[4]   Article 31.
[5]   Article 33 provides that the subject matter of a patent may be anything that can be made or used.

18.13 The operation of the Patent Co-operation Treaty serves to eliminate a measure of the duplication of searches and examinations which would otherwise face an international applicant. Ultimately, however, the decision as to whether to grant or refuse a particular application is one for the national authorities.

The European Patent Convention

18.14   Further rationalisation of the patent system has been carried out within Europe. The European Patent Convention operates under the auspices of the Patent Co-operation Treaty. This Convention was opened for signature in 1973, and has subsequently been ratified by Belgium, France, Germany, Luxembourg, the Netherlands, Switzerland and the UK. The Convention establishes the European Patent Office (located in Munich) and the concept of a European Patent. The title, however, is something of a misnomer. An applicant is required to specify those countries in which it is intended that the patent will apply and, assuming the application is successful, the end product will be the award of a basket of national patents. Effectively, the role of the Convention and the European Patent Office is to centralise the process for the award of national patents, with the costs to applicants rising in line with the number of countries in which protection is sought. As the European Commission has commented, one consequence of this process has been that 'the additional costs of protection for each designated country are prompting businesses to be selective in their choice of countries, with effects that run counter to the aims of the single market'.[1]

[1]   Green Paper *Community Patent and the Patent System in Europe*, available from http://europa.eu.int/comm/internal_market/en/intprop/indprop/paten.pdf.

18.15   Applications for patent protection may be addressed to the European Patent Office. Once again, the applicant must indicate those countries to which they wish the patent to extend.[1] Subsequently, all the examining procedures will be conducted by the European Patent Office, which will then proceed also to make the decision whether to grant the patent. Although some differences of procedure and style can be identified between the practice of the UK Patent Office and its European counterparts, the principles which will be applied are virtually identical. The British law relating to patents is to be found today in the Patents Act 1977. This statute was introduced in part to update domestic law, but principally to enable the UK to ratify the European Patent Convention. The Act provides that judicial notice is to be taken of decisions of the European Patent Office authorities and, as will be discussed below, decisions made within the European Patent Office have proved extremely influential in the domestic system. In one of the leading UK cases, the view was expressed strongly that: The decisions of the European Patent Office have been cited extensively in UK patent cases with the view expressed that:

> It would be absurd if, on the issue of patentability, a patent application should suffer a different fate according to whether it was made in the United Kingdom under the Act or was made in Munich for a European Parliament (United Kingdom) under the Convention.[2]

[1]   Article 79.
[2]   Per Nicholls J in *Gale's Application* [1991] RPC 305.

The Community Patent

18.16 Although the European Patent Convention (the Munich Convention) is sometimes linked with the EC, the two organisations are distinct. In the 1970s, it was the intention of the then EC member states that the Munich Convention should be followed shortly by the establishment of a Community Patent and the Community Patent Convention (the Luxembourg Convention) was signed in 1975. This sought to establish a unitary patent system operating throughout the EC. The system would, however, be administered through the European Patent Office. In spite of the conclusion in 1989 of a further Agreement (the Luxembourg Agreement), the Convention has never entered into force, having been ratified by only seven of the current member states (Denmark, France, Germany, Greece, Luxembourg, the Netherlands and the UK). Recently, however, as will be discussed, the European Commission has sought to become more involved in the field. During 1997, the Commission published a Green Paper *Community Patent and the Patent System in Europe*.[1] This document seeks views on future EC action in the field of intellectual property law exploring the possibility that a new EC patent regime might be established by Regulation. In spite of regular appearances on the agenda of meetings of the Council of Ministers the Regulation has not been adopted[2] with the Council meeting of 25 and 26 March 2004 concluding that:

> agreement on the Community Patent is now long overdue and the European Council calls for further efforts to complete work on this proposal.

A follow-up document to the Green Paper, published in 1999,[3] indicated the intention to bring forward proposals for a directive on the patentability of software. The intention was to provide a more favourable environment for software patents than that then perceived as being provided under the European Patent Convention. Subsequent case law developments which will be discussed in more detail in the next rendered the need for reform considerably less urgent and the text of the directive which was agreed by the Council of Ministers in May 2004 does no more than require member states to adhere to the principles laid down by the European Patent Convention authorities.[4]

[1] COM (97) 314 final.
[2] The draft regulation is available from http://europa.eu.int/comm/internal_market/en/indprop/patent/index.htm.
[3] 'Promoting innovation through patents. The follow-up to the Green Paper on the Community Patent and the Patent System in Europe', available from http://europa.eu.int/comm/international_market/en/intprop/indprop/99.htm.
[4] The text of the common position on the Directive is available from http://europa.eu.int/comm/internal_market/en/indprop/comp/index.htm.

18.17 Although the Community Patent Convention is not in force and the proposed directive has yet to appear, the provisions of EC law are of considerable significance in the field of intellectual property rights. In particular, the EC's competition policy will prevent the owner of a patent from using the rights conferred thereby to impede the flow of goods between member states. Effectively, if a product has been lawfully marketed in one member state, it may be bought and sold in other states, irrespective of any patent rights which might otherwise apply in those territories.[1]

[1]   See Chapter 25.

Intellectual property and international trade

18.18   The Trade Related Aspects of Intellectual Property Rights (TRIPS) Protocol[1] to the General Agreement on Tariffs and Trade (GATT) seems likely to lead to an expansion in the application of the patent system. The Protocol requires signatories to make patents:

> ... available for any inventions, whether products or processes, in all fields of technology, provided that they are new, involve an inventive step and are capable of industrial application ... patents shall be available and patent rights enjoyable without discrimination as to the place of invention, the field of technology and whether products are imported or locally produced.[2]

This provision was included at the behest of the developed world, and was prompted by concern that companies were suffering losses through audio, software and video piracy in developing countries, with little legal recourse because concepts of intellectual property law were not recognised by national laws. Effectively, TRIPS requires these states to introduce intellectual property statutes as the price for benefiting from the free trade provisions of the GATT. From the legal perspective, the fact that the Protocol requires that patents be made available for 'any inventions whether products or processes in all fields of technology' has been seen in many quarters as requiring the opening up of patent systems to software-related inventions.

[1]   Adopted in 1994 and entering into force on 1 January 1995. The text of TRIPS is available from http://www.wto.org/wto/intellec/1-ipcon.htm.
[2]   Article 27.

What may be patented?

18.19   A patent may be awarded in respect of an invention. The invention may relate to either a new product or to a novel process. The Patents Act 1977 does not define the word invention, but it does specify attributes that any invention must possess. These require that:

(a)   the invention is new;
(b)   it involves an inventive step;
(c)   it is capable of industrial exploitation; and
(d)   the grant of a patent for it is not excluded.[1]

As will be discussed extensively below, the categories of excluded subject matter are of great significance in the case of software-related inventions. Initially, however, attention will be paid to the positive attributes which must be possessed in order for a product or a process to be considered patentable.

¹   Section 1(1).

Novelty

18.20   The question of novelty is assessed against the existing state of human knowledge. Account will be taken of any material within the public domain which might indicate that the concept of the claimed invention did not originate with the particular applicant. It is not necessary that all the details of the alleged invention should have previously appeared in a single document. The test which will be applied is sometimes referred to as the 'mosaic' test. The analogy might also be drawn with a jigsaw puzzle. This consists of a number of pieces. Once completed, the subject matter will be readily identifiable, as will the manner in which the constituent pieces fit together. Such a result might not have been apparent to someone who merely saw a pile of unassembled pieces.

18.21   An indication of the complexity of the task of determining whether a claimed invention is novel or whether key elements have been anticipated in earlier products or publications can be taken from the case of *Quantel Ltd v Spaceward Microsystems Ltd*.¹ This concerned a challenge to the validity of a patent awarded in respect of a computer-based device permitting the production of graphical images for display on television screens. The end products of the system can be viewed every day in the captions and graphical montages which appear on almost all television programmes.

¹   [1990] RPC 83.

18.22   A competing product having been placed on the market, proceedings were instituted alleging breach of patent. In defending this action, the defenders alleged, inter alia, that the patent had been incorrectly awarded to a development that was not novel. A variety of material was presented in support of this contention, including a thesis submitted by an American student and deposited in the library of Cornell University. Although the validity of the patent was ultimately upheld by the court, when account is taken of the number of such works produced each year and the very limited publicity afforded to them, the incident demonstrates the magnitude of the task of determining whether an alleged invention is truly novel. The case also provides an excellent illustration of the fact that the grant of a patent may be only the first step for the inventor, who may be faced with a challenge to its validity in the course of any subsequent legal proceedings.

18.23   A further aspect of novelty concerns the question of whether details of the alleged invention might previously have been brought into the public domain by the applicant. Any significant disclosure of the features of an invention prior to the submission of an application for a patent will lead to its rejection. The Patent Office advise inventors:

If you are thinking of applying for a patent you should not publicly disclose the invention before you file an application because this could be counted as prior publication of your invention. Any type of disclosure (whether by word of mouth, demonstration, advertisement or article in a journal), by the applicant or anyone acting for them, could prevent the applicant from getting a patent. It could also be a reason for having the patent revoked if one was obtained. It is essential that the applicant only makes any disclosure under conditions of strict confidence.[1]

[1]   http://www.patent.gov.uk/dpatents/canipub.html.

Inventive step

18.24   The application of this test is as much a matter of art as of science and is linked to a considerable extent with the criteria of novelty. The Patents Act 1977 states that an invention:

> ... shall be taken to involve an inventive step if it is not obvious to a person skilled in the art, having regard to any matter which forms part of the state of the art.[1]

It is very much a question of fact whether the advance involved in a particular invention would have been 'obvious'. Again, the attempt has to be made to apply the test without engaging in the use of hindsight, but by reference to the state of the art at the time the invention was made.

[1]   Section 3.

18.25   An excellent example of a situation where the requirement of an inventive step was not satisfied can be seen in the case of *Genentech Inc's Patent*.[1] A research programme conducted by Genentech resulted in the identification and mapping of elements of DNA (one of the basic building-blocks of life, the universe and everything). The research furthered the knowledge of this basic structure and could be used as the basis for the production of anti-coagulant drugs. Genentech sought to patent the results of its efforts, the application ultimately failing when the Court of Appeal held that the work did not involve an inventive step. Mustill LJ referred to Genentech's activities in the following way:

> ... they won the race. The goal was known and others were trying to reach it. Genentech got there first.[2]

Whilst the achievement of a goal (equivalent, perhaps, to setting a new world record in a sporting event) would constitute evidence of novelty, if the target was widely known, winning of the race might tell no more than that the winner was richer or more determined or luckier than others working in the same area. To this extent, therefore, the expenditure of time and effort in making a breakthrough will not, of itself, be conclusive evidence of the existence of an inventive step.[3]

[1]   [1989] RPC 147.
[2]   [1989] RPC 147 at 251.
[3]   [1989] RPC 147 at 278.

18.26 Such arguments are of considerable relevance in the information technology field, where vast sums of money are being expended by large research units throughout the world, all pursuing the goal of faster, more powerful computing devices. A distinction can be drawn between this situation, where the goal can be expressed only in abstract terms, and that applying in *Genentech*,[1] where the target of the research was much more precisely defined. Even on this restricted analysis, the situation appears a little inequitable. The achievement of the goal of running a mile in less than three minutes might not be inventive, but would certainly be meritorious and deserving of recognition. The problem will be encountered in a number of areas and the traditional precepts of intellectual property may not fit well with developments in information technology, yet the effect of denying access to intellectual property rights is to deny any form of legal recognition and protection for the work in question.

[1] *Genentech Inc's Patent* [1989] RPC 147.

18.27 Also at issue in the *Genentech*[1] litigation was the identification of the notional persons 'skilled in the art' – those persons to whom the making of the steps leading to the claimed invention would have been 'obvious'. It was recognised that, in respect of advanced areas of technology, the collected knowledge of a team of researchers might be the relevant factor rather than the knowledge possessed by any particular individual. The question also arises whether the person or persons 'skilled in the art' should themselves be credited with possessing any inventive qualities. In the case of *Valensi v British Radio Corpn Ltd*,[2] it was stated that:

> ... the hypothetical addressee is not a person of exceptional skill and knowledge, that he is not to be expected to exercise any invention nor any prolonged research, inquiry or experiment. He must, however, be prepared to display a reasonable degree of skill and common knowledge of the art in making trials and to correct obvious errors in the specification if a means of correcting them can readily be found.[3]

[1] *Genentech Inc's Patent* [1989] RPC 147.
[2] [1973] RPC 337.
[3] [1973] RPC 337 at 377.

18.28 A more expansive view of the abilities of the skilled person was adopted by Mustill LJ in *Genentech*. In a comment which is especially relevant in relation to developments in information technology, he held that:

> Where the art by its nature involves intellectual gifts and ingenuity of approach, it would, I believe, be wrong to assume that the hypothetical person is devoid of those gifts.[1]

[1] *Genentech Inc's Patent* [1989] RPC 147 at 280.

Capability for industrial application

18.29 The final requirement which must be satisfied in order for a patent application to proceed is that the invention involved should be capable of industrial application. This requirement is, in many respects, at the heart of the patent system. However novel an idea might be, it will be of little practical benefit if it cannot usefully be applied. Application may take two forms, with the subject matter of the patent application referring to a product or a process (sometimes referred to as apparatus and means). In many instances, applications will combine the two elements. A helpful illustration is provided in Laddie J's judgment in the case of *Fujitsu Ltd's Application*:[1]

> ... it may be useful to consider what the position would be in a case where someone had invented a new way of mowing grass which involved designing a new type of motor with micro sensors and blade adjustment motors on it, the sensors being used to determine both the softness of the grass to be cut and the height of it above the ground and then produced an output which operated the motors so as to adjust the height of the cut, the angle of the blades and the speed at which they rotated ... considerations of novelty aside, such a device would be patentable and, so it seems to me, would be the mowing method itself.

[1]   [1996] RPC 511.

18.30   In a software context, the claim may often be that the equipment operating in accordance with the program's instructions constitutes a novel product, whilst the algorithmic steps prescribed by the implementing programs represent a novel process. Virtually any product will be capable of being sold or otherwise disposed of and, in this respect, will satisfy the applicability test. With a process, slightly different considerations will apply. If the end result of the application of the process will be a product, it is likely that the process will be considered capable of industrial application. An illustration of the kind of development which will be excluded from patent protection can be found in the provisions of the Patents Act 1977 which states that:

> ... an invention of a method of treatment of the human or animal body by surgery or therapy or of diagnosis practised on the human or animal body shall not be taken to be capable of industrial application.[1]

Thus, the intangible concept is not patentable. In the event, however, that new surgical tools or equipment are invented to facilitate the application of the new techniques, these will, assuming the other statutory criteria are complied with, be regarded as patentable.

[1]   Section 4(2).

Matters excluded from patent protection

18.31   In addition to defining the elements that must be found in an invention, the Patents Act 1977 lists a number of features which will not qualify for the grant of a patent. Section 1(2) (which mirrors art 52 of the European Patent Convention) provides that patents are not to be awarded for:

(a) a discovery, scientific theory or mathematical method;
(b) a literary, dramatic, musical or artistic work or any other aesthetic creation whatsoever;
(c) a scheme, rule or method for performing a mental act, playing a game or doing business, or a program for a computer; or
(d) the presentation of information.

18.32 Given the appearance of the phrase 'a program for a computer' in this listing, it may appear surprising that the topic should be of any significance in a text on information technology law. Matters, however, are not so straightforward. After reciting the list of prohibited subject matter, both the Patents Act 1977 and the European Patent Convention continue:

> ... but the foregoing provision shall prevent anything from being treated as an invention for the purposes of this Act only to the extent that a patent or an application for a patent relates to that thing *as such* (emphasis added).

18.33 In his judgment in *Fujitsu Ltd's Application*,[1] which was subsequently affirmed by the Court of Appeal,[2] Mr Justice Laddie analysed the rationale behind a number of the statutory exceptions. The prohibition against the grant of a patent to a discovery illustrates perfectly the problems inherent in this area. The obvious objection to awarding a patent for a discovery, for example, of a new mineral, is that there is no discernible inventive step. However, as was pointed out in the judgment:

> ... most inventions are based on what would be regarded by many people as discoveries. Large numbers of highly successful and important patents in the pharmaceutical field have been and continue to be based upon the discovery of new strains of micro-organisms which exist naturally in the wild.[3]

Recognising this fact, the statutory prohibition against the grant of a patent is restricted to the case where the application relates to the discovery 'as such'.[4]

---

[1] 1996 RPC 511.
[2] (1997) Times, 14 March.
[3] [1996] RPC 511 at 523.
[4] Patents Act 1977, s 1(2).

18.34 In principle, such an approach must be correct. Its practical application has proved more difficult with particular problems surrounding the treatment of what are frequently referred to as 'software-related inventions'. In part, the problem may lie with the fact that both the Patents Act 1977 and the European Patent Convention were enacted in the 1970s. At that time, it was considered that computer programs could be separated from the hardware components and should be excluded from the patent system. Both the report of the Banks Committee in the UK and the initial Guidelines for Examiners produced by the European Patent Office make this point clearly. Over the last 20-odd years, the nature of computer programs has changed and expanded, and the division between software and hardware has become a matter of chance as much as one of technology. It would be absurd if an invention were to be denied a patent on the basis, for example, that its 'on/off' switch was controlled by software embedded in a microprocessor chip. Equally, it is clear beyond doubt that a computer program taken in isolation is not patentable. As with so many areas of the law, the difficult task is to determine where the boundary lies between permitted and prohibited subject matter.

18.35 To complicate matters further, as the relevance of the obvious prohibition has declined, so it has also become apparent that software-related inventions are vulnerable to challenge under a range of the statutory exceptions. Applications have been rejected on the basis that they relate to a mathematical method, a method of doing business, the presentation of information and a method for performing a mental act, all of which are excluded from the award of a patent. It is difficult to think of any other form of technology whose nature and range of application is sufficiently chameleon as to bring it within so many of the statutory prohibitions. Not unnaturally, those seeking patent protection for software-related inventions have sought to lay as much emphasis as possible on the task performed by the invention, and as little as possible on the contribution made by computer programs. The criterion applied by both the European Patent Office and the UK authorities is to require that the claimed invention produced a 'technical contribution' to the state of the art (also referred to as a 'technical effect' or 'technical application'). The next question, of course, is whether the mere presence of a technical contribution can outweigh the explicit prohibition against patentability?

Patenting software

18.36 At a symposium held by the Patent Office in 1994 on the topic of 'Software Related Innovation', speakers from the Patent Office queried whether the list of statutory exclusions provides genuine assistance to the Patent Office and the courts, or whether reliance upon the need to demonstrate novelty, inventiveness and industrial application would suffice. A similar query has been posited by the European Commission in its Green Paper on the Community Patent,[1] which refers to the possibility of deleting the specific prohibition against the patentability of computer programs found in the European Patent Convention,[2] so that whilst:

> ... the requirement that the invention be of a 'technical' nature should be maintained but once such a feature was present, a program which is recorded on a medium and puts the invention into effect once it was loaded up and started would become patentable.[3]

[1]   COM (97) 314 final.
[2]   Article 52(2). The Convention is described in more detail at para 18.14ff above.
[3]   COM (97) 314 final at 17.

18.37 Notwithstanding the present prohibitions, there is no doubt that software-related inventions can be patented. In the UK, approximately 100 patent applications in their name are published each year. In proceedings before the

European Patent Office, this figure rises to 100 per month.[1] The report of the Parliamentary Office of Science and Technology on 'Patents, Research and Technology'[2] indicates that 'in the last 10 years the EPO has granted around 10,000 patents for software-related inventions, and has refused only 100 applications'.[3] Even more substantial figures are quoted for the number of patents awarded in the US although, in part because the existence of the statutory prohibitions requires that software-related inventions be catalogued by reference to their field of application rather than the software component, any calculation is a somewhat subjective assessment. There is no doubt, however, that patents have a significant role to play in the field of information technology.

[1] I am grateful to Mr J Houston, Intellectual Property Rights Officer of the University of Strathclyde, for the provision of these statistics.
[2] March 1996.
[3] Page 31. The Follow-up to the Green Paper on the Community Patent refers to the existence of 13,000 patents in Europe.

18.38   The determination of when an application relates to something more than prohibited subject matter has proved one of the most difficult aspects of the law, and will be discussed in detail in Chapter 19. In one respect, software-related inventions have proved uniquely vulnerable to challenge on this ground. The attainment of a satisfactory definition of computer programs has proved elusive and, in most of the cases which have arisen under the Patents Act 1977, the 'objectionable' features of a software-related invention could justify refusal on the grounds that the application refers to a mathematical method, a means for doing business, a scheme for performing a mental act or a method for presenting information.

The process of obtaining a patent

The application

18.39   The act of making an invention will confer no rights upon an inventor. A person wishing to secure protection is required to make application for a patent and to pursue this through all the stages of the patent procedure.[1] The key components of the process are described in the following paragraphs. Reference throughout is to the procedures and terminology applying under the UK system. Comparable procedures will be applied in respect of applications submitted under the European and Community Patent Conventions.

[1] Where an invention is made in the course of employment, the employer will be regarded as the inventor for the purpose of making a patent application.

Specification and statement of claim

18.40   The key elements of any patent application are the provision of a specification and a statement of claim(s).[1] The specification consists, essentially, of a description of the invention. It will describe the state of the technical art in the field and indicate the improvements which the invention makes and the manner in which this is accomplished. The specification should be formulated in such a manner as to permit the product to be made or the process operated by 'a person skilled in the art'.

¹   Section 14(2).

18.41 The specification serves to indicate what may be regarded as the inventor's opinion regarding the optimum embodiment of its principles. Beyond this, claims for protection may be made regarding the functioning of the product or process – effectively, what the invention does. The drafting of these claims is critical to the success of a patent. Any claim alleging infringement of a patent will relate to the claims rather than to the specification. If the claims are drawn too broadly, the patent application may be rejected on the grounds that the applicant is seeking protection either for matters which have not been disclosed in the specification or for matters which are not novel or inventive. If the claims are drawn more narrowly, the patent may well be awarded, but prove worthless as competitors evade its scope by making minor changes to the design of the invention. In many cases, an applicant will submit a considerable number of claims, commencing with extremely broad references to the technology at issue with subsequent claims narrowing down the level of protection, ending with a claim to protection for the invention 'substantially as described'.

18.42 An example of a failure in this regard has been reported concerning the patents granted to what has become the market-leading telephone modem. Modems play a vital role in the transfer of data between computers.¹ Just as with human telephone conversations, a basic requirement of data transmissions is the ability to identify when a communication has been completed and thereupon terminate the connection. This is referred to as the escape sequence. A particular sequence had been developed in which the initiating modem would transmit three + signs. Such a transmission would be most unlikely to occur in the course of a message and would signal to a compatible receiving modem that the communication had concluded. In this, as in many other areas of the intellectual property field, the question of compatibility is critical. Although it was not selected at random, the 3+s message possessed no unique qualities. The commercial success of the modem produced consumer demand for modems which transmitted and recognised this sequence. In laying claim to a patent for the modem design, the developers failed to claim in respect of the specific escape sequence. This proved a costly error. The resulting patent protection certainly prevented competitors from copying the specific design features of the modem, but the same effect, that of transmitting and receiving data communications, could readily be achieved using alternative and non-infringing means. Having done this, the absence of a claim in respect of the escape sequence left competitors free to utilise this, thereby acquiring compatibility with the market-leading product to their own commercial advantage.²

¹   *Guardian*, 9 February 1989.
²   See also the discussion as to compatibility and copyright at para 20.150 below.

18.43 The lodging of an application with the Patent Office serves to initiate the procedures leading to the grant of a patent. Until the Patent Act 1902, although substantial procedural requirements had to be observed, a patent would be awarded without the invention being subjected to any form of scrutiny. From 1902, increasingly stringent procedures have been introduced, whereby an application will be examined with a view to making a determination whether it complies with the statutory criteria. Under the Patents Act 1977, a two-stage process operates, with applications being subjected to preliminary and substantive examinations.

Preliminary examination

18.44 The first purpose of the preliminary examination is to ensure that the application complies with all the formal requirements of the legislation.[1] If this is the case, the examiner will turn to consider the merits of the application. At the stage of the preliminary examination, the examiner's main task is to identify those documents and information sources which it is considered are likely to prove of assistance in applying the criteria of novelty and inventiveness. Having identified relevant documents, the examiner is to scrutinise the documents to such extent as is considered will serve a purpose in determining the application.[2] The results of the preliminary investigation are to be reported to the Comptroller of Patents and to the applicant.[3]

[1] Patents Act 1977, s 17(2).
[2] Section 17(4)–(5).
[3] Section 17(2).

18.45 This initial report will be non-judgmental. It may indicate grounds for objecting to or refusing the grant of a patent. In such circumstances, it might become apparent to an applicant that the chances of the application being granted are minimal and the decision taken to pursue the matter no further.

Publication of the application

18.46 Unless notice of withdrawal is given, details of the specification and claims will be published 'as soon as possible' after the expiry of 18 months from the date of application.[1] In most cases, an applicant will receive the report of the preliminary examination before the application is due to be published. Whilst publication will have no detrimental effect in the event that the patent is ultimately granted, if the application is unsuccessful, the consequence will be that the inventor will have disclosed information to the public without securing any benefit in return. Equally seriously, publication may adversely affect the prospects of any modified application which the inventor might wish to make. Under the present US system, no details of an application are published until the patent is ultimately awarded. Although this may seem fairer to the applicant, problems have been encountered with what are referred to as 'submarine patents'. Even assuming a relatively straightforward application, it will be quite normal for the process to take two to three years. With more complex cases, perhaps including modification of the original application, this period may increase to ten years or even longer. The essence of a submarine patent is that, originally describing what has been described as 'science fiction technology', it lurks unseen in the patent office awaiting the widespread application of the technology by third parties (perhaps being modified better to describe their applications). At this time, the patent surfaces with claims of patent infringement being fired at any users.

[1]   Patents Act 1977, s 16.

Substantive examination

18.47   In the event that the applicant wishes the process to continue, a request must be made for a substantive examination.[1] It is at this stage that the examiner will make a full study of whether the claimed invention is novel, involves an inventive step, is capable of industrial application and does not fall within one of the prohibited categories. The request for a substantive examination must be made within six months of the date of publication.[2]

[1]   Patents Act 1977, s 18(1).
[2]   Patents Rules 1995, SI 1995/2093, r 33.

18.48   Although, as has been said, the determination of whether an invention is novel has to be made by reference to any material in the public domain, it would be unreasonable to expect patent examiners to be aware of every book or article deposited in any library anywhere in the world. The basic tool for examiners will be collections of patents previously awarded in the world's major patent offices.

18.49   It is at the stage of the substantive examination that a decision will be made regarding the patentability or otherwise of the invention. The examiner will make a report to the Comptroller of Patents. In the event that this report makes objection to aspects of the application, the applicant must be afforded the opportunity to make observations or to amend the application so as to take account of the examiner's objections. In the event that the applicant fails adequately so to do, the Comptroller may refuse the application.[1]

[1]   Patents Act 1977, s 18(3).

Third-party involvement

18.50   The Patents Act 1977 contains no provisions for the formal involvement of third parties in the processes leading to the grant or refusal of a patent. It is provided, however, that in any interval between publication of the application and the decision on grant a third party may submit written observations to the Comptroller, who must take these into account in reaching a decision.[1]

[1]   Section 21.

Award of a patent

18.51   In the event that a patent is awarded, the Comptroller is required to cause a notice to this effect to be published in the Official Journal (Patents). The maximum term of validity of a patent is 20 years, commencing from the date when the application is first submitted.[1] It should be noted, however, that a patent is not awarded for such a period. Protection will be awarded for an initial period of four years, thereafter annual applications will require to be made (accompanied by a fee) to retain the patent's validity. Only a small percentage of patents remain in force for the full 20-year period, the average lifespan of a patent being in the region of eight years.[2] By this time, it will have become apparent either that the patent has been overtaken by newer technologies or that the invention is of limited practical utility.

[1]   Patents Act 1977, s 20.
[2]   For an excellent analysis of the lifespan of patents, see Phillips and Frith *An Introduction to Intellectual Property Law* (2nd edn, 1990, Butterworths).

Infringement of patents

18.52   The definition of infringement is of critical importance. Under the terms of the Patents Act 1977, infringement may be either direct or indirect. Direct infringement occurs when a party, without the consent, express or implied, of the proprietor of the patent 'makes, disposes or offers to dispose of, uses, keeps, or imports' a product constituting the subject matter of the patent. Similar prohibitions apply in the event that the patent covers a process.[1]

[1]   Section 60(1).

18.53   Indirect infringement occurs where a party supplies or offers to supply any equipment which constitutes an essential part of the invention in the knowledge (or having reasonable grounds to believe) that infringement will result.[1]

[1]   Patents Act 1977, s 60(2).

Establishing infringement

18.54   The question whether a subsequent product infringes the provisions of a patent is essentially one of fact. It will seldom be the case that the subsequent product is an exact copy of a patented object. In the event that any infringement is innocent, with the product being the result of the competitor's own researches, it is unlikely that every detail of the original will be replicated. Should the subsequent producer have been aware of and seek to evade the provisions of the patent, it is again likely that differences of detail will be introduced in an effort to conceal the fact of infringement.

18.55   In the event that products are not identical, the task for the court is to examine the patent specification and statement of claim in order to identify the essential features or integers possessed by the patented product. These are then compared with those of the competing product. If the latter replicates the essential elements, infringement may be established even though the product may differ in other respects. An example of the operation of this principle can be seen in the case of *Beecham Group Ltd v Bristol Laboratories Ltd.*[1] Here, the plaintiffs held a patent for a pharmaceutical product possessing a particular chemical structure. The defendant company produced a product possessing a slightly different structure, but the evidence established that the latter product became converted to the patented product upon being absorbed into the bloodstream. In these circumstances, it was held that there was a patent infringement.

[1] [1978] RPC 153.

18.56   In the case of *Catnic Components Ltd v Hill and Smith Ltd,*[1] the plaintiffs had been granted a patent in respect of a design of lintel. The patent made specific reference to the fact that the support member was to be vertical. The defendants subsequently produced a lintel possessing most of the features of the original design, but with the change that the support was angled slightly from the vertical. The alteration made the design slightly less effective, although the difference was of no practical significance. It was held that the similarity between the two designs was sufficient for infringement to be established.

[1] [1982] RPC 183.

18.57   The fact that the addition of further integers increases the efficiency of the product will not necessarily defeat a claim of infringement. As was stated by Bower LJ in the case of *Wenham Gas Co Ltd v Champion Gas Lamp Co Ltd,*[1] 'the superadding of ingenuity to a robbery does not make the operation justifiable'. More difficult issues may arise in the event that the subsequent product substitutes or modifies some of the essential integers of the patented product. Here, the determination of whether there is any infringement will be influenced strongly by any expert evidence presented by the parties. If it can be established that it would have been obvious to the mythical 'workman, skilled in the art', presented with details of the modification at the date of publication of the patent, that the substitution of one feature for another would not have had a significant effect on the operation of the patented invention, infringement may be established.

[1] [1891] 9 RPC 49.

Remedies for infringement of patent

18.58   Four basic forms of remedy may be available to the holder of a patent. At the initial stage of legal proceedings, an interdict may be sought to prevent the defender continuing with the alleged infringement. When the dispute comes to trial, three further remedies may be applicable. An order may be sought requiring the delivery up to the patentee of any infringing copies. In terms of financial compensation, the patentee may seek either an accounting of profits from the infringer or an award of damages.

Revocation of patents

18.59   A patent may be revoked by the court or the Comptroller on the application of any person if it is established:

1. that the invention is not a patentable invention;
2. that the patent was granted to a person or persons who were not the only persons qualified to obtain such a grant. Such an action may only be brought by a person or persons who would have been entitled to be granted the patent or to have shared in such a grant. The action must be brought within two years from the date of the patent grant unless it is established that the patent holder was aware that he or she was not entitled to the proprietorship of the patent;
3. the specification does not disclose the invention sufficiently clearly and completely for it to be performed by a person reasonably skilled in the art;
4. the matter disclosed in the patent specification is more extensive than that disclosed in the patent application; or
5. the protection conferred under the patent has been extended by an amendment which should not have been allowed.[1]

[1]   Patents Act 1977, s 72.

18.60   Although it is possible that a challenge to the validity of a patent may be brought in isolation, it will more commonly be raised as an issue in the course of proceedings by the patent holder alleging infringement. Effectively, therefore, the trial may provide the forum for reconsideration of the question of whether the application for patent protection should be granted.

18.61   This possibility is particularly relevant in the information technology sector, where substantial criticism has been made of the abilities of patent offices to identify all materials relevant to determinations of novelty and inventiveness. To this extent, acquisition of a patent may mark only the first stage in a continuing battle to establish its validity and enforce its terms.

Are patents worth the effort?

18.62   The processes for obtaining a patent are frequently lengthy and expensive. Although the UK Patent Office introduced a 'fast track' process in 1995, which aimed to make a decision on the patentability of an application within 12 months,[1] the patent process will normally occupy a period in excess of two years. Fees must be paid at all stages of the patent process.[2] In addition, the complexity of the processes may compel applications to make use of the services of patent agents – something which is recommended by the Patent Office.

[1]   http://www.patent.gov.uk/dpatents/pataccel.html.
[2]   For current details, see http://www.patent.gov.uk/sservice/ukpatnt.html.

18.63   Faced with these factors, coupled with the requirement in the European and UK systems that details of an invention be published prior to the decision being taken whether to award a patent, it might be queried where the value of the patent system lies for those working in the software field. Given the pace of technical development, it will certainly be the case that, for many applications, the technology will be rendered obsolete before the patent is awarded. The US case of *Microsoft v Stac* provides perhaps the best example of the value of the patent system.[1]

[1]   For details of the case, see http://www.vaxxine.com/lawyers/articles/stac.html.

18.64   At issue in the case was a patent describing novel techniques for the practice of data compression. As the name suggests, this technique is used to reduce the amount of storage space necessary to hold data. A recent application of compression technology can be seen with the MP3 system. MP3 is an audio compression format that enables audio files to be stored and transferred on a computer with a relatively small file size. Typically, three minutes of music recorded in digital format would require some 30MB of storage space. Use of the MP3 mathematical techniques, which are themselves patented in the US[1] and the source of potential litigation, reduces the space required to about 3MB. Such a reduction makes it feasible to place musical tracks on, and download from, the Internet.

[1]   See http://www.mp3.com/news/095.html.

18.65   In the particular case, Stac held two US patents for a compression system which was sold under the name 'Stacker'. Interestingly, especially given the controversy which has existed concerning the eligibility of software-related inventions for patentability within the UK, one of the patents was originally issued in the UK to a British company, Ferranti, and was subsequently assigned to Stac. Microsoft wished to incorporate a compression system in a new version of their operating system. Negotiations followed with Stac but these proved unsuccessful, largely because Microsoft were unwilling to offer any payment for the use of the Stac system.[1] When the new version of the operating system appeared on the market, it did contain a compression system. It transpired that it was based on the Stac system. Microsoft's claim was that this had been used initially, but they had subsequently devised their own code. In copyright law, as will be discussed below,[2] this claim may well have succeeded and might at least have resulted in extensive litigation. As the techniques were protected by patents, all that Stac had to establish was that Microsoft had used these. In a jury trial, Stac were awarded $120m in compensation.[3]

[1]   For details of Stac's claim, see http://www.vaxxine.com/lawyers/articles/stac.html.
[2]   See discussion of *Computer Associates v Altai* 982 F 2d 693 (1992) at para 20.150 below.
[3]   Ultimately, the two companies signed a cross-licensing agreement. Stac received $43m in cash from Microsoft and Microsoft invested $39.9m in non-voting Stac stock (about 15%of the company's shares) – a total payout of $83m.

18.66   The litigation brought by Stac marked, at least until the anti-trust litigation brought by the US authorities, the most significant legal finding against Microsoft. As such, it is eloquent testimony to the strength of a patent. Software patents have been, and remain, an extremely controversial subject, especially in the US.

Objections appear to be based on a number of grounds. The system, it is argued, is inequitable in the situation where different people are working independently in the same field. The first one to obtain a patent is then in a position to stop others exploiting their own work. As can be seen from the example of Alexander Graham Bell and Elisha Grey cited at para 17.7 above, this is not a new phenomenon. A further ground of objection is founded in the perception that the inability of the Patent Offices to make comprehensive searches in the field has resulted in the award of patents in respect of technology which is not truly novel or inventive. This is a more difficult ground to assess. It may be noted that examination is a relatively novel feature of the patent system. Until the twentieth century, the system was effectively one of registration. The fact that a patent is granted is not conclusive evidence of its validity. It may be challenged at any time. Against this, it should be stated that the onus of proving a patent to be invalid lies with the challenger, and patent litigation can be prolonged and expensive. These issues will be considered in more detail in Chapter 19, which will consider the manner in which patent law has evolved in relation to patents for software-related inventions.

Chapter 19

Patents and software

Early software patents

19.1   The first UK cases involving the eligibility of software-related inventions for patent protection arose under the Patents Act 1949. The continuing relevance of cases decided under the 1949 Act has been the subject of some debate. The Patents Act 1977's definitions of the concept of an invention have been described in Chapter 18. The 1949 Act contained a simpler definition which looked for 'any manner of new manufacture'.[1] Although some commentators have expressed the view that the categories of qualifying and prohibited subject matter introduced in the 1977 Act represented a codification of existing precedent, it was stated by Purchas LJ in *Genentech Inc's Patent*[2] that the 1977 Act must be 'viewed in the context of a departure from much of the authority and usage of previous patent law'.

[1]   Section 101.
[2]   [1989] RPC 147 at 197.

19.2   Given the date of its passage, it is not surprising that the Patents Act 1949 contains no mention of computer programs. As will be discussed, however, the approach of making special reference to programs has itself proved problematic. Although cases decided under the 1949 Act may now possess limited precedential value, the issues raised and the approaches adopted remain of more than historical interest, not least because recent developments in Europe and the US appear to signal a reversion to the standards and criteria applied in cases brought under the 1949 legislation.

Developments under the 1949 legislation

19.3   The first case in which software was involved was that of *Slee and Harris's Application*.[1] The applicants in this case submitted two patent applications

392

relating to linear programming. The technicalities of the process involved need not concern us greatly. Effectively, the applicants' program allowed a computer to solve simultaneous linear equations more quickly than had previously been possible. The first application related to a method for operating and the second to means for controlling computers.

¹   [1966] RPC 194.

The method claims

19.4   As originally submitted, the patent application contained a claim relating to:

> A method of operating data processing apparatus, to produce a solution matrix for a plurality of simultaneous linear functions, comprising controlling iterative processing on a set of data representations of the simultaneous linear functions in such manner that an iteration is initiated while a previously initiated iteration is still proceeding so that a plurality of iterations proceed concurrently at one or more stages of the processing.

This claim was rejected on the basis that the term 'data processing apparatus' was inadequately defined. A further ground of objection was one which is often raised concerning modern patents, that it was not clear whether the patent might be infringed by a person using pen and paper to perform the calculations. In the effort to overcome this objection, a modified claim was submitted referring to:

> A method of operating a computer to produce a solution matrix for a plurality of simultaneous linear functions which method is a modification of the 'Simplex' method and comprises controlling the iterative processing in such manner that after the initiation of at least one of the iterations, and while that iteration is still proceeding, a further iteration is initiated and proceeds concurrently with the first mentioned iteration during the remainder of the first mentioned iteration.

19.5   The second claim, it was held, related to a method of operating a known machine. The end product was data in the form of intellectual information. The question then arose whether information could be classed as a product, a conundrum which arises again and again in the context of information technology law. Reference was made to the case of *GEC's Application*,¹ in which it was held that a method was a manufacture if it resulted 'in the production of some vendible product'. This point was discussed in more detail in the Australian case of *NRDC's Application*.² Here it was held that:

> ... what is meant by a 'product' in relation to a process is only something in which the new and useful effect may be observed. Sufficient authority has been cited to show that the 'something' need not be a 'thing' in the sense of an article, it may be any physical phenomenon in which the effect, be it creation or merely alteration, may be observed: a building (for example), a tract or stratum of land, an explosion, an electrical oscillation. It is, we think, only by understanding the word 'product' as covering every end produced, and treating the word 'vendible' as pointing only to the requirement of utility in practical affairs, that

the language of Morton J.'s 'rule' may be accepted as wide enough to convey the broad idea which the long line of decisions on the subject has shown to be comprehended by the Statute (of Monopolies).[3]

1   (1943) 60 RPC 1.
2   [1961] RPC 134.
3   [1961] RPC 134 at 138.

19.6   In the case of the present application,[1] it was held:

... the product of the present method, the end produced, is as I have said, intellectual information. This is quite different from any notion of 'product' appearing from the Australian judgment.[2] This judgment referred to 'any physical phenomenon in which the effect (of the process) may be observed'. Illustrations given were: a building, land, an explosion, an electrical oscillation. Although the judgment states that the word 'product' should be understood as covering 'every end produced', I venture to think, with respect in view of the reference to physical phenomena, and in view of the illustrations cited, that an end product comprising merely intellectual information is not within the meaning given to the word 'product' by the learned Australian Court.[3]

Increasingly, of course, information is now a vendible product and it might be that a different view would be taken were a similar case to come before the courts.

1   *Slee and Harris's Application* [1966] RPC 194.
2   *NRDC's Application* [1961] RPC 134.
3   [1966] RPC 194 at 197.

19.7   Although the initial claims failed, a final modified submission was considered to be acceptable in principle.[1] This referred to:

A computer having slow and quick-access storage, when programmed to solve a linear programming problem by an iterative algorithm the iterative algorithm being such that:

(a)   data representations are transferred, portion by portion, from slow-access storage to quick-access storage;

(b)   after at least one of the said transfers the transferred data representations are transferred back and forth, without intermediate transfer to slow-access storage, between the quick-access storage and the arithmetical unit of the computer where they are processed in accordance with at least two iterations of the iterative algorithm; and

(c)   the processed data representations are transferred from quick-access to slow-access storage.

This claim, it was held:

... is directed to a machine which has been set into such a condition that it can proceed to solve a particular program by undertaking a series of specified steps. It may be regarded as a machine which has been temporarily modified. No objection should in my view be raised by the Comptroller against such a claim on the ground that the invention concerned is not within the statutory definition.[2]

Essentially, it was considered that a computer running one program should be classed as a different machine from the same hardware running a different program.

¹ The hearing in *Slee and Harris* was conducted on the assumption that the developments described were novel and inventive.
² *Slee and Harris's Application* [1966] RPC 194 at 198.

The means claim

19.8 The second application, commencing a practice which remains relevant today, linked the programs involved to the operation of the hardware. The application, it was claimed, related to:

> Linear programming means for use in controlling data processing apparatus so that it effects iterative processing on a set of data representations, which means are formed in such manner as to cause the initiation of an iteration while a previously-initiated iteration is still proceeding, so that a plurality of iterations will proceed concurrently at one or more stages of the processing.

19.9 The programs required to accomplish this, it was recognised, could be recorded on any form of storage device. In the event a computer had optical character reader capabilities, it would even be possible to write the program on a sheet of paper. The programs constituted, it was held, more than an idea, being something which:

> ... physically coordinates with a computer to control the latter to operate in a particular way. The means can, therefore, be likened to a cam, shaped according to certain formulaes so that, when fixed into a machine, it controls the latter in a certain way.

The equipment holding the programs was, it was held, to 'be regarded as a machine which has been temporarily modified'.¹ On this basis, the application was to be regarded as containing patentable subject matter and it was referred back to the Examiner for a determination whether it satisfied the criterion of novelty required for the grant of a patent. Ultimately, a patent was awarded to the applicant.

¹ *Slee and Harris's Application* [1966] RPC 194 at 198.

Developing the concept

19.10 The concept of a linkage between hardware and software was developed further in the case of *Badger Co Inc's Application*.¹ The software involved in the case operated in the area of Computer Assisted Design (CAD). The only novelty in the application lay in the software elements. The application was rejected in the Patent Office on the ground that it did not contain patentable subject matter and an appeal was made to the Patent Appeals Tribunal. The Tribunal considered that the application related to two distinct aspects of the design process; the first concerned with the collection of data and the second with the setting up of machinery necessary for processing. The analogy was drawn with a chemical process which would involve the preparation of raw materials followed by the 'provision of the conditions necessary to secure the required conversion'.

1   [1969] FSR 474.

19.11   Following the decision in *Slee and Harris*,[1] it was held that the raw data involved in the present application could not constitute a product. Setting up the computer to perform the necessary work, however might be acceptable:

> [I]t is apparent that this purpose is the common characteristic of computer operation in that the function of the apparatus is required to follow the sequence of operations for which it is programmed. If, of course, the conditioning is procured by some alteration of the mechanism, the appropriate form of monopoly claim would be to the mechanism so modified. If, on the other hand, it is procured by imposing some hitherto unknown order of sequential operation, involving no mechanical change in the apparatus, inventiveness could presumably only reside in the manner of activation of known mechanism, and it would be in relation to the departure from any known pattern of operation that the subject matter test would have to be applied.[2]

Again, we have here the notion of a computer being temporarily modified through the loading and operation of a program.

1   *Slee and Harris's Application* [1966] RPC 194.
2   *Badger Co Inc's Application* [1969] FSR 474 at 476.

19.12   The next case to be considered is that of *Gever's Application*.[1] The applicant had developed a method of using a computer to file details of trade marks. The system would be used to facilitate any searches that might be required to determine questions of similarity or prior registration. Effectively, a proposed name would be entered and the equipment would search for any occurrences found in its records. The equipment was also programmed to search for modifications which would produce a similar result, either in terms of spelling or phonetics. Thus it would highlight instances where the letter 'I' had been substituted for a 'Y', 'ci' for 'si' and any instances where a single letter had been replaced by a double, for example 's' by 'ss'.

1   [1970] RPC 91.

19.13   The application was intended to run on standard computer equipment, with the programs responsible being stored on punch cards. Graham J, sitting in the Patent Appeals Tribunal, held that the application referred to patentable subject matter. Referring to the example of the lathe utilised in *Slee and Harris's Application*,[1] he stated:

> It is to my mind clear that a newly invented lathe, the tool of which is constrained by a cam to take a certain path in cutting ... is a method of manufacture. It is equally clear that such a cam could be made the subject of a subsidiary claim in a claim for a patent for the lathe. As sold, or as it lies on the table, of course, such a cam would have only a potential usefulness, but it seems to me right

that a claim should be able to be made to such a cam because it is in the circumstances novel and inventive and produces a useful result when it is placed in the machine for which it is designed.[2]

The punched cards utilised in order to instruct the computer to act in a particular way must be regarded in the same manner. If the card was shaped in such a way as a form of equipment, such as the cam, it would be patentable. How, the judge asked:

> ... can it make any difference that the card is punched instead of being contoured? It is to my mind properly to be regarded as a manner of manufacture since it is shaped in a particular way, namely by having holes in it at certain specified positions which ensure that it is capable when it is placed in its machine of controlling that machine in accordance with pre-determined directions.[3]

1   *Slee and Harris's Application* [1966] RPC 194.
2   *Gever's Application* [1970] RPC 91 at 98.
3   [1970] RPC 91 at 98.

19.14   The same approach was adopted by the Tribunal in the case of *Burroughs' Corpn's (Perkins') Application*.[1] This application concerned a method for transmitting data between computer terminals. Accepting that the application referred to patentable material, the court held that:

> If the bare method or idea is also clothed by the patentee in his specification with a practical garment in the shape of apparatus enabling that method or idea to be realised in practice it should no longer be regarded as a naked conception, for it has found a practical embodiment in the apparatus. It is then a method of new manufacture.[2]

1   [1974] RPC 147.
2   [1974] RPC 147 at 158.

19.15   Essentially, the distinction as identified by the courts in the decisions considered above can be stated as being one between a computer program and a computer programmed to operate in a particular way. In part, the development of this approach may have been assisted by the then state of programming technology. Reference has been made in a number of the passages cited above to the programs being implemented in the form of punched cards. This is a form of programming which is virtually obsolete, but it had the advantage, from the point of view of those seeking to make application for patents, that the function of the computer would be dictated by the physical shape of the cards which held the program. In the final case decided under the Patents Act 1949, that of *International Business Machines Corpn's Application*,[1] the court applied these principles in the context of the emerging tendency to store computer programs on disk or magnetic tape.

1   [1980] FSR 564.

19.16   The circumstances of this case differed from those discussed above. Here, a patent had been awarded and the proceedings related to a challenge by the applicants to its validity. The patent referred to a program designed to determine the optimum time for buying and selling stocks and shares. Its first claim referred to:

> A data handling system suitable for establishing prices for a given kind of fungible goods as hereinbefore defined in an auction market as hereinbefore defined, comprising data storing means suitable for storing data representing buy orders for the goods and representing sell orders for the goods, order entering means suitable for entering data representative of individual buy and sell orders including price information in said data storage means, comparing means which in use read out and compare the prices of buy and sell orders from the data storage means, by pairs chosen by progressing sequentially and simultaneously through a descending sequence of the buy orders and an ascending sequence of the sell orders by price, and means arranged to be controlled by said comparing means so as to select the price at which the goods are to be sold in dependence on the price or prices of the last compatible pair of orders which are matched and so as to select each pair of said buy and sell orders to be executed as a sale at a transaction price.

Dismissing IBM's claim that any novelty lay only in the intellectual concepts involved, the Tribunal held that:

> As we understand it, a programme is a series of instructions which are fed to the other equipment in the data processing system to produce a desired result. It is possible to have a computer in which a number of different programmes are stored to be used as and when required. Alternatively a particular programme may be fed into a computer from outside. These programmes, written in a language the computer can understand, have taken different physical forms. These forms have included punched cards, punched tape, printed directions which can be optically scanned and now, more commonly, magnetic information stored on tape, wire or drums. It is not suggested that before [the patent holder] came along there ever had been a computer programmed to carry out the operations required in conducting his system. The Superintending Examiner has found, and this we entirely accept, that once [the patent holder] conceived his idea any competent computer programmer could have told him how to programme a standard computer so as to produce the desired result. As matters stand, however, until Mr. Nymeyer came along there was no reason to suppose that anyone would have thought of writing the appropriate programme and building it into a computer or otherwise putting it into a physical form suitable for use with a standard computer.
>
> A computer programmed to carry out [the] system must we think be considered as being an apparatus having novel characteristics but IBM say that in as much as it can be said that by the introduction of this new programme a change may have been brought about this is not a change in manufacture. Counsel for IBM put it in this way that such 'newness' as there may be is purely intellectual. This cannot in our view be right. There must be different holes in the card or different magnetic patterns on the tape, or some other automatic control imposed to ensure that the computer carries out the particular operation required.[1]

---

[1] *International Business Machines Corpn's Application* [1980] FSR 564 at 572.

19.17   After surveying all of the previous UK authorities and considering the first US cases concerned with software-related inventions to reach the level of the Supreme Court,[1] the Tribunal concluded that:

> We proceed upon the basis that the only thing that was novel in connection with the present application was (the) concept of the way in which a price could be fixed, but what he seeks to claim as a manner of new manufacture is a method involving operating or controlling a computer in which, so far as the contested claims are concerned, the computer is programmed in a particular way or programmes in physical form to control a computer so that it will operate in accordance with his method. The method is embodied in the programme and in the apparatus in physical form and in our view the superintending examiner was right in concluding that the claims should be allowed to proceed ... an inventive concept, if novel, can be patented to the extent that claims can be framed directed to an embodiment of the concept in some apparatus or process of manufacture.[2]

[1]   For discussion of US authorities, see para 19.108ff below.
[2]   *International Business Machines Corpn's Application* [1980] FSR 564 at 573.

19.18   The decision in *International Business Machines Corpn's Application*[1] was the last to be delivered under the Patents Act 1949. Indeed, by the time the Tribunal delivered its judgment the legislation had been replaced by the Patents Act 1977. As discussed above, this statute was introduced with the intention both to update domestic patent law and to enable to UK to accede to the European Patent Convention. The steps leading to the enactment of the 1977 Act began a decade earlier with the appointment of a Committee, chaired by Mr M Banks (the Banks Committee), and with terms of reference:

> To examine and report with recommendations upon the British patent system and patent law, in the light of the increasing need for international collaboration in patent matters, and, in particular, of the United Kingdom Government's intention to ratify the recent Council of Europe Convention on patent laws.[2]

[1]   [1980] FSR 564 at 573.
[2]   Cmnd 4407, 1970.

The Committee on Reform of the Patent System

19.19   The Banks Committee's report was published in 1970, with a chapter being devoted to an examination of the position of computer programs.[1] This concluded that that the situation was characterised by considerable uncertainty, but indicated that the majority of the evidence submitted to the Committee was hostile to the notion that programs should qualify for patent protection.[2] This view was shared by the Committee, which put forward reasons of both principle and utility for denying protection. In terms of principle, it was argued that no significant distinction existed between programs and methods of mathematical calculation, which had always been excluded from protection. Practical problems were also identified, the Committee commenting:

... were programs to be patentable, very real and substantial difficulties would be experienced by the Patent Office in searching applications for program patents even were the search material available in suitably classified form. The issues of novelty and obviousness would be so difficult of determination that patents of doubtful validity would be likely to issue.[3]

1   Cmnd 4407, 1970, Chapter 17.
2   Chapter 17, para 479.
3   Chapter 17, para 483.

19.20   Although it appears that this comment is at odds with much of the case law described above, it should be noted that in almost all of the cases, the legal argument was restricted to the question whether an application was entitled to be considered for the award of a patent. The cases, typically, were not concerned with the question whether the software developments were truly novel. As will be discussed, one of the major arguments advanced against the application of the patent system to software-related inventions has concerned the difficulty in establishing the true state of the technical art. Especially in the US, a number of fairly high-profile patent awards have been subject to heavy criticism – in at least one case resulting in the revocation of the patent – on the ground that the technology described was well known to those working in the field. Thirty years of advances in database technology do not appear to have done much to resolve the concerns voiced by the Banks Committee.

19.21   In the event, the Banks Committee recommended that:

A computer program, that is: a set of instructions for controlling the sequence of operations of a data processing system, in whatever form the invention is presented e.g. a method of programming computers, a computer when programmed in a certain way and where the novelty or alleged novelty lies only in the program, should not be patentable.[1]

1   Cmnd 4407, 1970, Chapter 17, para 487.

19.22   Such a view clearly conflicts with the judgment of the Patent Appeals Tribunal in the *International Business Machines Corpn's Application* decision,[1] and represents a hardening of attitudes towards the award of patents for software-related inventions. It was not considered, however, that the presence of software components in an otherwise qualifying invention should exclude the latter from patent protection. The report drew a distinction between:

... applications for programs *per se* and for inventions of the kind claimed as a computer controlled steelworks ... which involve the use of a program. The invention should then be patentable if it does not reside merely in the details of the program.[2]

1   [1980] FSR 564 at 573.
2   Cmnd 4407, 1970, Chapter 17, para 486.

19.23   Although such a distinction may be totally supported, it will be seen that once again the seeds of doubt as to the application of patent protection have been planted. Two propositions can be culled from the report of the Banks Committee. A program per se should never, at least under the UK and European regimes, be accepted as the basis for a patent. Equally, an invention that would otherwise be considered patentable is not to be barred from protection merely because a program is utilised somewhere in its operations. Inevitably, problems arise at the margins, and especially in the situation where the product functions in a novel and inventive manner, but where this is due in large measure to the operation of the programs contained therein.

The Patents Act 1977 and the European Patent Convention

19.24   As indicated in Chapter 18, after specifying the positive attributes which must be evidenced in a patent application, the Patents Act 1977 provides that:

> ... the following (among other things) are not inventions for the purposes of this Act, that is to say anything which consists of—
>
> (a)   a discovery, scientific theory or mathematical method;
> (b)   a literary, dramatic, musical or artistic work or any other aesthetic creation whatsoever;
> (c)   a scheme, rule or method for performing a mental act, playing a game or doing business, or a program for a computer; or
> (d)   the presentation of information.[1]

Although the first draft of the European Patent Convention was silent on the point, the final text contains a virtually identical list of prohibited subject matter.[2] This, it is reported, was as the result of representations made by the UK delegation. In both the Act and the Convention, however, the list of non-qualifying subject matter is followed by the proviso that the prohibition applies only to the extent that the application relates to that item 'as such'. It is the interpretation of this latter provision that has been at the heart of the litigation in this area. Typically, as in the cases brought under the Patents Act 1949, the claim has been made that what should be protected is the end product of the program's operation, ie what the software plus hardware components accomplish, rather than the manner in which this is done.

[1]   Section 1(2).
[2]   Article 52.

19.25   To complicate matters further, it has become apparent that software-related inventions are vulnerable to challenge under a range of the statutory exceptions. Applications have been rejected on the basis that they relate to a mathematical method, a method of doing business, the presentation of information and a method for performing a mental act, all of which are excluded from the award of a patent. It is difficult to think of any other form of technology whose nature and range of application is so chameleon-like as to bring it within so many of the statutory prohibitions.

19.26 The Patents Act 1977 was enacted in order to enable the UK to ratify the European Patent Convention and provides, most unusually, that judicial notice is to be taken of decisions of the European authorities.[1] It is further provided that:

> ... the following provisions of this Act ... are so framed as to have, as nearly as practicable, the same effects in the United Kingdom as the corresponding provisions of the European Patent Convention ...[2]

Given this, it is not surprising that it should be stated by Nicholls LJ in *Gale's Application*:[3]

> It would be absurd if, on the issue of patentability, a patent application should suffer a different fate according to whether it was made in the United Kingdom under the Act or was made in Munich for a European Parliament (United Kingdom) under the Convention.[4]

[1]   Section 91.
[2]   Section 130(7).
[3]   [1991] RPC 305.
[4]   [1991] RPC 305 at 323.

19.27 In spite of this recognition, concerns have been raised that software-related applications have been treated more harshly before the UK courts. The concerns are twofold. First, as was suggested by counsel for the Comptroller of Patents in the *Fujitsu* case:[1]

> ... there are recent decisions of the EPO Technical Board of Appeal in which the question of what constitutes a technical advance or contribution seems to have been rather more flexibly interpreted than has hitherto been the case.[2]

Additionally, concern has been expressed that different criteria might be adopted in dealing with challenges based upon the prohibition against the award of a patent for a scheme or method for performing a mental act. Given the increasing use of expert systems and neural networks, this is likely to prove a significant area of development in the coming years.

[1]   *Fujitsu Ltd's Application* [1996] RPC 511. The decision was affirmed by the Court of Appeal, [1997] RPC 608.
[2]   [1996] RPC 511 at 521.

The quest for a technical contribution

19.28 Although the term 'technical contribution' does not appear in either the Patents Act 1977 or the European Patent Convention, it has achieved pivotal significance since being introduced in Guidelines for Examiners drawn up by the European Patent Office, and adopted by the European Patent Office Board of Appeal in the case of *Vicom*.[1] This approach was endorsed by the English courts in the case of *Merrill Lynch*.[2]

[1]   *Vicom Systems Inc's Application* [1987] 2 EPOR 74.
[2]   *Merrill Lynch's Application* [1989] RPC 561.

19.29   In the original Guidelines prepared for the assistance of examiners in the European Patent Office, it was stated:

> If the contribution to the known art resides solely in a computer program then the subject matter is not patentable in whatever form it might be presented in those claims. For example, a claim to a computer characterised by having the particular program stored in its memory or to a process for operating a computer under control of the program would be as objectionable as a claim to the program *per se* or the program when recorded on magnetic tape.[1]

<hr>

[1]   OJ 1/1978.

19.30   By 1985, it was recognised that a fuller exposition was required concerning the European Patent Convention's application to inventions which made use of computer programs. As is the case under the UK legislation, there is no doubt that a computer program per se is not patentable. The prevailing opinion would suggest that this would be the case regardless of the specific prohibition contained in art 52, this being of a declaratory nature. In view of the increasing importance of computer programs, it was considered desirable to offer more precise guidance both to inventors and to the examiners in the European Patent Office. To this extent, new Guidelines[1] were promulgated which seek to make it clear that the essential prerequisite for the grant of a patent is the making of a 'technical' invention, ie a requirement that there be some tangible end product. Thus, although the revised Guidelines provide that:

> A computer program claimed by itself or as a record on a carrier is unpatentable irrespective of its content. The situation is not normally changed when the computer program is loaded into a known computer.[2]

it is recognised also that inventions in which a computer program constitutes an essential element may qualify for patent protection, subject to the application of the Convention's general rules. The Guidelines continue:

> If, however, the subject matter as claimed makes a technical contribution to the known art, patentability should not be denied merely on the ground that a computer program is involved in its implementation. This means, for example, that program controlled machines and program controlled manufacturing and control processes should normally be regarded as a patentable subject matter. It follows also that, where the claimed subject matter is concerned only with the program controlled internal working of a known computer, the subject matter could be patentable if it produced a technical effect.

The aim of the new approach, it is stated, is to produce a workable system from the standpoint of the European Patent Office (particularly in relation to the search and examination requirements) whilst 'responding to the reasonable desires of industry for a somewhat more liberal line than that adopted in the past'.

<hr>

[1]   The current guidelines were published in 2003 and are available from http://www.european-patent-office.org/legal/gui_lines/index.htm
[2]   Paragraph 22.

19.31   The first significant case following from the adoption of the new European Patent Office Guidelines was the decision of the European Patent Office Technical Board of Appeal in the case of *Vicom/Computer-Related Inventions* in July 1986.[1] This ruling has been of pivotal importance, being cited in virtually every subsequent European Patent Office and UK decision. Discussion of the question how far software-related inventions might be patentable under the Patents Act 1977 must therefore commence with discussion of this case.

[1]   *Vicom Systems Inc's Application* [1987] 2 EPOR 74.

Computer programs in the courts

The decision in Vicom

19.32   The *Vicom* application[1] related to the use of a computer for image processing purposes. Data representing the image, in the form of electrical signals, would be processed by the computer so as to enhance the quality of the image as displayed on the computer monitor. It was accepted by the applicant that the process could be operated using a standard computer. This application was rejected by the examiner on the grounds both that it sought protection for a computer program and on the basis that it related to a mathematical method. The electrical signal, it was argued, could be represented in mathematical terms, likewise the processed signal.

[1]   *Vicom Systems Inc's Application* [1987] 2 EPOR 74.

19.33   Appealing against this refusal, the applicants claimed that:

> A novel technical feature clearly exists in not only the hardware, but also in the method recited in the claims presented by this appeal. The invention, furthermore confers a technical benefit namely a substantial increase in processing speed compared with the prior art.
>
> Digital filtering in general and digital image processing in particular are 'real world' activities that start in the real world (with a picture) and end in the real world (with a picture). What goes on in between is not an abstract process, but the physical manipulation of electrical signals representing the picture in accordance with the procedures defined in the claims. There is no basis in the EPC [European Patent Convention] for treating digital filters differently from analogue filters.
>
> The appellants have thus made a new and valuable contribution to the stock of human knowledge and patent protection for this contribution cannot be denied merely on the basis that the manner in which the invention is defined would appear to bring it within the exclusions of Article 52(3) EPC.[1]

[1]   *Vicom Systems Inc's Application* [1987] 2 EPOR 74 at 77–78.

19.34   Acting on a suggestion from the examiner, amended claims relating both the apparatus and means were submitted for consideration by the Board of

Appeal. This held that the claims referred to patentable subject matter. In respect of the program objection it was held that:

> Generally, claims which can be considered as being directed to a computer set up to operate in accordance with a specified program (whether by means of hardware or software) for controlling or carrying out a technical process cannot be regarded as relating to a computer program ...
>
> Generally speaking, an invention which would be patentable in accordance with conventional patentability criteria should not be excluded from protection by the mere fact that for its implementation modern technical means in the form of a computer program are used. Decisive is what technical contribution the invention as defined in the claim when considered as a whole makes to the known art.[1]

[1] *Vicom Systems Inc's Application* [1987] 2 EPOR 74 at 80-1.

19.35 It was further recognised that a mathematical method could not be protected directly. When the formula existed in isolation, there could be no question of it being granted a patent. Where the formula was applied, however, different considerations arose. It was stated that:

> ... if a mathematical method is used in a technical process, that process is carried out on a physical entity (which may be a material object but equally an image stored as an electronic signal) by some technical means implementing the method and provides as its end result a certain change in that entity. The technical means might include a computer comprising suitable hardware or an appropriately programmed general purpose computer.[1]

[1] *Vicom Systems Inc's Application* [1987] 2 EPOR 74 at 79.

19.36 What was required was that the mathematical method should be applied within a specific technical context which, being capable of industrial application, would qualify for patent protection. In this event, the mathematical methods could freely be used by third parties for any purpose other than the specified form of image processing. Such an approach overcomes one of the major concerns which has been expressed by opponents of software patents – especially in the US – that a patent could be infringed by a party working out calculations with pen and paper.

19.37 The Board, therefore, was of the opinion that even if the idea underlying an invention may be considered to lie in a mathematical method, a claim directed to a technical process in which the method is used does not seek protection for the mathematical method as such.[1]

[1] *Vicom Systems Inc's Application* [1987] 2 EPOR 74 at 79.

19.38 In respect of the claims relating to the apparatus, it was conceded that the process could be conducted using conventional computing equipment. The Board of Appeal held, however, that:

> ... a claim directed to a technical process which process is carried out under the control of a program (be this implemented in hardware or in software), cannot

be regarded as relating to a computer program as such within the meaning of Article 52(3) EPC [European Patent Convention], as it is the application of the program for determining the sequence of steps in the process for which in effect protection is sought. Consequently, such a claim is allowable under Article 52(2)(c) and (3) EPC.

In arriving at this conclusion, the Board has additionally considered that making a distinction between embodiments of the same invention carried out in hardware or in software is inappropriate as it can fairly be said that the choice between these two possibilities is not of an essential nature but is based on technical and economical considerations which bear no relationship to the inventive concept as such.

Generally speaking, an invention which would be patentable in accordance with conventional patentability criteria should not be excluded from protection by the mere fact that for its implementation modern technical means in the form of a computer program are used. Decisive is what technical contribution the invention as defined in the claim when considered as a whole makes to the known art.[1]

[1] *Vicom Systems Inc's Application* [1987] 2 EPOR 74 at 79.

19.39   A number of significant features can be identified from the decision in *Vicom*.[1] The applicants' argument might well be noted that they had made 'a new and valuable contribution to the stock of human knowledge'. Protecting such work is at the core of the patent system. In terms of the decision of the Board of Appeal, there is recognition that what an invention does is more important than the manner in which it is achieved. As was stated in the decision, and as is increasingly the case, the distinction between hardware and software implementation of a concept is a matter of choice.

[1] *Vicom Systems Inc's Application* [1987] 2 EPOR 74.

19.40   Software-related inventions returned to the European Patent Office Board of Appeal in 1987 in the case of *Koch and Sterzel*.[1] Here, a patent had been awarded in respect of a 'diagnostic X-ray system operative in response to control signals from a stored program digital computer to generate an X-ray beam and to produce an image of the object through which the X-ray beam passes'.[2] The validity of the patent was challenged by two competitor companies, which argued that its subject matter differed from the state of the art only through the involvement of a novel computer program. The decision in *Vicom*,[3] it was suggested, was erroneous in that an application should not be accepted where the elements of novelty and inventiveness lay only in prohibited subject matter; in this case a computer program. Support for this contention was found in a decision of the German courts, to the effect that:

> ... a teaching is not technical if in its essence it states a rule that can be carried out without employing controllable natural forces other than human brainpower, even if the use of technical means appears expedient or indeed the only sensible and hence the necessary procedure, and even if reference is made to these technical means in the claims or description.[4]

[1] [1988] EPOR 72.
[2] EP0001640.

3   *Vicom Systems Inc's Application* [1987] 2 EPOR 74.
4   [1988] EPOR 72 at 74.

19.41   We will return to this concept in discussing the impact of the prohibition against patenting schemes or rules for performing a mental act. In *Koch and Sterzel*, the Board of Appeal rejected the German approach holding that:

> ... an invention must be assessed as a whole. If it makes use of both technical and non-technical means, the use of non-technical means does not detract from the technical character of the overall teaching. The European Patent Convention does not ask that a patentable invention be exclusively or largely of a technical nature; in other words, it does not prohibit the patenting of inventions consisting of a mix of technical and non-technical elements.[1]

The alternative approach, it was suggested, could result in a situation where technical aspects of an invention which were themselves novel and inventive would be denied patent protection because they were connected with non-technical aspects such as computer programs.

1   [1988] EPOR 72 at 74.

19.42   The question of where novelty is required to reside was a key issue in the next authority to be considered, the UK case of *Merrill Lynch's Application*.[1] The case was first considered in the Patents Court prior to publication of the European Patent Office's decision in *Vicom*,[2] with the decision of the Appeal Court following after this landmark opinion.

1   [1989] RPC 561, reported at first instance at [1988] RPC 1.
2   *Vicom Systems Inc's Application* [1987] 2 EPOR 74.

Merrill Lynch

19.43   If *Vicom*[1] constitutes a landmark decision under the European Patent Convention, the decision in *Merrill Lynch's Application*[2] plays a similar role in UK patent law. The factual content of this case was very similar to that at issue in *International Business Machines Corpn's Application*.[3] Merrill Lynch had developed what was referred to as 'a data processing system for making a trading market in securities and for executing orders for securities transactions'. The application of computerised trading systems in stocks and shares has proved controversial in a number of areas. Some of the blame for the 'crash' of stock exchanges on 'Black Monday' has been apportioned to the operation of systems whereby a fall in share prices automatically triggers the sale of shares which produces a further drop in prices, more selling and a continuation of a downward spiral. Such considerations were not at issue in the present case, which was concerned solely with the question of whether a patent might be awarded in respect of one such system.

1   *Vicom Systems Inc's Application* [1987] 2 EPOR 74.
2   [1989] RPC 561, reported at first instance at [1988] RPC 1.
3   [1980] FSR 564.

19.44   The system devised by Merrill Lynch related to:

> ... business systems and, more specifically, to an improved data processing
> based system for implementing an automated trading market for one or more
> securities. The system retrieves and stores the best current bid and asked prices;
> qualifies customers' buy/sell orders for execution; executes the orders; and
> reports the trade particulars to customers and to national stock price reporting
> systems. The system apparatus also determines and monitors stock inventory
> and profit for the market maker.[1]

The specification went on to state that the programs involved could be
implemented on a wide range of data processing equipment. Effectively, what
the application was claiming was that a general-purpose computer could operate
the computer programs to produce novel effects.

[1]   *Merrill Lynch's Application* [1989] RPC 561 at 569.

19.45   The application was rejected within the Patent Office on the basis that
the subject matter of the alleged invention fell within the prohibition of s 1(2) of
the Patents Act 1977. The principal patent examiner held that the effect of this
section was such that it would prevent the award of a patent in the situation
where the program was incorporated in some other object (the computer) but
where the novelty and inventive step resided in the elements of the program
rather than in any of the other attributes of the subject matter.

19.46   This reasoning, which was upheld by Falconer J in the Patents Court,
was challenged before the Court of Appeal. The critical issue concerned the
interpretation of the concluding passage of s 1(2) of the Patents Act 1977 stating
that the prohibitions against patentability extended only 'to the extent that a
patent or application for a patent relates to that thing as such'. It was the
applicant's contention that the claim related to apparatus operating in accordance
with the requirements of the program and, therefore, was for more than the
program as such.

19.47   Subsequent to the decision of Falconer J at first instance,[1] the Court of
Appeal delivered its judgment in the case of *Genentech Inc's Patent*,[2] which also
took account of the decision of the European Patent Office Board of Appeal in
the case of *Vicom's Application*.[3] Although the subject matter of this case concerned
developments in genetic engineering, the issue of the extent of the prohibition
against patentability was also discussed, in this case in the context of a discovery.

[1]   *Merrill Lynch's Application* [1988] RPC 1.
[2]   [1989] RPC 147.
[3]   *Vicom Systems Inc's Application* [1987] 2 EPOR 74.

19.48   As described previously, Genentech had identified elements of DNA and
obtained patents for applications based upon this research. These patents were
revoked by order of Whitford J sitting in the Patents Court on the ground, inter
alia, that the identification of the make-up of the DNA was in the nature of a
discovery. Having made the discovery, its application was obvious. The only

novelty, therefore, lay in the act of discovery. As discoveries cannot be patented, the patent was invalid.

19.49 This interpretation of the legislation was rejected by the Court of Appeal. Although the decision to revoke the patent was upheld on other grounds, it was acknowledged that many developments in the pharmaceutical field could be regarded in the same light. Once it is discovered, for example, that a particular drug has a beneficial effect on stomach ulcers, its application is very obvious. Dillon LJ commented:

> Such a conclusion, when applied to a discovery, would seem to mean that the application of the discovery is only patentable if the application is itself novel and not obvious, altogether apart from the novelty of the discovery. That would have a very drastic effect on the patenting of new drugs and medicinal or microbiological processes.[1]

[1]   *Genentech Inc's Patent* [1989] RPC 147 at 239–240.

19.50   The Court of Appeal in *Genentech*[1] were referred to the decision of Falconer J in *Merrill Lynch*.[2] Indicating their disagreement with the reasoning applied (although concurring with the ultimate result of the case), the court held that so long as the subject matter of the application as a whole satisfied the requirements for patentability, it would not matter that the requisite novelty and inventiveness resided in non-qualifying elements. Effectively, the test concerns what the invention does as opposed to the manner in which this is accomplished.

[1]   *Genentech Inc's Patent* [1989] RPC 147 at 239–240.
[2]   *Merrill Lynch's Application* [1988] RPC 1.

19.51   Applying the reasoning of the *Genentech* decision[1] and that of the European Patent Offices Technical Board of Appeal in *Vicom*,[2] the Court of Appeal affirmed that an invention could be patentable where the novel or inventive elements lay entirely in a computer program. The decision of the Patent Office to refuse Merrill Lynch's application was upheld, however, on another ground. Even though the incorporation of the program in the computer equipment might serve to take it outwith the prohibition against the grant of patents for computer programs, attention had to be paid to the nature of the resulting application. In the present case, the result:

> ... whatever the technical advance may be, is simply the production of a trading system. It is a data processing system for doing a specific business, that is to say making a trading market in securities. The end result, therefore, is simply 'a method ... of doing business', and is excluded by section 1(2)(c) [of the Patents Act 1977] ... A data processing system operating to produce a novel technical result would normally be patentable. But it cannot, it seems to me, be patentable if the result itself is a prohibited item under section 1(2). In the present case it is such a prohibited item.[3]

[1]   *Genentech Inc's Patent* [1989] RPC 147.
[2]   *Vicom Systems Inc's Application* [1987] 2 EPOR 74.
[3]   *Merrill Lynch's Application* [1989] RPC 561 at 569.

19.52 It may be noted that Merrill Lynch subsequently obtained a patent for broadly the same application from the US Patent Office.[1] The case demonstrates that not only must the invention produce some technical contribution – in itself no easy thing to define – but the end product must not constitute prohibited subject matter. In cases such as *Koch and Stertzel*,[2] where the programs control the operation of some product, this test is fairly easily established. In the situation where the effects are either internal or affect information – echoing back to the debate in *Slee and Harris*[3] whether information can constitute a product – the prognosis for the grant of a patent is much less favourable.

1   This patent survived a challenge in the US courts. See discussion at paras 19.76–19.77 below.
2   [1988] EPOR 72.
3   *Slee and Harris's Application* [1966] RPC 194.

19.53 A number of cases in both the UK and before the European Patent Office have discussed these issues and will be considered below. In general, applications relating to software have fared less well before the UK courts. In more than half of the cases brought before the European Patent Office Board of Appeal, applications have been declared patentable. Of six reported cases brought before the UK authorities, in only one[1] was an application declared to constitute patentable subject matter, a determination at first instance, which was reversed before the Court of Appeal. In large measure, this may be explained by the strengths of the cases brought before the respective tribunals but, as will be discussed, there has been a perception that in some respects the criteria applied by the UK courts are more restrictive than those adopted within the European Patent Office.

1   *Gale's Application* [1991] RPC 305.

19.54 The following sections will consider the development of case law in the UK and before the European Patent Office. For the UK, the latest decision is that of the Court of Appeal in the case of *Fujitsu's Application*.[1] Subsequent to this decision, matters have moved on apace at the European and international level, with the EU indicating support for an extension of the availability of patents for software-related inventions. The Trade Related Aspects of Intellectual Property Rights (TRIPS) agreement negotiated as part of the 1994 General Agreement on Trade in Services has also influenced recent case law of the European Patent Office, with the 1999 decision in IBM's application[2] perhaps signalling a sea change in the role of the patent system.

1   [1997] RPC 608.
2   *International Business Machines Corpn's Application* [1980] FSR 564.

Gale's Application

19.55 In the case of *Gale's Application*,[1] Mr Gale had developed a new algorithm and sought a patent in respect of an invention entitled 'Improvements and means whereby a binary manipulative system may derive a square root'. Effectively, Gale had devised a simplified process for the calculation of square roots. This process could be implemented in a number of ways. Certainly, where it was intended that the calculations be made by a computer, it would have been possible to store them on a computer disk or tape. As such, the provisions of s 1(2) of the Patents Act 1977 would undoubtedly come into play. In his patent application, Gale sought to overcome this obstacle by describing the operation of the mathematical process as implemented on a ROM (read only memory) chip. Such a device, he argued, could be distinguished from a computer program in that its physical form was dictated by the specific function that it was designed to perform. Although the difference might be apparent only upon the most minute inspection, a chip produced to Mr Gale's specifications would have an appearance distinct from any other piece of circuitry.

¹   [1991] RPC 305.

19.56   This argument did not commend itself to the Principal Examiner in the Patent Office, who rejected the application on basis that it related to a program for a computer. There was, he ruled, no distinction between a segment of ROM with a program held on it and a disk holding the same data. The latter would not be patentable and neither, in his opinion, should the former. Such a scenario had also been posited by Dillon LJ in *Genentech*, and the view expressed that:

> It would be nonsense for the Act [Patents Act 1977] to forbid the patenting of a computer program, and yet permit the patenting of a floppy disc containing a computer program, or an ordinary computer when programmed with the program; it can well be said, as it seems to me, that a patent for a computer when programmed or for the disc containing the program is no more than a patent for the program as such.¹

¹   [1989] RPC 147 at 240.

19.57   In the Patents Court, Aldous J surveyed the case law under Patents Act 1977 referring to the *Merrill Lynch*¹ and *Genentech*² decisions. From this, he concluded that the relevant criterion was whether there was more to the claimed invention than unpatentable subject matter, in the present case whether Gale's application concerned more than a program for a computer:

> ... the first task of the court is to construe the claim as that is where the invention is defined. If the claim properly construed is drafted so as to relate to any of the matters disqualified by section 1(2) then the invention is not patentable. If however the claim is drafted to a process or technique or product and the basis of such process technique or product is a disqualified matter, the court should go onto consider whether the claimed invention is in fact no more than a claim to an invention for a disqualified matter. It is a question of fact to be decided in each case, but if the claimed invention is more than a claim to an invention for a disqualified matter then it qualifies as a patentable invention.
>
> In deciding that question of fact it is always important to consider whether the claimed invention is part of a process which is to be used in providing a technical result. If it is, then the claim cannot be said to be an invention relating to no more than one of the disqualified matters. Similarly, where a claim is directed to a product, it is important to consider whether the product claimed is a new technical product or merely an ordinary product programmed in a

different way as in the latter case the claim is in reality to the programme and therefore could not relate to a patentable invention.[3]

Applying this test, it was held that a distinction could be drawn between a computer program and the electronic circuitry specified in the patent application. The circuitry involved was a manufactured item which was dedicated to one function. In the situation where a program was held on a computer disk, the disk served merely as a storage device. In the present case, the program was used as the basis for altering the physical structure of the circuitry, which could then be used to implement the program. Accordingly, the decision of the Principal Examiner that the application fell into one of the prohibited categories under the Act was reversed, and the case was returned to the Patent Office in order for a substantive examination to be made concerning the issues of novelty and inventiveness.

[1]   *Merrill Lynch's Application* [1989] RPC 561 at 569.
[2]   *Genentech Inc's Patent* [1989] RPC 147.
[3]   *Gale's Application* [1991] RPC 305.

19.58   The decision in *Gale* was criticised by a number of commentators, principally on the basis that no significant distinction exists between a disk as a storage device for a program and a segment of ROM. The decision was subsequently appealed successfully by the Comptroller of Patents.[1] Delivering the leading judgment in the Court of Appeal, Nicholls LJ, whilst accepting that an invention would not necessarily be debarred from the grant of a patent where the novelty lay in a computer program (or a discovery or any other prohibited subject matter), disagreed that the form in which the series of instructions making up the program were stored was of any significance for patent purposes:

> To be used in a computer, a series of instructions has to be recorded in a physical form which a computer can understand. Typically, but by no means always, the instructions will be recorded either on a disc inserted in the computer when required or, in the case of sequences of instructions routinely or frequently required, in a ROM which normally is inserted in a computer and not removed. Plainly, however, if the instructions qua instructions are not patentable, a claimant's position is not improved by claiming a disc on which those instructions have been recorded or a ROM in which they have been embodied. The disc or ROM is no more than an established type of artefact in which the instructions are physically embedded. It is merely the vehicle used for carrying them.[2]

[1]   *Gale's Application* [1991] RPC 305.
[2]   [1991] RPC 305 at 325.

19.59   The analogy was drawn with compact discs used for the storage of pieces of music. Each disc will differ physically from other discs holding a different musical composition. These physical differences, however, related only to the use of the disc for its normal purpose, the differences being created through the use of conventional production techniques. Attempts to create distinctions on this basis would, it was held, 'exalt form over substance'.

19.60 Although the Court of Appeal was unanimous in the view that the prohibition against the patentability of a computer program could not be circumvented by implementing it in hardware, Parker LJ indicated that he had found the issue to be 'of considerable difficulty'[1] and that '(i)n the course of arguments it appeared to me from time to time that the contentions in favour of patentability should be accepted in preference to those against'.[2] The effect of Mr Gale's chip was, he stated, to allow computers to calculate square roots both faster and to a greater degree of accuracy than had hitherto been possible. Ultimately, however, the fact that the same effect might equally well have been achieved using software and would certainly have been unpatentable in this form proved fatal to the application.

[1] *Gale's Application* [1991] RPC 305 at 328.
[2] [1991] RPC 305 at 330.

19.61 In some respects, the refusal of a patent might appear somewhat inequitable. As a result of Mr Gale's activities, the prospect of a better form of calculator existed. Nicholls LJ noted that:

> Although a computer program as such is not patentable, this is not to say that the instructions comprised in such a program, when recorded in a suitable medium, attract no protection. In this country the writer of the instructions, considered simply as a sequence of instructions, has a measure of protection for the product of his skill and effort, but it lies elsewhere, namely, in the law of copyright.[1]

The copyright system will be considered in more detail in subsequent chapters. Although at the time the decision was delivered in *Gale* the received wisdom was that this branch of intellectual property law provided extensive protection (extending to what was often referred to as the 'look and feel' of software), subsequent decisions have raised the question whether copyright does provide adequate protection for the skill and effort of the developer.

[1] *Gale's Application* [1991] RPC 305 at 326.

Hitachi's Application

19.62 *Hitachi's Application*[1] concerned a development in the area of compiler programs. Today, most computer programs are initially written in source code. Depending upon the computer language used, this may bear close similarities to the normal use of English. In order to be understood by a computer, the source code has to be converted into machine or object code. Special programs known as compilers are available to perform this task.

[1] [1991] RPC 415.

19.63 Computers can operate on the basis of two forms of instructions, known as scalar and vector. The latter was, at least in the late 1980s, a relatively new development which enabled processing to be conducted at much higher speeds than were possible with their scalar equivalent. The source code of most programs was written in the scalar format. Hitachi's development was a form of compiler that would, in addition to converting source to object code, convert scalar instructions into their vector equivalent. This would obviate the need for the programmer to return to the source code and make the necessary changes by hand. Hitachi sought patents for this development, relating both to a computer programmed with the compiler and to the method of operation employed. It was argued that the claims related to a technical process in that the computer as programmed was operating on a physical entity in the form of the source code program. Such a view, it was argued, was supported by the European Patent Office's decision in *Vicom*.[1] This view was rejected by the Principal Examiner in the Patents Office, who held that although the *Vicom* case had indeed involved the mathematical processing of electronic signals, this had involved three elements:

> ... firstly a mathematical method, secondly numbers – these being the things upon which the mathematical method operates, secondly numbers – these being the things upon which the mathematical method operates – and thirdly the representation of images by the numbers, the third element being the element that converted the first two into a patentable invention. In the present application, in my view, the compiler program takes the place of the mathematical method, and the thing that the compiler operates upon, i.e. the thing that corresponds to the numbers of Vicom, is the source program. Thus, if the analogy between the present application and Vicom is set up in the way I have just indicated, there is no element in the present application that is analogous to the third element in Vicom, because the present application does not state what the source program represents, and indeed I think it stand alone and cannot properly be said to represent anything other than itself.[2]

[1] *Vicom Systems Inc's Application* [1987] 2 EPOR 74.
[2] *Hitachi's Application* [1991] RPC 415 at 417.

19.64 Additionally, it was held, the processing involved in *Vicom*[1] could be used for a variety of further purposes, some of which, as in the case of the image processing, could be put to industrial application whilst others, such as the use of the mathematical techniques for the purpose of making economic forecasts, would not. In the present case, the compiler, which was at the heart of the application, could only realistically work upon computer source code. As was concluded, 'this renders specious any separation of the data that the compiler operates upon and the source program, since they are one and the same'. Hitachi's claims, accordingly, were rejected as referring only to unpatentable subject matter.[1]

[1] *Vicom Systems Inc's Application* [1987] 2 EPOR 74.
[2] *Hitachi's Application* [1991] RPC 415 at 417.

When is a program more than a program?

19.65 The clear message from cases such as *Vicom*[1] is that in determining whether a software-related invention is patentable, a critical determinant will be what the application achieves. In a case such as *Koch and Sterzel*,[2] this may be relatively easy to identify. The end product in this case could be classed as a better X-ray machine. It is often suggested that the person who invents a better mousetrap will find the world waiting to pay a fortune for the device. It must surely be of little significance if the improved mousetrap relies on a computer program rather than a piece of cheese. More difficult cases arise when, as in *Hitachi*,[3] it is difficult to identify tangible elements as resulting from the operation of the program. A number of cases decided before the European Patent Office involving the computer company IBM illustrate the problem. In *IBM/Homphone Checker*,[4] the application referred to a novel method for correcting homophone errors in a document, for example, the use of the word 'where' when the context of the document required 'wear'. Such a facility is an important feature of speech recognition systems, but is also a process which is carried out (often imperfectly) within the brain of an author. The application, it was held, related only to known and standard apparatus, and was described in functional terms corresponding to the mental steps which would be carried out by a human performing the same text processing operations. Holding it unpatentable, the Board of Appeal ruled that:

> Since the only conceivable use for a computer program is the running of it on a computer, the exclusion from patentability of programs for computers would be effectively undermined if it could be circumvented by including in the claim a reference to conventional hardware features, such as processor, memory, keyboard and display, which in practice are indispensable if the program is to be used at all. In the opinion of the Board, in such cases, patentability must depend on whether the operations performed involve an inventive step in a field not excluded from patentability.[5]

[1] *Vicom Systems Inc's Application* [1987] 2 EPOR 74.
[2] [1988] EPOR 72.
[3] *Hitachi's Application* [1991] RPC 415 at 417.
[4] [1990] EPOR 181.
[5] [1990] EPOR 181 at 183.

19.66 A further decision relating to an application from IBM, *IBM Corpn/ Reading Age*,[1] is more explicit. This application concerned a system for checking automatically the text of a document in order to highlight words having a reading age higher than that specified for its readers. The system would go on to present a list of alternative formulations which would meet the appropriate age requirements. Again, the equipment could be seen as replicating functions traditionally carried out by human editors. Although the particular application was rejected, the Board of Appeal held that such a development might be patentable if the technical manner in which the process was conducted involved an advance on the state of the art *even though* (emphasis added) the steps taken might correspond to those performed in the mind of a human.

[1] [1990] OJEPO 384.

19.67 *IBM/Semantically Related Expressions*[1] involved an application by IBM, who sought to patent a system for automatically generating a list of expressions semantically related to an input linguistic expression, together with a method for displaying such a list, ie a form of thesaurus. The actions of the computer in this case were considered to operate in the field of linguistics rather than to produce a technical contribution to the known art.

¹   [1989] EPOR 454.

19.68   The computer's functions were all conventional, described as consisting of:

> ... storing data; comparing input data with an index for finding an address location; storing the address; accessing it with a memory; decoding the addressed data; utilising the decoded data as an address for accessing another memory; displaying the addressed data.¹

¹   *IBM/Semantically Related Expressions* [1989] EPOR 454 at 458.

19.69   Beyond the technicalities of its performance, all that the computer did was to compare data, in the form of a word, with other data already programmed into a segment of its memory and display the results of any matches. To this extent, its operations were comparable with a person 'searching' his or her memory for an alternative form of expression. The Board of Appeal concluded:

> It remains, of course, true that internally a computer functions technically and this applies also to its display device. However, the effect of this function, namely the resulting information about the existence of semantically related expressions, is a purely linguistic, that is, non-technical result. The appellant agrees that the claimed system can be implemented by pure software and this implementation is the only one described and preferred. No new reconfigured hardware has been shown to be used in this case. As said before, the two memories can be different sections of a single (conventional) memory. In the opinion of the Board, this new reconfiguration by software is not a technical contribution here.¹

¹   *IBM/Semantically Related Expressions* [1989] EPOR 454 at 460.

19.70   In a further case, *IBM/Data Processor Network*,¹ the application involved the interconnection of a series of computers in such a manner as to facilitate communications between programs and data held in the various computers. Obviously, the basis for the claimed invention lay in the computer programs which controlled these operations. It was accepted that:

> The proposed improved communication facilities between programs and files held at different processors within the known network do not involve any changes in the physical structure of the processors or the transmission network. The necessary control functions for this purpose, referred to as 'mirror transaction' in the description of the present application, are effected by appropriate software.²

In spite of this, it was the opinion of the Board of Appeal that:

> ... an invention relating to the coordination and control of the internal communication between programs and data files held at different processors in a data processing system ... and the features of which are not concerned with

the nature of the data and the way in which a particular application program operates on them, is to be regarded as solving a problem which is essentially technical. Such an invention therefore is to be regarded as an invention within the meaning of Article 52(1) EPC [European Patent Convention].[3]

1   [1990] EPOR 91.
2   [1990] EPOR 91 at 94.
3   [1990] EPOR 91 at 95.

19.71   In yet another application involving IBM, *IBM/Computer Related Invention*,[1] an application was accepted which referred to a method for causing a computer to display automatically one of a number of predetermined messages relating to the machine's status. The view was taken that:

> ... giving visual indications automatically about conditions prevailing in the apparatus or system is basically a technical problem.

The application proposed a solution to a specific problem of this kind, namely providing a visual indication about events occurring in the input/output device of a text processor. The solution included the use of a computer program and certain tables stored in a memory to build up the phrases to be displayed.[2]

1   [1990] EPOR 107.
2   [1990] EPOR 107 at 110.

19.72   The distinction between this successful application and the unsuccessful claim in *IBM/Semantically-Related Expressions*[1] appears slight. The Board of Appeal were of the view that the present application was more than a computer program, but it is not clear why a development which automatically displays information regarding a computer system's state of health should be so regarded whilst a development which automatically displays the synonyms of a word inputted by a user should be rejected.

1   *IBM/Semantically Related Expressions* [1989] EPOR 454.

19.73   Final reference will be made to another IBM application, this time involving a development in what is referred to as text clarity.[1] This consisted of a method by which a computer program would scan text in order to identify incomprehensible or obscure linguistic expressions and suggesting alternative formulations. Many authors could benefit greatly from such a facility.

1   *IBM/Text Clarity Processing (T38/86)* [1990] EPOR 606.

19.74   Once again, the Board of Examiners sought to identify whether the claimed invention produced any technical effect. It used, it was held, technical means to substitute for human intellectual acts, but once the steps required to perform the act have been identified, their implementation involved 'no more than the straightforward application of standard techniques'[1] which would be obvious to a person skilled in the technical art. On this basis, there was no inventive step. The Board of Examiners concluded:

Since the only conceivable use for a computer program is the running of it on a computer, the exclusion from patentability of computer programs would be effectively undermined if it could be circumvented by including in the claim a reference to conventional hardware features ... which in practice are indispensable if the program is to be used at all.[2]

[1]   *IBM/Text Clarity Processing (T38/86)* [1990] EPOR 606 at 611.
[2]   [1990] EPOR 606 at 613.

19.75   Although the case law of the European Patent Office as discussed above does not appear totally consistent, the number of successful applications, coupled with some of the dicta of the Board of Examiners, created a sense that the criteria were being applied more flexibly. This was the case not just in respect of the prohibition against the award of patents for computer programs, but also in respect of the prohibition against the award of a patent in respect of a scheme or method for performing a mental act. Given that the effect of many computer programs is to automate processes which would previously have required human intervention, this can be a substantial obstacle to the award of a patent.

Schemes or methods for performing a mental act

19.76   Two relevant UK cases on this point concern applications by Wang and Raytheon. In *Wang*,[1] the claimed invention related to a novel form of expert system. This was held to be unpatentable on the ground that it related to nothing more than a computer program. Reference was also made in the case to the statutory prohibition against the grant of a patent in respect of a scheme or method for performing a mental act. Counsel for Wang argued that the phrase 'scheme, rule or method for performing a mental act' only applied to methods which were capable of being performed in the human mind. The operation of the expert system, although seeking to produce results similar to those arrived at by a human expert, utilised steps and procedures which would not be replicated by such a person. This interpretation was rejected by Aldous J (as he then was), who held that:

Just as a claim to a disk containing a program can be in fact a claim to an invention for a computer program, so can a claim to steps leading to an answer be a claim to an invention for a method for performing a mental act. The method remains a method for performing a mental act, whether a computer is used or not. Thus a method of solving a problem, such as advising a person whether he has acted tortuously, can be set out on paper, or incorporated into a computer program. The purpose is the same, to enable advice to be given, which appears to me to be a mental act. Further, the result will be the advice which comes from performance of a mental act. The method may well be different when a computer is used, but to my mind it still remains a method for performing a mental act, whether or not the computer program adopts steps that would not ordinarily be used by the human mind.[2]

[1]   [1991] RPC 463.
[2]   [1991] RPC 463 at 473.

Image identifying

19.77 The decision in *Wang*[1] was approved in the subsequent case of *Raytheon's Application*.[2] At issue in this case was a method of automatically identifying objects such as ships. The image of the object's silhouette would be captured by some form of imaging device, such as a camera, and transformed into digital format. The digitised image would then be processed by a standard computer. This process involved making a comparison with a library of images stored on the computer in order to select the most appropriate match. A patent was sought for the process, but was rejected within the Patent Office on the grounds that the application related to no more than a method for performing a mental act using a computer. This interpretation was upheld in the Patents Court, where Mr Julian Jeffs QC (sitting as a deputy judge) held that the phrase 'a mental act' had to be construed in its normal sense. This was equated with the possibility of explaining in words how a mental act had been performed. Thus:

> I have long known that seven eights are fifty-six. By an analytical process I could demonstrate how that result is derived. It is certainly a mental process. But if I meet a friend in the street and I recognise him, it is hard to explain in words precisely why. No doubt the act of recognition could to some extent be analysed and expressed in words, but no combination of words would enable a total stranger to pick my friend out of a crowd. To move on to a more abstract conception, if I smell an orange, I know that it is an orange. I recognise it by such a process of comparison calling up the smell of oranges that I have smelt in the past, but no words could be formulated that would enable someone to recognise the smell of an orange who has never smelt one. Yet in recognising the orange I have no doubt that I am performing a mental act. It would no doubt be possible to devise an apparatus which would achieve the same result by a process of chemical analysis. Such an alternative process of recognition would not be a mental act and the apparatus might well embody one or more inventions. There would be a technical advance, but that is not what is happening in the present invention.[3]

[1]   [1991] RPC 463.
[2]   [1993] RPC 427.
[3]   [1993] RPC 427 at 432.

19.78 The approach developed in *Wang*[1] and *Raytheon*[2] would deny protection to any software-related innovation performing a function which, *in principle*, could be carried out within the human brain even though this would not reflect the normal process of human reasoning. This approach sits uneasily with at least some of the jurisprudence of the European Patent Office and, during the 1990s, concerns were raised in a number of forums concerning the state of UK law and whether the stated objective to ensure compatibility with the case law of the European Patent Office was being met. The most recent UK decision is that of *Fujitsu's Application*. The scrutiny of the High Court[3] and Court of Appeal[4] was welcomed, not least by the patent authorities, it being commented before the High Court that:

> ... in recent years the Comptroller has found himself in some difficulty in applying these statutory exclusions for two reasons. The first is that, whilst the

authorities appear to distinguish clearly between inventions which provide a 'technical advance' and are thus patentable and those which do not and, accordingly, are not, in practice it is often very difficult to determine whether a particular invention does as a matter of fact involve the sort of technical contribution or result alluded to in the cases. That difficulty, he suggested, has been compounded by the fact that there are recent decisions of the E.P.O. Technical Board of Appeal in which the question of what constitutes a technical advance or contribution seems to have been rather more flexibly interpreted than has hitherto been the case. The second reason is that strict application of the guidance laid down in the authorities leads to the exclusion from patentability of a considerable number of inventions which do in reality appear to provide a substantial contribution to the sum of technical knowledge. He said that the present case raises starkly and clearly the effect of these two exclusions. Since they have become of considerable importance and controversy when applied to software-related inventions and there is a relatively large number of applications in which their scope has to be considered, the Comptroller is anxious, if at all possible, to have the guidance of the court to assist him in the future on the scope and application of the exclusions.[5]

It is not clear whether these hopes have been realised, although more recent developments in the European Patent Office and the EU may, if not rendering the issue otiose, change significantly the nature of the questions.

[1]   [1991] RPC 463.
[2]   [1993] RPC 427.
[3]   [1996] RPC 511.
[4]   [1997] RPC 608.
[5]   [1996] RPC 511 at 521–522.

Fujitsu's Application

19.79   The technology at issue in *Fujitsu*[1] will be familiar to anyone with a recollection of chemistry lessons at school and the use of three dimensional lattices to depict molecular structures. Fujitsu's invention sought to bring this concept into the age of virtual reality, allowing chemists to depict and manipulate crystal structures on a computer screen. The effect would be to allow the analysis of the properties of new compounds without the need to create these in the real world. The novelty in the claimed invention lay only in the relevant computer programs.

[1]   *Fujitsu Ltd's Application* [1996] RPC 511.

19.80   The patent application was rejected in the Patent Office on two grounds: first, that the application related to a program for a computer; and secondly, that it constituted a method for performing a mental act – that of visualising molecular structure.

The computer program exception

19.81   Relying on the *Vicom* decision,[1] Counsel for Fujitsu suggested that what was required to bring prohibited subject matter, such as computer programs or schemes for performing mental acts, within the patent system was that these should be tied to some technical application. In the present case,[2] as in *Vicom*, the technical component was that the application resulted in the manipulation of images. In *Vicom*, images of physical objects were processed; in the present case, images of molecular structure.

[1]   *Vicom Systems Inc's Application* [1987] 2 EPOR 74.
[2]   *Fujitsu Ltd's Application* [1996] RPC 511.

19.82   After surveying relevant UK and European Patent Office authority, Laddie J concluded that four propositions could be drawn relating to the patentability of software-related inventions:

1. The types of subject-matter referred to in section 1(2) [of the Patents Act 1977] are excluded from patentability as a matter of policy. This is so whether the matter is technical or not.

2. The exclusion from patentability is a matter of substance not form. Therefore the exclusion under section 1(2) extends to any form of passive carrier or recording of excluded subject matter. Thus, merely because a piece of paper is in principle patentable (save to the extent that it lacks novelty), it is not permissible, for example, to record a literary work (section 1(2)(b)) or a computer program (section 1(2)(c)) on a piece of paper and then seek patent monopoly for the paper bearing the recorded work. Similarly it is not permissible, without more, to seek protection for a computer program when it is stored on a magnetic medium or when merely loaded into a computer.

3. Prima facie a computer running under the control of one program is a different piece of apparatus from the same computer when running under the control of another program. It follows that a claim to a computer when controlled by a program or to a method of controlling a computer by a program or to a method of carrying out a process by use of a computer so controlled can be the subject of patent protection. However, because the court is concerned with substance not form, it is not enough for the designer of a new program to seek protection for his creation merely by framing it in one of these terms. The court or patent office must direct its attention not to the fact that the program is controlling the computer but to what the computer, so controlled, is doing.

4. Therefore a data processing system operating to produce a novel result would not be deprived of protection on the ground that it was a program as such. On the other hand, even if the effect of the program is to make the computer perform in a novel way, it is still necessary to look at precisely what the computer is doing, i.e. at the nature of the process being carried out. If all that is being done, as a matter of substance, is the performance of one of the activities defined under section 1(2) as unprotectable, then it is still unprotectable.

On the basis of these criteria, he concluded:

> ... just as it would be possible to obtain a patent, considerations of novelty aside, for a faster chip or a more effective storage medium or a computer containing such a chip, there is no reason in principle or logic why modification of the computer to achieve the same speed or storage increase by means of software should be excluded from protection.[1]

Attention must therefore be focused on what the claimed invention achieves rather than the manner in which it accomplishes this.

¹ *Fujitsu Ltd's Application* [1996] RPC 511 at 530.

19.83 At first instance, it is unclear whether the *Fujitsu* application was regarded as constituting nothing more than a computer program. Holding that 'prima facie, they avoided the program exclusion', Laddie J continued:

> The real issues it seems to me is whether the application also avoids the other exclusions ... If it does not, the application will fail. Whether in those circumstances, the grounds of failure are stated to be that the invention is only for a program or that it is, for example, a method for performing a mental act is a matter of semantics.¹

¹ *Fujitsu Ltd's Application* [1996] RPC 511 at 532.

19.84 The issue was considered in more detail in the Court of Appeal. Here, Aldous LJ held that the application should be rejected on this basis. Comparing the claimed invention with that at issue in *Vicom*,¹ he concluded that:

> In VICOM, the technical contribution was provided by the generation of the enhanced display. In the present case, the combined structure is the result of the directions given by the operator and use of the program. The computer is conventional as is the display unit. The displays of crystal structures are provided by the operator. The operator then provides the appropriate way of superposition and the program does the rest. The resulting display is the combined structure shown pictorially in a form that would in the past have been produced as a model. The only advance is the computer program which enables the combined structure to be portrayed quicker.²

¹ *Vicom Systems Inc's Application* [1987] 2 EPOR 74.
² *Fujitsu Ltd's Application* [1997] RPC 608 at 618–619.

19.85 It might be suggested that a quicker method of producing a display of molecular structure should be regarded as patentable in the same way as would a better mousetrap or a method for producing better quality images. Certainly, the comments made regarding the conventional nature of the computer and the fact that 'virtual reality' displays are substituting for traditional three dimensional models might be ground for challenge on the issues of novelty and inventiveness, but the distinction drawn with the situation in *Vicom*¹ exacerbates rather than clarifies the issue what is required to produce a technical effect.

¹ *Vicom Systems Inc's Application* [1987] 2 EPOR 74.

Schemes or methods for performing a mental act

19.86 Holding that the application related to no more than a scheme or method for performing a mental act, Laddie J stated that:

> In VICOM,¹ the Board explained that a mathematical method could be distinguished from a patentable process based on it in that the former involved

an abstract concept in which numbers were worked on to produce new numbers whereas in a patentable process a physical entity was worked on and a new physical entity was produced. Very similar concepts apply to the distinction between methods for performing mental acts and processes methods or apparatus based upon such acts. Excluded mental acts must include those mental activities which involve a significant level of abstraction and intellectual generality. Rules as to the planting of potatoes in which the operator is instructed to measure and evaluate matters such as the type of soil, location, weather and availability of irrigation is a method for performing a mental act. Directions to plant one seed potato every metre is not. It is a precise process.

In this case, Fujitsu's application leaves it to the operator to select what data to work on, how to work on it, how to assess the results and which, if any, results to use. The process is abstract and the result of use of it is undefined. What is produced is not an inevitable result of taking a number of defined steps but is determined by the personal skill and assessment of the operator. As such it consists in substance of a scheme or method for performing a mental act and is unpatentable.[2]

1   *Vicom Systems Inc's Application* [1987] 2 EPOR 74.
2   *Fujitsu Ltd's Application* [1996] RPC 511 at 532.

19.87   The decision in *Fujitsu*[1] provides no specific answer to the definitional questions raised above. It does appear to support a restrictive view of the scope of patentability. In some respects, the result seems somewhat paradoxical. A computer-controlled potato-planting machine which plants a potato every metre might be patentable. Were the identical machine to have more sophisticated software allowing account to be taken of factors such as soil conditions, weather and the presence of other crops, no patent could be awarded, even though this second machine might appear more technologically advanced and deserving of protection. Again, reference to the role of the Fujitsu system in presenting information for the operator to act upon might be compared with many other pieces of machinery. The example might be presented of a novel form of navigational aid incorporated on an aircraft flight deck. This might present the pilots with information as to height, speed and direction of flight. Assuming that the device made use of mechanical components, there would be no bar to its patentability.

1   *Fujitsu Ltd's Application* [1996] RPC 511 at 532.

The Commission Green Paper on the Patent System

19.88   Reference has been made in the previous chapter to the attempts by the European Commission to revive the Community Patent Convention. In its Green Paper on 'Promoting innovation through patents: Green paper on the Community patent and the patent system in Europe',[1] the Commission sought views on the application of the patent system in the field of computer software. Whilst restating the current prohibition against the patentability of software as such, it recognises that:

Faced with the increasing importance of software, the European Patent Office and the national Patent Offices of some Member States have in recent years granted thousands of patents protecting logical models composed of basic ideas and principles that constitute 'technical solutions to technical problems'. These patents were not granted for the software *per se* but in respect of software-related inventions consisting of hardware and software.[2]

1 (1997) Available from http://europa.eu.int/comm/internal_market/en/intprop/indprop/
   paten.pdf.
2 Chapter 4(2).

19.89 The Commission notes that the TRIPS agreement provides that patents should be available for 'any inventions, whether products or processes, in all fields of technology' (art 27). This formulation does not exclude software and some commentators have argued that the present approach of the European Patent Convention contravenes the TRIPS agreement. The current US patents law makes no specific mention of computer programs and practice in the courts and Patent Office has indicated an increasing willingness to award patents for software-related inventions in situations where the role of the hardware component was extremely peripheral to the technology at issue. Japan has also adopted a favourable attitude towards the patentability of software-related inventions, with draft Guidelines indicating that patents should be awarded to inventions which involve a high degree of 'technological creativeness using the laws of nature'.

19.90 A follow-up document published by the Commission in 1999[1] takes matters a stage further. Problems were identified with the working of the European Patent Convention it being reported that:

There are significant disadvantages, such as differences in court judgments, inherent in such a practice which lacks transparency in terms of the text of the Munich Convention. Thus, opinions differ between the EPO and certain German courts on the one hand, and the British courts on the other; this means that the same invention is protected in some Member States and not in others, a situation which is *damaging* [emphasis in original] to the proper operation of the internal market.[2]

This situation means that, although the Munich Convention and the national laws of Member States do not permit the patentability of computer programs as such, there are about 13 000 European patents covering software! It would also appear that, owing to extensive ignorance of the current legal situation in Europe, about 75% of these patents are held by very large non-European companies. European industry is very interested in this type of protection; however, most SMEs in the programming sector are not aware that, by filing patent applications in a certain way, patent protection can be obtained for this type of invention. With investments of almost $40 000 million annually in developing information technology and software programs, the economic importance of this sector is obvious.[3]

1 Available from http://europa.eu.int/comm/internal_market/en/intprop/indprop/8682en.pdf.
2 Section 3.2.1.
3 Section 3.2.1.

19.91 Whilst it was recognised that inventions would be patentable where the use of computer programs resulted in a technical contribution to the state of the art, the refusal to grant protection to the program per se, constituted a significant limitation to the level of protection. As was stated:

> An important consequence of the difference of protection is the scope of the conferred rights and the means of enforcement: in the United States, the holder of a patent covering a program may directly attack the distributor of counterfeit programs distributed via a medium ('direct infringement'), whereas in Europe, since the protection is limited to the technical invention which uses the program, the distributor of a diskette is only the accomplice, but not the author of the infringement ('contributory infringement'); the sole author of the infringement is the user who uses the program on the diskette and only he can be sued. The harmonisation of legislation on this question must ensure that rights are *implemented effectively* [emphasis in original] throughout the Community.[1]

[1]   Section 3.2.1.

19.92 With the support of the European Parliament, the Commission recommended that software should be brought unequivocally within the scope of the patent system. Two initiatives, it was suggested, should be pursued. First, a directive should be introduced aimed at harmonising member states' laws regarding the patentability of software. A precedent for such action lies in the field of biotechnology, where a Directive was introduced to overcome problems with the European Patent Convention's prohibition against the award of a patent for developments in this field.[1] Secondly, the member states who were signatory to the Patent Convention should propose the removal of computer programs from the art 52 list of prohibited subject matter.

[1]   Directive 98/44/EC on on the legal protection of biotechnological inventions, OJ 1998 L 213/13

19.93 The proposal that the European Patent Convention should be amended to remove the prohibition against the patentability of computer programs was discussed and rejected at a diplomatic conference held in 2000. There were perhaps two reasons for this decision. First, it was considered that a decision regarding the future of the programs prohibition should not be taken in isolation from the other Convention grounds of exclusion such as discovery or mathematical method. Also, in February 1999, the European Patent Convention Board of Appeal published its decision in the case of yet another application from IBM.[1] This decision signalled significant changes of emphasis and direction concerning the manner in which software-related inventions will be treated within the European Patent Office, removing much of the impetus for more radical change to the Convention itself. The case is important not just for its findings in relation to the operation of the patent system, but also as providing an excellent illustration of the manner in which the activities of the World Trade Organization and the provisions of the TRIPS agreement are exercising a profound influence over the interpretation of systems of intellectual property law.

[1]   Case T0935/97 [1999] RPC 861. A virtually identical decision was handed down in July 1998 in case T1173/97 concerning another application by IBM.

IBM's Application

19.94　At issue in this case was an application for a patent for developments in relation to the use of 'windows' as a means for presenting information on a computer monitor. The advantage of IBM's programs, it was claimed, was that it rearranged the information held in one window so that it remained visible even when another window was opened on top of it. The application was rejected by the examiner on the ground that it related to a program per se and an appeal made to the Board of Appeal.

19.95　IBM's appeal was based on a number of grounds. It was argued that:

> ... the reason for the exclusion of computer programs as such from patent protection under the European Patent Convention was because there was already adequate and clear protection in the form of copyright, but that if the claims sought to protect something which would not attract copyright protection then the objection to patentability must fall. It was also argued that this approach was consistent with TRIPS. The appellants further argued that since the European Patent Office allowed a claim defining an invention by way of a technical feature, even if that feature was embodied in a computer program, once such an intellectual construction had been accepted as an invention, the provisions of Article 52 of the EPC were satisfied and would no longer justify constraining the applicant as to how to claim the invention.[1]

The issue concerning the availability of copyright for developments such as the IBM software was not pursued by the Board of Appeal. Whilst there is no doubt that computer programs are protected by copyright, this does not extend to the underlying concepts.

[1]　Case T0935/97 [1999] RPC 861 at 862.

19.96　The TRIPS agreement provides that computer programs are to be protected by copyright. It requires also, however, that 'patents shall be available for any inventions, whether products or processes, in all fields of technology, provided they are new, involve an inventive step and are capable of industrial application'.[1] There is no equivalent to the European Patent Convention's list of prohibited subject matter.

[1]　Article 5.

19.97　It is national states (and the EU) who are signatories to TRIPS. The Agreement, therefore, is not binding upon international organisations such as the European Patent Office. The Board of Appeal held, however, that its provisions should be taken into account:

> ... since it is aimed at setting common standards and principles concerning the availability, scope and use of trade-related intellectual property rights, and therefore of patent rights. Thus TRIPS gives a clear indication of current trends[1].

[1]　Case T0935/97 [1999] RPC 861 at 868.

19.98   Reference was made also to developments in the US and Japanese Patent Offices, which had adopted a more liberal approach towards the grant of patents for software-related inventions. Whilst recognising that these offices worked under legal provisions different from those applying in Europe, the developments, it was considered, 'represent a useful indication of modern trends' which 'may contribute to the further highly desirable (worldwide) harmonisation of patent law'. The clear implication would appear to be that the European Patent Office was out of step with other major offices in its treatment of software-related inventions.

19.99   Turning to the substance of the particular application, reference was made to the fact that computer programs were excluded only to the extent that the invention related to the program 'as such'. This formulation, it was held, indicated that the 'legislators did not want to exclude from patentability all programs for computers'. In previous decisions, the European Patent Office had laid stress on the requirement for a technical contribution. In the present case, attention focused on the interpretation of the phrase 'as such'. This phrase, it was held:

> ... may be construed to mean that such programs are considered to be mere abstract creations, lacking in technical character. The use of the expression 'shall not be regarded as inventions' seems to confirm this interpretation.
>
> This means that programs for computers must be considered as patentable inventions when they have a technical character.[1]

[1]   Case T0935/97 [1999] RPC 861 at 870.

19.100   The question, therefore, was to determine when a computer program constituted more than a more abstract creation and exhibited a technical character in its own right, independent of linkage with tangible objects. What was required was that the program should have the potential to cause the occurrence of a technical effect. Consequently, it was held:

> ... a patent may be granted not only in the case of an invention where a piece of software manages, by means of a computer, an industrial process or the working of a piece of machinery, but in every case where a program for a computer is the only means, or one of the necessary means, of obtaining a technical effect within the meaning specified above, where, for instance, a technical effect of that kind is achieved by the internal functioning of a computer itself under the influence of said program.
>
> In other words, on condition that they are able to produce a technical effect in the above sense, all computer programs must be considered as inventions within the meaning of Article 52(1) of the EPC [European Patent Convention], and may be the subject-matter of a patent if the other requirements provided for by the EPC are satisfied.
>
> ... Once it has been clearly established that a specific computer program product, when run on a computer, brings about a technical effect in the above sense, the Board sees no good reason for distinguishing between a direct technical effect on the one hand and the potential to produce a technical effect, which may be considered as an indirect technical effect, on the other hand.[1]

[1]   Case T0935/97 [1999] RPC 861 at 871.

19.101 It was recognised that the Guidelines for Examiners stated that a 'computer program claimed by itself or as a record on a carrier is not patentable'. For the future, however, the Board's decision was that:

> ... a computer program claimed by itself is not excluded from patentability if the program, when running on a computer or loaded into a computer, brings about, or is capable of bringing about, a technical effect which goes beyond the 'normal' physical interactions between the program (software) and the computer (hardware) on which it is run.[1]

[1] Case T0935/97 [1999] RPC 861 at 877.

19.102 Although the Board of Appeal argued that their decision was consistent with previous European Patent Office case law (subject to one decision which was distinguished from the present case), there is no doubt that the effect of the decision has been to increase the profile of the patent system as a vehicle for protecting software developments significantly. In the 'follow-up to the Green Paper on the Community patent' the Commission note that whilst some 13,000 software-related patents had been awarded by the European Patent Office:

> ... owing to extensive ignorance of the current legal situation in Europe, about 75% of these patents are held by very large non-European companies.

19.103 The argument is effectively that US and Japanese software companies expect to be able to obtain patents and make successful application to the European Patent Office. European companies, especially in the small and medium-size sector, tend to look at the headline prohibition on the European Patent Convention and decide that patents are not available.

19.104 The new European Patent Office approach seems to meet the objectives of the Commission's Green Paper and follow-up document. As indicated in the Green Paper, the major effect of the extension of the patent system to computer programs per se will be to increase the rights of the patent holder. In the situation where the patent relates only to the implementation of the programs within a computer system, a party who supplied copies of the software would not be guilty of patent infringement – although there might be a case of breach of copyright. Where the software is itself patented, the supply of copies will be unlawful. In the particular case, provision of software causing the manipulation of windows displays as described in the patent will be unlawful, even though the code used to implement this may be totally different from that utilised by IBM. To this extent, the scope of protection is very much greater than that which can be obtained under the law of copyright.

19.105 Following the decision in *IBM*,[1] a Practice Note was issued by the UK Patent Office.[2] This traced the development of case law in the UK and under the European Patent Convention. After surveying the UK precedents, it was indicated that in all of the cases discussed above:

... the courts were not able to identify any substantive technical contribution in any of these authorities and as a result they rejected the applications for that reason. Consequently, they did not elaborate on the position in the event there is such a contribution.

1   Case T0935/97 [1999] RPC 861.
2   Available from http://www.patent.gov.uk/snews/notices/practice/programs.html.

19.106   The principles applied, however, were it was suggested, the same as those adopted in the European Patent Office. As a consequence, the decision in *IBM*[1] was seen as 'fully consistent with UK case law'. At the level of practice, however, changes would be required and the Note indicated that the:

> Patent Office's practice will in future be to accept claims to computer programs, either themselves or on a carrier, provided that the program is such that when run on a computer it produces a technical effect which is more than would necessarily follow merely from the running of any program on a computer and which is such that claims to the computer when programmed would not be rejected under section 1(2)(c) [of the Patents Act 1977] under the existing practice.

1   Case T0935/97 [1999] RPC 861.

19.107   Whilst it has been argued above that the criteria applied by the UK courts have been, in some significant respects, more restrictive than those of their European Patent Office counterparts, it does seem clear that the patent system is going to play a much more important role in protecting software developments than has hitherto been the case within Europe. It is perhaps ironic that some 20 years after the UK court handed down its decision in respect of IBM's application under the Patent Act 1949, and after two decades of statutory and judicial word games, we should have returned to what might be considered the original start point.

1   *International Business Machines Corpn's Application* [1980] FSR 564.

US patent law

19.108   In the preceding sections, reference has frequently been made to developments within the US. As was indicated, the US authorities have over a period of years adopted a liberal approach towards the grant of patents for software-related inventions. Given the extensive references made to US law and practice in the Commission Green Paper and follow-up document, and also the views expressed by the European Patent Office Board of Appeal regarding the desirability of international harmonisation, some brief consideration of key US decisions may provide a helpful conclusion to this chapter.

19.109   The basis of patent law within the US is found in the Constitution, which empowers the Congress to 'promote the progress of science and the useful arts'.[1] Title 35 of the US Code gives effect to this providing, inter alia, that:

Whoever invents or discovers any new and useful process, machine, manufacture, or composition of matter, or any new and useful improvement thereof, may obtain a patent therefor.[2]

No specific mention is made in the statute of computer programs and the US legislation might be considered analogous to the provisions of the Patents Act 1949.

[1]   Article 1.
[2]   Section 101.

19.110   Questions relating to the patentability of software-related inventions have come before the Supreme Court on a number of occasions. These cases are, perhaps, of limited significance in themselves, but are important in respect of the signals that they transmit to the US patent authorities and to the lower courts.

19.111   The first case to be considered is that of *Gottschalk v Benson.*[1] This concerned the alleged invention of a method for converting what were referred to as 'binary-coded decimal numbers' into their 'pure binary' equivalents. The distinction between the two forms of notation is that the former convert each decimal component separately, whilst the latter make the conversion as a unit. Thus the binary-coded decimal equivalent of the number 53 would be expressed as 0101 0011 whilst its pure binary equivalent will be 110101.

[1]   34 L Ed 2d 273 (1972).

19.112   The mathematical formulae by which this conversion might be accomplished manually are well known, but the contested application described a novel method by which this could be accomplished using a computer program and claimed a patent in respect of all applications of the process. No reference was made to any particular form of computer on which the program was intended to operate.

19.113   The application was rejected in the Patent Office, whose decision was reversed by the Court of Customs and Patent Appeals. Their finding was in turn reversed by the Supreme Court.[1] Delivering the judgment of a unanimous court, Douglas J referred to dicta in the earlier Supreme Court case of *Mackay Co v Radio Corpn,*[2] to the effect that:

> ... (w)hile a scientific truth, or the mathematical expression of it, is not a patentable invention, a novel and useful structure created with the aid of knowledge of scientific truth may be.[3]

The requirement was that the theory or discovery or other unpatentable subject matter must be put to some practical and useful end. In the present case, the result of granting a patent would be to confer a monopoly prohibiting any future use of the mathematical formula involved in a situation where the application referred to no substantial practical application other than the operation of a computer program.

¹   *Gottschalk v Benson* 34 L Ed 2d 273 (1972).
²   306 US 86 (1939).
³   306 US 86 at 94 (1939).

19.114   Having determined that the particular application did not qualify for the grant of a patent, comment was made concerning the possible extension of the patent system to cover computer programs. Such a decision was held, however, to be one for the legislature rather than the courts.

19.115   The next case to be considered is that of *Parker v Flook*.¹ This case concerned the application of a computer program in the process of catalytic conversion. During such processes, it was normal practice to monitor operating conditions. The existing technology would permit this to occur automatically, the process being monitored against predetermined limits with alarms being triggered in the event that these were exceeded. It was recognised that fixed alarm limits were of limited value at some stages in the process, such as the initial start-up, where the limits might safely be exceeded for brief periods of time.

¹   57 L Ed 2d 451 (1978).

19.116   The applicant's claimed invention operated in three stages. First, it monitored a variety of operating conditions, for example, temperature and pressure; secondly, it applied an algorithm (a step-by-step procedure for solving a mathematical problem) to calculate a new alarm limit; and, finally, it reset the system to operate at the new levels. The only novelty in the applicant's system lay in the second step. The protection sought extended to any application of the algorithm in a process of catalytic conversion of hydrocarbons, a claim which encompassed a substantial range of activities.

19.117   The application was rejected in the Patent Office, but was upheld by the Court of Customs and Patent Appeals.¹ This distinguished the case of *Gottschalk v Benson*² on the basis that it applied only to situations where the application claimed all applications of the formulae. In the present case, the claims referred to a limited class of application. This decision was appealed to the Supreme Court which, by a majority of 6-3, upheld the initial decision of the Patent Office. Although it stopped short of denying the possibility of patent protection to any computer-related invention, the majority held that where the only novelty in the application lay in a mathematical formula (or any other form of unpatentable subject matter), a claim could not succeed.

¹   *Parker v Flook* 57 L Ed 2d 451 (1978).
²   *Gottschalk v Benson* 34 L Ed 2d 273 (1972).

19.118   This approach was criticised by the dissenting minority of the court, who argued:

> The issue here is whether a claimed process loses its status of subject-matter patentability simply because one step in the process would not be patentable subject matter if taken in isolation.¹

Subject to the question of whether the remaining elements of the claimed invention would satisfy the requirements of novelty and inventiveness, the minority were, therefore, in favour of the grant of a patent.

1   *Parker v Flook* 57 L Ed 2d 451 at 463 (1978).

19.119   The arguments of the minority in *Parker*[1] appear comparable with the approach adopted under the UK and European patent systems. Although the arguments were unsuccessful in *Parker*, they were to meet with more success in the final case to be considered, that of *Diamond v Diehr*.[2] Once again, the application related to the use of a computer to control a manufacturing process, in this case for the production of rubber products.

1   *Parker v Flook* 57 L Ed 2d 451 (1978).
2   67 L Ed 2d 155 (1981).

19.120   A difficulty which had faced producers of rubber products was that of determining the length of time for which the rubber should be held in a mould. The applicants claimed invention involved the process of continually monitoring the temperature inside the mould, feeding the measurements into a computer, which would, using an established mathematical equation, calculate the optimum time for the production process and would, at the appropriate time, transmit a signal causing the mould to open. Once again, the application was initially rejected within the Patent Office on the basis that it involved the use of a mathematical formula and, as such, was barred from protection. Once again, a successful appeal was made to the Court of Customs and Patent Appeals, whose decision was, on this occasion, upheld by a 5-4 majority in the Supreme Court.[1]

1   *Diamond v Diehr* 67 L Ed 2d 155 (1981).

19.121   The basis of the majority's decision in *Diamond*[1] lies in the arguments of the minority in *Parker*.[2] The composition of the court being the same in both cases, the reversal of the result was based on the 'defection' of two of the majority from *Parker*, the court's distinguishing of the two cases being somewhat unconvincing. In the view of the majority, the applicant's claim was in respect of an improved process for the production of rubber products. The claim had to be considered as a whole. In this situation:

> ... it is inappropriate to dissect the claim into old and new elements and then to ignore the presence of the old elements in the analysis. This is particularly true in a process claim because a new combination of steps in a process may be patentable even though all the constituents of the combination were well known and in common use before the combination was made.[3]

1   *Diamond v Diehr* 67 L Ed 2d 155 (1981).
2   *Parker v Flook* 57 L Ed 2d 451 (1978).
3   67 L Ed 2d 155 at 167 (1981).

19.122   Although care must be taken to avoid the possibility that a skilled draftsman might attempt to evade the prohibition against the grant of a patent to a program per se by linking the program to an insignificant specific application, the present case did not fall into this category and, accordingly, the claim should not be barred from the award of a patent.

US Patents after Diamond v Diehr

19.123 The decision of the Supreme Court in *Diamond*[1] served to open the way for the inclusion of software within the patent system. Subsequent cases before lower courts have shown a considerable willingness to extend the process. An illustration of this may be taken from the decision of the Delaware District Court in the case of *Paine, Webber, Jackson and Curtis, Inc v Merrill Lynch, Pierce, Fenner and Smith, Inc.*[2]

[1]   *Diamond v Diehr* 67 L Ed 2d 155 (1981).
[2]   564 F Supp 1358 (1983).

19.124 At issue in the action was a patent which had been awarded in respect of a financial management system which permitted funds to be switched between a variety of accounts in such a way as to maximise the financial benefit accruing to the account holder. The various forms of account involved were totally orthodox. Merrill Lynch's innovation was to automate the transfer procedures, and a patent was awarded in respect of the data processing methodology and apparatus devised to implement the system. The validity of this patent was challenged by the plaintiffs, who argued that its subject matter was barred from patent protection.

19.125 Dismissing this claim, the District Court held that a patent could be awarded when its subject matter did not consist solely of a mathematical algorithm. The word 'algorithm', it was held:

> ... has been a source of confusion which stems from the different use of the term in the related, but distinct fields of mathematics and computer science. In mathematics, the word algorithm has attained the meaning of a recursive computational procedure and appears in notational language defining a computational course of events which is self-contained, for example, $A^2 + B^2 = C^2$. In contrast, the computer algorithm is a procedure consisting of operations to combine data, mathematical principles and equipment for the purpose of interpreting and/or acting upon a certain data input. In comparison to the mathematical algorithm which is self-contained, the computer algorithm must be applied to the solution of a specific problem.[1]

[1]   *Paine, Webber, Jackson and Curtis, Inc v Merrill Lynch, Pierce, Fenner and Smith, Inc* 564 F Supp 1358 at 1366–1367 (1983).

19.126 Referring to the Supreme Court decision in *Gottschalk v Benson*,[1] it held that the word algorithm had to be interpreted restrictively so as to encompass only procedures intended to solve a mathematical problem. In the present case:

> ... the patent allegedly claims a methodology to effectuate a highly efficient business system and does not restate a mathematical formula ... Nor are any of the recited steps in the claims mere procedure for solving mathematical problems.[2]

The patent, accordingly, was held valid.

1   *Gottschalk v Benson* 34 L Ed 2d 273 (1972).
2   *Paine, Webber, Jackson and Curtis, Inc v Merrill Lynch, Pierce, Fenner and Smith, Inc* 564 F Supp 1358 at 1368 (1983).

19.127   A significant point to note in the court's decision is its reference to the program effecting 'a highly efficient business system'. In the US, as in the UK and Europe, a method of doing business will not qualify for patent protection. The court admitted that the:

> ... patent effectuates a highly useful business method and would be unpatentable if done by hand. The CCPA, however, has made it clear that if no Benson algorithm exists, the product of a computer program is irrelevant, and the focus of analysis should be on the operation of the program on the computer.[1]

The wheel would thus appear to have turned full circle. From a situation where computer programs might be debarred from protection simply because they were computer programs, there is now authority for saying that an invention that would normally be unpatentable may qualify for protection if it is incorporated in a computer program.

1   *Paine, Webber, Jackson and Curtis, Inc v Merrill Lynch, Pierce, Fenner and Smith, Inc* 564 F Supp 1358 at 1369 (1983).

19.128   During the 1980s and 1990s, the final Court of Appeals for patent-related matters has been the Court of Appeals for the Federal Circuit. In a number of significant decisions, this court has shown considerable willingness to declare inventions patentable. Three cases are of particular importance.

Re Hiroyuki Iwahashi

19.129   In *Re Hiroyuki Iwahashi*[1], the Court of Appeals accepted that an application for a voice recognition system was patentable. The system operated on the basis of a simple mathematical calculation, with the results obtained being subjected to the application of a specific formula. The court held:

> The claim as a whole certainly defines apparatus in the form of a combination of interrelated means and we cannot discern any logical reason why it should not be deemed statutory subject matter as either a machine or a manufacture.[2]

1   888 F 2d 1370 (1989).
2   888 F 2d 1370 at 1375 (1989).

19.130   It is now accepted in the US that a distinction is to be drawn between mathematical algorithms and any other form of step-by-step process. The latter, when described in a patent application, will not serve as any bar to patentability. Where a mathematical algorithm is described in the application's claims:

> ... the claim as a whole must be further analyzed. If it appears that the mathematical algorithm is implemented in a specific manner to define structural

relationships between the physical elements of the claim (in apparatus claims) or to refine or limit claim steps (in process claims), the claim being otherwise statutory, the claim passes muster.[1]

[1]   *Re Walter* 618 F 2d 750 at 767.

Arrhythmia Research Tech v Corazonix Corpn

19.131   At issue in *Arrhythmia Research Tech v Corazonix Corpn*[1] was a system for analysing electrocardiograph signals emanating from patients who had suffered a heart attack. The benefit claimed for the system was that the mathematical analysis performed allowed the identification and treatment of patients who were vulnerable to a condition known as ventricular tachycardia.

[1]   958 F 2d 1053 (1992).

19.132   The application's subject matter was held to be patentable. Although the mathematical formula was critical to the working of the system, the claim did not 'wholly pre-empt' its use. In determining applications for software-related inventions:

> It is of course true that a modern digital computer manipulates data, usually in binary form, by performing mathematical operations ... But this is only *how* the computer does what it does. Of importance is the significance of the data and their manipulation in the real world, i.e. *what* the computer is doing.[1]

In the particular 'invention is properly viewed as an electrocardiograph analysis process' and was entitled to the grant of a patent.

[1]   *Arrhythmia Research Tech v Corazonix Corpn* 958 F 2d 1053 at 1057 (1992)).

Re Alappat

19.133   Alappat had devised a method to cause an oscilloscope to present its signal in the form of a smooth, continuous waveform, eliminating the apparent discontinuities, jaggedness or oscillation which were a feature of existing machines. The results were achieved by the application of mathematical calculations to the raw data involved. An application was rejected in the Patent Office but accepted by the Court of Appeals.[1] 'Mathematics', it was held, 'is not a monster to be struck down or out of the patent system, but simply another means whereby technological advance is achieved'.[2]

[1]   *Re Alappat* 33 F 3d 1526 (1994).
[2]   33 F 3d 1526 at 1570 (1994).

19.134   Again, as was stated by Rader J:

> ... inventors are their own lexicographers. (they) may express their inventions any manner they see fit, including mathematical symbols and algorithms.

Whether an inventor calls the invention a machine or a process is not nearly as important as the invention itself. Thus, the inventor can describe the invention in terms of a dedicated circuit or a process that emulates that circuit. Indeed, the line demarcation between dedicated circuit and a computer algorithm accomplishing the identical task is frequently blurred and is becoming increasingly so as the technology develops. In this field, a software process is frequently with a hardware circuit.[1]

[1]   *Re Alappat* 33 F 3d 1526 at 1583 (1994).

State Street Bank and Trust Co v Signature Financial Group Inc

19.135   This final US decision to be considered marked another significant extension in the scope of materials which might be protected under the patent system. Signature were the assignee of a patent entitled 'Data Processing System for Hub and Spoke Financial Services Configuration'.[2] State had initially sought to negotiate a licence for the use of patented technology, but, when negotiations broke down, instituted proceedings alleging that the patent was invalid as failing to identify patentable subject matter. State were successful at trial, but the decision was reversed by the Court of Appeals.[1]

[1]   *State Street Bank and Trust Co v Signature Financial Group Inc* 149 F 3d 1368 (1996).
[2]   US Patent 5,193,056.

19.136   The patent's abstract states that it relates to:

A data processing system is provided for monitoring and recording the information flow and data, and making all calculations, necessary for maintaining a partnership portfolio and partner fund (Hub and Spoke) financial services configuration. In particular, the data processing system makes a daily allocation of assets of two or more funds (Spokes) that are invested in a portfolio (Hub). The data processing system determines the percentage share (allocation ratio) that each fund has in the portfolio, while taking into consideration daily changes both in the value of the portfolio's investment securities and in the amount of each fund's assets. The system also calculates each fund's total investments based on the concept of a book capital account, which enables determination of a true asset value of each fund and accurate calculation of allocation ratios between the funds. The data processing system also tracks all the relevant data, determined on a daily basis for the portfolio and each fund, so that aggregate year-end data can be determined for accounting and for tax purposes for the portfolio and for each fund.

Essentially, the system can be described as a method for managing financial services. Before the District Court, it was held that the patent was invalid as relating both to a mathematical algorithm and a method for doing business.

19.137   Referring to previous authorities discussed above, the Court of Appeals reiterated that mathematical algorithms were considered non-patentable only to the extent that they constituted abstract ideas. Once some 'useful, concrete and tangible result' could be demonstrated, the subject matter became patentable. In *Arrhythmia*,[1] this took the form of a method for transforming electrocardiograph signals through the application of mathematical formulae in order to monitor the condition of a patient's heart. In the present case, it was stated:

> ... we hold that the transformation of data, representing discrete dollar amounts, by a machine through a series of mathematical calculations into a final share price, constitutes a practical application of a mathematical algorithm, formula, or calculation, because it produces 'a useful, concrete and tangible result' – a final share price momentarily fixed for recording and reporting purposes and even accepted and relied upon by regulatory authorities and in subsequent trades.[2]

[1] *Arrhythmia Research Tech v Corazonix Corpn* 958 F 2d 1053 (1992).
[2] *State Street Bank and Trust Co v Signature Financial Group Inc* 149 F 3d 1368 at 1373 (1996).

19.138 In this respect, the decision does little more than restate previous dicta of the court. In respect of the finding that the patent was invalid as referring to a method for doing business, the court was blunt:

> We take this opportunity to lay this ill-conceived exception to rest. Since its inception, the 'business method' exception has merely represented the application of some general, but no longer applicable legal principle, perhaps arising out of the 'requirement for invention – which was eliminated by §103. Since the 1952 Patent Act, business methods have been, and should have been, subject to the same legal requirements for patentability as applied to any other process or method.[1]

[1] *State Street Bank and Trust Co v Signature Financial Group Inc* 149 F 3d 1368 at 1375 (1996).

19.139 In its judgment against Signature, the District Court had argued that:

> If Signature's invention were patentable, any financial institution desirous of implementing a multi-tiered funding complex modelled (sic) on a Hub and Spoke configuration would be required to seek Signature's permission before embarking on such a project. *This is so because the '056 Patent is claimed [sic] sufficiently broadly to foreclose virtually any computer-implemented accounting method necessary to manage this type of financial structure* (emphasis in original).[1]

The Court of Appeals held that the application had to be judged by reference to the criteria of novelty, inventiveness and industrial application rather than by its area of application. Even if the effect of the patent was as the District Court had suggested, this 'has nothing to do with whether what is claimed is statutory subject matter'. Effectively, the decision removes the business method ground of exclusion from US law.

[2] *State Street Bank and Trust Co v Signature Financial Group Inc* 149 F 3d 1368 at 1376– 1377 (1996).

Where next for software patents?

19.140 It was suggested at the beginning of this chapter that the patent system was based largely on the notion of national patents. This is likely to remain the case, and even the proposed Community patent would exist alongside, rather than replace, national patents. The increasingly global nature of commerce and industry is serving to bring about an increasing degree of harmonisation and, as shown in the discussion above of the most recent European Patent Office case law, the TRIPS Agreement is providing a legal basis for harmonising initiatives. The trend throughout the world is clearly to accept that software should be brought within the ambit of the patent system. In some senses, there is almost an element of competition between states as to who can provide the strongest protection. As was said in the US case of *Lotus v Paperback*:

> It is no accident that the world's strongest software industry is found in the United States, rather than in some other jurisdiction which provides weaker protection for computer programs.[1]

[1]   740 F Supp 37 (1990).

19.141 It is now 20 years since patent law was reformed by the Patents Act 1977. At that time, although the status of computer programs was certainly discussed in the preceding report of the Banks Committee,[1] it was not a matter of massive importance. In the intervening years, not only has the technology permeated into every aspect of life, the development of microprocessors has rendered almost redundant distinctions between hardware and software – to the extent that the term computer program is seldom used today. From a situation of existing as a rather small adjunct to the industrial society, information technology has become pivotal to the information society. Software development has changed from a craft to an industry. The turnover and profits of software companies such as Microsoft dwarf those of the vast majority of industrial enterprises. The development of satisfactory forms of protection is a matter of great importance.

[1]   Cmnd 4407, 1970. See para 19.19ff above.

19.142 As will be discussed in the next chapters, one of the legislative trends of the 1980s was to provide that computer programs are protected under the law of copyright. Certainly copyright provides an acceptable and appropriate form of protection for most computer programs which do not possess significant elements of novelty or originality. Copyright, however, particularly given precedents in the US and the UK placing limits on the scope of protection against non-literal copying, is less suitable as a vehicle for protecting innovative works. Competitors can readily discern the underlying – and unprotected – ideas and replicate these without the necessity to engage in literal copying of any of the code used in the original. In such situations, the attractions of the patent system are apparent. In return for disclosing details of the techniques employed, the patent holder secures monopoly protection against reproduction of the novel ideas.

19.143   When the topic of the patentability of computer programs was discussed by the Banks Committee in the 1970s, the issue was agreed to be finely balanced. Ultimately, the Committee recommended against eligibility on grounds both of principle and practice. In terms of principle it was argued that no significant distinction existed between programs and methods of mathematical calculation which had always been excluded from protection.

19.144   These arguments cannot be discounted. It may have been preferable had the relatively hard line against patentability advocated by Banks been enforced by the courts. Once the dam had been broken by the EPC decisions in *Vicom*[1] and *Genentech*,[2] the line has proved impossible to hold. In *Fujitsu*,[3] Mr Justice Laddie commented that the distinction between the prohibition against programs and that relating to methods for performing a mental act was 'a matter of semantics'. In respect of many of the decisions and distinctions drawn, it may be suggested that the issue of patentability has been submerged in a semantic sea. Whilst accepting that there may be reasons of principle why no software patents should be issued, it is more difficult to accept at this level that an image processing system should qualify whilst a virtual reality system would not.

[1]   *Vicom Systems Inc's Application* [1987] 2 EPOR 74.
[2]   *Genentech Inc's Patent* [1989] RPC 147.
[3]   *Fujitsu Ltd's Application* [1996] RPC 511.

19.145   With its decisions in IBM, the Board of Appeal has sent clearer signals than previously regarding the approach which European and national examiners should take towards software-related inventions. It might be argued that such a significant change should have been made at a political level through the forum of a diplomatic conference. In a statement made at the end of the 2000 Conference Dr Roland Grossenbacher, Chairman of the Administrative Council of the European Patent Organisation argued that:

> The Conference's decision took account of the process of consultation on the future of legal protection in this field, and in no way challenges the existing practice of the Office and its boards of appeal, or that of national patent authorities and courts. As before, computer-implemented inventions can be patented if they involve a new and inventive technical contribution to the state of the art. Technical solutions for use in data processing or for carrying out methods of doing business therefore remain patentable.
>
> This follows from the concept of invention itself, which draws a clear distinction between technical solutions and non-technical methods. On this basis, patents cannot be granted for computer programs or business methods which are not of a technical nature.[1]

[1]   http://www.european-patent-office.org/news/pressrel/2000_11_29_e.htm.

19.146   Although the decision not to make provision for the computer program exclusion in isolation is supportable, the general failure of law makers to act over the past decade does mark something of an abdication of responsibility. Clearer policy guidance would allow the technical and judicial authorities to concentrate upon the merits of an application rather than playing word games.

19.147   Even were the question of the status of software-related inventions to be unequivocally resolved, there would, of course, remain the practical difficulty identified by the Banks Committee of determining issues of novelty and inventiveness in an area of rapidly changing technology. Certainly, much of the controversy in the US where software patents appear to be much more readily available has centred on the argument that patents have been awarded to developments that were not truly novel or inventive. Against this it must be remembered that the award of a patent is by no means conclusive as to questions of validity. Any patent may be challenged by any person at any time. Indeed, the very notion of examining patents for novelty and inventiveness prior to award is a comparatively recent development in our law.

Chapter 20

Copyright protection

Introduction

20.1   Although there is an increasing willingness to bring software-related inventions within the ambit of the patent system, only a small proportion of computer programs will display the necessary degree of novelty and inventiveness to qualify for protection. Virtually every program will, however, qualify for the award of copyright. In addition to software being protected by copyright, information recorded in electronic format such as email messages, multimedia packages and web pages will also be protected by copyright.

20.2   The essence of copyright can be deduced from the name itself. The owner of copyright in a work possesses the right to copy and, by inference, the right to prevent others from copying. Until the invention of moveable-type printing by Gutenberg in 1450, the issue of copying of a work was of no legal importance. The beginning of mass publishing of literary works brought with it new forms of regulation and control. Initially in the UK, use of the new technology was controlled by a requirement that printing be restricted to authorised printers and that the publication of individual books be licensed by the Crown. This scheme continued until 1695. With its abolition, petitions were presented to Parliament at the behest of the Stationers' Company, which had enjoyed an effective monopoly of publishing but which would now be subjected to competition. Responding to these representations, the first copyright Act, the Statute of Anne, was enacted in 1709. This Act granted the author (or assignee) the exclusive right to reproduce the work. In respect of existing works, this right would subsist for 21 years, with new works being protected for up to 28 years subject to these being registered with the Stationers' Company. The registration scheme was a comparatively short-lived component of the UK copyright regime, although it continues to be a feature of the US system.

20.3   The copyright system has developed over the centuries and has expanded far beyond its initial domain of books. In 1734, engravings became the first form of artistic work to be protected under the terms of the Engraving Copyright Act. In 1814, sculptures were brought within the copyright system by the Sculpture Copyright Act, and the Dramatic Copyright Act 1833 extended protection still further to encompass the public performance of musical and dramatical compositions. The Fine Art Copyright Act 1862 marked a significant recognition of the intervention of technology, with protection being extended to photographs. Study of the various copyright statutes enacted in the twentieth century indicates a steady expansion in the range of subject matter covered, normally following close on the heels of technological developments. In the Copyright Act 1911, reference is made to:

> ... any record, perforated roll, cinematography film or other contrivance by which the work may be mechanically performed or delivered.[1]

[1]   Section 1(2)(d).

20.4   The Copyright Act 1956 extended protection to television and radio broadcasts made by the BBC or the Independent Television Authority.[1] During the 1980s, albeit motivated as much by the desire to introduce significant criminal sanctions as by uncertainty whether the subject matter was protected under existing provisions of copyright law, the Copyright (Computer Software) (Amendment) Act 1985 brought its subject matter unequivocally within the ambit of copyright law.[2] The Copyright, Designs and Patents Act 1988 consolidated provisions relating to existing legal categories and also introduced provision for the protection of satellite broadcasts.[3] As was the case with the Patents Act 1977, a variety of motives prompted the introduction of the new legislation. The previous statute, the Copyright Act 1956, had been subjected to piecemeal amendment and a need could be identified for a consolidating piece of legislation, coupled with a measure of reform to take account of specific problems which had been encountered concerning the extent to which protection might be extended towards functional works such as the design of product components. These problems were manifested in the decision of the House of Lords in the case of *British Leyland Motor Corpn Ltd v Armstrong Patents Co Ltd*.[4] Finally, reform of the UK's copyright system, in the shape of the introduction of a system of 'moral rights', was required to permit ratification of the 1971 and 1979 revisions to the Berne Convention.

[1]   Section 14.
[2]   Section 1.
[3]   Section 6.
[4]   [1986] AC 577.

20.5   Although the Copyright, Designs and Patents Act 1988 remains the major statute in the copyright field, a measure of reform has been introduced pursuant to the requirements of the EC's Directive 'on 'the Legal Protection of Computer Programs'.[1] Effect has been given to the Directive's requirements by the Copyright (Computer Programs) Regulations 1992,[2] which make a number of amendments to the text of the 1988 Act. A further European Directive, ' on the legal protection of databases', introducing a sui generis form of protection for the contents of electronic databases was adopted in 1996 and required to be adopted within member states by 1 January 1998.[3] As discussed in more detail in chapter 22, implementation of this Directive introduced some new elements into domestic law designed to cope with the new challenges posed by the Internet. Further changes to domestic law have also been required to satisfy the requirements of the Directive 'on the harmonisation of certain aspects of copyright and related rights in the information society'.[4] The provisions of this directive are discussed in chapter 21.

[1] Directive 91/250/EC, OJ 1991 L 122, p 42.
[2] SI 1992/3233. Despite their title, these regulations were introduced under the authority of the European Communities Act 1972 as opposed to the Copyright, Designs and Patents Act 1998.
[3] Directive 96/9/EC, OJ 1996 L 77/20.
[4] Directive 2001/29/EC, OJ 2001 L 167/10.

Copyright basics

20.6 In contrast to the patent and trade mark systems, the copyright regime is noteworthy for a near complete lack of procedural formalities. The substantive requirements will be considered in more detail below, but at the outset it may be stated that protection begins at the moment that a work is recorded in some material form. Copyright lasts during the lifetime of the author and continues for a period of 70 years after the author's death. During this time, civil and criminal penalties may be imposed upon a party who, without the consent of the copyright owner, reproduces all or a substantial part of the work or engages in one or more of a list of other prohibited acts.

Creation and ownership of copyright protected works

What works are protected by copyright?

20.7 Copyright, it is provided in the Copyright, Designs and Patents Act 1988, is a 'property right' which subsists in three categories of original work:

•   literary, dramatic, musical or artistic works;
•   sound recordings, films, broadcasts or cable programmes; and
•   the typographical arrangement of a published work.[1]

[1] Section 1.

20.8 Although there were debates in the 1970s and 1980s whether computer programs were a proper subject for protection under the copyright system, there is now near universal recognition that they should be protected on the same basis as literary works. The Copyright, Designs and Patents Act 1988, the EC Directive on the Legal Protection of Computer Programs,[1] the Berne and WIPO Copyright Conventions and the TRIPS Agreement all provide that computer programs are to be protected on this basis.

[1]   Directive 91/250/EC.

20.9   As enacted, the Copyright, Designs and Patents Act 1988 provided simply that the term 'literary work':

> ... means any work, other than a dramatic or musical work, which is written, spoken or sung, and accordingly includes—
>
> (a)   a table or compilation; and
> (b)   a computer program.[1]

[1]   Section 3(1).

20.10   In common with many other aspects of the subject, the term 'computer program' is not defined in the legislation. This may have been a matter of limited importance in 1988, but is becoming more significant in our digital age. A computer program may be developed which will itself cause images to be displayed on screen. Many computer games will fall into this category and the technique is increasingly used to create or enhance images in feature films. Recent examples include the films 'Titanic' and 'Gladiators', whilst the film 'Toy Story 2' is reported to be the first production which exists entirely in digital format. No actors were involved, with all the images being produced within a computer environment. Copies of the film are recorded on computer storage media and projected directly from this. As will be discussed in more detail below, in such instances it is difficult to tell where the computer program ends and the film begins.

20.11   In the course of producing a computer program, a good deal of other material may be developed. The process may begin with a general formulation of the intended purpose of the program. Subsequently, a detailed specification may be written down describing all the functions and manner of operation to be provided in the completed work. This may take the form of a flow chart depicting the structure and sequence of the operations to be carried out. Drawings may also be made depicting various aspects of the screen displays to be produced.

20.12   It is almost certain that such preparatory works would have been protected under the original formulation of the Copyright, Designs and Patents Act 1988. As will be discussed at various stages below, the UK requires a very low degree of originality or literary merit in order to award copyright protection, and there is little doubt that even a few scribbles on a piece of paper would be protected. The situation was less clear in other EU member states, and the Directive on the Legal Protection of Computer Programs made special provision for the protection of such materials.[1] In implementing the measure, the Copyright (Computer Programs) Regulations 1992[2] added a new section 3(1)(c) to the 1988 Act, referring to:

> (c) preparatory design material for a computer program.

1   Directive 91/250/EC, art 1(1).
2   SI 1992/3233.

20.13   In some respects, the amendment may create more problems than it solves. Where the preparatory work is in the form of lines of code and written descriptions of the intended functions, there will be no problem in offering protection on this basis. The preparatory material may also take the form of flow charts or drawings of possible screen displays. In the Copyright, Designs and Patents Act 1988, the term 'artistic work' is defined as including 'any painting, drawing, map, chart or plan'.[1] Whilst it may be that artistic copyright will continue to exist in these elements, the rationale for protecting plans and drawings as something which they clearly are not appears somewhat obscure.

1   Section 4(2).

20.14   The issue of the relevance of protecting software as a literary work is becoming more important with the increasing numbers of multimedia works and the mass of graphical material available on the WWW. With material of this kind, it appears more relevant to focus attention on the informational content rather than to underlying programs. It may be that in addition to protection as literary works, certain forms of digitally recorded information may also be protected under other headings of copyright law.

Computer programs as audio or visual works

Sound recordings

20.15   A sound recording is defined in the legislation as:

> ... a recording of sounds from which the sounds may be reproduced ... regardless of the medium on which the recording is made or the method by which the sounds are produced or reproduced.[1]

In many instances, the digitised squawks and screams emanating from a computer game will not satisfy any criterion of originality for the grant of copyright protection. There would appear no reason to doubt that where the audio content is more sophisticated, this will not benefit from protection in its own right.

1   Section 5(1).

Digital sampling

20.16   The practice of digital sampling is commonplace in the musical industry. With the introduction of digital technology, it has become possible to represent any sound as a unique digital code. In this respect, a CD is not unlike a computer program whose contents are decoded by the associated player. For the listener, the change from the previous, analogue, method of recording is claimed to lie in a more accurate production coupled with greater durability in the recording medium. For those involved in the production processes, other forms of activity become possible. Any information that can be recorded in digital format can be processed. This might be utilised to eliminate defects or extraneous sounds in a recording. The process of digital sampling is another and controversial application.

20.17 As the name would suggest, digital sampling involves recording a small portion of an existing work. This will encompass not only the musical element but will also capture the particular style of the musician involved. The ability to process digital information means that this material may be modified or may be merged imperceptibly with other materials to produce a new work.

20.18 The copyright implications of this new practice raise few issues of principle but many extensive practical problems. There can be no doubt that the making of a recording of a protected musical work will constitute an infringement of copyright. The practical problem will be to establish whether the portion copied represents a substantial portion of the work. Although the criterion is qualitative rather than quantitative,[1] reproduction of a few bars of music may not suffice.

[1] See para 27.14 below.

20.19 A further issue may arise when the sampled work is modified. Here, it might be possible that the composer or performer involved might seek recourse under the new system of moral rights established by the Copyright, Designs and Patents Act 1988.[1] Amongst these is the right to object to any failure to identify a person as the author of the work[2] or to any derogatory treatment of the work.[3] Treatment will be regarded as derogatory if it amounts to 'distortion or mutilation of the work or is otherwise prejudicial to the honour or reputation of the author'.[4] It will, of course, be a question of fact whether this is the case.

[1] See para 27.22ff below.
[2] Section 77.
[3] Section 80.
[4] Section 80(2)(b).

Computer programs as photographs or films

20.20 Two issues are of relevance in this context: first, the question whether an image generated through the operation of a computer program might be classed as a photograph; and, secondly, whether moving images might be classed as films.

20.21 In the Copyright, Designs and Patents Act 1988, a photograph, which is protected as an artistic work, is defined as:

> ... a recording of light or other radiation on any medium on which an image is produced or from which an image may by any means be produced, and which is not part of a film.[1]

This provision will effectively be limited to the situation where a single screen display (or a number of discrete displays) is produced by a computer program. With the advent of digital cameras, it is quite possible for images to be recorded directly onto a computer disk and viewed on a computer monitor. The difficulty with the 1988 definition will concern the question whether the working of such cameras involves the making of 'a recording of light or other radiation'.[2]

1   Section 4(2).
2   See also discussion of the case of *R v Fellows* [1997] 2 All ER 548 at para 15.16 above.

20.22   In respect of films, the Copyright, Designs and Patents Act 1988 refers to 'a recording on any medium from which a moving image may by any means be produced'.[1] This definition is wider than that which applied under the Copyright Act 1956, which made reference to:

> Any sequence of visual images recorded on material of any description (whether translucent or not) so as to be capable, by the use of that material, either of being shown as a moving picture, or of being recorded on other material (whether translucent or not) by the use of which it can be so shown.[2]

The adoption of an amended definition was intended to eliminate any doubt as to whether a copy of a film on video tape would be protected. The form of words used in the 1988 Act appears wide enough to cover the storage of moving images on a computer disk or tape.

1   Section 5(1).
2   Section 13(1).

20.23   The availability of this form of visual copyright would be highly attractive to the owners of copyright in many computer programs. As will be discussed below, there is doubt how far the provisions of literary copyright will confer protection in the event that a second program replicates aspects of the functioning and appearance of an earlier work but does so using a different form of code. The point was made by Sir Robert Megarry V-C in one of the early interlocutory cases involving copyright in programs that:

> If I may take an absurdly simple example, 2 and 2 make 4. But so does 2 times 2, or 6 minus 2, or 2 per cent of 200, or 6 squared divided by nine, or many other things. Many different processes may produce the same answer and yet remain different processes that have not been copied one from another.[1]

Protecting the result achieved by a computer program rather than (or in addition to) the manner in which it is produced offers a potentially significant extension in protection.

1   *Thrustcode Ltd v WW Computing Ltd* [1983] FSR 502 at 506.

20.24   Beyond the situation where an image is produced through the operation of what is clearly a computer program lie developments in the field of interactive video. Such products, which are increasingly being used in the educational sector, enable a large number of film images to be processed in accordance with input from a user to produce a continuous display. Typically, a court case might be depicted with the flow of events being influenced by the suggestions and commands entered by the user. Interactive video calls for extensive use both of computer programs and of film images. Although the point has not been at issue in any legal proceedings, allocation of copyright interests promises to be a matter of considerable complexity.

20.25　In addition to the issue of content, the nature of data transfers involved with online services such as those provided on the WWW is such that the database might be regarded as a cable programme service with individual items of data classed as cable programmes.[1]

1　See *Shetland Times v Wills* 1997 SLT 669.

The requirement of originality

20.26　Semantically, the word 'original' found in the copyright legislation might be equated with the requirement of novelty applying under the patents regime. In reality, the requirement of originality has been construed as requiring only that the work is that of the author, ie has not been copied from any other source. In *University of London Press Ltd v University Tutorial Press Ltd*,[1] Petersen J held that:

> The word 'original' does not mean that the work must be an expression of original or inventive thought. Copyright Acts are not concerned with the originality of ideas, but with the expression of thought, and, in the case of 'literary work', with the expression of thought in print or writing. The originality which is required relates to the expression of the thought. But the Act does not require that the expression must be in an original or novel form but that the work must not be copied from another work – that it should originate from the author.[2]

1　[1916] 2 Ch 601.
2　[1916] 2 Ch 601 at 608–609.

20.27　Under the UK's copyright system, the most crass and unedifying piece of prose (or the most error-ridden computer program) is as entitled to the benefit of copyright protection as the most illustrious example of the species (although it may fare less well in the marketplace). This approach is to be contrasted with that applying in Germany, where the application of strict qualitative criteria resulted, prior to the EC Directive on the Legal Protection of Computer Programs,[1] in an estimated 95% of computer programs being denied protection on the ground that they were not original. The Directive would appear to endorse the UK position on the legal protection of computer programs, stating in its Preamble that 'no tests as to the qualitative or aesthetic merits of the program should be applied' and providing subsequently that:

> A computer program shall be protected if it is the author's own intellectual creation. No other criteria shall be applied to determine its eligibility for protection.[2]

¹   Directive 91/250/EC.
²   Article 1(3).

20.28   The phrase 'intellectual creation' is more reflective of the civil law's system of authors' rights than the common law notions of copyright, and it might prove sufficiently vague to allow a measure of discretion in this area. It remains uncertain, therefore, whether the Directive on the Legal Protection of Computer Programs will secure its objective of eliminating 'differences in the legal protection of computer programs offered by the laws of the Member states (which) have direct and negative effects on the functioning of the common market as regards computer programs'.¹

¹   Directive 91/250/EC, Preamble.

Ownership of copyright

20.29   The author of a work will, subject to one exception, be the first owner of any copyright which may subsist in it.¹ Where a work is the product of two or more authors, any copyright arising will be the joint property of the authors.² The criterion for determining the existence of joint authorship is whether the individual contributions of the authors can be distinguished.³ In this case, each author will possess individual copyright in his or her portion of the work. This may be a matter of some significance in the software field, where in the case of a program intended for use in a specific area of business, production may require both programming skills and knowledge of the subject area. Unless suitable contractual arrangements are negotiated, the result could be the existence of two separate copyrights, each useless without the other.

¹   Copyright, Designs and Patents Act 1988, s 11(1).
²   Section 10(3).
³   Section 10(1).

Employee-created works

20.30   An exception to the principle that the author is the first owner of copyright in a work applies where the work is created in the course of the author's employment. In this event, copyright will, subject to any contractual provision to the contrary, vest in the employer.¹ This approach marks a change from the position under previous copyright statutes, where the employer's rights in respect of employee-created works were limited in the situation where the work was created for publication in a newspaper, magazine or other periodical.² Although the employer would possess copyright in the publication containing the work, all other rights in respect of it would remain with the author. Thus, the inclusion of the work in a database would require the author's permission. Today, many newspapers make copies of previous issues available in the form of an electronic database. Under the provision described above, the consent of the author of every piece of information appearing in the database would have been required. Responding to lobbying on the part of media interests, the Copyright, Designs and Patents Act 1988 eschews any exceptions to the general rule conferring unrestricted copyright on the employer.

1   Copyright, Designs and Patents Act 1988, s 11(2).
2   Copyright Act 1956, s 4(2).

Computer-generated works

20.31   Computers are frequently used to assist in the production of a work. In many instances, this will not affect copyright in the work at all. This book, for example, was typed on an Apple Macintosh®™ computer using Microsoft Word®™ software. In this, and in many other situations, the computer is merely a tool and the author of the text acquires full copyright in the completed work. In *Express Newspapers plc v Liverpool Daily Post and Echo plc*,[1] another case determined at interlocutory level, the plaintiff ran a competition 'Millionaire of the Month' in its newspaper. A number of other national newspapers operated similar competitions. In each case, the key feature was that competitors would have to check the newspaper each day to see whether numbers allocated to them matched winning numbers. The defendant republished all the winning numbers with the obvious intention that readers could participate in the competitions run by other publishers without having to purchase copies of the newspaper. In defence to an action alleging copyright infringement, the defendant claimed that as the numbers were selected by a computer program they were not entitled to protection. Dismissing this defence, Whitford J (as he then was) held that a great deal of skill and labour had been required to develop the computer program (not least to ensure that too many winning numbers were not selected). As with the word processing example cited above, the computer was no more than a tool giving effect to the intentions of its human controller.

1   [1985] 1 WLR 1089.

20.32   In other instances, the role of the computer may move beyond that of recording a user's work and may serve to embellish the creation. An example concerns the practice of digital sampling.[1] Other applications in the musical field might concern the use of electronic synthesisers. Without delving into the technical details concerning the manner in which these products function, it is sufficient to note that the involvement of the computer is at a qualitatively greater level than that occurring in word processing applications.

1   See para 20.16 above.

20.33   A further situation which may raise questions of the ownership of copyright might apply where a database or expert system program is acquired. The program will require the addition of data by the user and the combination of the program and the user supplied data will produce a new product in the form of the processed output. Again, this finished product will owe a considerable amount to the underlying program.

20.34 The Copyright, Designs and Patents Act 1988 contains a provision which appears to be unique in copyright statutes. It introduces a specific category of computer-generated work and provides:

> In the case of a literary, dramatic, musical or artistic work which is computer-generated, the author shall be taken to be the person by whom the arrangements necessary for the creation of the work are undertaken.[1]

The concept of a computer-generated work is defined as one where 'the work is generated by computer in circumstances such that there is no human author of the work'.[2]

[1]   Section 9(3).
[2]   Section 178.

20.35 It is unclear when this provision might be applicable. Few, if any, works will be created by a computer in the absence of any human involvement. In circumstances such as those identified above, human involvement will be required. The question which may have to be determined by a court in the event of any dispute is whether the input of any of the parties is sufficiently substantial to qualify them for sole ownership of copyright (as will almost certainly be the case with a piece of text produced on a word processor) or whether there might be joint ownership of copyright? In many instances, the enabling computer programs may be sold under the terms of a contract which prescribes the use to which a completed work may be put. Typically, the purchaser of the program will be entitled to use it for his or her own purposes but prohibited from selling or disposing of any work thereby created without the further agreement of the supplier.

20.36 In determining whether there is no human author of a work, two issues may be relevant. The first would be whether there is no human involvement of any kind in the production of the work. It is difficult to conceive of situations where the computer will act entirely on its own initiative. Once the possibility of some human intervention is accepted, the statutory provision might appear otiose. The general criterion for a literary or other work to be protected requires that it be the author's 'original' work. Although the requirement of originality has little application in the general field, the concept of computer-generated works can have meaning only if this is interpreted so as to exclude a human computer operator from qualifying for authorship where they make no intellectual contribution to the work. An example of such a situation might be where a computer program operates to produce a drawing on a completely random basis, with the operator's only contribution being to initiate its operation. In this case, the operator, or a person who instructed that person to carry out the task, will become owner of the computer-generated work.

Commencement and duration of protection

20.37 Copyright protection commences at the moment that a work is recorded in a material form. In the Copyright (Computer Software) (Amendment) Act

1985, it was specifically provided that this would 'include references to the storage of that work in a computer'.[1] The Copyright, Designs and Patents Act 1988 contains a more general formulation, referring to a recording being made 'in writing or otherwise'. There would appear no doubt that this would include the direct entry of a work into a computer. In contrast to the approach adopted under the patent system, no formalities attach to the grant of copyright. Although some differences of detail may exist concerning the protection offered to published and unpublished works, as a matter of principle, the question whether a work is intended to be published is immaterial. Again, inclusion of the well-known copyright symbol © in a work is not required to obtain protection under domestic law, although it is featured in the Universal Copyright Convention adopted in Geneva in 1952.[2]

[1] Section 2.
[2] The Universal Copyright Convention was developed in large part in order to bring the US into the worldwide copyright regime. A particular feature of US copyright law was its requirement that works be registered with its Copyright Office as a condition for the award of full copyright protection. This clearly put obstacles in the way of foreign copyright owners. The Convention allows for the copyright symbol to substitute for registration requirements.

20.38 The duration of copyright will depend upon the particular form of the work. In the case of a literary, dramatic or musical work, copyright will subsist during the lifetime of the author and for a period of 70 years after the author's death.[1] In the event that the work is computer-generated, copyright will last for 50 years from the end of the calendar year in which the work is produced.[2] The same period of protection extends to films, sound recordings and broadcasts,[3] whilst a shorter period of 25 years is applicable to the typographical arrangements of a published work.[4]

[1] Copyright, Designs and Patents Act 1988, s 12(1). The only exception to this rule applies in favour of the work *Peter Pan*. Copyright in this work was bequeathed upon the author's death to the Great Ormond Street Children's Hospital, with the revenue accruing from royalty payments etc constituting a significant portion of the hospital's income. J M Barrie having died in 1937, copyright would normally have expired at the end of 1987. In what may be a unique provision, s 301 and Sch 6 of the Act provide, not inappropriately given the nature of the work's main character, that elements of the copyright in Peter Pan will never die.
[2] Section 12(3).
[3] Section 13.
[4] Section 15.

20.39 The lifespan of copyright is clearly much greater than that of a patent, although it must be doubted whether a period of protection which, depending upon the age and longevity of the author, may subsist for a century or longer is of any practical significance in the information technology field. Given the pace of technological development, it is unlikely that any piece of software will retain commercial value for more than a few years, although, as the publicity surrounding the Millennium Bug evidenced, many programs have enjoyed a longer lifespan than originally expected. Even in the case of the author's own word processing package, Microsoft Word, the copyright notice refers to versions of the program dating back to 1983.

Infringement of copyright

20.40   As discussed in the preceding chapters, the award of a patent serves to confer upon the successful applicant a monopoly in respect of the exploitation of its subject matter. Although judicial references have been made to copyright conferring a monopoly – in the case of *Green v Broadcasting Council of New Zealand*,[1] Lord Bridge, delivering the judgment of the Privy Council, stated that '(t)he protection which copyright gives creates a monopoly' – it is generally accepted that the copyright owner possesses only the exclusive right to perform certain acts in respect of the work. These comprise the rights:

- to copy the work or any substantial part of it;[2]
- to issue copies of the work to the public;[3]
- to perform, show or play the work in public;[4]
- to broadcast the work or include it in a cable programme service;[5] and
- to make an adaptation of the work or do any of the above in relation to an adaptation.[6]

The act of copying is defined as involving the reproduction of the work, or a substantial part of the work in any material form.[7] This is to include 'storing the work in any medium by electronic means'.[8] Thus, for example, the use of some form of scanning device to transform text into electronic format will constitute an infringement of copyright in the original text.

[1]   [1989] 2 All ER 1056.
[2]   Copyright, Designs and Patents Act 1988, s 16(1)(a).
[3]   Section 16(1)(b).
[4]   Section 16(1)(c).
[5]   Section 16(1)(d).
[6]   Section 16(1)(e).
[7]   Section 17(2).
[8]   Section 17(3).

To issue copies of the work to the public

20.41   The owner of copyright in a work has the right to determine whether copies of that work might be made available to the public. This right extends only to the first occasion upon which the work is made available and not to any subsequent dealings in the work by way of importation, distribution, sale, hire or loan.

20.42   In most cases, a person who has lawfully come into possession of a copy of a protected work will have the right either to resell the copy or to make it available to members of the public on a rental basis. The Copyright, Designs and Patents Act 1988 provides an exception to this rule in the case of the rental of computer programs, sound recordings and films.[1] Essentially, such works may be hired only under the terms either of an order made by the Secretary of State or according to the provisions of a licensing scheme devised by the copyright owners and approved by the Copyright Tribunal. Either procedure will prescribe terms upon which the rental may occur and the royalty that will be payable to the copyright owner. The justification for this provision lies with the ease with which copies of software may be made. To this extent, the provisions for royalty payments can be seen as offering some compensation for losses which may result from such activities.

¹   Section 66.

To perform, show or play the work in public

20.43   The acts of performing or showing the protected work in public are reserved to the copyright owner. The issue of what is a public performance is not defined in the legislation. It would seem clear, however, that the operation of a computer game program within, for example, a public house or an amusement arcade would constitute an infringing act if committed without the consent of the copyright owner.

To broadcast the work or include it in a cable programme service

20.44   As will be discussed in Chapter 21, there is some authority for the proposition that a website is to be classed as a cable programme service with individual pages being classed as cable programmes.

To make an adaptation of the work or do any of the above in relation to an adaptation

20.45   In respect of computer programs, it is provided that adaptation 'means an arrangement or altered version of the program or a translation of it'.¹ Producing, for example, a version of a program originally designed to run under Microsoft Windows to operate on Apple computers will, in the absence of authorisation from the copyright owner, constitute unlawful adaptation.

¹   Copyright, Designs and Patents Act 1988, s 21(4).

The nature of copying

20.46   A popular saying is to the effect that if enough monkeys are given enough typewriters, eventually one monkey will hit the keys in such an order as to reproduce the works of Shakespeare. Discounting the inconvenient fact that the works of Shakespeare are out of copyright, and considerable uncertainty whether a monkey could own copyright, the end product would not infringe copyright for the reason that it represents an independent composition.

20.47   The question whether one work infringes copyright in an earlier work is determined on the basis of objective criteria. It is not necessary that the act should have been deliberate. A number of cases have been brought in which the allegation has been made (and sometimes established) that a musical work was derived from an earlier composition which might well have been heard by the second composer, who retained a subconscious memory of the melody. The fact that the copying or plagiarism was unintentional will not serve as a defence. The key factors which will have to be established by a party alleging copyright infringement are that the alleged copyist would have had access to the work and that there are substantial similarities between the works which are not explicable by factors other than copying.

20.48   In situations where two are more people are working on the same topic, for example, a history of the Second World War, it is likely that similarities will exist between the finished works. In a non-fictional work, the ending must be the same and there is likely to be consensus regarding the key events of the conflict. Greater levels of similarity may raise suspicions that one author has relied too heavily on the work of the other.

20.49   In the US copyright system, a distinction is drawn between ideas – which are not protected by copyright – and particular forms of expression. The, so called, idea/expression dichotomy features prominently in many cases concerned with copyright infringement in software. Generally, however, although providing a useful sound bite, the idea/expression dichotomy can offer only limited assistance in determining whether copyright infringement has occurred.

Applying copyright principles to software

20.50   In the early days of computers, little attention was paid to the topic of intellectual property law. Computers were rare creatures. Generally, the machines would not be sold to a user but rather supplied under the terms of a rental agreement, which would also make extensive provision for the manufacturer to supply technical support staff to minister to the needs of the sensitive machines. The software to run on a particular computer could be obtained only from the manufacturer of the hardware and, therefore, the possibilities for copyright infringement were limited. A US anti-trust decision in the 1960s which compelled the computer giant IBM to separate its hardware and software divisions marked a change in the situation, and the emergence of the PC has totally transformed the position. Although, in many cases, computers may come with a range of software packages pre-installed, a vast range of independent software developers provide application packages capable of running on PCs and, to a lesser extent, other computers such as Apple Macs.

20.51   In discussing the extent to which activities relating to software might contravene copyright law, three categories of potential infringement can be considered. The first two relate to what is called literal copying of software. Here, the program code is directly copied. In the first instance, this may be done for commercial gain, and will be discussed under the heading of software piracy. As indicated above, the act of using software necessitates the making of a copy of the work. This creates problems for the relationship between copyright owner and user, and has led in part to the emergence of software licences. These documents, which are an almost inevitable companion to mass-produced software packages, typically confer use rights, but at the expense of seeking to oblige the user to accept other provisions limiting or excluding liabilities in the event the software fails to operate in a satisfactory manner and thereby causes some form of injury or damage to the user. Although the Copyright, Designs and Patents Act 1988 as enacted was silent on all questions concerned with users rights other than the somewhat nebulous concept of fair dealing, implementation of the EC Directive on the Legal Protection of Computer Programs [1] has brought about significant changes. Although the extent of some of the rights remains unclear, lawful users of software acquire a number of entitlements, ranging from a right to use software to the ability to reverse engineer and decompile, albeit in limited circumstances.

[1]   Directive 91/250/EC.

20.52   The third category of infringement raises the most interesting legal issues. It concerns the situation where two programs exhibit similarities at the level of screen displays but not at the level of code. Although the phrase has rather fallen out of legal favour, the argument might be put in terms that one program has copied the 'look and feel' of another. This topic might also be considered at two levels. In the first, and more common, case the alleged infringer will have had some access to the original program's code. Typically, a programmer will have worked on the development of one package, moved to another employer and been involved with the development of a competing program. In the second category, the parties will act much more at arm's length, with the only access obtained by the alleged infringer being to the working copy of the program.

Software piracy

20.53   The term 'software piracy' encompasses a range of forms of conduct. The Business Software Alliance (BSA), an organisation which includes most of the major Western software producers amongst its membership, has identified a range of forms of conduct:

- *Multiple Installation*
  This is where you install more copies of a software program than you have licences. For example, if you by 10 single-user licences for a product yet install it onto 20 machines, you are using 10 illegal copies.
- *End-User Piracy*
  Similar to multiple installation, this involves an end-user (or company employee) copying programs illegally or using unlicensed software in the work place.
- *Client/Server Piracy*
  Occurs when a program is run off a server (rather than from individual PCs) and is accessed by more end-users than the company has bought licenses for.

- *On-line Piracy*
  This happens when software is downloaded from the web and installed but not paid for. There are other types of software piracy (grey software, counterfeit software etc).[1]

[1] http://www.bsa.org/uk/types.

20.54 Essentially, any conduct which can be considered an infringement of copyright will come within these definitions. As the term 'piracy' would suggest, there is little doubt that the conduct at issue is unlawful. A considerable number of studies have sought to assess the scale of the problem. Most have been conducted by or on behalf of organisations such as the BSA. The eighth and most recent study was conducted by the International Planning and Research Corporation on behalf of the BSA and the Software and Information Industry Association.[1] Published in 2003, the study provides a detailed overview of the state of software piracy in 2002.

[1] Available from http://www.bsa.org.

20.55 The study indicated that the global piracy rate in 2002 was 39%. Although indicating that nearly four out of every ten software packages in use were unauthorised copies, the figures for piracy have declined markedly over recent years, the comparable figure for 1994 being 49%. Wide variations exist between countries and regions in respect of the level of piracy. The 'distinction' of topping the piracy charts falls to Vietnam, with a 95% rate. Other significant offenders are China, with a 92% rate, and Russia at 89%. In general, Eastern Europe is the region with the highest rate of pirate software at 71%. At the other end of the table, the US posts a rate of 23%, the UK stands only slightly higher at 26%, with Western Europe generally averaging at 30%.

20.56 In economic terms, the total loss is estimated at $13bn. Given the scale of software use within North America and Europe, it is not surprising that the regions with the highest financial losses were North America and Western Europe. A further estimate of the impact of piracy can be taken from a further study produced for the BSA by Price Waterhouse in 1998.[1] This calculated that:

> Reducing software piracy rates by realistic levels from the 1996 Western European average of 43 per cent for PC business software to the corresponding U.S. average of 27 per cent, and equivalent reductions in other software categories would generate as many as 258,651 more jobs and $13.9bn additional tax revenues by the year 2001, in addition to forecast market growth.

[1] Available from http://www.bsa.org/uk/studies/europe_study98.pdf.

20.57 Clearly, such figures can be no more than estimates, and many of the calculations appear to be based on the perhaps unlikely premise that in the absence of pirate copies of software, users would pay the full price for legitimate programs. It is perhaps noteworthy that in the 1999 Global Software Piracy Report, in presenting reasons for the reduction in piracy, the following factors were identified:

1. Software companies have struggled to keep up with the development of the worldwide PC marketplace and have an effective legal sales presence in all areas of the world. As they have made progress and established a global presence, software becomes easier to purchase legally.
2. Software companies have increased the availability of user support for their products outside of the U.S. This increased user support has promoted the purchase of legal software.
3. Legal prices of software have declined significantly in 1996 and 1997, narrowing the difference between legal and illegal versions.
4. The BSA and SIIA have promoted the need to purchase legal versions of software and the importance of intellectual property rights. This has included high profile legal proceedings against companies using illegal software.
5. In an increasingly global marketplace, a company's risks of being found with illegal software extend to more than the legal implications, impacting their business practices and credibility.
6. Increased government cooperation to provide legal protection for intellectual property and to criminalize software piracy also assisted in the downward trend in piracy rates.

Although there can be little doubt that most people making counterfeit copies of software will be aware that their conduct is in breach of copyright law, a number of the other activities identified in the BSA definition are less obviously wrongful. As will be discussed in the following section, however, copyright law affords very limited rights to those seeking to use software.

User rights in respect of software

20.58 Whilst the application of provisions of copyright law to software-based products is less contentious than is the case with the application of the patent system, the principles of the copyright system were designed for application in the literary and artistic fields. Information technology products operate in the practical arena, and it may be argued that fundamental concepts such as reproduction or adaptation require to be applied in a modified form in such circumstances. Two particular difficulties can be identified.

20.59 The essence of copyright is that it prohibits the copying of a work without the consent of the copyright owner. In the case of most works, this does not impinge upon a third party's normal use of the work. The purchaser of a book can read it without requiring to make any form of copy. Likewise, a television broadcast can be watched and an audio cassette listened to without the need for any form of copying. Software (and indeed other digital products, such as CDs) operates in a different manner. Any form of use requires that the contents of the work be copied from a storage location to be processed within the equipment. Normal use requires copying, a fact which creates complications not just in the field of copyright but also, through the widespread use of software licences, in the area of liability.

Fair dealing

20.60 Much is written and spoken of concerning the right of a user to copy a work to such extent as is justified under the heading of 'fair dealing' for the purposes of research or private study.[1] Few of these expressions receive any form of definition in the legislation. The concept of fair dealing will undoubtedly permit a degree of copying of a protected work, but the supplementary question 'how much?' cannot be definitively answered. At one time, the UK publishing industry suggested that the copying of up to 10% of a book might be regarded as fair dealing. This was, however, an informal indication which was subsequently withdrawn. It would not appear that the extent of copying permitted under this heading has been at issue in any case.

[1] Copyright, Designs and Patents Act 1988, s 29.

20.61 Whilst the concept of private study is not one which will be of great practical significance in the software field, that of research is potentially much more so. It is to be noted that the word 'research' precedes the phrase 'private study' in the Copyright, Designs and Patents Act 1988. It would appear to follow, therefore, that its application is not restricted to the area of individual research, but will extend into the commercial sphere.

20.62 In the case of a traditional literary work such as a book or article, the acts which encompass fair dealing can readily be identified. Clearly, researchers must be able to read the work and to quote small portions of it in any work which they themselves might compile. In the course of this task, they may copy portions of the work, perhaps by means of a photocopier, although infringement may occur equally well if the work is copied by hand. It must be accepted that the concept of fair dealing in a literary work cannot extend to the making of a copy of the complete work. Different considerations may apply in respect of software.

20.63 Two arguments can be put forward in support of such a proposition. First, whilst it is a very simple task to copy portions of a book – indeed it is much easier to copy a part than the whole – the reverse is the case with respect to a computer program. A second argument operates at a utilitarian level. The user of a book would generally be considered as having no legitimate need to take a second copy of the work in case the original suffers damage. This view would be justified on the basis that although the cosmetic appearance of a book may easily be harmed, for example, through the spillage of a cup of coffee, the damage will seldom be such as to prevent its continued use. Software is a much more fragile creature and, especially if research is being conducted as to its make-up, terminal damage may easily result. In such an event, the making of a back-up copy might appear a reasonable precaution.

20.64 In concluding the examination of the fair dealing exception, the point must be stressed that any of the actions referred to above will be sanctioned only to the extent that they are carried out in connection with research. It is specifically provided that decompilation of a program will not be permitted under the fair use provisions.[1] Assuming that a copy of software may legitimately be made for research purposes, its status will change in the event that the research ends and the copy is put to operational use.

[1]   Copyright, Designs and Patents Act 1988, s 29(4). See para 20.75 below.

A use right for software?

20.65   Reference has previously been made to the fact that copying or adapting a protected work constitutes an infringement of copyright.[1] This raises one significant issue in relation to software. Whenever a computer program is operated, the process requires that its contents be copied from the storage disk upon which it normally resides into the hardware's memory. The act of using software in its normal manner is capable, therefore, of constituting a breach of copyright.

[1]   See para 20.40 above.

20.66   Prior to 1992, this was arguably the case, although it is submitted that a persuasive case could have been made out for implying at least a basic use right. Substantial precedent exists for such judicial creativity under patent law, where it has been held that the purchaser of a patented product may exercise all the normal rights of an owner, including the right to resell, unless specific notice has been given of restrictions.[1] With most software products, the response of producers to the uncertain state of the law was to seek to incorporate the terms of a licence into the contract with the end user. The status of software licences will be considered in more detail in the context of liability issues. Essentially, the licence would grant permission for the use of software in specified circumstances, but would frequently couple this with clauses limiting or excluding liability in the event the performance of the software was defective. In 1992, the provisions of the Copyright Designs and Patents Act 1988 were amended in order to implement the provisions of the EC Directive on the Legal Protection of Computer Programs.[2] The Copyright (Computer Programs) Regulations 1992[3] add a new s 50C to the 1988 Act, providing that:

> It is not an infringement of copyright for a lawful user of a copy of a computer program to copy or adapt it, providing that the copying or adapting—
>
> (a)   is necessary for his lawful use; and
> (b)   is not prohibited under any term or condition of an agreement regarding the circumstances under which his use is lawful.

[1]   See, for example, *National Phonograph Co of Australia v Menck* (1911) 28 RPC 229.
[2]   Directive 91/250/EC.
[3]   SI 1992/3233.

20.67   In the European Commission's explanatory memorandum to the 1989 proposal for the Directive, it was argued that it was not clear:

... whether the practice of so-called, 'shrink wrap licensing' where use conditions are attached to a product which is, to all intents and purposes 'sold' to the user, constitutes a valid licence in all circumstances and in all jurisdictions.

It is therefore proposed that ... (w)here 'sale', in the normal sense of the word occurs, certain rights to use the program must be taken to pass to the purchaser along with the physical copy of the program.[1]

whilst the Preamble to the Directive on the Legal Protection of Computer Programs[2] states that:

Whereas the exclusive rights of the author to prevent the unauthorized reproduction of the work have to be subject to a limited exception in the case of a computer program to allow the reproduction technically necessary for the use of the program by the lawful acquirer.

Whereas this means that the acts of loading and running necessary for the use of a copy of a program which has been lawfully acquired ... may not be prohibited by contract.

It may be queried how far the text of the Directive implements this. Article 4 makes it clear that the copyright owner retains the right to authorise the:

... permanent or temporary reproduction of a computer program by any means and in any form, in part or in whole. Insofar as loading, displaying, running, transmission or storage of the computer program necessitates such reproduction, such acts shall be subject to authorization by the rightholder.

whilst art 5 provides for an exception to this provision stating that:

In the absence of specific contractual provisions, the acts referred to in Article 4 ... shall not require authorization by the rightholder where they are necessary for the use of the computer program by the lawful acquirer in accordance with its intended purpose.

[1]   COM (88) 816 final – SYN 183, paras 3.4–3.5.
[2]   Directive 91/250/EC.

20.68   In implementing the Directive on the Legal Protection of Computer Programs,[1] the UK government substituted the term 'lawful user'[2] for the original 'lawful acquirer'. Another change was to substitute reference to 'lawful use'[3] for the Directive's 'intended use'. These changes undoubtedly complicate matters. The concept of 'lawful use', in particular, is defined as applying where a person has '(whether under a licence to do any act restricted by the copyright in the program or otherwise) ... a right to use the program'.[4] This formulation relates to the status of the user as much as to the nature of the application, thereby producing a somewhat circular effect. Although there seems no doubt that the Directive sought to confer a use right, it is less clear whether the UK implementing legislation secures this and it is possible that the issue may some day have to be resolved before the courts.

[1]   Directive 91/250/EC.
[2]   Copyright, Designs and Patents Act 1988, s 50A.
[3]   Section 50A.
[4]   Section 50A(2).

20.69 Although a basic use right will now be implied, difficulties may arise in a number of areas. Increasingly, computers are being networked. The communications facilities provided by such a development means that one copy of a program may be used by a considerable number of different persons. Depending upon the nature of the program and the network, use may be either simultaneous or successive. A further difficulty may arise in the situation where a user has two computers, typically, one at home and one at work. In this case, the user may well wish to use the same software (perhaps a word processing program) on both computers. In these situations, the need and justification for licences will continue.

Error correction

20.70 It is received wisdom that every computer program contains errors or 'bugs'. In accordance with the requirements of the EC Directive on the Legal Protection of Computer Programs,[1] it is provided that an authorised user may copy or adapt a program 'for the purpose of correcting errors in it'.[2] This provision might appear to give a user carte blanche to copy a program in the quest to discover errors. An alternative, and perhaps preferable, view is that the right will extend only in respect of particular errors which have been discovered by the user in the course of running the program in a normal manner. Even on this basis, uncertainties remain as to the extent of the user's rights. Computer programs are not like other literary works. A typing or grammatical error occurring in a book may be corrected without the act having any impact upon the remainder of the work. The relationship between the various elements of a computer program is much more complex. If an error is discovered in the course of running a program, its cause may lie almost anywhere in the program. If the source of a particular error is detected and a correction made, it cannot be certain that the effects of the change will not manifest themselves in an unexpected and undesirable fashion elsewhere in the program. There is, indeed, a school of thought in software engineering that suggests that when errors are detected, rather than amending the program, operating procedures should be changed to avoid the conditions which it is known cause the specific error to occur.

[1] Directive 91/250/EC.
[2] Copyright, Designs and Patents Act 1988, s 50C(2).

Back-up copies

20.71 Computer programs are invariably supplied on some storage device, such as a disk or tape. Such storage media are notoriously fragile and it is all too possible that their contents might be accidentally corrupted or erased. In such circumstances, it might not appear unreasonable for a user to seek to take a second, or back-up, copy of the work, with the intention that this will be stored in a safe location and brought into use in the event that the original copy of the software be destroyed.

20.72   As enacted, the UK Copyright, Designs and Patents Act 1988 (in contrast to several other copyright statutes) made no mention of the possibility that a user might make a back-up copy of a program which had been lawfully acquired. Although, once again, it is possible to argue that such a term must be implied into any relevant contract, the argument is more tenuous than that relating to the implication of a basic use right.

20.73   Implementation of the provisions of the Directive on the Legal Protection of Computer Programs[1] has brought about a measure of reform, the Copyright, Designs and Patents Act 1988 now providing that a back-up copy may be made by a user where this is 'necessary ... for the purposes of his lawful use'.[2] It is unclear how useful this provision might be. The making of a back-up copy will invariably be a wise precaution, but it is difficult to envisage any situation where the presence of a second copy is 'necessary' for the functioning of the original.

[1]   Directive 91/250/EC.
[2]   Copyright, Designs and Patents Act 1988, s 50A(1).

20.74   Some small measure of consolation may be offered to a user by the fact that the copyright owner may not validly restrict or exclude the operation of the provisions regarding the making of back-up copies.[1] It is doubted, however, whether the new provisions will alter significantly either the law or the practice in this area.

[1]   Copyright, Designs and Patents Act 1988, s 296A(1)(b).

Reverse engineering and decompilation

20.75   When software is supplied to a customer, it will be in a form known as object or machine-readable code. If this were to be viewed by a user, it would appear as a series (a very long series) of zeros and ones. Obtaining sight of these digits will give little indication as to the manner in which the program is structured. Although it is possible for a program to be written in object code, much more programmer-friendly techniques are available and almost universally utilised. A number of what are referred to as 'high level' languages exist – examples are BASIC and FORTRAN. These allow programmers to write their instructions in a language which more closely resembles English, although the functional nature of computer programs limits the variations in expression which are a hallmark of more traditional literary works.

20.76   Most users, of course, will be concerned only with what a program does rather than the manner in which this is accomplished. Some, however, may have different motives. The practice of reverse engineering has a lengthy history in more traditional industries and, typically, involves the purchase and dismantling of the products of a competitor. In the computer context, reverse engineering

463

may involve study of the operation of a computer program in order to discover its specifications. This is essentially a process of testing and observation and might involve pressing various keys or combinations of keys in order to discover their effects. The technique known as decompilation may be used as part of this process. Normally involving the use of other computer programs to analyse the object code, the technique seeks to reproduce the original source code.

20.77 The two leading English authorities on the topic of reverse engineering point are *LB (Plastics) Ltd v Swish Products Ltd*[1] and *British Leyland Motor Corpn v Armstrong Patents Co Ltd*.[2] Although in the *LB Plastics* case the alleged infringers had obtained a degree of access to the product drawings, in neither case was it argued that these had been reproduced directly. Instead, the case was based on the contention that by reproducing the finished object, respectively furniture drawers and a vehicle exhaust system, the provisions of s 48(1) of the Copyright Act 1956 had been breached. This provided inter alia: 'that copyright in a two-dimensional work, the product drawings, will be infringed by converting these into a three dimensional form, the product.'

[1] [1979] RPC 551.
[2] [1986] RPC 279.

20.78 In *LB (Plastics)*,[1] the plaintiff designed and produced a drawer system. The key feature was that the drawers could be supplied to customers (generally, furniture manufacturers) in what was referred to as 'knock-down' form. This offered considerable benefits at the transportation and storage stages, whilst the design facilitated swift and easy assembly of the drawers by the final producer. The concept proved commercially successful and some time later the defendant introduced a similar range of products. It was alleged that this was achieved by copying one of the plaintiff's drawers.

[1] *LB (Plastics) Ltd v Swish Products Ltd* [1979] RPC 551.

20.79 In the High Court, Whitford J accepted that the resulting product infringed the plaintiff's copyright in two of the original product drawings. Although this ruling was reversed by the Court of Appeal, which held that an insufficient causal link existed between the drawings in question and the defendant's product, it was reinstated by the House of Lords.[1] A significant factor underpinning the judgment would appear to have been the recognition that although the defendant was required by commercial dictates to ensure that their drawers were functionally compatible with those produced by the plaintiff, this could have been attained in ways which required less in the way of replication of the original design.

[1] *LB (Plastics) Ltd v Swish Products Ltd* [1979] RPC 551.

20.80 The decision in *LB Plastics*[1] was approved in the subsequent case of *British Leyland Motor Corpn v Armstrong Patents*.[2] Here, the plaintiff manufactured motor vehicles. The multitude of parts which make up each vehicle were produced in accordance with detailed designs drawn up by the plaintiffs. The defendant specialised in the manufacture of spare parts, in the particular case an exhaust system, which would be offered for sale to motor vehicle owners. In order to allow the replacement systems to be fitted to the plaintiff's vehicles, their design required to be virtually identical to that of the original component. This was achieved by taking an example of the plaintiff's exhaust system and examining its shape and dimensions.

1   *LB (Plastics) Ltd v Swish Products Ltd* [1979] RPC 551.
2   [1986] RPC 279.

20.81   The plaintiff's exhaust system was not itself eligible for copyright protection; neither was protection available under the law of patents or of registered designs.[1] The court's attention was directed, therefore, to the question whether copyright subsisted in the original engineering designs and, if so, whether the defendant's conduct constituted an infringement.[2] Holding in favour of the plaintiff on the issue of copyright infringement, the court (Lord Griffiths dissenting on the basis that although the majority's opinion was in line with precedent, the case was one which justified the application of the 1966 Practice Direction) held that the defendant's conduct amounted to indirect copying of the designs, constituting a breach of s 48(1) of the Copyright Act 1956. This provides that the conversion of a two-dimensional work into one of three dimensions will constitute reproduction.

1   The Copyright, Designs and Patents Act 1988 introduced the concept of a design right which will apply to drawings such as those at issue in *British Leyland Motor Corpn v Armstrong Patents* [1986] RPC 279. This right will substitute for copyright but, significantly, does not extend to any aspects of the design which enable the finished article to be 'connected to, or placed in or around or against, another article so that either article may perform its function' (s 213(3)).
2   The plaintiff's action ultimately failed on a second ground, the House of Lords holding that their claim to copyright was defeated by the right of a purchaser of their vehicle to obtain spare parts as economically as possible. The relationship between the provisions of intellectual property and competition law is assuming some significance in EC law. Recent dicta would suggest that whilst a refusal to grant competitors licences in respect of the use of intellectual property rights will not constitute an abuse of art 82 of the Treaty of Rome, any element of discrimination may render the conduct an abuse of a dominant position.

20.82   A further relevant case on this point is that of *Plix Products Ltd v Frank M Winstone*,[1] a case heard before the High Court of New Zealand whose decision was upheld on appeal to the Privy Council. This case concerned the design of containers designed for the transport of kiwi fruits. During the 1960s and 1970s, the plaintiff designed and produced a number of containers which offered significant advantages in respect of the safe storage and transportation of the fruit. The New Zealand kiwi fruit industry is subject to tight regulation, with the New Zealand Kiwi Fruit Authority having power to prescribe, inter alia, standards of packing. This power was exercised, with the standards being based on the plaintiff's designs. The defendants wished to penetrate this potentially lucrative market. Being aware of the potential intellectual property pitfalls, they sought to avoid infringement by engaging a designer who had no knowledge of the plaintiff's product. The designer was given the Fruit Authority's standards together with samples of kiwi fruit and instructed to produce an appropriate design. Strict instructions were given that the project was not to be discussed with any other party and that no examination should be made of any existing product. Effectively, therefore, the designer was given a set of written specifications and instructed to begin work on a clean sheet of paper. Perhaps not surprisingly, the end result was a series of designs which, when put into production, resulted in a container extremely similar in appearance to the plaintiff's.

¹ [1986] FSR 63.

20.83 Holding that the plaintiff's copyright had been infringed, the High Court of New Zealand ruled that copyright in an artistic design could be infringed by a party who had been provided with a written or verbal description of the work in the event that the description provided was sufficiently detailed to convey the form (expression) of the work as opposed to outlining the concept.[1] An illustration of the latter situation can be taken from the case of *Gleeson and Gleeson Shirt Co Ltd v H R Denne Ltd*.[2] Here, the plaintiff had designed a novel form of clerical shirt. The design proved commercially successful. A competing firm was asked by one of its clients whether it could produce a similar product. To this end, a general description of the shirt was given to one of its employees who had previously produced shirts containing similar features (although not in a single specimen). The resulting product was alleged to infringe the plaintiff's copyright in the artistic designs relating to its shirt. Dismissing this claim, it was held that the instructions given related only to the underlying ideas and that the application of the employee's own skill and knowledge had resulted in the creation of an independent piece of work. A second factor which appeared to influence the Court of Appeal in reaching this conclusion was the fact that the drawings upon which the plaintiff's copyright was founded were more in the nature of sketches than designs intended to serve as the blueprint for production. To this extent, the notion of an 'idea' and its distinction from 'expression' becomes blurred. As was stated in *Plix Products*:

> There are in fact two kinds of 'ideas' involved in the making of any work which is susceptible of being the subject of copyright. In the first place there is the general idea or basic concept of the work. This idea is formed (or implanted) in the mind of the author. He sets out to write a poem or a novel about unrequited love or to draw a dog listening to a gramophone ... Then there is a second phase – a second kind of 'idea'. The author of the work will scarcely be able to transform the basic concept into a concrete form – i.e. 'express' the idea – without furnishing it with details of form and shape. The novelist will think of characters, dialogue, details of plot and so forth. All these modes of expression have their genesis in the author's mind – these too are 'ideas'. When these ideas ... are reduced to concrete form, the forms they take are where the copyright resides.[3]

Even so, the distinction between protected and unprotected aspects of a work remains obscure. A significant factor relates to what might be termed the 'added value' element introduced by the author. Where the idea is expressed in simplistic or general terms (as with the sketches in *Gleeson*), a considerable degree of reproduction may be considered legitimate. In the event, however, that the expression is 'ornate, complex or detailed', the would-be plagiariser must beware, as 'the only product he can then make without infringing may bear little resemblance to the copyright work'.[4]

1   *Plix Products Ltd v Frank M Winstone* [1986] FSR 63.
2   [1975] RPC 471.
3   [1986] FSR 63 at 93.
4   [1986] FSR 63 at 94.

20.84   Although the cases of reverse engineering are of considerable relevance to the present topic, one major point of distinction may be identified. It will be recalled that the legislation specifically provides that computer programs are to be protected as a species of literary work. Although no criterion of literary merit is applied, the protection must extend to a particular combination of letters and numbers. As stated above, in the situation where access is obtained to these, it is arguable that a claim for breach of copyright will succeed even though the literary aspects of the second work bear little resemblance to the original. Where there is no question of access, merely the assertion that the operation of the second program replicates the 'look and feel' of the original, and where there is little evidence of literal similarity, it is difficult to argue that the traditional reverse engineering cases referred to above have any applicability. In each case, the cornerstone of the copyright owner's claim has been that, albeit indirectly, protected drawings have been reproduced. In the event that the operation of a computer program is studied and the attempt made to replicate its functions, there may be no substantial similarity between the two sets of code which make up the programs.

20.85   A closer analogy with computer software may be found with the case of *Green v Broadcasting Corpn of New Zealand*.[1] The plaintiff, Green, had been author, producer and presenter of a popular British television show, 'Opportunity Knocks'. The show operated according to a specific format and considerable use was made of catchphrases. Some years later, a programme with the same title was produced in New Zealand, making use of the same formats and catchphrases. With the interpolation of a new presenter, the programme, it might be stated, mimicked the 'look and feel' of the original. Upon discovering this, Mr Green instituted proceedings alleging, inter alia, that the later programme infringed his copyright in the original production. This action was rejected in the High Court of New Zealand, which held that, in the absence of evidence that scripts for the programmes had been reduced to writing, details of the dialogue could not be regarded as protected. An alternative head of claim concerned the dramatic format of the original programme, the various items which were included and the order in which they appeared. This claim was also rejected, the court referring to the views of a US commentator to the effect that:

> Formats are thus an unusual sort of literary creation. Unlike books, they are not meant for reading. Unlike plays, they are not capable of being performed. Unlike synopses, their use entails more than the expansion of a story outline into a script. Their unique function is to provide the unifying element which makes a series attractive – if not addictive – to its viewer.[2]

With minimal substitution of terminology, these sentences would seem to describe exactly the nature and role of many items of computer software. Whilst the case would not provide authority for the proposition that the reproduction of every aspect of a user interface will be sanctioned, it does suggest that a considerable degree of commonality may be permitted.

¹ [1989] RPC 469.
² R Meadow 'Television Formats – The Search for Protection' (1970) 58 Californian LR 1169 at 1170.

Reverse engineering and computer programs

20.86 Computer programs can be divided into two broad categories – operating systems and application programs. An operating system, the best known examples are perhaps MSDOS or Microsoft Windows, contains the basic instructions necessary for a computer to operate. A very simple analogy might be made with a railway system. The gauge of the track and the height and width of tunnels and bridges might be regarded as equivalent to an operating system. They set down basic parameters which must be respected by anyone wishing to build a train to operate on the system. If the track gauge is 4ft 8ins, no matter how technologically advanced an engine might be, it will be quite useless if its wheels are set seven feet apart. In the computer field, programs such as word processing and spreadsheet packages constitute the equivalents of railway engines. They work with the operating system to perform specific applications and must respect its particular requirements.

20.87 A producer intending to develop an applications package for use on a particular operating system must be aware of its functional requirements. In most instances, the information necessary will be made available by the producer of the operating system, whose own commercial interests will be best served by the widest possible availability of applications to run on the system. In the event that the information is not readily available – or that it is suspected that only partial information has been made available – the attempt may be made to reverse engineer the operating system.

20.88 A second occasion for the use of reverse engineering occurs at the level of applications packages. Programs such as word processors and spreadsheets store data in a particular format. In the case of basic text, a widely used standard exists – ASCII (American Standard Code for Information Interchange). The text of most word processed documents is a much more complex creature. Particular fonts, type size and line spacing will be used. Portions of the text may be printed in italics or may be emboldened or underlined. These matters are not standardised. A producer intent on developing a new word processing program may wish to discover the codes used by rival producers so that conversion facilities may be built into the new product. From a commercial perspective, existing users are more likely to change to a new program if they can still use documents created using their existing program.

20.89 The final form of reverse engineering is the most controversial. Here, the object of the reverse engineering is to discover information about the user interface of an applications package, which may then be used as the basis for the attempt to produce a substantially similar package. In early court cases on the point in the US, it was often asserted that the intent was to reproduce the 'look and feel' of the original package.

20.90 Given that a lawful user cannot be prevented from using a program for its normal purpose, some aspects of reverse engineering must be considered legitimate. A user who operates the program in a normal fashion in order to study its various aspects will not infringe copyright. Subject to strict conditions, a user will also be given the right to attempt to decompile a program's object code when this is done in order to produce a further program which will be interoperable with the copyright owner's. This would apply with respect to the first and second forms of reverse engineering discussed above. The right cannot be excluded by contract, but will apply only where the information required has not been made 'readily available' by the copyright owner. The term 'readily available' appears imprecise. It would not seem to require that the information be supplied free of charge. The levying of excessive charges would obviously be incompatible with the provision, but the question will arise what level is to be so considered. In most cases where interchange information is used in, for example, the word processing programs referred to above, it would appear that this is done under the terms of cross-licensing agreements between the parties involved. A second issue raises more technical questions. Producers of operating systems will normally find it in their own commercial interest to make the information available to those who wish to produce applications to run on the system. In some case, the producer of an operating system will also produce applications packages. The best known example is Microsoft. Although sufficient information concerning its operating system is made available to other producers, the systems have a number of what are referred to as 'undocumented calls' and it is frequently asserted that these are used by Microsoft's own applications packages. The situation might be compared with producing a road map of the British Isles which omitted all reference to motorways. A motorist who relied totally on the map would certainly be able find a route between Glasgow and London, although the journey might take considerably longer than one making use of the motorway network. Returning to the computer context, it may be queried whether the provision of incomplete information will resurrect the decompilation right. Against this, it may be noted that the legislation makes no mention of the quality of the interconnection which is to be enabled. If comparison is made with the patent system, which requires that an inventor disclose details of the manner in which the invention functions, the duty here is to disclose an effective manner of performing the invention, and not necessarily the optimum method. Any claim relating to the sufficiency of disclosure above and beyond that necessary to achieve interoperability might more reasonably lie under the heading of competition law.

20.91 The activities carried out in reliance on the decompilation right are to be restricted to the minimum necessary to obtain the information.[1] Again, this may be a difficult matter to determine. It might be that the user can determine which elements are essential to their legitimate goals only after the entire program has been decompiled. A further restriction imposed upon the user provides that information derived from the decompilation may not be passed on to any third party except where this is done in order to produce the new interoperable program.[2]

1   Copyright, Designs and Patents Act 1998, s 50B(3)(b).
2   Section 50B(3)(c).

20.92   The final restriction concerns the format of the finished program. This, it is provided, is not to be substantially similar in its expression to the original.[1] This is not to be implied as meaning that the program may not compete with the original. The producer of a word processing program may decompile existing programs to discover details of their format so as to permit the new program to accept text files produced using the earlier program. What is not permitted is the production of a program which infringes copyright in the original. The question how far copyright extends to the appearance and manner of functioning of computer programs is discussed below.

1   Copyright, Designs and Patents Act 1998, s 50B(4).

Literal and non-literal copying

20.93   The question when a basic idea is refined sufficiently to become a protected work is one of the most difficult issues in the field of copyright law. In the US, what is invariably referred to as the 'idea/expression dichotomy' has assumed statutory form, with the US Code providing:

> In no case does copyright protection for an original work of authorship extend to any idea, procedure, process, system, method of operation, concept, principle or discovery, regardless of the form in which it is described, explained, illustrated or embodied in such work.[1]

1   Title 17 USC at 102(b) (1982).

20.94   The EC Directive on the Legal Protection of Computer Programs[1] applies this principle in the specific context of computer programs, providing that:

> ... protection ... shall apply to the expression in any form of a computer program. Ideas and principles which underlie any element of a computer program ... are not protected by copyright.[2]

For the UK, although Lord Hailsham indicated in *LB (Plastics) Ltd v Swish Products Ltd* that 'it is trite law that there is no copyright in ideas', he continued 'But, of course, as the late Professor Joad used to observe, it all depends on what you mean by "ideas"'.[3] The notion of a formal separation between ideas and expressions is found nowhere in UK copyright law. Indeed, although the UK has incorporated most aspects of the directive into national law – even where, as in the case of the application of protection to preparatory material, it is arguable that no specific provisions were required, no attempt was made to include this formulation in the implementing regulations.

1   Directive 91/250/EC.
2   Article 1(2).
3   [1979] RPC 551 at 629.

20.95   The main justification for refusing protection to an idea lies in the belief that ideas as such are too intangible, too ethereal, to be protected. It is only when a thought or an idea is committed to paper or some other form of recording device, or even spoken in a public forum, that any evidence becomes available of the existence of what might be a protected interest. Even where this occurs, policy considerations operate to limit the scope of protection. Many legal journals (and academic CVs) would be much thinner if the first person to conceive of the notion of writing a learned article on the idea/expression dichotomy in copyright law had been granted a monopoly concerning the subject. The approach adopted under the law both of patent and of copyright has been to regard ideas as an unprotected step along the road to the protection of some concrete or practical manifestation of the concept. The grant of a patent requires a description of a practical application of the idea, whilst copyright law serves to protect a particular sequence of letters, words, figures or symbols which constitute the application or expression of the underlying idea.

20.96   A second area of difficulty concerns the extent of the protection offered under copyright. There is no doubt that direct or literal copying of the work will constitute infringement. A less certain matter concerns the extent of the protection in respect of what is sometimes referred to as 'non-literal copying'. During the 1980s and early 1990s, this was regarded as the most critical issue in intellectual property law. From a high-water point of perceived protection in 1990, the effect of subsequent decisions in the UK and the US has been to reduce the scope of protection. The increasing use of graphical interfaces and the application of text and graphic-rich applications such as multimedia products and, indeed, the WWW has brought with it a switch in emphasis from indirect protection of the underlying code to direct protection of the end product. Given the ease with which material held in electronic format may be copied, attention has also tended to switch from the exercise of the exclusive rights which are pivotal to the copyright regime to the issue how copyright may be managed in the interests of both owners and users. An indication of the scale of the issue and the problems can be taken from a WIPO estimate presented to the European Commission's Legal Advisory Board that some 90% of the costs incurred in producing a multimedia product made up of existing materials were related to the management of the intellectual property interests involved.

20.97   From a legal perspective, there is no doubt that the complete reproduction of software packages will constitute infringement of copyright. In other cases, elements of an earlier work may be reproduced. A typical scenario will see an employee changing jobs and subsequently producing software which incorporates routines from earlier works, the copyright in which will, of course, vest in the original employer. The issues involved here essentially concern the questions whether a substantial amount of the previous work has been reproduced and whether any similarities can be explained by reasons other than that of deliberate copying. Particularly in the case of computer programs, a variety of producers may be operating in the same field. In such a situation, and especially given the technical constraints which may operate, close similarities between two works may occur in the absence of deliberate copying or plagiarism. Similarities in the educational background of different programmers might also result in the production of substantially similar portions of program.

Fair and unfair use of an earlier work

20.98   Beyond those situations in which it may be apparent that a protected work has been copied, translated or adapted, situations may arise in which it is clear that the work has been used in the course of producing another work, but where the conduct cannot equivocally be regarded as involving any of the acts prohibited in the legislation. In a variety of cases concerned with literary works, the courts have adopted a broad view as to the scope of copyright protection, extending it to conduct which is regarded as involving the inequitable exploitation of the work of another – what might in everyday language be referred to as 'plagiarism'.

20.99   In the case of *Harman Pictures NV v Osborne*,[1] the plaintiff owned the screen rights in respect of a book dealing with the Charge of the Light Brigade. Negotiations had taken place with a view to the defendants acquiring the rights. The negotiations came to nothing, but some time later the defendants indicated their intention to produce a film on the same theme. The screenplay for the film was written by the first defendant. The plaintiff sought an injunction to prevent the film's distribution, alleging that the screenplay infringed their copyright.

[1]   [1967] 2 All ER 324.

20.100   Comparison of the screenplay with the book revealed points both of similarity and dissimilarity. The defendant did not deny having knowledge of the plaintiff's work, but argued that their screenplay had been based upon a much wider variety of sources.

20.101   Whilst accepting that it was permissible for a later author to make use of an existing work, it was held that this could not be utilised as a substitute for the expenditure of independent effort. As was stated by Sir William Page Wood V-C in the case of *Jarrold v Houlston*:[1]

> I take the illegitimate use, as opposed to the legitimate use, of another person's work on subject matters of this description to be this: If, knowing that a

person whose work is protected by copyright has, with considerable labour, compiled from various sources a work in itself not original, but which he has digested and arranged, instead of taking the pains of searching into all the common sources and obtaining your subject matter from them, you avail yourself of the labour of your predecessor, adopt his arrangements, adopt moreover the very questions he has asked or adopt them with but a slight degree of colourable variation, and thus save yourself pains and labour by availing yourself of the pains and labour which he has employed, that I take to be an illegitimate use.

In the present case, the issue was whether the defendant had worked independently to:

... produce a script which from the nature of things has much in common with the book, or did he proceed the other way round and use the book as a basis, taking his selection of incidents and quotations therefrom, albeit omitting a number and making some alterations and additions by reference to the common sources and by some reference to other sources?[2]

Considering these matters, Goff J determined that the similarities between the two works were sufficient to justify the grant of an interlocutory injunction, with terms preventing the defendants from 'exhibiting, releasing or distributing any film of or based on (the screenplay)'.[3]

[1] (1857) 3 K&J 708 at 716–717.
[2] *Harman Pictures NV v Osborne* [1967] 2 All ER 324 at 334.
[3] [1967] 2 All ER 324 at 337.

20.102 The question of the use which can be made of an earlier work was again at issue in the case of *Elanco Products Ltd v Mandops Agricultural Specialists Ltd*.[1] Elanco had invented and secured patent protection for a herbicidal product. During the currency of the patent's validity, both the plaintiff and independent research institutions had made extensive studies of the herbicide's application. Some of the information derived from these studies was incorporated in the form of instructions which were supplied with the product.

[1] [1980] RPC 213.

20.103 Upon the expiry of the patent, the defendant commenced production and marketing of the herbicide. Initially, they produced an accompanying instructional leaflet that was a virtual copy of the plaintiff's. The plaintiff objected to this action, alleging that it infringed copyright in their compilation of instructions, and the leaflet was withdrawn. A revised version was produced which also brought objections. When a third version was still considered objectionable, the plaintiff sought an injunction. Although the final version of the defendant's leaflet used terminology different from that of the plaintiff's, it was alleged that it remained based upon their material, thereby constituting an infringement of their copyright.

20.104 Holding in favour of the plaintiff, Goff LJ agreed that there was an arguable case of copyright infringement:

> It may well be that if the respondents had in fact at the start simply looked at the available information ... and from that decided what they would put in their literature and how they would express it, the appellants would at least have had considerable difficulty in bringing home any charge of infringement, even, having regard to the evidence, if the results had been extremely similar and the selection of items had been the same. But they chose, on the evidence as it stands at the moment, to proceed by making a simple ... copy, and then they proceeded to revise it. It may well be that the result produced that way is an infringement.[1]

Concurring, Buckley LJ ruled:

> As I understand the law in this case, the defendants were fully entitled to make use of any information, of a technical or any other kind which was in the public domain, for the purpose of compiling their label and their trade literature, but they were not entitled to copy the plaintiffs' label or trade literature thereby making use of the plaintiffs' skill and judgement and saving themselves the trouble, and very possibly the cost, of assembling their own information, either from their own researches or from sources available in documents in the public domain, and thereby making their own selection of information to put into that literature and producing their own label and trade literature.[2]

[1] *Elanco Products Ltd v Mandops Agricultural Specialists Ltd* [1980] RPC 213 at 228.
[2] [1980] RPC 213 at 231.

20.105 In one significant respect, the decision in *Elanco*[1] must be approached with a measure of caution. The fact that the defendant had originally produced a near total copy of the plaintiff's work must have cast a shadow over their subsequent conduct. One aspect of the case would, however, appear apposite in a software context. As is the case with much software, the literary works were functional in nature. Unlike the situation where works are created with a view to the reader's entertainment, their purpose was to provide instruction. In the situation where a user has become familiar with the instructions issued by one producer, the use of semantic variations may result in unnecessary confusion. Whereas diversity of expression may be a valuable attribute in literature, its virtues are less obvious in a more technical arena.[2]

[1] *Elanco Products Ltd v Mandops Agricultural Specialists Ltd* [1980] RPC 213.
[2] Some recognition of the different status of product instructions can be seen in the case of *Wormell v RHM Agriculture (East) Ltd* [1987] 3 All ER 75. Once again, a pesticide product was at issue, with the purchaser alleging that its failure to eradicate weeds rendered it unmerchantable in terms of s 14 of the Sale of Goods Act 1979. Although this action failed, the court accepted that the adequacy or otherwise of instructions constituted a relevant factor in determining questions of merchantability. This approach may be contrasted with the general refusal of the courts to consider claims that the quality of a written work is of unacceptable quality.

The rise and fall of look and feel protection

20.106 With the emergence of the PC, the possibilities for copyright infringement increased dramatically. As has been discussed above, in the situation where one party makes a complete or literal copy of a program, there is no doubt that infringement has occurred. A more difficult issue arises where there is an element of independent creative activity on the part of the second producer.

20.107 Starting in the late 1970s, a number of cases of this nature were raised in courts in the UK and the US. The disputes can reasonably be placed into two categories. In the first, a person or persons would have been employed to work on the development of a particular computer program. The employment would come to an end and the individual, either in his or her own right or as an employee of another company, would be involved in the development of a similar program. The program might well be written in a different computer language, providing limited evidence of literal similarities, and would often incorporate additional features or refinements not found in the original. The contention on the part of the original copyright owner would be that a substantial part of the original program had been copied into the new version.

20.108 A second category of case, which to date has arisen only in the US, would see parties acting very much at arm's length. The alleged infringer will have had the opportunity to see a copy of the original program in operation and will have set out to create from scratch a competing product which will replicate all or parts of the on-screen appearance of the original.

The computerised pharmacist

20.109 In the first category of disputes, there is no doubt that the individual responsible for the development of the allegedly infringing product will have had access to all significant elements of the original program. The English case of *Richardson v Flanders*,[1] which was the first case concerned with software copyright to reach the stage of trial in the High Court, might be considered as a typical example of the species.

[1] [1993] FSR 497.

20.110 At issue in this case was a computer program designed for use by pharmacists. The program, which was developed to run on the then popular BBC microcomputers, performed a number of tasks. Principally, when the computer was attached to a printer it would automate and simplify the task of preparing dosage instructions to be supplied with medicines. The program's other major function was to assist in stock-keeping by keeping a record of the drugs dispensed. The program was marketed by the plaintiff, who had also performed a significant amount of work on the original program. Subsequently, the first defendant was employed to work on the project. It was accepted that all relevant copyrights in the work belonged to the plaintiff.

20.111 The program achieved considerable commercial success. Relationships between the plaintiff and the defendant were not so happy. The defendant resigned from his position, although he continued to perform some work for the plaintiff as an independent contractor for a further period of time. With the advent of the IBM PC, one of the plaintiff's major customers expressed interest in a version of the program capable of running on this machine and which could be sold on the Irish market. Following discussions, the plaintiff decided not to proceed with the project but suggested that the defendant might be willing to perform the work. The program was completed and was sold in Ireland. The defendant subsequently contacted the plaintiff offering him the rights to market the product in the UK. These discussions proved fruitless and the defendant proceeded to market a modified version of the program in the UK. At that stage, the plaintiff initiated proceedings alleging that the new product infringed copyright in his original program.

20.112 Because of the fact that the programs had been developed to run on different computers, examination of the code used would have revealed few evidences of similarities. The programs did perform the same functions and had very similar appearances when operating on their respective hardware.

20.113 In the absence of any relevant UK precedent, the judge placed considerable reliance on US authority, notably the case of *Computer Associates v Altai*.[1] The court, it was held, should conduct a four-stage test designed to answer the questions.[2] This would seek to answer the following questions:

1. Whether the plaintiff's work was protected by copyright.
2. Whether similarities existed between the plaintiff's and the defendant's programs.
3. Whether these were caused by copying or whether other explanations were possible.
4. In the event that copying was established, whether the elements copied constituted a significant part of the original work.

Given what has been said above regarding the willingness of UK courts to confer copyright protection on a work, it is not at all surprising that the first question could be answered quickly and definitively in the affirmative. Consideration of the other issues was a more difficult task.

[1]   982 F 2d 693 (1992). See para 20.150 below.
[2]   *Richardson v Flanders* [1993] FSR 497.

20.114 Examining the operation of the original program, the judge identified 13 aspects of the functioning of the original program leading to the printing of the label for a drug container. This program also offered a stock control function and some 17 other features allowing a pharmacist to customise the program in accordance with any particular requirements. When the same analysis was applied to the revised program, 17 points of similarity were identified between the two programs which would require further investigation to determine whether they were the product of copying.

20.115 These similarities were identified from an examination of the screen displays and key sequences. The judge did not attempt to compare the underlying codes. Although an expert witness for the plaintiff had presented an analysis of alleged similarities between the source codes of the two programs, the judge indicated that he found this 'extremely difficult to understand'. Counsel for the plaintiff failed to pursue an invitation to attempt further explanation, and the analysis formed no part of the final decision.

20.116 One obvious cause of similarities, that of deliberate copying, was rejected by the judge. It was accepted, however, that the defendant must have retained considerable knowledge of the plaintiff's program and that if similarities resulted from the unconscious use of this material, infringement might be established.

20.117 Examining the similarities between the two programs, most were considered explicable by reasons other than copying. The two programs, for example, presented dates in a similar format. Conventions for the presentations of dates are well established and the fact that two works utilise a similar format is more likely to be caused through adherence to such conventions rather than by copying.

20.118 In a second aspect, the original program had presented the pharmacist with the option of placing a date other than the current date on a label. This feature was reproduced in the revised program. Although the judge held that it was likely that this had been copied from the original, he held that, given there were a very limited number of ways in which the idea could be expressed, the fact that the two programs utilised very similar approaches did not establish infringement.

20.119 In total, six of the 17 similarities identified by the judge were considered explicable by reasons other than copying. The remaining 11 items it was considered, with varying degrees of conviction, might have been copied from the original program. Eight of these, however, referred to matters which in the opinion of the judge did not amount to a substantial part of the program. One element found in both programs gave users an indication that their instructions have been accepted. In both programs, the message 'operation successful' would appear on the screen and the computer would emanate a double-beep sound. This aspect of the original program, it was held, 'lacks originality and cannot have required any significant skill or effort to devise it'.

20.120 Ultimately, infringement was established in respect of only three of the points of similarity, comprising editing and amendment functions and the use of dose codes. The similarities in respect of the editing function were perhaps especially noticeable as it operated in the same idiosyncratic (and probably erroneous) manner in both programs. The dose code facility allowed the user to abbreviate certain instructions regarding the dosage and the manner in which the medication was to be taken. Thus in both programs, use of the abbreviation

AC (Ante cibum) would cause the instruction 'before food' to be printed on the label. Although a number of the abbreviations were held to be obvious, the fact that 84 out of 91 codes found in the original program were reproduced in an identical format in the later version, with only minor changes in another five, was held to raise an inference of copying.

20.121 Although copyright infringement was ultimately established, the plaintiff's victory was heavily qualified.[1] The copying was described as constituting 'a fairly minor infringement in a few limited respects and certainly not ... slavish copying'. Although some of the processes adopted clearly differ from those in *Computer Associates*,[2] the effect of the judgment is similar in recognising that for functional works, external forces may well be the cause of similarities, thereby excusing conduct that might otherwise appear to constitute a breach of copyright.

1   *Richardson v Flanders* [1993] FSR 497.
2   *Computer Associates v Altai* 982 F 2d 693 (1992). See para 20.150 below.

Agricultural software

20.122 Allegations of copyright were again before the High Court in the case of *Ibcos Computers v Barclays Mercantile Highland Finance*.[1] Again, there was a background of the major defendant having worked for the plaintiff on the development of a software product intended for use by agricultural dealers, which was marketed under the name ADS. On leaving its employment, he developed a further and competing product which was marketed under the name of Unicorn. The plaintiff alleged that sufficient features of this were copied from the original to constitute an infringement of copyright.

1   [1994] FSR 275.

20.123 In determining the criteria which would be applied in determining the question whether infringement had occurred,[1] Jacobs J was somewhat critical of the extensive references to the US decision in *Computer Associates*[2] and warned against 'overcitation of US authority based on a statute different from ours'. The approach to be adopted was for the court to determine whether there was a sufficient degree of similarity between the two works which, coupled with evidence of access to the original work, would establish an inference of copying. The onus would then switch to the defendant to establish that the similarities were explicable by causes other than copying. Evidence that 'functional necessity' served to narrow the range of options open to the defendant would be relevant. Trivial items may well provide the most eloquent testimony. As was said in *Bilhofer v Dixon*:

> It is the resemblances in inessentials, the small, redundant, even mistaken elements of the copyright work which carry the greatest weight. This is because they are the least likely to have been the result of independent design.[3]

1   *Ibcos Computers v Barclays Mercantile Highland Finance* [1994] FSR 275.

2   *Computer Associates v Altai* 982 F 2d 693 (1992).
3   [1990] FSR 105 at 123.

20.124   In the present case, evidence was presented that the same words were misspelled in the same manner, the same headings were used in the two programs and both shared the same bit of code which served no useful purpose for the functioning of the program. Beyond this, there were considerable similarities at the level of the code itself. In respect of one element of the programs, it was held that:

> ... there are 22 identical variables, 8 identical labels, 1 identical remark, 31 identical code lines and one identical redundant variable. This to my mind plainly indicates copying and enough in itself to constitute a significant part.[1]

1   *Ibcos Computers v Barclays Mercantile Highland Finance* [1994] FSR 275 at 308.

20.125   The court recognised in *Ibcos*[1] that copyright protection must extend beyond the literal aspects of the program code to aspects of 'program structure' and 'design features'. In the case of the former element, it was held that copyright subsisted in the compilation of individual programs which made up the ADS system. Although some differences existed between ADS and Unicorn, it was held that the defendant had taken 'as his starting point the ADS set and that set remains substantially in Unicorn'. Although the two programs had a different visual appearance and it was recognised that 'Unicorn is undoubtedly to the user a much friendlier program than ADS was at the time', the defendant, it was held had taken 'shortcuts by starting with ADS and making considerable additions and modifications'.

1   *Ibcos Computers v Barclays Mercantile Highland Finance* [1994] FSR 275.

Financial markets

20.126   The most recent UK decision was delivered by the High Court in April 1999, in the case of *Cantor Fitzgerald International v Tradition UK Ltd*.[1] Both companies involved in the case operated in the financial services market. The plaintiff had developed a computer package which was used in the course of its bond-broking activities. Much of the work in respect of this had been carried out by its Managing Director, a Mr Howard, and a team of programmers appointed by him. The Managing Director was dismissed in 1991. He subsequently secured employment with the defendants, in large part because of his suggestion that he could develop a similar system for them. On taking up employment, he secured the recruitment of three other members of the plaintiff's programming team.

1   [2000] RPC 95.

20.127   The defendant obtained computers of the same type as those used by the plaintiff, and the employees (who were also defendants in the litigation) began work. In a period of less than three months, a working system was produced. Action alleging copyright infringement and breach of confidence was initiated by the plaintiffs, who argued that it would have been impossible for the programs involved to have been written from scratch in the time available.

20.128 Initially, the programmers denied that they had had access to any other plaintiff's source code. When the process of discovery highlighted evidence suggesting copying of certain modules, the truth emerged that the programmers had taken a copy of the plaintiff's source code with them. The defendant dropped its initial denial of any copyright infringement and the case proceeded on the basis of how extensive the copying had been.

20.129 Expert witnesses were appointed by both parties. The witness for the plaintiff was subjected to severe criticism by the trial judge, Pumphrey J, who opined that the witness had held back relevant information and had acted as an advocate for the plaintiff rather than as an objective and impartial expert. The defendant's witness, on the other hand, was regarded as 'an admirable expert'. His conclusions were perhaps surprising, and were summarised by the judge:

> The Tradition system comprises some 77,000 lines of source code divided into some 363 'modules'. A total of 2,952 lines of code are admitted to have been copied, of which some are repeated copies of a single block of code. In addition Dr McKenzie has identified some 1,964 lines of code which he says are questionable, although he says that the majority of the questionable code was probably not copied. This means that if the admissions are exhaustive, the copied code represents 2 per cent of the system by number of lines. If all the questionable code is included as well, the figure is about 3.3 per cent.[1]

[1]   *Cantor Fitzgerald International v Tradition UK Ltd* [2000] RPC 95 at 102.

20.130 Faced with this report, the plaintiff restricted its claim of copying to 35 of the systems modules. The question, therefore, was whether what was copied constituted a substantial part of the original program. It also made two claims alleging breach of confidence in respect of the techniques used for developing programs of the kind at issue and also in respect of the code itself, arguing that if the programmers had used their access to the plaintiff's code to 'increase their confidence' in the accuracy of their new work, that would of itself constitute misuse of confidential information, regardless whether the code was subsequently copied.

The copyright infringement claims

20.131 Initial reference was made to the decision of Jacobs J in *Ibcos Computers v Barclays Mercantile Highland Finance*[1] laying down the steps to be followed in deciding an action for infringement of copyright:

(1)   What are the work or works in which the plaintiff claims copyright?
(2)   Is each such work 'original'?
(3)   Was there copying from that work?
(4)   If there was copying has a substantial portion of that work been reproduced?

[1]   [1994] FSR 275.

20.132   The situation in *Cantor*[1] was in many respects more complex than in *Ibcos*.[2] Although the start point may have been the same, it was more questionable both whether the end product could be regarded as the product of copying of a substantial part of the original programs and, indeed, whether what had been copied satisfied the criterion of originality required for copyright to come into existence. Pumphrey J expressed some doubt whether the application of criteria developed in a literary context was a proper approach when dealing with a functional product such as software:

> A program expressed in a computer language must not contain errors of syntax (or it will not compile) and it must contain no semantic errors. Computers do not have the capacity to deduce what the author meant when they encounter errors in the kind of software with which this action is concerned. If the software contains semantic errors it will produce the wrong answer or no answer at all: it may merely fail to run. The only opportunity that the programmer gets to express himself in a more relaxed way is provided by the comments in the code, which are for the benefit of the human reader and are ignored when the code comes to be compiled.[3]

1   *Cantor Fitzgerald International v Tradition UK Ltd* [2000] RPC 95 at 102.
2   *Ibcos Computers v Barclays Mercantile Highland Finance* [1994] FSR 275.
3   [2000] RPC 95 at 130.

20.133   It might be suggested from this that every line of code in a program should be considered essential for its operation and, therefore, that any copying would involve reproduction of a substantial part of the original. The Australian case of *Autodesk v Dyson*[1] was cited as authority for this proposition. For the UK, however, whilst every aspect of a program was essential at the technical level, the determination of substantiality required to be made by reference to the level of skill and effort expended in the creation of the original work. This was to be determined at a qualitative level:

> In the general case it is well established that a substantial part of the author's skill and labour may reside in the plot of a novel or play; and to take that plot without taking any particular part of the particular manner of its expression may be sufficient to amount to copyright infringement.[2]

For software, it was suggested:

> It seems to be generally accepted that the 'architecture' of a computer program is capable of protection if a substantial part of the programmer's skill, labour and judgment went into it. In this context, 'architecture' is a vague and ambiguous term.[3]

1   [1992] RPC 575.
2   *Cantor Fitzgerald International v Tradition UK Ltd* [2000] RPC 95 at 134.
3   [2000] RPC 95 at 134.

20.134   Two possible meanings were identified for the term, the first relating to the overall description of the system at a high level of abstraction. It could also mean, as was at issue, the overall program structure. Here, functions which it was agreed between the parties were essential elements of the particular software package were grouped into programs with copyright being recognised in the 'compilation of the programs'.

20.135   In spite of the somewhat reprehensible nature of the programmer's work in *Cantor*[1] (which included documenting plans to alter code so as to disguise the fact that it had originated in the plaintiff's program), only a very limited degree of copyright infringement was established. The defendant had accepted liability for the points of similarity identified by its expert witness and in all other respects the finding of the court was that there was no infringement. Similarities were considered either to relate to insubstantial pieces of work or to be explicable by reasons other than copying.

[1]   *Cantor Fitzgerald International v Tradition UK Ltd* [2000] RPC 95.

The breach of confidence claim

20.136   The judgment in respect of the claims of breach of copyright follows what appears to be a general trend to limit the scope of copyright protection to little more than direct or literal copying. As such, it might appear to leave a copyright owner with limited protection. The alternative claim relating to breach of confidence fared better. Although it was held that the techniques used in the development of the original programs were not sufficiently novel or unusual to be regarded as trade secrets and entitled to protection on this basis, it was found, albeit without any detailed explanation, that the use of the original code as an aide memoire constituted breach of confidence.

Arm's length reproduction

20.137   In all of the cases which have been brought before a UK court, there has been some previous contact between the parties. To find situations where parties have dealt more or less at arm's length, reference needs to be made to US authority. Three cases are worthy of consideration. First is the decision of the Massachusetts' District Court in the case of *Lotus Development Corpn v Paperback Software International and Stephenson Software Ltd.*[1] This case can be regarded as marking the high-water point of copyright protection in the US. An alternative and more restrictive approach to copyright protection was applied by the Court of Appeals for the Second Circuit in the case of *Computer Associates v Altai.*[2] Finally, the decision of the Court of Appeals for the First Circuit (and a subsequent appeal to the Supreme Court) in the case of *Lotus Development Corpn v Borland,*[3] although applying different reasoning from that of the court in *Computer Associates*, also signified a retrenchment in the level of protection afforded to copyright owners.

[1]   740 F Supp 37 (1990).
[2]   982 F 2d 693 (1992).
[3]   49 F 3d 807 (1995).

Problems with spreadsheets

20.138 Credit for the 'invention' of electronic spreadsheet packages tends to be given to Daniel Bricklin, a student at Harvard Business School in the late 1970s. Building on his work there, he produced the first commercial package, 'Visicalc'. As originally produced, Visicalc would run on Apple computers. Although a version was produced for use on IBM machines, this did not prove particularly successful. The deficiencies in the 'Visicalc' program prompted Michael Kapor and Jonathon Sachs to produce the first version of '1-2-3'. Although the basic idea of an electronic spreadsheet was taken from Visicalc, 1-2-3 expressed it in a different and more versatile way. Lotus 1-2-3 acquired considerable commercial success, a factor which contributed to the creation of a considerable number of competing packages, generally referred to as clones. A variety of actions were raised by Lotus alleging copyright infringement with two, against Paperback and Borland, proceeding to the trial stage. As discussed below, the *Borland* litigation[1] eventually proceeded to the Supreme Court, but it was the action against Paperback and its spreadsheet package 'VP-Planner' which was to constitute the first significant precedent.[2]

[1] *Lotus Development Corpn v Borland* F 3d 355 (1995).
[2] *Lotus Development Corpn v Paperback Software International and Stephenson Software Ltd* 740 F Supp 37 (1990).

20.139 Development of what was to become the contentious VP-Planner began in 1982. Originally, this was developed in ignorance of the features of 1-2-3, but in 1983 its developer, James Stephenson, saw a copy of 1-2-3 in operation. By 1984, recognising the commercial success of 1-2-3, he came to the conclusion that VP-Planner, in order to be a commercial success, would have to be 'compatible' with 1-2-3.[1] Compatibility, it was determined, would require that the arrangement and names of commands and menus found in 1-2-3 would have to be replicated in VP-Planner. This would allow users to transfer data between the systems and also permit a user familiar with 1-2-3 to switch to VP-Planner without any need for retraining.

[1] *Lotus Development Corpn v Paperback Software International and Stephenson Software Ltd* 740 F Supp 37 (1990) at 69.

20.140 The goal of compatibility was realised in the final version of VP-Planner, and some stress was laid upon this facility in publicity material. Thus, it was stated:

> VP-Planner is designed to work like Lotus 1-2-3, keystroke for keystroke ... VP-Planner's worksheet is a feature for feature workalike for 1-2-3. It does macros. It has the same command tree. It allows the same kind of calculations, the same kind of numerical information. Everything 1-2-3 does, VP-Planner does.[1]

Although the two systems' appearance was not identical, with 'VP-Planner' indeed containing a number of additional features, the works were, it was stated by the judge, 'substantially, indeed strikingly similar'.

¹   *Lotus Development Corpn v Paperback Software International and Stephenson Software Ltd* 740 F Supp 37 (1990) at 69–70.

20.141 In the present proceedings,[1] which were originally joined with an identical action against the producer of another 1-2-3 lookalike, it was argued that the defendants infringed Lotus's copyright in the program 1-2-3. The feature[2] which serves to distinguish the present case from the earlier decisions of *Whelan*[2] and *Broderbund*[3] is that there was no prior relationship between the parties and no question of the alleged copier having access to anything other than a commercially available copy of the software.

¹   *Lotus Development Corpn v Paperback Software International and Stephenson Software Ltd* 740 F Supp 37 (1990) at 69–70.
²   *Whelan v Jarlow* 797 F 2d 1222 (1986).
³   *Broderbund Pixellite v Unison World* 648 F Supp 1127 (1986).

20.142 The first matter which needed to be determined in the proceedings concerned the criteria which should be applied in deciding whether any infringement of copyright had occurred. In the US District Court in Massachusetts, Judge Keeton adopted a three-stage test in order to distinguish the unprotected idea from the protected expression:

> FIRST, in making the determination of 'copyrightability', the decisionmaker must focus upon alternatives that counsel may suggest, or the court may conceive, along the scale from the most generalized conception to the most particularized, and choose some formulation – some conception or definition of the 'idea' – for the purpose of distinguishing between the idea and its expression ...
>
> SECOND, the decisionmaker must focus upon whether an alleged expression of the idea is limited to elements essential to expression of the idea (or is one of only a few ways of expressing the idea) or instead includes identifiable elements of expression not essential to every expression of the idea.
>
> THIRD, having identified elements of expression not essential to every expression of the idea, the decisionmaker must focus on whether those elements are a substantial part of the allegedly copyrightable 'work'.[1]

¹   *Lotus Development Corpn v Borland* F 3d 355 (1995) at 60–61.

20.143 In attempting to apply these tests, which are essentially a more detailed version of those adopted in the *Whelan*[1] and *Broderbund*[2] cases, Judge Keeton indicated that he found the phrase 'look and feel' to be of little assistance in determining the extent of the copyrightable elements.[3] The phrase, he suggested, represented a conclusion and was of little assistance to a judge attempting to progress towards that goal. Acting upon this hint, the plaintiffs presented their case with reference to the alleged reproduction of the 'user interface' of 1-2-3. This was defined as including elements such as 'the menus (and their structure and organisation), the long prompts, the screens on which they appear, the function key assignments, (and) the macro commands and language'. The question to be answered was, therefore, whether the plaintiff's user interface constituted an idea or was a means of expression.

[1]   797 F 2d 1222 (1986).
[2]   648 F Supp 127 (1986)
[3]   *Lotus Development Corpn v Paperback Software International and Stephenson Software Ltd* 740 F Supp 37 (1990) at 60–61.

20.144   The concept of an electronic spreadsheet was, it was held, unprotectable on the basis that:

> ... the core idea of such a spreadsheet is both functional and obvious, even to computer users who claim no technical competence ... It does not follow, however, that every possible method of designing a metaphorical spreadsheet is obvious, or that no form of expressing the idea of the spreadsheet metaphor can possible have such originality in pressing beyond the obvious as is required for copyrightability, or that no special form of metaphorical spreadsheet can possibly be a distinctive expression of a particular method of preparing financial information.[1]

[1]   *Lotus Development Corpn v Paperback Software International and Stephenson Software Ltd* 740 F Supp 37 (1990) at 65.

20.145   Certain features of such spreadsheets were, it was held, intrinsic to the concept of a spreadsheet and, indeed, to many other forms of computer program. The notion of what was referred to as a 'moving cursor menu' fell into this category. It was pointed out, however, that the idea could be expressed in a number of ways and that other spreadsheets available on the market utilised a format different from that found in 1-2-3. The conclusion was drawn from this that:

> ... a menu command structure is capable of being expressed in many if not an unlimited number of ways, and that the command structure of 1-2-3 is an original and non-obvious way of expressing a command structure.[1]

On this basis, the 1-2-3 menu structure met the requirements of the second element of the three-stage test for copyrightability. The question then arose as to whether the 'structure, sequence and organization' of the 1-2-3 menu system constituted a substantial part of the work as a whole. The judge was in no doubt that this was the case, a conclusion strengthened by the fact that the defendants had gone to considerable lengths to imitate it, conduct evidencing their own view as to its significance.

[1]   *Lotus Development Corpn v Paperback Software International and Stephenson Software Ltd* 740 F Supp 37 (1990) at 68.

20.146   In respect of the issue of infringement, although there were some differences in particular forms of expression between the two packages, Visicalc using the term 'replicate' rather than the perhaps more obvious 'copy' used in the Lotus package. In terms of arranging functions in a list of available commands, Visicalc ordered these in order of predicted use whilst Lotus adopted an alphabetical structure. Nonetheless, Judge Keeton was in no doubt that infringement had occurred. The copying was described as being 'overwhelming and pervasive' so that from 'the perspective of both an expert and an ordinary viewer, the similarities overwhelm differences'.[1]

[1] *Lotus Development Corpn v Paperback Software International and Stephenson Software Ltd* 740 F Supp 37 (1990) at 69.

20.147 In addition to basing their defence on a denial of copyright infringement, the defendants presented a number of arguments based upon considerations of public policy. Effectively, these were based on the argument that 1-2-3 had become a de facto industry standard. This status, it was argued, meant that its features must be made available to anyone wishing to utilise them. Rejecting these claims, Judge Keeton ruled:

> ... one object of copyright law is to protect expression in order to encourage innovation. It follows, then, that the more innovative the expression of an idea is, the more important is copyright protection for that expression. By arguing that 1-2-3 was so innovative that it occupied the field and set a de facto industry standard, and that, therefore, defendants were free to copy plaintiff's expression, defendants have flipped copyright on its head. Copyright protection would be perverse if it only protected mundane increments while leaving unprotected as part of the public domain those advancements that are more strikingly innovative.[1]

[1] *Lotus Development Corpn v Paperback Software International and Stephenson Software Ltd* 740 F Supp 37 (1990) at 79.

20.148 The argument that standardisation was to be encouraged as protective of the public interest fared no better, Judge Keeton opining that there was no evidence proving that standardisation, except when achieved by law, was necessarily supportive of the public interest. It was further pointed out that the presence on the market of a number of other non-compatible spreadsheets contradicted the defendant's assertion of the existence of a de facto standard.

20.149 With hindsight, the decision in *Lotus v Paperback*[1] can be seen as marking the high-water point of copyright protection for software. Throughout the judgment, references are made to the concepts of 'innovation'. Lotus's user interface, we are told, is an 'original and non-obvious way of expressing a command structure'. Traditionally in copyright law, the requirement of originality has been restricted to the demand that the work should not have been copied from elsewhere. The novelty of the subject matter has never been an issue. By introducing these requirements, the decision has been referred to as involving the 'patentisation' of copyright.

[1] *Lotus Development Corpn v Paperback Software International and Stephenson Software Ltd* 740 F Supp 37 (1990).

Compatibility requirements

20.150 An alternative, and more restrictive view, as to the scope of copyright protection was adopted by the US Court of Appeals for the Second Circuit in the case of *Computer Associates Inc v Altai Inc.*[1] Both parties were involved in designing and producing computer software products. At issue was a program, marketed by the plaintiffs under the name of 'ADAPTER'. ADAPTER was supplied as an integral part of a larger software product, and was designed to permit computer programs written in a variety of computer languages to operate on particular brands of IBM computers.[2]

[1]   982 F 2d 693 (1992).
[2]   For a detailed description of the products involved in this litigation, reference should be made to the decision of the District Court reported at 775 F Supp 544 (1991).

20.151   The defendants, Altai, determined to produce a program that would fulfil similar functions. An employee of the plaintiff was recruited to perform this task, although the fact that he had worked on the development of the ADAPTER program was unknown to the defendant. The employee brought with him copies of the source code of ADAPTER, these having been made and retained in violation of his contract of employment with the plaintiff. Again, the defendant was unaware of this fact.

20.152   After a period of time, the defendant's program was completed and marketed under the name 'OSCAR'. It may be a source of no surprise that it bore great similarities to ADAPTER, subsequent investigations revealing that around 30% of its code had been copied from the earlier program. Rather more surprisingly, OSCAR was marketed for some three years before the plaintiff became aware of the fact that much of its work had been copied[1] and instituted proceedings alleging breach of copyright and infringement of trade secrets.

[1]   This may be explained by the fact that neither ADAPTER nor OSCAR was supplied independently, but only as part of larger suites of programs.

20.153   At trial, the defendant did not contest the original infringement and damages of $364,444 were awarded against them.[1] To this extent, the case appears similar to *Cantor Fitzgerald*.[2] Where the case differs is that the defendant immediately dropped the original program and appointed a new team of programmers to develop a new version. In spite of the fact that none of the new team had any knowledge of the original program, the plaintiff argued that the programs they created violated its copyrights. The plaintiff also alleged that the new version of OSCAR remained substantially similar to 'ADAPTER' and, as such, also infringed their copyright. This claim was rejected by the judge and an appeal was lodged on this issue.

[1]   *Computer Associates Inc v Altai Inc* 982 F 2d 693 (1992).
[2]   *Cantor Fitzgerald International v Tradition UK Ltd* [2000] RPC 95.

20.154   In determining whether copyright infringement had occurred, the Court of Appeals utilised a three-stage approach, referred to as an 'Abstraction-Filtration-Comparison'.[1] Apart from sharing a similar number of steps, the application of this test was to prove to have few similarities with the approach adopted in *Lotus v Paperback*.[2]

[1]   *Computer Associates Inc v Altai Inc* 982 F 2d 693 (1992).

Abstraction

20.155   The abstraction element of the *Computer Associates*[1] test involves the court in determining the manner in which the original and the allegedly infringing programs were produced. Effectively requiring a form of reverse engineering, the first task is to identify the original concept involved. The next step would be to divide the program into a number of discrete segments. Having identified the segments and the tasks that they are to perform, the relationship between these will be charted in organisational or flow charts. It is at this stage that the work will move from the conceptual to the practical, with the lines of code being written to implement the plans described above. The code would be written as source code and subsequently compiled into object code.

1   *Computer Associates Inc v Altai Inc* 982 F 2d 693 (1992).

Filtration

20.156   The result of the abstraction process will be a detailed understanding of the various elements which make up the program. The filtration step seeks to identify those elements which will fall outside the scope of copyright protection. Efficiency is a major virtue in most aspects of life and where certain procedures and processes are regarded as being the most efficient available, the fact that two works are substantially similar may, it was held, 'as likely lead to an inference of independent creation as it does to one of copying'.[1]

1   *Computer Associates Inc v Altai Inc* 982 F 2d 693 at 708 (1992).

20.157   The Court of Appeals also recognised that external constraints might play a major role in forming the shape of a computer program. Five factors were specifically identified. The 'mechanical specifications' of items of equipment upon which the program was intended to run would exert considerable influence. Where the program was intended to operate in conjunction with other computer programs, the dictates of compatibility would again be a dominant factor. The design standards of computer manufacturers and the demands of customers were identified as further factors which might shape the format of a particular program, with reference finally being made to the existence of widely-accepted programming practices.

20.158   The final factor to be taken into account in the filtration process would seek to identify any elements which might be regarded as falling within the public domain. No attempt was made to define the boundaries of this topic, but it would appear applicable in the situation where routines are widely utilised and publicised.

Comparison

20.159   The previous stages may have sifted out various aspects of the original program. The remains, what the court described as the 'golden nugget',[1] would require to be compared with the allegedly infringing process. This examination will contain two elements, first to determine whether copying has occurred and, secondly, whether this represents a substantial portion of the protected work.

[1]   *Computer Associates Inc v Altai Inc* 982 F 2d 693 at 710 (1992).

20.160   In the present case,[1] the Court of Appeals affirmed the trial judge's finding that there had been no infringement. Most of the similarities between the amended OSCAR program and ADAPTER were explicable and justifiable by reference to the functional demands of the program or involved matters which fell into the public domain. Any remaining similarities, it was held, related to minor portions of the work and hence did not involve reproduction of a substantial part of the protected work.

[1]   *Computer Associates Inc v Altai Inc* 982 F 2d 693 (1992).

Policy considerations

20.161   Although, in the subsequent case of *Lotus Development Corpn v Borland International Inc*,[1] Judge Keeton expressed the view that the decisions in *Lotus v Paperback*[2] and *Computer Associates*[3] were not inconsistent, there appears little doubt that they do represent significant divergences in approach regarding the proper role of copyright in respect of computer programs. The decision in *Lotus v Paperback* might be regarded as triumphalist in tone. In one passage, Judge Keeton indicated his agreement with the plaintiff's contention that:

> ... the tremendous growth and success of the US software industry is the direct result of the creative and original efforts of its software developers, laboring under the protection of the copyright laws.
> ... It is no accident that the world's strongest software industry is found in the United States, rather than in some other jurisdiction which provides weaker protection for computer programs.[4]

[1]   799 F Supp 203.
[2]   *Lotus Development Corpn v Paperback Software International and Stephenson Software Ltd* 740 F Supp 37 (1990).
[3]   *Computer Associates Inc v Altai Inc* 982 F 2d 693 (1992).
[4]   740 F Supp 37 at 75 (1990).

20.162   By way of contrast, the Court of Appeals recognised significant problems in applying principles of copyright law. Referring to the arguments advanced on behalf of the present plaintiff, it commented:

> CA and some *amici* argue against the type of approach that we have set forth on the grounds that it will be a disincentive for future computer program research and development. At bottom, they claim that if programmers are not guaranteed broad copyright protection for their work, they will not invest the

extensive time, energy and funds required to design and improve program structures. While they have a point, their argument cannot carry the day. The interest of the copyright law is not in simply conferring a monopoly on industrious persons but in advancing the public welfare through rewarding artistic creativity, in a manner that permits the free use and development of non-protectable ideas and processes.[1]

---

[1] *Computer Associates Inc v Altai Inc* 982 F 2d 693 at 711 (1992). See also the discussion of the case of *Feist Publications Inc v Rural Telephone Service Co Inc* 111 Sup Ct Rep 1282 (1991).

20.163   Continuing, doubt was expressed as to the utilisation of the copyright system in the field of computer programs, the court quoting with approval the trial judge's comment that:

> In the context of computer programs, many of the familiar tests of similarity prove to be inadequate, for they were developed historically in the context of artistic and literary, rather than utilitarian, works.[1]

Pursuing the point, the Court of Appeals itself commented:

> To be frank, the exact contours of copyright protection for non-literal program structure are not clear. We trust that as future cases are decided, those limits will become better defined. Indeed, it may well be that the Copyright Act serves as a relatively weak barrier against public access to the theoretical instances behind a program's source and object codes. This results from the hybrid nature of a computer program, which, while it is literary expression, is also a highly functional, utilitarian component in the larger process of computing.[2]

---

[1] *Computer Associates Inc v Altai Inc* 982 F 2d 693 at 713 (1992).
[2] 982 F 2d 693 at 712 (1992).

20.164   In tone, if not necessarily in legal content, it is difficult to reconcile the *Lotus*[1] and *Computer Associates*[2] approaches. The developments in the availability of patents described in Chapter 18 may result in a greater emphasis being placed upon this branch of intellectual property law, an approach endorsed by the Court of Appeals, which commented:

> Generally, we think that copyright registration – with its indiscriminating availability – is not ideally suited to deal with the highly dynamic technology of computer science. Thus far, many of the decisions in this area reflect the court's attempt to fit the proverbial square peg in a round hole ... patent registration, with its exacting up-front novelty and non-obviousness requirements, might be the more appropriate rubric of protection for intellectual property of this kind.[3]

---

[1] *Lotus Development Corpn v Paperback Software International and Stephenson Software Ltd* 740 F Supp 37 (1990).
[2] *Computer Associates Inc v Altai Inc* 982 F 2d 693 (1992).
[3] 982 F 2d 693 at 712 (1992).

Spreadsheets again. The last word?

20.165   Paralleling its action against Paperback,[1] Lotus instituted proceedings against another competitor, Borland.[2] The trial was also heard before Judge Keeton and the judgment, which demonstrated substantial evidence of the use of the 'cut and paste' functions on a word processor, was also in favour of the plaintiff. Procedural complexities, however, meant that the case was not concluded until 1992, some two years after the *Paperback* decision was delivered. Unlike *Paperback*, and perhaps encouraged by the subsequent decision in *Computer Associates v Altai*,[3] Borland did pursue an appeal and, on Thursday 9 March 1995, the US Court of Appeals for the First Circuit issued a judgment overturning the original decision.[4]

[1]   *Lotus Development Corpn v Paperback Software International and Stephenson Software Ltd* 740 F Supp 37 (1990).
[2]   *Lotus Development Corp v Borland International Inc* 788 F Supp 78 (D Mass 1992).
[3]   982 F 2d 693 (1992).
[4]   49 F 3d 807 (1995).

20.166   A number of interesting points arise from the Court of Appeals decision. The court considered and was somewhat critical of the 'Abstraction-Filtration-Comparison' approach which, it argued, was at least impliedly based on the premise that some elements of copyrightable expression existed. This test, it was suggested, was appropriate where non-literal copying was involved, but could be 'misleading' in a case such as the present where the fact that literal elements in the form of menu structures had been copied was not at issue. What had to be decided was whether what had been copied was protected by copyright. The majority of the court held that the Lotus menu structure was not protected. In reaching this conclusion, they applied a prohibition in the US copyright law against protecting a 'method of operation'. The Lotus menu, it was held, did not merely describe the manner in which the program functioned, but provided the 'means by which users control and operate Lotus 1-2-3'. As such, Borland were free to copy the Lotus menu structure. An analogy was drawn with the control buttons on a video recorder. No one, it was suggested, could copyright the 'play', 'record' or other functions inscribed on the relevant buttons. Menu commands in a computer program performed the same function.

20.167   It may be doubted whether any UK court would be as cavalier in its rejection of the existence of copyright. As will be discussed in Chapter 21, following the decision of the Supreme Court in the case of *Feist v Rural*,[1] the US courts have taken a more critical view of the requirement of originality than is the case in the UK. Delivering a concurring judgment, however, Boudin CJ made a number of trenchant criticisms of the state of US copyright law which are of relevance also in a UK context. Applying copyright law to computer programs, he held, 'is like assembling a jigsaw puzzle whose pieces do not quite fit'. The computer program, he held:

> is a means for causing something to happen; it has a mechanical utility, an instrumental role, in accomplishing the world's work. Granting protection, in

other words, can have some of the consequences of patent protection in limiting other people's ability to perform a task in the most efficient manner. Utility does not bar copyright (dictionaries may be copyrighted), but it alters the calculus.[2]

In terminology reminiscent of the decision in *Feist v Rural*, he acknowledged that the use of Lotus's work by others might deprive Lotus of 'a portion of its reward', but pointed out that 'the provision of reward is one concern of copyright law, but it is not the only one'. Specific reference was made to the investment of users in acquiring expertise in the operation of a program and to the need to ensure that they did not remain 'captives of Lotus'.

[1]   111 S Ct 1282 (1991).
[2]   *Lotus Development Corpn v Borland Int'l* 49 F 3d 807 at 819 (1995).

20.168   The decision of the Court of Appeals[1] provides further evidence of judicial scepticism and concern at the application of copyright provisions in a software context. It may indeed be the case that the much-vaunted flexibility of the copyright system is approaching the limits of plasticity. Although elements of the decision are based on elements of US law that are not replicated in the UK's copyright regime, two issues are of general significance. First, the court appears to treat conduct where reproduction occurs in the course of building upon an earlier work as different from reproduction as an end in itself. It has been suggested that an appeal by the defendants in *Lotus v Paperback*[2] would have failed on this basis, although the founder of the paperback software company has expressed the view on the Internet newsgroup, 'misc.int-property', that his firm's product was qualitatively superior to Lotus '1-2-3'. The second message that might be taken from *Lotus* is recognition that all software is not the same. A distinction has to be drawn between products, such as that issue in *Computer Associates*,[3] whose value rests in the tasks which they accomplish and the functional efficiency achieved and those applications packages where the value lies in more aesthetic aspects involving interaction between the product and its user. It may well be that the notion of a single test for determining issues of infringement is a false goal and that a variety of tests will be required to deal with a variety of applications.

[1]   *Lotus Development Corpn v Borland Int'l* 49 F 3d 807 (1995).
[2]   *Lotus Development Corpn v Paperback Software International and Stephenson Software Ltd* 740 F Supp 37 (1990).
[3]   *Computer Associates Inc v Altai Inc* 982 F 2d 693 (1992).

20.169   In their turn, Lotus sought to appeal against the decision of the Court of Appeals. For the first time, the Supreme Court of the US granted certiorari in respect of a software copyright case and a definitive ruling was eagerly awaited by all concerned with the issues. A substantial number of briefs amicus curiae were submitted to the court. Unfortunately, by the time the dispute reached the Supreme Court,[1] Lotus had been taken over by IBM and members of the family of one of the Supreme Court Justices (Stevens) owned shares in this company. The Justice, therefore, took no part in the court's deliberations and, unfortunately, the remaining eight judges were evenly divided on the merits of the appeal. In this circumstance, the Supreme Court did not deliver an opinion allowing the decision of the Court of Appeals to stand.

¹   *Lotus Development Corpn v Borland Int'l* 133 L Ed 2d 610 (1996).

Conclusions

20.170   The inconclusive and rather unsatisfactory ending to the litigation in *Lotus v Borland*[1] might have raised expectations that many further copyright disputes would be brought. In fact, this has proved not to be the case and copyright litigation has, at least in the US, almost dried up. A variety of reasons might be advanced for this state of affairs. The emergence of the patent system as a vehicle for the protection of software has undoubtedly 'siphoned off' many forms of software. If a software producer can obtain a patent, not only is the level of protection increased, but also the task of establishing infringement is considerably simplified. An example of the complexity which frequently accompanies copyright litigation can be taken from the case of *Cantor Fitzgerald v Tradition*.[2] The main trial hearing in this case occupied 28 days of court time. *Richardson v Flanders*[3] was only slightly shorter at 26 days. In *Cantor*, the conduct at issue took place in Spring 1991. Eight years elapsed before the case reached trial. In the case of *Lotus v Borland*, by the time the case reached the Supreme Court,[4] Lotus had been taken over by IBM and Borland were no longer active in the spreadsheet market. Beyond benefiting layers and academic textbook writers, it is difficult to asses what the litigation achieved.

¹   *Lotus Development Corpn v Borland* F 3d 355 (1995).
²   *Cantor Fitzgerald International v Tradition UK Ltd* [2000] RPC 95.
³   *Richardson v Flanders* [1993] FSR 497.
⁴   *Lotus Development Corpn v Borland Int'l* 49 F 3d 807 (1995).

20.171   Apart from legal factors, the emergence of Windows as a standard operating system has served to impose a measure of uniformity on software developers. It is clearly in the interests of operating system producers such as Microsoft to encourage as many hardware and software producers as possible to build their own operations around the particular operating system. Rather than relying on copyright to prevent third party use of programs, this involves placing the information necessary to interact with an operating system into the public domain.

20.172   The issue of compatibility also arises between competing applications developers. In the early days of word processing software, the capabilities of the programs were limited. Most data was represented in accordance with the American Standard Convention for Information Interchange (ASCII) and, as such, it would be relatively easy for a document produced by one package to be opened by another. Further, it was comparatively rare for documents to be exchanged in electronic format. With more sophisticated packages and the massive increase in the electronic dissemination of information, it becomes necessary in their mutual interests for producers to exchange the data necessary to allow documents to be transported between different applications. To an extent, co-operation has replaced litigation.

20.173   Although copyright litigation in respect of non-literal aspects of copyright may have diminished, the importance of the subject remains high. As with most other aspects of life, the emergence of the Internet has created new issues and problems. Chapter 21 will look at some of the issues associated with the development and application of copyright principles within the information society.

Copyright in the information society

Introduction

21.1   Issues of intellectual property have been at the forefront of much of the debate concerning the legal impact of the 'information superhighway'. An indication of the relative importance and complexity of the issues involved can be taken from a WIPO estimate that no less 90% of the total investment in a multimedia product was expended in dealing with intellectual property issues.[1] In its 'Follow-Up to the Green Paper on Copyright and Related Rights in the Information Society' the Commission have estimated that:

> The market for copyright goods and services ranges Community-wide from between 5 and 7% of the GNP. This market is comprised of a large variety of products and services, containing protected subject matter, ranging from traditional products, such as print products, films, phonograms, graphic or plastic works of art, electronic products (notably computer programs) to satellite and cable broadcasts, CD and video rental, theatres and concert performances, literature and music, art exhibitions and auctions.[2]

For the UK, the Prime Minister has indicated that the country's cultural sector is a greater source of revenue that the steel industry.[3]

[1]   'The Information Society: Copyright and Multimedia', Proceedings of a meeting held under the auspices of the Legal Advisory Board, Luxembourg, 16 April 1995.
[2]   COM (96) 568 final, p 6.
[3]   http://www3.europeparl.eu.int/omk. Debates of Tuesday 9 February 1999.

21.2   Whilst managing intellectual property rights is complex and time consuming for those who wish to remain within the law, the ease with which digital information may be copied renders the owners of copyright in literary, artistic and musical works vulnerable to the making and dissemination of unauthorised copies of a work in electronic format. If the invention of the printing press resulted in a move from an oral to a written tradition at the price of chaining information to the pages of a book, the information revolution frees information in the sense that it may be readily transferred without the need for linkage to paper or any other form of storage device.

21.3 To date, the attempt has generally been made to bring technological applications within the scope of the intellectual property system, most notably in the field of copyright. As has been discussed in Chapter 20, copyright has proved an extremely flexible instrument, having been extended from literary works through sound recordings, films, terrestrial broadcasts, satellite and cable broadcasts and onto computer programs. Even the most flexible tool, however, has limits to its elasticity, and as the Information Society becomes more and more entrenched, so the relevance of the system, especially with its notion of exclusive rights, becomes open to challenge. This chapter will look at some of the emerging issues in the attempt to consider whether, and to what extent, copyright principles have a future in the Information Society?

The Directive on Copyright in the Information Society and the Copyright and Related Rights Regulations 2003

21.4 A Green Paper *Copyright and Related Rights in the Information Society* was published by the Commission in July 1995.[1] This was followed by a proposal for a directive 'on the harmonisation of certain aspects of copyright and related rights in the Information Society' which was submitted by the Commission to the European Parliament in January 1997.[2] A number of aspects of the proposal were criticised in the Parliament, and an amended proposal was tabled in May 1999.[3] The Directive was finally adopted in May 2001[4] with member states being obliged to implement its provisions by 22 December 2002. In common with a number of other member states the UK failed to meet this deadline with implementation occurring through the medium of the Copyright and Related Rights Regulations 2003[5] which entered into force on 31 October 2003. The Regulations make a number of changes to the provisions of the Copyright, Designs and Patents Act 1988.

[1]   COM (95) 382 final.
[2]   OJ 1998 C 108, p 6.
[3]   COM (1999) 250 final.
[4]   Directive 2001/29/EC, OJ 2001 L 167/10 (the Directive on Copyright in the Information Society).
[5]   SI 2003/2498.

21.5 The Explanatory Memorandum to the original proposal for a directive[1] contains useful background statistics on the importance of the IP sector for European economies. It proceeds to identify discrepancies in the level of protection offered within the member states, not so much at the level of fundamental principles, but in respect of detailed implementation and the provision of exceptions. Thus, all member states accept that the right holder possesses the exclusive right to reproduce material, but differ in respect of issues such as whether a temporary reproduction will constitute infringement. Variations occur also in respect of concepts such as fair dealing and the provision of special regimes for the educational sector.

¹ Available from http://europa.eu.int/comm/internal_market/en/intprop/intprop/1100.htm.

21.6 Beyond the issue of reproduction, significant issues concern the extent of rights to distribute a work or to communicate its contents to the public. With the development of 'on demand' services for the delivery of digital information in the form of audio or video material, lacunae exist between provisions relating to private communications and broadcasting. The Directive on Copyright in the Information Society¹ sets out to make provision for these matters and to harmonise existing national provisions, keeping always in line with the provisions of the Berne Convention and the 1996 WIPO Treaty on Copyright and Performances and Phonograms. In essence the Directive is evolutionary rather than revolutionary in its contents. As recital 5 indicates:

> Technological development has multiplied and diversified the vectors for creation, production and exploitation. While no new concepts for the protection of intellectual property are needed, the current law on copyright and related rights should be adapted and supplemented to respond adequately to economic realities such as new forms of exploitation

¹ Directive 2001/29/EC.

21.7 Reflecting this approach, the initial articles of the Directive on Copyright in the Information Society¹ do little more than confirm existing copyright realities, especially as they have developed in the UK. Article 2 provides authors, performers, producers and broadcasters with the exclusive right to prohibit direct or indirect, temporary or permanent reproduction of the protected work by any means or in any form. Article 3 provides for similar exclusive rights in respect of the communication of all or part of a work to the public by wire or wireless means. It is specifically provided that the provision is to extend to the situation where the works are communicated in such a way that 'members of the public may access them from a place and at a time individually chosen by them', for example, over the Internet. Article 4 provides for authors to enjoy the exclusive right to control the distribution of works to the public by sale or otherwise.

¹ Directive 2001/29/EC.

Caching

21.8 The most controversial section of the Directive on Copyright in the Information Society¹ is contained in art 5:

> 1. Temporary acts of reproduction referred to in Article 2, which are transient or incidental [and] an integral and essential part of a technological process and whose sole purpose is to enable:
>
> (a) a transmission in a network between third parties by an intermediary, or

(b) a lawful use of a work or other subject-matter to be made,
    and which have no independent economic significance, shall be exempted
from the reproduction right provided for in Article 2.

¹   Directive 2001/29/EC.

21.9   Recital 33 indicates the intent behind this provision:

The exclusive right of reproduction should be subject to an exception to allow
certain acts of temporary reproduction, which are transient or incidental
reproductions, forming an integral and essential part of a technological process
and carried out for the sole purpose of enabling either efficient transmission in
a network between third parties by an intermediary, or a lawful use of a work
or other subject-matter to be made. The acts of reproduction concerned should
have no separate economic value on their own. To the extent that they meet
these conditions, this exception should include acts which enable browsing as
well as acts of caching to take place, including those which enable transmission
systems to function efficiently, provided that the intermediary does not modify
the information and does not interfere with the lawful use of technology, widely
recognised and used by industry, to obtain data on the use of the information.
A use should be considered lawful where it is authorised by the rightholder or
not restricted by law. The terms in italics represent changes which were made to
the original proposal following objections in the European Parliament that the
measure gave insufficient weight to the interests of right owners.

21.10   A range of situations might be envisaged in which this provision will be
applicable. The act of viewing information on a third party's web page will
involve the making of a temporary copy of that data on the user's own equipment.
The nature of the Internet, again, will mean that transient copies of email messages
will be made at various stages of the message's journey through cyberspace.
Such copying falls within the criteria 'integral' and 'essential'. The practice of
caching, which is specifically referred to in the recital,¹ raises more difficult
issues and the inclusion of the phrase 'an integral and essential part' might be
seen as robbing the provision of much of its meaning.

¹   Directive 2001/29/EC, recital 33.

21.11   Caching involves the making of copies of materials originating on another
site on a local machine. A user seeking access to the materials will be presented
with a local copy, rather than having the request transmitted over the Internet to
the original host site. Typically, the materials copied will be those for which
there is the greatest demand, and the practice serves both to speed access for the
user and reduce traffic over what is often a congested Internet. The problem that
may be faced under the directive's provisions is that although the use of caching
may be advantageous, it cannot be considered essential.

21.12   The legality of caching is also provided for in the Electronic Commerce
Directive.¹ This introduces the concept of an 'information society service'. This
is defined as 'any service normally provided for remuneration, at a distance, by

electronic means and at the individual request of a recipient of services'.[2] The provisions of the Directive will be discussed in more detail in Chapter 28. In respect of the practice of caching, however, it provides that:

> Where an Information Society service is provided that consists in the transmission in a communication network of information provided by a recipient of the service, Member States shall provide in their legislation that the provider shall not be liable, otherwise than under a prohibitory injunction, for the automatic, intermediate and temporary storage of that information, performed for the sole purpose of making more efficient the information's onward transmission to other recipients of the service upon their request, on condition that:
>
> (a) the provider does not modify the information;
> (b) the provider complies with conditions on access to the information;
> (c) the provider complies with rules regarding the updating of the information, specified in a manner consistent with industrial standards;
> (d) the provider does not interfere with the technology, consistent with industrial standards, used to obtain data on the use of the information; and
> (e) the provider acts expeditiously to remove or to bar access to the information upon obtaining actual knowledge of one of the following:
>   – the information at the initial source of the transmission has been removed from the network;
>   – access to it has been barred; or
>   – a competent authority has ordered such removal or barring.[3]

[1] Directive 2000/31/EC, OJ 2000 L 178/1.
[2] Directive 98/48/EC, OJ 1998 L 217/218.
[3] Article 13.

21.13 In most cases, it may be assumed that the creator of a material on the WWW will seek its wide distribution, and the practice generally raises few objections. The Electronic Commerce Directive[1] goes on to make further provisions relating to the need to ensure that cached copies are kept up to date and that access to these does not impinge with the original user's ability to monitor access to the material. This last point will be of particular importance where a website is commercial in nature. Increasingly, such sites carry advertising material and the advertising income may be dependent upon evidence being supplied of the number of persons accessing and using the site.

[1] Directive 2000/31/EC.

Copy protection

21.14 The use of copy protection devices was a feature of many early software products. A wide range of techniques was utilised in the attempt to ensure that only an authorised user could make use of software. In some cases, anti-copying techniques would have been embedded in the software itself, in other cases physical devices were used. The absence of a uniform approach between producers meant that there was almost invariably a non-protected version of software available on the market and, given that the use of such devices normally made software more difficult to use, market forces compelled most producers to abandon such tactics. With devices such as Digital Video Discs (DVDs) there are signs that the technique is returning to favour. Here, manufacturers of discs embed a code corresponding to the region of the world in which the disc is marketed. DVD players are also coded in a similar manner, so the effect is intended to be that only discs marketed in one region can be played on equipment marketed in that area. A variety of techniques can be used to overcome this form of protection and the directive sets out to provide legal sanctions against such acts.

21.15 Article 6 of the Directive on Copyright in the Information Society[1] provides that:

> 1. Member States shall provide adequate legal protection against the circumvention of any effective technological measures, which the person concerned carries out in the knowledge, or with reasonable grounds to know, that he or she is pursuing that objective.
>
> 2. Member States shall provide adequate legal protection against the manufacture, import, distribution, sale, rental, advertisement for sale or rental, or possession for commercial purposes of devices, products or components or the provision of services which:
> (a) are promoted, advertised or marketed for the purpose of circumvention of, or
> (b) have only a limited commercially significant purpose or use other than to circumvent, or
> (c) are primarily designed, produced, adapted or performed for the purpose of enabling or facilitating the circumvention of, any effective technological measures.

Measures will be considered effective when:

> the use of a protected work or other subject-matter is controlled by the rightholders through application of an access control or protection process, such as encryption, scrambling or other transformation of the work or other subject-matter or a copy control mechanism, which achieves the protection objective

Section 296 of the Copyright Designs and Patents Act 1988 already provided a copyright holder who publishes work in an electronic form which is copy-protected with a right of action against a person who:

> (a) makes, imports, sells or lets for hire, offers or exposes for sale or hire, or advertises for sale or hire, any device or means specifically designed or adapted to circumvent the form of copy-protection employed, or
> (b) publishes information intended to enable or assist persons to circumvent that form of copy-protection, ...

This provision with its limitation to devices 'specifically designed or adapted' is rather more restrictive than the Directive's provisions which refer to an articles primary purpose.[2] Accordingly whilst retaining the original formula in respect of computer programs (which are outside the scope of the Directive) the regulations introduce a number of somewhat complex provisions – new sections 296ZA (circumvention of technological measures), 296ZD (rights and remedies in respect of devices and services designed to circumvent technological measures) and 296ZE (remedy where effective technological measures prevent permitted acts).[3]

1 Directive 2001/29/EC.
2 Albeit in a slightly different context, see the discussion of *CBS Songs Ltd v Amstrad Consumer Electronics plc* at para 21.26 below where the fact that a twin cassette deck had some legitimate uses provided a defence to a claim of copyright infringement even though it might be argued that most purchasers would use the equipment for unlawful purposes.
3 SI 2003/2498, reg 24.

21.16 With traditional forms of literary work it is customary to incorporate copyright details in the printed text. Where work is distributed in electronic format rights management information would see details identifying copyright owners being embedded in a digitised work and a facility included to record the use made of the work. This would facilitate the tasks of establishing copyright and the extent of any infringing use of the work. As the Directive on Copyright in the Information Society's[1] recitals indicate:

(55) Technological development will facilitate the distribution of works, notably on networks, and this will entail the need for rightholders to identify better the work or other subject-matter, the author or any other rightholder, and to provide information about the terms and conditions of use of the work or other subject-matter in order to render easier the management of rights attached to them. Rightholders should be encouraged to use markings indicating, in addition to the information referred to above, inter alia their authorisation when putting works or other subject-matter on networks.

(56) There is, however, the danger that illegal activities might be carried out in order to remove or alter the electronic copyright-management information attached to it, or otherwise to distribute, import for distribution, broadcast, communicate to the public or make available to the public works or other protected subject-matter from which such information has been removed without authority. In order to avoid fragmented legal approaches that could potentially hinder the functioning of the internal market, there is a need to provide for harmonised legal protection against any of these activities.

1 Directive 2001/29/EC.

21.17 To guard against this, art 7 requires that:

Member States shall provide for adequate legal protection against any person performing without authority any of the following acts:

(a) the removal or alteration of any electronic rights-management information; or

(b) the distribution, importation for distribution, broadcasting, communication or making available to the public, of copies of works or other subject matter protected under this Directive[1] or under [the Database Directive[2]] from which electronic rights-management information has been removed or altered without authority, if such person knows, or has reasonable grounds to know, that by so doing he is inducing, enabling or facilitating an infringement of any copyright or any rights related to copyright as provided by law, or of the sui generis right provided for in [the Database Directive].

¹   Directive on Copyright in the Information Society, Directive 2001/29/EC.
²   Directive on 'the legal protection of databases', Directive 96/9/EC, OJ 1996 L 77/20 (the Databases Directive).

21.18   In order to implement this provision, the regulations add a further new section (296ZG) to the Copyright, Designs and Patents Act 1988. This provides that an offence will be committed by:

a person(D) who knowingly and without authority, removes or alters electronic rights management information which—

(a)   is associated with a copy of a copyright work, or
(b)   appears in connection with the communication to the public of a copyright work, and
(c)   where D knows, or has reason to believe, that by so doing he is inducing, enabling, facilitating or concealing an infringement of copyright.[1]

Offences will also be committed by parties concerned with the importation, distribution or communication to the public of copies from which electronic rights information has been removed.

¹   SI 2003/2498, reg 25.

Private copying in the digital age

21.19   In many jurisdictions, a measure of tolerance has traditionally been extended in respect of copying activities carried out by private individuals. In some European jurisdictions, such conduct is specifically authorised, often in parallel with the imposition of some form of levy on the costs of recording devices such as cassette tapes, the proceeds of which will go to authors' rights organisations to be distributed or used for the benefit of copyright owners, thereby providing at least some compensation for losses caused by copying.

21.20   Although at one stage it was proposed to introduce a similar scheme in the UK, the objection has always been that the devices can be used for lawful as well as for infringing purposes. An individual might, for example, use a cassette recorder and tape to record his or her own compositions rather than to make a copy of a third party's work. In such a situation, it is difficult to identify equitable grounds for requiring payment to be made to copyright owners.

21.21   Even though the UK does not legitimise domestic copying,[1] a measure of tolerance is shown by the fact that the criminal penalties applicable in the event of copying for commercial purposes do not extend to private persons. Such an approach can be justified in the context of analogue copying. It would be a rare person who has not infringed copyright at some stage through over-zealous use of a photocopier. Most readers will be familiar with the limitations of the copying technology. A photocopy of an article in a journal or a chapter of a book will invariably be of lower quality than the original. Slight movement of the page as the copy is being made will cause blurring of lines, the size of the book being copied and the paper being used in the photocopier may differ, again with adverse consequences for the appearance of the copy. Problems will be exacerbated if a photocopy is itself copied and by the time the process is repeated over a few generations of copies, the final version will be virtually indecipherable. Similar factors will apply when a cassette copy is made of a musical recording or television or film production. In general, with equipment normally available to the domestic copyist, the copying process is a laborious one and the results inferior in quality to the original work.

[1]   Save in the case of use of a video recorder to record a television broadcast 'solely' in order to allow it to be viewed at a more convenient time (Copyright, Designs and Patents Act 1988, s 70).

21.22   Where information is recorded in digital format, the task of the copier is very much easier. A copy of a digital work will be identical in terms of quality to the original, and the same result will apply no matter how many generations of copies are produced. The speed with which copies may be made is also generally increased, whilst the emergence of the Internet makes it possible for a program to be placed on a website and copied by tens or even hundreds of thousands of users around the world. The popular encryption program PGP was released to the world in this manner in order to pre-empt attempts by the US authorities to prevent its distribution. Not even the might of the US could put the technological genie back in that particular bottle. Today, much debate focuses on the presence on the Internet of copies of audio recordings in MP3 format. As will be discussed below, one legal response to the problem has been to seek to impose liability on commercial third parties whose equipment or facilities are regarded as facilitating the infringing acts of private individuals. The question arises also what should be the level of liability imposed on the individual's concerned?

21.23   The Directive on Copyright in the Information Society[1] contains provisions which, if adopted, may require significant changes to present UK law and practice, recital 38 stating that:

> Member States should be allowed to provide for an exception or limitation to the reproduction right for certain types of reproduction of audio, visual and audio-visual material for private use, accompanied by fair compensation. This may include the introduction or continuation of remuneration schemes to compensate for the prejudice to rightholders. Although differences between those remuneration schemes affect the functioning of the internal market, those differences, with respect to analogue private reproduction, should not have a significant impact on the development of the information society. Digital private copying is likely to be more widespread and have a greater economic impact. Due account should therefore be taken of the differences between

digital and analogue private copying and a distinction should be made in certain respects between them.

¹ Directive 2001/29/EC.

21.24 It would seem that this provision empowers rather than requires member states to introduce licensing or similar schemes. Regulation 26 of the Copyright and Related Rights Regulations 2003¹ provides for an extension of the scope of criminal offences. Previously an offence was committed only when a copyright infringer acted in the course of a business. The Copyright, Designs and Patents Act 1988 is now amended to provide that:

> (2A) A person who infringes copyright in a work by communicating the work to the public—
> (a) in the course of a business, or
> (b) otherwise than in the course of a business to such an extent as to affect prejudicially the owner of the copyright,
>   commits an offence if he knows or has reason to believe that, by doing so, he is infringing copyright in that work.²

¹ SI 2003/2498.
² Section 107.

Third-party liability for copyright infringement

21.25 In terms of the question whether infringement of copyright has occurred, there is little doubt that the individual responsible for copying a work in electronic format will incur liability where this act is done without the authority of the copyright owner. An individual who downloads a copy of a software program or the text of an article from a bulletin board or other form of online service will infringe copyright. A constant thread in discussions of audio, video or software piracy has concerned the impossibility, and indeed the desirability, of bringing proceedings against thousands if not millions of individual infringers. Much attention has been paid to the possibility of holding liable those parties who provide the equipment or facilities used for infringing acts.

21.26 The question how far an ISP may be held responsible for the activities of its users is of considerable significance for the industry. In the UK, the decision of the House of Lords in the case of *CBS Songs Ltd v Amstrad Consumer Electronics plc*¹ is a relevant precedent. The respondents in this case produced audio equipment. Included in their range was a hi-fi unit containing two cassette decks. This feature allowed a user to copy the contents of one cassette tape onto another, a prospect which caused considerable concern to the owners of copyright in works recorded on cassette, a sector of the audio market which had hitherto enjoyed a considerable degree of immunity from the ravages of home copying. The concern was exacerbated by a further feature which allowed the contents of a tape to be copied in half of the normal playing time. Action was brought alleging that Amstrad had, by their production of the equipment and the use of marketing strategies[2] described by Lord Templeman as being 'deplorable', 'cynical' and 'open to severe criticism',[3] purported to authorise users to make copies of protected works in disregard of the rights of the copyright owners and in breach of the provisions of the Copyright Act 1956. This contention was rejected by the House of Lords. The critical issue, it was held, was whether equipment could be put to legitimate as well as to illegitimate purposes. Where this was the case, even the most ambiguous marketing strategy could not be regarded as purporting to authorise its use for illegal purposes. 'By selling the recorder', it was held, 'Amstrad may facilitate copying in breach of copyright but do not authorise it'.[4] A similar approach can be seen in the earlier case of *CBS Records v Ames Records and Tapes*,[5] where a record library which lent out records and simultaneously offered blank cassette tapes for sale at a reduced price was held not to have purported to authorise customers to make infringing copies.

1   [1988] AC 1013.
2   One advert claimed that the system 'features "hi-speed dubbing" enabling you to make recordings from one cassette to another, record direct from any source and then make a copy and you can even make a copy of your favourite cassette'.
3   [1988] AC 1013 at 1053.
4   [1988] AC 1013 at 1053.
5   [1982] Ch 91.

21.27   Applying these principles in the context of Internet-based activities, it would seem that an ISP whose facilities were used by customers for purposes which would constitute infringement of copyright – for example, through the posting of MP3 audio files – will not be liable. This conclusion is strengthened by the provisions of the Electronic Commerce Directive,[1] which states that:

> Where an Information Society service is provided that consists in the storage of information provided by a recipient of the service, Member States shall provide in their legislation that the provider shall not be liable, otherwise than under a prohibitory injunction, for the information stored at the request of a recipient of the service, on condition that:
>
> (a)   the provider does not have actual knowledge that the activity is illegal and, as regards claims for damages, is not aware of facts or circumstances from which illegal activity is apparent; or
>
> (b)   the provider, upon obtaining such knowledge or awareness, acts expeditiously to remove or to disable access to the information.[2]

1   Directive 2001/31/EC.
2   Article 14. The implications of the requirement in para (b) are discussed in more detail in the context of defamatory material in Chapter 31.

21.28   Even more helpfully for ISPs, the Electronic Commerce Directive goes on to provide that no obligation is to be imposed on ISPs requiring that they monitor the contents of their site with a view to determining whether material might be considered unlawful.[1] This accords with the UK position but reg 27 of the Copyright and Related Rights Regulations 2003[2] adds a new s 97 the Copyright, Designs and Patents Act 1998 to provide that:

(1) The High Court (in Scotland, the Court of Session) shall have power to grant an injunction against a service provider, where that service provider has actual knowledge of another person using their service to infringe copyright.

(2) In determining whether a service provider has actual knowledge for the purpose of this section, a court shall take into account all matters which appear to it in the particular circumstances to be relevant and, amongst other things, shall have regard to—

(a) whether a service provider has received a notice through a means of contact made available in accordance with regulation 6(1)(c) of the Electronic Commerce (EC Directive) Regulations 2002 (SI 2002/2013); and

(b) the extent to which any notice includes
(i) the full name and address of the sender of the notice;
(ii) details of the infringement in question.

[1]   Directive 2001/31/EC, art 15.
[2]   SI 2003/2498.

Intellectual property in the twenty-first century

21.29   In our fast-changing societies it is tempting to conclude that history has few lessons to teach us. Much depends, perhaps, on whether we see change as evolutionary or revolutionary. Prior to considering where and how intellectual property should develop it is perhaps useful to look back to consider how and why the systems developed. The first intellectual property statutes were motivated very much by economic and trade considerations. In the English patent system, for example, invention took second place to the need to overcome by force of law the obstacles placed by local tradesmen against those seeking to apply techniques and technologies, established in other countries but novel in England. In order to encourage foreigners to ply their trade in the country, a monopoly in respect of the particular technology would be conferred. As the system developed, the monopoly element became increasingly abused. Exclusive rights were conferred in respect of the manufacture and sale of well-established goods. A particularly unpopular patent related to the manufacture of playing cards. The abuses of the patent system played a part in the enactment of the Statute of Monopolies in 1624 which limited the grant of patents to the situation where a new product or process was invented. From there the patent system developed along well-known lines with the national dimension of the system remaining very much applicable today.

21.30   A similar trend can be mapped in respect of the copyright system. Essentially a product of the invention of the printing press, this seeks to protect a range of interests associated with the creation and publication of literary, musical and dramatic works. If we look back to the world's first copyright statute, the Statute of Anne of 1709 we see that its scope is limited to the direct and complete reproduction of books. The statute is a very short instrument but one which repays examination. Its Preamble recites the reasons behind the statute's introduction:

> Whereas Printers Booksellers and other Persons have of late frequently taken the Liberty of printing reprinting and publishing or causing to be printed, reprinted or published Books and other Writings without the consent of authors or proprietors of such Books and Writings to their very great Detriment and too often to the ruin of them and their Families. For preventing therefore such Practices for the future and for the Encouragement of learned Men to compose and write useful Books ... (capitalisation and (lack of) punctuation as in original).

21.31   A number of other features of the legislation deserve brief comment. In the event of infringement, although any infringing copies were to be handed over to the copyright owner for destruction, the financial penalties imposed on the infringer took the form of a penalty payable to the Crown. The copyright owner, also, was not free to demand such price as was thought fit for the book. The Statute of Anne 1709 allowed any person to make complaint to one or more high officials (including the Archbishop of Canterbury and the Lord Chief Justice) that the price demanded by a bookseller or printer was 'too high and unreasonable'. In the event the complaint was upheld, the price would be reduced to a specified amount. Any subsequent attempt to charge a higher price would be punishable by fine. It is interesting to speculate how such a provision might be applied in the context of today's software and information products.

21.32   In general it may be stated that the approach in the Statute of Anne 1709 is more consistent with the attempt to balance competing interests rather than to confer exclusive rights. It seeks specifically to promote learning. Over the centuries, the range of works protected by copyright has expanded steadily as has the protection afforded to copyright owners and the extent of their remedies. Less and less emphasis is put on the educative goals of the system or on the rights of those who seek to use the protected works.

21.33   Whilst the basic notion that a work should not be copied for commercial gain remains valid, the application of copyright law is hindered by the fact that digital technology operates in a different manner than its analogue equivalent. Although one motive behind statues such as the United States Digital Millennium Copyright Act and the Directive on Copyright in the Information Society[1] is to confer a measure of legal immunity on users and service providers it is difficult to see why a user's freedom to act in a reasonable manner should depend upon exceptional provisions.

[1]   Directive 2001/29/EC.

21.34   The problem may not be one only for users. Another aspect of digital technology is that it puts extensive copying facilities in the hands of private individuals. The existence of systems such as Napster and MP3 provides eloquent testimony to this. Enforcement of intellectual property rights against instances of blatant copying has proved difficult. Whilst there will always be those users who wish to obtain something for nothing, a perception of imbalance between the rights afforded to producers and users can only encourage disregard of the law. It may be that just as software companies have reduced levels of piracy in part through offering added value in the form of upgrades and customer support services to legitimate users of software packages, so the wider information industries might require to make use of similar techniques. The purchaser of a music CD might, for example, qualify for reduced price admission or preferential access to concerts performed by the artist(s) involved.

21.35 At a more legalistic level, in the English case of *R v Gold*[1] the House of Lords had to consider the question whether the transitory holding of data in part of the memory of a computer system satisfied a requirement that data be 'recorded or stored'. Holding that this was not the case, the court ruled that the process required 'a degree of continuance'. It may be that the implementation of a similar approach could resolve at least some of the issues arising in respect of digital information. In general terms there requires to be recognition that whilst an author or other inventor may choose to keep a work out of the public domain, once the decision has been taken to make it available rights have to be balanced against those of other parties, especially those who invest time or money in order to use the work. As is often noted in the context of human rights law, rights are accompanied by responsibilities. It is difficult either in law or in practice to see that these are currently in balance in the intellectual property field.

[1]   [1988] 1 AC 1063.

Chapter 22

Protection of databases

Introduction

22.1 From 1 January 1998, a new form of intellectual property right has been established in UK law. Implementing the provisions of the EC Directive of 11 March 1996 on 'the legal protection of databases',[1] the Copyright and Rights in Databases Regulations 1997[2] may reduce the level of copyright protection available to database owners, substituting this with a new, sui generis, right effective against the extraction and/or re-utilisation of a substantial part of the database contents.

[1] Directive 96/9/EC, OJ 1996 L 77/20 (the Database Directive).
[2] SI 1997/3032.

What is a database?

22.2 The concept of a database is one which does not receive specific mention in the UK's copyright legislation. The term tends to be used with specific reference to computers, the dictionary defining it as a '(l)arge body of information stored in a computer which can process it and from which particular bits of information can be retrieved as required'. The initial draft of the EC's Database Directive adopted a similar approach, limiting its application to:

> ... a collection of work or materials arranged, stored and accessed by electronic means, and the electronic materials necessary for the operation of the data base such as its thesaurus, index or system for obtaining and presenting information.[1]

[1] COM (92) 393 final, art 1.

22.3 Although there might be pragmatic reasons for limiting the scope of legislation, there is no reason in principle why more traditional forms of data

509

storage, such as a card index file, should not also be classed as a database. In the final version of the Database Directive,[1] and in the Copyright and Rights in Databases Regulations 1997, which implement the provisions of the Directive for the UK, a broader definition applies, referring to:

> ... a collection of independent works, data or other materials which:
>
> (a) are arranged in a systematic or methodical way; and
> (b) are individually accessible by electronic or other means.[2]

[1] Directive 96/9/EC.
[2] SI 1997/3032, reg 3.

22.4 The Preamble to the Database Directive expands on this definition somewhat, stating that:

> Whereas the term 'database' should be understood to include literary, artistic, musical or other collections of works or collections of other material such as texts, sound, images, numbers, facts, and data; whereas it should cover collections of independent works, data or other materials which are systematically or methodically arranged and can be individually accessed; whereas this means that a recording or an audio-visual, cinematographic, literary or musical work as such does not fall within the scope of this Directive.[1]

[1] Directive 96/9/EC, recital 17.

Examples of databases

22.5 Starting with non-automated systems, a telephone directory can be classed as a database. Here, data in the form of names, addresses and telephone numbers are arranged in alphabetical order, and may be retrieved by users through opening the directory at the appropriate page. Card index systems, such as those catalogue systems which used to occupy significant areas of floor space within libraries, also function in a similar manner. On the basis of the definition cited above, one might even class the contents of the library itself as a database.

22.6 With the dawning of the digital revolution and the ability to record and store any form of information in electronic format, the range and commercial value of databases has increased dramatically. Introducing the proposed regulations in Parliament, the Minister of State stated that:

> The database sector is a major United Kingdom industry. Estimates of the size of the UK database market range up to £10 billion but even that may be an underestimate. It is growing at more than 11% a year. About 350 firms are believed to be active in the sector, 30 of which are large suppliers and the rest small and medium-sized enterprises. UK suppliers have a share of the wider European Union market which has been put at more than 50%.[1]

[1] 4th Standing Committee on Delegated Legislation, 3 December 1997.

22.7 Many electronic databases are accessible on an online basis. Most lawyers will, for example, be familiar with the 'Lexis' database. Located in Dayton,

Ohio, this represents the world's largest collection of case law and statutory material. The parallel 'Nexis' service provides access to electronic copies of the contents of a vast range of newspapers and journals. Also on the market is a wide range of CDs. Such capacity devices typically have a storage capacity of around 650MB of data. A 500-page book would occupy somewhere in the region of 2.5MB. A single CD could, therefore, contain the text of some 300 volumes, although this figure would drop if pictures and illustrations were to be embedded in the text.

Databases and new technology

22.8   Traditionally, one of the basic requirements for a functional database has been that its contents are stored in accordance with a predetermined structure. A similar requirement applies to many automated databases, where data is stored in predetermined fields. With developments in retrieval software and what are referred to as relational databases, it is less and less necessary for information to be stored in accordance with a predetermined structure. In general, the tendency is to allow users maximum flexibility in using a database rather than requiring searches to be formulated in accordance with predetermined structures. Once again, the telephone directory may provide an apposite example. With a paper directory, a user can search effectively only by means of the structure devised by the publisher – effectively in alphabetical order by reference to subscribers surnames. CD directories typically allow searches by reference to any item of data – or to a combination of items. Reverse searching is a popular feature which allows names to be identified from telephone numbers or a listing produced of all subscribers resident in a particular street.[1]

[1]   See, for example, British Telecom's (BT) online directory at http://www.bt.com/phonenetuk/ and the more extensive service at http://www.192.com/.

22.9   Where a database comprises an amalgam of data and retrieval software, it will be necessary for the software to compile indexes of words used in the data, such indexes being used in subsequent acts of retrieval. Such a system is likely to come within the definition. More problematic issues will arise where the retrieval software is separate from the data being searched. The WWW, for example, consists of tens of millions of individual items of data controlled by millions of users. It is difficult to think of a less structured network than the WWW, yet search engines such as Alta Vista provide increasingly sophisticated searching facilities. Whilst it must be likely that many items on the WWW will qualify for copyright protection in their own right, others may not, for example, law reports or copies of statutes from countries which regard such materials as being in the public domain. It may be that the list of materials identified by a search engine as meeting the user's request will itself constitute a database. In this instance, there might be a further issue, discussed below – who is to be considered owner of any resulting database right?

Legal protection of databases before the Database Directive[1] and the Copyright and Rights in Databases Regulations 1997[2]

22.10 The rationale behind the Database Directive lies in the belief that 'databases are at present not sufficiently protected in all member states by existing legislation'.[3] This may certainly have been the case in some other member states, notably Germany, which have required strict qualitative criteria for the award of copyright, but it is less applicable in a UK context. The basis for the legal protection of databases lies in the copyright system. As we have seen, s 3 of the Copyright, Designs and Patents Act 1988 defines a literary work so as to include 'a table or compilation'. Although there is little precedent on the point, there seems little doubt that a database would fall within the latter category.

1 Directive 96/9/EC.
2 SI 1997/3032.
3 Recital 1.

22.11 Copyright in respect of the contents of a database may arise in two ways. First of all, the individual pieces of work located therein may qualify for copyright protection in their own right. An example might be of a database consisting of a collection of poems. Each poem, it may be assumed, will be protected by copyright. Additionally, the database may qualify for protection in its own right, a matter which may acquire particular importance if portions of the subject material are not so protected, for example, because the author has been dead for more than 70 years or, in the case of collections of factual material, because the nature of the data excludes copyright protection. The names of individual companies, for example, will be unlikely to be protected by copyright, but a compilation such as the FTSE 100 will enjoy protection as a compilation. Again, as was at issue in the case of *Ladbroke (Football) Ltd v William Hill (Football) Ltd,*[1] although the names of individual football teams will not be protected by copyright, a compiled fixture list will be eligible for protection.

1 [1964] 1 WLR 273.

22.12 Discounting the issue whether the contents of a database might qualify for protection in their own right, the issue arises whether the degree of effort which accompanies the compilation of a database is sufficient to qualify for such a grant. Traditionally, a major element of the task facing the compiler of a database has been to determine the order in which the material is to appear and subsequently giving effect to this concept. Using modern technology, text can be scanned and converted into digital format. Whereas traditional compilations such as directories will require to be carefully structured to make it easy for users to find particular items of information, the utilisation of appropriate software will mean that the entire contents of a database may be scanned with reference to a particular word or phrase. In such a case, there is less need for the database compiler to expend effort in arranging the layout of the database.

22.13   It is also one of the features of many computerised services that they seek to take advantage of the processing and storage capabilities of computers in order to present a comprehensive collection of materials. The goal of a legal database such as Lexis is to provide a transcript of every High Court decision delivered in the English courts. Similarly, the website of the Scottish Courts Administration[1] provides the text of every High Court and Court of Session judgment. This is to be contrasted with the more traditional law reports which contain only a comparatively small number of decisions, and where some skill and labour will be expended by the publishers to determine which cases are of sufficient importance to warrant a place in a particular volume.

[1]   http://www.scotcourts.gov.uk/pages/opinions_intro.htm.

The 'sweat of the brow' doctrine

22.14   In the event that a database seeks to provide a comprehensive coverage of its chosen subject area, it may be difficult to evidence any originality in the selection process. It is here that a significant divergence exists between the UK approach and that adopted in almost every other copyright system. As has been stated, the UK system imposes minimal qualitative requirements relating to originality. In the case of a compilation, the traditional justification for extending protection has been the effort that has gone into selecting the works to be incorporated therein; what has been referred to in the US as the 'sweat of the brow' doctrine. This approach is well illustrated in the case *of Waterlow Publishers v Rose*.[1] The plaintiff, under contract to the Law Society, had published listings, arranged geographically, of English solicitors and barristers in a publication, the *Solicitors' Diary and Directory*. A listing of all solicitors was supplied to the plaintiff by the Law Society, and this was used to send out forms seeking further information about areas of specific expertise.

[1]   [1995] FSR 207.

22.15   Prior to 1984, a company owned by the defendant had been contracted to print copies of the directory. Following a take-over of the plaintiff, this work was transferred to another firm. The defendant thereupon determined to publish a similar work, the *Lawyers' Diary* which would compete with the plaintiff's publication. The defendant's manner of work was to commence with the *Solicitors' Diary*, which constituted the only comprehensive public listing of the names and addresses of solicitors. A copy of the entry in the *Solicitors' Diary* would be sent out to the individuals concerned and they would be asked to reply either confirming the accuracy of the information or making any changes that were felt desirable. The plaintiff alleged that this method of work meant that the resultant publication infringed their copyright.

22.16   In deciding the case, the court had to consider first the question whether copyright subsisted in the compilation of names, addresses and other information published in the *Solicitors' Diary* and, secondly, whether the defendant's conduct constituted infringement. Although it was recognised that the nature of compilations was such that it might be difficult to identify a single person as author, the fact that the plaintiff was identified as publisher established a presumption that copyright was owned by it. Regarding the issue of infringement, the Court of Appeal held that:

> Mr Rose argued that he only used the existing directory to get in touch with the solicitors and that his work was then based upon the forms returned to him ... There were something like 50,000 forms and the names and addresses to which they were sent were all obtained from the Solicitors' Diary 1984 ... In my judgement that goes beyond lawful use of an existing publication and amounted to an infringement of the plaintiff's copyright.[1]

1 *Waterlow Publishers v Rose* [1995] FSR 207 at 221.

22.17 The effect of this and of similar decisions is that extensive copyright protection is afforded to databases compiled in the UK. A similar approach had been followed in the US, until the landmark Supreme Court case of *Feist Publications Inc v Rural Telephone Service Co Inc*[1] signalled a significant change of direction.

1 111 S Ct 1282 (1991).

22.18 The case concerned the extent of copyright protection in a telephone directory. The respondent, Rural, was a telephone service provider which was required under the terms of its operating licence to publish a directory of its subscribers. A substantial number of service providers operate in the US, each publishing directories covering a small geographical area. The appellant, Feist, was a publishing company which specialised in publishing directories which covered a wider geographical area than that of a typical small-scale provider such as Rural. It entered into negotiations seeking licences to publish from 11 different telephone utilities. Only Rural refused permission.

22.19 Despite Rural's refusal, Feist went ahead with the publication, extracting the necessary information from Rural's directory. Although it added some items of information and attempted to verify other items independently, 1,309 entries in the Feist directory were identical to their Rural counterparts. More damningly, four of these were fictitious entries inserted by Rural in order to provide a means of detecting unauthorised copying.

22.20 Rural's action alleging copyright infringement succeeded before the lower courts. The Supreme Court took a different view.[1] Infringement, it was held, could occur only when what was copied was protected under the copyright regime. Although the level of originality required as the basis for protection was low, there was 'a narrow category of works in which the creative spark is utterly lacking or so trivial as to be virtually non-existent'. Rural's telephone directory, it was held, fell into this category. Its selection of listing 'could not be more obvious'. Rural, it was held, 'expended sufficient effort to make the ... directory useful, but insufficient creativity to make it original'.

1 *Feist Publications Inc v Rural Telephone Service Co Inc* 111 S Ct 1282 (1991).

22.21 The decision in *Feist*[1] produced considerable comment and controversy within the US and, as was discussed in Chapter 20, prompted a significant tightening up of the criteria for the award of copyright generally. Certain aspects of the court's reasoning are potentially significant for the UK system. In particular, the court explicitly rejected the notion that the expenditure of effort, the 'sweat of the brow', could suffice for the grant of copyright. Even so, the court makes it clear that only a modicum of creativity is required. Although copyright does not subsist in an alphabetical listing of subscribers, subsequent cases have held that 'yellow pages'-type listings, where subscribers are grouped according to the nature of their business or profession, will attract protection.

[1]   *Feist Publications Inc v Rural Telephone Service Co Inc* 111 S Ct 1282 (1991).

22.22 A further illustration of the new US approach can be found in the case of *ProCD v Zeidenberg*.[1] As was stated in the case report:

> Plaintiff spent millions of dollars creating a comprehensive, national directory of residential and business listings. Plaintiff compiled over 95,000,000 residential and commercial listings from approximately 3,000 publicly available telephone books. The listings include full names, street addresses, telephone numbers, zip codes and industry or 'SIC' codes where appropriate. Plaintiff sells these listings on CD-ROM discs under the trademark 'Select Phone TM', as well as under other trade names and trademarks.[2]

The plaintiff's pricing strategy was to sell copies of the CD at a low price for consumer use, but levy higher rates for those seeking to make commercial use of the product. The defendant purchased a copy of the consumer CD which retailed for less than $100. Using its own retrieval software, it placed a copy of the plaintiff's listings on an Internet site, from where it allowed users to extract up to 1,000 listings free of charge. More extensive access, typically for commercial purposes, could be obtained at a cost less than that charged by the plaintiff. The site was soon attracting up to 20,000 visitors a day and, fearing significant adverse effects on sales of its CD, the plaintiff sought an injunction preventing its continued operation. Although at first instance the injunction was refused, the Court of Appeals eventually found in favour of the plaintiff on the ground that the defendant was bound by the terms of a licence accompanying the CD which prohibited its use for commercial purposes, it was common ground that no copyright subsisted in the data itself.

[1]   86 F 3d 1447 (1996).
[2]   86 F 3d 1447 at 1447 (1996).

22.23 More recently, litigation has been initiated by the legal database supplier, Lexis, against an Internet-based company, Jurisline.[1] In the US, Lexis markets compilations of law reports in CD format. Jurisline admittedly copied the contents of these CDs and placed the material on a website. Access to the site is free of charge, with the intention being that the site's costs will be met by advertising. As in the *ProCD* case,[2] the CDs in question are supplied subject to the terms of a licence which restricts the use to which the materials may be put. It appears, however, that the terms of the licence are not made accessible to the user until after the CD is purchased.[3] An additional argument advanced on behalf of Jurisline is to the effect that Law Reports in the US are regarded as being in the public domain so that:

> ...the limitations built into Lexis' licensing agreement attempt to control an 'essential facility' in violation of federal antitrust law.
>
> Lexis may not use a contract to take public domain material such as court opinions – which are explicitly not covered by the federal copyright law – and create a level of protection that is tantamount to a federal copyright.[4]

1　The Jurisline site is at http://www.jurisline.com.
2　*ProCD v Zeidenberg* 86 F 3d 1447 (1996).
3　See discussion of the validity of software licences at para 26.73 below.
4　Cited in D Wise 'Lexis Battles Web Upstart' *New York Law Journal*, 8 February 2000.

22.24　At the time of writing, the case appears to be in its early stages, but already it indicates the complexity of some of the issues involved. Whilst there is little scope for originality in the production of a comprehensive collection of law reports, denial of protection for the efforts and investment required to gather the material together might dissuade commercial publishers from making the initial effort. Such a decision would deny copyists their raw material, but would also produce the same effect for the public.

22.25　As indicated in *ProCD*,[1] one of the consequences of the *Feist*[2] decision has been the emergence of a new market in the US for CD and Internet-based compilations of telephone directories. Selling for a few dollars, these will contain hundreds of millions of names and numbers, often providing additional facilities such as a reverse search option allowing a persons address to be identified from a telephone number. In the UK, BT has continued to assert copyright in telephone directories and has threatened copyright actions against parties planning to introduce competing products. This situation has now changed, not through the operation of copyright law but as a result of the actions of the Director General of Telecommunications, who inserted a clause in BT's licence requiring them to make directory information available to third parties.[3]

1　*ProCD v Zeidenberg* 86 F 3d 1447 (1996).
2　*Feist Publications Inc v Rural Telephone Service Co Inc* 111 S Ct 1282 (1991).
3　See http://www.oftel.co.uk/dq998.htm.

22.26　A major goal of the Database Directive[1] is to eliminate obstacles to the creation of a single market by harmonising the level of protection afforded to databases. Although not explicitly stated in the Preamble, there was undoubtedly the feeling that the UK's 50% share of the EU database market was due in part to the fact that strong legal protection provided an incentive for database producers to locate their businesses in the UK. An alternative explanation might refer to the advantages of working in the English language and the larger market available to such databases.

1　Directive 96/9/EC.

The new regime

22.27 The provisions of the Database Directive[1] can be grouped into three categories. First, it makes provision regarding the application of copyright to the contents of databases; secondly, it provides for the extent of and exceptions to such copyrights. Finally, a new sui generis right is established to benefit some databases which are excluded from the copyright regime.

[1] Directive 96/9/EC.

Copyright and databases

22.28 Article 1 of the Database Directive[1] provides that:

> ... databases which, by reason of the selection or arrangement of their contents, constitute the author's own intellectual creation shall be protected as such by copyright.

The key phrase in this provision refers to work being 'the author's own intellectual creation'. This term is not defined further. In the implementing UK regulations, it is provided that:

> For the purposes of this Part, a literary work consisting of a database is original if, and only if, by reason of the selection or arrangements of the contents of the database the database constitutes the author's own intellectual creation.[1]

[1] Directive 96/9/EC.
[1] SI 1997/3032, reg 6 introducing a new s 3A(2) into the Copyright, Designs and Patents Act 1988.

22.29 The formula that work will be protected when it is the author's 'own intellectual creation' is also used in the EC Directive on 'the legal protection of computer programs',[1] which provides that these are to be protected as literary works. When the Directive was implemented into UK law, this phrase was not included. Introducing the regulations in Parliament, however, the Minister of State commented that:

> Some people felt that no amendment of the [Copyright, Designs and Patents Act 1988] was needed to introduce the test and that the current test for the originality of literary works was enough.
>
> The Government do not share that view. The Directive is clear. It requires copyright protection for databases 'which by reason of selection or arrangement of their contents, constitute the author's own intellectual creations'.
>
> This is intended to exclude so-called sweat of the brow databases – that is, ones that involve time, money or effort but no intellectual creation, such as the white pages telephone directory.[1]

[1] Directive 91/250/EC, OJ 1991 L122/42 (the Software Protection Directive).
[2] 4th Standing Committee on Delegated Legislation, 3 December 1997.

22.30   Assuming this view is correct, it gives rise to the suggestion that the UK has failed to implement the Database Directive[1] adequately. If the view is incorrect, the effect of the regulations has been to introduce unnecessary complexity into copyright law. Prior to implementation of the Directive, s 3(1) of the Copyright, Designs and Patents Act 1988 provided that the term 'literary work' was to encompass:

> ... any work, other than a dramatic or musical work, which is written, spoken or sung, and accordingly includes:
> (a)   a table or compilation;
> (b)   a computer program; and
> (c)   preparatory design material for a computer program.[2]

[1]   Directive 96/9/EC.
[2]   Section 3, as amended by the Copyright (Computer Programs) Regulations 1992, SI 1992/3233.

22.31   This is now amended to read:

> ... any work, other than a dramatic or musical work, which is written, spoken or sung, and accordingly includes:
>
> (a)   a table or compilation other than a database;
> (b)   a computer program;
> (c)   preparatory design material for a computer program; and
> (d)   a database.[1]

For the purposes of this Part, a literary work consisting of a database is original if, and only if, by reason of the selection or arrangements of the contents of the database the database constitutes the author's own intellectual creation.[2]

[1]   Copyright, Designs and Patents Act 1988, s 3(1).
[2]   SI 1997/3032, reg 6, introducing a new s 3A into the Copyright, Designs and Patents Act 1988.

22.32   Given that databases were hitherto regarded as a form of compilation, this approach might not be considered entirely satisfactory, and it is unclear where the division between the two categories lies. The Preamble to the Database Directive recites that:

> ... as a rule, the compilation of several recordings of musical performances on a CD does not come within the scope of this Directive, both because as a compilation, it does not meet the requirements for copyright protection and because it does not represent a substantial enough investment to be eligible under the *sui generis* right.[1]

Under previous UK law, there is little doubt that such a work would benefit from protection as a compilation. The question which will be discussed below is whether implementation of the Directive will alter this situation.

[1]   Directive 96/9/EC, recital 19.

Licensing and databases

22.33   In the first draft of the Database Directive,[1] provision was made for database owners to be required to grant licences to users in certain circumstances:

> If the works or materials contained in a database which is made publicly available cannot be independently created, collected or obtained from any other source, the right to extract and re-utilize, in whole or substantial part, works or materials from that database for commercial purposes shall be licensed on fair and non-discriminatory terms.[1]

It was also provided that licenses should require to be issued:

> ... if the database is made publicly available by a public body which is either established to assemble or disclose information pursuant to legislation or is under a general duty to do so.[2]

[1]   Directive 96/9/EC.
[2]   COM (92) 393 final, art 8(1).
[3]   Article 8(2).

22.34   At least in respect of the first category, compulsory licences would only be available in very limited circumstances. It might be commented, in particular, that in most cases where only one party could obtain data, this might fall into the category of confidential information or be regarded as a trade secret, and would certainly not be made available to the public. In the event, the proposal was dropped following objections from Parliament, although it is provided that the issue is to be kept under review by the Commission, which is to report to the Council and Parliament within the first three years of the Database Directive's[1] operation, indicating whether the operation of the new regime:

> ... has led to abuse of a dominant position or other interference with free competition which would justify appropriate measures being taken including the establishment of non-voluntary licensing arrangements.[2]

[1]   Directive 96/9/EC.
[2]   COM (92) 393 final, art 16(3).

22.35   Extensive provisions are made in the Copyright, Designs and Patents Act 1988[1] for the handling of licensing agreements between copyright owners and those wishing to make use of their materials. The Copyright Tribunal is established to determine disputes as to the nature and extent of such schemes. The regulations extend the scope of the statutory provisions and of the Tribunal's jurisdiction to matters relating to database licences.[2]

[1]   See Chs VII and VIII.
[2]   SI 1997/3032, reg 25.

Other copyright changes

22.36   A number of other changes are made to the provisions of the Copyright, Designs and Patents Act 1988. In order to implement the provisions of the software protection Directive,[1] amendments were made by the Copyright (Computer Programs) Regulations 1992,[2] which had the effect of allowing the lawful user of a program to perform acts which might otherwise be restricted by copyright. In particular, this would sanction such copying of the program as was necessary for its use. Similar considerations will apply with electronic databases (whether online or held on disc) and the regulations add equivalent authorising provisions to the 1988 Act. Any attempt contractually to restrict or exclude the operation of these rights is now declared void.[3]

[1] Directive 91/250/EC.
[2] SI 1992/3233.
[3] Regulation 9, inserting a new s 50D into the Copyright, Designs and Patents Act 1988.

The new database right

22.37 Implementation of the Database Directive[1] will have the effect of removing the protection of copyright from certain databases. Balancing this, a new database right is created which will arise when:

> ... there has been a substantial investment in obtaining, verifying or presenting the contents of the database.[2]

The maker of the database will be the first owner of the database right except in the case where the work is created by an employee, in which event the employer will own the right.[3]

[1] Directive 96/9/EC.
[2] SI 1997/3032, reg 13.
[3] Regulation 14.

22.38 It is not clear how much investment will be required to justify application of the adjective 'substantial'. The Database Directive's[1] assertion that a musical compilation will not require substantial investment has been cited above. Dependent upon the popularity of the music involved, it may be, however, that a high price will need to be paid to obtain the necessary copyright licences.

[1] Directive 91/250/EC.

22.39 The database right is not presently found in any international agreements, although WIPO have proposed a draft treaty which would establish such a right. Pending the adoption of this instrument (which has been the subject of considerably hostility from certain quarters in the US, where it is seen as marking a retreat from the principles of free access to data enshrined in the *Feist*[1] decision), protection is limited to individuals or undertakings who are nationals of, or incorporated in a state within, the European Economic Area (EEA).[2] Assuming that the effect of the changes to the Copyright, Designs and Patents Act 1988 discussed above do have the effect of taking databases outwith the scope of copyright protection, the effect will be to reduce the level of protection afforded to databases owned by non-EEA nationals or undertakings, without conferring the compensatory benefit of the new database right. To this extent, non-EEA database owners may be significant losers under the new regime. This may cause difficulties where databases are maintained on the WWW. Implementation of the Database Directive[3] in the UK might have the effect of removing some such databases from the copyright regime, but where the database is controlled by a non-EEA national, the compensatory database right will not be available. The effect of the new regime will, therefore, be to reduce the level of protection afforded within the UK to, for example, US-based database providers.

[1] *Feist Publications Inc v Rural Telephone Service Co Inc* 111 S Ct 1282 (1991).
[2] SI 1997/3032, reg 18.
[3] Directive 96/9/EC.

22.40 It is immaterial for the existence of this right, which is stated to be a 'property right' whether the database or its contents are protected by the law of copyright. The right will be infringed by a person who:

> ... without the consent of the owner ... extracts or re-utilises all or a substantial part of the contents of the database.[1]

This may take the form either of a single act or a succession of smaller extractions. Where conduct by a lawful user would not infringe the database right, it is provided that any term or condition which seeks to restrict this will be null and void. The traditional copyright exemption permitting such use as comes under the heading of fair dealing is restated in modified form for the new right. This provides that:

> Database right in a database which has been made available to the public in any manner is not infringed by fair dealing with a substantial part of the database for the purposes of illustration for teaching or research, other than teaching or research for a commercial purpose, provided that the source is indicated.[2]

[1] SI 1997/3032, reg 16.
[2] Directive 96/9/EC, art 9, as implemented by SI 1997/3032, reg 20.

22.41 Infringement of the database right will expose the perpetrator to actions for damages, injunctions or accounting of profits as specified in s 96 of the Copyright, Designs and Patents Act 1988.[1] Significantly, however, although the Database Directive[2] confers considerable discretion on member states as to the nature of the rights and remedies adopted in respect of the new right, the 1988 Act's provisions relating to criminal penalties do not extend to infringements of the database. Also unavailable are the rights of seizure of infringing copies and the right to demand delivery up. It may be that such rights are of limited relevance to online databases but, as has been discussed, the right extends to a wide range of electronic and manual products.

[1] SI 1997/3032, reg 23.
[2] Directive 96/9/EC.

Duration of the right

22.42   The right will come into existence when a database is made available to the public and will subsist for a period of 15 years. It is provided, however, that:

> Any substantial change to the contents of a database, including a substantial change resulting from the accumulation of successive additions, deletions or alterations, which would result in the database being considered to be a substantial new investment shall qualify the database resulting from that investment for its own term of protection.[1]

The application of this provision should be non-problematic where databases (perhaps a telephone directory) are issued on an annual basis. Its application to online databases may be more contentious, and the provision cited above was amended from earlier proposals to try to cover the situation where a database was subject to continual minor amendment. The example might be taken of an online database of law reports such as Lexis. In most areas, cases are stored for the last 50 years. If reports are added on a daily basis, each day will see a database which is very slightly different from the earlier one. On a rough and ready calculation, the change from one day to another will be in the region of 0.0001% of the total database. This can surely not be considered substantial. As additions accumulate and are accompanied, perhaps, by changes to the structure of the database itself, it must be likely that the criteria will be satisfied before the expiry of the 15-year period. Assuming continuing development of the database, it will obtain perpetual protection.

[1]   Directive 96/9/EC, art 10(3), as implemented by SI 1997/3032, reg 17.

22.43   In practice, it must be likely that the issue of whether the contents of a database remain protected by the database right will be significant only when legal proceedings are brought alleging infringement. A database might, for example, be made available to the public in the year 2000 and subjected to continual minor amendments. In 2020, the database owner might institute proceedings against a third party alleging breach of the database right. In this event, evidence could be submitted to the court of the state of the database in 2000 compared with its 2015 incarnation. In the event this indicated substantial additional investment, the court would have to conclude that a new period of protection began in 2015 and that infringement had occurred.

The database right in the courts

22.44   Although the right has been in existence for almost six years it was only in February 2001 that the first case concerned with the extent of the right reached the High Court. At issue in the *British Horseracing Board Ltd, the Jockey Club and Weatherbys Group Ltd v William Hill Organization Ltd*[1] was the legality of the defendant's practice of taking information from a database maintained by the claimants relating to horses and riders scheduled to compete in horse races and using this for the purpose of its betting operations.

[1]   [2001] 2 CMLR 12.

22.45   The databases in question were extremely large and subject to a process of continual updating. It was estimated that some 800,000 entries were added or revised each year. The cost of the work was put at some £4m annually.

22.46   The database had been used by the defendant and other betting operators for a number of years. No complaint had been made regarding this. As with so many other aspects of life, the emergence of the Internet, in the particular case as a medium for betting, changed circumstances. William Hill published information concerning horses and riders competing in particular races taken from the database on its website only for the claimants to allege that this constituted unauthorised extraction and re-utilisation of protected material. As was stated in the judgment:

> BHB's case is that it owns database right in the BHB Database and that William Hill is making unlicensed use of that data in its internet business. It says that what William Hill takes from the SIS RDF is derived by SIS from the BHB Database. It says that William Hill's activities constitute breaches of BHB's database right in two ways. First, it says that each day's use by William Hill of data taken from the SIS RDF is an extraction or re-utilisation of a *substantial* part of the contents of its database contrary to Article 7(1) of the Directive [Database Directive[1]]. Secondly, it says that, even if the individual extracts are not substantial, nevertheless the totality of William Hill's actions amount to repeated and systematic extraction or re-utilisation of *insubstantial* parts of the contents of the database contrary to Article 7(5).[2]

[1]   Directive 96/9/EC.
[2]   *British Horseracing Board Ltd, the Jockey Club and Weatherbys Group Ltd v William Hill Organization Ltd* [2001] 2 CMLR 12 at 232.

22.47   In its defence, William Hill argued that: its conduct did not offend the concept which it described as 'database-ness'. As the judgment states:

> ... one must distinguish between the data or information within a database and the characteristics which give rise to the new type of protection. Database right does not protect the information within a database *per se*. It is crucial that BHB cannot use any database right which it may own to prevent William Hill, or anyone else, from making use of any facts within its Database. Taking the facts, and only the facts, can never infringe database right, whether one fact is taken or all of them. What is protected is ... the 'database-ness' of the collection of information.[1]

Expanding upon the definition of the concept it was suggested that:

> Since no right is created in the works, data or other materials, the 'database-ness' of a database must lie in the fact that the independent materials are arranged in a systematic or methodical way, and are individually accessible ... the acts amounting to infringement of a database must in some way take unfair advantage of this 'database-ness'. Any acts which do not make any use of the arrangement of the contents of the database, nor take advantage of the way in which the maker has rendered the contents individually accessible, cannot infringe the database right.[2]

1   British Horseracing Board Ltd, the Jockey Club and Weatherbys Group Ltd v William Hill
    Organization Ltd [2001] 2 CMLR 12 at 232
2   [2001] 2 CMLR 12 at 232.

22.48   This is perhaps the crux of the debate. Whilst early database software packages required that great attention be paid to the structure and layout of the database, modern techniques permit searching to be carried out independently of structure. The idea that a predetermined structure was necessary for the establishment of protection was rejected by Mr Justice Laddie who ruled that:

> nothing in the Directive [Database Directive[1]] supports the second part (the) submission relating to 'database-ness' which runs together two entirely distinct concepts, namely the feature of form which have to exist before a database will be recognised as existing and the features of content or investment which are protected once a database is held to exist. Thus a database consists of a collection of data brought together in a systematic or methodical way so as to be individually accessible by electronic or other means. In much the same way a literary work in copyright has to 'written, spoken or sung' before it is recognised as suitable for protection but infringement is not restricted to acts of writing, speaking or singing. A collection of data in the mind of an author does not qualify for protection until it is put into a form where it is searchable. But the fact that it has to take this form before database right can apply to it does not mean that the database right protects that form. Indeed the Recitals to the Directive are quite explicit that the form of a database is what is protected by copyright not by the sui generis right ...[2]
>
> These recitals make it clear that infringement of the new right is not avoided by taking the contents and rearranging them. On the contrary, what has to be protected is not primarily the form but the investment which went into 'obtaining, verifying or presenting the contents' of the database as made clear, not only by art 7(1) but also Recital 40 (see paragraph 31 above). It is for this reason that substantial investment in verification (where the form is substantially unchanged) still qualifies for database right in accordance with Recital 55 (see paragraph 36 above). In such a case, the infringer takes advantage of the relevant investment if he makes use of the accuracy of the data in the database, not because he takes it in a particular form.[3]

It was successfully argued that the taking amounted to repeated and systematic extraction and/or re-utilisation of insubstantial parts of the database, Laddie J rejecting the argument that the constant updating of the database meant that it was not one database but a series of works:

> Although this is an attractive argument, I do not think it is right. The Directive has to be construed to make sense. This argument starts from the assumption that all databases have to be considered as discrete 'frozen' products, rather like separate editions of a book, each with a discrete period of protection. So, a database which is modified over time is to be broken down into a series of steps, each of which is protected by database right. However that would cause serious difficulties. If a database which is under constant revision is to be considered as a series of discrete protected works, how is one to know where one ends and the next begins? Presumably the size of the steps would be determined by the amount of effort needed to trigger the operation of art 10(3), yet it will be virtually impossible in any case either to determine where

the starting point is in the creation of the series of databases or to define the size of the steps ...

There is nothing in the Directive which suggests that it was not to apply to dynamic databases in just the same way as it applies to ones which are built and modified in discrete, well defined steps. Many of the most valuable databases are those which are under constant revision ...

In my view the BHB Database is a single database which is in a constant state of refinement. It seems to have been so regarded by all the witnesses. An attempt to split it into a series of discrete databases, besides being impossible to do, would not reflect reality. Its contents change with time and without any obvious break. So too, the term of protection changes. As new data are added, so the database's term of protection is constantly being renewed. However an unlicensed third party who takes only older data from it only faces a database right which runs from the date when all of that older data was present in the database at the same time. This does not render art 10(3) meaningless. First it emphasises that the term keeps being renewed as the database is renewed. Secondly it makes clear that if someone takes an existing database and adds significantly to it, he obtains protection for the database incorporating his additions. This would be so even if the new author is not the same as the author of the original database ...[4]

---

[1] Directive 96/9/EC.
[2] *British Horseracing Board Ltd, the Jockey Club and Weatherbys Group Ltd v William Hill Organization Ltd* [2001] 2 CMLR 12 at 232.
[3] [2001] 2 CMLR 232 at 234.
[4] [2001] 2 CMLR 232 at 241.

22.49 Repeated references in the judgment make it clear that the purpose of the new right is to protect investment rather than creativity. In determining whether a substantial part of the data base had been extracted account was to be taken of qualitative and quantitative aspects. No hard and fast rule could or should be laid down for the task of balancing quantitative and qualitative aspects. As was stated:

No useful purpose would be served by trying to assess this issue first on a quantitative basis and then, separately, on qualitative basis. They should be looked at together.[1]
the importance of the information to the alleged infringer is not irrelevant. In some cases, of which this is an example, the significance of the information to the alleged infringer may throw light on whether it is an important or significant part of the database[2]

---

[1] *British Horseracing Board Ltd, the Jockey Club and Weatherbys Group Ltd v William Hill Organization Ltd* [2001] 2 CMLR 12 at 236.
[2] [2001] 2 CMLR 232 at 235.

22.50 An appeal was lodged against the decision.[1] The trial judge, it was argued had interpreted the EC Database Directive,[2] the source of the UK Regulations,[3] incorrectly giving too wide a meaning to the database right and what it protected. Thus, it was argued:

information which might have been thought to have entered the public domain and to be freely usable could prove to be derived from a database the right in which was protected even though the user was unaware of that ultimate source and right. Other national courts had adopted narrower approaches to database right and there had so far been no European Court of Justice ruling on the interpretation of the Database Directive.[4]

1 [2001] EWCA Civ 1268.
2 Directive 96/9/EC.
3 SI 1997/3032.
4 [2001] EWCA Civ 1268 at para 40.

22.51 Although indicating support for the initial decision, the Court of Appeal determined that the matter should be referred to the European Court of Justice for a preliminary ruling, stating that 'the points made were of wide importance' and that domestic courts could not resolve the issues with complete confidence.[1] It noted that courts in some other member states appeared to have adopted a narrower interpretation of the Database Directive.[2]

1 [2001] EWCA Civ 1268 at para 45.
2 Directive 96/9/EC.

22.52 In total 11 questions have been referred to the European Court[1] seeking its views on a wide range of issues relating to the scope of the Database Directive.[2] At the time of writing, the case is still before the European Court.

1 OJ 2002 C 180/14.
2 Directive 96/9/EC.

Conclusions

22.53 Since the US Supreme Court moved away from the 'sweat of the brow' doctrine in its decision in *Feist*,[1] the UK (and to an extent Commonwealth jurisdictions) have been isolated in terms of the extent of copyright protection. Copyright has been held to extend to subjects such as a football fixture list whilst the threat of copyright litigation was used by BT during the latter years of the twentieth century to deter parties who were planning to publish competing telephone directories in CD format. There is perhaps little doubt that the British Horse Racing Board could have succeeded in an action for copyright infringement under the old UK regime. The fact the case has been litigated to the extent it has may be indicative that, as was stated by Mr Justice Laddie:

> These propositions dovetail with a more general point, namely that database right is to be construed so as to be narrower than the protection which used to be afforded to compilations under English copyright law.[2]

1 *Feist Publications Inc v Rural Telephone Service Co Inc* 111 S Ct 1282 (1991).
2 *British Horseracing Board Ltd, the Jockey Club and Weatherbys Group Ltd v William Hill Organization Ltd* [2001] 2 CMLR 12 at 232.

22.54 Given the increasing economic importance of the informational content of databases this is a rather paradoxical conclusion. As has been the case in other areas, there is a degree of tension between the common and civil law legal traditions. It is arguable that if the UK afforded too much protection to works possessing little or no literary worth, other member states afforded too little protection. The result, in the form of the Database Directive,[1] has been a compromise. Only time, and perhaps the deliberations of the European Court of Justice, will show whether the compromise will be a successful one.

[1]   Directive 96/9/EC.

Chapter 23

Trade mark issues

Introduction

23.1 Along with patents and copyright, trade marks constitute a key component of the system of intellectual property rights. In the UK, the system originated in the Trade Marks Registration Act 1875. The present law is to be found in the Trade Marks Act 1994, which was introduced in order to enable the UK to comply with its obligations under the 1988 EC Directive 'to approximate the laws of the Member States relating to trade marks'.[1] The 1993 Council Regulation 'on the Community trade mark'[2] established a Community Trade Mark to operate in parallel with national systems. At the international level, the Madrid Agreement Concerning the International Registration of Marks provides for a system of international registration of trade marks.[3]

[1] Directive 89/104/EC, OJ 1989 L 40/1 (the European Trade Mark Directive).
[2] Regulation 40/94/EC, OJ 1994 L 11/1. Although dated '94' the Regulation was adopted on 20 December 1993.
[3] The text of the Agreement is available from http://www.wipo.org/eng/madrid/texts.htm.

23.2 As defined in the Trade Marks Act 1994, a trade mark is:

... any sign capable of being represented graphically which is capable of distinguishing goods or services of one undertaking from those of other undertakings.

A trade mark may in particular, consist of words (including personal names), designs, letters, numerals or the sale of goods or their packaging.[1]

Details of trade marks are recorded in the Register of Trade Marks, a document which is open to public inspection.

[1] Section 1(1).

23.3 The scope of this definition is broader than might initially appear to be the case. In our digital age, virtually everything is capable of being represented in graphical form. The process of 'sampling', for example, would allow any sound to be depicted in graphical format. A trade mark has been awarded for the distinctive sound of the telephone which features in advertising for the Direct Line Insurance company. In similar vein, the Chanel No 5 perfume smell has been trade marked under the description:

> The scent of aldehydic-floral fragrance product, with an aldehydic top note from aldehydes, bergamot, lemon and neroli; an elegant floral middle note, from jasmine, rose, lily of the valley, orris and ylang-ylang; and a sensual feminine base note from sandal, cedar, vanilla, amber, civet and musk. The scent also being known by the written brand name No 5.

23.4 This latter description illustrates a difficulty with the system. Although the description may identify the ingredients used, it makes no reference to the relative proportions of the ingredients or to the manner of manufacture. It would be possible to perform a chromatographic analysis and provide a much more detailed and specific description of the product. This might also prove useful to would-be counterfeiters. In the particular instance cited, inspection of the Register of Trademarks would be of little assistance to anyone wishing to determine whether a product infringed the Chanel trade mark. This could only be determined by an inspection of samples of the perfumes involved. What is protected may not be apparent from scrutiny of the register.

23.5 In terms of their manner of issuance, trade marks fall somewhere between patents and copyright. Registration of the trade mark (in the UK, responsibility for the system vests in the Patent Office) is an essential requirement. This distinguishes the system from the copyright regime, where the right arises as soon as work is recorded in some manner. Although there are provisions relating to what form of marks may or may not be used, these requirements fall short of the exacting requirements of novelty and inventiveness applied under the patent system. The Register of Trademarks is divided into 42 categories and an applicant will be required to specify those in respect of which he or she would wish the trade mark to apply. A sliding scale of fees will apply, depending on the number of categories applied for.

23.6 Once accepted for registration, a trade mark will be valid indefinitely. The first trade mark was issued in 1876 in respect of the red triangle symbol found on containers of Bass beer and remains valid to this day. The two main threats to trade mark owners are that the mark will fall into disuse or, at the other end of the spectrum, will become so widely used on account of the proprietor's failure or inability to take action against infringers, that it takes on a generic meaning rather than 'distinguishing goods or services of one undertaking from those of other undertakings'. The word 'aspirin', for example, was once a registered trade mark (and remains so in France) owned by the German Bayer company. The trade mark rights in the UK were lost in the First World War, and the term may now be used to describe any painkiller containing the drug aspirin.

23.7 At the international level, the Madrid Agreement provides that the owner of a trade mark in one signatory state may request the national authority to present an application for international registration to the International Bureau WIPO, indicating those countries in which recognition of the mark is sought. The International Bureau, in turn, notifies each state referred to which must give notice of a refusal to accept the trade mark, generally within a period of 12 months. The effectiveness of the international system is limited by the fact that many significant countries, including the US, are not signatory to its various constituent agreements and protocols.

Effect of trade marks

23.8 As with other forms of intellectual property, trade marks constitute 'property rights' conferring upon the proprietor the exclusive right to certain forms of use of the mark.[1] A trade mark will be infringed in two main situations:

> Where an identical or similar mark is used in respect of goods or services which are identical or similar to those forming the subject of the trade mark and where there is a consequential likelihood of confusion on the part of the public.
>
> Where the identical or similar mark is used; where the goods or services are not identical or similar to those forming the subject of the trade mark but where the trade mark has a reputation in the United Kingdom and where its reproduction 'takes unfair advantage of, or is detrimental to the distinctive character or repute of the trade mark.'[2]

[1] Trade Marks Act 1994, s 2.
[2] Section 10.

23.9 In the first situation, dispute is likely to centre upon the issue whether an allegedly infringing mark is sufficiently similar to confuse members of the public. Thus the name 'OXOT' has been held to infringe the trade mark 'OXO'. In most cases, the fact that the mark is used in respect of different categories of goods or services will defeat a claim of infringement. Where the trade mark has widespread recognition, infringement may occur when the use of the name (or a similar name) is regarded as seeking to benefit unfairly from association with the brand name or is likely to reduce its standing. In one US case, use of the name 'Dogiva' for dog biscuits was held actionable on the first of these grounds by the proprietors of the trade mark 'Godiva', representing the well-known Belgian chocolates.

Passing off

23.10 By no means every name or indication of origin can be protected under the law of trade marks. Although US practice appears to be somewhat more liberal, in the UK popular names and geographic indicators cannot be protected as trade marks, as these are considered insufficiently descriptive of the origin of goods or services. Thus, a name such as McDonald cannot be protected by trade mark although, as is the case with regard to the well known fast food supplier of that name, trade marks encompass almost every other aspect of the business from the 'Golden Arches' symbol through styles of writing and design to the names of individual dishes, for example, 'BigMac'. On occasion, in deciding on the eligibility of a name submitted for trade mark registration, the Patent Office has had recourse to documents such as telephone directories in order to determine whether a name is in common usage.

23.11 A trader finding that it is unable to register its name as a trade mark will not be deprived of legal protection. The doctrine of 'passing off' is a common law creation located in the law of tort and is based on the premise that 'nobody has any right to represent his goods as the goods of somebody else'. The action is effectively one of unfair competition and will lie where a competitor markets goods or services in such a manner that the public are likely to be confused as to their origins. In the case of *Erven Warnink v Townend*,[1] Lord Diplock identified five requirements for a successful action:

(1) a misrepresentation
(2) made by a trader in the course of trade,
(3) to prospective customers of his or ultimate consumers of goods or services supplied by him,
(4) which is calculated to injure the business or goodwill of another trader (in the sense that this is a reasonably foreseeable consequence) and
(5) which causes actual damage to a business or goodwill of the trader by whom the action is brought or ... will probably do so.

Although the doctrine of passing off is limited to use of a name in a manner which will harm commercial interests, recent decisions under the Internet domain name dispute resolution procedures indicate that protection may extend to private interests in respect of the practice sometimes described as 'cybersquatting'.[2]

[1] [1979] FSR 39.
[2] See para 23.47 below.

Trade marks and information technology

23.12 As with many other forms of products and services, information technology products are likely to seek the protection of trade mark law. Many product names are trade marked – Apple and Microsoft, for example, are both registered trade marks, together with symbols such as the famous Apple logo. In these situations, the application of trade mark law raises no novel issues.

23.13 With the emergence and increasing commercialisation of the Internet, many businesses have sought to establish a presence in cyberspace. Typically, they will seek to register a domain name which incorporates their real-life identity. British Airways, for example, can be found at http://www.britishairways.com. In some cases, businesses which exist wholly or primarily on the Internet have sought to register aspects of the domain name structure as a trade mark, an example being Amazon.com, where the .com element is part of the registered mark. The UK Patent Office has published notices on 'Practice on Trade Marks Incorporating the Word Net'[1] and on 'Registration of Internet Domain Names as Trade Marks'.[2] The notices indicate that in deciding whether a mark should be registered, elements such as http, www, .com, .co.uk are to be discounted in determining the eligibility of the mark. The term will then fall to be judged on normal criteria. Initially, applicants should show that the mark is distinctive of their business or that goods or services have been supplied under the name in such a manner as to show factual distinctiveness.

[1]   Available from http://www.patent.gov.uk/snews/notices/tmnet.html.
[2]   Available from http://www.patent.gov.uk/snews/notices/tmnames.html.

23.14   Where novel issues have arisen is in the relationship between trade mark rights and the allocation of Internet domain names.[1] As the systems of allocating domain names developed, the responsible agencies adopted a first come, first served policy. As the commercial attractiveness of the WWW has increased, so more and more commercial organisations have sought to develop a presence. The impact of a web presence will obviously be enhanced by use of the organisation's trading name, something which may well be protected by trade marks. What many have discovered is that, whether by accident or design, the name is already in use. In such instances, consideration may well be given to the possibility of raising an action alleging infringement of the trade mark. Unfortunately, the application of trade mark law to the operation of the Internet is not without its difficulties.

[1]   See Chapter 2 for a description of the function of Internet domain names and the manner in which these are allocated.

23.15   Problems are exacerbated by a number of features of the system of Internet domain names. In many instances, the names of undertakings may be shared by many individuals. There are in excess of 2,000 Macdonalds listed in the Glasgow telephone directory alone. Although the existence of sub-domains such as .co and .ltd means that the same name might be used in these various sectors, there may not be enough sub-domains to go around. Even where domain names identical to a trade mark have been obtained by another commercial undertaking, there may be no question of infringement when this undertaking's activities are conducted in different sectors. Again, domain names cannot incorporate a distinctive type font or style of presentation of a name or identifying badges or signs.

23.16   Additional problems exist in respect of the generic top level domain names such as .com. These may be obtained by anyone from anywhere in the world. This global system sits uneasily with the trade mark system which, albeit with mechanisms for international co-operation, is still based on the notion of national rights. It may well be the case that the same trade mark is owned by different persons or undertakings in different states. An example is Budweiser beer. Although this is currently the subject of a dispute between US and Czech-based brewers, for historical reasons, the name has been used by two distinct parties.

23.17 In considering the relationship between trade marks (and other legal rights such as passing off) and domain names, consideration will first be given to a number of cases which have been brought before the courts in the UK. Following this, reference will be made to the dispute resolution procedure adopted by Internet regulatory agencies.

Internet-related trade mark disputes

23.18 Most of the disputes which have reached the courts have concerned the question whether use or possession of a domain name including a trade mark constitutes infringement. Two situations might arise, the first concerned with cases of domain name hijacking as discussed above, and the second with the more problematic case of honest concurrent usage.

DOMAIN NAME HIJACKING

23.19 As indicated above, domain registries have (and to a considerable extent, continue to) operated on the basis of accepting the first application for registration of a particular domain name. This has been open to exploitation by street- (or Internet-) wise users, who have sought to register large numbers of popular names. Names such as Macdonalds, Hertz and Rolex were issued to applicants with no connection with the well-known firms. The practice of seeking a domain name corresponding with a well-known organisation is generally referred to as 'domain name hijacking'. As the commercial usage of the Internet has increased, so the benefits of obtaining a domain name which is readily identifiable with the owner's business has become recognised. It is reported that one domain name (business.com) has been sold for no less than $150,000,[1] with a number of firms conducting online auctions for the sale of attractive domain names.[2]

[1] http://www.news.com.News/Item/0,4,11230,00.html.
[2] See, for example, http://www.part.to/index.html.

23.20 In the case of a number of the names mentioned above, the return of these to their 'rightful' owners has been accompanied by the making of payments to charity. Other 'hijackers' have acted from less altruistic motives. The first Internet-related dispute to come before an English court provides an illustration. In *Harrods v Lawrie*,[1] the plaintiff successfully asked the High Court to order the defendant to give up all claim to the domain names Harrods.com and Harrods.co.uk. It was noted that the defendant had also registered the names ladbrokes.com and cadburys.com. A spokesman for Harrods suggested:

> There can be only two purposes in him registering the name. One is to demand money from us to relinquish it, and the other to stop us using it. Either purpose is, we think, illegal and we believe that the existing laws of this country should

be sufficient to establish that a company may protect its name and reputation on the Internet.

[1]   (1997) Telegraph, 14 January.

23.21   The decision in this case was handed down in the absence of the defendant and is of very limited precedential value. A non-Internet related case which may be of relevance in illustrating the issues involved is that of *Glaxo plc v Glaxowellcome Ltd*.[1] Here, a merger had been proposed between two pharmaceutical companies, Glaxo and Wellcome. The news was announced in a press release on 23 January 1995, which stated that the new company would trade under the name Glaxo-Wellcome plc. The following day, one of the defendants, who acted as a company registration agent registered a company under the name Glaxowellcome Ltd. The defendant's normal business was to create 'shell' companies which would be sold for a fee of £1,000. The plaintiffs discovered the details of the registration which would have prevented their own use of the name. The defendants refused to sell the rights in the name for their standard fee, but indicated 'without prejudice' that this might be arranged for a fee of £100,000. The plaintiffs alleged that the defendants were guilty of the tort of 'passing off' and sought an order requiring the defendants to change the name of their company to something 'which did not contain the names "Glaxo" or "Wellcome" or any other confusingly similar words'.

[1]   [1996] FSR 388.

23.22   This order was granted in the High Court, Lightman J holding that the plaintiffs were not obliged to follow the statutory procedures for challenging the registration of a company name with the Registrar of Companies, proceedings which could well be lengthy. The court, he stated:

> ... will not countenance any such pre-emptive strike of registering companies with names where others have the goodwill in those names, and the registering party then demanding a price for changing the names. It is an abuse of the system of registration of companies' names[1]

and granted an injunction 'specifically requiring the company and subscribers to take all such steps as lie within their power to change or facilitate the change of name'.

[1]   *Glaxo plc v Glaxowellcome Ltd* [1996] FSR 388 at 391.

23.23   A more significant and directly relevant decision is that of the Court of Appeal in *British Telecommunications plc, Virgin Enterprises Ltd, J Sainsbury plc, Marks & Spencer plc and Ladbroke Group plc v One in a Million*.[1] The defendant, One in a Million, together with four other companies, acted as dealers in Internet domain names. Included in the names registered by them were:

ladbrokes.com	bt.org
sainsbury.com	virgin.org
sainsburys.com	marksandspencer.co.uk
j-sainsbury.com	britishtelecom.co.uk
marksandspencer.com	britishtelecom.net
cellnet.net	britishtelecom.com

The plaintiff companies alleged that the defendants' conduct constituted both threats to engage in and completed acts of passing off and trade mark infringement. Judgment was granted in their favour in the High Court, with the judge concluding that:

> The history of the defendants' activities shows a deliberate practice followed over a substantial period of time of registering domain names which are chosen to resemble the names and marks of other people and are plainly intended to deceive. The threat of passing-off and trademark infringement, and the likelihood of confusion arising from the infringement of the mark are made out beyond argument in this case, even in which (sic) it is possible to imagine other cases in which the issue would be more nicely balanced. The result is that the plaintiffs in all five actions are entitled to final injunctions.[2]

1   [1999] FSR 1. The decision at first instance is reported at [1998] FSR 265.
2   [1998] FSR 265 at 273.

23.24   The Court of Appeal upheld the initial judgment in all respects. In respect of the allegation that the defendant had engaged in passing off, it was argued that the mere act of registering names was not sufficient. As indicated above, the tort requires that members of the public be deceived as to the source of origin. Until some attempt was made to use the names, it was argued, there would be no deception. This contention was rejected. Delivering the judgment of the court, Lord Justice Walker identified the criteria that should be applied by a court in deciding whether to grant relief:

> Whether any name is an instrument of fraud will depend upon all the circumstances. A name which will, by reason of its similarity to the name of another, inherently lead to passing-off is such an instrument. If it would not inherently lead to passing-off, it does not follow that it is not an instrument of fraud. The court should consider the similarity of the names, the intention of the defendant, the type of trade and all the surrounding circumstances. If it be the intention of the defendant to appropriate the goodwill of another or enable others to do so, I can see no reason why the court should not infer that it will happen, even if there is a possibility that such an appropriation would not take place. If, taking all the circumstances into account the court should conclude

535

that the name was produced to enable passing-off, is adapted to be used for passing-off and, if used, is likely to be fraudulently used, an injunction will be appropriate.[1]

1   *British Telecommunications plc, Virgin Enterprises Ltd, J Sainsbury plc, Marks & Spencer plc and Ladbroke Group plc v One in a Million* [1999] FSR 1 at 8.

23.25   The judge proceeded to examine the activities of the defendant in some detail. A considerable number of instances were identified when names of well-known companies had been registered and subsequently offered for sale. One instance might be quoted as typical:

> ... a letter dated 17 September 1996 to Intertan UK Limited stated: 'Further to our telephone conversation on Friday, 13 September 1996, I confirm that I have the domain name tandy.co.uk available for sale or hire. Additionally, I have also the other following domain names that may interest you:
>
> > intertan.co.uk
> > tandy.net
> > intertan.net
> > tandyuk.com
> > intertanuk.com
>
> As discussed, I would like these domain names to go to Tandy, as we have a mutual business relationship in the past.
>
> I would be willing to offer you all six domain names for the sum of £15,000 plus VAT. This is a small one-off price to pay for a unique corporate identity on a medium that is the fastest growing information service in the world, the Internet.'[1]

1   *British Telecommunications plc, Virgin Enterprises Ltd, J Sainsbury plc, Marks & Spencer plc and Ladbroke Group plc v One in a Million* [1999] FSR 1 at 21.

23.26   After considering a number of similar cases where he considered there was an express or implicit threat to sell the domain names to a third party, Walker LJ described the defendants' conduct:

> In my view there was clear evidence of systematic registration by the appellants of well-known trade names as blocking registrations and a threat to sell them to others. No doubt the primary purpose of registration was to block registration by the owner of the goodwill. There was, according to Mr Wilson (counsel for the defendants) nothing unlawful in doing that. The truth is different. The registration only blocks registration of the identical domain name and therefore does not act as a block to registration of a domain name that can be used by the owner of the goodwill in the name. The purpose of the so-called blocking registration was to extract money from the owners of the goodwill in the name chosen. Its ability to do so was in the main dependent upon the threat, expressed or implied, that the appellants would exploit the goodwill by either trading under the name or equipping another with the name so he could do so.[1]

1   *British Telecommunications plc, Virgin Enterprises Ltd, J Sainsbury plc, Marks & Spencer plc and Ladbroke Group plc v One in a Million* [1999] FSR 1 at 22.

23.27   In respect of a number of the domain names, the defendant argued that there could be other legitimate holders of the name:

> Mr Wilson pointed to the fact that there are people called Sainsbury and Ladbroke and companies, other than Virgin Enterprises Ltd, who have as part of their name the word Virgin and also people or firms whose initials would be BT.[1]

Even the defendant had to concede that this argument could not apply in respect of the name marksandspencer.co.uk. The court was also unimpressed with the arguments relating to the other companies. Once again, the pattern of the defendants' behaviour was damming.

[1]   *British Telecommunications plc, Virgin Enterprises Ltd, J Sainsbury plc, Marks & Spencer plc and Ladbroke Group plc v One in a Million* [1999] FSR 1 at 23.

23.28   A number of the plaintiffs also brought action alleging trade mark infringement. Section 10(4) of the Trade Marks Act 1994 defines what constitutes use of a trade mark:

> For the purposes of this section, a person uses a sign if, in particular, he—
>
> (a) affixes it to goods or the packaging thereof;
> (b) offers or exposes goods for sale, puts them on the market or stocks them for those purposes under the sign, or offers or supplies them under the sign, or offers or supplies services under the sign;
> (c) imports or exports goods under the sign; or
> (d) uses the sign on business papers or in advertising.

23.29   In *One in a Million*,[1] Walker LJ took the view that the use was in connection with the defendant's business of supplying services. Counsel for the defendant argued that in order to constitute infringement there had to:

> ... be a trade mark use in relation to goods or services, in the sense that it had to denote origin. He also submitted that the use had to be confusing use.[2]

These issues are potentially significant in the Internet context. In the present case, the defendant's conduct again told against them, it being held that:

> I am not satisfied that Section 10(3) [of the Trade Marks Act 1994] does require the use to be trade mark use nor that it must be confusing use, but I am prepared to assume that it does. Upon that basis I am of the view that threats to infringe have been established. The appellants seek to sell the domain names which are confusingly similar to registered trade marks. The domain names indicate origin. That is the purpose for which they were registered. Further they will be used in relation to the services provided by the registrant who trades in domain names.
> Mr Wilson also submitted that it had not been established that the contemplated use would take unfair advantage of, or was detrimental to the distinctive character or reputation of the respondents' trade marks. He is wrong. The domain names were registered to take advantage of the distinctive character and reputation of the marks. That is unfair and detrimental.[3]

[1]   *British Telecommunications plc, Virgin Enterprises Ltd, J Sainsbury plc, Marks & Spencer plc and Ladbroke Group plc v One in a Million* [1999] FSR 1.

² [1999] FSR 1 at 25.
³ [1999] FSR 1 at 25.

23.30 The issue of 'trade mark use' and the possibility of confusion were discussed in more detail in the Scottish case *of Bravado Merchandising Services Ltd v Mainstream Publishing (Edinburgh) Ltd.*[1] An author had written a book about the pop group 'Wet Wet Wet'. The group had trade marked its name in categories relating to printed matter. The book's title was *A Sweet Little Mystery – Wet Wet Wet – The Inside Story.* It was alleged that this constituted trade mark infringement.

¹ [1996] FSR 205.

23.31 Delivering judgment, Lord McCluskey made frequent reference to the criterion whether the name was used 'in a trade mark sense'. He pointed out that:

> ... a travel writer who wrote an article about a fortnight's hill walking in the Lake District might well, if he had been unlucky enough, give it the title 'Wet Wet Wet'.

Such usage would be descriptive of the topic and would not constitute use in a trade mark sense. In the present case, however:

> The repeated reference to 'Wet' has nothing to do with moisture or political timidity. On the contrary, the use of 'Wet Wet Wet' is avowedly and obviously a use of the name which the group has registered. Accordingly, even if the use is appropriate to indicate the subject matter of the book on whose cover it appears that use does not thereby cease to be used in a trade mark sense.[1]

¹ *Bravado Merchandising Services Ltd v Mainstream Publishing (Edinburgh) Ltd* [1996] FSR 205 at 213.

23.32 If use of a trade mark as the title of a book constitutes trade mark use, there can be little doubt that use as a domain name would be similarly regarded. Lord McCluskey went on, however, to consider the defence provided by s 11(2) of the Trade Marks Act 1994. This sanctions:

> ... the use of indications concerning the ... intended purpose of goods or services ... provided the use is in accordance with honest practice in industrial or commercial matters.

In the present case, the use of the trade mark was to indicate the subject matter of the book. The judge commented that:

> In the course of the discussion, as I noted earlier, such names as Ford, Disney and Guinness were discussed. It would be a bizarre result of trade marks legislation, the primary purpose of which is to 'guarantee the trade mark as an indication of origin', if it could be used to prevent publishers from using the protected name in the title of a book about the company or product. If that had been the intention of Parliament, I would have expected it to be made plain.[1]

¹ *Bravado Merchandising Services Ltd v Mainstream Publishing (Edinburgh) Ltd* [1996] FSR 205 at 216.

23.33 Accordingly, the claim of trade mark infringement was dismissed. It is perhaps unlikely that a defendant such as 'One in a Million' could satisfy the Trade Marks Act 1994, s 11(2) defence, but the issue may be more open in the case where a site contains material about a trade mark owner. If the author's book could legitimately use the group's name as its title, the same might be said of a website containing information or comment about the group. On the same basis, someone establishing a website to discuss the current US antitrust litigation involving Microsoft might well wish to include reference to the company in the domain name.

HONEST CONCURRENT USE

23.34 In the cases discussed above, there appears little doubt that the parties seeking to register the domain names were acting, at the least, in bad faith and without possessing any colourable title to use of the name. Other circumstances may be less clear cut, with two or more parties possessing rights in respect of a name. The problem may arise in a number of ways. With 42 categories of goods and services in the Trademark Register, the same name may have been allocated to a number of persons. The existence of many national trade mark regimes is likely to result in further duplication, whilst in the case of trade marks which can be used as human surnames, tens of thousands of persons may have an entitlement to the name.

23.35 A number of actions have reached the courts involving disputes between parties as to the right to a particular Internet domain name. Many of the disputes have also involved the organisations responsible for the administration of the system of domain names and, as will be discussed in the telecommunications module, these have devised a bewildering range of policies in the attempt to limit their exposure in trade mark disputes. If a name is retained following a challenge from a trade mark owner, there is the possibility that the registered owner may regard them as jointly liable with the name holder. If the name is withdrawn following a complaint, an action may be brought by the registered owner alleging breach of contract. The case of *Pitman Training Ltd v Nominet UK*[1] is illustrative of the situations which are likely to arise.

[1]   [1997] FSR 797.

23.36 The Pitman publishing company was established in 1849 and expanded to cover a range of publishing and training activities. In 1985, the various divisions of the business were sold, the publishing business being acquired by Pearsons, the second defendant in the present case, and the training business by the plaintiff. An agreement was reached at that time providing for the continued use of the Pitman name by the new owners.

23.37 In February 1996, a request was submitted to Nominet UK, the organisation which administers much of the .uk domain name system, by an ISP, Netnames, acting on behalf of the publishing company and seeking registration of the names 'pitman.co.uk' and 'pitman.com'. The application was accepted. Although the publishers had plans to establish a website and reference to its new domain names was used in some of their advertising, it does not appear that any significant use was made of the Internet.

23.38 In March 1996, another ISP acting on behalf of the plaintiff, Pitman Training, made a totally independent request for the allocation of the domain name 'pitman.co.uk'. Under the allocation rules operated by Nominet, a system of 'first come, first served' applied. Under this provision, the plaintiff's request should have been rejected. Owing to some administrative mishap, however, the request was accepted and the original registration was removed and reallocated to the plaintiff, who promptly made extensive use of the name, sending out significant mailings and publishing adverts inviting email responses to the 'pitman.co.uk' address. From a commercial perspective, the exercise was not successful. Only two replies had been received by the date of the trial.

23.39 It was not until December 1996 that the second defendant discovered that its domain name had been withdrawn. It made complaint to its ISP, requiring reinstatement of its name. Prolonged negotiations followed, involving all of the parties to the case but without an acceptable solution being reached. Finally, on 4 April 1997, Nominet, applying their 'first come, first served' rule, indicated that the domain name would be removed from the plaintiff and re-allocated it to the second defendant. Matters then switched to the High Court.

23.40 On 11 April, a consent order was made restraining Nominet from transferring the domain name pending a full hearing or further order. In May 1997, the matter returned to the High Court, where the Vice-Chancellor held that the injunction should be withdrawn on the basis that the plaintiff had not demonstrated a reasonable prospect of succeeding in its action. As was stated:

> It is trite law and, of course, common ground that interlocutory relief in an action can only be granted in support of some viable cause of action. If a plaintiff cannot show a reasonably arguable cause of action against a defendant the plaintiff cannot obtain any interlocutory relief against that defendant however convenient the grant of that relief might appear to be.[1]

[1] *Pitman Training Ltd v Nominet UK* [1997] FSR 797 at 806.

23.41 In terms of intellectual property, the plaintiff's main ground of action was that the defendant had committed the tort of passing off. This contention was not accepted by the judge. The name Pitman had been used for publishing for almost 150 years. The agreement at the time of the break-up of the original company provided for its continued use in this context. Indeed, it was suggested, given the terms of the agreement, if any party was guilty of passing off it was more likely to be the plaintiff. He concluded:

> That there may be some confusion experienced by some members of the public is undoubtedly so. But that confusion results from the use by both companies, PTC and Pitman Publishing, of the style Pitman for their respective trading purposes. No viable passing off claim against Pitman Publishing arising out of

the future or past use by Pitman Publishing of the 'pitman.co.uk' domain name has, in my judgment, been shown.[1]

[1]   *Pitman Training Ltd v Nominet UK* [1997] FSR 797 at 807.

23.42   In many respects, it may be considered that the problems of trying to apply national trade mark law in the context of the Internet are intractable. Final reference may be made to the case of *Prince PLC v Prince Sports Group*.[1] The plaintiff was a UK company providing a range of computer consultancy and training services. The defendant was a major US-based sports goods manufacturer which possessed US and UK trade marks in respect of the use of the name Prince for sports goods.

[1]   [1998] FSR 22.

23.43   In 1995, the plaintiff applied for and was awarded an Internet domain name as Prince.com. In 1997, the defendant became aware of this fact and its attorneys wrote a letter to the plaintiff, indicating that a failure on its part to relinquish rights in the name would constitute trade mark infringement and impliedly threatening legal proceedings:

> Dear Sirs:
>
>   We represent Prince Sports Group, Inc, with respect to trademark and other intellectual property matters. Prince is the owner of the famous PRINCE trademark, which has been used in connection with tennis rackets, squash rackets, other sporting items and clothing for at least the past 20 years in the United States. Prince is the owner of several US registrations for the PRINCE mark, many of which are incontestable, eg, Registration Nos 1,049,720; 1,074,654; 1,111,008; 1,103,956; 1,233,680; 1,284,452; 1,290,202; and 1,290,217. Our client has also registered the PRINCE mark in many other countries throughout the world, including the United Kingdom.
>
>   Through extensive sales and advertising under the PRINCE mark and the excellent quality of our client's products, the PRINCE mark has become an asset of immeasurable goodwill and value to our client.
>
>   It has come to our client's attention that you have registered "PRINCE.COM" as a domain name with Network Solutions Inc, (NSI) thereby preventing our client from registering its house mark and trade name as a domain name. We are writing to advise you that your company's use and registration of PRINCE as a domain name constitutes infringement and dilution of our client's trademark rights in PRINCE, as well as unfair competition, under the Lanham Act, 15 USC 1051 et seq.
>
>   This matter can be amicably resolved by an assignment of the PRINCE.COM domain name to Prince Sports Group, Inc, in accordance with the procedures of NSI and an agreement not to use PRINCE as part of any new domain name you may select. While we are willing to wait for your orderly transition to a new domain name, we must have your immediate written agreement to assign the PRINCE.COM domain name to Prince Sports to avoid litigation.
>
>   We look forward to hearing from you or your attorneys in the very near future.[1]

[1]   *Prince PLC v Prince Sports Group* [1998] FSR 21 at 24.5.

23.44 The plaintiff considered that the letter related to proceedings in the UK. Under UK trade mark law, an unjustified threat to institute infringement proceedings is actionable, s 21 of the Trade Marks Act 1994 providing that:

(1) Where a person threatens another with proceedings for infringement of a registered trade mark other than—
    (a) the application of the mark to goods or their packaging;
    (b) the importation of goods to which, or to the packaging of which, the mark has been applied; or
    (c) the supply of services under the mark
    any person aggrieved may bring proceedings for relief under this section

(2) The relief which may be applied for is any of the following—
    (a) a declaration that the threats are unjustifiable;
    (b) an injunction against the continuance of the threats; or
    (c) damages in respect of any loss he has sustained by the threats.

23.45 The plaintiff sought all three remedies plus a further declaration that its conduct did not constitute trade mark infringement. It achieved significant but not total success. Although the plaintiff's letter made extensive reference to US trade marks and to provisions of US law, it was considered that it could also reasonably be understood as relating to proceedings in the UK. The threat of action did not come under the headings in s 24(1) of the Trade Marks Act 1994. Although the plaintiff's business involved the supply of services, the threat of action was general in its terms. The court therefore awarded the remedies under s 24(2)(a) and (b). It rejected the request for a more extensive declaration of non-infringement, holding that such a determination was not appropriate for interim proceedings. As regards damages, the court was of the view that the plaintiff had not suffered any financial loss sufficient to sustain a claim for damages.

[1] *Prince PLC v Prince Sports Group* [1998] FSR 21.

The Uniform Dispute Resolution Rules and cybersquatting

23.46 A feature of early disputes concerned with rights relating to domain names was the attempt by domain name registries such as Network Solutions and Nominet to devise policies designed to render them immune from legal action. In many respects, the agencies were put in difficult legal positions. In the *Pitman* case[1] discussed at para 23.36ff above, for example, the domain name registry, Nominet, was threatened with legal action by one party unless the name was re-assigned and with action by the other in the event it was. A classic example of a 'no win' situation.

[1] *Pitman Training Ltd v Nominet UK* [1997] FSR 797.

23.47 With the emergence of ICANN as the co-ordinating body for the system of domain names, a new approach has been adopted to the problem of trying to resolve domain name disputes without invoking national courts. Any organisation wishing to act as a registry in respect of the generic domain names[1] is obliged to conduct business according to the 'Uniform Domain Name Dispute Resolution Policy'.[2] This requires applicants for domain names to submit to mandatory dispute resolution procedures before approved dispute resolution service providers in the event of any claim that:

(i)   your domain name is identical or confusingly similar to a trademark or service mark in which the complainant has rights;

(ii) you have no rights or legitimate interests in respect of the domain name; and

(iii) your domain name has been registered and is being used in bad faith.

The onus is on a complainant to establish all of these heads of claim.[3]

[1]   See discussion at para 2.9 above.
[2]   Available from http://www.icann.org/udrp/udrp.htm.
[3]   Uniform Dispute Resolution Rules, r 4a.

23.48   There are currently four organisations offering dispute resolution services under the ICANN rules.

> The Asian Domain Name Dispute Resolution Centre[1]
>
> CPR Institute for Dispute Resolution[2]
>
> The National Arbitration Forum[3]
>
> The World Intellectual Property Organisation[4]

Whilst the National Arbitration Forum describes itself as the 'largest provider of domain name dispute resolution in North America', the largest provider globally is the World Intellectual Property Organization. The latter has received more than 6,000 complaints concerning the use of domain names.

[1]   http://www.adndrc.org/adndrc/index.html
[2]   http://www.cpradr.org/ICANN_Menu.htm
[3]   http://www.arbforum.com/domains/
[4]   http://arbiter.wipo.int/domains/

23.49   An early decision of the WIPO dispute resolution panel in the case of *Jeanette Winterson v Mark Hogarth* illustrates how these requirements might be applied. In this case, the complainant, a well known author, objected to the registration of the domain names:

> jeanettewinterson.com
>
> jeanettewinterson.net
>
> jeanettewinterson.org

by the respondent, a Cambridge University academic.[1]

[1] A copy of the decision can be obtained from http://arbiter.wipo.int/domains/decisions/index.html.

23.50   In circumstances similar to those at issue in the *One in a Million* case,[1] the registrant had registered a range of domains making use of the names of well-known authors. Contact had been made with a number of these; in the case of one, Joanna Trollope, a letter was sent to her literary agent indicating the intent to auction the names to third parties, but giving the author a right of 'first refusal' to acquire the names for a fee of 3% of her 1999 gross book sales. Similar communications were made to the complainant.

[1] *British Telecommunications plc, Virgin Enterprises Ltd, J Sainsbury plc, Marks & Spencer plc and Ladbroke Group plc v One in a Million* [1999] FSR 1.

23.51   Responding to complaints to the effect that:

> The Complainant also contends that the Respondent has no rights to or legitimate interests in respect of the domain names in issue, that the Complainant has not consented to use of the Mark by the Respondent and that the Respondent has registered and is using the domain names in bad faith.

The respondent stated that:

> ... he registered the domain names in issue in the belief that JEANETTE WINTERSON was not a trade mark or a service mark and that the domain names in issue were registered with a view to developing a website devoted to the work of the Complainant.

It was held by the panel that the Uniform Domain Name Dispute Resolution Policy required that a complainant establish all three grounds specified, namely, use of an identical or confusingly similar mark, in breach of a trade or service mark in which the respondent has no rights and in circumstances evidencing bad faith.

23.52   It is clear that the name used is effectively identical to the complainant's name. More significant was the finding of the panel in respect of the next ground. Here, it was ruled that:

> The Rules do *not* require that the Complainant's trademark be registered by a government authority or agency for such a right to exist.

The complainant being resident in England, it was ruled, English law had to be applied to determine the extent of rights. The doctrine of passing off, it was held could also be invoked:

> 6.11   There are a number of English cases dealing with passing-off the names of well-known individuals and personalities, which all – as may be expected – turn on the facts. These include, the Uncle MAC case [*Mcculloch v Lewis A May (Produce Distributors) Ltd* [1947] 2 All ER 845]: the KOJAK case [*Taverner Rutledge v Trexpalm* (1975) FSR 479]: the

WOMBLES case [*Wombles Ltd v Wombles Skips Ltd* [1977] RPC 99]: the ABBA case [*Lyngstad v Anabas Products* [1977] FSR 62]: and the Teenage Mutant Ninja Turtles case [*Mirage Studios v Counter Feat Clothing Co Ltd* [1991] FSR 145]. The case for decision here does not concern whether or not passing-off has occurred *but* whether the Complainant (Jeanette Winterson) has rights in her name sufficient to constitute a trade mark for the purposes of para. 4a of the Policy.

6.12 In the Panel's view, *trademarks* where used in para. 4a of the Policy is not to be construed by reference to the criteria of registrability under English law [the ELVIS PRESLEY case] but more broadly in terms of the distinctive features of a person's activities. In other words, akin to the common law right to prevent unauthorised use of a name. Thus, applying English law the Complainant clearly would have a cause of action to prevent unauthorized use of the Mark JEANETTE WINTERSON in passing-off.

The other tests being satisfied, the panel ordered that the registrations should be transferred to the complainant.

23.53 The decision in this case appears in line with the authorities cited. The complainant was a well-known and successful author and the effect of the registrations complained of would satisfy the criteria for the award of a remedy by the English courts. The English courts have never, however, accepted that any general right to personality exists which can be infringed by use of a name or other indications of identity.[1] It must remain an open question whether any action would lie against registrations such as those reported to have been made in the name of the Prime Minister's youngest son ('leoblair.com' and 'leoblair.co.uk').

[1] See discussion in Cornish *Intellectual Property* (3rd edn, 1996, Sweet and Maxwell) paras 16.33–16.34.

23.54 Some time after the development of dispute resolution schemes for WWW sites within the generic top level domains a similar scheme has been adopted to deal with disputes within the .uk top level domain. Operated by the domain name registry, Nominet, a panel of around 30 experts will be appointed to act as adjudicators with individual cases being heard by a single person.[1] The basis for any complaint is that there was 'abusive registration of a domain name'. This encompasses a Domain Name which either:

    i.   was registered or otherwise acquired in a manner which, at the time when the registration or acquisition took place, took unfair advantage of or was unfairly detrimental to the Complainant's Rights; OR

    ii.   has been used in a manner which took unfair advantage of or was unfairly detrimental to the Complainant's Rights.

Beyond substituting the perhaps more pejorative term 'abusive registration' for the ICANN criterion of 'bad faith' the substance of the policy is broadly similar.

[1] http://www.nic.uk/ref/drs-policy.html.

23.55 The first decision under the new procedure was delivered in 2001. The pharmaceutical company Eli Lilley was successful in its application to have rights in the domain xigris.ci.uk transferred to it. Eli Lilley had obtained a European Community Trade Mark in the name Xigris in 1999. The domain name had been registered by an ex-employee in June 2001. No representations were made by the employee in response to Eli Lilley's complaint and although there was no evidence available as to the purpose for which the registration might have been made, the expert held that the circumstances surrounding the case were such that a prima facie case of abuse had been made out and that in the absence of any attempt at explanation, the request for transfer should be granted.[1]

[1]   The full text of the decision can be obtained from http://www.nic.uk/DisputeResolution/ Decisions/EliLillyAndCompany-v-DavidClayton.html

23.56   In total, more than 1,600 disputes have been referred to the UK dispute resolution service. The roll call of complainants includes some of the best-known names in the UK's commercial and public life, featuring organisations such as Harrods, Vodaphone, Barclays Bank, Nokia, the Royal Marines and Interflora. It appears almost to be the case that an incident of cybersquatting is an integral consequence of commercial success.

Conclusions

23.57   With the emergence of global and national dispute resolution procedures, trade mark disputes involving the use of domain names appear to have largely vanished from the legal system. Although most disputes are settled, statistics from the dispute resolution organisations do show that the majority of decisions reached are in favour of the complainant. Given the nature of many of the incidents referred which involve blatant hi-jacking of the name of a business, this rate is not in itself a source of surprise. What may be a greater cause for concern is the fact that the law applied in a number of instances appears to be almost but not quite trade mark law. In one sense, disputes are being hi-jacked from the courts to tribunals which are strongly supported by commercial pressures. The approach, especially concerning the allocation of generic domain names, may represent a way forward for dispute resolution in what is an increasingly globalised society but great care needs to be taken to ensure that it acquires a considerable measure of legitimacy and is not seen as the captive of particular interest groups.

Chapter 24

Protection of semiconductor chip designs

Introduction

24.1 A conducting material is one which will allow an electric current to pass through it. Most metals fall into this category. At the other end of this spectrum are materials such as ceramics, glass or rubber, which will not transmit electricity. These are referred to as insulators. In their pure form, materials such as silicon, germanium and selenium will not conduct electricity. The great virtue of these materials from the standpoint of computer producers is that when impurities are added to the materials, the flow of electricity will be permitted to a certain and predictable extent. This renders them very suitable as electronic circuits and allows them to replace the valves and transistors which were required in earlier generations of computers. Today, semiconductor chips, often referred to as silicon chips, serve as one of the key building blocks of any computer. Their small size has also meant that they can be used to control the operation of a vast range of appliances, from washing machines to telephones.

24.2 As any computer user will be aware, the quest over the years has been to produce chips which are more and more powerful and which also take up less space than previous designs. In 1965, the scientist Gordon Moore coined the eponymous law which stated that the power of microchips would double every 18–24 months. Although the remorseless growth in numbers means that the sequence of exponential growth came to an end before the end of the century, increases in processing power continue in spite of frequent predictions that chip design is reaching the limits of physical capacity. In order to squeeze more transistors onto a chip, each element of circuitry requires to be smaller and at current levels can be as narrow as 90 nanometres. An average human hair is some 100 times thicker.

24.3 It has been a recurring theme in the intellectual property field that it is easier to emulate than to innovate. This is certainly the case with semiconductor chip design – more frequently referred to as topography. The task of developing an architecture to maximise processing capability in as small a physical space as possible is a massively expensive one which very few firms have the resources or expertise to conduct at the highest level. As has been stated:

> ... the development of such topographies requires the investment of considerable resources, human, technical or financial, whilst topographies of such products can be copied at a fraction of the cost needed to develop them independently.[1]

On a small scale, devices exist to copy the make-up of a completed chip. On a larger scale, techniques of reverse engineering will permit the replication of the mask designs fairly readily. These can then be used to produce identical chips.

[1]   OJ 1987 L 24/36.

24.4   The performance of a semiconductor chip is dictated by its physical layout. In the early days of chip development, the main method of manufacture commenced with a blank piece of silicon. A protective covering known as a mask would be placed over the chip which would then be immersed in acid. The acid would etch patterns into those parts of the chip which were not protected by the mask. The chip would then be removed and a second mask fitted. This would be to a different pattern so that when the chip was again placed in acid, further patterns would be etched onto its surface. The process would be repeated until the complete circuitry was etched onto the surface of the chip.

24.5   As may be deduced, the above process was somewhat convoluted. More modern techniques involve effectively the use of lasers which, operating in accordance with instructions contained in computer programs, burn the required circuitry onto the surface of the chip.

The emergence of legal protection

24.6   The extent of the legal protection conferred upon the producer of a semiconductor chip was initially a matter of some uncertainty. Whilst it may well have been the case that any design drawings and the masks used in the production process would benefit from copyright protection as would the software used to control the operation of the laser, the status of the finished product was less clear. In cases where there was sufficient novelty, it might be that the product could be protected by means of a patent, but it was argued that most of the development work involved was of a developmental rather than an inventive nature.

24.7   The UK copyright legislation was one of the few statutes which offered the possibility of extending copyright protection to the three-dimensional reproduction of a two-dimensional work.[1] Under the Copyright Act 1956, it was provided that copyright in an artistic work (the drawings upon which the semiconductor chip design was first plotted) would be infringed by its conversion into a three-dimensional form (the semiconductor chip).[2] An objection did, however, exist to this argument. Under s 9(8) of the Copyright, Designs and Patents Act 1988, it is provided that:

> ... the making of an object of any description which is in three dimensions shall not be taken to infringe the copyright in an artistic work in two dimensions, if the object would not appear, to persons who are not experts in relation to objects of that description, to be a reproduction of the artistic work.

The relationship between the detailed technical drawings and the finished chip might well, it was argued, be lost on a non-expert.

[1] See *LB (Plastics) Ltd v Swish Products Ltd* [1979] RPC 551, discussed at para 20.77ff above.
[2] Section 3.

24.8   The impetus for legal reform in this area resulted from developments in the US which, responding to concerns from the US chip producers who dominated the global market, enacted the Semiconductor Chip Protection Act in 1984. This established a sui generis form of protection for chip designs. It is not proposed to consider the provisions of the US legislation, but its impact extended virtually throughout the world. The Act provided that protection would extend to US citizens and to the citizens of countries whose domestic law provided a level of protection equivalent to that applying within the US. The consequence for any state which failed to introduce legislation would be that, from the end of 1987, its national chip designers would be deprived of protection within the world's largest market for information technology products. The Semiconductor Chip Protection Act might be seen as a form of 'gunboat diplomacy'.

24.9   The tactic proved effective as states rushed to introduce protection for semiconductor chips. Within the EC, a Directive on 'the legal protection of topographies of semiconductor products' was introduced by the Council of Ministers in 1986.[1] This required member states to introduce appropriate legislation by 7 November 1987. Implementation in the UK took the form of the Semiconductor Products (Protection of Topography) Regulations 1987. These regulations defined 'topography' as the design, in whatever form it is expressed, of:

(a)   the pattern fixed or intended to be fixed, in or upon a layer of semiconductor product;

(b)   the pattern fixed, or intended to be fixed, in or upon a layer of material in the course of, and for the purpose of, the manufacture of a semiconductor product; and

(c)   the arrangement of the layers of a semiconductor product in relation to one another. [2]

[1] Directive 87/54/EEC, OJ 1987 L 24, p 36.
[2] SI 1987/1497. The Regulations have been substituted by the provisions of the Design Right (Semiconductor Topographies) Regulations 1989, SI 1989/1100, reg 2.

24.10   Protection thus extends either to designs or to the completed product. The maker of the topography has the exclusive right to make the semiconductor product involved or to reproduce any of the design materials such as masks. The Copyright Act 1956 was amended in order to exclude topographies from the protection offered to artistic works.[1]

¹   SI 1987/1497, reg 9(1).

24.11   The 1987 regulations[1] introduced a free-standing topography right, distinct from other forms of intellectual property. Following the House of Lords decision in the case of *British Leyland Motor Corp v Armstrong Patents Co Ltd*,[2] a need was recognised for the establishment of a new form of protection in respect of industrial designs. The Copyright, Designs and Patents Act 1988 accordingly created the concept of the design right.[3] This right, as implemented in a slightly modified form by the 1989 regulations,[4] constitutes the current regime for semiconductor protection.

¹   SI 1987/1497.
²   [1986] 1 All ER 850.
³   Part III.
⁴   SI 1989/1100.

Nature of design right

24.12   In common with copyright, design right is stated to be a property right which subsists in an original design.[1] The UK legislation contains no definition of originality, but the EC Directive provides that:

> The topography of a semiconductor product shall be protected in so far as it satisfies the conditions that it is the result of its creator's own intellectual effort and is not commonplace in the semiconductor industry. Where the topography of a semiconductor product consists of elements that are commonplace in the semiconductor industry, it shall be protected only to the extent that the combination of such elements, taken as a whole, fulfils the above mentioned conditions.[2]

This criterion appears more strict than that applying under the copyright regime, and it may be that the application of the traditionally liberal UK approach will produce a divergence in approach, requiring the intervention of the European Court of Justice.

¹   Copyright, Designs and Patents Act 1988, s 213(1).
²   Directive 87/54/EEC, art 2(2).

Ownership of design right

24.13   The designer of a topography will be the first owner of the resulting design right, subject to a number of exceptions:

1. Where the work is created in pursuance of a commission, the party issuing the commission will be the right holder.
2. Where the work is produced in the course of employment, ownership will vest in the employer.[1]

In both cases, contrary provisions may be made by agreement between the parties. Further, design rights will be awarded only if the party classed as owner is a citizen of an EC member state or, where a body corporate, is established or carries on substantial business activity in such a country.[2]

[1]   SI 1989/1100, reg 5.
[2]   Regulation 4.

24.14   Where a topography design is created by means of the operation of a computer program, ownership of the design right will vest in the person by whom the arrangements necessary for the creation of the design were undertaken.[1]

[1]   Copyright, Designs and Patents Act 1988, s 214(2).

24.15   Where a topography is designed outside the EC, no rights will arise under the UK legislation (although foreign design rights may be recognised on the basis of reciprocity).[1] This is subject to an exception where the first marketing of articles made to the design is by a qualifying person who is exclusively authorised to market the product in every EC member state.[2]

[1]   Copyright, Designs and Patents Act 1988, s 256.
[2]   Section 220, as amended by SI 1989/1100, reg 4(4).

Duration of topography right

24.16   The new form of protection expires ten years from the end of the year in which the topography was first made available for sale or hire anywhere in the world.[1] In determining when this occurs, no account is taken of any marketing conducted, subject to an obligation of confidence in respect of information about the product.[2] In the event that it was not commercially exploited, protection ceases 15 years after the date of its creation.[3]

[1]   SI 1989/1100, reg 6.
[2]   Regulation 7.
[3]   Regulation 6.

Extent of topography right

24.17   The owner of the design right in a topography has the exclusive right to reproduce the design (or a substantial part thereof),[1] whether by making the article (or one substantially similar) or a design document intended to be used as the basis for manufacture of an infringing product.[2] This is a broad form of protection effective against parties who produce finished chips, reproduce masks or enter details of the design to some other format to serve as the basis for a production process.

[1]   SI 1989/1100, reg 8(5).
[2]   Regulation 8(1).

Exceptions to the right

24.18 A limited amount of reverse engineering is permitted under the terms of the Copyright, Designs and Patents Act 1988 and regulations. It is provided that the owner's rights will not apply where the design is reproduced either privately for non-commercial purposes or where the reproduction is carried out in order to analyse or evaluate the design or to analyse, evaluate or teach the 'concepts, systems or techniques embodied in it'.[1] The information acquired from these exercises may be used in order to create another semiconductor topography so long as this is not substantially similar to the original design.[2]

[1] SI 1989/1100, reg 8(1).
[2] Regulation 8(4).

24.19 Further exceptions to the right apply in respect of elements of the original design which enable the semiconductor product to be connected to another object in order to enable either to perform its intended function.[1] The scope of this provision may be limited to the physical components necessary to allow a semiconductor product to be connected to another chip or other section of a computer. Where programs are stored in a semiconductor, decompilation of these for the purposes of ensuring inter-operability may be sanctioned under exceptions to the scope of copyright,[2] but it is unlikely that reproduction of elements of the topography itself will be required in order to attain this purpose.

[1] Copyright, Designs and Patents Act 1988, s 213(3)(b).
[2] See para 27.42 below.

Recognition of foreign design rights

24.20 In line with the approach adopted in the US, the Directive and the UK legislation provide that protection will be available to non-EC nationals only on a reciprocal basis. A list of the qualifying countries is contained in the Schedule to the 1989 regulations.[1] The Directive makes provision for the Commission and Council to co-ordinate an EC response to the extension of protection to non-member states.[2]

[1] SI 1989/1100.
[2] Directive 87/54/EEC, art 3.

Directive provisions not implemented in the UK

Marking of semiconductor products

24.21 Although the provisions are not mandatory, and have not been adopted within the UK, the Directive empowers member states to provide that semiconductor products containing protected topographies should carry an indication to this effect in the form of a capital T.[1]

[1] Directive 87/54/EEC, art 9.

Registration of protected topographies

24.22 In certain regimes, principally the US, registration has been a feature of the copyright system. The Directive sanctions the application of this approach in the semiconductor field, so that rights in semiconductor topographies will not come into existence or will cease to be valid unless an application is made for registration within two years from the date of the first commercial exploitation of the product.[1]

[1]   Directive 87/54/EEC, art 4.

The WIPO Treaty

24.23 Brief reference must finally be made to the Treaty on Intellectual Property in Respect of Integrated Circuits adopted by the World International Patent Organization in 1989.[1] The Treaty agrees a level of protection for semiconductor topographies somewhat more limited than that applying under the directive and the UK legislation. To date, the Treaty has been signed by eight states, but ratified by only one (Egypt).[2] It will enter into force upon being ratified by five states, but seems unlikely to have significant impact upon UK law and practice.

[1]   Text available at http://www.wipo.org/eng/iplex/wo_top1_.htm.
[2]   http://www.wipo.org/eng/ratific/s-ic.htms.

Conclusions

24.24 Whilst semiconductor chips are undoubtedly pivotal to the information technology industry, it cannot be said that the sui generis protection afforded to their designs has had a similar impact upon the legal environment. The legislation does not appear to have been at issue in any reported UK case. In some respects it may be criticised as being unduly influenced by the manufacturing technology in use in the 1980s when the US and EC rushed to legislate. As has been discussed in other contexts, legislation drafted speedily in response to particular concerns has seldom proved successful. Where the true significance of the legislation may lie is in its origin as a device to exert pressure on law makers in the developing world to take action to protect the economic interests of First World developers. In some respects a comparison may be drawn with the current controversies concerning the regulation of transborder data flows under the European Data Protection Directive[1] although the semiconductor legislation is more overtly economic in nature.

[1]   Directive 95/46/EC.

Chapter 25

Competition, standards and intellectual property

Introduction

25.1   In the case of *Lotus v Paperback*,[1] Judge Keeton expressed considerable scepticism as to the defendant's argument that the existence of de facto standards made compatibility with the acknowledged market-leading product a commercial imperative. The protection afforded by copyright, he held, must prevail, even though the effect of this was effectively to prevent the later party from entering onto the market.

[1]   *Lotus Development Corpn v Paperback Software International and Stephenson Software Ltd* 740 F Supp 37 (1990). See para 20.137ff above.

25.2   Reference has previously been made[1] to the incursions upon copyright owners' rights provided for in the EC Directive on the legal protection of computer programs.[2] In this chapter, fuller consideration will be given to the impact of European law upon the exercise of intellectual property rights. Reference will also be made towards the status and role of both de facto and official standards in the field of information technology.

[1]   See para 20.65 above.
[2]   Directive 91/250/EC, OJ 1991 L 122, p 42.

Copyright and competition

25.3   One of the basic tenets of the EC is that there shall be free movement of goods and services between member states. Article 36 of the EC Treaty provides for an exception to this in respect of prohibitions 'justified on grounds of ... the protection of industrial and commercial property'.

25.4   Whilst the provisions of the Treaty do not impact upon the existence of intellectual property rights, the European Court has held that the provisions of arts 81 and 82 (formerly arts 85 and 86), dealing with anti-competitive agreements between undertakings and conduct which is abusive of a dominant position, may restrict the extent to which they can be exercised.

25.5   One of the most significant actions concerning the application of art 86 of the EC Treaty within a computer context concerned proceedings instituted by the Commission against IBM. Unfortunately, from a legal perspective, the proceedings did not reach the stage of a Decision, but the factual situation is of some interest. The following passage is taken from the Commission's Fourteenth Report on Competition Policy, published in 1985.

In this proceeding, the Commission had alleged that IBM held a dominant position in the common market for the supply of the two key products of System/370 (the central processing unit and the operating system), so that IBM was able to control the markets for the supply of all products compatible with this system. In the statement of objections, IBM was alleged to have abused this dominant position:

(i)   by failing to supply other manufacturers in sufficient time with the technical information needed to permit competitive products to be used with System/370 ('interface information');
(ii)   by not offering System/370 central processing units ('CPUs') without a capacity of main memory included in the price ('memory bundling');
(iii)   by not offering System/370 CPUs without the basic software included in the price ('software bundling'); and
(iv)   by discriminating between users of IBM software, ie refusing to supply certain software installation services ('installation productivity options' – IPOs) to users of non-IBM CPUs.

While not admitting the existence of a dominant position, nor position nor any abuse thereof, IBM has now undertaken to offer its System/370 CPUs in the EEC either without main memory or with only such capacity as is strictly required for testing, and to disclose in a timely manner, sufficient interface information to enable competing companies in the EEC to attach both hardware and software products of their design to System/370. IBM will also disclose adequate and timely information to competitors to enable them to interconnect their systems or networks with IBM's System/370 using Systems Network Architecture. For interfaces to hardware products, information will be made available by IBM within four months of the date of announcement of the product concerned or at the general availability of the product, if earlier. For interfaces between software products, the information will now be made available as soon as the interface is reasonably stable, but no later than general availability.

> These undertakings do not extend to interfaces between two specific products of a subsystem, which are those most likely to reveal product design. This exception will not, however, exclude competition from suppliers who themselves offer products as a subsystem.
>
> The undertaking will have the effect of substantially improving the position of both users and competitors in the markets for System/370 products in the EEC. As a result, competition in the common market can be expected to be strengthened and made more effective. Users will now be given the possibility of a choice between different suppliers at an earlier time. They may also be free to choose from a wider selection of products because other manufacturers will now have the incentive to develop new products in the knowledge that the essential interface information will be made available.

---

[1] *Lotus Development Corpn v Paperback Software International and Stephenson Software Ltd* 740 F Supp 37 (1990). This case is discussed at para 20.138 above.

25.6 The IBM situation may be considered somewhat unusual on account of the dominant position enjoyed by this company, at least at the time in question. In other cases, the existence of copyright or patent rights in a product will confer an extremely dominant position upon the intellectual property right holder in respect of the subject matter of the right, but this person or company may not possess a dominant position in the market per se. Again, a distinction can be drawn between the situation as found in IBM, where information is required to enable functional compatibility, and the situation epitomised in the production of cloned versions of popular software packages, where compatibility offers commercial benefits but is not required in order to permit the software to operate. It might be argued, however, that the standards arguments advanced by the defendant in the US case of *Lotus v Paperback*[1] and summarily dismissed by the judge would have received at least more measured consideration had they been advanced before the European Court.

Decisions of the European Court

25.7 An illustration of the manner in which the provisions of competition policy will not prevent the exploitation of intellectual property rights can be taken from the case of *Volvo v Veng*.[1] Volvo produce motor vehicles; Veng specialised in the supply of replacement body panels for use in the repair of damaged vehicles. As part of this business, Veng imported into the UK panels for the front wing of the Volvo 200 series of motor car. Volvo instituted proceedings before the UK Patents Court alleging breach of its registered design right in the panels in question. In their defence, Veng argued, inter alia, that Volvo's refusal to grant them a licence upon reasonable terms to manufacture the components in question constituted an abuse of a dominant position.

[1]   [1988] ECR 6211.

25.8   The question of the compatibility of Volvo's conduct with the requirements of art 86 of the EC Treaty was referred to the Court of Justice for a preliminary ruling. Holding that there was no infringement of art 86, the court reiterated that in the absence of Community standardisation or of laws, the determination of the existence and extent of intellectual property rights was one for the member states. It went on:

> It must also be emphasized that the right of the proprietor of a protected design to prevent third parties from manufacturing and selling or importing, without its consent, products incorporating the design constitutes the very subject matter of his exclusive right. It follows that an obligation imposed upon the proprietor of a protected design to grant to third parties, even in return for a reasonable royalty, a licence for the supply of products incorporating the design would lead to the proprietor thereof being deprived of the substance of his exclusive right, and that a refusal to grant such a licence cannot in itself constitute an abuse of a dominant position.[1]

[1]   *Volvo v Veng* [1988] ECR 6211 at 6235.

25.9   The court went on to state, however, that the right of the proprietor was not total. In particular, it was indicated that art 86 of the EC Treaty might be invoked in response to:

> ... certain abusive conduct such as the arbitrary refusal to supply spare parts to independent repairers, the fixing of prices for spare parts at an unfair level or a decision no longer to produce spare parts for a particular model even though many cars of that model are still in circulation, provided that such conduct is liable to affect trade between Member States.[1]

[1]   *Volvo v Veng* [1988] ECR 6211.

Television listings

25.10   It is clear from the above comments that ownership of any of the species of intellectual property rights does not confer complete freedom of action upon the proprietor. The decision of the European Court of Justice in the case of *Radio Telefis Eireann (RTE) v European Commission*,[1] which brought to an end prolonged litigation concerning the plans of an independent publisher, Magill, to publish a weekly guide to television listings in Ireland, is of considerable significance. The case highlights the conflict between the rights of a copyright holder and the obligations imposed under the provisions of competition law.

[1]   [1995] All ER (EC) 416.

The Irish television market

25.11 In the Republic of Ireland and some parts of Northern Ireland, the population are able to choose from six television channels: the four available on the British mainland broadcast by the British Broadcasting Corporation (BBC) and by Independent Television (ITP) and, in addition, RTE and RTE2, which are broadcast by Radio Telefis Eireann (RTE) within the Irish Republic. At the time of the case, in neither part of Ireland were there available any comprehensive guides to all the channels. Each company (BBC, IBA and RTE) distributed its own separate guide in which copyright was claimed under the respective UK Copyright Act 1956 and Irish Copyright Act 1963, which prevent reproduction by any third party. Exclusive rights to publish and distribute weekly programme schedules were retained, although newspapers were provided with programme details to allow them to print daily schedules.

25.12 In May 1986, Magill Publications produced a magazine containing weekly programme schedules for all the television channels available in Ireland. The ITP, BBC and RTE successfully applied to an Irish court for an injunction to prevent continued publication of this guide on the ground that it infringed the copyright in the companies' programme schedules. These were held to be the result of a process of planning, preparation and the use of expert appraisal of content and layout and, as such, entitled to protection as compilations.

25.13 Prior to this decision, Magill had registered a complaint with the European Commission under arts 85 and 86 of the EC Treaty, arguing that the ITP, BBC and RTE were abusing a dominant position by refusing to allow third parties to publish their television listings. This complaint was investigated by the Commission, which issued a Decision on 21 December 1988.[1] This upheld Magill's complaints, finding that the ITP, BBC and RTE did hold a dominant position within art 86, that third parties were being prevented from competing by the existence of the monopoly enjoyed by the broadcasting companies and, further, that by claiming copyright an economic monopoly had been reinforced by a legal monopoly. The Commission rejected the argument that copyright was justified and stated its view that copyright was being used to prevent free competition. The broadcasting companies were ordered to permit reproduction of their programme schedules by granting licences to third parties. The three organisations involved brought an appeal against this decision before the European Court.

[1] Decision 89/205/EEC, OJ 1989 L 78, p 43.

25.14 A number of the arguments concerned the definition of the relevant market. In respect of the claim that the invocation of the appellants' intellectual property rights constituted an abuse under art 86 of the EC Treaty, it was argued that action taken to protect the subject of their intellectual property right could not constitute an abuse, and claimed that the Treaty did not affect such rights as were given in the member states. The existence of copyright allowed them to retain an exclusive right to reproduce the subject of the copyright protection.

25.15 The Commission rejected this view of the scope of copyright. The national rules granting copyright to television schedules, it was argued, allowed broadcasting companies to gain an unlawful monopoly on the production of weekly guides and prevented the publication of any competing guide. To this extent, the existence of copyright would obstruct the achievement of a single market in broadcasting services. To resolve the conflict between copyright and competition, the Commission indicated that the correct approach was to identify the 'specific subject matter' of the intellectual property right, which might qualify for special protection and which might justify an exception to the Community rules on competition.

25.16 The Commission first asserted that the television guides were not 'secret, innovative or related to research' and stated that the only reason for retaining copyright was to 'reserve a monopoly'. The sole reason for refusing to authorise the Magill guide was to prevent the publication of a competing product. The fact that programme information was distributed by the broadcasting companies to daily newspapers which do not compete with weekly guides was held to be arbitrary and discriminatory. A copyright holder could not choose to allow reproduction of its daily information and yet seek to prevent publication of a competing weekly guide. Enforcement of copyright was being used to restrict competition.

25.17 A distinction was drawn between the *Volvo* case[1] discussed at para 25.7ff above and the situation presently at issue. In the former case, the manufacturer reserved to itself the exclusive right to manufacture spare parts, ie no third parties were authorised to utilise the designs. By way of contrast, the television companies involved had authorised newspapers and other periodicals to publish their listings on a daily basis. This rendered their refusal to offer licences to Magill arbitrary. It was further pointed out that whilst the market for spare parts fell within the main part of a motor manufacturer's activities, the publishing of details of television broadcasts was an activity separate and downstream from that of broadcasting, which constituted the raison d'être of the appellants. Finally, the Commission pointed out that the effect of the appellants' conduct was to prevent the appearance of a new product (a general listings magazine) for which there was public demand. In the *Volvo* case, the products were available to the public whilst considerable competition remained both between independent repairers and from other manufacturers.

[1] *Volvo v Veng* [1988] ECR 6211.

25.18 After presenting this analysis the Commission commented significantly, if ambiguously, to the effect that:

> ... its analysis of the abuse of copyright applies also to situations different from that at issue in this case, in the area of computer software for example.[1]

[1] *Independent Television Publications v EC Commission* Case T-76/89 [1991] 4 CMLR 745 at 761.

25.19 Comparable conduct in this context might involve the owner of copyright in an operating system attempting to invoke copyright law to prevent a third party producing an applications package designed to function with the operating system. It might also extend to the situation where the owner of copyright in, for example, a word processing program, attempts to prevent a third party using aspects of their programs in a spreadsheet application. The existence of specific provisions in the software directive may mean, however, that the implications of the *Magill* decision[1] may be somewhat limited.

---

[1] *Independent Television Publications v. Commission of the European Communities* [1991] CMLR 745.

The Decision of the Court of First Instance[1]

25.20 The Court of First Instance upheld the Commission's Decision in all respects. Referring to previous decisions, it held that the reconciliation between the provisions of intellectual property law, which remained a matter for national authorities,[2] and the Treaty provisions relating to the free movement of goods and the maintenance of competition, required that a distinction be drawn between legitimate and illegitimate aspects of the exercise of the rights. Although in principle it was accepted that:

> ... the two essential rights of the author, namely the exclusive right of performance and the exclusive right of reproduction are not called in question by the rules of the [EC] Treaty.[3]

the court went on to state:

> ... while it is plain that the exercise of the exclusive right to reproduce a protected work is not in itself an abuse, that does not apply when, in the light of the details of each individual case, it is apparent that the right is exercised in such ways and circumstances as in fact to pursue an aim manifestly contrary to the objectives of Article 86. In that event, the copyright is no longer exercised in a manner which corresponds to its essential function ... which is to protect the moral rights in the work and to ensure a reward for the creative effort, while respecting the aims of, in particular, Article 86 [of the EC Treaty].[4]

---

[1] Separate judgments were issued against the three broadcasting companies involved. In all relevant respects, the judgments were identical. References in this section are to the court's judgment in the case involving Independent Television Publications.

[2] Subject now to a partial exception in the case of the Commission Directive on the Legal Protection of Computer Programs and Data, 91/250/EC, OJ 1991 L 122, p 42.

[3] *Warner Bros Inc v Christiansen* [1988] ECR 2605 at 2629.

[4] *Independent Television Publications v Commission of the European Communities* [1991] CMLR 745 at 767.

25.21 The concept of a distinction between the essential functions of intellectual property rights and any remaining attributes is one which may prove easier to define in principle than in practice. In terms of its application to software, whilst there is no doubt that a copyright owner may take action to prevent the direct copying of their work, it might be that attempts to prevent non-literal reproduction might infringe art 86 of the EC Treaty. Again, and always assuming that the copyright owner is accepted as occupying a dominant position, a refusal to issue licences to third parties to produce programs that were functionally compatible with the original might be considered unlawful.

The opinion of the Advocate General

25.22 An appeal was lodged by the television companies against the Court of First Instance's ruling. In 1994, the Advocate General (Gulmann) delivered an opinion supporting the appeal. After analysing relevant case law concerning the relationship between the Community's competition policy and the system of intellectual property rights he concluded that:

> The specific subject matter of copyright does unreservedly include a right to refuse to grant licences and the imposition of a compulsory licence pursuant to art 86 constitutes interference with the specific subject matter.[1]

1   [1991] 4 CMLR 745 at para 53.

25.23 It was only in the situation where an intellectual property right holder sought to exercise rights to prevent the development of a work which did not compete with the subject matter of the right that there would be any prospect that the provisions of art 86 of the EC Treaty could overrule this basic aspect of the copyright system. Continuing, the Advocate General addressed an argument advanced by the Commission that a distinction should be drawn between literary and artistic works and functional products such as computer programs. Concern was expressed by the Commission that a failure to grant licences in the software field could prevent effective competition and argued that the solution to such a problem should lie with legislation rather than a strained interpretation of the Treaty. Accordingly, he recommended that the decision of the Court of First Instance should be reversed.

The decision of the court

25.24 Notwithstanding the strong recommendations of the Advocate General, the Court of Justice affirmed the judgment of the Court of First Instance. Whilst:

> ... in the absence of Community standardisation or harmonisation of laws, determination of the conditions and procedures for granting protection of an intellectual property right is a matter for national rules. Further, the exclusive right of reproduction forms part of the author's rights, so that refusal to grant a licence, even if it is the act of an undertaking holding a dominant position, cannot in itself constitute abuse of a dominant position.[1]

In 'exceptional circumstances', however, it was held that the exercise of an exclusive right might constitute abusive conduct. This was the case in the present action, with the court determining that the appellant's conduct was such as to

561

prevent a new form of product appearing on the market. Stress was laid also on the fact that the market for TV guides constituted a secondary market to the appellant's broadcasting operations. Under these situations, a breach of art 86 of the EC Treaty had occurred.

¹ [1991] 4 CMLR 745 at para 49.

25.25 More difficult questions will arise concerning the extent to which the right owner might be compelled to permit the production of competing products, for example, the spreadsheet at issue in the US case of *Lotus v Paperback*.¹ In the situation where the later program has involved a considerable amount of independent work and where the utilisation of particular structures and sequences within the program is dictated by consumer preferences, it is at least arguable that the invocation of copyright or other rights might constitute a breach of art 86 of the EC Treaty. Thus, where a product has become a de facto standard, the endeavour to restrict its application to the original producer might be considered abusive. To some extent, this may provide the resolution to the difficulties identified above in respect of the utilisation of proprietary information within the standard-making process.

¹ *Lotus Development Corpn v Paperback Software International and Stephenson Software Ltd* 740 F Supp 37 (1990). See para 20.137ff above.

Computerised reservation systems

25.26 Almost all airline reservations are made through computerised reservation systems. The value of these to their owners may be gauged by the fact that in a number of cases, the reservation service has been valued more highly than the planes and other items of equipment owned by the company.

25.27 The cost of creating the reservation systems is so great that only the largest airlines can afford to engage in this activity, with smaller companies being compelled to rent space on these systems. Control over the contents and manner of operation of a reservation system constitutes a powerful marketing weapon. The flights of one airline may be presented in a manner which makes them more noticeable to a user.

25.28 In an attempt to minimise the distortions of competition that might arise from the control and use of reservation systems, the EC adopted a regulation containing a mandatory code of conduct for the use of these products.¹

¹ Regulation 2299/89/EEC, OJ 1989 L 220, p 1.

Scope of the regulation

25.29 The regulation applies to all computerised reservation systems offered for use within the Community. Two parties are identified in this respect.¹ A 'system vendor' is any entity involved in the provision of a system, whilst the term 'parent carrier' refers to an airline which, jointly or individually, owns such a system.

¹   Regulation 2299/89/EEC, art 2.

Conditions of supply

25.30   Effectively, the regulation seeks to ensure that there is no discrimination between users of a system. Subject to any external technical constraints, a system vendor must make the system available to any air carrier on a non-discriminatory basis.¹ The regulation contains provision relating to the manner in which flight information is to be displayed.² These are designed to ensure that no bias is shown in favour of the flights of one carrier.

¹   Regulation 2299/89/EEC, arts 3 and 9.
²   Annex.

25.31   Further obligations are imposed in respect of airlines which operate their own system. These may not require that travel agents or other users make use of their own or any other specified system. This is, however, subject to any conditions which may be imposed in contracts relating to the issuing of tickets.

Agreements for standardisation

25.32   Although art 85 prohibits agreements between undertakings which have as their object or effect the prevention, restriction or distortion of competition within the common market, and, in particular, those which 'limit or control production, markets, technical development or investment',¹ provision is made for exemption in respect of agreements whose effects are beneficial to the consumer. One such exception has been provided in respect of agreements whose sole object is the 'development or uniform application of standards or types'.² The operation of this provision was discussed in a Decision concerning an agreement relating to the use of the 'Unix' operating system.³ The agreement was entered into between nine computer companies, who formed what was referred to as the XOpen Group. The main goal of the group was to create industry standards relating to the Unix system, thereby overcoming some of the difficulties that existed through the availability of different and incompatible versions of Unix. The Commission Decision stated that this goal:

> ... was to be achieved by the creation of an open industry standard consisting in a stable but evolving common application environment.⁴

further:

> The Group will define this software environment by selecting existing interfaces; it has no primary intent of creating new interfaces. The Group will proceed, in due time, to the standardisation of selected interfaces by appropriate national and international standards organisations.⁵

¹   Regulation 2299/89/EEC, art 85(1)(b).

²   Article 4(2)(a). Regulation 17/62. Official Journal 1959–62, 87.
³   Decision 87/69/EEC, OJ 1987 L 35, p 36.
⁴   OJ 1987 L 35, para 9.
⁵   OJ 1987 L 35, para 10.

25.33 The agreement provided for the admission of new members to the group, for the taking of decisions affecting its conduct by a majority of its members in a vote and for the exchange of information between the parties subject to the imposition of obligations of confidence. Supplementary issues covered included the joint ownership of copyright in any documents produced as a result of the group's activities. Members of the group would not be obliged to produce items which conformed to the group's formulations.

25.34 Prior to reaching a decision as to whether the agreement qualified for an exemption under the provisions of art 85(3),[1] the Commission conducted an assessment of the likely impact of its provisions upon the competitive situation. It was recognised that the success of the group's efforts would be likely to prove attractive to software producers, who would be presented with a wide range of hardware upon which their equipment could operate. This would obviously benefit the members of the group, but concern was expressed at the position of non-members. Although the standards adopted by the group would be published and could be freely used by any third party, members would retain a competitive advantage in that their involvement in the standard production process would allow them to make plans for their implementation prior to the stage of formal publication. The Commission argued:

> The advantage in question is different in nature from the competitive advantage which the participants in a research and development project naturally hope to get over their competitors by offering a new product on the market; they hope that their new product will result in a demand from users but their competitors are not prevented from developing a competing product, whereas in the present case non-members wishing to implement the standard cannot do so before the standard becomes publicly available and, therefore, are placed in a situation of dependence as to the member's definitions and the publication thereof.[2]

¹   Regulation 2299/89/EEC, art 85(3).
²   OJ 1987 L 35, para 32.

25.35 Concern was expressed at the possibility that membership of the group might be used as a means of discriminating against competitors. It was recognised, however, that the group was both entitled and commercially obliged to maintain controls over membership. A situation of open membership would, it was accepted, 'create practical and logistic difficulties for the management of the work and possibly prevent appropriate proposals being passed'.[1] Overall, the benefits potentially available from the agreement, especially the availability of a wider range of software and enhanced interchangeability between items of hardware from different manufacturers,[2] were considered to outweigh the competitive disadvantages, and the agreement was granted an exemption under art 85(3),[3] subject to the imposition of an obligation to notify the Commission of any changes in the membership of the group and to report annually on any cases in which an application for membership was refused.

1   OJ 1987 L 35, para 45.
2   OJ 1987 L 35, para 44.
3   Regulation 2299/89/EEC, art 85(3).

Intellectual property rights and standards

25.36   Considerable effort is being expended by the EC in the standard-making field. In its Communication on 'Standardization and the Global Information Society',[1] the Commission argued that:

> Standards are not only a technical question. They determine the technology that will implement the Information Society, and consequently the way in which industry, users, consumers and administrations will benefit from it.

In large measure, this is prompted by the recognition that the development of European standards will assist to make the Single Market a reality. Linked to standardisation is the topic of certification, where an independent party certifies that a product conforms with specified standards.

1   COM (96) 359.

25.37   Much of the standard-making work is being conducted within the information technology field. The European Telecommunications Standards Institute has been established to develop standards, principally concerned with issues of compatibility in the telecommunications sector. At a wider level, the European Committee for Electrotechnical Standardisation (CENELEC) has promulgated a number of standards in the area of information technology. The EC's 'Tedis' programme was introduced to assist in the development of standards in the field of electronic trade.[1]

1   See http://cwis.kub.nl/~frw/people/hof/tedis.htm.

25.38   In a Decision of 1986 on standardisation in the field of information technology and telecommunications,[1] the Council recognised a need for standards or equivalent measures to 'ensure the precision required by users for exchange of information and data and systems interoperability',[2] and indicated that the Community standardisation bodies would be invited to pursue initiatives in this area.[3] To date, more than 150 standardisation orders have been submitted to CENELEC and ETSI.

1   Decision 87/95/EEC, OJ 1987 L 36, p 31.
2   Article 2(b).
3   Article 4.

25.39   In addition to encouraging the production of standards, the 1986 Decision attempts to encourage their use by providing that public procurement agencies must make reference to any relevant European standards when seeking tenders for the supply of such equipment.[1]

[1] Decision 87/95/EEC, art 5.

25.40 The near-universal availability of copyright in respect of the software controlling the operation of information technology products, coupled with the possibility that patents may be awarded, poses considerable problems for those involved in standardisation.

25.41 Problems may arise in two respects. First, the inclusion of material protected by intellectual property rights, perhaps details of an interface, may serve to increase the value of the right holder if anyone wishing to utilise the standard will have to come to an agreement regarding the use of those aspects covered by the intellectual property right.

25.42 A second problem is especially acute in respect of patents, where the duration of the award process may result in a number of years passing between an application being submitted and the details of the patent being publicised. In a field characterised by rapid technical development, there is a real danger that parties may discover that they have innocently been violating the terms of a patent.[1]

[1] The fact that standard-making processes may themselves occupy a number of years will minimise this possibility.

25.43 One approach to this topic is found in the policy of ETSI, which requires as a condition of membership that an undertaking is given to licence the use of any intellectual property rights for standardisation purposes. The Commission, in their recent communication on intellectual property rights and standardisation,[1] establishes a number of principles which it is recommended should be followed by standard-making bodies. Essentially, these envisage that the standard-making bodies will make reasonable efforts to identify the existence and ownership of intellectual property rights which may exist in a particular area, and that the latter party should either indicate a refusal to allow their property to be utilised for such a purpose or negotiate reasonable licence agreements. Where conformance with standards is rendered mandatory by some provision of Community or national law, there is an obligation upon the law maker to ensure that access to the standard is available to all parties on a non-discriminatory basis.

[1] COM (92) 445 final.

25.44 It is uncertain how effective these provisions might be in respect of information technology. Perhaps ominously, the communication notes that:

> In the telecommunications area an argument has been made by some that the advances in technology are so rapid and the degree of involvement of intellectual property rights so great that existing ... rules are inadequate.[1]

In this, as in other areas of the subject, the application of established legal principles to the products of the information age appears to create considerable tensions and difficulties.

[1]   At para 4.8.6.

Chapter 26

Contractual liability for defective software

Introduction

26.1 Software is undoubtedly the driving force of the information society.[1] By any standards, the sector is a major contributor to national economies and employment and it should be borne in mind that these figures relate to only one part of the information technology industry. The traditional notion of a computer is that it consists of a monitor, processing unit, keyboard and sundry peripherals such as the ubiquitous mouse. Most people will recognise such a device when they see one. It is less easy to recognise a motor car or video recorder as a computer, yet a modern motor car is in many respects a sophisticated computer system to the extent it has been calculated that the 'chip cost of a new car is now greater than the metal cost'.[1] A vast range of objects, from domestic appliances to nuclear power stations, is dependent on microprocessors. In many cases, these are, quite literally, built into a structure. Worldwide, it is estimated that there are some 20 billion embedded chips in use, a fact which cased great concern in the context of the Millennium Bug. In has been reported that:

> All buildings built between 1984 (the year when building services started to computerise) and 1996/7 (the period when most new buildings were fitted with systems that were millennium compliant) are likely to be affected by the millennium bug. Bovis Construction Group, one of the biggest building contractors has written to the owners of 870 buildings it has built since 1984 warning them integral systems ranging from ventilation and heating to intruder alarms and connections to the electricity supply network may fail. This is because many building systems use microchips to identify dates for switching machinery on and off and to alert maintenance staff of the need for servicing.[2]

---

[1] http://www.scl.org/members/emagazine/vol9/iss3/vol9-iss3-peter-cochrane-art.htm.
[2] Cited in evidence to the House of Commons Select Committee on Science and Technology.

26.2   As the importance of software increases, so does the level of societal vulnerability in the event of any failure. In purely economic terms, losses are potentially massive. Although it is tempting to take the example of the Millennium Bug as a case where the degree of risk was exaggerated, even what might be regarded as a false alarm proved an extremely costly exercise. The British Bankers Association estimated that UK banks spent £1bn checking and repairing systems. British Telecom budgeted for expenditure of £300m. Worldwide, costs were estimated at some £400bn. To put these figures into perspective, these figures exceed the total financial cost of the Vietnam War.[1]

[1]   *The Sunday Times*, 10 August 1997. The cost of the Vietnam War has been estimated at some £370bn.

26.3   Matters could, of course, have been significantly worse in the event extensive problems had materialised. One estimate suggested that the effect of the bug would cause 8% of Western European companies to fail. The prospect of global recession was frequently raised in reports. Additionally, as indicated above, the application of information technology in a vast range of applications conjured up the spectre of hospital patients dying because of failures of medical devices; trains, planes and automobiles crashing; massive power cuts; and shortage of food and drink due to failures in retailers' distribution systems. Fortunately, the predictions of computer doom proved unfounded, but the incident may have served a useful, albeit expensive, purpose in bringing home the extent of our society's dependence on information technology. What the incident also achieved was to highlight the fact that where losses arise through the improper operation of systems and equipment, considerations of legal liability will not be far behind.

26.4   To date, comparatively few cases concerned specifically with issues of software quality have reached the stage of court proceedings. A variety of explanations may be proposed for this state of affairs. Although parties may not wish to litigate when the answer is certain, excessive uncertainty as to the very basis upon which a court may decide will itself inhibit litigation. Some of the most basic questions concerning the application of provisions of contractual and non-contractual liability in the information technology field admit of no easy or certain answer. With one exception, all of the cases which have reached the stage of High Court proceedings have concerned relatively high-value contracts for software which has either been developed under the terms of a specific contract (bespoke software) for one or a small number of clients or which has been modified extensively to suit the needs of a particular customer (customised software). To date, there have been no cases concerned with the extent of the liabilities which will apply to mass-produced or standard software packages such as word processing or spreadsheet programs. A further factor complicating such cases is the invariable presence of a software licence. The role of these documents in respect of intellectual property issues has been discussed previously. In respect of liability considerations, the terms of the licence inevitably seek to limit or exclude the producer's liabilities in the event the performance of the software does not match the user's expectations.

Forms of liability

26.5 Two main strands of liability run through the field of private law. The law of contract confers rights and imposes duties upon contracting parties. Whilst the nature and extent of these may be determined in large part by the expressed wishes of the parties, these may be constrained by the provisions of statutes such as the Sale of Goods Act 1979 and the Unfair Contract Terms Act 1977. It is, of course, a basic tenet of the common law that contractual rights can be enforced only by those who are a party to the contract. In the situation where no contract exists, attention must turn to non-contractual remedies. Until recently, the basis of these has rested in the law of tort/delict. The prerequisite for a successful action in tort is evidence of negligence on the part of the defender (absent exceptional circumstances where strict liability has attached to this party's actions). The passage of the Consumer Protection Act 1987 has radically transformed the non-contractual position. Based on the provisions of an EC Directive on 'the approximation of the laws, regulations and administrative provisions of the member states concerning liability for defective products',[1] this serves to impose a strict liability regime whereby the producer of a product is held liable for personal injury or damage to non-commercial property resulting from the presence of a defect within the product, irrespective of any fault on their part.

[1]   Council Directive 85/374/EEC, OJ 1985 L 210, p 29.

The nature of software defects

26.6   Prior to considering issues of legal liability, it might be helpful to attempt a brief analysis of the nature of the differences which exist between software and the tangible products with which society and the law are more familiar. Defects in a traditional product such as a motor car may originate in one of two ways. Design defects relate to some failure at the design stage, with the consequence that the failure node will be exhibited in every species of the product. A more commonplace form of defect is introduced during the production stage. It might be, for example, as happened in the case of *Smedleys v Breed*,[1] discussed below,[2] that a caterpillar found its way into a can of peas somewhere within the canning process. Such defects will be restricted to one or to a limited number of examples of the product. In the *Smedleys* case, for example, only four caterpillars or other foreign bodies had been reported from an annual production of 3.5 million cans.

[1]   [1974] AC 839.
[2]   See para 27.78ff below.

26.7   If a party is trying to establish that a product fails to comply with relevant quality requirements, the task is almost invariably simpler where defects arise in production. In most cases, what a claimant will seek to establish is that compared with other examples of a product, the one at issue is of inferior quality. The case might be put, for example, that 3,499,996 cans of peas did not contain foreign bodies. The four that did should, therefore, be considered exceptional (or exceptionally bad). Evidential burdens are more extensive when all examples of the product exhibit the same properties. A prime example is in the pharmaceutical field, where adverse reactions to a product are generally caused because of the properties of the drug rather than through contamination of a particular tablet or bottle of medicine.

26.8 Where software is concerned, the nature of the digital copying process is such that there can be a high degree of confidence that every copy of software will be identical. If particular copies are corrupted, the likelihood is that they will not work at all, so that any defect becomes apparent before any damage is caused. If a customer should wish to establish that a copy of a word processing program which has been purchased is not of satisfactory quality, argument will have to proceed by reference to word processing programs produced by other producers and to general standards. Although the task can be accomplished, it is a significantly more onerous burden than that faced by a person claiming the existence of a production defect.

26.9 A more general difference may be identified at the level of the testing which may be carried out in respect of a product. With a product such as a motor car, it is possible to test every component so as to provide definitive information about its properties. Often, however, testing entails destruction of the item involved and, even where this is not the case, it will seldom be commercially feasible to test every specimen of the product. In production, it is possible that some components will be of inferior quality to those tested. Only a portion of products will be possess any particular defect and these may not be the ones which are selected for inspection. The conclusion from this analysis is that it is possible to test one item exhaustively, but that the results have limited applicability regarding other items of the same type.

26.10 The situation is radically different where software is concerned. It is impossible to test even the simplest program in an exhaustive fashion. This is because of the myriad possibilities for interaction (whether desired or not) between the various elements of the program. In the world of popular science, much publicity has been given in recent years to what is known as the chaos theory. This suggests that every event influences every other event; that the beating of a butterfly's wings has an impact upon the development of a hurricane. On such an analysis, totally accurate weather forecasting will never be practicable because of the impossibility of taking account of all the variables affecting the climate. The theory's hypothesis is reality in a software context. Although software can and should be tested, it has to be accepted that every piece of software will contain errors which may not materialise until a particular and perhaps unrepeatable set of circumstances occurs. It is commonplace for software to be placed on the market in the knowledge that it contains errors. Early users, in effect, act as unpaid testers. As faults are reported to the producer, fixes will be developed and incorporated in new versions of the software.[1]

26.11 Especially where software is used in safety-critical functions, it is sometimes advocated that where an error is discovered, it is preferable to devise procedures to prevent the circumstances recurring than to attempt to modify the software. The argument is that any change to the software may have unanticipated consequences resulting in another error manifesting itself at some time in the future. The cause of a massive failure which paralysed sections of the US telecommunications system in 1991 was ultimately traced to changes which had been made in the call-routing software.[1] The software contained several million lines of code. Three apparently insignificant lines were changed and chaos ensued. By way of contrast, the operators of London's Docklands Light Railway, whose trains are driven under computer control, took the decision that they would not make any changes to the software after it had passed its acceptance tests. The result was that for several years trains stopped on an open stretch of line, paused for a few seconds and then continued with their journey. It had been intended to build a station at the site. After the software was accepted the plans were abandoned, but the trains remained ignorant of this fact.

¹   Most of the examples of software failure cited in this chapter have been culled from the columns of comp.risks, an Internet-based newsgroup which chronicles the failures of safety-critical systems and the risks they pose to the public.

Forms of software

26.12 As indicated above, software is supplied in a variety of situations and under a range of conditions. Viewed across the spectrum, at one end we can identify bespoke or made-to-measure software products. The cost of these may run into many millions of pounds, with the essential feature being that the supplier agrees to design and develop software to suit the needs of a particular customer, or a comparatively small number of identified customers. The software will be supplied under the terms of a written agreement negotiated between the parties. Perhaps not surprisingly, given the costs involved, almost all of the software-related disputes which have reached the courts have been concerned with such forms of contract.

26.13 At the far end of the software spectrum are standard software packages. In this category, identical copies will be supplied to users – perhaps tens or even hundreds of thousands in number – often via a substantial distribution chain and at a cost ranging from tens to thousands of pounds. There will seldom be any written agreement negotiated in advance between the parties, with the producer attempting to introduce a set of terms and conditions through the device of a licence. As will be discussed below, the validity of software licences is open to challenge on a number of grounds.

26.14 A final and more nebulous category of software is referred to as having been 'customised'. This involves the supplier modifying existing software, developed either by themselves or a third party, better to suit the requirements of a particular customer. The degree of customisation may vary from making very minor adjustments to a single package, to developing a unique system based on a combination of a number of existing packages. With developments in 'object oriented engineering' it may be expected that the range of customised products will increase substantially as developers base their operations on a 'pick and mix' philosophy.

The legal status of software and software contracts

26.15 Throughout this book, use has been made of terms such as 'software industry' and of software being 'produced'. Such terms are in common use. The pages on the Microsoft website describing its software packages are titled 'products',[1] whilst the Price Waterhouse study discussed in the context of copyright law[2] is titled 'The Contribution of the Packaged Software Industry to the European Economies'. The fact that terms are in popular usage does not, of course, mean that their legal interpretation will be the same, and over the years much legal ink has been spilled in discussion of the question whether contracts for the supply of software should be regarded as a species of goods or as a form of services.

[1] http://www.microsoft.com/office/products.htm.
[2] See para 20.56 above.

26.16 Much of the discussion regarding status has focused on two decisions of the Court of Appeal. In *Lee v Griffin*,[1] the Court of Appeal was faced with a contract under which a dentist undertook to make a set of dentures for a patient. A dispute subsequently arising, the court was faced with the question of the contract's proper categorisation. Holding the contract to be one of sale, the court held that the essential test was whether anything that could be the subject matter of a sale had come into existence. In the event, for example, that an attorney was engaged to draw up a deed for a client, it was held that the contract would be one for services. In other situations, however:

> I do not think that the test to apply to these cases is whether the value of the work exceeds that of the materials used in its execution; for, if a sculptor were employed to execute a work of art, greatly as his skill and labour, assuming it to be of the highest description, might exceed the value of the marble on which he worked, the contract would in my opinion, nevertheless be a contract for the sale of a chattel.[2]

On this basis, it would appear that the supply of software on some storage device such as a disk or CD would be classed as involving goods. The increasingly common situation where software is supplied electronically, typically being downloaded from a website, could not, of course, come within the definition.

1   (1861) 1 B&S 272.
2   (1861) 1 B&S 272 at 278.

26.17   The distinction between goods and services was again at issue before the Court of Appeal in the case of *Robinson v Graves*.[1] The contract here was one whereby an artist agreed to paint a portrait of his client's wife. On the basis of the situation hypothesised in *Lee v Griffin*,[2] it would appear that such a transaction should be regarded as one of sale. In the event, however, it was held that it should be regarded as one for services. In reaching this conclusion, the court sought to identify the prime purpose of the contract. In the oft-quoted words of Greer LJ:

> If the substance of the contract ... is that skill and labour have to be exercised for the production of the article and ... it is only ancillary to that that there will pass from the artist to his client or customer some materials in addition to the skill involved in the production of the portrait, that does not make any difference to the result, because the substance of the contract is the skill and experience of the artist in producing the picture.[3]

1   [1935] 1 KB 579.
2   (1861) 1 B&S 272.
3   [1935] 1 KB 579 at 587.

26.18   Although the court in *Robinson*[1] did not overrule, or even distinguish, the earlier authority, it must be doubted how far the two approaches can truly be considered compatible. It would appear that the decision in *Robinson* has been the more influential in recent years but, even so, its application in a software context has not been without its difficulties. Whilst it would seem to suggest that contracts for the development of bespoke software should be regarded as services, standard software exhibits many of the attributes associated with goods.

1   *Robinson v Graves* [1935] 1 KB 579.

26.19   In the final analysis, the precise categorisation of software contracts may be a matter of limited practical significance. In most of the cases which have come before the courts, the dispute has centred on the interpretation of a specific contract between the parties. The court's task is to determine what the contract said rather than concern itself unduly with categorisations. Even where no detailed contract exists, there is little difference between the relevant statutory provisions. The Sale of Goods Act 1979 implies terms relating to title description and quality. The Supply of Goods and Services Act 1982 implies requirements that the supplier should exercise reasonable skill and care and that any goods ultimately supplied will comply with identical requirements relating to title, description and quality as those required under the Sale of Goods Act 1979. Faced with this convergence between the statutory provisions, it is not surprising that Staughton LJ delivering judgment in the case of *Saphena Computing Ltd v Allied Collection Agencies Ltd* was able to state:

> It was, we are told, common ground that the law governing these contracts was precisely the same whether they were contracts for the sale of goods or for the

supply of services. It is therefore unnecessary to consider into which category they might come.[1]

1   [1995] FSR 616 at 652.

26.20 In the case of *St Albans District Council v ICL*,[1] the Court of Appeal were braver – or more foolhardy. Here, Sir Iain Glidewell posed the question 'Is software goods?' He continued:

> If a disc carrying the program is transferred, by way of sale or hire, and the program is in some way defective, so that it will not instruct or enable the computer to achieve the intended purpose, is this a defect in the disc? Put more precisely, would the seller or hirer of the disc be in breach of the terms of quality or fitness implied by s.14 of the Sale of Goods Act [1979].[2]

There was, he recognised, no English or indeed any common law precedent on this point. An analogy was drawn, however with another form of informational product:

> Suppose I buy an instruction manual on the maintenance and repair of a particular make of car. The instructions are wrong in an important respect. Anybody who follows them is likely to cause serious damage to the engine of his car. In my view the instructions are an integral part of the manual. The manual including the instructions, whether in a book or a video cassette, would in my opinion be 'goods' within the meaning of the Sale of Goods Act and the defective instructions would result in breach of the implied terms.
>   If this is correct, I can see no logical reason why it should not also be correct in relation to a computer disc onto which a program designed and intended to instruct or enable a computer to achieve particular functions has been encoded. If the disc is sold or hired by the computer manufacturer, but the program is defective, in my opinion there would prima facie be a breach of the terms as to quality and fitness for purpose implied by the Sale of Goods Act.[3]

1   [1996] 4 All ER 481. Reported at first instance at [1995] FSR 686.
2   [1996] 4 All ER 481 at 492.
3   [1996] 4 All ER 481 at 493.

26.21 As will be discussed, this statement will have implications for all of those involved in the information market. In the case of *Wormell v RHM Agriculture Ltd*,[1] the Court of Appeal recognised that where instructions for use were supplied along with a product, the sufficiency and adequacy of these should be taken into account in considering questions of the product's merchantability. *St Albans District Council v ICL*[2] appears, however, to be the first occasion in which instructions per se were subjected to the qualitative requirements of the Sale of Goods Act 1979. It remains uncertain, however, how extensive liability will be. The analogy drawn with a motor instruction book may be appropriate. In the circumstances described, where following the instructions will result in serious damage, there could be little argument that the book is not fit for its purpose. The decision becomes much closer if the complaint is that the book describes an inefficient method for performing work. Another problematic case might be where an instruction is so obviously wrong that no reasonable person would follow it. Equivalents in a software context might be inefficient methods of saving word processed documents or defects which require a user to 'work around' them. Further cases will be required before we can attempt a plausible answer to the question of what these qualitative requirements mean in a software context.

1   [1987] 3 All ER 75.
2   [1996] 4 All ER 481.

26.22   There is, of course, the increasing possibility that software might be downloaded over the Internet so that no tangible objects change hands. Indeed, in the present case, the practice for installing software was that an ICL engineer would visit, load the software from disk and retain the disk. In such cases, there could be no transfer of goods. In such situations, it was indicated, in determining the extent of the parties' obligations:

> The answer must be sought in the Common Law. The terms implied by the Sale of Goods Act ... were originally evolved by the Courts of Common Law and have since by analogy been implied by the courts into other types of contract.
> ...
> In the absence of any express term as to quality or fitness for purpose, or of any term to the contrary, such a contract is subject to an implied term that the program will be reasonably fit for, i.e. reasonably capable of achieving the intended purpose.[1]

1   *St Albans District Council v ICL* [1996] 4 All ER 481 at 494.

26.23   Given the existence of a specific contract between the parties, these comments must be regarded as obiter dicta rather than as binding precedent. They do appear, however, to be in line with a judicial trend to imply requirements that software be fit for its purpose into contracts unless the terms make clear provision to the contrary. Any ambiguities will be interpreted contra proferentem, with the case of *Salvage Association v CAP Financial Services*[1] providing a good illustration of how restrictive this doctrine may be. The key issue, therefore, must be to determine what concepts, such as fitness and the newly introduced requirement that goods be of 'satisfactory quality', might mean in an informational context.

1   (9 July 1993, unreported), CA. The case is reported at first instance at [1995] FSR 654.

Implied terms in software contracts

26.24   The Sale of Goods Act 1979 provides for three conditions to be implied into a contract of sale. Although there is room for argument whether software is generally sold by virtue of the fact that intellectual property rights will remain with the original owner, the Supply of Goods and Services Act 1982 provides that the implied terms will extend to any other contract for the supply of goods. Although interpretative problems may remain in the situation discussed above, where software is supplied over, for example, the Internet, the categorisation of contracts as forms of sale or rental or loan is of no significance. Reference throughout this section will be to the provisions of the Sale of Goods Act 1979, as amended by the Sale and Supply of Goods Act 1994.

26.25 One of the cornerstones of English commercial law has been the doctrine of caveat emptor ('let the buyer beware'). Traditionally, no provisions relating to the quality of goods has been implied into contracts of sale. In previous eras, this approach was not as inequitable as it might appear in the twenty-first century. Goods were simple in nature and composition, and it was a feasible task for a buyer to make an assessment of their condition and suitability. As goods became more sophisticated, it became increasingly difficult for an inexpert customer to examine them. Even if a potential buyer were to wish to do this, the reaction of the seller of a computer could well be predicted in the event a customer were to produce a screwdriver and seek to disassemble the equipment. The notion of the implied term has been developed, first by the courts and now enshrined in statute, as a means for protecting the interests of the consumer. In general law, of course, an implied term is overridden by any contrary express agreement made between the parties. Often such an express term will seek to reduce or exclude the liability of the seller in the event the performance of the goods is inadequate. Again, the first attempts to control these contractual tactics were made by the courts, with Parliament intervening in 1977 with the passage of the Unfair Contract Terms Act 1977. The following sections will consider the extent of the obligations implied by law into contracts for the supply of software. Attention will then be paid to the extent to which these might validly or lawfully be reduced by the application of devices such as licences or contractual terms.

Title in software

26.26 By virtue of s 12 of the Sale of Goods Act 1979, a seller must guarantee that he or she possesses the right to sell the goods and that full title to the goods will be transferred to the buyer, except for such limitations as are brought to the buyer's attention prior to the contract of sale. In terms of the usage of the goods, it is provided that the buyer is to enjoy 'quiet possession'. This entails that the buyer's freedom to deal with the goods in such manner as might be desired is not to be restricted by virtue of any rights retained by the seller or by some third party. In many cases concerned with software, the sale will be made by a retailer, with the producer retaining ownership of copyright in the work and remaining an interested third party.

26.27 The major limitations imposed upon the buyer's freedom to deal with software are found in the copyright legislation. As has been seen, the mere use of software might constitute a breach of copyright. The buyer's right under s 12 of the Sale of Goods Act 1979 is always subject to the caveat that the use proposed is lawful. The terms of the European Directive on the Legal Protection of Computer Programs[1] might have implications for the operation of s 12. Under the Directive, a number of forms of behaviour concerned with software, for example, modification for the purpose of error correction, will be permitted unless the terms of a contract or licence provide otherwise. Where the copyright owner intends to exercise this option and seeks to do so by means of a licence document whose contents are not disclosed to the buyer until after the contract of sale is concluded, the failure to give prior notice might place the seller in breach of s 12.

[1]   Directive 91/250/EC, OJ 1991 L 122/42.

Description

26.28   Section 13 of the Sale of Goods Act 1979 provides that where a sale is by description, there is to be an implied condition that the goods will correspond with this description. In the course of many contracts of sale, a variety of claims may be made concerning the attributes of the product involved. Not all such elements will be incorporated into the final contract. Many laudatory phrases, typically used in promotional materials, will be regarded as too general. A claim that a product is 'user-friendly' might, for example, be regarded as insufficiently precise to be considered as a description, although in such cases it may be that an action will lie on the ground of misrepresentation.

26.29   Claims of compatibility with other products, typically that a piece of software will operate on a specified piece of hardware, might be regarded as descriptive. Equally, lists of the features possessed by a product will be considered as part of its description, although even here the matter may not be beyond doubt. In the case of a popular laser printer, for example, the product specification made reference to a printing speed of four pages per minute. The statement appears true, but what is not made clear is that the printer can only print four copies of the same page in any given minute. The printing process requires that data regarding the contents of any page be transmitted from the computer to the printer. This process takes some time, with the result that the speed for printing a multi-page document slows to little more than a single page per minute. One factor which is relevant throughout all the discussion of liability is the absence of clearly defined industry standards and conventions. In the absence of these in respect of speed of printing or many other attributes concerned with the functioning of information technology systems, it may be difficult to establish liability in respect of claims that are accurate but potentially misleading.

Quality requirements

26.30   The Sale of Goods Act 1979 requirements relating to product quality are so well known that little exposition is required. Two partially overlapping conditions will be implied into a contract of sale. Goods must be of satisfactory quality and reasonably fit for any particular purpose for which they are supplied.[1] The requirement that goods supplied be of satisfactory quality was introduced in 1995 in substitution for the concept of merchantable quality. The notion of merchantable quality can be traced back to the Middle Ages. It assumed statutory form for the first time in the Sale of Goods Act 1893 and was retained in the Sale of Goods Act 1979. The latter statute also introduced a new definition, providing that goods would be of merchantable quality if they are:

> ... as fit for the purpose or purposes for which goods of that kind are commonly bought as it was reasonable to expect having regard to any description applied to them, the price (if relevant) and all the other relevant circumstances.[2]

[1] Section 14.
[2] Section 14(6).

26.31 The law relating to sale of goods was the subject of a report by the Law Commissions in 1987.[1] This expressed concerns at the suitability of the venerable concept of merchantability to deal with the complexities inherent in many modern products. Beyond the issue of whether the terminology itself was not unduly archaic, the notion of a general requirement of fitness for purpose (as opposed to the more specific instantation in the second implied term) was developed in an era of comparatively simple products, which would either work or fail to work. With a modern product, such as a motor car or a software product, the manner or quality of performance is of at least as much importance.

[1] A Joint Report was published: Law Com no 160, Scots Law Com no 104, Cm 137.

26.32 Acting on the Law Commissions' recommendations, the Sale and Supply of Goods Act 1994 substituted the requirement that goods be of satisfactory quality. The definition of the new requirement retains echoes of its predecessor. It is now provided that:

> ... goods are of satisfactory quality if they meet the standard that a reasonable person would regard as satisfactory, taking account of any description of the goods, the price (if relevant) and all the other relevant circumstances.[1]

The statute goes on, however, to list a number of specific factors which are to be taken into account in determining whether goods are of satisfactory quality:

> ... the following (among others) are in appropriate cases aspects of the quality of goods:
>
> (a) fitness for all the purposes for which goods of the kind in question are commonly supplied;
> (b) appearance and finish;
> (c) freedom from minor defects;
> (d) safety, and
> (e) durability.

[1] Sale of Goods Act 1979, s 14.

26.33 A number of points from this new definition may be of considerable significance in a software context. Problems have arisen in the past where an object is fit for only some of its normal purposes.[1] An integrated spreadsheet/word processing/database package, for example, might perform satisfactorily in two modes but be unworkable in the third. A design package may be satisfactory for external designs but unsuited for internal design. It is now stated clearly that products must be fit for all the purposes for which they are commonly supplied. Products of the kind mentioned above will fail to meet the statutory requirement. Producers will be well advised to give greater care to the descriptions of their products and, at the risk of blunting their marketing strategy, make clear any design limitations applying to the product.

[1]   *Aswan Engineering v Lupdine* [1987] 1 WLR 1.

26.34 A number of the other features of the definition of satisfactory quality will also be relevant in a computer context. The criteria relating to appearance and finish might be invoked in respect of the user interface and screen displays of a software product. Perhaps the biggest source of problems may arise with the specific mention of 'freedom from minor defects'. Given that all software products contain defects, this may be of considerable significance. It must be stressed, however, that the Sale of Goods Act 1979 does not require that goods be perfect. The standard relates to the expectations of a 'reasonable person'. The major impact may lie in the fact that the specific mention of minor defects may be expected to draw a court's attention to this aspect of an allegedly defective product. Assessment of software product causes particular difficulties. With most products, defects are likely to be introduced at the production stage. If a complaint relates to the allegedly defective performance of a television set, the item at issue can normally be compared with other examples of the same model produced by the same manufacturer. Given the fact that all copies of a software product are likely to be identical, the only basis for comparison will be with the products of competitors. This creates problems in comparing like with like.

26.35 The decision as to whether a product is satisfactory is a factual one. A variety of factors may be taken into account. The question of price is one which is of considerable weight in many cases. In *Rogers v Parish*, Mustill LJ stated that '(t)he buyer was entitled to value for his money'.[1] In the vast majority of cases, one might reasonably expect that a more expensive product will be of better quality than a lower-priced alternative. This approach may break down to some extent in the context of software. The physical components make up such a small part of the value of a package that it is unlikely that any significant variation might be expected here. The point can also be made that it is easier and cheaper to emulate than to innovate. On this basis, and ignoring possible intellectual property complications, it might not be unreasonable to expect a lower-priced derivative package to attain a similar level of quality to that of the original. The speed of development in the entire information technology field also makes difficult the task of determining issues of quality and value for money. A product which might have been regarded as of acceptable quality if sold for

£500 on 1 January might be regarded much less favourably if sold for the same amount (or even a lower price) on the following 31 December.

[1] [1987] 2 All ER 232 at 237.

26.36 Further problems may arise in determining the proper purpose of an item of software. Difficulties may be exacerbated by a lack of customer knowledge, as epitomised in the first software disputes to reach the courts, *MacKenzie Patten v British Olivetti*.[1] In this case, the plaintiff, a small firm of solicitors, entered into an agreement for the supply of a computer in the apparent belief that this would be able to access court schedules held on a computer at the Old Bailey. This notwithstanding the fact that neither computer possessed any form of communications capability. It is also the case, of course, that design limitations are not as apparent in software products as may normally be the case. Under the provisions of the Sale of Goods Act 1979, a customer wishing to receive the benefit of the fitness for purpose condition is obliged to inform the seller if it is intended to put the product to some unusual purpose. No specific mention need be made if the product is intended to be put to its normal use. 'Normal' in this sense may be interpreted in two ways. First, consideration must be given to the normal uses of a product of the type in question. Thus, a screwdriver is to be used to insert and remove screws. Use as a crowbar would not be classed as normal. A second element might relate to the scale of the intended use. Most products might be intended for a specific sector of a market. A low-cost and low-powered electric drill might be suitable for occasional use in domestic circumstances, but would not be fit for intensive use by a professional builder or joiner. With most products of this kind, design limitations will be apparent. A customer putting a product to excessive use might not receive the court's sympathy in the event of a claim that the product was not fit for its purpose. With software products, design limitations will be much less transparent. A disc retailing at £10,000 will look no different from a blank disc worth a few pence. The development of cheap personal computers has led to the marketing of 'cut-down' versions of computer programs originally designed for the commercial market. Intended for domestic use, these may be marketed on the back of the original but may lack some of its features and capabilities. This may render the program unfit for use at a commercial level of activity. The limitations will not be as apparent as with the electric drill, and sellers may be faced with a dilemma. If they do not make them clear to potential buyers, they may run the risk that a naïve and inexperienced business user may purchase the product and find it unsuitable, whilst drawing excessive attention to the limitations of the product might not be advisable in marketing terms.

[1] (1985) 48 MLR 344.

Remedies for breach of the implied terms

26.37 In the event of a breach of any of the implied terms, the buyer's claim may be to reject the goods supplied as failing to conform with the contractual requirements. It follows that if the goods are validly rejected, the buyer will released from any obligation to pay for them. If the seller's breach of contract has resulted in the buyer suffering any further loss, the rejection of the goods may be accompanied by a claim for damages.

26.38   The right to reject will be lost where the buyer's conduct indicates acceptance of the goods. The Sale of Goods Act 1979 provides that the buyer is to be given a reasonable opportunity of examining them. This may occur before or after the sale.[1] One factor which may arise in software contracts, given the near certainty that every copy of a particular package will be identical, concerns the problem whether the opportunity to examine a copy in the seller's premises will debar the right of rejection, even though a different copy is supplied to the customer.

[1]   Section 34(1).

26.39   The Sale of Goods Act 1979 provides further that the right to reject will cease when the buyer does any act which is inconsistent with the seller's continuing ownership or by the lapse of a 'reasonable time'.[1] In respect of the first of these elements, it might be queried whether the act of completing and returning a licence agreement accompanying the software might be regarded as an act inconsistent with the seller's ownership. In the case of many popular software programs, the disks are contained in an envelope inside the packaging. The envelope bears a legend to the effect that opening it signifies acceptance of a licence agreement. The validity of such techniques will be explored in more detail in the next chapter, but the buyer may be put in the position where taking the steps that are physically necessary to use the software might involve an act which is inconsistent with the seller's title. Given that the buyer's right to use the software will otherwise be severely restricted, such a view would appear harsh but by no means illogical.

[1]   Section 35(1).

26.40   More difficult still is the question of what will be considered a reasonable time to examine the goods. In the case of *Bernstein v Pamsons Motors (Golders Green) Ltd*,[1] a new motor car was sold to the plaintiff. Some three weeks after delivery, the car suffered a major and potentially dangerous breakdown on a motorway. Examination revealed that a blob of sealing compound had somehow found its way into the vehicle's lubrication system during the course of manufacture. During the course of the engine's short life, the object floated around the system until the occasion when it caused an obstruction, blocking the flow of oil to the severe detriment of the engine.

[1]   [1987] 2 All ER 220.

26.41   Under the terms of the Sale of Goods Act 1979, goods are accepted when the buyer retains them beyond a reasonable length of time without intimating any complaint to the seller. In this case, it was held that the passage of three weeks sufficed to prevent the buyer from rejecting the vehicle. A purchaser, it was held, was entitled to such time as was required to make a general examination of the goods. Although this time would vary depending upon the complexity of the goods, no account would be taken of the nature of the particular defect in question.

26.42   The implications of this case for software purchasers are not hopeful. Although particular defects may not manifest themselves for a considerable period of time, it seems unlikely that a general examination of software, of the kind sanctioned in *Bernstein*[1] would occupy a substantial period of time. It must be stressed, however, that the fact that the right to reject is lost does not imply that the buyer possesses no remedies. In the event that goods are unmerchantable or are not fit for their purpose, a remedy will remain in damages. The situation at issue in *Bernstein* is again relevant in a software context. The engine of the motor car suffered significant damage in the incident. The seller was willing to repair those components which had identifiably been affected. The customer, however, expressed the fear that the stresses incurred during the incident might have affected other components, rendering them more likely to fail in the future. This fear served to reduce significantly the customer's confidence in the vehicle. Although the judge accepted that the vehicle was not of merchantable quality and an award of damages was made, it is arguable that this provided an inadequate remedy. In the software context, it might be argued that a customer who discovered significant defects in a software product might justifiably fear that efforts on the supplier's part to correct these might create further problems, alternatively, that other defects might be lying in wait. The fact that software is not susceptible of exhaustive testing, coupled with its intangible nature, makes the issue of customer confidence a significant one.

[1]   *Bernstein v Pamsons Motors (Golders Green) Ltd* [1987] 2 All ER 220.

26.43   The fact that a buyer no longer possesses the right to reject goods for non-conformity with contractual obligations does not mean that no remedies are available. An action for damages will always be competent. In respect of the product itself, the measure of damages will reflect the difference between the value of the goods as supplied and the cost of acquiring goods which will conform with the contractual obligations. The implications of this may be significant. An example might be taken of a seller who, having been informed of the buyer's requirements, supplies a system for £4,000. In the event that the system proved not to be fit for that purpose and evidence indicated that a sum of £10,000 might be required in order to meet the requirements, the measure of damages would reflect this difference. This may not be an unlikely scenario in the information technology field. One of the criticisms made in the inquiry into the failures of the London Ambulance Service's computer system was that the cost of the system was approximately half of that which might have been expected for such a significant project.

Software quality and the courts

26.44   Having outlined the general principles applicable in any contractual action relating to the quality of goods supplied, attention will be paid in the remainder of this chapter to the approach adopted by the courts in the limited number of cases which have reached the High Court or Court of Appeal. Initially, examination will be made of the application of the quality requirements. It is a feature of software contracts that the attempt is normally made to limit or even to exclude liabilities which would normally arise under the application of the law of contract. Such provisions are subject to judicial scrutiny under the provisions of the Unfair Contract Terms Act 1977. In respect both of quality requirements and the validity of exclusion clauses a variety of judicial approaches can be identified and even nearly 20 years after the first case reached the Court of Appeal, it remains difficult to lay down precise guidelines concerning the nature and extent of liability. In some respects the situation may be characterised as similar to that applying in respect of the categorisation of contracts as involving goods and services where two precedents exist rather uneasily in the cases of *Lee v Griffin*[1] and *Robinson v Graves*.[2]

[1] *Lee v Griffin* (1861) 1 B&S 272.
[2] *Robinson v Graves* [1935] 1 KB 579.

Questions of time

26.45 The inclusion of the word 'reasonable' or 'reasonably' in the statutory requirement indicates that a customer may not be entitled to expect perfection. This may be relevant in two respects. The first concerns the condition in which the goods are delivered and the second, the broader question of the level of quality ultimately attained by the product. In the case of *Eurodynamic Systems v General Automation Ltd*,[1] the High Court was faced with a dispute concerning, inter alia, the quality of an operating system for a computer. Steyn J stated that:

> The expert evidence convincingly showed that it is regarded as acceptable practice to supply computer programmes [sic] (including system software) that contain errors and bugs. The basis of the practice is that, pursuant to his support obligation (free or chargeable as the case may be), the supplier will correct errors and bugs that prevent the product from being properly used. Not every bug or error in a computer programme can therefore be categorised as a breach of contract.

[1] (6 September 1988, unreported), QBD.

26.46 It is not, of course, only with software that a product may originally be supplied suffering from minor defects. Although the continued presence of these after the supplier has been offered the opportunity of repair will eventually lead to a finding that the product is not of satisfactory quality, the courts have tended to require that this opportunity be given. In the Scottish case of *Millars of Falkirk Ltd v Turpie*,[1] a new car was sold to the defendant. Immediately upon taking delivery, he discovered an oil leak emanating from the power-assisted steering unit. Upon being notified, the sellers attempted to repair the defect. This attempt proving unsuccessful, the defendant refused to pay for the vehicle and purported to reject it. Holding that he was not entitled so to do, the Court of Session ruled that although the car as supplied was not of merchantable quality, the seller must be granted a reasonable opportunity to repair the defect. 'Many new cars', it was stated, 'have on delivery to a purchaser, some defects, and it was not exceptional that a car should come from the manufacturer in the condition of the defender's new car on delivery'.[2] As the buyer had failed to allow this, the breach of contract was on his part.

[1]   1976 SLT (Notes) 66.
[2]   1976 SLT (Notes) 66 at 67.

26.47   Given the received wisdom that all software contains defects, it would appear that a customer will have to extend reasonable tolerance towards their supplier if or when minor defects manifest themselves. This is well illustrated by the case of *Saphena Computing v Allied Collection Agencies Ltd*,[1] the first software dispute to reach the Court of Appeal. The appellant, Saphena Computing, was a small firm specialising in the supply of third-party hardware and software, either produced or customised by themselves. The respondent was engaged in the business of debt collection. Under an initial contract between the parties, it was agreed that Saphena would supply a quantity of software. The software was ordered in January 1985 and installed between February and April. Despite initial teething problems, it was functioning satisfactorily by May 1985. In August 1985, a second contract was made for the supply of further software. It was intended that this would upgrade the defendant's system. Upon installation of the system, a degree of modification was required as a result of difficulties in attaining compatibility with the existing system and through changes in the defendant's requirements.

[1]   [1995] FSR 616.

26.48   Although attempts were made to remedy the problems, it was common ground between the parties that the system was not operating in a satisfactory manner by February 1986. On 11 February, a telephone conversation took place between representatives of the parties. In the course of this, it was agreed that the relationship should be terminated. Unfortunately, untangling the legal consequences was to prove no simple matter, and when the dispute went to trial proceedings before the High Court lasted for 17 days.

26.49   Subsequent to the termination of the contract, another programmer was contracted to work on the system. In the course of this work, the source code of the programs produced by the plaintiff was copied. Responding to this action, the plaintiff instituted proceedings alleging breach of copyright in its programs. It was further claimed that the defendant had acted wrongfully in terminating the contract and that the plaintiff was entitled to the price of the goods or services supplied under the contract. This latter contention was challenged by the defendant, who counterclaimed for damages, alleging that the software supplied was not to be considered fit for its purpose. The plaintiff succeeding in all significant aspects of its claim, the defendant appealed to the Court of Appeal, which unanimously affirmed the findings of the lower court. In particular, it was held, there was an implied term as to the fitness for the purpose for which the software was required. It had to be reasonably fit for such purposes as had been notified to the suppliers before the orders were placed or were notified subsequently and accepted by the supplier. These obligations had not fulfilled by the supplier at 11 February when the relationship was terminated. Although the software was usable at this stage, it was not entirely fit for the defendant's purposes. There remained faults which required correction. However, the defendant was not entitled, at that stage, to terminate the agreement on this basis. Software, it was held by Staughton LJ:

> ... is not a commodity which is delivered once, only once, and once and for all, but one which will necessarily be accompanied by a degree of testing and modification.[1]

[1] *Saphena Computing v Allied Collection Agencies Ltd* [1995] FSR 616 at 652.

26.50 Thus, it would not be a breach of contract to deliver software in the first instance with a defect in it. In this respect, software must be distinguished from other products, in that the concept of delivery is a much more fluid one. In part, this is due to the necessary interaction between supplier and customer:

> Just as no software developer can reasonably expect a buyer to tell him what is required without a process of feedback and reassessment, so no buyer should expect a supplier to get his programs right first time.[1]

The eradication of defects may be a lengthy and laborious process. In the absence of specific provisions relating to acceptance tests and procedures, it is debatable as to how long the buyer must allow this process to continue. Certainly, the message from *Saphena* would indicate that the buyer must exercise caution and restraint before seeking to terminate a contractual relationship. In this instance, the effect of termination was that:

> ... the defendant thereby agreed to accept the software in the condition in which it then was and, by agreement, put it out of the plaintiff's power to render the software fit for its purpose. The original agreements were thereby varied by deleting the fitness term.[2]

In the event, the plaintiff was held entitled to payment of a reasonable sum in respect of their work on the software and were freed from the requirement to conduct any further work on the system. The defendant's counterclaim for damages in respect of losses caused by the alleged unfitness of the software was dismissed.

[1] *Saphena Computing v Allied Collection Agencies Ltd* [1995] FSR 616 at 652.
[2] [1995] FSR 616 at 618

26.51 The final question before the court concerned the extent of the defendant's right to seek themselves to rectify the defects. To effect this process, they would require access to the programs' source code. Although the plaintiff's contractual conditions made it clear that the source code remained their property, in view of the circumstances under which the agreement had been cancelled, the court held that the defendants must be allowed such access to this as would enable them to cure the defects in the software. In so far as the defendant had gone beyond this by copying portions of the code, they were acting in breach of copyright.

26.52 The principle lesson which might be taken from the *Saphena* case[1] is that there is need for precision in the drafting of contractual provisions. In this case, the court had to find its way through a number of written agreements, coupled with evidence of verbal negotiations and promises which were considered to have also constituted part of the agreement. In spite of these factors, the parties do not appear to have addressed the basic question of what level of quality was to be expected, how conformity with this was to be established and what periods of time would be appropriate for testing and the rectification of errors.

1   *Saphena Computing v Allied Collection Agencies Ltd* [1995] FSR 616 at 652.

Problems with the Community Charge

26.53   Although it was held in *Saphena*[1] that the customer could not expect software to work perfectly from the moment it was supplied, the next case to be considered, *St Albans District Council v ICL*[2] illustrates that this cannot provide a defence in a situation where software proves incapable of meeting its basic purposes.

1   *Saphena Computing v Allied Collection Agencies Ltd* [1995] FSR 616 at 652.
2   [1996] 4 All ER 481. Reported at first instance at [1995] FSR 686.

26.54   The background to the case began with the introduction of a new form of local taxation, the Community Charge. This tax, more commonly known as the poll tax, proved one of the less popular forms of taxation in recent British history. In fiscal terms, the tax is no longer operative, but thanks to the litigation in *St Albans*[1] it has made a significant contribution to information technology law. The case was concerned with the acceptability of hardware and software supplied to the plaintiff for the purpose of administering the operation of the tax. The case is undoubtedly the most significant precedent in the field of information technology law and deserves detailed consideration.

1   *St Albans District Council v ICL* [1996] 4 All ER 481.

26.55   The key element of the poll tax was that, subject to a very limited number of exceptions, all those aged 18 or above living in a local government district were required to pay an identical sum. No account was taken of a taxpayer's income, so that a person earning £100,000 would pay the same as a person earning £10,000. In administrative terms, this approach simplified the task of the local authorities. Effectively, all that was required was to calculate the income required, the number of persons liable to pay the tax and divide the one by the other.

26.56   If ever a task could be seen as made for the computer, this was surely it, and apparently without exception, local authorities invested heavily in IT systems to administer the tax. Many of the authorities, St Albans included, entered into contracts with the computer supplier ICL, who promoted an IT system referred to as 'The ICL Solution'. At the time the contract was signed, the elements of the system required to cope with the specific demands of the Community Charge had not been completed or tested. This fact was promoted as a positive benefit to the authority. The developers would use a 70-strong development team to produce the necessary software and by entering into the contract, the Council would be able 'to input into the development process in order to be sure that this product meets your specific requirements'.

26.57 The contract, valued at some £1.3m, was concluded subject to ICL's standard terms and conditions, which excluded all liability for consequential loss and limited liability for other losses to a maximum of £100,000. The system was delivered to the council timeously but, as envisaged in the contract, the software required was to be delivered and installed in stages as various elements were completed and in line with legislative requirements relating to the introduction of the new tax. Initial elements were to be completed in Autumn 1988, with the full system being operable by February 1990.

26.58 One of the first tasks which needed to be conducted by local authorities was to calculate the number of persons in their area liable to pay the tax. Many local authorities were politically opposed to the new system, and in order to prevent them delaying its introduction, the legislation provided a rigid timetable for the various actions required with penalties being imposed upon recalcitrant authorities. St Albans Council was, therefore, faced with the requirement to complete its count by a certain date. Once the figure had been calculated, the legislation provided that it could not be altered.

26.59 The calculation was carried out using the ICL system in early December 1989 and a figure of 97,384.7 was produced. Unfortunately, the version of the software used had a bug and, for some unknown reason, a new release which would have cured the problem was not installed on the Council's computers prior to the calculation. The correct figure, it was subsequently discovered, was almost 3,000 lower at 94,418.7. The financial effects were significant. The council were effectively caught in a double-edged trap. Their income was reduced because the 3,000 phantom taxpayers would clearly not produce any income. To compound matters, part of the Community Charge income was destined to be transferred to the larger Hertfordshire County Council and this figure was also calculated on the basis that St Albans' taxpaying population was greater than it actually was. When the accounts were finally completed, it was calculated that the loss to St Albans was over £1.3m.[1]

---

[1] In the event, ICL were held liable for only some two-thirds of the amount, it being held that the remainder could be recouped from taxpayers by increasing the rate of tax in the next financial year.

26.60 Although the defendants did not dispute the fact that the software involved in the calculation had been defective, they argued that their obligation was merely to supply a system which would be fully operative at the end of February 1990. Until then, as was recognised in the contract, the system would be in the course of development. Save where it could be shown that the supplier had acted negligently, it was argued, the case of *Saphena v Allied Collection Agencies*[1] provided authority for the proposition that 'the plaintiffs had impliedly agreed to accept the software supplied, bugs and all'. This contention was rejected, with Nourse LJ stating in the Court of Appeal that:

> Parties who respectively agree to supply and acquire a system recognising that it is still in the course of development cannot be taken, merely by virtue of that recognition, to intend that the supplier shall be at liberty to supply software which cannot perform the function expected of it at the stage of development at which it is supplied.[2]

In the particular case, it was of critical importance that the system should have been able to provide an accurate population count in December 1989.

1   [1995] FSR 616.
2   *St Albans District Council v ICL* [1996] 4 All ER 481.

26.61   The defendant's arguments relating to the protection conferred by its exclusion clause will be considered in more detail below. Although it might be argued that the defect in *St Albans*[1] was considerably more serious than the failures in *Saphena*,[2] the tenor of the judgment does seem to be much more 'user friendly' than was the case in the earlier judgment.

1   *St Albans District Council v ICL* [1996] 4 All ER 481.
2   *Saphena Computing v Allied Collection Agencies Ltd* [1995] FSR 616.

Water privatisation

26.62   ICL was also the defendant in the most recent case concerned with software quality, *South West Water Services Ltd v International Computers Ltd*.[1] Once again, the origins of the case lay in politics, on this occasion the privatisation of the English water companies. Following the establishment of the Office of the Water Regulator, a formula was devised which would limit the ability of the companies to increase charges to customers. The intention was that the companies would only be able to maintain their profits through efficiency gains. The plaintiff identified its billing system as a candidate for such savings. The introduction of a new IT system, it was considered, would allow 46 employees to be made redundant.

1   [1999] Masons CLR 400.

26.63   A prolonged contractual process then followed although, as was the case in *St Albans*,[1] external factors, in the form of scheduled reviews to be conducted by the Regulator, imposed immutable deadlines for the accomplishment of a working system and its associated cost savings. One false start ensued, with a contract being entered into with a major supplier who quickly discovered that the project could not be completed on time. The contract was cancelled by South West Water (SWW).

1   *St Albans District Council v ICL* [1996] 4 All ER 481.

26.64   A new call for tenders was initiated on the basis of a User Requirements Specification (URS) drawn up by SWW. The defendant entered into negotiations on the basis of customising a package (Custima) developed by a third party, Creative Computer Systems (CCS), in which it held a 30% stake. The Custima package would require to be customised to meet the user's requirements. The extent of customisation required was at the heart of the subsequent legal dispute. In his findings of fact, the judge held that:

> In my view the problem started here. Although SWW never agreed with ICL or CCSL any specification other than in conformity with the URS, ICL proceeded on the basis that in the end it would be able to persuade SWW that it did not need to provide what was specified in the URS.[1]

[1] *South West Water Services Ltd v International Computers Ltd* [1999] Masons CLR 400 at 402.

26.65 Essentially, it would appear, the supplier was very keen to obtain the contract, not least because with the existence of a considerable number of privatised utilities, it saw prospects of a lucrative market in selling further versions of the system. The customer's specifications were seen as being unnecessarily rigorous and it was hoped that it could be persuaded to accept a more realistic approach, one which would involve significantly less work in customising the Custima software.

26.66 Following extensive discussions, a contract was awarded to ICL in September 1994, with the completed system being scheduled for delivery on 31 October 1995. The contract was costed at some £3.6m. Expert evidence before the court was of the view that the timetable was a tight one. Progress was poor, with several deadlines for delivery of component parts being missed. Even though a delay in completion until the end of March 1996 was agreed between the parties, by early in that month it was clear that the timetable would not be met and the customer served notice terminating the contract. An action was brought seeking recovery of sums paid under the contract plus compensation for additional losses. The claims were based on allegations both of misrepresentation and of breach of contract. These contentions were rejected by the supplier, who argued that its entry into the contract had followed misrepresentations from the customer regarding the amount of work that would be required in order to customise the software to suit its needs. It was also contended that exclusion clauses in the contract served to limit the extent of its liability.

26.67 In the event, the customer succeeded on all counts. A key factor in the failure of the contract was identified as lying in the lack of a properly structured agreement between ICL and CCS. The need for what was described as a 'seamless relationship' between these parties had been identified as critical by the customer. In its absence, there could be no guarantee that the effort required to customise the software would be forthcoming. It was argued on behalf of ICL that there could be no representation as, at the time relevant statements were made, there had been the intention to conclude such a contract. The judge disagreed, holding that there was no evidence to support such an assertion. Records of discussions between ICL and CCS indicated clearly that the latter would not have been willing to enter into a contract on the basis of the arrangements proposed by ICL. Even if the representation had originally been made in the belief it was warranted, there was ample evidence to show that ICL must have been aware before the conclusion of the contract that it did not continue to be valid.

26.68   In respect of ICL's claim that the customer had misled them as to the amount of work required, the judge was not able to accept that the evidence supported this. In any event, it was clear that:

> Not only were ICL not mislead but ICL were in fact the experts whose duty it was to evaluate the project and use their skill, with the assistance from (CCS) in making proposals as to how the project was to be carried out.[1]

Whilst this falls short of imposing duties to advise, counsel or warn customers regarding the merits and suitability of their wares, it does suggest that suppliers cannot, as was indicated in this case, remain silent concerning what are considered to be unrealistic expectations on the part of the customer in the belief that it could subsequently be persuaded to adopt a more realistic view as to its requirements.

[1]   *South West Water Services Ltd v International Computers Ltd* [1999] Masons CLR 400 at 402.

The Monday software package

26.69   In *SAM Business Systems Ltd v Hedley & Co*,[1] the claimant supplied the defendants, a small firm of stockbrokers, with a software package called Interset. The software was intended to replace an existing system called ANTAR which it was feared (perhaps wrongly) was not 'year 2000 compliant'. Following some negotiations, the contract was signed in October 1999 and it was estimated that a period of 12 weeks would be required to install the software and transfer the defendant's processing operations from its old system. The nature of the software and the installation process was described in the following terms:

> Buying InterSet is not as simple as going into a shop and buying a shrink wrapped package, but it is not a bespoke system. The customer can make choices between certain modules and certain services, but it is sold as a developed system.

[1]   [2002] EWHC 2733 (TCC), [2003] 1 All ER (Comm) 465.

26.70   In pre-contractual negotiations, the customer alleged, the sellers stated that the system would cost no more than £180,000 with a money-back guarantee in the event it failed to work in a satisfactory manner. Although no particular figures were specified in any of the contractual documents the case proceeded on the basis that this was the appropriate figure relating to the supply and installation of the software and some items of associated hardware. The licence for supply and use of the software was costed at £116,000. Half of this sum was to be paid at the time the contract was entered into with two further payments to be made when the software was installed and finally when it had been accepted. Under the terms of the contract the customer was given a period of 30 days to test the software to ensure conformity with specification. In the event defects were discovered, these were to be reported. If they were not rectified within 90 days, the customer would have the option to reject the software and obtain a refund of all sums paid. This, it was stated, represented the full extent of the supplier's liability.

26.71 The migration to the new system proved an unhappy experience for all concerned. The salient facts will be considered in more detail below but in February 2001, some 17 months later, the defendants decided to abandon their efforts to make the new system work and had decided instead to outsource their processing operations to another company. By this stage the defendants had paid a total of £183,000 reflecting payments in respect of the licence, the purchase of some items of hardware and a sum of approximately £14,000 in respect of a separate maintenance contract. The final licence instalment had not been paid. Further negotiations took place between the parties but in June 2001 the claimant commenced proceedings claiming some £310,000 partly in respect of the outstanding licence fee but principally for what was described as 'post-installation maintenance'. A total of 785 hours of work was alleged to have been expended in this manner. The defendant counterclaimed seeking nearly £790,000 reflecting a total refund of all sums paid for Interset plus damages reflecting 'increased cost of working, write-offs, fines and additional charges, mitigation costs, and loss of profits'.

26.72 As has been typical in cases involving liability for software, the judgment can be split into two components concerning the questions whether the software supplied complied with contractual and legal requirements relating to quality and, in the event that the answer to this question was in the negative, whether clauses limiting or excluding the supplier's liability complied with the requirements of unfair contract terms legislation. In respect of the quality requirements the court accepted the submission of counsel for the defendants to the effect that:

> Subject to the validity of SAM's purported exemption clauses, it cannot be disputed that the licence agreement would be subject to implied terms to the effect that: InterSet would be constructed and installed at Hedley's premises with all proper and professional care and skill; InterSet would be reasonably fit for the purposes for which Hedley's required it; InterSet would be of satisfactory quality; InterSet would properly and efficiently perform all the required functions; InterSet would perform all such functions in such a way as to enable Hedley's to fulfil its professional obligations to its clients and its statutory duties as required by the FSA; SAM would efficiently carry out the migration and processing of the ANTAR data.[1]

[1] *SAM Business Systems Ltd v Hedley & Co* [2002] EWHC 2733 (TCC), [2003] 1 All ER (Comm) 465 at [50].

Was the software satisfactory?

26.73 From early stages, the attempts to introduce Interset proved difficult and doubtless frustrating for both parties. The judgment charts a familiar if depressing path through the detritus of a failed commercial relationship lasting for some 18 months. The software was supplied timeously but errors continually manifested themselves to the extent that the defendant was warned by the financial services regulator for failing to comply with its requirements regarding record keeping and accounting and was also fined by the Inland Revenue for late payment of Stamp Duty taxes arising from transactions. Although the suppliers acknowledged that there were some bugs in the software which required to be corrected it was argued also that the defendant's staff were largely to blame for failures. The system did mark a substantial change from the defendant's existing package which operated under the DOS operating system, making use solely of keystrokes for command and control purposes. Interset operated under Microsoft Windows and provided the now ubiquitous graphical user interface. As was concluded by the judge:

> what was being presented to Hedleys was a system with a very high degree of automation, a system that was going to be operable by ordinary people, and not technically qualified people.[1]

> [1]   *SAM Business Systems Ltd v Hedley & Co* [2002] EWHC 2733 (TCC), [2003] 1 All ER (Comm) 465 at [21].

26.74   This was to be a matter of some importance as one of the claimant's chief arguments was to the effect that the system had been installed and was working effectively in a considerable number of other business environments. A prime cause of any failure to operate in a satisfactory manner for the defendants was allegedly 'because the staff at Hedley's were not trained for the work or were otherwise incompetent'. Although it was acknowledged that the staff's IT knowledge was limited and somewhat dated to the extent that:

> [t]he staff used their old ... system competently but they did not know how to use a mouse[1]

the staff were considered to have been committed to the successful implementation of the new system. Provision of training was a contractual responsibility of the claimant and was considered to have been inadequate, the judge commenting critically that the claimant's trainer, a former primary schoolteacher:

> gave her evidence in a curiously deadpan manner. Perhaps it was due to nervousness, but if she taught in that manner I can understand that she might have difficulty in communicating computer skills.[2]

> [1]   *SAM Business Systems Ltd v Hedley & Co* [2002] EWHC 2733 (TCC), [2003] 1 All ER (Comm) 465 at [5].
> [2]   [2002] EWHC 2733 (TCC) at [83].

26.75   The fact that Interset was used successfully elsewhere was considered to be a matter of limited significance.

> I am no more impressed by it than if I were told by a garage that there were 1,000 other cars of the same type as the one I had bought where there was no complaint of the defect that I was complaining of so why should I be complaining of a defect? We have all heard of Monday cars, so maybe this was a Monday software programme.[1]

Given that it is received wisdom that all copies of software are identical, this is at first sight a rather puzzling comment. Certainly, there should be few if any instances of what can be classed as production defects in copies of software. Linked with the issue of training, however, indication can be seen of some of the complex interactions which impact upon the user's ability to use software effectively. Many of the applications of Interset software were in larger organisations, the claimant's publicity referring to the fact

> SAM's customers are a mixture of household names and well respected city and international businesses using InterSet to process up to £80bn of STP settlements a day on the domestic and international exchanges.
>
> Major InterSet installations include Deutsche Bank, HSBC, ING Barings, Lloyds Bank and NatWest Bank. But also there is a range of smaller and more specialised firms taking advantage of commercial terms which make InterSet an affordable solution for any securities trading business.

At the time of the case, the evidence was that only one other stockbroking firm was using the system and in general it appears that most users had staff with greater IT skills than those possessed by the defendant's.

¹ *SAM Business Systems Ltd v Hedley & Co* [2002] EWHC 2733 (TCC), [2003] 1 All ER (Comm) 465 at [103].

26.76 A litany of complaints is reported in the judgment¹ and the claimant expended very significant amounts of staff time in seeking to either rectify problems or establish work round procedures whereby operators could avoid undesirable results. The decision of the Court of Appeal in the case of *Saphena v Allied Collection Agencies*² was cited as authority for the proposition 'that in a bespoke system bugs were inevitable'. The later decision of the Court in the case of, *St Albans District Council v ICL* was also referred to, Lord Justice Nourse here ruling that:

> Parties who respectively agree to supply and acquire a system recognising that it is still in the course of development cannot be taken, merely by virtue of that recognition, to intend that the supplier shall be at liberty to supply software which cannot perform the function expected of it at the stage of the development at which it is supplied.³

¹ *SAM Business Systems Ltd v Hedley & Co* [2002] EWHC 2733 (TCC), [2003] 1 All ER (Comm) 465.
² [1995] FSR 616.
³ [1996] 4 All ER 481 at 487.

26.77 The systems involved in both *Saphena*¹ and *St Albans*² were referred to as 'bespoke' systems and therefore distinguishable from the customised system supplied to the present defendant. This is perhaps putting matters too strongly. In *Saphena* the supplier's business was described as consisting of providing 'hardware obtained from others, and software comprising some standard items and others specially written'. In *St Albans* the tax collection system at issue had also been supplied to a number of other local authorities. Where a better distinction perhaps lay was in the state of development of the system. In *St Albans* the software was being developed in parallel with the enactment of the legislation establishing the tax which it was designed to help collect. Upgrades and revisions were continually being supplied to the users and indeed the fluid nature of the software posed serious problems in trying to replicate and explain the nature of the error which gave rise to the litigation. Interset, however:

> was sold as a developed system allegedly already working well in other places. This is a much stronger case than the St Albans case against toleration of bugs. I am in no doubt that if a software system is sold as a tried and tested system it should not have any bugs in it and if there are any bugs they should be regarded as defects. Of course, if the defects are speedily remedied without charge, it may be that there will be no consequential damage.[3]

1   *Saphena Computing v Allied Collection Agencies Ltd* [1995] FSR 616.
2   *St Albans District Council v ICL* [1996] 4 All ER 481 at 487.
3   *SAM Business Systems Ltd v Hedley & Co* [2002] EWHC 2733 (TCC), [2003] 1 All ER (Comm) 465 at [19].

26.78   This seems an eminently correct ruling although as was recognised in the judgment:

> SAM, like some others in the computer industry seem to be set in the mindset that when there is a 'bug' the customer must pay for putting it right. Bugs in computer programmes are still inevitable, but they are defects and it is the supplier who has the responsibility for putting them right at the supplier's expense.[1]

In line with these arguments, the sums claimed by the claimant in respect of the time and effort incurred in seeking to modify the software was rejected. The defendant was held to have been entitled to take the view that the software contract had not been completed in a satisfactory manner and the claimant's claim for additional payments was rejected. Unfortunately, from its perspective, however, it was also necessary to consider the effectiveness of the claimant's exclusion clauses which effectively limited its liability to providing a refund of sums paid in the situation that the customer followed the contractual procedures regarding rejection. As will be discussed below, the defendant failed in this task rendering victory in respect of the claim of defectiveness pyrrhic.

1   *SAM Business Systems Ltd v Hedley & Co* [2002] EWHC 2733 (TCC), [2003] 1 All ER (Comm) 465 at [19].

Exclusion or limitation of liability

26.79   In the previous sections, consideration was given to the nature and extent of the liabilities which may arise pursuant to the production, supply and use of software. Although the argument that software should be treated in the same manner as any other product is a weighty one, it must also be conceded that software producers may be exposed to a greater degree of risk than their more traditional counterparts. First, if one copy of a software product exhibits defects, it must be extremely likely that all copies will be so tainted. With manufactured products generally, most defects are introduced at the production stage and affect only a portion of the products in question. A finding that one copy of a software package is unmerchantable might, by way of contrast, leave its producer liable to every purchaser. A further problem is that many losses resulting from software defects will be economic in nature. Such losses may not only be extensive but are also extremely difficult to quantify and, accordingly, to insure against. A spreadsheet program, for example, may be used for domestic accounting purposes, where the degree of financial exposure in the event of error may be minimal, or in the course of preparing a multi-million pound construction contract, where any error might threaten the financial viability of a contracting party.

26.80   Few would argue that the state of the law relating to software liability is in a satisfactory state. Uncertainty feeds upon uncertainty and perception appears more significant than reality. The producer's fear that it may be exposed to crippling legal actions has resulted in an almost universal practice of seeking to exclude some and place limits on the extent of their liabilities in respect of other forms of loss resulting from the operation (or non-operation) of their software. The validity of such clauses[1] has been at issue in most of the disputes which have reached the courts.

[1]   In this section, the term 'exclusion clause' will be used to refer both to clauses which seek to exclude and those which limit the extent of liability. Most terms under discussion fall into the latter category.

26.81   An initial point to note is that in order to be effective, a clause must be incorporated into the contract. The rules relating to this are to be found in common law rather than statute, and require that reasonable steps be taken to bring the existence of the clause to the notice of the other contracting party. This may be accomplished in a number of ways, with a major factor being whether the software is supplied pursuant to a written contract signed by both parties. In such cases, there will generally be little doubt that the exclusion clause forms part of the contract, and discussion will focus on the effect of the provisions of the Unfair Contract Terms Act 1977 and the Unfair Terms in Consumer Contracts Regulations 1994.[1]

[1]   SI 1994/3159.

26.82   More difficult issues arise when software (typically standard) is supplied through less structured channels. Such software is typically supplied subject to what is generally referred to as a 'shrink wrap licence'. The term appears to date from early forms of consumer software, mainly computer games. These were typically supplied on an audio cassette, with the terms of a very basic licence printed on the cellophane wrapping of the cassette. Today, licences tend to be printed on substantial booklets (often making separate provisions to accommodate the legal requirements of a range of countries in which the software is sold) included inside packaging. The validity of these is subject to some debate.

Enforceability of shrink wrap licences

26.83   Many contracts, of course, are made other than by means of a signed document; a typical example might relate to the purchase of a piece of standard software from a shop. In this situation, the legal requirement will be that reasonable steps should be taken to bring the existence of any contractual provisions to the notice of the other party prior to the conclusion of the agreement.[1] It is not required that he or she should be aware of all of the details or of the legal implications arising from the contract. An example can be taken from a railway ticket. The ticket will contain reference to the carrier's conditions of carriage but will not itself contain details of these. The presence on the ticket of a notice referring the customer to the conditions will suffice to incorporate them into the contract. Returning to the software context, the display of a clause on the outside of the packaging (or perhaps on a notice displayed in the seller's premises) will serve to give the customer notice of its existence. It is increasingly the case that software is supplied over the Internet. The practice has implications in respect of a number of areas of the law, not least, as will be discussed below, in the field of taxation. From a licensing perspective, use of the Internet may simplify the supplier's task of establishing customer awareness of and agreement to the licence terms. It is a simple matter to cause either a set of the terms or at least reference to their existence to be displayed with the customer required to 'click' on a button marked 'I accept' before the transaction can proceed.

[1] See *Thornton v Shoe Lane Parking Ltd* [1971] 2 QB 163, where the display of exclusion clauses inside a car park was held to be ineffective, the contract having been concluded at the point when the customer entered into the premises.

26.84 Assuming that the terms of the licence, including its provisions restricting liability, become incorporated into the contract, attention must again turn to the effect of the Unfair Contract Terms Act 1977 and the Unfair Terms in Consumer Contracts Regulations 1999.[1] To date, all litigation concerned with the effectiveness of exclusion or limitation clauses in software contracts has occurred in the context of commercial transactions. The increasing use of software within the home must increase the importance of the consumer sector and initially, therefore, consideration will be given to the potential application of the legislation in this regard.

[1] SI 1999/2083.

Consumer contracts

26.85 Somewhat confusingly, different definitions of the term 'consumer' are found in the Unfair Contract Terms Act 1977 and 1999 regulations.[1] The Act provides that a person deals as a consumer if:

(a) he neither makes the contract in the course of a business nor holds himself out as doing so; and

(b) the other party does make the contract in the course of a business.[2]

Additionally, where goods are supplied under the contract, these must be of a kind ordinarily used for private use or consumption. It would seem that computer games must satisfy this requirement. Although the status of other forms of software, such as word processing or accounting packages or Internet access software, may at one stage have been debatable, it would seem that they are now sufficiently widely used to be classed as consumer products. This issue may not arise under the regulations, which make no reference to the nature of goods, requiring only that they be obtained for non-business purposes.[3]

[1]   SI 1999/2083.
[2]   Section 12(1).
[3]   Section 2.

26.86   In respect of statutory requirements relating to title, description or quality, the Unfair Contract Terms Act 1977 provides that exclusion or limitation will not be permitted.[1] In the case of consumer contracts falling under the ambit of the Sale of Goods Act 1979, the prohibition is even more extensive. Here, the Consumer Transactions (Restrictions on Statements) Order 1976[2] provides that any attempt at restriction or exclusion will constitute a criminal offence. An offence will also be committed when any form of guarantee is offered other than those provided for in the Sale of Goods Act 1979, unless it is made clear that this is offered in addition to, rather than in substitution for, the consumer's rights under the legislation. It appears common practice amongst the suppliers of computer games to display notices restricting the buyer's rights to the supply of a replacement game in the event that the original is defective. In the event that the contract is regarded as one involving the sale or supply of goods, the display of such notices will render the supplier involved liable to criminal prosecution.

[1]   Section 6.
[2]   SI 1976/1813.

26.87   In terms of their scope, the 1994 regulations are broader,[1] applying to any term in a non-negotiated contract for goods or services other than those defining the main subject matter or relating to the adequacy of the price. Such terms will not be binding on the consumer if they are determined to be unfair. An unfair term is one which:

> ... contrary to the requirements of good faith causes a significant imbalance in the parties' rights and obligations under the contract to the imbalance of the consumer.[2]

This is a somewhat nebulous criterion. Schedule 2 to the regulations contains an 'indicative and non-exclusive list of the terms which might be considered unfair'. These include clauses purporting to limit the legal rights of consumers in the event of unsatisfactory performance. A further illustration stigmatises clauses:

> ... making an agreement binding on the consumer whereas provision of services by the supplier or seller is subject to a condition whose realisation depends on his own will alone.

It might be that this provision could be invoked in the event that a software producer seeks to link a right to use software to the acceptance of restrictive terms within a licence.

[1]   SI 1994/3159.
[2]   Unfair Contract Terms Act 1977, s 4(1).

26.88 A further aspect of the 1999 regulations[1] may be of considerable significance. Although many forms of exclusion clause have long been regarded as of dubious quality, the difficulties facing individual litigants have prevented these being challenged before the courts. The regulations establish a role for the Director General of Fair Trading providing that the Director is to consider any complaint that a contract term is unfair and may then seek an injunction preventing the continued use of the term (or any similar term) in consumer contracts.[2]

[1] SI 1999/2083.
[2] Regulation 10.

Non-consumer contracts

26.89 In the case of non-consumer contracts for supply of goods, as well as any contracts where standard form contracts are used, limitation or exclusion clauses will be valid only in so far as they satisfy the statutory requirement of reasonableness.[1] The Unfair Contract Terms Act 1977 lists a number of factors that are to be taken into account in deciding any such question.[2] These include the strength of the parties' respective bargaining positions, the practice of the trade or profession involved and whether the customer was given the option of contracting on terms which did not seek to exclude liability.

[1] Section 8.
[2] Section 11 for England and Wales, s 24 for Scotland and Sch 2 applying throughout the UK.

The nature of a standard form contract

26.90 The term 'standard form contract' is not defined in the Unfair Contract Terms Act 1977. In the Scottish case of *McCrone v Boots Farm Sales*,[1] it was held that a standard form contract existed where a party invariably sought to do business on terms which did not differ to any material extent. It was immaterial whether these were reduced to writing or were, at least in part, agreed orally. Such an approach has been upheld in subsequent cases with the courts being willing to overlook minor variations where it can be shown that a party will generally do business only on the basis of a substantially identical set of terms and conditions

[1] 1981 SLT 103.

26.91 The definition of standard form contracts in a software context was considered in the case of *Salvage Association v CAP Financial Services Ltd*.[1] At issue here was a contract for the computerisation of the plaintiff's accounting system. The project proved unsuccessful, and after a number of broken completion dates the plaintiff terminated its agreement with the defendant and sought damages. Much of the dispute centred on the applicability and enforceability of clauses limiting the defendant's liability in the event of breach of contract. In respect of the question whether the clauses were to be classed as standard form contracts, Thayne Forbes J analysed the history of the contract, pointing to the fact that extensive negotiations had taken place between the parties prior to its conclusion. Although the terms of the agreement 'closely followed CAP's standard terms of contract', this fact was not to be taken to mean that the contract was a standard form one. Six factors were identified as relevant to the determination:

(i)   the degree to which the 'standard terms' are considered by the other party as part of the process of agreeing the terms of the contract;
(ii)   the degree to which the 'standard terms' are imposed on the other party by the party putting them forward;
(iii)   the relative bargaining power of the parties;
(iv)   the degree to which the party putting forward the 'standard terms' is prepared to entertain negotiations with regard to the terms of the contract generally and the 'standard terms' in particular;
(v)   the extent and nature of any agreed alterations to the 'standard terms' made as a result of the negotiations between the parties; and
(vi)   the extent and duration of the negotiations.

Applying these criteria he concluded that:

> In this case SA had considered the various drafts of the contract that had been sent by CAP and had taken legal and other advice on all the proposed terms in order to decide what alterations it wished to make. To the extent that SA sought changes and additions to the draft terms, CAP largely agreed them. I am satisfied that the terms of the second contract were not imposed on SA by CAP, but were fully negotiable between parties of equal bargaining power and that CAP was prepared to engage in a meaningful process of negotiation with SA as to those terms. The process of negotiation between the parties took place over a considerable period of time.

The contract was not, therefore, a standard form contract although, as will be discussed below, its terms were struck down on the basis that they constituted an unreasonable attempt to evade liability for negligence.

[1]   (9 July 1993, unreported), CA. The case is reported at first instance at [1995] FSR 654.

26.92   A different conclusion was reached in *St Albans District Council v ICL*.[1] Here, the Council published a call for tenders, negotiated – albeit fairly incompetently – with a number of potential suppliers, engaged in further negotiations with ICL and concluded a contract, one clause of which stated that it was subject to ICL's standard terms and conditions. As was stated by Nourse LJ in the Court of Appeal:

> Scott Baker J (the judge at first instance) dealt with this question as one of fact, finding that the defendant's general conditions remained effectively untouched in the negotiations and that the plaintiffs accordingly dealt on the defendant's written standard terms for the purposes of s 3(1) (see [1995] FSR 686 at 706). I respectfully agree with him.

[1]   [1996] 4 All ER 481.

26.93   A similar decision was reached in *South West Water v ICL*.[1] Once again, the customer had initially argued that the agreement should be made on the basis of its own standard terms and conditions. The defendant countered by submitting a contract governing a previous agreement between the parties. This was subject to some negotiation, but it was agreed that the limitation clauses in the contract were taken from ICL's standard terms. Considering the nature of the agreement Toulmin J made reference to the leading textbook, *Chitty on Contracts*. This stated that:

> Since in any event, no two contracts are likely to be completely identical, but will at least differ as to subject-matter and price, the question arises whether variations or omissions from or additions to standard terms thereby render them 'non-standard' and they do not whether all the terms become standard terms.[2]

Referring to the decision in *St Albans*[3] described above, it was held that the contract was a standard form contract.

[1]   [1999] Masons CLR 400.
[2]   (27th edn, 1994, Sweet and Maxwell) para 14-056.
[3]   *St Albans District Council v ICL* [1996] 4 All ER 481.

26.94   In some respects, the conclusion may be seen as a surprising one. A water authority is a substantial party and the decision makes several references to the fact that discussions between the parties were extensive. Evidence from ICL concerning one meeting was to the effect that:

> It was a take it or leave it session. They [SWW] were very hard negotiators but we took the decision to proceed as it was too good a long term opportunity to walk away from.

Perhaps the most significant factor was the fact that the contract signed between the parties was silent on what was described as the 'very obvious circumstance' what should happen in the event of a total failure to deliver a workable system. The judge concluded:

> The reason it was not covered is because the parties used a standard ICL contract which was only slightly adapted. Those standard ICL terms were not appropriate where substantial development work was required to adapt the basic system, as in this case.[1]

[1]   *South West Water v ICL* [1999] Masons CLR 400.

The requirement of reasonableness

26.95   In determining whether clauses limiting or excluding liability can be considered fair and reasonable, the Unfair Contract Terms Act 1977 provides initially that regard is to be had to 'the circumstances which were or ought reasonably to have been, known to or in the contemplation of the parties when the contract was made'.[1] It provides further that account is to be taken of:

(a) the resources which he could expect to be available to him for the purpose of meeting the liability should it arise; and

(b) how far it was open to him to cover himself by insurance.

Schedule 2 to the Act continues to provide a set of 'Guidelines' to be taken into account. These include:

• The strength of the parties respective bargaining positions.
• The general practice of a particular trade or profession.
• Whether the goods are made, processed or adapted to the special order of the customer.

[1] Section 11.

26.96 In determining the question of the reasonableness of the limitation clauses, particular reference was made to the statutory reference to the resources likely to be available to the party seeking to rely on the clause, and how far it was open to him to cover himself by insurance. In the case of *Photo Production Ltd v Securicor Transport Ltd*, Lord Wilberforce stated with reference to the Unfair Contract Terms Act 1977:

> ... in commercial matters generally, when the parties are not of unequal bargaining power, and when risks are normally borne by insurance, not only is the case for judicial intervention undemonstrated, but there is everything to the said, and this seems to have been Parliament's intention, for leaving the parties free to apportion the risks as they think fit and for respecting their decisions.[1]

[1] [1980] AC 827 at 843.

26.97 In *Salvage Association v CAP Financial Services Ltd*,[1] it was accepted that the parties were of equal bargaining power. There had been genuine negotiations and the plaintiff had at all relevant times the realistic option of giving its business to another producer. A number of factors, however, operated to justify a finding that the limitation clause was unfair. First reference was made to the discrepancy between the contractual limit of £25,000 and the defendant's general acceptance of liability up to £1m. Additionally, whilst the losses claimed by the plaintiff were covered under an insurance policy taken out by the defendant, albeit one which was subject to a £500,000 excess, it was accepted by the court that the plaintiff would have been unable to obtain insurance cover against losses of the kind incurred at other than a prohibitive price.

[1] (9 July 1993, unreported), CA.

26.98 The decision of the Court of Appeal in *St Albans District Council v ICL*[1] provides further evidence of a judicial willingness to scrutinise the terms of contracts entered into by large organisations. Following the introduction of the Community Charge legislation, the plaintiff, in common with all other local authorities, was under considerable pressure to introduce new computer systems capable of coping with the administrative demands of the new tax. After an initial call for tenders, the choice of supplier was effectively between the defendant and IBM. Assessing various elements of the competing bids, including the terms and conditions associated with each, the decision was made to accept the defendant's tender and:

> Immediately commence negotiations with ICL to ensure the best possible deal can be secured for the authority.

[1] *St Albans District Council v ICL* [1996] 4 All ER 481.

26.99 The negotiations do not appear to have been conducted by the Council with great expertise. Following submission of a draft contract based upon a Council official's previous employment with London Transport, everything proceeded on the basis of ICL's standard terms and conditions (again out of date in respect of the level of liability accepted). As the deadline for the introduction of the new tax approached, the council were under some pressure to conclude the agreement. When concerns were raised concerning the limitation on liability clause, the defendant's response was to indicate that unless the contract was concluded by the following Monday, there could be no guarantee that the system would be delivered in time for the introduction of the tax, a consequence which could have dire financial consequences for the authority. A letter from the defendant stated:

> With regard to ICL's contractual terms and conditions ... our offer is based on these standard terms and conditions, and given the tight time-scale, I would advise you to make use of them.
>
> These standard ICL conditions are accepted by over 250 local authorities, and in no way detracts from the business partnerships.[1]

[1] *St Albans District Council v ICL* [1995] FSR 686 at 695.

26.100 The plaintiff promptly signed the contract. Given these circumstances, it is not surprising that the court held that the contract was a standard form contract and that it did not satisfy the statutory criterion of reasonableness. In reaching this decision, the Court of Appeal approved the judgment of Scott Baker J at first instance, where he identified as determining factors, the points that:

(1) the parties were of unequal bargaining power;
(2) the defendants have not justified the figure of £100,000, which was small, both in relation to the potential risk and the actual loss;
(3) the defendants were insured; and
(4) the practical consequences.

I make the following observations on the fourth point, which follows on in a sense from the third. On whom is it better that a loss of this size should fall, a local authority or an international computer company. The latter is well able to insure (and in this case was insured) and pass on the premium cost to the customers. If the loss is to fall the other way it will ultimately be borne by the local population either by increased taxation or reduced services. I do not think it unreasonable that he who stands to make the profit (ICL) should carry the risk.[1]

[1] *St Albans District Council v ICL* [1995] FSR 686 at 711.

26.101 The decisions of the Court of Appeal in the cases of *St Albans District Council v ICL*[1] and *South West Water v ICL*[2] cast significant doubt on the effectiveness of contractual provisions whereby software suppliers sought to limit the extent of their liabilities in the event software failed to operate in a proper manner. A further decision of the court in the case of *Watford Electronics Ltd v Sanderson CFL Ltd*[3] may signal a less interventionist policy on the part of the judiciary. Albeit of less precedential value, the decision of the High Court in *SAM Business Systems Ltd v Hedley & Co*,[4] discussed at para 26.69ff above, also provides useful guidance concerning the application of the statutory criteria.

[1]   [1995] FSR 686 at 711.
[2]   [1999] Masons CLR 400.
[3]   [2001] EWCA Civ 317, [2001] 1 All ER (Comm) 696.
[4]   [2002] EWHC 2733 (TCC), [2003] 1 All ER (Comm) 465.

26.102 In *Watford Electronics v Sanderson CFL Ltd*,[1] the supplier, Sanderson, undertook to provide an integrated software system to control all aspects of the customer's business. Unfortunately the project was not completed to the satisfaction of the customer and legal proceedings were initiated seeking damages of some £5.5 million. At trial the judge found that the supplier was in breach of its obligations to supply a system of reasonable quality. The supplier's conditions of contract limited its liability to the cost of any defective goods supplied. The bulk of the customer's claim related to losses of profit resulting from the failure of the system to operate in a satisfactory manner. The trial judge ruled that this clause was invalid under the provisions of the Unfair Contract Terms Act 1977 which provide that exclusion clauses found in standard form contracts will be valid only in so far as they can be considered fair and reasonable. The present clause, it was held, could not be so regarded.

[1]   [2001] EWCA Civ 317, [2001] 1 All ER (Comm) 696.

26.103 The Court of Appeal took a different view. The customer, it was held, was an experienced and established business. There had been extensive negotiations between the parties. It was noted that the customer used a very similar form of exclusion clause in contracts with its own customers. The conclusion reached was that:

> Where experienced businessmen representing substantial companies of equal bargaining power negotiate an agreement, they may be taken to have had regard to the matters known to them. They should, in my view be taken to be the best judge of the commercial fairness of the agreement which they have made; including the fairness of each of the terms in that agreement. They should be taken to be the best judge on the question whether the terms of the agreement are reasonable. The court should not assume that either is likely to commit his company to an agreement which he thinks is unfair, or which he thinks includes unreasonable terms., Unless satisfied that one party has, in effect, taken unfair advantage of the other – or that a term is so unreasonable that it cannot properly have been understood or considered - the court should not interfere.
> ... In the present case the parties did negotiate as to the price. Mr Jessa, on behalf of Watford, secured substantial concessions on price from Mr Broderick. The parties negotiated, also, as to which of them should bear the risk (or the

cost of insurance against the risk) of making good the loss of profits, and other indirect or consequential loss, which Watford might suffer if the product failed to perform as intended. Mr Jessa was less successful in obtaining from Mr Broderick the concession which he wanted. The most that he could get was an undertaking that Sanderson would use its best endeavours to allocate appropriate resources to ensuring that the product performed according to specification. But, for the reasons which I have sought to explain, that was worth something to Watford; and Mr Jessa decided that he would be content with what he could get. In my view it is impossible to hold, in the circumstances of the present case, that Sanderson took unfair advantage of Watford; or that Watford, through Mr Jessa, did not properly understand and consider the effect of the term excluding indirect loss.[1]

The exclusion clause was therefore upheld and the supplier's appeal was upheld.

[1]   *Watford Electronics Ltd v Sanderson CFL Ltd* [2001] EWCA Civ 317, [2001] 1 All ER (Comm) 696 at [55]–[56].

26.104   Although the judgments in the present case[1] do not refer to the decisions in *St Albans*[2] and *South West Water*,[3] the tone does differ markedly. It may be noted that especially in the *St Albans* case, negotiations between the parties appear to have been conducted in a rather ineffective manner. Owing to an error, indeed, the contract limited liability to a sum less than that which the supplier would normally have accepted. External factors also placed the customer under considerable pressure to conclude the agreement. It may be that in these circumstances, the present court would also have declared the exclusion clause to be unfair. *Watford v Sanderson* does indicate, however, that where it appears that genuine negotiations have taken place and where it is clear that the customer has freely determined to enter into a contract in awareness of the nature and significance of exclusion clauses, the courts will be slow to interfere.

[1]   *Watford Electronics Ltd v Sanderson CFL Ltd* [2001] EWCA Civ 317, [2001] 1 All ER (Comm) 696.
[2]   *St Albans District Council v ICL* [1995] FSR 686 at 695.
[3]   *South West Water v ICL* [1999] Masons CLR 400.

26.105   A similar approach was taken by the High Court in the case of *SAM Business Systems Ltd v Hedley & Co*[1] discussed at para 26.69ff above. Here the contract provided in part that:

> 30 days from delivery of the application software by SAM, acceptance tests will be completed by the client in order to test the application software ... Client will advise SAM of any instances where the application software fails to achieve the stated acceptance criteria. Such advice shall be in writing ... Any individual software component reissued by SAM ... may be subjected to retesting by client for a further 30 days ... If, having followed these procedures, and within 90 days from the original date of delivery, there remain acceptance criteria correctly notified by client according to the procedures outlined above but not achieved by the application software, client shall be entitled to initiate procedures for rejecting the application software. In the event that SAM consider the rejection of the application software to be unreasonable, SAM shall have the right to request client to enter into arbitration via an independent third party, and client shall not unreasonably refuse this request.

> In the absence of a valid written advice from client, detailing unacceptable behaviour of the application software, and referencing a particular acceptance criterion not attained, the application software will be deemed accepted.
>
> In the event of the application software not being accepted according to the obligations and procedures outlined in sections 2.9 and 2.10, client shall have the right at its entire discretion to rescind this agreement and to be repaid all sums which have previously been paid to SAM in respect of the licence under this agreement. This shall be the sole and exclusive remedy available to client in the event of the application software not being accepted.

Effectively, therefore the customer's rights were limited to a refund of the purchase price.

¹ [2002] EWHC 2733 (TCC), [2003] 1 All ER (Comm) 465.

26.106 Given that the terms were part of the supplier's written terms of business there was little doubt that the Unfair Contract Terms Act 1977 should apply. The judgment gives extensive and helpful consideration to the extent to which the various criteria identified as components of the requirement of reasonableness may be relevant in cases such as the present. A key factor to be taken into account was whether it would have been feasible for the customer to have obtained similar software without the accompaniment of exclusion clauses. The evidence before the court was to the effect that '(t)he only way to get the software they needed was by contracting on terms that made rigorous exclusions of liability because those were the terms on which all suppliers were contracting'.¹ The parties it was accepted, were not in a equal bargaining position:

> Hedley's had to get a system in a short space of time that was Year 2000 compliant or go out of business. But that was a difficulty of their own making. If they had woken up to the problem earlier, as most people did, they would not have had a problem as to time. On the other hand, SAM no doubt wanted the work to make a profit, but there is no evidence that they would have gone out of business if they did not get the work.²

There was no evidence that the customer had made any effort to negotiate regarding the terms of the contract although it appeared that, given the degree of financial exposure to which it might have been exposed, the supplier's attitude towards any request that the exclusion clause be excluded would have been 'We did not have to take on this contract. Having taken it on on our terms, why should the contract be re-written to expose us to a huge risk and possibly put us out of business?' On the basis of this hypothesis, the judge continued:

> That is a freedom of contract attitude that would have been entirely acceptable in the nineteenth and early twentieth centuries. Can it survive since Parliament intervened at the behest of the Law Commission in 1977?³

¹ *SAM Business Systems Ltd v Hedley & Co* [2002] EWHC 2733 (TCC), [2003] 1 All ER (Comm) 465 at [70].
² [2002] EWHC 2733 (TCC) at [70].
³ [2002] EWHC 2733 (TCC) at [70].

26.107 Ultimately, the answer to this question was in the affirmative. The contract, it was held, had to be considered as a whole. Although certain of the clauses considered in isolation would have been considered unreasonable, the overall conclusion was that the contract provided for a fair apportionment of risk between the parties. The judge concluded:

> Not forgetting my duty to look at each term individually, it is important to look at each in relation to the whole contract. Before contract, SAM says, 'We think our system is marvellous and will do everything you need, but if you are not satisfied you can ask for your money back'. The contract, signed by Hedley's after they have had a few days to think about it but without any attempt to negotiate on their part, says, 'So far as possible we exclude any liability for our system, but if you are not satisfied and you go through the right machinery, you can have your money back'. Having regard to the enormous potential liabilities, that seems to me to be a reasonable arrangement in the circumstances existing between the two parties. The big question is, 'Not having gone through the contractual arrangements for getting their money back, can Hedley's nonetheless get their money back or recover any other damages?'
>
> If SAM had not offered what Mr. Tustain on 4 October, 1999 called 'a standard money back guarantee on licence', I would have regarded the exclusion of liability and entire agreement clauses as quite unreasonable though I would have regarded the limitation of liability to the amount of money paid under the licence agreement as reasonable. But on the evidence before me and in all the circumstances to which I have referred (which would not necessarily exist with other contracts signed on the same terms) I find that all of the terms to which objection is taken in the contract were reasonable. The parties were of equal bargaining power in terms of their relative size and resources. Hedley's were in a difficult position of their own making because of their lateness in tackling the problem of Year 2000 compliance. The evidence from SAM is that other companies like theirs had similar exclusion clauses, but on the other hand, Hedley's did not even try to negotiate for terms more favourable to them.[1]

The end result of the litigation might be considered as a draw. The suppliers were not able to recover additional costs incurred in seeking to place the software into a satisfactory state and the customers were similarly unsuccessful in securing reimbursement of losses caused through the failure of the software to operate in a satisfactory manner.

[1] *SAM Business Systems Ltd v Hedley & Co* [2002] EWHC 2733 (TCC), [2003] 1 All ER (Comm) 465 at [71]–[72].

Conclusions

26.108 In the early days of software, it was commonplace for suppliers to seek totally to exclude all liabilities relating to their products. A 1993 version of the standard licence used by a major software producer stated that:

> LIMITED WARRANTY AND DISCLAIMER OF LIABILITY
>
> THE SOFTWARE AND ACCOMPANYING WRITTEN MATERIALS (INCLUDING INSTRUCTIONS FOR USE) ARE PROVIDED 'AS IS' WITHOUT WARRANTY OF ANY KIND. FURTHER, (Producer) DOES NOT WARRANT, GUARANTEE OR MAKE ANY REPRESENTATIONS REGARDING THE USE OF, OR THE RESULTS OF USE, OF THE SOFTWARE OR WRITTEN MATERIALS IN TERMS OF CORRECTNESS, ACCURACY, RELIABILITY, CURRENTNESS, OR OTHERWISE. THE ENTIRE RISK AS TO THE RESULTS AND PERFORMANCE OF THE SOFTWARE IS ASSUMED BY YOU. IF THE SOFTWARE OR WRITTEN MATERIALS ARE DEFECTIVE YOU, AND NOT (Producer) OR ITS DEALERS, DISTRIBUTORS, AGENTS OR EMPLOYEES, ASSUME THE ENTIRE COST OF ALL NECESSARY SERVICING, REPAIR OR CORRECTION.
>
> THE ABOVE IS THE ONLY WARRANTY OF ANY KIND, EITHER EXPRESS OR IMPLIED, INCLUDING BUT NOT LIMITED TO THE IMPLIED WARRANTIES OF MERCHANTABILITY AND FITNESS FOR A PARTICULAR PURPOSE, THAT IS MADE BY (Producer) ON THIS ... PRODUCT.

26.109 The world has moved on and more recent versions are somewhat more 'generous', guaranteeing that the software will perform 'substantially in accordance with the accompanying Product Manual(s) for a period of 90 days'. In general, as was indicated at the outset of the chapter, clauses excluding liability have largely been replaced by those seeking to limit the extent of liability. In a number of cases, it has been accepted that it is easier and more cost-effective for a software producer to obtain insurance cover in respect of claims which might be made by customers, than it is for customers to obtain cover against more speculative risks associated with the failure of an automation project intended to bring future gains in efficiency and productivity. There may be cases where exclusion clauses may be upheld, but the range of these may be diminishing. In *South West Water v ICL*, in rejecting the defendant's attempts to limit liability to a partial refund in the case of a total failure of the project, it was held that:

> In some cases such a clause might be reasonable to reflect the balance of risk in a developing project, but there is no evidence that this is the case here.[1]

Given the vital role played by software in the modern world, it must be right that issues of liability should be assessed by the standards and criteria applied to industrial products rather than to those of a niche market within the services sector. Whilst the cases of *Watford Electronics Ltd v Sanderson CFL Ltd*[2] and *SAM v Hedley*[3] produce results which are more favourable to the producer than was the case in the ICL cases, the emphasis remains on the criterion of fairness. Especially in situations in which its functioning is critical to the survival of the customer's business it is not unreasonable that every effort should be made to ensure both that the software itself is suitable and that arrangements – in the form of contractual safeguards or the acquisition of insurance cover – are in place to guard against the risk of failure. Caveat emptor has not returned to business contracts but neither is a supplier expected to act as nanny to its customers.

1   [1999] Masons CLR 400.
2   [2001] EWCA CIV 317.
3   *SAM Business Systems Ltd v Hedley & Co* [2002] EWHC 2733 (TCC), [2003] 1 ALl ER (Comm) 465.

Chapter 27

Non-contractual liability

Introduction

27.1   Chapter 26 has considered some of the issues which may arise between parties who contract for the production, supply and use of software products. The all-pervasive nature of software applications means that the effects of any failure may not be limited to contracting parties. A pedestrian may be knocked down by a car whose software-controlled brakes have failed or a passenger may be on a plane whose fly-by-wire computer system malfunctions. In the first of these situations, the pedestrian will have no contract with anyone, whilst in the second, the passenger's contract will be with the airline and subject to the limits on liability contained in the Warsaw Convention. There will be no contractual relationship with the plane's producer. In such events, the focus of attention switches to the topic of non-contractual liability. In this chapter, attention will be paid first to the tort of negligence. Next, consideration will be given to the possible implications of the system of strict product liability introduced under the Consumer Protection Act 1987.

Tortious liability

27.2   A number of features can be identified as prerequisites for a successful claim in tort:

1. a duty of care must be owed to the claimant by the defending party;
2. there must be a breach of that duty;
3. loss must result from that breach;
4. the loss must not be too remote a consequence of the breach; and

5.   the loss must be of a nature which is accepted as giving rise to a claim for compensation.

Brief consideration will now be given to each of these elements and as to the significance which they possess in the software field.

Duty of care

27.3   The starting point in the law of tort is the requirement that a duty be owed between the parties. In the UK, the scope of such duties is defined by reference to the neighbour principle. Under this, everyone owes a duty of care towards his or her neighbour. As defined by Lord Atkins in the seminal case of *Donoghue v Stevenson*, the word 'neighbour' encompasses those:

> ... persons who are so closely and directly affected by my act that I ought reasonably to have them in contemplation as being so affected when I am directing my mind to the acts or omissions which are called in question.[1]

[1]   [1932] AC 562 at 580.

27.4   It follows from this that tortuous duties do not extend to the world at large. Indeed, it was only in 1932 that it was finally accepted that the manufacturer of a product owed any duty towards the ultimate user in the event that the latter suffered injury because of a defect in the product. Within continental jurisdictions, the extent of the duty of care tends to be formulated more widely. Thus, the French and German Civil Codes provide, respectively:

> Any act whatever of man which causes damage to another obliges him by whose fault it occurred to make reparation.[1]

> A person who, intentionally or negligently, injures unlawfully the life, body, health, freedom, property or any other right of another person is bound to compensate him for any damage arising therefrom.[2]

[1]   Article 1382.
[2]   Article 823.

27.5   The application of this rule will not generally pose problems for a party claiming against a software producer. Software is a flexible tool, however, and may be put to uses which were not expected by the producer. Cases have been cited where spreadsheet packages, intended for use in the making of financial calculations, have been used by heart surgeons in the course of major operations. In the event that a failure in the package resulted in injury or death to the patient, it might well be argued that this category of person was outwith the reasonable contemplation of the software producer.

Breach of duty

27.6   Not every act which causes loss to another will give rise to an action in tort. Save in exceptional circumstances, some element of fault must also be present. This is most frequently expressed in terms of negligence – a failure to observe that standard of care which would be observed by a reasonable person placed in the position of the defending party.

27.7   The concept of the reasonable man is a flexible one which will be adjusted to take account of the nature of and the particular circumstances under which an action occurred. In the event, for example, that the activities of a member of a profession are called into question, the requisite standard will be that of the reasonable member of that profession. Some difficulty may be anticipated in the software field in that, given the relative novelty of the subject, professional bodies have yet to acquire the recognition and status afforded to those representing the more traditional professions such as law or medicine. This has posed problems within the US, where the doctrine of professional malpractice requires the observance of a higher duty of care on the part of members of recognised professions. In a number of cases, the courts have refused to accept the concept of computer malpractice.[1]

[1]   See *Chatlos Systems Inc v National Cash Register Corpn* 479 F Supp 738 (1979).

27.8   Such difficulties are unlikely to arise in the UK, where a more pragmatic approach prevails. Under this, questions as to the requisite standard of care are essentially factual ones, which may be resolved through the production of expert witnesses who can speak to the level of performance that they would expect of a party in the position of the defender. Although it is not unusual for expert witnesses to come to different opinions, reports of proceedings in a number of computer-related disputes appear to demonstrate an unusually high level of divergence. In the case of *Missing Link Software v Magee*,[1] a case concerned with alleged infringement of copyright, the expert witnesses' disagreements prompted the judge to comment of one report where the expert had indicated that he had attempted to express his views in as moderate a fashion as possible:

> In the course of eight or nine pages the following expressions may be found: 'effect of misleading the court in a major way'; 'fundamental errors'; 'conclusions which are at best fanciful and in my opinion not worthy of serious consideration'; 'no grounds whatsoever for the conclusions reached'; 'no person of reasonable common sense'; 'displays an inability to read a program'; 'cannot distinguish between'; 'this is a ridiculous inference to draw'; 'an error of which even a schoolboy would be ashamed'; 'attempting to mislead the court'; 'this is another absolutely basic error'; 'paragraph 17 and 18 are of course based on the same fundamental error'; 'sheer and utter nonsense' ... One shudders to think what he might have said if he had really let himself go.

[1]   [1989] FSR 361.

27.9   The absence of a consensus regarding even basic aspects of software development must render difficult the task of a judge in determining whether any aspect of the work might have been tainted by negligence. The sheer pace of technological development also creates substantial problems. The example of the Millennium Bug provides a relevant illustration. Certainly, it would be considered negligent today to supply software which was not capable of coping with a date in the year 2000, but the question may still arise in legal proceedings as to when a reasonable software producer should have been aware of the problem. One of the first recorded uses of the term Millennium Bug was in 1989.[1] A search of the Nexis database, which contains the full text of leading UK newspapers, indicates that the first use of the phrase 'millennium bug' occurred in early 1995.

[1]   Cited in P Neumann *Computer-Related Risks* (1995, ACM Press).

Application of the concept of negligence to software

27.10   As has been stated previously, the quest for perfect software has proved as successful as the hunt for the Loch Ness monster. Cynics might suggest that neither exist. In the real world, the producer's compliance with generally observed industry standards may be sufficient to comply with tortuous requirements. A number of formal standards do exist in the information technology field, although it may be doubted how far these may assist in the task of identifying negligent conduct. An international standard, ISO 9126, identifies six quality characteristics which might be applied in determining questions of software quality. These comprise: functionality, reliability, usability, efficiency, maintainability and portability.

27.11   Although identification of critical qualities is of value, the standard provides no assistance in answering the legal question 'how much?'. Other standards may provide more precise guidance. ISO 9127, for example, is entitled 'User documentation and cover information for consumer software packages' and provides detailed guidance regarding the information which should be supplied on the outer cover of a software package. This is considered important to enable 'potential purchasers to assess the applicability of the package to their requirements'. Items covered include the intended purpose of the software, any hardware and software requirements, any design restrictions and information about any licence provisions. Studies suggest, however, that few producers meet this standard.[1] Given this, it may be difficult to argue that a failure to observe the standard would constitute negligence. In the Scottish case of *Kelly v Mears and Partners*,[2] a failure by an architect to follow the provisions of a British Standard Code of Practice was held not to constitute professional negligence. The terms of the Code, it was held, had no evidential value in their own right and could be relied upon only in so far as it was referred to in evidence by witnesses speaking as to the professional standard applicable to the particular case.

[1]   *Personal Computer World*, April 1989.
[2]   1983 SC 97.

27.12   The standard of the reasonable man will normally be determined by reference to that generally prevailing in the trade or profession. This may not always be conclusive. A professional journal has reported an instance whereby a factory employee was killed by a robot. Safety devices were available, including an electronic beam which caused the robot to cease working if a person approached too close. The report indicated that this feature was offered at extra cost. The reason advanced as to why it was not fitted as standard was that the producer had:

> ... polled customers for their reactions. But because there have been so few problems of safety until recently, customers haven't felt the need for it. [The Producer] knows of no other robot manufacturer that includes the safety device as a standard.[1]

Without attempting to analyse the particular issues involved, the example illustrates a difficulty with leaving decisions as to the level of safety devices to members of the industry involved.

[1]   (1985) 10 Communication of the Association of Computing Machinery 3.

Liability for use of information technology

27.13   A number of instances have been documented of humans being injured or even killed by coming into contact with computer-controlled products. Robots have killed factory workers, computer-controlled X-ray machines have exposed hospital patients to excessive doses of radiation, computer-controlled ambulance despatch systems have failed, causing delays in the arrival of ambulances. The list could go on and on.

27.14   Save in the most extreme case, it may be considered unlikely that a decision to use technical devices will, of itself, constitute negligence. Significant issues may concern the manner in which the technology is introduced and applied. A British Standard[1] which provides a guide to specifying user requirements for a computer-based system contains detailed guidance as to the information which users should provide to and seek from potential suppliers of computer systems. Although the dividing line between the user's and the supplier's obligations may be unclear, the standard makes it clear that a user cannot abdicate all responsibility.

[1]   BS 6719, 1986.

27.15   A particular requirement imposed upon those responsible for computer systems must be to ensure that those responsible for using the technology are adequately trained. In the case of *The Lady Gwendolen*,[1] a ship had radar installed but the owners took no steps to ensure its proper use by the crew. A collision resulted, largely as a consequence of the crew's failure in this regard, and the owners were held liable in negligence for damage caused to the other vessel owing to their failure to secure the satisfactory use of radar. The message from this case is clear. It is not enough for an employer to install an effective information technology system. Steps must also be taken to ensure that employees are trained in its operation and, on a continuing basis, to ensure that proper procedures are followed.

[1]   [1965] P 294.

27.16 Evidence of the problems that may arise in this respect can be taken from the report of the inquiry into the London Ambulance Service.[1] This inquiry was conducted following a number of well-publicised failures in a recently installed computer system controlling the despatch of ambulances. Matters subjected to critical comment in the report include the selection of a supplier with limited experience of work in the field, of the haste with which the system was introduced (which did not allow for sufficient testing of the various components), the failure to provide adequate training and the absence of contingency plans to cope with system failures.

[1] South West Thames Regional Health Authority (February 1993).

27.17 A further issue that may arise concerns the question of whether extensive reliance is placed on information technology products. An instance has been reported from the US of a situation where an accountant used an established tax calculation program in the course of preparing a client's tax returns. A fault in the software meant that the client made an overpayment of $36,800. Although this sum was eventually repaid, the loss of interest amounted to some $700.[1] A similar bug has been reported in a tax package developed to assist UK taxpayers in dealing with the new self-assessment system. The package was supplied free of charge to registered users of an existing personal finance package, thereby creating problems due to the lack of consideration in the event a customer sought to claim under the law of contract. Media reports indicate that the producer has offered to refund any penalties imposed by the Inland Revenue for inaccurate returns. The indications, however, are that the bug will result in over- rather than under-payment.

[1] *The Risks Digest*, available from http://catless/ncl.ac.uk/Risks.

27.18 In this example, the relationship between the client and the accountant would be a contractual one. The requirements as regards negligence, however, will be equivalent to those applying in the non-contractual situation. It might be argued that a failure to check the output from a computer system might constitute negligence. Against this, many aspects of life today are so complex that the use of computers provides the only cost-effective means of conducting business. The report indicates that the accounts making up the tax return in question were more than half an inch thick. In such situations, there may be little option other than to place reliance upon the computer's output. Especially where the user operates in a professional capacity, it may be argued that a failure to detect major errors in output would amount to negligence.

Liability for failure to use information technology

27.19 If the application of information technology may expose the user to the risk of liability, so a failure to take advantage of the technology might also amount to negligence. Once again, reference to prevailing practice in the particular area of activity will furnish assistance. If use of technical aids is not commonplace, then a failure on the part of a particular defendant is unlikely to constitute negligence. There may, however, be exceptions to this rule. The US case of *The T J Hooper*[1] provides an illustration of such a situation. Here, two barges were lost in a storm at sea. The storm had been forecast and a warning broadcast on the radio. Unfortunately, the tugs towing the barges did not have radio sets installed and so the opportunity to take shelter was lost. Holding the tug owners liable for the resultant loss, it was determined that the failure to provide a radio constituted a negligent omission. Although the evidence before the court fell far short of establishing that it was common practice to install radio equipment on tugs, the particular owner was held liable, the court commenting that '(a)whole calling may have unduly lagged in the adoption of new and available devices'. To this extent, producers and others may be considered under a continuing duty to keep up to date with technical developments and to modify their standards accordingly.

[1]   60 F 2d 737 (1932).

27.20   As the global usage of information technology products expands, so it might be reasonable to expect that their application will become the rule rather than the exception in more and more areas of activity. It has been suggested that a failure to use computers in the course of activities such as air traffic control would amount to negligence.[1] The suppliers of a computerised legal retrieval service have suggested in publicity materials that a failure by a lawyer to make use of their system might constitute professional negligence. To date, these issues have not been tested in court. It may be that a distinction should be drawn between the situation where technology is used to substitute for human action, for example, where automated equipment is used to perform tasks in a factory that would require humans to be exposed to some form of danger and those, as with the examples cited above, where the technology provides assistance to humans.

[1]   C Tapper *Computer Law* (1989, Longman).

27.21   In terms of legal principle, the application of information technology raises no novel issues in the field of negligence. The rapid pace of technical development may pose practical problems. As discussed in the previous section, reliance upon unstable or immature technology might be held negligent, whilst excessive delay in adopting proven technical aids might also be so regarded.

Causation

27.22   To establish liability, a claimant must establish that the breach of the duty was the proximate cause of the resulting damage. In many respects, this requirement raises factual rather than legal problems. During 1987, for example, problems were encountered with a number of medical linear accelerators being used to treat patients suffering from cancer. The operation of the machines was controlled by software. Owing to an undetected flaw in the software, if the operator inserted an unusual but possible series of commands, the machine subjected the patient to a massive overdose of radiation. A number of the patients subsequently died.[1]

1   H Bassen, J Silverberg, F Houston et al *Computerised Medical Devices*, Proceedings of the Seventh Annual Conference of IEEE Engineering in Medicine and Biology Society, 1985, p 180.

27.23   Assuming that the negligence can be established in such a case, there would appear little doubt that a causal link between the operation of the equipment and the injury could be established. A more recent incident occurring in the UK raises more complex issues. Once again, it concerned equipment being used to provide radiation treatment to cancer patients. In this case, however, an operator error resulted in patients receiving up to 30% less radiation than intended. Whilst an overdose of radiation will cause physical injury to the recipient, a shortfall will not of itself cause injury, but may have the effect of depriving the patient of possible benefit. A spokesman for the Department of Health was quoted as conceding that 'There is no doubt that negligence was involved'.[1] Although a £2 million settlement has recently been negotiated between the Health Authority involved and around 100 of the patients affected, a report on the incident stated that 'it was virtually impossible to say whether those who had died would have survived had it not been for the mistake'.[2] Particularly given the insidious nature of the disease, the existence of a causal link between negligence and injury would be very difficult to establish in court.

1   *Independent*, 7 February 1992.
2   *Independent*, 22 April 1997.

27.24   A further illustration of this point can be taken from the case of *R v Poplar Coroner, ex p Thomas*.[1] The Court of Appeal reversed an order that an inquest be held into the death of a young woman. The woman had suffered from asthma throughout her life. In April 1989, she suffered a serious attack and a call was made to the ambulance service. The 999 call produced only a recorded message: 'There is no one here at present. Please hold on and we will answer your call as soon as we can.' By the time contact was made with the ambulance service and an ambulance arrived, over half an hour had elapsed and the patient was dead. A post-mortem examination and report indicated that prompt treatment would have saved the patient's life.

1   [1993] 2 All ER 381.

27.25   Under the provisions of the Coroners Act 1988, an inquest may be held only in specified circumstances, including where there is reasonable ground to suspect that death was 'unnatural'.[1] The coroner refused to hold an inquest in this case on the basis that the death was not unnatural. This view was upheld by the Court of Appeal.[2] Referring to the dicta of Lord Salmon in *Alphacell Ltd v Woodward*, to the effect that:

... who or what has caused a certain event to occur is essentially a practical question of fact which can best be answered by ordinary common sense rather than by abstract metaphysical theory.[3]

1   Section 8(1).
2   *R v Poplar Coroner, ex p Thomas* [1993] QB 610.
3   [1972] 2 All ER 475 at 490.

27.26   Dillon LJ recognised that a variety of scenarios could be postulated under which an ambulance might arrive too late to save such a patient. Included in his examples was the possibility that:

... a newly installed computer installed by the ambulance service to handle emergency calls more efficiently malfunctioned as newly installed computers are prone to.[1]

From the perspective of the provisions of the Coroners Act 1988, however, the illness must be regarded as the 'cause' of death. Asthma being a relatively common medical condition, the death was not, he considered, unnatural.

1   *R v Poplar Coroner, ex p Thomas* [1993] QB 610 at 628.

27.27   In many cases, the result of a failure on the part of an information technology system will be to deprive a person of some form of warning. An example might be the failure on the part of a computer-controlled fire alarm to sound when a fire occurred. In such a situation, there might well be an argument that the alarm was not of satisfactory quality or fit for its purpose, but in the event that injury or damage occurred, it would be difficult to argue that the failure of the alarm was the proximate cause.

Remoteness of damage

27.28   The test of causation is essentially a factual one. Common sense dictates, however, that some limits must be placed upon the extent of a negligent party's responsibilities. Illustrations of the extreme consequences following the application of the 'but for' test belong in the history rather than the law books. The test of remoteness sets legal boundaries determining the forms of damage and the categories of injured party to whom an admittedly negligent party may be liable.

27.29   The relationship between the issues of causation and remoteness is close, and similar issues may arise under both headings. In the example of the delayed arrival of an ambulance, the defence to an action by a patient might be based either on the absence of a causal link or on the ground that the injury was too remote a consequence of the original negligence.

27.30   Once again, the test of reasonable foresight will come into play, with a defendant being held liable only for losses of a kind which it was reasonably foreseeable could spring from his or her negligent acts or omissions. In the event that damage of a particular kind could have been anticipated, full liability will be incurred even though the extent of the damage might not have been foreseen. The literature on computer viruses is replete with plaintive tales of students creating and disseminating viruses by way of a practical joke, only to discover that the consequences of their action were much more serious. Once the intent to cause a little harm can be established, the perpetrator will be liable for the full amount of damage, even though the scale is much greater than might have been intended or expected.

Novus actus interveniens

27.31   One factor which may serve to terminate a party's liabilities on the ground of remoteness may arise where a third party intervenes in the chain of events leading from negligent act to injury or damage. In some instances, the third party will serve merely as a conduit whose involvement will not diminish the original actor's responsibilities. A party may, for example, develop a computer virus and put infected disks into circulation. If the virus spreads, it will be through the action of third parties using the disks. In the event that the intermediary acts negligently or intentionally in propagating the virus, liability may be incurred on this basis, but it must be doubted whether this will diminish in any way the liability of the originator of the virus towards those whose computers are affected.

27.32   More complex issues arise where the involvement of the third party contributes in larger part towards the ultimate injury. Where a complex information technology system is supplied which requires a high degree of skill on the part of its users, injury to a third party resulting from the negligent operation of the system would normally be considered too remote to impose liability upon the supplier. Although there appears no authority on the point, it might be argued that the supplier would remain liable in the event he or she should have been aware that the user would not be able to obtain staff of a sufficient level of expertise to operate the product in a reasonably safe manner. Again, a failure to supply adequate instructions for the use of the product might leave the supplier exposed to an action by an injured third party.

Compensatable loss

27.33   The final requirement for a successful claim in tort requires that the particular form of loss suffered by the claimant should be recognised at law. In principle, damages may be claimed under the law of tort in respect of any form of damage. During the 1970s and early 1980s, the distinction between contractual and tortuous liability appeared to be steadily eroded. In the case of *Junior Books v Veitchi*, Lord Roskill commented that:

I think today the proper control lies not in asking whether the proper remedy should lie in contract or instead in tort, not in somewhat capricious judicial determination whether a particular case falls on one side of the line or the other, not in somewhat artificial distinctions between physical or economic loss when the two sometimes go together and sometimes do not (it is sometimes overlooked that virtually all damage including physical damage is in one sense financial or economic for it is compensated by an award of damages) but in the first instance in establishing the relevant principles and then in deciding whether a particular case falls within or without those principles.[1]

[1] [1983] 1 AC 520 at 545.

27.34 The effect of such an approach was at least to accept the possibility that damages might be awarded in tort in respect of defects which served to diminish the value of a product, rather than requiring that the product cause injury damage to persons or property. More recently, however, the courts have retreated substantially from such a proposition. In the case of *CBS Songs Ltd v Amstrad Consumer Electronics plc*,[1] the House of Lords considered and rejected the proposition that the manufacturer of audio equipment, in this case a hi-fi unit with two cassette decks, owed a tortuous duty of care to the owners of copyright in musical works whose interests, it was alleged, would be adversely affected in the event that users of the equipment used its facilities to make unauthorised copies of pre-recorded cassette tapes. Delivering the judgment of the court, Lord Templeman was critical of the approach in *Junior Books*[2] and the earlier case of *Anns v Merton London Borough Council*,[3] stating that since these decisions:

... a fashionable plaintiff alleges negligence. The pleading assumes that we are all neighbours now, Pharisees and Samaritans alike, that foreseeability is a reflection of hindsight and that for every mischance in an accident-prone world someone solvent must be liable in damages.[4]

[1] [1988] AC 1013.
[2] *Junior Books v Veitchi* [1983] 1 AC 520.
[3] [1978] AC 728.
[4] [1988] AC 1013 at 1059.

27.35 In particular, the courts are today extremely reluctant to award compensation for economic loss.[1] The concept of economic loss is not easily or precisely defined. It may consist of a sum representing the diminished value of a product which is considered to be defective, or it may represent lost profits resulting from an inability to perform what would otherwise be a profitable activity. An example might be found in the case of a person who negligently cuts off a factory's electricity supply causing cessation of production. Certainly, the party will be held liable for any form of physical damage which may be caused to the factory or its assets, but will not be held responsible for the lost profits which may result from the breakdown in production. Although the case of *Junior Books*[2] remains as precedent for the proposition that economic loss might be compensated in the event that the relationship between the parties is akin to one based in contract, it must be questioned how far this approach will be followed in any future decisions.

1   See *D & F Estates v Church Comrs for England* [1989] 2 All ER 992 and *Murphy v Brentwood District Council* [1990] 2 All ER 908.
2   *Junior Books v Veitchi* [1983] 1 AC 520.

27.36   In many instances, the arguments that have persuaded the courts to backtrack from the award of damages for economic loss outside the contractual relationship will apply with particular force to information technology. Comparatively few products operate in the safety-critical field, most being concerned with more mundane tasks where the consequence of a failure will be some form of economic loss. The example of the tax calculation program cited at para 27.17 above provides an excellent illustration. Thousands of copies of such a product may be sold, they may be used in a large number of situations and their operation may result in exposure to a great variety of risks ranging from minor inconvenience to the substantial losses referred to in the example. In this and in many other situations it might be unreasonable to hold the producer liable. Another example cited from the US may further evidence the point. In this, proceedings were initiated against the Lotus Corporation alleging that a defect in their spreadsheet had resulted in a building contractor submitting a tender which was too low. The contract was awarded, only for the contractor to discover that the work could be carried out only at a loss.

27.37   This action was withdrawn before trial but the case provides some evidence of the range of situations in which a basic software product might be used and of the impossibility for the producer to anticipate the extent of potential losses. A final example might be cited from the author's own experience. Students on a postgraduate course were required to submit a sizeable number of items of assessment. The marks attained were entered into a spreadsheet program to calculate the final mark. Two different departments used two different makes of spreadsheet. When the figures were rounded up or down to the nearest whole number, the result in the case of one student was that there was a disagreement between the spreadsheets. One gave a pass mark of 50% and the other a fail at 49%. Analysis of the possible legal consequences of such a result might occupy most of this book. Could either of the spreadsheets be considered wrong? Should the users have been aware of this possibility? Should all marks be double-checked? Assuming the student was denied a degree because of an incorrect output, would any form of compensation be available? Fortunately for the student, and unfortunately for the legal profession, this incident ended with the higher mark being selected.

Defences

27.38   In the event that liability can prima facie be identified under the law of tort, attention must be paid to the defences which may be available, and as to the forms of loss or damage which may be compensated. An obvious defence to any action in tort will consist of the claim that the claimant has failed to establish any of the factors outlined above adequately. Two further defences should receive specific mention.

Contributory negligence

27.39 Contributory negligence should, perhaps, be regarded as a plea in mitigation rather than as a defence per se. Under its ambit, the defender admits a degree of culpability but argues that the claimant was also partially responsible for the damage. Contributory negligence may be an appropriate plea in the event that a claim relates to the inadequacy of instructions supplied with a product. Save in the event that the instructions are simply erroneous, any loss may result from a combination of their deficiencies and the claimant's failure either to comprehend their proper message or to realise that they provided an unsafe basis for reliance and, therefore, that the product should not be used pending clarification.

27.40 Another area where contributory negligence may be relevant would be in the situation where the claimant failed to take precautions such as ensuring that back-up copies were maintained of programs or data. Dependent upon the nature of the activity and the risks involved, further measures might be required to guard against the risk of software or hardware failure. Where computers are utilised in aircraft, for example, a party could be guilty of at least contributory negligence if adequate provision were not made against the possibility of failure. In most cases, this involves the provision of two or even three independent systems, each of which can enable the plane to operate safely.

Volenti non fit injuria

27.41 The underlying basis of the doctrine of volenti is that acts which would otherwise give rise to legal liability will not do so in the event that they are directed against a person who has consented to accept that particular risk of injury. The application of the doctrine is most prominent in the sporting field. Under normal circumstances, the act of punching another party would undoubtedly constitute a tort (and render the perpetrator liable to criminal prosecution). A boxer, however, by agreeing to enter into a contest with another, must be taken as accepting the risk of injury. With volenti, however, it is important to recognise the limitations of the consent. A party will be taken to have accepted only those risks which are inherent to the sport itself. If a boxer strikes a blow outside the rules of the sport, his opponent will be entitled to raise an action in tort.

27.42 The above sporting example is an illustration of a situation where consent to a risk may be implied from the very fact of participating in an undertaking. Such situations will be rare. In the normal course of life, people are entitled to assume that their interests will not be adversely affected by the negligence of others. It may be that if a hacker secures access to a computer system only to find that, owing to a defect in the victim computer, his or her own system is damaged, volenti will provide a complete defence to any claim for compensation which might be raised.

Measure of damages

27.43 The purpose of an award of damages under the law of tort is, in so far as is possible, to return the injured party to the position occupied prior to the occurrence of the negligent act. This approach is to be contrasted with the position under the law of contract, where the purpose of an award of damages is to put the innocent party in the position that would have been occupied had the contract been completed. In the event, for example, that A contracts to provide B with a piece of software for £50,000, if A fails to deliver the software so that B has to obtain the product elsewhere at a cost of £100,000, this latter figure will be the appropriate amount of an award. Under the law of tort, if A negligently destroys B's software which cost £50,000 when new but will now cost £100,000 to replace, the maximum measure of damages will be £50,000. To this extent, contractual damages may be more extensive than their tortuous equivalent.

Exclusion of tortuous liability

27.44 A further aspect of this topic relates to the extent to which a party may give notice of a refusal to accept liability for losses arising in the course of a non-contractual relationship. The issues involved here are similar to those applying in the context of contractual exclusion clauses. Couched this time in terms of the tortuous duty of care, it might be argued that if a party announces an unwillingness to accept any responsibility for the fate of another, this will serve to prevent the creation or continuance of any duty of care. An illustration here might see the provision of a notice on the screen of a computer program warning users against placing reliance upon the program's output. Alternatively, the provision of a notice warning of a risk, for example, a 'beware of the dog' sign, might be seen as fulfilling a duty of care.

27.45 Under the provisions of the Unfair Contract Terms Act 1977, any attempt to exclude tortuous liability in respect of personal injury or death resulting from a negligent act will be invalid.[1] This is not to say that a claim for compensation in respect of such an occurrence will succeed. The provision of a suitable warning notice may well discharge the duty of care. What will be necessary in this case is that the notice be sufficiently brought to the attention of the other party at a stage where this party retains genuine freedom to determine whether to proceed with a particular course of action, accepting the consequential risk of loss. In the case of software, this would require that a prominent notice appear as soon as a user begins to operate the system.

[1]   Section 2.

Product liability and software

27.46 The entry into force of the product liability provisions of the Consumer Protection Act 1987 has brought about major changes in the non-contractual liability regime in the UK. The Act, which was introduced pursuant to the requirements of an EC Directive[1] on the 'approximation of the laws, regulations and administrative provisions of the member states concerning liability for defective products',[2] serves principally to introduce a system of no fault liability in respect of certain forms of injury and damage.

[1] In most respects, the Directive and the Act utilise terminology that is substantially similar. Where this is the case, specific references will be to the provisions of the Act.
[2] Directive 85/374/EEC, OJ 1985 L 210/26.

27.47 The rationale behind the Directive[1] can be found in its Preamble which asserts that:

> ... liability without fault on the part of the producer is the sole means of adequately solving the problem, peculiar to our age of increasing technicality, and of a fair apportionment of the risks inherent in modern production.
>
> Thus, public policy demands that the burden of accidental injuries caused by products should be placed upon the producer and be treated as a cost of production arguing that the producer can best afford and meet these costs. A further factor in this calculation lies in the relative ease with which a producer should be able to obtain insurance cover against any costs incurred in this manner.

[1] Directive 85/374/EEC.

27.48 Removing the requirement that a claimant establishes negligence effectively places a defending producer in the position of an insurer. In some respects, the Consumer Protection Act 1987 equates the non-contractual liability of a producer with the contractual liability of a supplier under the Sale of Goods Act 1979, although this is restricted to incidents of injury or damage and does not afford the consumer with any rights where the product is of poor quality. This marks a fundamental change in the common law approach, although the Directive[1] requires fewer changes in civil law-based systems, which have increasingly in consumer cases tended to impose either strict liability or apply a presumption of fault, thereby shifting the onus of proof on to the defendant. Although the doctrine of res ipsa loquitur permits a similar approach to be followed in the UK, this has operated only in restricted circumstances.

[1] Directive 85/374/EEC.

Scope of the legislation

Parties liable

27.49 A number of parties involved in the production or distribution chain may incur liability under the provisions of the Directive[1] and the Consumer

Protection Act 1987. An action may be brought against the producer of the finished product – or any persons who, by putting a name or brand mark on goods produced by a third party, hold themselves out as being the producer. Action may also be taken against the producer of any component incorporated into the product where it is claimed that that component is defective. In the case that a product is imported into the EC, the importer will be liable in the event it proves defective.[2]

[1] Directive 85/374/EEC.
[2] Section 1(2).

27.50 Any supplier of the product may also incur liability under the Consumer Protection Act 1987. This liability, however, will arise only in the event that it is asked by an injured consumer to identify one or more of the parties referred to in the preceding paragraph and, without reasonable excuse, fails so to do.[1] This provision is likely to be of relevance only where products are imported or carry no brand or other identification marks.

[1] Section 2(3).

Products

27.51 The Consumer Protection Act 1987 and the Directive[1] apply in respect of products. A further EC directive was proposed which would apply approximately equivalent provisions in respect of the liability of service providers.[2] This directive was withdrawn for revision following the adoption of the new doctrine of subsidiarity, although the Commissions' Consumer Action Plan 1999–2001'[3] indicates the intention to bring forward a new proposal.

[1] Directive 85/374/EEC.
[2] COM (90) 482 final – SYN 308.
[3] COM (98) 696.

27.52 For the purposes of the Directive, a product is defined as:

All movables, with the exception of primary agricultural products and game, even though incorporated into another movable or immovable ... 'Product' includes electricity.[1]

[1] Directive 85/374/EEC, art 2.

27.53 The Consumer Protection Act 1987 utilises different terminology, defining a product as 'any goods or electricity'.[1] Assuming the application of the Sale of Goods Act 1979 definition whereby the word 'goods' encompasses 'all personal chattels other than things in action and money',[2] the British and European definitions appear virtually identical. The question as to their application to software has, however, produced significant disagreement between the UK and the Community authorities. In a consultative document published by the UK Department of Trade and Industry concerning the introduction of legislation on this topic, it was stated:

Special problems arise with those industries dealing with those products concerned with information such as books ... and computer software. It has been suggested that it would be absurd for printers to be held liable for faithfully reproducing errors in the material provided to them that by giving bad instructions ... indirectly causes injury.[3]

By contrast, Lord Cockfield, in responding to a written question in the European Parliament concerning the application of the directive to software, stated unequivocally that:

Under article 2 of (the) directive ... on liability for defective products[4] ... the term product is defined as all movables, with the exception of primary agricultural products (not having undergone initial processing) and game, even though incorporated into another movable or into an immovable. Consequently the directive applies to software in the same way, moreover, that it applies to handicrafts and artistic products.[5]

Neither comment can be regarded as definitive of the status of software under the respective instruments. It may be that questions as to the scope of the Directive and as to the conformity of national implementing legislation will have to be determined before the European Court of Justice.

[1]   Section 1(2).
[2]   Section 61(1).
[3]   'Implementation of the EC Directive on Product Liability, Department of Trade and Industry' (1985) para 47.
[4]   Directive 85/374/EEC.
[5]   OJ 1989 C 114/42.

27.54   Issues of product liability concerning the operation of information technology products may arise in two respects. In the present chapter, consideration will be given to the liability that may arise where software is used to control the operation of some other product. Numerous examples could be cited – it is an unusual car or aircraft which does not possess its quota of microprocessors. Even mundane household objects such as washing machines and video recorders may be so equipped. In this situation, the question of whether the software is itself a product is of limited significance. The plane or the car or the washing machine will undoubtedly be so regarded and the issue to be discussed will be the manner in which that product functions, taking account of the role of any software.

Damage

27.55   Only limited categories of damage may be compensated. Compensation may be claimed in respect of personal injury or in respect of damage to any property which is of a kind ordinarily intended for private use or consumption and which is used for such a purpose. A de minimis rule applies, with the effect that the damage must be costed at a minimum of £275. Finally, the producer will incur no liability in respect of damage to the product itself or to any other product of which it constitutes a component part.[1] Thus, in the event that the software controlling the operation of a motor car's anti-lock braking system fails, causing an accident, no compensation will be payable in respect of the damage to the vehicle itself.

¹ Consumer Protection Act 1987, s 5.

27.56 The Directive provides that national legislation may impose an overall ceiling of €70m on the liability of a producer in respect of damage arising from identical items.¹ This option was not exercised in the Consumer Protection Act 1987, so that a producer may be held liable for any amount of damage resulting from defective products.

¹ Directive 85/374/EEC, art 16(1).

Defectiveness

27.57 A producer will incur liability only when a product is defective. A product will so stigmatised if 'it does not provide the level of safety that persons generally are entitled to expect'.¹ In determining questions of defectiveness, account is to be taken of the manner in which the product is marketed, any normal or intended uses and any instructions supplied to the user. Account is also to be taken of the state of the art in respect of products of that kind, both the Consumer Protection Act 1987 and Directive² providing that a product is not to be characterised as defective merely because a safer product subsequently becomes available.³

¹ Section 3(1), art 6(1).
² Directive 85/374/EEC.
³ Section 3(2), art 6(2).

27.58 In considering the level of safety that may legitimately be sought by persons coming into contact with a product, it may be argued that they expect complete safety. Although a degree of risk may attach to almost any activity, be it a plane journey or the carving of a joint of meat, the passenger and the carver are surely entitled to expect that they will arrive safely at their intended destination. The effect of the approach adopted in the legislation would appear to be to establish a presumption of defectiveness in the event that injury or damage occurs connected with the operation of a product. The onus is then upon the producer to demonstrate that the cause was something other than a defect in the product. In the event, for example, that a cook cuts his or her hand whilst carving the meat, it is arguable that any defectiveness lies with the user rather than the product. In this context, the adequacy of any instructions supplied for the use of a product may be of considerable significance. Disregard by users of warnings concerning design limitations in a product's capabilities might result in them being regarded the author of their own misfortune in the event they suffer injury or damage.

27.59 More significant in the information technology field is the provision that the performance of a product in safety terms is to be judged against contemporary products. To illustrate this provision, we might take the example of cars designed in 1970 and 1990 being driven at the same speed. If the cars' brakes were to be applied simultaneously, one would expect the more modern design of brakes to stop the car in a shorter distance. If the difference in stopping distances marked the difference between hitting an object or stopping short, the older car would not be considered defective on this count. Given the pace of developments in information technology, this provision might be of considerable importance, although its application may not prove a simple matter.

27.60 The possibility of drawing comparison with the general level of performance reasonably to be expected from a product of the kind in question will apply only in respect of risks which are inherent to the activity involved, but which are extrinsic to the product itself which performs at the level that a user might reasonably expect. On this basis it might be argued that as every computer program possesses defects, every product so controlled will be defective and that a user is entitled to expect only a defective product. This argument appears to run counter to the basic philosophy of the product liability regime. As described above, the directive proclaims that:

> ... liability without fault on the part of the producer is the sole means of adequately solving the problem, peculiar to our age of increasing technicality, and of a fair apportionment of the risks inherent in modern production.[1]

[1]   Directive 85/374/EEC, Preamble.

27.61   In many areas of activity, there are statistically verifiable risks associated with product failure. An aircraft will be certified for public use not on the basis that its components will never fail, but that it is extremely unlikely that this will occur. If it is calculated that one accident will occur per 10 million hours of flight because of some defect introduced at the design or production stage, it would not appear open to a producer to utilise the defence subsequent to an accident that its occurrence was in line with the statistical predictions.

27.62   On this basis, a defence would be available to a motor car manufacturer that the state of technical knowledge would not permit the production of a braking system capable of stopping a car travelling at 50 mph within 30 feet. In the situation where the car's brakes had failed, it would not be open to the producer to claim that it was not possible to produce a braking system with a failure rate of less than one in 100,000 applications. In the same manner, a software producer should not be heard to argue that a product fails no more often than its competitors.

Defences

27.63   The basic defence to a claim under the product liability legislation will consist of the assertion that the product was not defective at the time it left the producer's control.[1] As indicated above, this will normally be an issue of fact. In one respect, the position of a software producer will be less tenable than is the case with more tangible products. Software will not deteriorate with the passage of time. The possibility that a user may have introduced a defect by mishandling the product will also have limited application in respect of software. To a greater extent than with other products, the state of a software-based product at the moment an accident occurs can be considered equivalent to its state at the moment that the product left the producer's control.

[1] Consumer Protection Act 1987, s 4(1)(d) and Directive 85/374/EEC, art 7(b).

Compliance with legal requirements

27.64 Additionally, it will be a defence for the producer to establish that the defect resulted from compliance with any requirement imposed by or under any enactment or with any Community obligation.[1] Effectively, this will require evidence that the producer was legally required to produce to particular specifications and that the defect lay in the specifications. Few, if any, legal requirements exist in the software field, although they are more prevalent in the area of information technology products concerning such matters as electromagnetic emissions and electrical safety. Even here, the regulations are more likely to prescribe standards – leaving the manner in which these are attained to the producer – than to prescribe particular aspects of product design.

[1] Consumer Protection Act 1987, s 4(1)(a) and Directive 85/374/EEC, art 7(d).

Conformity with specification

27.65 A more relevant provision applies in the situation where a product is produced for incorporation into another product. In this instance, the legislation provides the component producer with a defence that the defect:

> ... was wholly attributable to the design of the subsequent product or to compliance by the producer of the product in question with instructions given by the producer of the subsequent product.[1]

[1] Consumer Protection Act 1987, s 4(1)(f). Directive 85/374/EEC, art 7(f) is in similar terms.

27.66 Where a product is to incorporate software, the production of which is the responsibility of a sub-contractor, it might be that the latter will be able to use this defence where the requirements are laid down by the main producer and where any defect lies in these. A simple example might see a software company being required to develop a controlling program to work in certain temperatures, being told that it is to recognise temperatures of between -10 and +40°C. If the control system fails in temperatures of -20°C, it would appear inequitable to hold the software producer liable. The presence of the word 'wholly' in the statutory provision must limit its application. In the report of the Inquiry into

629

the London Ambulance Service, where the system specifications were drawn up by the customer, it is stated that:

> The (specification) is very detailed and contains a high degree of precision on the way in which the system was intended to operate. It is quite prescriptive and provided little scope for additional ideas to be incorporated from prospective suppliers.[1]

Interpretative difficulties may also be anticipated in the not uncommon situation where the two parties co-operate on the production of requirements, but where the contract for the work itself sees these being 'imposed' by the main producer.

[1]   South West Thames Regional Health Authority (1993) para 3017.

Development risks

27.67   This defence represents perhaps the most controversial element of the new product liability regime. As contained in the Directive, the development risks defence allows for the producer to demonstrate that although the product failed to provide the requisite level of safety:

> ... the state of scientific and technical knowledge at the time when he put the product into circulation was not such as to enable the existence of the defect to be discovered.[1]

The Consumer Protection Act 1987 adopts different terminology, providing that the defence will be available where:

> ... the state of scientific and technical knowledge at the relevant time was not such that a producer of products of the same description as the product in question might be expected to have discovered the defect if it had existed in his products while they were under his control.[2]

[1]   Directive 85/374/EEC, art 7(e).
[2]   Section 4(1)(e).

27.68   By substituting the phrase 'might be expected to have discovered' for the original 'enable the existence of the defect to be discovered', the UK legislation might be seen as extending the scope of the defence. This was the view of the Commission, which initiated legal proceedings against the UK authorities alleging that the change in terminology constituted a failure to implement the provisions of the Directive[1] fully, having the effect of 'transforming the strict or no-fault liability introduced by art 1 of the Directive into liability founded on negligence on the part of the producer'.[2] This claim was rejected by the Court of Justice in the case *European Commission v United Kingdom*.[3] The Directive's requirements relating to the defence, it was held, were:

> ... not specifically directed at the practices and safety standards in use in the industrial sector in which the product is operating, but, unreservedly, at the state of the scientific and technical knowledge, including the most advanced level of such knowledge, at the time when the product in question was put into circulation.

Second, the clause providing for the defence in question does not contemplate the state of knowledge of which the producer in question actually or subjectively was or could have been appraised, but the objective state of scientific and technical knowledge of which the producer is presumed to have been informed.[4]

1   Directive 85/374/EEC.
2   [1997] All ER (EC) 481 at 484.
3   [1997] All ER (EC) 481.
4   [1997] All ER (EC) 481 at 494–495.

27.69   The only additional feature which might limit the producer's exposure would be whether knowledge of risks might be accessible to the producer. The Advocate General in his opinion cited the example of a Manchurian researcher discovering information about a potential danger but where at the relevant time the information was published only in an obscure Chinese journal.

27.70   The UK provision, it was held, also referred to objective standards. The Commission's criticisms, it was ruled:

> ... selectively stresses particular terms used in s 4(1)(e) [of the Consumer Protection Act 1987] without demonstrating that the general legal context of the provision at issue fails effectively to secure full application of the directive [Directive 85/374/EEC].[1]

1   *European Commission v United Kingdom* [1997] All ER (EC) 481 at 495.

27.71   The decision of the court provides useful guidance on the interpretation of the Directive.[1] It is perhaps surprising that in the ten years in which the legislation has been in force, not a single case relating to the product liability regime has reached the High Court. Given the absence of any case law on the application of the defence – indeed no cases have been reported under any of the product liability provisions of the Consumer Protection Act 1987 – any comment must be speculative. For a variety of reasons, it is suggested, the defence should have little application in respect of software defects.

1   Directive 85/374/EEC.

27.72   Accepting that the Court of Justice's interpretation will be followed in the UK, it may further be noted that the defence refers to a particular type of defect rather than to its occurrence in a particular product. Thus, the defence will have no application in the event of failures of quality control. A producer's method of ensuring that mass-produced goods adhere to their design specifications can never be absolute, for 'the possibility remains of a rogue product and of an undiscoverable defect arising in this way'.[1] Such a producer will, knowingly, but without negligence, put into circulation defective products. The individual defects would, however, have been susceptible to discovery and the defence does not apply to defects that were foreseeable but undiscoverable in the current state of knowledge governing the principles of quality control.

1   C Newdick 'The Development Risks Defence of the Consumer Protection Act' (1988) 47 CLJ 455 at 469.

27.73 Assuming that the defence will have no application in respect of the frailties of quality control systems, when may it apply? Two categories of defect might be anticipated. First, those which result from some property or characteristic of the product which was not foreseen at the time of production. An example might be found in the case of drugs whose side-effects might only become apparent when they are prescribed in conjunction with other drugs, or where they are used for a long period of time. A second situation arises where the defect is foreseeable but the claim is that the technology does not permit the elimination of risk. This might typically relate to failures in a quality control system, where it could be claimed that economic considerations rendered the complete elimination of defects impracticable.

27.74 Most software defects will come within the first of the above categories. A producer must know that any software produced will possess defects. Whatever procedures and tools are used to create and validate the program, 100% accuracy cannot be guaranteed. Whilst it might, of course, be argued that a drug manufacturer must realise that there is a very high probability that any drug will prompt adverse side-effects in some patients, the two situations are not precisely comparable. In particular, given that software is purely a creation of the human intellect, any defects are man-made. Although the production of modern drugs may require a vast application of human skill and knowledge, the base building blocks are natural products. To this extent, defects are the manifestation of existing physical properties.

27.75 The onus is on the producer to establish the development risks defence. In practical terms, it would be virtually impossible to establish that nowhere had there been a warning as to possible defect. Additionally, consideration will have to be given to the weight to be attached to any piece of evidence. Scientific and technical opinions may be conflicting and contradictory. In the recent controversy concerning the supply of contaminated blood products to haemophiliacs, resulting in large numbers of persons contracting the AIDS virus, it was alleged that a scientific paper warning of the risks was rejected for publication in a scientific journal. It was further alleged that had the paper been published, screening for the virus might have been introduced and the haemophiliacs safeguarded. The case illustrates two aspects of the problems which may face the courts. First, would such a paper be regarded as forming part of the corpus of available scientific knowledge; secondly, as the reason for its non-publication presumably lay in a difference of opinion between experts as to the validity and relevance of the information, could a producer be expected to rely on it, or be held liable for failing so to do?

27.76 In civil cases, issues are decided on the basis of the balance of probabilities. The approach for a producer must be to produce expert witnesses who will testify to the fact that the danger was not foreseeable. As seen earlier,[1] it will be a rare event for them to agree and the court will be faced with the task of determining which opinion it should accept.

---

[1]   See para 27.8 above.

27.77   It must be likely that software defects will fall into the second category. In most cases, the consequences of a defect will be foreseeable, the producer's argument being that current validation and verification techniques are incapable of ensuring the identification and eradication of all defects in software. Given the intangible nature of software, a producer would be unable to detect and extract defective products from the production line.

27.78   In the past, inevitable deficiencies in a quality control process have not been held to excuse the producer. In the case of *Smedleys Ltd v Breed*,[1] the House of Lords rejected an appeal by a food producer and retailer against conviction under the Food and Drugs Act 1955. Although the terminology of the 1955 Act is not precisely comparable with that of the Consumer Protection Act 1987, the issues and principles involved are sufficiently similar to justify consideration of this decision.

[1]   [1974] AC 839.

27.79   The genesis of this case lay in the presence of a green caterpillar in a can of peas. This unadvertised ingredient proved unwelcome to the purchaser, a Mrs Voss, although it was asserted that:

> This innocent insect, thus deprived of its natural destiny, was in fact harmless, since, prior to its entry into the tin, it had been subjected to a cooking process of 22 minutes duration at 250° Fahrenheit, and, had she cared to do so, Mrs Voss could have consumed the caterpillar without injury to herself, and even, perhaps, with benefit.[1]

[1]   *Smedleys Ltd v Breed* [1974] AC 839 at 845, per Lord Hailsham.

27.80   Under the provisions of the Food and Drugs Act 1955, a defence would be available where the presence of a foreign body was an 'unavoidable consequence of the process of collection or preparation'.[1] Evidence was led as to the firm's quality control procedures. These consisted of a mixture of mechanical checks and human inspections. The efficiency of these might be gauged from the fact that only four complaints had been received relating to an annual production of some 3.5 million cans. This statistically impressive performance availed the firm not at all. It was stated that the caterpillar could have been discovered had the inspection been targeted in its particular direction. This was considered to be the critical issue and even though it would not have been economically feasible or commercially practicable to have conducted more extensive tests, the defence was not available.[2]

[1]   Section 3(3).
[2]   *Smedleys Ltd v Breed* [1974] AC 839. A similar reasoning is found in the decision of the French Court of Cassation in a case involving the supply of contaminated blood for transfusion purposes. Although the defects were considered to be undetectable, the development risk was held to be applicable only in cases where some undiscoverable external factor caused the damage. Cited in the Commission Green Paper *Liability for Defective Products* COM (1999) 396 final, p 23.

27.81 The analogy with software production is clear, even though it might be argued that the software production process is not comparable with that of canning peas. Application of the principles laid down in *Smedleys*[1] will, it is submitted, render the development risks defence of little utility to software producers. Even in the event that this precedent might not be considered in point, a further argument can be advanced against the application of the defence. Software is the creation of the human intellect. It represents the ideas and aspirations of its creator. To this extent, any defects in software are man-made. This position is to be contrasted with more tangible products. Although considerable amounts of human ingenuity may be involved in the development of, for example, a new drug and a cocktail of ingredients of staggering complexity may be created, the ingredients are natural substances and, although the drug may display undesired side-effects, these arise from natural causes. Although the producer might be stigmatised for failing to anticipate dangers, he or she cannot be said to have created them. With software, the producer is put in the position of creator. The act of creation involves responsibility. In such a circumstance, it is submitted, the producer cannot disclaim knowledge of his or her creature's properties.

[1]   *Smedleys Ltd v Breed* [1974] AC 839.

Conclusions

27.82 To date, there has been almost no litigation concerned directly with the non-contractual liability of software producers or suppliers. It seems unlikely that this can continue. Whilst the requirement that a claimant establish negligence may be a barrier to claims based in negligence, there appears steadily increasing recognition that software is to be regarded as a product and hence will be subject to the product liability regime. Although the limitation to situations where software causes injury or damage to non-commercial property is a significant one, the ever-expanding range of software applications must make a similar expansion in litigation a not unreasonable prospect.

Chapter 28

International and European initiatives in ecommerce

Introduction

28.1   Reference has been made in Chapter 1 to the scale of ecommerce. Although it is frequently difficult to distinguish hype from reality, there is no doubt that an increasing range of contracts will be concluded using some form of electronic communication. In many cases concerned with services, delivery and perhaps performance will also take place within an electronic environment.

28.2   In the context of traditional business activities, it is often stated that the three attributes most critical to commercial success are 'location, location and location'. It is regarded as one of the hallmarks of ecommerce that issues of location, at least at the physical level, are of no significance. Paradoxically, however, when consideration is given to legal issues, location returns very much to the forefront. The most important questions concern the determination when and where a contract is made and which laws and tax regimes will govern the transaction.

International initiatives

28.3   Given the international nature of the topic, it is not surprising that many of the activities in the field of ecommerce have been initiated by international organisations. The United Nations Commission on International Trade Law (UNCITRAL) adopted a model law on ecommerce in 1996, whilst in December 1999, the OECD agreed Guidelines on Electronic Commerce.[1] The goal of the guidelines, it is stated:

> ... is that consumers shopping on-line should enjoy transparent and effective protection that is not less than the level of protection that they have in other

areas of commerce. Among other things, they stress the importance of transparency and information disclosure.

¹   Available from http://www.oecd.org/news_and_events/release/guidelinesconsumer.pdf.

28.4   The model law and the guidelines have no binding force. In focusing on regulatory activity, attention must concentrate on the activities of the EU and of national legislatures. EU involvement in the field of ecommerce can be traced primarily to a Commission Communication, 'A European Initiative in Electronic Commerce', published in April 1997.¹ Itself building on earlier information society initiatives, this outlined a programme for regulatory action across a range of topics. In what might be considered chronological order, action was required in order to ensure that organisations were enabled to establish electronic businesses in any of the member states, that legal barriers to electronic trade should be removed, that provision should be made for the manner in which contracts should be negotiated and concluded. Finally, legislation might be required in the field of electronic payments.

¹   Available from http://www.cordis.lu/esprit/src/ecomcom.htm.

28.5   The mechanics of ecommerce constitute one aspect of the regulatory task. It was also recognised that other more general principles would require to be applied in the context of commercial applications. Issues such as data protection arise whenever personal data is transmitted and received. Again, as will be discussed in Chapter 29, the use of cryptographic techniques as a means for enhancing security, both to preserve privacy and to enhance consumer and business confidence in the integrity of electronic communications, raises significant and controversial regulatory questions.

28.6   Although it is tempting to regard ecommerce as a new phenomenon, this is to neglect a significant existing market sector – that dealing with mail order or catalogue selling. Especially in the US, there is a substantial tradition of sales being conducted on this basis – dating back to the Wild West days beloved of cyberspace analogists. Given the federal nature of the US Constitution, such sales also occurred across state boundaries. The oft-cited Uniform Commercial Code was first promulgated in 1940 to provide means to overcome jurisdictional and substantive problems arising when a supplier located in one jurisdiction contracted with a customer in another. Subject to some variations, it provides a common body of rules applicable throughout the 50 states. Recent (and highly controversial) developments in the US have resulted in proposals to amend the venerable provisions of the Uniform Commercial Code to take account of the special nature of software sales.¹ Most initiatives seeking to amend the Code are the joint product of two bodies, the American Law Institute (ALI) and the National Conference of Commissioners on Uniform State Laws (NCCUSL). Originally, it was proposed to table an amendment to art 2 of the Code. This provision deals with the law relating to the sale of goods. During 1999, a division occurred between the two drafting bodies, with the ALI taking the view that the proposal as drafted was too heavily weighted in favour of the interests of software developers and suppliers. The NCCUSL proceeded with the proposal which was changed into a stand-alone statute, the Uniform Computer Information Transactions Act.[2] The measure has been passed to the 50 states although has been enacted only in two (Maryland and Virginia).

[1] For a vast range of materials and comments on the proposed new law, see http://www.2bguide.com/legart.html.
[2] Text available from http://www.law.upenn.edu/bll/ulc/ucita/cita10st.htm.

EU initiatives

28.7 A number of measures adopted or proposed by the EU are relevant to any discussion of ecommerce. Three are of particular relevance. The Distance Selling Directive[1] and substantive law elements of the Electronic Commerce Directive[2] will be discussed in the present chapter. The Electronic Commerce Directive also contains provisions relating to the legal recognition of electronic contracts in cases where national laws require that contracts be concluded in a particular form. These matters, which are also covered in the Directive on 'a Community framework for electronic signatures',[3] will be discussed in Chapter 29.

[1] Directive 97/7/EC.
[2] Directive 2000/31/EC.
[3] Directive 99/93/EC, OJ 2000 L 13/12.

The Distance Selling Directive

28.8 The market for distance selling through catalogues is a well-established one, especially in remote areas where retail outlets are few and far between. The sector is particularly well established in the US, and it is anticipated that businesses with experience of these forms of transactions will be well placed to benefit from the move to ecommerce. Over the last decade, the telephone, fax machine and, most recently, email and the WWW have been used to solicit consumer contracts. One of the most important European legal instruments is the Directive on 'the protection of consumers in respect of distance contracts'.[1] The Directive applies to all forms of distance selling, but contains some provisions relating specifically to the use of electronic communications. A number of these have been supplemented by the terms of the draft Electronic Commerce Directive.[2] The Distance Selling Directive required to be implemented within the member states by June 2000.[3] The Preamble makes its rationale clear:

> Whereas the introduction of new technologies is increasing the number of ways for consumers to obtain information about offers anywhere in the Community and to place orders; whereas some Member States have already taken different or diverging measures to protect consumers in respect of distance selling, which has had a detrimental effect on competition between businesses in the internal market; whereas it is therefore necessary to introduce at Community level a minimum set of common rules in this area.[4]

1   Directive 97/7/EC, OJ 1997 L 144 (the Distance Selling Directive). A further proposal for a directive concerns the distance selling of financial services, COM (98) 468 final of 14.10.98.
2   Directive 2000/31/EC.
3   Two consultation papers have been published by the Department of Trade and Industry seeking views on the UK's implementation policy. The first, published in June 1998, is available from http://www.dti.gov.uk/CACP/ca/distcon.htm, and the second, published in November 1999, from http://www.dti.gov.uk/cacp/ca/distance/index.htm.
4   Recital 4.

28.9   The Distance Selling Directive defines the term 'distance contract' as:

> Any contract concerning goods or services concluded between a supplier and a consumer under an organized distance sales or service-provision scheme run by the supplier, who, for the purpose of the contract, makes exclusive use of one or more means of distance communication up to and including the moment at which the contract is concluded.[1]

Annex 1 contains an illustrative list of communication technologies. In addition to traditional categories, such as letters and press advertisements, reference is made to the use of systems of videotext, email and facsimile transmission.

1   Directive 97/7/EC, art 2(1).

28.10   The Distance Selling Directive's provisions commence at the stage where the consumer's entry into a contract is solicited, the principal requirement here being that promotional techniques must pay due regard to the consumer's privacy, conform to the 'principles of good faith' and provide 'clear and unambiguous information' regarding the nature of any product or service, its price and the identity of its supplier.[1] In the case of telephone communication, the supplier is obliged to make its identity, and the fact that the call is commercial in nature, clear at the commencement of a call.[2]

1   Directive 97/7/EC, art 4(2).
2   Article 4(3).

28.11   The Distance Selling Directive also provides that two forms of technology, automated calling systems and fax machines, may be used only with the prior consent of the consumer – what might be referred to as an 'opt-in' system.[1] Automated calling systems involve the use of a computer system to call numbers and on answer play a pre-recorded message to the recipient. Such technologies are effectively prohibited in the UK as their use would require a licence from OFTEL, which has indicated objections to the practice. In the case of other forms of communication, it is provided that these are to be made only when the consumer has not indicated a clear objection to receipt of solicitations.[2] The operation of an 'opt-out' system would be compatible with this requirement.

1   Directive 97/7/EC, art 10(1).
2   Article 10(2).

28.12   The rationale behind the selection of specific prohibited technologies is not clear. Recital 17 of the Distance Selling Directive[1] asserts that the consumer's right to privacy should extend to 'freedom from certain particularly intrusive means of communication'. It is difficult to argue, however, that a pre-recorded telephone message is intrinsically more intrusive than other forms of telephone canvassing. Unsolicited faxes also are unlikely to be seen as invasive of privacy, and a perhaps more persuasive basis for restricting these lies in the fact that the recipient of a fax incurs cost in terms of the paper and ink used for its reproduction. This was, perhaps, more of a factor with previous generations of fax machines which required the use of special (and expensive) paper.

[1]   Directive 97/7/EC.

The provision of information to the consumer

28.13   Assuming that discussions between supplier and consumer extend beyond the initial contact, there is clear need to ensure that the latter is made aware of the terms and conditions associated with a particular contract. The Distance Selling Directive[1] provides for two approaches, the first of which is outwith the scope of the present study, requiring the grant of a 'cooling off' period following the conclusion of the contract.[2] More relevant are provisions requiring that the consumer be given information as to terms. Article 4 specifies the items of information which must be given. These relate primarily to the identity of the supplier, the nature and cost of the goods or services and any arrangements for delivery. These are relatively easily satisfied in traditional mail order or catalogue sales, but in respect of electronic communications, recital 13 states that:

> Whereas information disseminated by certain electronic technologies is often ephemeral in nature insofar as it is not received on a permanent medium; whereas the consumer must therefore receive written notice in good time of the information necessary for proper performance of the contract.

[1]   Directive 97/7/EC.
[2]   Article 6.

28.14   Whilst the comment regarding the transient nature of information displayed on, for example, a website is basically true, the text of an email message can be as locatable as any written message. It would seem somewhat Luddite were a party engaging in ecommerce to be required to supply confirmation details on paper. The Distance Selling Directive requires that confirmation be supplied in writing or:

> ... in another durable medium available and accessible to him.[1]

It may be that the transmission of an email which may be stored on the consumer's computer would satisfy this requirement. This is the view which has provisionally been adopted by the Department of Trade and Industry, which has commented in its second consultation paper:

We consider that confirmation by electronic mail would meet the definition of confirmation in 'another durable medium available and accessible to [the consumer]', where the order has been made by means of e-mail. We have not however specified this in the Draft Regulations since the Directive is not specific on the point, and only a court can determine the meaning of the wording.[2]

[1]   Directive 97/7/EC, art 5.
[2]   Paragraph 3.9.

The Electronic Commerce Directive and Regulations

28.15   The proposal for a directive on 'legal aspects of electronic commerce' was introduced in November 1998.[1] The proposal was debated in the European Parliament[2] and following its comments, an amended proposal was introduced in September 1999,[3] becoming law on its adoption by the Council of Ministers in May 2000.[4] It is implemented in the UK by the Electronic Commerce (EC Directive) Regulations 2002[5] The regulations follow very closely the wording and format of the Directive.

[1]   OJ 1999 C 30.
[2]   A copy of the report and proceedings is available from http://www.ispo.cec.be/ecommerce/legal/legal.html.
[3]   COM (99) 427 final.
[4]   Directive 2000/31/EC, OJ 2000 L 178/1 (the Electronic Commerce Directive). The text of the measure can be obtained from http://europa.eu.int/comm/internal_market/en/media/eleccomm/index.htm.
[5]   SI 2002/2013.

28.16   The scope of the measure is broad ranging. It applies to what are referred to as 'Information Society Services'. These are defined in Directive 98/34/EC, laying down a procedure for the provision of information in the field of technical standards[1] which refers to:

... any service normally provided for remuneration, at a distance, by electronic means and at the individual request of a recipient of services.

For the purposes of this definition three fundamental requirements apply:

'at a distance' means that the service is provided without the parties being simultaneously present;

'by electronic means' means that the service is sent initially and received at its destination by means of electronic equipment for the processing (including digital compression) and storage of data, and entirely transmitted, conveyed and received by wire, by radio, by optical means or by other electromagnetic means; and

'at the individual request of a recipient of services' means that the service is provided through the transmission of data on individual request.

It is specifically provided that the definition is not to apply to radio or television broadcasting services. A television 'shopping channel' will, therefore, not be governed by the Directive. Beyond this, however, the Commission have commented that:

> The Directive covers all Information Society services, both business to business and business to consumer, and services provided free of charge to the recipient e.g. funded by advertising or sponsorship revenue and services allowing for on-line electronic transactions such as interactive tele-shopping of goods and services and on-line shopping malls.
>
> Examples of sectors and activities covered include on-line newspapers, on-line databases, on-line financial services, on-line professional services (such as lawyers, doctors, accountants, estate agents), on-line entertainment services such as video on demand, on-line direct marketing and advertising and services providing access to the World Wide Web.[2]

[1]   OJ 1998 L 204/37, as amended by Directive 98/48/EC, OJ 1998 L 217/18.
[2]   'Commission welcomes final adoptions of legal framework Directive.' http://europa.eu.int/comm/internal_market/en/media/eleccomm/2k-442.htm.

28.17   No authorisation is generally required in connection with the establishment of an information society service. Article 5 of the Electronic Commerce Directive[1] provides that:

1.   Member States shall lay down in their legislation that access to the activity of Information Society service provider may not be made subject to prior authorisation or any other requirement the effect of which is to make such access dependent on a decision, measure or particular act by an authority.

This provision is subject to an exception where authorisation will be required in connection with the establishment of any business in a sector, ie legal or financial services firm.

[1]   Directive 2000/31/EC.

Substantive law issues

When and where is a contract made?

28.18   In order for a contract to be concluded, it is required that there should be an unconditional offer and acceptance. In many instances, of course, there may be several iterations of offer and counter-offer before the parties reach agreement on all important matters concerned with the contract.

28.19   In the situation where a customer purchases goods in a shop, there is little problem in determining the question where a contract is made. The question when the contract is concluded is a little more problematic. In the situation where goods are displayed in retail premises, it is normally the case that the display constitutes an invitation to treat. An offer to purchase will be made by the customer which may be accepted (or rejected) by the seller. There are sound reasons for such an approach, not least due to the possibility that goods might be out of stock or that the wrong price tag may have been placed on an item by mistake (or through the action of some third party). In practical terms, it can be said that a contract will typically be concluded when the customer's offer of payment is accepted by the seller.

28.20 Subject to any other mechanism agreed between the parties, it is generally the case that acceptance becomes effective when it is communicated to the offeror. Clearly, in the case of a face-to-face transaction this occurs at the point where the acceptor indicates – whether by words or actions – that the offer is acceptable. Matters become rather more complex when the parties to the transaction are at a distance. Here, two sets of rules have been developed depending on the nature of the communications technology employed. The rule relating to postal contracts form a well-established feature of the legal system. Here, it is provided that the contract is deemed to have been concluded at the moment the acceptance is placed into the postal system. The main rationale for such an approach is that once the message has been posted, it moves out of the control of the sender. The effect of this is, of course, that a contract will be concluded before the offeror is aware of the fact of acceptance. It is also the case that having been posted, an acceptance cannot be withdrawn even though this may have been brought to the attention of the offeror prior to delivery of the acceptance.

28.21 The postal rule is to be contrasted with another rule relating to the use of forms of technology which might be classed as involving 'instantaneous communication'. In *Entores Ltd v Miles Far East Corpn*,[1] the question at issue was where a contract made following communications by telex should be regarded as having been concluded. The plaintiffs, who were located in London, had made an offer which had been accepted by the defendants in Amsterdam. Holding that the contract was made when the acceptance was received by the plaintiffs in London, Parker LJ held that where:

> ... parties are in each other's presence or, though separated in space, communication between them is in effect instantaneous, there is no need for any such rule of convenience. To hold otherwise would leave no room for the operation of the general rule that notification of the acceptance must be received. An acceptor could say: 'I spoke the words of acceptance in your presence, albeit softly, and you did not hear me'; or 'I telephoned to you and accepted, and it matters not that the telephone went dead and you did not get my message' ... So far as Telex messages are concerned, though the despatch and receipt of a message is not completely instantaneous, the parties are to all intents and purposes in each other's presence just as if they were in telephonic communication, and I can see no reason for departing from the general rule that there is no binding contract until notice of the acceptance was received by the offeror.[2]

[1]   [1955] 2 All ER 493.
[2]   [1955] 2 All ER 493 at 498.

28.22 This view was endorsed by the House of Lords in the case of *Brinkibon Ltd v Stahag Stahl und Stahlwarenhandel GMBH,*[1] although it was recognised by Lord Wilberforce that the result might have to be reviewed in the event it could be established that there was:

> ... some error or default at the recipient's end which prevents receipt at the time contemplated and believed in by the sender ... No universal rule can cover all such cases; they must be resolved by reference to the intentions of the parties, by sound business practice and in some cases a judgement where the risks should lie.[2]

[1] [1982] 1 All ER 293.
[2] [1982] 1 All ER 293 at 296.

28.23 In the context of the present work, the key question will be whether emails and other forms of message transmitted over the Internet will be classed as coming under the postal rule, or whether the provisions relating to instantaneous communications will apply. Although the issue of determining when an email contract is concluded might appear to be of the 'number of angels on a pinhead' category, this is not always the case especially when, as in the *Entores*[1] and *Brinkibon*[2] cases, transactions possess an international dimension. In such cases, the questions will arise which law will govern the transaction and which courts will have jurisdiction in the event of a dispute. In the event that a contract is silent on the point, the location where a contract is concluded will be a major factor in determining the choice of law question. This issue will be considered in more detail below.

[1] *Entores Ltd v Miles Far East Corpn* [1955] 2 All ER 493.
[2] *Brinkibon Ltd v Stahag Stahl und Stahlwarenhandel GMBH* [1982] 1 All ER 293.

28.24 In terms of speed of transmission, email might generally be equated with fax or telex transmission. In the event of problems or congestion on the networks, messages may be delayed by hours or even days and, in terms of the nature of transmission, the more accurate parallel may be with the postal system. An email message will be passed on from point to point across the network, with its contents being copied and forwarded a number of times before being delivered to the ultimate recipient. There is no single direct link or connection between sender and receiver.

28.25 The Electronic Commerce Directive provides what appears to be a somewhat complex mechanism for determining the moment at which a contract is concluded. It is stated that:

> Member States shall lay down in their legislation that, save where otherwise agreed by professional persons, in cases where a recipient, in accepting a service provider's offer, is required to give his consent through technological means, such as clicking on an icon, the contract is concluded when the recipient of the service has received from the service provider, electronically, an acknowledgment of receipt of the recipient's acceptance.[1]

[1] Directive 2000/31/EC, art 11.

28.26 Such an approach would pose problems for the UK system which, as stated above, sees offers emanating from the customer rather than the supplier. There appears also to be an element of unnecessary complication by adding the requirement of acknowledgment of receipt of acceptance as a condition for the conclusion of a contract. The original proposal was even more prolonged, stating that the contract would not be concluded until acknowledgment was made of receipt of the acknowledgment! Receipt of acceptance would seem quite sufficient for this legal purpose. An alternative, and perhaps preferable, approach is advocated by the International Chamber of Commerce, whose draft Uniform Rules for Electronic Trade and Settlement propose that:

> An electronic offer and/or acceptance becomes effective when it enters the information system of the recipient in a form capable of being processed by that system.[1]

Albeit intended primarily for business to business contracts rather than the EU's consumer contract focus, this approach seems to achieve the legal requirements in a rather simpler fashion. Simplest of all, however, would be the UK approach, which would allow the seller to combine acceptance of the customer's offer with acknowledgment of the terms of the transaction.

[1]   Article 2.1.1.

28.27   A further obligation is proposed in the EC Electronic Commerce Directive. Member states are required to ensure that national laws require that:

> ... the service provider shall make available to the recipient of the service appropriate means that are effective and accessible allowing him to identify and correct handling errors and accidental transactions before the conclusion of the contract. Contract terms and general conditions provided to the consumer must be made available in a way that allows him to store and reproduce them.[1]

Whilst the provision is well meaning, it is difficult to identify how the result might be achieved. The provisions relating to the moment of formation of contract discussed above require that 'the service provider is obliged to immediately send the acknowledgment of receipt'. We can assume that in most cases, this will be transmitted automatically. This affords very little time for the customer to identify and seek to correct any mistakes which have been made.

[1]   Directive 2000/31/EC, art 11(2).

28.28   An alternative approach would be to provide consumers with a 'cooling off' period within which a contract might be terminated. The Distance Selling Directive provides for a seven-day period, beginning with the date upon which goods supplied under the contract were received by the consumer.[1] The provision does not, however, apply to contracts for the provision of services where 'performance has begun with the consumer's agreement, before the end of the seven day working period'. This will exclude contracts for the electronic delivery of software. Exemption is also provided in respect of contracts 'for the supply of audio or video recordings or computer software which were unsealed by the consumer'. The legitimate concern in all these cases is that the consumer would have the ability to copy the material before returning the originals to the supplier and seeking a refund of the purchase price.

1   Directive 97/7/EC, art 6.

Choice of law issues

28.29   As has been stated frequently, location is irrelevant in ecommerce. It is also the case that the largest body of sites offering to supply goods or services is in the US. A consumer located in the UK and wishing to engage in ecommerce is almost inevitably going to require to deal with US-based companies. International trade, which hitherto has been almost exclusively the preserve of large commercial operators, is assuming a significant consumer dimension.

28.30   In any situation where buyer and seller are located in different jurisdictions, two key legal issues will arise. The first is to determine which legal system will govern the transaction and the second to determine which courts will be competent to hear disputes arising from the transaction. In many cases, it will be the case that the parties make explicit contractual provision for both matters. In a contract between parties in Scotland and France, for example, it might be provided that French law will govern the transaction but that disputes may be raised in the French or the Scottish courts, the latter being required to decide the case according to the relevant principles of French law.

28.31   In general, parties have (subject to the legal systems chosen having some connection with the subject matter of the contract) complete freedom to determine choice of law issues. Different rules apply where consumers are involved. Problems arise also where the parties fail to make explicit provision for issues of jurisdiction. In this case the matter may fall to be decided by the courts.

28.32   As discussed above in the context of contract formation, the question when and where a contract is concluded is a major factor in determining which legal system is to govern the transaction. Where transactions are conducted over the Internet, the question is not always easy to answer. The Global Top Level Domain name .com gives no indication where a business is located. Even where the name uses a country code such as .de or .uk there is no guarantee that the undertaking is established in that country. It is relatively common practice, based in part upon security concerns, to keep web servers geographically separate from the physical undertaking. A website might, for example, have an address in the German (.de) domain. Its owner, however, might be a UK-registered company.

28.33   The question whether an Internet-based business can be regarded as having a 'branch, agency or establishment' in all the countries from which its facilities may be accessed is uncertain. The OECD has pointed out in the context of tax harmonisation that the notion of permanent establishment, which is of major importance in determining whether an undertaking is liable to national taxes, may not be appropriate for ecommerce.[1]

1   See discussion at para 30.13 below.

28.34 Within Europe, the Brussels[1] and Rome[2] Conventions make special provision for consumer contracts. The latter provides that a supplier with a 'branch, agency or establishment' in the consumer's country of residence is to be considered as domiciled there. Further, consumers may choose to bring actions in either their country of domicile or that of the supplier, whilst actions against the consumer may be brought only in the consumer's country of domicile.

1   C 189 of 28 July 1990.
2   OJ 1980 L 266/1.

28.35 The Brussels Convention builds on the Rome Convention's provisions and provides that an international contract may not deprive the consumer of 'mandatory rights' operating in the consumer's country of domicile. The scope of mandatory rights is not clear cut but, given the emphasis placed on the human rights dimension in many international instruments dealing with data protection, it is argued that any attempt contractually to deprive consumers of rights conferred under the Council of Europe Convention and the EC Electronic Commerce Directive[1] would be declared ineffective on this basis.

1   Directive 2000/31/EC.

28.36 More recent developments may complicate matters. The Electronic Commerce Directive[1] provides that transactions entered into by electronic means should be regulated by the law of the state in which the supplier is established. This approach is justified on the basis of supporting the development of the new industries, recital 8 stating that:

> ... in order to effectively guarantee freedom to provide services and legal certainty for suppliers and recipients of services, such Information Society services should only be subject to the law of the Member State in which the service provider is established.

At the same time, however, the Commission have adopted, in the form of a Regulation 'on jurisdiction and the recognition and enforcement of judgments in civil and commercial matters',[2] amendments to the Brussels and Rome Conventions which would have the effect of subjecting all consumer contracts to the law of the consumer's domicile.[3] This approach is justified on the basis that the consumer is regarded as the weaker party in any contract with a business organisation.

1   Directive 2000/31/EC.
2   Regulation 44/2001/EC, OJ 2001 L 12/1.
3   Article 15.

28.37 There appears to be an inescapable conflict between choice of law provisions designed to favour the development of ecommerce, by making more predictable the nature of the liabilities incurred by service providers and giving priority to the interests of consumers by maximising their access to local courts and tribunals. The Explanatory Memorandum to the draft Regulation stated that:

> The Commission has noted that the wording of Article 15 has given rise to certain anxieties among part of the industry looking to develop electronic commerce. These concerns relate primarily to the fact that companies engaging in electronic commerce will have to contend with potential litigation in every Member State, or will have to specify that their products or services are not intended for consumers domiciled in certain Member States.

The intention was announced to review the operation of art 15 two years after the Regulation's entry into force. In the shorter term, public hearings on the subject were announced and were held in Brussels in November 1999. The hearings attracted an audience of several hundred persons[1] and produced several hundred pages of comments and suggestions.[2] No consensus was – or perhaps could be – reached and the position remains one where different Commission Directorates appear to be promoting different policies.

[1]   Available from http://europa.eu.int/comm/scic/conferences/991104/participants.pdf.
[2]   Available from http://europa.eu.int/comm/scic/conferences/991104/contributions.doc.

Alternative dispute resolution

28.38   One possible palliative for jurisdictional problems is to try to obviate the need for formal legal proceedings. Two provisions in the Electronic Commerce Directive[1] seek to facilitate this. Article 16 requires member states and the Commission to encourage the drawing up at Community level of codes of conduct designed to contribute to the implementation of the substantive provisions of the directive. Such codes, which will be examined by the Commission to ensure their compatibility with Community law, might provide a valuable unifying force throughout the EU. Article 17 obliges member states to:

> ... ensure that, in the event of disagreement between an Information Society service provider and its recipient, their legislation allows the effective use of out of court schemes for dispute settlement, including appropriate electronic means.

[1]   Directive 2000/31/EC.

28.39   Although a number of online dispute resolution services have been established, these have mainly been in the US and do not appear to have attracted significant custom. In the UK, the 'Which Web Trader' scheme operated by the Consumers Association,[1] requires participating traders to observe a code of practice but, in the event of a dispute with a consumer, makes it clear that recourse will have to be sought through the courts.

[1]   Available from http://www.which.com/webtrader/consumer_guide.html.

28.40   In 1998, the Commission adopted a 'Communication on the out-of-court settlement of consumer disputes'.[1] A Commission Working Document on the creation of an European Extra-Judicial Network (EEJ-NET)[2] was published in March 2000. This notes that:

> The continuing expansion of economic activity within of the internal market inevitably means that consumers' activities are not only confined to their own country. Greater cross border consumption has arisen due to an increase in consumer travel and the emergence of new distance selling technologies like the Internet. This increase in cross border consumption, especially with the ever-increasing expansion of electronic commerce and the introduction of the Euro, is invariably likely to lead to an increase in cross border disputes. It is, therefore, necessary and desirable to create a network of general application which will cover any kind of dispute over goods and services.

The Commission is now proposing the establishment of a network of National 'Clearing Houses'. These organisations will give consumers wishing to pursue complaints against suppliers located in their jurisdiction information about available facilities for dispute resolution. The Clearing Houses will also assist their own national consumers who are in dispute with a supplier in another member state by liaising with the relevant Clearing House to provide information about dispute resolution procedures. A further Green Paper on alternative dispute resolution in civil and criminal law was published by the Commission in 2002.[3]

[1]   COM (98) 198 final.
[2]   Available from http://europa.eu.int/comm/dg24/policy/developments/acce_just acce_just06_en.pdf.
[3]   COM (2002) 196 final.

Conclusion

28.41   The scope of the Electronic Commerce Directive[1] is broad ranging and is generally non-controversial. Even matters such as the procedure for concluding a contract may cause theoretical rather than practical problems. The major criticism that might be made of the EU's activity in the field of ecommerce is that initiatives are dispersed across a range of measures. As well as complicating the task of determining what the law is in a particular respect, there is the potential for internal conflict as has been discussed in relation to the issue of choice of law.

[1]   Directive 2000/31/EC.

28.42   Perhaps the key message which can be taken from the initiatives discussed in this chapter is that in most cases, the application of traditional legal provisions will be quite adequate in order to regulate ecommerce. The key issue is perhaps the negative one that legal requirements should not impede the operation of ecommerce. This issue primarily arises in the context of formal or procedural requirements that a contract be concluded or evidenced in writing. The issue to what extent such requirements might be satisfied in an electronic environment has become entangled with the topic of encryption. Both topics will be considered in Chapter 29.

Cryptography, electronic signatures and the Electronic Communications Act 2000

Introduction

29.1   An issue which is often identified as a factor deterring consumers from participating in ecommerce is the fear that information transmitted over the Internet might be intercepted by computer hackers. Where the data takes the form of, for example, credit card information, the potential for loss is obvious. Reality does not necessarily accord with perception. To date, no instances have been recorded of data being intercepted in transmission, although there are numerous instances of fraud conducted by parties involved in ecommerce. Rather than seeking to intercept messages, for anyone wishing to engage in criminal conduct, it is a much simpler matter to set up a website offering to supply goods or services at attractive prices, solicit orders with payment by credit card and make off with a rich harvest of numbers.

29.2   In addition to concerns relating to the security of payment systems, the ease with which electronic data might be modified without leaving any discernible trace raises concerns regarding the legal status of contracts evidenced only in such format. The situation is not, of course, unique to electronic data. Forgery is a well-established, if disreputable, profession. Whilst most contracts can be constituted in such manner as the parties think fit, there are obvious problems in permitting large contracts with obligations continuing over many years to be concluded in a relatively informal manner. Two parties might well enter into a verbal agreement for the sale and purchase of property. With the passage of time, memory of what was agreed may fade and both parties will at some stage die. The land, of course, goes on forever and either the parties or their successors may at some time have to determine just what was agreed. Taking account of such problems, there have long been requirements in the law that some agreements be reduced to written form and authenticated by the signature of the party or parties responsible for the creation of documents.

29.3 Along with the proposals for a directive on 'legal aspects of electronic commerce',[1] a draft electronic signatures directive was published by the Commission.[2] This was adopted slightly before the Electronic Commerce Directive,[3] final approval being given in December 1999 to a Directive 'on a Community framework for electronic signatures'.[4] Although member states were given until 19 July 2001 to implement the measure,[5] with the enactment of the Electronic Communications Act 2000 in May 2000, the UK would appear to have met all its obligations under the Directive.

[1]   OJ 1999 C 30.
[2]   OJ 1998 C 325.
[3]   Directive 2000/31/EC.
[4]   Directive 99/93/EC, OJ 2000 L 13/12 (the Electronic Signatures Directive).
[5]   Article 13.

29.4   The main purpose of the Electronic Signatures[1] and Electronic Commerce[2] Directives and the Electronic Communications Act 2000 is to encourage the development of electronic equivalents to written documents and manual signatures. In considering the impact of the Directives and the Act, consideration might usefully be divided into three sections. First, a brief account will be given of the background to the Electronic Communications Act 2000, a measure which will be pivotal to many of the developments described in this chapter. Next, an examination will be made of provisions relating to requirements for writing. This may relate both to the contractual situation and to other cases, such as the submission of tax returns. Finally, consideration will be given to requirements for signature. The notion of electronic or digital signatures has become inextricably linked with the use of cryptographic techniques and this section will commence with a brief description of this somewhat complex topic.

[1]   Directive 99/93/EC.
[2]   Directive 2000/31/EC.

Background to the Electronic Communications Act 2000

29.5   After a number of false dawns and extensive consultation exercises, an Electronic Communications Bill was introduced into the House of Commons in November 1999. The Bill, it was stated in the Second Reading debate:

> will be Britain's first 21st century law. It was the first Bill referred to in the Queen's Speech, it was the first to be introduced; and, tonight, it will become the first to receive Second Reading. It will bring our statute book into the 21st century, provide a sound legal basis for electronic commerce and electronic government, and help to build consumer and business confidence in trading on the Internet.[1]

[1]   Patricia Hewitt, Minister for Small Business and E-Commerce, 340 HC Official Report (6th series) col 4, 29 November 1999.

29.6   In the event, the need to introduce emergency legislation to suspend the operation of Northern Ireland's power-sharing Executive meant that the measure was not to be the first statute of the twenty-first century. Once this honour had been removed, some of the sense of urgency which had accompanied the early stages of the Bill seemed to be dissipated and it was not until 25 May 2000 that the measure received the Royal Assent.

29.7 The genesis of the measure can be traced to a Consultation Paper published by the previous administration, in March 1997, on the 'Licensing of Trusted Third Parties for the Provision of Encryption Services'. In April 1998, the Department of Trade and Industry published a statement on 'Secure Electronic Commerce'. This marked the first occasion when the term Electronic Commerce was used in an official statement. It was indicated that:

> 2. The Government places considerable importance on the successful development of electronic commerce. It will, if successfully promoted, allow us to exploit fully the advantages of the information age for the benefit of the whole community.
> 3. The Government is committed to the successful development and promotion of a framework within which electronic commerce can thrive. Electronic commerce, as indicated below, is crucial to the future growth and prosperity of both the national economy and our businesses. Although the prime economic driver for electronic commerce may currently lie with business-to-business transactions, it is clear that consumers (whether ordering books or arranging pensions) will also directly benefit.

Although the statement used the term electronic commerce, its contents were almost exclusively concerned with security issues:

> To achieve our goals, however, electronic commerce, and the electronic networks which it relies, have to be secure and trusted. Whether it be the entrepreneur E-mailing his sales information to a potential supplier or the citizen receiving private advice from their doctor; the communications need to be secure. In a recent DTI survey 69% of UK companies cited security as a major inhibitor to purchasing across Internet.[1]

[1]   Available from http://www.dti.gov.uk/cii/ana27p.html.

29.8 Security can have a number of components and the statement referred approvingly to BS7799, which was referred to as the 'national standard on information security'. As well as organisational and technical measures, however, the statement focused on encryption policy. As discussed above,[1] this has been, and remains, a contentious political issue and the paper was criticised widely as appearing to promote a scheme of mandatory key escrow.

[1]   See para 16.5 above.

29.9 The next significant event occurred in March 1999, when a Consultation Paper, 'Building Confidence in Electronic Commerce', was published.[1] This indicated that 'The Government is committed to introducing legislation in the current Parliamentary session'. Comments were sought within a three-week period. Although cryptography policy again featured prominently in the document, significant provisions were also introduced concerning procedural issues of ecommerce, specifically relating to the removal of requirements that contracts be concluded in writing or be accompanied by a signature.

[1]   Available from http://www.dti.gov.uk/cii/ana27p.html.

29.10   The Paper was the subject of critical comment by the House of Commons Select Committee on Trade and Industry.[1] Two hundred and fifty-two comments were made by other organisations.[2] In July 1999, a further consultation document, 'Promoting Electronic Commerce', was published. Although a draft Bill (now referred to as the Electronic Communications Bill) was appended to this paper, the commitment to introduce legislation in the 1998–99 parliamentary session was abandoned, apparently because of the refusal by the opposition to allow it to be certified as non-controversial and thereby permitted to continue its progress over two sessions. Comments this time were requested to be submitted by October 1999. A further report was tabled by the Select Committee in November 1999[3] and the Electronic Communications Bill was introduced in the House of Commons on 18 November, receiving its Second Reading on 29 November.

[1]   Tenth Report of the Select Committee on Trade and Industry (1998–99), available from http://www.parliament.the-stationery-office.co.uk/pa/cm199899/cmselect/cmtrdind/648/64802.htm.
[2]   A summary of responses is available from http://www.dti.gov.uk/cii/elec/conrep.htm.
[3]   Fourteenth Report of the Select Committee on Trade and Industry (1999–2000), available from http://www.parliament.the-stationery-office.co.uk/pa/cm199899/cmselect/cmtrdind/862/86202.htm.

29.11   As the legislative proposals have developed, the main changes have been in respect of the controls imposed over those operating cryptographic services. Concerns were expressed in many quarters that those using encryption would be required to lodge copies of their keys with agencies, from where they might be passed on to the law enforcement or national security agencies. It would appear that this is now off the legislative agenda. In a speech delivered in September 1999, Patricia Hewitt, the newly appointed Minister for Small Firms and E-Commerce, proclaimed that:

> Let me confirm that mandatory key escrow is NOT part of the bill. Many of you will have taken part in the campaign against mandatory key escrow – the previous cross-party policy to coerce people to give copies of the keys to their encrypted mail to a third party. This issue assumed such importance that the PIU set up a special taskforce to look at it. Back in May the PIU concluded that these plans were not going to work.
>   Let me repeat what the Prime Minister said last week:
>
>> 'No company or individual will be forced, directly or indirectly, to escrow keys.'
>
> The Electronic Communications Bill is not about key escrow. Mandatory key escrow is off the agenda.

29.12   In the event, the provisions relating to the interception of encrypted messages were removed from the Electronic Communications Bill and transferred

653

to the Regulation of Investigative Powers Bill. To emphasise the rejection of mandatory key escrow, the Electronic Communications Act 2000 provides that there shall be no power 'to impose a requirement on any person to deposit a key for electronic data with another person'.[1]

[1]   Section 14(1).

29.13   The removal of the provisions relating to interception seems to have drawn the teeth from most of the opposition to the Bill. The remaining provisions have been generally welcomed, with Bill Gates, the President of Microsoft, referring to it as a 'model for Europe'.[1] This may be somewhat exaggerated as, in many respects, the legislation provides only a framework which will require to be filled in by secondary legislation.

[1]   Cited in 340 HC Official Report (6th series) col 41, 29 November 1999.

29.14   The Electronic Communications Act 2000 contains three parts. Part I contains provisions relating to the use of encryption, Pt II is designed to facilitate ecommerce, whilst Pt III contains miscellaneous provisions, mainly concerned with a change to the telecommunications licensing regime. This topic is largely outwith the scope of the present work, with the Bill trying to resolve a procedural problem which has been identified by OFTEL. All telecommunications activities require to be conducted under the terms of a licence. Licences are divided into two categories, individual and class. Many class licences may apply to hundreds or even thousands of users. If the Director General of Telecommunications proposes to amend the terms of a class licence, this will require to be notified to the Competition Commission unless all licence holders indicate agreement to the change. Experience suggests that with large numbers of licences, obtaining a 100% response rate is virtually impossible. Some licence holders may, unknown to the Director General, have gone out of business or may simply fail to reply to communications. It is now proposed that the requirement to obtain approval prior to making a change is to be replaced by a provision that change may be made without reference to the Competition Commission where no licence holder has intimate objection to the proposal.

Requirements for writing

29.15   In a 1990 report, 'Preliminary study of legal issues related to the formation of contracts by electronic means', UNCITRAL identified four reasons which had historically prompted a requirement that contracts be concluded in writing. These were the desire to reduce disputes, to make the parties aware of the consequences of their dealings, to provide evidence upon which third parties might rely upon the agreement and to facilitate tax, accounting and regulatory purposes.

29.16   A wide range of statutory provisions make provision for information to be supplied 'in writing', for example, company accounts. In a number of instances, specific statutory provision has been made for the acceptance of computer-generated information. In the taxation field, for example, electronic copies of invoices will be accepted for purposes connected with Value Added Tax. As will be discussed, the Electronic Communications Bill seeks to pave the way for greater acceptance of electronic information as satisfying requirements for writing. At present, however, statutory requirements will be subject to the terms of the Interpretation Act 1978, which defines writing as including:

> ... typing, printing, lithography, photography and other modes of representing or reproducing words in a visible form, and expressions referring to writing are construed accordingly.[1]

A document which exists solely in digital form, for example, an email message stored on the hard disk of the recipient's computer, will not be capable of coming within this definition as the electronic impulses representing its contents are not visible.

[1]   Schedule 1.

29.17   It seems clear that the 1978 definition was introduced at a time when communication between computers was limited and, as with other statutory definitions of that era relating to concepts of recording and storage, is ill suited to the modern age. The UN Model Law on Electronic Commerce introduces the concept of 'a data message', which is defined as:

> ... information generated, sent, received or stored by electronic, optical or similar means including, but not limited to, electronic document interchange (EDI), electronic mail, telegram, telex or telecopy.[1]

and goes on to provide that:

> Where the law requires information to be in writing, that requirement is met by a data message if the information contained therein is accessible so as to be usable for subsequent reference.[2]

[1]   Article 2.
[2]   Article 6.

29.18   The desire to reduce requirements for paper-based documents is a feature of the Electronic Commerce Directive.[1] This provides that:

1.   Member States shall ensure that their legislation allows contracts to be concluded electronically. Member States shall in particular ensure that the legal requirements applicable to the contractual process neither prevent the effective use of electronic contracts nor result in such contracts being deprived of legal effect and validity on account of their having been made electronically.

2.   Member States may lay down that paragraph 1 shall not apply to the following contracts:
     (a)   contracts requiring the involvement of a notary;
     (b)   contracts which, in order to be valid, are required to be registered with a public authority;

> (c)   contracts governed by family law; and
> (d)   contracts governed by the law of succession.[2]

1   Directive 2000/31/EC.
2   Article 9.

29.19   The effect of this provision would be to ensure that most forms of ecommerce can be conducted without requiring to comply with any additional requirements relating to form. This general rule may, at the option of a member state, be subject to exceptions. The situations specified in the proposed directive relate to contracts which are regarded as being of special importance. In respect of these, national laws typically require that the terms of the contract be recorded in writing and signed by the contracting parties.

29.20   The Electronic Commerce Directive's provisions[1] are implemented in the Electronic Communications Act 2000. This provides ministers (including Scottish ministers) with a general power to modify any statute or statutory instrument:

> ... in such manner as he may think fit for the purpose of authorising or facilitating the use of electronic communications or electronic storage (instead of other forms of communication or storage) for any purpose mentioned in subsection (2).
>   (2) Those purposes are—

(a)   the doing of anything which under any such provisions is required to be or may be done or evidenced in writing or otherwise using a document, notice or instrument;

(b)   the doing of anything which under any such provisions is required to be or may be done by post or other specified means of delivery;

(c)   the doing of anything which under any such provisions is required to be or may be authorised by a person's signature or seal, or is required to be delivered as a deed or witnessed;

(d)   the making of any statement or declaration which under any such provisions is required to be made under oath or to be contained in a statutory declaration;

(e)   the keeping, maintenance or preservation, for the purposes or in pursuance of any such provisions, of any account, record, notice, instrument or other document;

(f)   the provision, production or publication under any such provisions of any information or other matter; and

(g)   the making of any payment that is required to be or may be made under any such provisions.[2]

The power is not to be invoked unless the minister is satisfied that the use of electronic communications provides at least an equal measure of certainty and security as can be garnered through the use of more traditional requirements.[3]

1   Directive 2000/31/EC.
2   Section 8.
3   Section 8(3).

29.21   A vast range of transactions might be affected by this power. It was indicated in Parliament that for England and Wales:

> The Lord Chancellor is exploring, with the assistance of the Law Commission and the Land Registry, what is necessary to allow conveyancing in particular to be done electronically.[1]

Much publicity has been given to the recognition of electronic signatures, but the power will also extend to permitting firms to supply accounts in electronic form and to give shareholders notice of meetings by email. It may well be that government will be major users of the provision in connection with oft-quoted targets that 25% of government services should be available electronically by 2002, 50% by 2005 and 100% by 2008. It is also indicated that 90% of routine government procurement should be conducted electronically by 2001.[2]

[1] HC Official Report, SC B (Electronic Communications Bill), col 73, 14 December 1999.
[2] Explanatory Notes to the Electronic Communications Bill.

29.22   The task of updating the statute book will be a massive one. It has been estimated that there are in the region of 40,000 references to paper signatures, documents and records.[1] The range of topics covered and the variety of expressions used in these statutes was considered to be such that it would be impracticable for a straightforward abolition of requirements for writing to be considered. What remains uncertain is the timetable for action. It was stated in Committee by the Minister for Small Businesses and E-Commerce that:

> I am keen for the powers provided under clause 8 to be used extensively to modernise the statute book as quickly as possible. As I said on Second Reading, my right hon. Friend the Minister for the Cabinet Office, who is responsible for e-government, is already working with other Government departments to ensure that each Department examines the statutes for which it is responsible in order to ascertain in which cases it can move rapidly to introduce electronic equivalents. A timetable for completing that has not yet been specified, but I am drawing to the attention of my colleagues in different Departments the need to move with considerable urgency. We are leading by example in my own Department, which is already preparing under clause 8 a draft order that relates to company law, to enable us to consult on it early in the new year and have it ready for introduction as soon as the Bill becomes law and clause 8 comes into effect.[2]

[1] 340 HC Official Report (6th series) col 41, 29 November 1999.
[2] HC Official Report, SC B (Electronic Communications Bill), col 75, 14 December 1999.

29.23   Concerns were expressed in Parliament that the provisions of s 8 of the Electronic Communications Act 2000 might be used to compel persons doing business with the government to engage in electronic communications. Section 8(6) provides, however, that any order made 'may not require the use of electronic communications or electronic storage for any purpose'. What may serve as a greater incentive for the use of electronic communications is the provision of some form of discount. Here, it is provided that regulations may make:

> Provision, in relation to cases in which fees or charges are or may be imposed in connection with anything for the purposes of which the use of electronic

communications or electronic storage is so authorised for different fees or charges to apply where use is made of such communications or storage.[1]

[1]   Section 6(4)(h).

29.24   It has recently been announced in the budget, for example, that taxpayers submitting income tax returns electronically will qualify for a (small) discount of £10.[1] Such reductions seem modest compared with the savings which can be accomplished through the use of electronic communications. It has been estimated that paper documentation and associated handling procedures can represent up to 10% of the total costs of goods. Costs savings on this element of up to 50% can be attained through a switch to electronic communications. Another producer has estimated that it costs $70 to process a paper purchase order as opposed to 93 cents when the order is submitted electronically. In other cases, the figures might be even higher. In June 1997, the National Audit Office criticised procurement practices within the Ministry of Defence, citing a case where £73.50 was spent processing an order for a padlock worth just 98p.[2]

[1]   Details can be found at http://www.inlandrevenue.gov.uk/ebu/info.htm.
[2]   'Improving the Procurement of Routine Items' (June 1997).

29.25   Implementation of the above statutory provisions will open the way for businesses, individuals and government agencies to make use of electronic communications for most aspects of their life and work. Whether they utilise this freedom will, of course, depend upon whether there is sufficient confidence in the integrity and reliability of systems of communication. As indicated at the beginning of this chapter, the use of systems of encryption is seen as playing an important role in this respect. The following sections will describe the nature of the technology and some of the practical and legal problems involved.

The nature of encryption

29.26   Techniques of encryption date back many centuries. An early user was Julius Caesar, who wrote his despatches from Gaul in what is now referred to as the Caesar code. This involves shifting letters an agreed number of spaces along the alphabet. For example, placing the two alphabets above each other with a shift of three would give:

```
ABCDEFGHIJKLMNOPQRSTUVWXYZ

DEFGHIJKLMNOPQRSTUVWXYZABC
```

and the letter C would become F, A become D and T, W so CAT would read FDW.

The Caesar code is an example of what is referred to as a substitution cipher. The other main form of encryption has involved a process of transposition. Effectively, this involves taking a phrase, such as:

> WET DAY IN GLASGOW

omitting spaces and placing the letters into blocks of five, producing:

> WETDA YINLA ASGOW

The letters in each block are then shuffled in a pre determined manner. If the first letter is moved to the fourth space, second to fifth, third to first, fourth to second and fifth to third we arrive at:

> TDAWE NLAYI GOWAS

29.27 Obviously, a real-life example would require to add far more in the way of complexity but, until recent times, all codes were based on substitution or transposition techniques. Throughout history, there has been a constant battle between those seeking to use encryption to preserve secrecy and those wishing to break the codes. Simon Singh recounts how a critical factor in the decision to try to execute Mary, Queen of Scots was the successful attempt by Hugh Walshingham, Queen Elizabeth's chief secretary, in deciphering coded messages exchanged between Mary and others conspiring to overthrow the English monarch.[1]

[1] *The Code Book* (1999, Fourth Estate). This book provides an excellent account of the history and nature of cryptography and has been drawn on heavily in the preparation of this chapter.

29.28 In the pre-computer age, the battle between code makers and breakers could well have been regarded as an intellectual pursuit akin to solving a crossword puzzle.[1] The advent of the computer served to change the situation. Much has been written concerning the British and US cryptographic operations during the Second World War. These led to the development of the world's first practical computing machines. Although limited by today's standards, the processing power of these computers transformed code breaking from what had been an intellectual pursuit into an exercise in number crunching. The analogy might be made with a combination lock on a safe and the contrast between the stereotypical image of a skilled safe breaker using a stethoscope to detect the correct combination and the random selection of numbers continued until the correct combination is achieved. Whilst the effort of trying several million possible combinations would be too great for humans, the task is comparatively simple for a computer.

[1]   A contest to solve *The Times* crossword puzzle in less than 12 minutes was used by the security service as a front for the quest to find suitable people to work on its attempt to break the German Enigma code.

29.29   In response to the vulnerability of traditional forms of encryption, modern systems place reliance upon mathematical techniques. One of the first of a new generation of cryptographic techniques was implemented in the US Data Encryption Standard, or DES. DES has been a source of some controversy since its inception in 1977, with allegations that its effectiveness was deliberately reduced at the behest of the US National Security Agency. The level of security is basically as great as the complexity of the encryption software. The analogy might be made with a combination lock. A lock with three dials provides some security, but one with five considerably more so. The original version of DES used what is described as a 56-bit key. This has some 70 quadrillion combinations. A massive figure for human calculators, but one which provides a more manageable challenge to modern computers. The selection of a 56-bit key is rumoured to have been influenced by the US National Security Agency. The agency is reported to possess the world's most powerful computers, machines capable of decoding messages encoded using a 56-bit key within a matter of hours. As computer technology develops, it has become more possible for other organisations to acquire the processing power required. In 1998, the Electronic Frontier Foundation, a civil liberties pressure group, claimed to have built a 'DES cracker' for $250,000 whilst, in yet another significant demonstration of the power of the Internet, it has been reported that messages have been successfully decoded using several thousand computers linked together over the Internet and operating throughout the night whilst their normal users slept.[1]

[1]   3,500 computers were linked over the Internet, searching possible key combinations at a rate of 1.5 trillion keys per hour. In total, 312 hours of processing were required to find the correct key.

29.30   DES – and other forms of substitution and transposition codes – are examples of single key or symmetric encryption systems. In the same way that the same key is used to open and lock a door, a message is encoded and decoded using the same key. So long as only the sender and recipient know the key, the system is reasonably secure. Apart from the vulnerability of codes to attack by code breakers, another significant point of weakness has concerned the fact that a single key is used to encode and to decode the message. If a sender wishes the recipient to be able to decipher his or her messages, it is necessary to deliver a copy of the key. The possibility that the key might be intercepted or misused creates another major point of vulnerability. Whilst systems such as DES might be used within closed networks of trusted parties – EDI agreements would be an obvious example – it can be of limited value in the wider world of ecommerce. Here, just as is the case in the High Street, the intention is that customers and suppliers who have no prior knowledge of each other can conduct business. Clearly, no sensible users of encryption would send a key to a party who they had not met previously.

29.31 A solution to this problem emerged with the development of public key or asymmetric cryptography. The concept was initially devised in 1976 by two mathematicians, Diffie and Hellman, and was brought to practical fruition by three further mathematicians, Rivest, Shamir and Adleman, after whom the RSA system is named. It has recently been reported that similar work had been conducted in the UK at the GCHQ, although details were withheld on grounds of national security.

29.32 The RSA system has proved controversial in a number of respects. Although the system was developed using public funds, the algorithms were patented (the patents expired in the year 2000) by a private company which marketed the software on a commercial basis. The system was first marketed in 1977, and required levels of processing power which effectively limited its use to large organisations and government departments. A modified form of public key encryption, still based on the RSA algorithms but suitable for use on personal computers, was developed by Phil Zimmerman and is generally referred to by the acronym PGP (Pretty Good Privacy). Zimmerman's original intention was reportedly to offer the system on a commercial basis. In 1991, however, he became concerned at legislative proposals being discussed in the US Congress which, if enacted, would have restricted the availability of encryption software. Zimmerman's response was to persuade a friend to place a copy of PGP on the Internet. From that date, the cryptographic genie has been well and truly out of the bottle and copies of PGP can be downloaded free of charge from a wide range of Internet sites.

29.33 For a number of years, Zimmerman faced threats of patent infringement action by RSA, but eventually the parties concluded a licence allowing the use of the RSA algorithms in non-commercial copies of PGP. This has been dropped. The US government also places restrictions on the strength of RSA software which may lawfully be exported from the US and threatened action against Zimmerman. Doubts were raised, however, whether causing a copy of PGP to be placed on the Internet constituted an act of exporting as defined in the relevant legislation and, given that the system could not be uninvented, the decision was taken to drop proceedings.

29.34 A user of either PGP or RSA software will generate two keys, a public and a private key. The act of generating the keys typically requires nothing more than random movements of the computer mouse. Messages can be encrypted using either key, but possession of the other key will be required in order to decrypt them. Although the mathematics are beyond the comprehension of mere lawyers, the system is claimed to be significantly more secure than single-key systems, although it also operates considerably more slowly.

29.35　If consideration is given to the nature of the public key system, strengths and weaknesses can be identified. The scenario might be postulated whereby A receives a message which purports to have been sent by B and encrypted using the latter's private key. Assuming A had details of the public key, the message can be decrypted and A can be certain that the message has not been tampered with following its encryption. A cannot, however, be certain that B has not let the private key fall into a third party's hands. Again, given the ease with which PGP software and email accounts can be acquired or forged, if A and B have not dealt previously, A cannot be confident that B is who he or she claims to be. A final weakness may be most relevant in the commercial context. B may be a company and the key used to encrypt a message ordering 100,000 widgets from A. A will have no means of knowing that the person sending the message on A's behalf is authorised to engage in such transactions.

29.36　The same issues will apply in the event that A replies to B encrypting the message with A's public key. Again, there can be confidence that the message has not been intercepted and amended in transit but less reliance upon the identity of the claimed sender. Indeed, given that the essence of the public key is that it is public, it might be a foolhardy person who would place too much credence on the origin of a message. From the point of view of the sender, he or she may be given details of a public key and told that it belongs to Ian Lloyd, a well-known supplier of memorabilia of Glasgow Celtic Football Club. Encouraged by the prospect of secure communications, credit card details may be transmitted with a view to acquiring a selection of materials. Unfortunately, the key may have been generated by a criminal seeking to acquire valid credit card numbers.

Enter trusted third parties

29.37　If the aim of encryption is to authenticate the accuracy of a transmission and to identify its sender, systems of public key cryptography score one out of two. To provide mechanisms for promoting trust in the identity and status of the parties involved, the involvement of trusted third parties (TTP), also referred to as certification agencies, has emerged. The TTP will seek evidence that the party sending a message is who he or she claims to be and will cause a certificate to that effect to be attached to a message. Even today, the market is significant with the market leader, Verisign,[1] reporting a turnover of $30m in 1998. For the UK, banks, some solicitors and accountancy firms and even the Post Office have expressed interest in acting as TTPs.

[1]　http://www.verisign.com/index.html.

29.38　The basic operation of TTPs is non-controversial and can be equated with traditional professions such as that of notary or even with the role of a witness to a document. TTPs will almost inevitably obtain information about their customers' keys and some offer what is referred to as a key recovery service. This effectively involves them keeping secure a copy of a private key. In the event that the user forgets the key or – perhaps more likely – details are destroyed by a disaffected or departing employee, the loss can be made good.

29.39 As with many issues concerned with the Internet, initial moves in the field came from the US. Here, enormous controversy followed proposals to introduce a new system of encryption, the Escrowed Encryption Standard, more commonly referred to as the 'Clipper Chip'. The attraction of this system, which would be based on public key cryptography, would be that any form of digitised data would be encrypted in such a way as to ensure a high level of security. The less welcome aspect of the system was that its structure would enable 'keys' to be made available to government agencies, enabling messages to be deciphered readily. Concerns were expressed whether the legal controls envisaged concerning release of the keys would provide adequate safeguards. Although legislation implementing the clipper proposals did not pass through Congress, it was announced in Autumn 1996 that export controls on encryption software would be reduced in return for an industry commitment to the introduction of a 'key recovery' system requiring that copies of all keys be held by a 'Trusted Third Party'. It would appear in this case that the prime motive was that the third party should be trusted by the government rather than by the contracting parties.

29.40 Much of the legislative debate in the late 1990s has concerned the role of TTPs and systems of key recovery and escrow. In March 1997, the Council of the OECD adopted 'Guidelines for Cryptography Policy'.[1] In a manner similar to that adopted in the field of data protection, the guidelines identify eight principles which should inform national legislation in this field:

1. Cryptographic methods should be trustworthy in order to generate confidence in the use of information and communications systems.
2. Users should have a right to choose any cryptographic method, subject to applicable law.
3. Cryptographic methods should be developed in response to the needs, demands and responsibilities of individuals, businesses and governments.
4. Technical standards, criteria and protocols for cryptographic methods should be developed and promulgated at the national and international level.
5. The fundamental rights of individuals to privacy, including secrecy of communications and protection of personal data, should be respected in national cryptographic policies and in the implementation and use of cryptographic methods.
6. National cryptographic policies may allow lawful access to plain text, or cryptographic keys, of encrypted data. These policies must respect the other principles contained in the guidelines to the greatest extent possible.
7. Whether established by contract or legislation, the liability of individuals and entities that offer cryptographic services or hold or access cryptographic keys should be clearly stated.

8.   Governments should co-operate to co-ordinate cryptographic policies. As part of this effort, governments should remove, or avoid creating in the name of cryptography policy, unjustified obstacles to trade.

A strong relationship can be identified between these principles and a number of those applying in the data protection field. Although the guidelines recognise the need for some legal controls over the use of cryptography, it is stressed throughout that these must 'respect user choice to the greatest extent'. To this extent, the guidelines are seen as moving away from the US-sponsored notion of mandatory key escrow, a move which is also followed in recent EU and UK legislation and proposals.

[1]   Available from http://www.oecd.org//dsti/sti/it/secur/prod/crypto1.htm.

29.41   It is not the purpose of this chapter to discuss in detail the political aspects of encryption policy. It is suggested, however, that both sides are failing to come to terms with the reality of modern life. Those advocating extensive powers for law enforcement agencies are, in many respects, looking back to a form of golden age when governments could exercise genuine control over communications. Terrestrial broadcasting was largely a state-controlled monopoly, and the limits of transmitter power meant that foreign broadcasts could be received only in border region. Postal and telecommunication services were also state-controlled, and international communications were conducted only on a small scale. The world has moved on and attempts to re-exert control are likely to be doomed to failure.

29.42   Those opposed to the interception of encrypted messages may suffer from a similarly dated view of the world, harking back to a golden era of individual anonymity. In many Western countries, this can be considered to have reached its apogee in the 1960s. The last 30 years have seen a massive increase in the amount of personal data recorded and processed. Privacy in the traditional sense has largely vanished. In part, this is as a result of public sector activity but a large and growing threat comes from the private sector. There has never been a situation in which all communications receive immunity from interception. Whilst there is certainly need for controls to be introduced concerning interception and decryption of encoded messages, the notion that individuals should be assured of absolute privacy for their communications has never been a feature of societal life.

The Electronic Signatures Directive

29.43   Although its provisions generally conjure up images of systems of public key encryption, the Electronic Signatures Directive[1] seeks to be technologically neutral. Its implementation would have the effect of providing for electronic equivalents to writing and signature to be accepted within the member states. The Directive is expressly stated to be unconcerned with contractual and other procedural requirements.[2] Its purpose is stated to be:

... to facilitate the use of electronic signatures and to contribute to their legal recognition. It establishes a legal framework for electronic signatures and certain certification-services in order to ensure the proper functioning of the internal market.[3]

¹ Directive 99/93/EC.
² See also the provisions of the Electronic Commerce Directive, Directive 2000/31/EC, discussed at para 28.27 above.
³ Article 1.

29.44 The Electronic Signatures Directive identifies two forms of signature: electronic and advanced electronic signatures. These are defined:

  1.   'electronic signature' means data in electronic form which are attached to or logically associated with other electronic data and which serve as a method of authentication; and
  2.   'advanced electronic signature' means an electronic signature which meets the following requirements:
       (a)   it is uniquely linked to the signatory;
       (b)   it is capable of identifying the signatory;
       (c)   it is created using means that the signatory can maintain under his sole control; and
       (d)   it is linked to the data to which it relates in such a manner that any subsequent change of the data is detectable.[1]

¹ Directive 99/93/EC, art 2(1).

29.45 The term 'electronic signature' is very broad. It would encompass, for example, the use of scanning equipment to create a digital image of a person's signature, with this image being reproduced at the end of a word-processed letter. Advanced forms of signature will require the use of some form of encryption. The Electronic Signatures Directive refers to this under the heading of 'secure-signature-creation device'. The technical attributes to be possessed by such devices are specified in Annex 3, whilst the Directive provides that member states may, acting in accordance with criteria to be specified by the Commission, establish mechanisms to verify the conformity of particular systems of encryption.[1]

¹ Directive 99/93/EC, art 3(4).

29.46 In terms of the legal status to be afforded to electronic signatures, the Electronic Signatures Directive provides that:

  1.   Member States shall ensure that advanced electronic signatures which are based on a qualified certificate and which are created by a secure-signature-creation device:
       (a)   satisfy the legal requirements of a signature in relation to data in electronic form in the same manner as a hand-written signature satisfies those requirements in relation to paper-based data; and
       (b)   are admissible as evidence in legal proceedings.
  2.   Member States shall ensure that an electronic signature is not denied legal effectiveness and admissibility as evidence in legal proceedings solely on the grounds that it is:

- in electronic form; or
- not based upon a qualified certificate; or
- not based upon a qualified certificate issued by an accredited certification-service-provider; or
- not created by a secure signature-creation device.[1]

[1]   Directive 99/93/EC, art 5.

29.47   An advanced electronic signature will give a considerable degree of assurance that the signature is that of a particular person. There cannot be assurance that its use has been authorised by the owner either generally or in the context of a particular transaction. It might be, for example, that an unauthorised third party has obtained a copy of a private key. Alternatively, a company may have a private key which is used by an employee to place an order for goods but where the employee is acting in excess of his or her authority. To overcome these difficulties, the notion has been advanced that the use of a signature should be certified by an independent agency. The Electronic Signatures Directive identifies criteria which must be met in what is called a 'qualified certificate':

(a)   an indication that the certificate is issued as a qualified certificate;

(b)   the identification of the certification-service-provider and the State in which it is established;

(c)   the name of the signatory or a pseudonym, which shall be identified as such;

(d)   provision for a specific attribute of the signatory to be included if relevant, depending on the purpose for which the certificate is intended;

(e)   signature-verification data which correspond to signature-creation data under the control of the signatory;

(f)   an indication of the beginning and end of the period of validity of the certificate;

(g)   the identity code of the certificate;

(h)   the advanced electronic signature of the certification-service-provider issuing it;

(i)   limitations on the scope of use of the certificate, if applicable; and

(j)   limits on the value of transactions for which the certificate can be used, if applicable.[1]

This is in effect creating a role for the TTPs, now known as certification-service-providers, discussed above. Annex 2 of the Directive specifies a wide range of technical and organisational attributes which must be demonstrated in order for a certificate issued by a service provider to be recognised as a qualified certificate.

[1]   Directive 99/93/EC, Annex 1.

29.48   The Electronic Signatures Directive makes it clear that no limitations are to be imposed upon the freedom of anyone to engage in the activity of a certification-service-provider. It is provided, however, that:

> Member States may introduce or maintain voluntary accreditation schemes aiming at enhanced levels of certification-service provision. All conditions related to such schemes must be objective, transparent, proportionate and non-discriminatory. Member States may not limit the number of accredited

certification-service-providers for reasons which fall within the scope of this Directive.[1]

It may well prove, of course, that a person wishing to engage in the business of certification-service-provider may find that commercial pressure may dictate that accreditation is sought.

[1] Directive 99/93/EC, art 3(2).

Electronic signatures and the Electronic Communications Act 2000

29.49 The Electronic Signatures Directive[1] requires to be implemented in the member states by July 2001. The UK met this timetable with the enactment of the Electronic Communications Act which received the Royal Assent on 25 May 2000. Reference has previously been made to the role of this statute in providing for electronic communications to be taken as satisfying requirements for writing. The Act provides also for recognition of electronic signatures and for the activities of what are referred to as cryptography service providers.

[1] Directive 99/93/EC.

Electronic signatures

29.50 The Electronic Communications Act 2000's provisions relating to the recognition of electronic signatures are rather more simple than those found in the Electronic Signatures Directive.[1] The Act eschews the distinction between 'electronic' and 'advanced electronic signatures', instead providing that:

> In any legal proceeding—
>
> (a) an electronic signature incorporated or logically associated with a particular electronic communication or with particular electronic data, and
> (b) the certification by any person of such a signature,
>
> shall each be admissible in evidence in relation to any question as to the authenticity of the communication or data or as to the integrity of the communication or data.[2]

The term 'electronic signature' is defined in terms similar to those found in the Directive:

> For the purposes of this section an electronic signature is so much of anything in electronic form as—
>
> (a) is incorporated into or otherwise logically associated with any electronic communication or electronic data; and
> (b) purports to be so incorporated or associated for the purpose of being used in establishing the authenticity of the communication or data, the integrity of the communication or data, or both.[3]

Effectively, the decision will be left to a court what weight to attach to any particular signature.

1 Directive 99/93/EC.
2 Section 7(1).
3 Section 7(2).

29.51 In the situation where a signature is required to validate a contract, the provisions of s 8 of the Electronic Communications Act 2000 will again be relevant. As is the case with requirements for writing generally, rather than providing for blanket recognition of electronic signatures, the Act provides that secondary legislation may be made in order to provide for:

> (c) the doing of anything which under any such provisions is required to be or may be authorised by a person's signature or seal, or is required to be delivered as a deed or witnessed by electronic means.[1]

1 Section 8(2).

Cryptography service providers

29.52 The final, and most controversial, element of the Electronic Communications Act 2000 concerns the provisions made for cryptographic service providers. This term is defined as encompassing:

> ... any service which is provided to the senders or recipients of electronic communications, or to those storing electronic data, and is designed to facilitate the use of cryptographic techniques for the purpose of—
>
> (a) securing that such communications or data can be accessed, or can be put into an intelligible form, only by certain persons; or
> (b) securing that the authenticity or integrity of such communications or data is capable of being ascertained.[1]

The service must either be provided from premises within the UK or be provided to persons carrying on a business in the UK. A German service provider marketing services to UK-based companies would come within the second element of this definition.

1 Section 6.

29.53 Anyone is entitled to establish a cryptography support service. Equally, there is no obligation imposed on users of encryption to involve such a service in their transactions. Especially in cases where parties have a background of previous dealings or operate as part of an EDI network, such third-party involvement may well be rendered otiose.

29.54 At present, no restrictions – and virtually no legislation – apply to the use of encryption or cryptography services. Maintenance of the status quo would not justify such flagship legislation. What is envisaged in Pt I of the Electronic Communications Act 2000 is the establishment of a voluntary register of accredited cryptography service providers along the lines provided for in the Electronic

Signatures Directive.[1] Whilst the decision to seek registration will be a voluntary one, the intention is that the existence of such a scheme will promote public confidence in what must be regarded as an embryonic profession.

[1]   Directive 99/93/EC.

29.55   The Electronic Communications Act 2000 provides in ss 2 and 3 that responsibility for the establishment of such a register is to vest in the Secretary of State (or such other body to whom performance of the task may be delegated). It has been indicated, however, that the intention is that the register should be operated on a voluntary basis. Section 16 provides that the provisions will come into force on such day as may be fixed by order, but that if no order is made within five years from the date of Royal Assent, the order making power will lapse.

29.56   Government speakers in the Commons indicated a strong desire that a voluntary scheme should be introduced as soon as possible. Discussions with the Alliance for Electronic Business resulted in the establishment of a non-statutory self-regulating scheme (tScheme) for Trust services'. The scope of the proposal is described as being 'to operate and enforce a voluntary approval scheme for trust services'. The overall objective is stated to be to provide a mechanism that will:

- set minimum criteria for trust and confidence;
- be responsible for:
    - the approval of electronic trust services against those criteria;
    - the monitoring of approved services;
    - provide a means of redress where services fall below those criteria;
- and thereby promote the benefits of using an approved electronic trust service.

[1]   Available from http://www.tscheme.org/.

29.57   Five organisations are currently approved for the provision of services. An indication of the nature of the likely requirements can be found in Annex 2 of the Electronic Signatures Directive[1] (with which the Electronic Communications Act 2000 is designed to be compatible). This refers to the need for demonstrable reliability of the systems, technologies and personnel involved in the provision of the service, the acceptance of liability for losses caused through errors in the service provision and the observance of a proper degree of confidentiality regarding details of the customer's business. Further indication regarding the criteria which might be applied can again be taken from the Alliance for Electronic Business Scheme, which states that:

> It is anticipated that the criteria will address business, management, operational and technical issues necessary for approval. Criteria will relate to both the services offered and the organisations offering them and will be based as far as possible on existing criteria in the marketplace.
>
> The actual criteria used for assessment will be a selection of elements from publicly available, and wherever possible international, technical or management standards. (e.g. ISO 9000, BS 7799, X.509, FIPS 140; and from other appropriate criteria published by bodies such as FSA and OFTEL).

In addition to adopting previously defined standards the organisation will, when necessary, create criteria not already existing in the marketplace. It is vital to the success of (the) scheme, and its take up by providers, that it does not duplicate existing approval and regulatory structures, but builds on their foundations.

The selection of criteria, termed an Approval Profile, will be unique for each different type of service. Criteria will be selected by reference to specific versions of standards, and reviewed periodically to ensure that the most relevant and appropriate criteria are applied, as the standardisation process and services develop. A list of the criteria selected, including any necessary identifying publication information (e.g. dates, versions, etc.) will be maintained and publicly available.

[1]   Directive 99/93/EC.

29.58   It is clear from the above that there can be no single scheme of certification. Given the vast range of transactions that may be carried out electronically, such an approach is necessary and desirable. It is to be expected and hoped that standards will emerge over time to give appropriate guidance to the courts and other agencies on what reliance might reasonably be placed upon a particular form of certificate. One thing does seem certain: accreditation will not be a cheap process for service providers. The Minister for Small Business and E-Commerce stated in Committee that:

> An estimate of the possible costs involved for a medium-sized company that is seeking approval for the issue of certificates would be between £10,000 and £30,000.[1]

[1]   HC Official Report, SC B (Electronic Communications Bill), col 37, 9 December 1999.

Conclusions

29.59   There seems little doubt that ecommerce will expand significantly in coming years. It is the author's view that this will take place in spite of concerns regarding lack of security. Consumers run the risk of falling victim to fraud in every aspect of life. The Internet is no better and no worse in this respect. Encryption is frequently used by service providers to enhance security. This is typically done in a manner which makes no demands on the consumer. The complexities of public key cryptography are such that its use is likely to remain restricted to the commercial sector and to techno-freaks.

29.60   A further development which may enhance consumer confidence in ecommerce relates to the acceptance by credit card providers of the risk of loss due to fraud on the Internet. Under s 75 of the Consumer Credit Act 1974, credit card providers incur joint and several liability with merchants in respect of any claim which a consumer may have in respect of misrepresentation or breach of contract relating to a transaction valued at between £100 and £30,000. This provision will apply to Internet transactions, although there is doubt whether it applies in a situation where a consumer resident in the UK contracts with a merchant located in some other country. In the event that the consumer's details are intercepted by a third party and subsequently misused, s 83 of the Act may be of assistance. This provides that the card holder is not liable for loss arising from third-party use of the credit facility by 'another person not acting as the debtor's agent'. Section 84 does provide that the consumer may be liable (up to a maximum of £50) for misuse of a 'credit token' during the period when it leaves the consumer's control until its loss is reported to the creditor. The term credit token is defined as a 'card, check voucher, coupon, stamp, form, booklet or other document or thing'. This can clearly relate to the physical card rather than the numbers contained thereon.

29.61 If the Internet creates the problem, it may also provide the solution. A growing number of credit card suppliers conduct business over the Internet. As described previously, this can result in very considerable cost savings. One card provider, Egg.com,[1] offers its customers a guarantee:

> To overcome any concerns you may have about shopping online, the Egg Card comes with its unique Internet guarantee that covers you when you are shopping with your Egg Card in the Egg Shopping Zone.
>
> Whenever you shop with your Egg Card online, we guarantee you will be covered against any fraudulent transactions carried out without your knowledge or consent, whatever the amount.
>
> With any of our shopping zone retailers, if you have a problem with any goods or services purchased with your Egg Card that are:
>
>> Not delivered
>> Damaged or faulty
>> Not of satisfactory quality
>> Not as described on the website
>
> You should first check the retailer's site as they often have their own money back or goodwill policies that go beyond your statutory rights and then contact their customer services department to request a refund or replacement item.
>
> In the unlikely event that you still cannot get a refund or replacement from the retailer, Egg will make sure your problem is resolved or you get your money back.

[1]   http://www.egg.com.

29.62 The guarantee is, of course, restricted in that it applies only in respect of activities carried out within the card company's own network of approved dealers. Again, the impression is given that the credit card company will be liable only after redress has been sought and refused by the supplier. Section 75 of the Consumer Credit Act 1974 gives the consumer the option which party to proceed against in the first instance.

29.63 The Commission and UK proposals regarding electronic signatures may be of greater relevance in the commercial sector, where many requirements of form currently restrict the extent to which companies can maximise the use of electronic communications. This may relate more, however, to undertakings' relations with the state rather than between themselves. The unanswered question in this – as in many other areas of IT law – is whether legal provisions will be relevant in the face of seemingly remorseless advances in technology?

Chapter 30

Tax and the Internet

Introduction

30.1   Although few things in life are inevitable, our exposure to death and taxes is generally claimed to constitute an exception to the general rule. Michael Faraday is reported to have answered a question concerning the utility of electricity: 'Sir, I do not know what it is good for. But of one thing I am quite certain, some day you will tax it.' As the scale of Internet usage and of ecommerce grows, so attention is increasingly being paid to tax implications.

30.2   The factor complicating the assessment and collection of taxes is (at least potentially) the global nature of ecommerce. The question, therefore, arises where a business is to be regarded as established for fiscal purposes? The notion of place of establishment is also of great significance in determining the question when and where a contract is to be regarded as having been concluded and which legal systems should regulate its performance. These issues will be considered in this chapter.

30.3   Although every state maintains its own system of taxation, considerable international harmonisation already exists, most notably in the form of the OECD Model Tax Convention. This provides the basis for more than 1,500 bilateral treaties between states providing for tax arrangements regarding each other's nationals. An OECD 'Discussion Paper on Taxation Issues',[1] prepared by its Committee on Fiscal Affairs, identified 'generally accepted tax principles of neutrality, efficiency, certainty, simplicity, effectiveness, fairness and flexibility' and affirmed that these should also apply in regimes established to deal with the new world of ecommerce.

[1]   Available from http://www.oecd.org/daf/fa/E_COM/discusse.pdf.

30.4   A similar view has been expressed in the UK in a joint policy paper prepared by the Inland Revenue and HM Customs and Excise.[1] This indicated approval of the proposition that UK businesses required:

673

- certainty about tax rules;
- neutrality between electronic and conventional commerce;
- no double or unintentional non-taxation;
- compliance costs should be as low as possible;
- no new taxes on electronic commerce; and
- the use of modern technology by our tax administrations to improve the service they offer their customers.

This view was restated in 'Electronic Commerce: The UK's Taxation Agenda', published by the Inland Revenue and HM Customs and Excise in November 1999.[2] This identified three areas where ecommerce and communications both offered opportunities and posed challenges to tax authorities:

- Tax administration.
- Compliance and tax evasion issues.
- Taxation rules per se.

[1] 'Electronic Commerce: UK Taxation Policy' Available from http://www.inlandrevenue. gov.uk/taxagenda/index.htm.
[2] Available from http://www.inlandrevenue.gov.uk/taxagenda/ecom.pdf.

30.5 Little consideration needs to be given to the first of these topics. It is possible at present for individuals and companies to submit tax returns in electronic format and to engage in email discussions with the tax authorities.

30.6 The remaining topics raise some issues of principle, although most problems may be identified at the practical level. In most respects, it is argued that the application of traditional provisions of tax law to ecommerce will provide appropriate treatment for ecommerce. The Inland Revenue has commented that:

> The Government does not believe that it is necessary at this stage to make any major changes to existing tax legislation and regulations or to introduce new taxes.[1]

[1] *Electronic Commerce: UK Taxation Policy* (1999).

30.7 The notion that businesses should not be fiscally penalised for engaging in ecommerce is one which receives widespread recognition. The US Congress passed the somewhat portentously titled Internet Tax Freedom Act in 1998. Although much media publicity concerning the measure spoke in terms of a tax-free regime in cyberspace, the reality was somewhat less dramatic, with the statute restricting itself to a prohibition against the imposition of any new state or local taxation, either upon Internet access or which imposed multiple or discriminatory taxes on e-commerce. The Act was given a limited life span of three years. In 2001, the Internet Tax Non-Discrimination Act extended its application until November 2003. Proposals for a permanent measure are currently stalled before the US legislature.

30.8 Whilst few changes may be required in relation to the principles of taxation policy, a number of issues may provide problems. Consideration may be divided into two sections, the first concerned with the liability of a service or product supplier to make payment to the UK authorities in respect of transactions carried out with UK citizens. The second concerns the liability of UK citizens to pay import duties or VAT in respect of goods or services obtained from a provider located outside the UK.

30.9 In most countries, citizens are liable for payment of a range of direct and indirect taxes on capital, income and consumption. In respect of income tax, perhaps the best-known form of direct taxation, the emergence of the Internet will, especially for employed persons taxed under the PAYE system, have no significant effect in respect of liabilities.

30.10 More difficult issues will arise in respect of direct taxation imposed upon businesses and individuals who generate income in respect of operations undertaken in two or more countries. Two issues arise. The first concerns the division between taxes based on the source of income and upon the residence of the taxpayer, and the second concerns the issue where a business may be considered to be established.

Source and residence taxation

30.11 In the situation where income is earned in one country by an individual resident or undertaking established in another the question inevitably arises of where taxes fall due to be paid. Resolution of this issue is the prime rationale behind the raft of bilateral tax conventions negotiated under the auspices of the OECD Model Tax Convention. These typically identify their purpose as 'the avoidance of double taxation and the prevention of fiscal evasion'. Two approaches are possible, providing for income to be charged either on the basis of its source or the residence of the individual or organisation concerned. In the situation where there is an approximate balance of income flow between countries, there is little financial consequence whether income is taxed on the basis of source or residence, although matters become more difficult when this is not the case.

Permanent establishment

30.12 In the first of these cases, the question which may have to be determined is whether an organisation which is conducting business over the Internet, for example, a bookshop soliciting orders from UK-based customers, can be regarded as having an establishment in the UK sufficient to render it liable to UK taxes. It is clear that the bookshop may be making a profit from its UK customers, but if the books are supplied from a warehouse in Seattle and if the company's computer system is also located there, a clear connection exists with the US. Whilst no new issues arise in respect of liability for taxes on capital, the emergence of a global banking system makes it much more feasible for individuals to invest capital abroad.

Establishment of electronic providers

30.13   In the situation where a person or business established in one country earns income in another, it is apparent that there will be two countries with a potential interest in taxing income. This might be taxed either at the point and in the country where it is earned or in the country of residence. One point which might be taken into account is that the rules of private international law do not permit enforcement of national tax obligations in another country. Different countries adopt different approaches and the prime purpose of tax treaties is to ensure that double taxation does not occur. Article 7 of the OECD Model Tax Convention provides that:

> The profits of an enterprise of a Contracting State shall be taxable only in that state unless the enterprise carries on business in the other Contracting State through a permanent establishment situated therein.

30.14   The notion of 'permanent establishment' is defined in art 5 of the Convention. It includes places of management, branches, offices, factories and workshops, but specifically excludes:

> The use of facilities solely for the purpose of storage, display or delivery of goods or merchandise belonging to the enterprise; and
> The maintenance of a stock of goods or merchandise belonging to the enterprise solely for the purpose of storage, display or delivery.

30.15   In the situation where a website permits customers to download data such as software, audio or visual works, the question may arise whether the database can be considered as a 'stock of goods or merchandise'. The commentary on the Convention indicates that the exceptions (six in total) seek to isolate activities which are preparatory or auxiliary to the purpose of a business from those which are more integral in their nature and significance. The OECD's Committee on Fiscal Affairs has undertaken to give more precise guidance concerning the application of art 5 within the context of ecommerce. It is unclear, for example, whether maintaining a website in a particular jurisdiction to which orders for goods or services might be submitted would class as a permanent establishment. The activity might be regarded as coming within one or both of the exceptions listed above, but appears to be integral to the seller's business. Further complexities can be identified:

> ... a server may be located in a building situated in a country where the enterprise has no other presence. Alternatively, it could be located on a portable computer used in different places within that building or moved from city to city by an itinerant employee, Further difficulties would arise where a number of mirror sites on different servers located in different countries would be used so that a customer could be directed to any site for any function depending on electronic traffic.[1]

1   'Electronic Commerce: The Challenge to Tax Authorities and Taxpayers', an informal round-table discussion between business and government held in connection with the OECD Electronic Commerce conference in Turku, Finland, 1997, available from http://www.oecd.org/daf/fa/e_com/turku_e.pdf.

30.16 Many of these possibilities exist already. With the reduction in telecommunications costs, many global businesses routinely switch customers' telephone calls to an office in a convenient (for the business) time zone. Anyone, for example, wishing to book a British Airways plane ticket between Glasgow and London and telephoning the airline outwith UK business hours may find the call dealt with by an agent in the US or India. Again, it is common for popular websites offering users the possibility to download materials to maintain facilities in a range of countries. An example of the international potentialities of even a comparatively simple-seeming electronic transaction can be seen in the following example, involving a French company specialising in the supply of food products such as wine from Cahors and nougat from Montelimar. It is reported that:

> The site has an intercontinental architecture: stock and order management activities and supplier relationship management are situated in France: the import/export organisation is based in Hong Kong for tax reasons and the Web pages are also created in Hong Kong, 4 times more cheaply than elsewhere (slightly under 3 Ecus, as against 10 Ecus in France or the United States) ... the site is hosted by an American server in Arizona essentially for reasons connected with bandwidth, freedom of encryption and the securitization of card payments ... The orders are delivered throughout the world by UPS.[1]

1   Cited in 'On-line services and data protection and the protection of privacy', a study prepared by Arete for DG15 of the European Commission, available from http://europa.eu.int/comm/dg15/en/media/dataprot/studies/servint.htm.

30.17 Although all of the jurisdictional and taxation issues in this example are doubtless capable of resolution, it does appear that food shopping has never been so complex. Faced with the flexibility which the Internet provides, it is to be expected that 'street-wise' traders will lose little time in structuring their electronic businesses in such a way as to minimise their liability for income tax.

Indirect taxation

30.18 In many developed countries, a shift has occurred over the last 20 years from a situation where taxes were levied primarily on income to tax at the point of consumption. The OECD has estimated that 30% of its member states' tax income now comes from indirect taxes. Two main forms of indirect taxation can be identified. Within Europe and all of the members of the OECD, other than Australia and the US, systems of Value Added Tax (VAT) operate. In the two other countries, the system of sales tax applies. Additionally; of course, certain forms of goods will attract excise taxes on being imported into a country. Principle examples will include alcohol and cigarettes.

30.19 In the situation where supplier and consumer are located in the same jurisdiction, the fact that a transaction is entered into or performed electronically should not impact upon liability for tax. More difficult issues arise where transactions occur across borders. This has been an issue of some significance in the US, where each of the states possesses the freedom to impose sales tax on goods supplied for use or consumption within its territory. The tax collection structure can indeed devolve to the level of local communities to the extent that some 2,300 local taxes exist. Faced with the problems for businesses of dealing with 50 different state laws, the Uniform Commercial Code was drawn up in 1898. Amended on many subsequent occasions, it provides a common set of principles which, when adopted in state law, ensures a uniform regulatory structure across the states. Interstate commerce is regulated at the Federal level, with the US authorising Congress to 'regulate Commerce with foreign nations and among the several States'. In the case of *Freeman v Hewitt*,[1] the Supreme Court ruled that:

> State taxation falling on interstate commerce ... can only be justified as designed to make such commerce bear a fair share of the cost of the local government whose protection it enjoys.

[1]   329 US 249 (1946).

30.20 In the case of *National Bellas Hess, Inc v Department of Revenue of the State of Illinois*,[1] the Supreme Court confirmed that this prohibited a state from requiring a mail order business established outwith its boundaries to collect and account for taxes due on purchases made by its citizens.

[1]   386 US 753 (1967).

30.21 The issue returned to the Supreme Court in 1992 in the case of *Quill Corpn v North Dakota*.[1] Once again, the constitutionality of a state tax law was at issue. The tax required to be collected and remitted by every 'retailer maintaining a place of business' in North Dakota. The word 'retailer' is defined as encompassing 'every person who engages in regular or systematic solicitation of a consumer market in the state'. It was argued on behalf of the North Dakota government that this definition was capable of applying to any organisation which advertised goods or services to its citizens. In the particular case, this would apply to mail order sales, but the principle would also clearly extend to ecommerce. The Supreme Court of North Dakota refused to follow the case of *Bellas Hess*[2] arguing that 'the tremendous social, economic, commercial and legal innovations of the past quarter century have rendered its holding obsolete'. In particular, it was argued that mail order sales had transformed from 'a relatively inconsequential market niche in 1967' to a market worth $183.3bn in 1989.

[1]   504 US 298 (1992).
[2]   *National Bellas Hess, Inc v Department of Revenue of the State of Illinois* 386 US 753 (1967).

30.22 By a majority, the Supreme Court affirmed its earlier ruling in *Bellas Hess*.[1] Whilst it recognised that a physical connection between a company and a state was not required to subject a corporation to state law, the constitutional prohibition against measures which might impede interstate commerce remained applicable to prohibit the imposition of an obligation to collect and remit sales and use taxes. It was suggested that the matter might be addressed by Congress, something that might appear a reasonable step given estimates that the annual loss of revenue to the states amounted to some $3.2bn. To date, however, no action has been taken and the enactment of the Internet Tax Freedom Act has, if anything signalled a move in the opposite direction. The legislation provided for a two-year moratorium on the imposition of new state taxes. Proposals have been tabled in 1999 which would have the effect of making the moratorium permanent. Significantly, the proposal was initiated by a Senator from the state of New Hampshire, which is one of only two states which does not impose any form of sales tax. The continuance of the moratorium might well have the effect of making such a location economically attractive to organisations wishing to develop an ecommerce business.

¹ *National Bellas Hess, Inc v Department of Revenue of the State of Illinois* 386 US 753 (1967).

VAT-related issues

30.23   To a considerable extent, the problems identified in the US with its systems of sales tax do not occur under the European Value Added Tax model. As indicated above, this style of tax is adopted by the overwhelming majority of OECD members. As opposed to the concept of a sales tax, which is levied once at the point of supply to the end user, VAT is chargeable at all stages throughout a supply chain. If a supply chain A-B-C-D can be identified, A will charge VAT on the supply of the goods or services to B. B will be entitled to reclaim this amount and must in turn charge VAT on the supply to C. The process will be repeated by C with the effect that ultimately only the end user, D, will bear the cost of the tax.

30.24   As with other aspects of ecommerce, a vital question will relate to the jurisdiction within which tax liabilities will arise. In the EU, the Sixth VAT Directive¹ established a common set of rules for determining where tax liabilities will arise. Generally, the applicable regime will be that in which the supplier is established. Cultural, artistic and entertainment services are liable for tax at the place of performance, whilst services relating to intangibles or intellectual services, a concept which includes agreements relating to copyright, licensing or professional services, are liable for VAT in the jurisdiction where the customer is established.

¹ Directive 77/388/EC, OJ L145/1. See also Directive 2002/38/EC OJ L128/41 which makes further provision for suppliers established outside the EU to make arrangements for payment of taxes.

30.25   As has been discussed above, the concept of establishment can raise complex issues in the information age. As is pointed out by the OECD, with the liberalisation of telecommunications regimes, a large number of companies can offer telecommunications services in a country without necessarily being resident in that territory. Until the loophole was closed in 1997, it was indeed the case that ISPs (such as CompuServe and America Online) based outside the EU were not responsible for charging VAT to their customers, thereby obtaining a significant competitive advantage over EU-based providers. With effect from 1 July 1997, the rules relating to VAT liability in respect of telecommunications services within the EU have provided for the location of the customer to be the determinant factor in assessing liability to VAT.

30.26   One significant issue which arises in the EU concerns the distinction between goods and services in the case where these are provided by a supplier established outside the EU. An example would be the provision of books or software from a supplier established in the US. Where goods are imported into the EU, there is liability to pay the VAT due in the country of importation. There are thus no issues of principle, although concern has been expressed at the ability of customs authorities to cope with volume of transactions. The relevant international instrument concerned with such issues is the 1999 Kyoto Convention on the simplification and harmonization of Customs procedures prepared by the World Customs Organization. Discussions are currently taking place with a view to adopting provisions to deal with the expected upsurge in the numbers of small-volume imports arising from the growth in ecommerce.

30.27   More difficult issues arise with regard to the importation of services. At present, an EU consumer obtaining a service from an external supplier is not liable to pay VAT. A Commission Communication explains that this situation has arisen because the volume and value of such transactions has historically been very low. This situation is changing, not least because many information-based products, such as software and audio works, can readily be supplied in digital form over the Internet. The strange situation, therefore, arises that a consumer purchasing a disc-based copy of a software program from a US-based supplier will be liable to pay VAT on the importation, whilst a more Internet-wise consumer can obtain exactly the same result through downloading the software without incurring liability to tax. The Commission have commented that:

> Turn-over relating to EU final consumption attributable to e-commerce (i.e. delivered to private individuals as opposed to companies) is difficult to estimate. This may reach a figure of 5 billion ECU by the year 2001 for all types of e-commerce – goods and services, ordered and paid for on-line, irrespective of the mode of delivery. Only a proportion of this total will be attributable to supplies from non-EU sources and only a further fraction of this will consist partly of 'direct' electronic commerce, i.e. services delivered on-line ...
>
> If the predicted increase in such services supplied to final consumers, who at present pay no VAT, reaches a level which is economically significant it may be necessary, in conjunction with the business community, to design mechanisms to tax such supplied.[1]

Consumers might be advised to make electronic transactions whilst the fiscal sun continues to shine. The UK's newly published taxation agenda indicates the intention to seek to close the loophole allowing consumer imports of services to escape liability to VAT.

1   'E-Commerce and Indirect taxation', Communication by the Commission to the Council of Ministers, the European Parliament and the Economic and Social Committee, 1998, available from http://www.ispo.cec.be/Ecommerce/legal/taxation.html.

The European Single Market and ecommerce

30.28   An interesting fiscal issue arose in the case of *R v Commissioners of Customs and Excise, ex p EMU Tabac SARL, the Man in Black Ltd and John Cunningham*,[1] a dispute referred by the Court of Appeal for a preliminary ruling from the European Court of Justice.

1   Case C296/95 (2 April 1998, unreported), available from http://curia.eu.int/jurisp.

30.29   EMU is a company incorporated in Luxembourg and the Man in Black Limited (MBL) in the UK. Both are subsidiaries of another company, the Enlightened Tobacco Company. Taking advantage of the fact that excise duties on tobacco are much lower in Luxembourg than in the UK, an operation was established whereby UK smokers could place cigarette orders with MBL, which would in turn make purchases from EMU and arrange for the cigarettes to be delivered to the UK. The UK tax authorities argued that the cigarettes were liable to tax on importation, the companies that they were covered by the exemptions applicable in respect of imports made by private individuals. A transaction conducted through an agent, it was argued, had to be considered in the same light as a transaction carried out by the principal. As individuals could, under Single Market rules as established in Directive 92/12/EEC,[1] themselves bring goods into the UK without liability to tax, the same result should apply to the present arrangement.

1   OJ 1992 L 6/1.

30.30   The European Court of Justice held that the UK was entitled to levy duty on the cigarettes. The provisions in art 8 of Directive 92/12/EEC sanctioning personal imports required that:

> ... transportation must be effected personally by the purchaser of the products subject to duty ... [A]t no point did the Community legislature intend Article 8 to apply in the event of the involvement of an agent.

30.31   An alternative approach has now evolved, making use of the Internet. A Greek company has established a website offering to supply cigarettes and other tobacco products to UK consumers at Greek prices. The site claims:

> By taking advantage of the European Common Market! In the same way you can buy a U.K. specification car in the Netherlands cheaper than in the UK, or tobacco and alcohol cheaper in Calais, you can also avoid paying the over-taxation by buying your cigarettes and tobacco mail-order from us![1]

The response to the question whether the transaction is legal is unequivocal:

> Absolutely! One of the benefits of being part of the European Union in the U.K. is that it allows free movement of goods between member countries. There is only one restriction about the quantity. The maximum order for cigarettes is 4 cartons and for tobacco is 1Kg.

[1]   http://www.cigishop.com/.

30.32   By avoiding the involvement of an agent, it is clearly hoped to bring the transactions within the scope of art 8 of Directive 92/12/EEC. Conceptually, it is difficult to identify reasons why this should not be the case. If the Single Market is to be effective, there should not be a distinction between the situation where a UK citizen buys cigarettes whilst on holiday in Athens and where the order is made over the Internet. It should be noted, however, that the Inland Revenue, in a 'Guide for International Post users',[1] have indicated the view that excise duty will remain payable on such transactions.

[1]   Available from http://www.hmce.gov.uk/notices/143.htm.

Alternative forms of taxation

30.33   As the EU and OECD reports recognise, practical difficulties are likely to meet attempts to enforce tax systems in respect of ecommerce. A number of alternative approaches have been canvassed, with some attention being paid to the notion of a 'bit tax'. In essence, this would involve charges being levied upon Internet users dependent on the volume of data transmitted to or from their equipment. The notion of such a tax was first proposed in a paper produced by Arthur Cordell and Thomas Ide for the Club of Rome in 1994.

30.34   Within Europe, the report 'Building the Information Society for Us All',[1] produced by a group of independent experts appointed by the Commission, suggested in 1996 that the Commission investigate:

> Appropriate ways in which the benefits of the Information Society (IS) can be more equally distributed between those who benefit and those who lose. Such research should focus on practicable, implementable policies at the European level which do not jeopardise the emergence of the IS. More specifically, the expert group would like the Commission to undertake research to find out whether a 'bit tax' might be a feasible tool in achieving such redistribution aims.

[1]   Available from http://meritbbs.unimaas.nl/publications/2-hleg.pdf.

30.35   A more detailed argument in favour of the 'bit tax' concept was prepared by the chairman of the group, Luc Soete.[1] The proposal was not generally well received, with objections being raised both to the level of 'surveillance' which might be required to collect data for billing purposes and also on the grounds that as well as catching commercial uses of the Internet, the tax would apply where, for example, a person distributed copies of holiday photos taken with a digital camera to friends and relatives. In some respects, the arguments are similar to those which have been raised concerning proposals to impose a levy on the cost of audio cassette tapes, the proceeds going to compensate copyright holders for losses caused by unauthorised domestic copying. The objection has been made that those users (admittedly perhaps a small minority) who make non-infringing use of tapes, should not be required to make payments to copyright owners. The Commission have indicated that it does not intend to move in this direction, it being stated that:

> While some commentators have suggested that there might be a need to look at alternative taxes such as a bit tax, the Commission is of the opinion that this is not appropriate, since VAT already applies to these transactions.[2]

The question remains, however, whether systems of taxation primarily designed to operate in an economy dominated by tangible goods, is well suited for the information society.

[1]   Available from http://merithbs.unimaas.nl/rmpdf/rm98_020.pdf.
[2]   'The European Initiative on Electronic Commerce', available from http://www.cordis.lu/esprit/src/ecomcom.htm.

30.36   Arguments in favour of a 'bit tax' have also been advanced by the United Nations in a report 'Globalization With a Human Face', published in July 1999.[1] This advocated levying a tax on data sent over the Internet, with the funds used to support the development of a telecommunications infrastructure in the least developed countries of the world. Statistics produced by NUA Internet Surveys[2] indicate a massive variation in access to and use of the Internet between the various regions of the world. Some 304.6 million people are estimated to make use of the Internet, with the geographic breakdown:

Africa	2.58 million
Asia/Pacific	68.9 million
Europe	83.35 million
Middle East	1.9 million
Canada and USA	136.86 million
Latin America	10.74 million

A tax of 1 cent per 100 emails, it was estimated, would yield an annual income of $70bn.

¹   Available from http://www.undp.org/hdro/99.htm.
²   Available from http://www.nua.ie/surveys/how_many_online/index.html.

30.37   The United Nations proposal (coupled with a further proposal for a tax on income from patents) has not received a warm welcome in the developed world, where it was described by the leader of the US Republican Party in Congress as 'an unnecessary and burdensome tax on the Internet'.

Conclusions

30.38   The term 'globalisation' is one of the buzzwords associated with the expansion of international trade. Its impact will be felt on national tax regimes as well as on all other aspects of life and society. The Internet makes it possible for operators in almost every area of activity to deal directly with an end user without the need for such traditional intermediaries as travel agents, import agencies, car dealers, tobacconists, off licences and so on. From a fiscal perspective, such operators offered the advantage that responsibility for the collection of taxes and duties could be placed on them. It is much more straightforward to collect tax in respect of 10,000 items from one person than to proceed against 10,000 individual purchasers.

30.39   A further significant change arises from the ability of vendors to target customers in a particular state without the need to maintain any form of physical establishment. The Greek cigarette case described at para 30.31 above provides an excellent example of such a situation. Other illustrations might refer to the ease with which Internet-based banks can transact with UK customers without the need for any UK branch structure. 'Offshore banking' is no longer the preserve of the wealthy. Further problems may arise with the emergence of 'smart cards' such as 'Mondex', which act as a kind of virtual wallet. A benefit claimed for these systems is that transactions are effectively anonymised. Users could download 'cash' from offshore bank accounts and pay for goods or services with the same anonymity as available with cash transactions. The supplier will, in turn, be able to upload credit to a similar bank account. Whilst it might be argued that this is no different from the present situation where goods might be paid for with paper money, logistical and security problems will make most customers wary of carrying too much money, whilst the supplier may be wary of retaining too much money in biscuit tins or under bedding. With electronic cash, however, the carrying of large amounts of digital money poses no logistical or security problem. Altogether, a book for the black economy, to the extent that it has been suggested that for many people, paying tax will be an optional matter. A hopeful conclusion for some individuals perhaps, but one with dire consequences for the employment prospects of the Chancellor of the Exchequer and for those who, due to the nature of their employment, will have to bear the burden of a shrinking tax base.

Chapter 31

Defamation

Introduction

31.1   The notion of freedom of expression is widely recognised as a fundamental human right, the European Convention on Human Rights providing, for example, that:

1.   Everyone has the right to freedom of expression. This right shall include freedom to hold opinions and to receive and impart information and ideas without interference by public authority and regardless of frontiers.[1]

As with other rights, however, the right cannot be absolute. The Convention goes on to provide that:

2.   The exercise of these freedoms, since it carries with it duties and responsibilities, may be subject to such formalities, conditions, restrictions or penalties as are prescribed by law and are necessary in a democratic society, in the interests of national security, territorial integrity or public safety, for the prevention of disorder or crime, for the protection of health or morals, for the protection of the reputation or rights of others, for preventing the disclosure of information received in confidence, or for maintaining the authority and impartiality of the judiciary.

[1]   Article 10.

31.2   Prohibitions against the publication of pornographic or obscene materials constitute an example of a case where restrictions and penalties might be justified on the ground of the protection of morals. The law relating to defamation constitutes a further example relating to the 'protection of the rights or reputations of others'. As with national rules relating to obscenity, considerable variations exist between states. In the US, for example, comments made concerning public figures will attract liability only if it can be shown that they were motivated by malice. This is a very difficult hurdle for any litigant to overcome. Although UK law recognises that certain forms of communication should benefit from a similar form of protection, as a general rule, no distinction is drawn between public

685

figures and private individuals. A consequence is that statements which might be made with impunity in the US could attract legal sanctions if published in the UK. Differences exist also between the UK and many continental legal systems. In the UK, defamation is almost entirely a matter for the civil courts, whereas in countries such as Germany it is primarily a criminal matter. Again, countries such as France offer protection under the law of privacy in the event information about an individual's private life is brought into the public domain.

31.3   Given the ease with which material may be published on the Internet and the range of dissemination which can readily be achieved, it is little cause for surprise that issues relating to the law of defamation have assumed considerable significance. Whilst in the early days of the Internet the response of users faced with the presence of unwelcome comments or allegations was to publish a forthright rebuttal and response, increasingly today the response is to turn to the legal system and seek a remedy under the law of defamation.

31.4   A number of significant issues arise in the attempt to apply the law of defamation to Internet-related behaviour. Whilst there is seldom doubt that a party who makes a defamatory allegation is liable to legal proceedings, the reality has often been, especially in jurisdictions such as those in the UK where the legal response takes the form primarily of an award of financial compensation, there has often been the issue that the individual concerned has limited financial assets. The tendency for those aggrieved by a publication has been to take action against some third party whose financial strength is likely to be greater than that of the individual responsible. As will be described below, the application of general principles of vicarious liability has meant that employers may be liable for the words of their employees uttered in the course of their employment. Traditionally newspapers and broadcasting corporations have also incurred substantial exposure to the risk of legal proceedings in respect of comments made in their columns or programmes. Given that the possibility for a considerable degree of editorial control generally exists, this is not generally contentious in itself. In the emergence of the Internet, most users acquire access to its facilities through the medium of an ISP. This party may well provide facilities for hosting web pages. As will be discussed, the question has arisen to what extent an ISP will be classed as equivalent to traditional media publishers and broadcasters for the purposes of the law of defamation.

31.5   In addition to issues of substantive law, the global reach of the Internet poses significant jurisdictional challenges. In the era of the printed word, the vast majority of a newspaper's circulation would be restricted to its country and jurisdiction of publication.[1] Similarly, most television and radio broadcasts have been received only in one national territory – although satellite broadcasting is changing this situation. With the Internet, the place of publication becomes a matter of little practical significance so that it is as easy for a UK-based browser to view the web version of the *New York Times* as its London equivalent. Questions where and when a defamatory comment is published have assumed considerable importance.

The existence of separate legal systems in Scotland and England has posed some difficulties in the past in respect of the law of defamation.

The nature of defamation

31.6   The term 'defamation' tends to be used as a generic descriptor for actions in which it is alleged that the making of untrue and unwarranted comments about an individual have tended to lower that person's standing in the eyes of right-thinking members of society. The question what sorts of comments would produce this effect is not easy to answer and will vary with changing social attitudes. Until the Second World War, it was not considered defamatory to accuse someone of being anti-Semitic. The term 'computer hacker' was originally used to describe someone who was particularly skilled in operating computers and finding solutions to problems. In this context, the phrase could not be considered defamatory. Today, of course, the generally accepted meaning has changed and the accusation that someone is a computer hacker might have legal consequences.

31.7   In English law, a distinction exists between libel and slander. The law of libel applies to comments which are recorded in some permanent form – in print or on tape, whilst slander is reserved for comments which are more transient in nature. In general, the law of libel operates on a stricter basis than that of slander, based in part on the assessment that statements which are recorded are likely to be more damaging to the subject than those which are not. Developments in recording and broadcasting technology have served to blur both the distinction between libel and slander and the rationale for distinct treatment. A statement on a live television broadcast might be heard by tens of millions of viewers and be far more damaging to the reputation of the subject than would be the case with a letter published in a local newspaper. In the case of broadcasting, the Defamation Act 1952 provided that the law of libel was to apply in respect of any statements made.

31.8   In the case of email and the contents of the Internet and WWW, it seems beyond question that there is a sufficient degree of recording to ensure that the law of libel will apply. Some doubt, perhaps, remains concerning the status of services such as chat rooms where the atmosphere at least is closer to a conversational forum and where no permanent record is maintained. In cases of slander a defence is available, commonly referred to as 'vulgar abuse'. The essence is that statements were made in the heat of an argument. The essence of the defence is that words, albeit defamatory in content, were neither intended as such nor would be so regarded by anyone listening to the exchange. Such a defence might seem appropriate in relation to many postings to Internet newsgroups, where the concept of the flame war is well established. Anyone perusing computer newsgroups will be aware that forthright expression is often the order of the day and that 'flame wars' in which discussion is reduced to a level of personal abuse, are not uncommon. One newsgroup, 'alt.flame', even specialises on this topic. Although the existence of a culture encouraging robust and blunt debate cannot affect the determination whether a message is defamatory, there may be an element of consent on the part of those participating in such fora. With newsgroups, although there would seem no doubt that postings are written and the range of dissemination is comparable (perhaps even wider) than that associated with the written word, the attitudes and practices coupled with the speed of communication are perhaps more akin to the spoken word.

Communication

31.9   In order to be actionable, it is necessary that a statement be communicated to at least one person other than the subject. The range of dissemination need not be wide. A letter or email to a third party will suffice, as would posting a comment on a public notice-board. Indeed, in terms of impact on an individual, a letter to an employer making false and defamatory comments might have far more serious consequences than a communication accessible to a wider audience. The Internet provides a superbly effective communications medium. Email permits cheap and swift communications of messages between individuals, whilst newsgroups allow anyone to express views on almost any topic under the sun and the WWW permits individuals to establish themselves as electronic publishers. Given the volume and variety of traffic carried by the Internet, it would be a source of considerable surprise were its contents to be free of defamatory comments. The essence of defamation is that a statement is published which is both inaccurate and likely to have the effect of lowering the standing of its subject in the eyes of right-thinking members of society.

Who is liable for defamatory comments?

Liability of the poster

31.10   There is no doubt that a person making a defamatory comment will incur liability. It has, for example, been reported that a student has been warned by the office of a government minister that postings to a politics newsgroup were considered to be defamatory, although no legal proceedings followed.[1] In addition to cases concerning the liability of service operators, which will be discussed below, in the US, a journalist has reportedly faced a legal bill in excess of $25,000 after settling a libel suit resulting from a posting which he made on the Internet.[2]

[1]   *The Times*, 3 July 1995.
[2]   *The Quill*, October 1994.

31.11   Although it may be stated that the poster of a defamatory message runs the risk of legal action, the task of identifying the party responsible may not be an easy one. Even if a message appears to originate from a particular individual, it may be necessary to establish that it is genuine. In the US case of *Stratton Oakmont v Prodigy*,[1] a message appeared to have been sent from a particular user's account. The user, however, denied that the message had been sent by him or from his equipment. In the particular case, the issue was not of great significance as the action proceeded against the service provider, who, it appears, had always been the major target of the litigation. In other cases, it may be necessary for a claimant to establish that a message was sent by the party whose identifiers appear. It appears that it is possible for a user's identity to be impersonated. Instances have been reported of forged email messages purporting to have originated from the White House. Another technical facility which may complicate any legal proceedings is the use of anonymous remailing services. These services, which may be based anywhere in the world, accept messages from users, strip out the details of the original poster and forward them to the addressee with no indication of the identity of the original poster. Such a technique makes it impossible to identify the author without the co-operation of the operator of the remailing service. Such co-operation may not readily be forthcoming, and considerable controversy surrounded attempts by the Church of Scientology to discover the identity of a user who posted documents relating to the organisation, allegedly in breach of copyright. On this occasion, the remailing service involved was based in Finland.[2]

[1]   (1995) 195 NY Misc LEXIS 229.
[2]   *Independent*, 4 March 1995.

31.12   Even in the event that a service provider does not actively refuse to cooperate with a complainant, legal complexities may arise. The decision of the Court of Appeal in the case of *Totalise v Motley Fool Ltd*[1] raises a number of interesting issues concerning the interaction between the requirements of data protection and other elements of law. Interactive Investor operated a business providing financial information to individual investors. The information was made available via a website. Included in the website was a bulleting board facility allowing users to post views and comments.

[1]   [2001] EWCA Civ 1897, [2002] 1 WLR 1233.

31.13   In order to access the website, users had to register and indicate acceptance of the operator's terms and conditions. These contained a data protection notice to the effect that the provider was:

> registered under the Data Protection Act 1998. All personal information you supply to us will be treated in accordance with that Act. We will collect and use your personal information in order to operate, enhance and provide to you the Information Services you request.
>
> We will not pass your personal information on to any other person except to our Service Providers, where it is necessary, to enable us to provide you with the Information Services you request from us.

31.14   One user, operating under the pseudonym 'Zeddust' posted comments which were defamatory of the claimant company. It complained to Interactive who removed the positing and suspended the user. Totalise then requested provision of information identifying the poster in order that it might initiate proceedings for defamation. This was refused by Interactive who stated that the supply of personal data would place it in breach of its terms and conditions and also of the requirements of the Data Protection Act 1998.

31.15 Totalise instituted proceedings seeking a court order requiring disclosure of the data. This was granted by a High Court judge who also made an order holding Interactive liable for the costs incurred by Totalise. An appeal was made on the issue of costs, they key question being whether Interactive had acted unreasonably in refusing to hand over the data without subjecting totalise to the expense of obtaining a court order (costs were assessed at just under £5,000)?[1]

[1]   *Totalise v Motley Fool Ltd* [2001] EWCA Civ 1897, [2002] 1 WLR 1233.

31.16 The Court of Appeal held that the behaviour was not unreasonable. The issues involved, it was ruled, were complex, especially with the addition of the Human Rights Act 1998 to the UK statute book. A balance had to be struck between the interests of the claimant in being able to secure a remedy and the right of the individual to respect for private life. Such a task was one for the courts and, it was held:

> It is difficult to see how the court can carry out this task if what it is refereeing is a contest between two parties, neither of whom is the person most concerned, the data subject; one of whom is the data subject's prospective antagonist; and the other of whom knows the data subject's identity, has undertaken to keep it confidential so far as the law permits, and would like to get out of the cross-fire as rapidly and as cheaply as possible. However the website operator can, where appropriate, tell the user what is going on and to offer to pass on in writing to the claimant and the court any worthwhile reason the user wants to put forward for not having his or her identity disclosed. Further, the Court could require that to be done before making an order. Doing so will enable the court to do what is required of it with slightly more confidence that it is respecting the law laid down in more than one statute by Parliament and doing no injustice to a third party, in particular not violating his convention rights.[1]

It is important to keep in mind that there was no appeal against the initial ruling that in this case the identifying data should be handed over to the claimant. The decision therefore, gives no sort of green light for the posting of defamatory comments under the shield of anonymity. It does provide, however, welcome recognition of the fact that privacy issues are important and are not to be discarded lightly in the face of competing claims.

[1]   *Totalise v Motley Fool Ltd* [2001] EWCA Civ 1897, [2002] 1 WLR 1233 at [26].

Employer's liability

31.17 As more and more companies make use of email as a method of communication between staff, so there will be increasing exposure to action on the basis of vicarious liability in respect of the use or misuse made of the communications network. In 1997, the Norwich Union insurance company reached a settlement in a libel action brought by a health insurance company, Western Provident Association. Under the terms of the agreement, Norwich Union agreed to pay £450,000 in damages and costs in respect of libellous messages concerning the association's financial stability which had been contained in email messages exchanged between members of the Norwich Union's staff.[1]

[1]   *The Times*, 18 July 1997.

31.18   The fact that a settlement was reached prior to trial means that the case is of no value as a legal precedent. The lesson for those engaging in email discussions is obvious – that although communications may be approached as a form of conversation, everything is recorded almost without limit of time and can be retrieved at a later date. A similar example of this phenomenon can be seen in the discovery of internal Microsoft emails during the legal investigations into their commercial practices conducted by the US Department of Justice. One significant factor limiting the extent of liability for defamatory communications made by employees may be that the vicarious liability applies only in respect of acts committed in the course of employment. In the Norwich Union case, the communications were clearly work-related but it is unlikely that an employer would be held liable in the event, for example, that employees used email facilities to exchange defamatory comments on subjects unconnected with work. To minimise the risks of liability, it would be advisable for employers to indicate clearly in contracts of employment or staff handbooks what uses may or may not be made of electronic communications.

31.19   Faced with concern at their potential liabilities for misuse of electronic communications, it is commonplace for employers to monitor use of the facilities. In the US, a number of actions have been reported of corporations being sued 'for millions of dollars' by employees alleging that fellow workers have been engaging in some form of electronic harassment involving the posting of abusive or offensive messages. It has been suggested that:

> Lawyers are bracing themselves for a wave of litigation as people catch on to the fact that they can redress grievances – and possibly become very rich – by producing e-mail evidence of prejudice based on gender, sexual preference, race, nationality or age. Proving cases that depend on spoken jests and casual remarks has always presented its difficulties in court. The beauty of e-mail is that all plaintiffs have to do is retrieve it from their company's computer systems and then print it out. Plenty of material is certain to be available in a country where 80 per cent of organisations use e-mail, and where it is expected that by the year 2000 more than one billion messages will be sent a week.[1]

[1]   *Independent*, 20 July 1997.

31.20   Faced with such exposure, employers may well be tempted to use packages to monitor email communications within the workplace. One such package, it is reported:

... system may be programmed to suit the offensiveness threshold of each particular firm. Thus it might be that a message between two secretaries that contained the words 'sex' or 'black' – or something profane – would immediately appear on their boss's computer screen for inspection.[1]

[1] *Independent*, 20 July 1997.

31.21 Under present UK law, it would appear that use of such a system would not be unlawful. Although the provisions of the Interception of Communications Act 1985 will govern the interception of email messages passing through a public telecommunications network, this statute does not apply to private networks. In the case of *Halford v UK*,[1] however, the European Court of Human Rights held that the Convention's requirements relating to protection of privacy had been breached where telephone calls made from work premises by a senior police officer had been 'bugged' on the authority of her Chief Constable. Argument on behalf of the UK to the effect that the telephones in question belonged to the employer, in this case the government, did not sway the court. It would appear that any monitoring of email might be challenged on this basis, although it is not clear whether the giving of notice to employees that phone calls or email messages might be monitored would remove their 'reasonable expectation' of privacy in their communications.

[1] [1997] IRLR 471.

Liability of ISPs

31.22 With the exception of the issue whether a defence should be available for those who post defamatory messages in the heat of a flame war, there can be little dispute that the author of such a posting should face the legal consequences. More controversial is the question how far the operators of an on-line service should incur liabilities akin to those of traditional publishers in respect of messages appearing on their systems.

31.23 The first UK case to reach the stage of High Court proceedings was that of *Godfrey v Demon*.[1] Although the case was settled prior to a full trial, preliminary hearings have raised a number of interesting and potentially significant issues concerned with the extent of an Internet Service Provider's liability for defamatory postings carried on its services.

[1] [1999] EMLR 542.

31.24 The plaintiff, Laurence Godfrey, is a UK-based lecturer in computer science, mathematics and physics. He appears to be a keen poster to Usenet, with reference being made in the court proceedings to a posting record of more than 3,000 messages. A number of Godfrey's postings, it was suggested by the defendant at a later stage in proceedings, were intended to provoke a violent response from other posters:

The words complained of were posted to a newsgroup. Newsgroup users have come to abide by an informal code of conduct known as 'netiquette', which is intended to introduce an element of restraint and moderation with regard to the content of postings. Those who persist in breaching netiquette are almost invariably exposed to irate (and sometimes offensive or aggressive) postings from aggrieved users: this practice is known as 'flaming'. As a regular newsgroup user, it is to be inferred that the Plaintiff would at all material times have known of the foregoing facts and matters.

---

1   *Godfrey v Demon* 1999 WL 33285490 at para 7.

31.25   Rather than perpetuating a flame war, Mr Godfrey had, on at least seven occasions, instituted proceedings against both posters and ISPs alleging that comments defamed him. The defence alleged that:

> ... the Plaintiff has cynically pursued the tactic of posting deliberately provocative, offensive, obnoxious and frequently puerile comments about other countries, their citizens and cultures; and has done so with a view to provoking others to trade insults which he can then claim are defamatory and seek to use as the basis for bringing vexatious libel actions against them and against access or service providers such as the Defendant.

---

1   *Godfrey v Demon* 1999 WL 33285490 at para 7.

31.26   The conduct at issue in the *Demon* case[1] was slightly different. A message purporting to come from Godfrey had appeared in the Newsgroup 'soc.culture.thai'. The message was a forgery, and in its tone and content was described by the judge as being 'squalid, obscene and defamatory of the plaintiff'. The basis for the defamation would lie in the argument that the plaintiff's standing in the eyes of right thinking members of society would be damaged if it was thought that he held the views attributed to him in the email. The defendant, Demon, is a well-known ISP. Messages in 'soc.culture.thai' could be accessed by its subscribers, the postings being held on Demon's servers for around 14 days.

---

1   *Godfrey v Demon* [1999] EMLR 542.

31.27   The posting at issue, which originated in the US, appeared in the newsgroup on 13 January 1997. On 17 January, Godfrey faxed the defendant's managing director with the demand that the posting be removed from Demon's servers. It was accepted by both sides that this could have been done. Although Demon acknowledged that the fax had been received, it appeared that it never reached its managing director's desk and the message remained on its site until routinely deleted after a fortnight. The plaintiff subsequently brought proceedings seeking damages in respect of the damage to his reputation caused by the defendant's actions. The defendant denied liability on two grounds. First, it was argued, its conduct was covered by the defence of innocent dissemination established under the Defamation Act 1996. Secondly, it was denied that there had been any publication of the comment by it. The plaintiff brought action before Moreland J in the High Court seeking as a preliminary step to strike out these defences as invalid.[1]

---

1   *Godfrey v Demon* [1999] EMLR 542.

Innocent dissemination

31.28   The Defamation Act 1996 was enacted in an attempt to update the law relating to defamation. It followed a study conducted by the Law Commission which recommended the introduction of a new defence of 'innocent dissemination'. The Act accordingly provides that:

> (1) In defamation proceedings a person has a defence if he shows that—
> (a)   he was not the author, editor or publisher of the statement complained of;
> (b)   he took reasonable care in relation to its publication; and
> (c)   he did not know, and had no reason to believe, that what he did caused or contributed to the publication of a defamatory statement.[1]

It is further provided that:

> In determining for the purposes of this section whether a person took reasonable care, or had reason to believe that what he did caused or contributed to the publication of a defamatory statement, regard shall be had to—
>
> (a)   the extent of his responsibility for the content of the statement or the decision to publish it;
> (b)   the nature or circumstances of the publication; and
> (c)   the previous conduct or character of the author, editor or publisher.

[1]   Section 1.

31.29   The section proceeds to define the terms 'author', 'editor' and 'publisher'. It is important to note that these definitions apply only for the purposes of the section. A publisher is defined as:

> ... a commercial publisher, that is, a person whose business is issuing material to the public, or a section of the public, who issues material containing the statement in the course of that business.[1]

It is further provided that for the purposes of the section a person will not be classed as an author, editor or publisher if the involvement with the work is 'only' in specified capacities. The relevant categories relate to involvement:

> (a)   in printing, producing, distributing or selling printed material containing the statement;
> (c)   in processing, making copies of, distributing or selling any electronic medium in or on which the statement is recorded, or in operating or providing any equipment, system or service by means of which the statement is retrieved, copied, distributed or made available in electronic form; or
> (e)   as the operator or provider of access to a communications system by means of which the statement is transmitted or made available, by a person over whom he had no effective control.[2]

[1]   Defamation Act 1996, s 1(2).
[2]   Section 1(3).

31.30   It was held by Moreland J that Demon was not to be considered as acting as a publisher in respect of the postings and therefore satisfied the first requirement of the defence.[1] The provisions, however, were cumulative, with Demon also being required to demonstrate that they had taken reasonable care and were unaware of the fact that their actions had caused the publication of a defamatory comment. From the recital of the facts presented above, it is clear that these elements constituted a much more substantial hurdle, and it is perhaps not surprising that the court held that the defence could not be sustained. The defamation action related only to the period after 17 January 1997, when the plaintiff's fax arrived and, as the defendant had taken no action to examine the matter, it was not in a position to demonstrate that reasonable care had been taken.

[1]   *Godfrey v Demon* [1999] EMLR 542.

31.31   The judge's finding[1] appears in line with the provisions of the Defamation Act 1996 and with the Law Commission's recommendation. In its Consultation Paper, the Law Commission had suggested:

> The defence of innocent dissemination has never provided an absolute immunity for distributors, however mechanical their contribution. It does not protect those who knew that the material they were handling was defamatory, or who ought to have known of its nature. Those safeguards are preserved, so that the defence is not available to a defendant who knew that his act involved or contributed to publication defamatory of the plaintiff. It is available only if, having taken all reasonable care, the defendant had no reason to suspect that his act had that effect.[2]

[1]   *Godfrey v Demon* [1999] EMLR 542.
[2]   'Reforming Defamation Law and Procedure' (1995) para 2.4

31.32   The fact that a faxed message of complaint attracted no response of any sort makes it difficult to see how Demon could have availed themselves of the defence of innocent dissemination. The more interesting and controversial question might relate to what could have been expected of the defendants if their administrative procedures had been more effective. It is clear from the calendar of events described above that the case concerned a period of around ten days. There would have been limited opportunity for the defendant to undertake in-depth inquiries. As noted above, the offending message entered the Internet via a US-based ISP. Without the active co-operation of this party, there may well have been little that the defendant could do to verify the true identity of the sender. Even with co-operation, with the proliferation of ISPs offering free access to the Internet with a minimum of registration procedures which could themselves be falsified with minimal effort. Given the time-scale and the technical constraints identified, it would appear that an ISP in receipt of a complaint regarding a posting would have little choice other than between doing nothing and removing the posting from its servers. The first action obviously carries the risk of an action for defamation, but the automatic removal of messages upon receipt of a complaint is something which carries its own problems and dangers.

31.33   It would appear that following the decision, a number of ISPs have adopted a policy of automatically withdrawing access to material in respect of which any form of complaint has been received. One case reported by the Campaign Against Censorship of the Internet appeared to go even further:

> Outcast magazine hadn't even done anything wrong: the solicitors alleged that Outcast might commit a libel at some unspecified time in the future, and that if they did, they would hold Netbenefit responsible. The ISP demanded a lawyer's guarantee against any such future wrongdoing, and when Outcast was unable to provide it within 3 hours, deleted the entire web site.[1]

¹   http://test.liberty.org.uk/cacib/.

31.34   To an extent, the nature of the Internet may provide such organisations with a means of self-help. The Campaign Against Internet Censorship found its site evicted from its UK-based ISP following a complaint from Dr Godfrey regarding its account of the Demon litigation. It is, however, a comparatively simple matter for an organisation put in such a position to find an alternative ISP; in the case of the Campaign Against Internet Censorship, one based in the US.

Publication at common law

31.35   Although Demon were not classed as publishers for the purpose of the defence of innocent dissemination, the definitions discussed above apply only to this defence. The issue arose also whether Demon might be classed as publishers under the general law of defamation. Once again, the court found against the company.[1] Reference was made to a number of authorities, the most relevant being the case of *Byrne v Deane*,[2] where the directors of a golf club were held liable as publishers in respect of a defamatory message placed by a third party on a notice board in the club. Here, the court held that:

> It is said that as a general proposition where the act of the person alleged to have published a libel has not been any positive act, but has merely been the refraining from doing some act, he cannot be guilty of publication. I am quite unable to accept any such general proposition. It may very well be that in some circumstances a person, by refraining from removing or obliterating the defamatory matter, is not committing any publication at all. In other circumstances he may be doing so. The test it appears to me is this: having regard to all the facts of the case is the proper inference that by not removing the defamatory matter the defendant really made himself responsible for its continued presence in the place where it had been put?[3]

¹   *Godfrey v Demon* [1999] EMLR 542.
²   [1937] 1 KB 818.
³   [1937] 1 KB 818 at 837.

31.36   In the present case, the conclusion was reached that:

> In my judgment the Defendants, whenever they transmit and whenever there is transmitted from the storage of their news server a defamatory posting, publish that posting to any subscriber to their ISP who accesses the newsgroup

containing that posting. Thus everytime one of the Defendants' customers accesses 'soc culture thai' and sees that posting defamatory of the Plaintiff there is a publication to that customer.

I do not accept (the) argument that the Defendants were merely owners of an electronic device through which postings were transmitted. The Defendants chose to store 'soc.culture.thai' postings within their computer. Such postings could be accessed on that newsgroup. The Defendants could obliterate and indeed did so about a fortnight after receipt.[1]

[1]   *Godfrey v Demon* [1999] EMLR 542 at 550.

31.37   Following the striking out of its defence in March 1999, it is difficult to identify what ground Demon might have had for opposing the plaintiff's claim. The case did return to the court in the following month when Demon sought leave to introduce evidence of the defendant's activities on the Internet which, it was claimed, demonstrated a history of postings whose nature appeared calculated to produce an intemperate response. Although permission was granted, this material could only have been relevant to the assessment of damages. It would also appear that at least some of the allegations made were unsubstantiated. In the event, a settlement was reached shortly before the case was scheduled to proceed to trial in Spring 2000. The terms of the settlement saw Demon making a payment to the plaintiff of some £250,000. Although this headline figure attracted a great deal of publicity, less publicised was the fact that all bar £15,000 represented the plaintiff's legal costs.

ISPs and the Electronic Commerce Directive

31.38   Although it has not been the subject of litigation provisions of the European Directive on Electronic Commerce[1] may provide some protection for ISPs. It provides in Article 12 that:

1. Where an Information Society service is provided that consists of the transmission in a communication network of information provided by the recipient of the service, or the provision of access to a communication network, Member States shall provide in their legislation that the provider of such a service shall not be liable, otherwise than under a prohibitory injunction, for the information transmitted, on condition that the provider:
    (a)   does not initiate the transmission;
    (b)   does not select the receiver of the transmission; and
    (c)   does not select or modify the information contained in the transmission.
2. The acts of transmission and of provision of access referred to in paragraph 1 include the automatic, intermediate and transient storage of the information transmitted in so far as this takes place for the sole purpose of carrying out the transmission in the communication network, and provided that the information is not stored for any period longer than is reasonably necessary for the transmission.

Article 15 provides further that:

Member States shall not impose a general obligation on providers, when providing the services covered by Articles 12 to 14, to monitor the information which they transmit or store, nor a general obligation actively to seek facts or circumstances indicating illegal activity.

[1]   Directive 2000/31/EC.

31.39   Implementing these provisions, the Electronic Communications (European Community) Regulations 2002[1] provide that:

19. Where an information society service is provided which consists of the storage of information provided by a recipient of the service, the service provider (if he otherwise would) shall not be liable for damages or for any other pecuniary remedy or for any criminal sanction as a result of that storage where—

(a)   the service provider—
(i)   does not have actual knowledge of unlawful activity or information and, where a claim for damages is made, is not aware of facts or circumstances from which it would have been apparent to the service provider that the activity or information was unlawful; or
(ii)   upon obtaining such knowledge or awareness, acts expeditiously to remove or to disable access to the information, and
(b)   the recipient of the service was not acting under the authority or the control of the service provider

[1]   SI 2002/2013.

31.40   The scope of protection extended under the provision is somewhat uncertain. In a scoping report on the law of defamation published in 2002,[1] the Law Commission comment:

There has been some debate on how far this test differs from the test under section 1 of the Defamation Act 1996. One view is that article 14 [of Directive 2000/31/EC] mirrors section 1 by providing that once an ISP is aware that material is defamatory and fails to act, the protection is lost. The other view is that it may provide wider protection: it is not enough for the ISP merely to know that the material is defamatory. They would also need to know that it was 'illegal' (or at least be aware of facts and circumstances from which the illegal activity was apparent). On this basis, the ISP would need to know that the material was not only defamatory but also libellous (i.e. that the potential defences of justification, fair comment or privilege were not available).[2]

The Commission's conclusion was to the effect that:

In order to resolve this question, one needs to ask what constitutes an 'unlawful activity' in defamation law. Under current English law, it is *prima facie* unlawful to publish a defamatory statement that refers to the claimant (though in some circumstances it may be open to a defendant to prove a defence, such as truth). On this basis, it would seem that an ISP has 'actual knowledge of unlawful activity' as soon as they become aware that a publication has taken place that would make reasonable people think less well of a third party. The provider does not need to be aware that the material is false.[3]

1   CP5 (special) Scoping study no. 2.
2   At para 2.18.
3   Paragraph 2.22.

31.41 It seems doubtful that the Electronic Commerce Directive[1] and the Regulations[2] clarify significantly the previously uncertain state of the law and, as indicated above, it appears that most ISPs adopt a 'safety first' policy whereby information is withdrawn. Whilst understandable, such a response and situation is not desirable and clarification of this area of the law would be beneficial.

1   Directive 2000/31/EC.
2   SI 2002/2013.

Single or multiple publications

31.42 With many traditional works, ascertaining the date of publication is a relatively straightforward matter. Different factors may apply in the case of on-line resources as was at issue in the case of *Loutchansky v Times Newspapers Ltd*.[1] Here the claimant sued the defendant newspaper in respect of a number of stories which suggested that he was linked to organised crime in Russia. In common with most other newspapers *The Times* publishes an 'online' edition with the added capability for readers to search an archive of previous editions. The stories relating to Mr Loutchansky appeared on the online edition.

1   [2001] EWCA Civ 1805, [2002] QB 783.

31.43 Actions for defamation require to be commenced within one year of the publication of the material complained of.[1] The action relating to the online publication was not raised within a year of the initial publication but it was argued on behalf of the claimant that publication in the context of an online work, occurred anew each time the material was accessed by a reader. This argument was accepted by the trial judge and endorsed by the Court of Appeal:

> It is a well established principle of the English law of defamation that each individual publication of a libel gives rise to a separate cause of action, subject to its own limitation period. *Duke of Brunswick v Harmer* (1849) 14 QB 185 provides a striking illustration of this principle. On 19 September 1830 an article was published in the *Weekly Dispatch*. The limitation period for libel was then six years. The article defamed the Duke of Brunswick. Seventeen years after its publication an agent of the Duke purchased a back number containing the article from the Weekly Dispatch's office. Another copy was obtained from the British Museum. The Duke sued on those two publications. The defendant contended that the cause of action was time barred, relying on the original publication date. The Court of Queen's Bench held that the delivery of a copy of the newspaper to the plaintiff's agent constituted a separate publication in respect of which suit could be brought.[2]

1   Limitation Act 1980, s 4A.
2   *Loutchansky v Times Newspapers Ltd* [2001] EWCA Civ 1805, [2002] QB 783 at [57].

31.44 By way of contrast, the courts in the US apply what is referred to as the 'single publication' rule. The basis of this was explained in the case *Ogden v Association of the United States Army*:

> it is the prevailing American doctrine that the publication of a book, periodical or newspaper containing defamatory matter gives rise to but one cause of action for libel, which accrues at the time of the original publication, and that the statute of limitations runs from that date. It is no longer the law that every sale or delivery of a copy of the publication creates a new cause of action.[1]

[1]   (1959) 177 F Supp 498 at 502.

31.45 Counsel for the newspaper did not seek to argue that its case was sustainable under the established UK position but sought to persuade the Court of Appeal that it should adopt the single publication rule on the basis that:

> The difficulties which [the multiple publication] rule poses for the new technology of the internet, and in particular for website publication by newspapers of back numbers, are obvious. Above all, every day during which a back number remains on a website potentially gives rise to a new publication of that issue, and therefore a new cause of action, whether by actual accessing of a defamatory article by an internet user, or (as the claimant argued was open to it) by reliance on an inference that someone must have accessed the article. The continuous and indefinite nature of that publication has the consequence that s 4A of the Limitation Act 1980 (which provides for a one year limitation period in cases of libel and slander) is rendered nugatory, and that the maintainer of the website is liable to be indefinitely exposed to repeated claims in defamation. If it is accepted that there is a social utility in the technological advances which enable newspapers to provide an internet archive of back numbers which the general public can access immediately and without difficulty or expense, instead of having to buy a back number (if available) or visit a library which maintains a collection of newspaper back numbers, then the law as it had developed to suit traditional hard copy publication is now inimical to modern conditions, and (as has always been the strength of the common law) must evolve to reflect those conditions. As is developed below, it must evolve also to accommodate the requirements of the European Convention and of the Human Rights Act 1998.[1]

In respect of the argument relating to the European Convention it was suggested that to expose publishers to the risk of litigation an indeterminate length of time after publication would constitute an unacceptable obstacle to the right of free expression. Maintaining a web archive, it was argued:

> was a valuable public service. If a newspaper defendant which maintained a website of back numbers was to be indefinitely vulnerable to claims in defamation for years and even decades after the initial hard copy and Internet publication, such a rule was bound to have an effect on the preparedness of the media to maintain such websites, and thus to limit freedom of expression.[2]

[1]   *Loutchansky v Times Newspapers Ltd* [2001] EWCA Civ 1805, [2002] QB 783 at [52].
[2]   [2001] EWCA Civ 1805 at [71].

31.46   The Court of Appeal was not convinced.

> We accept that the maintenance of archives, whether in hard copy or on the
> internet, has a social utility, but consider that the maintenance of archives is a
> comparatively insignificant aspect of freedom of expression. Archive material
> is stale news and its publication cannot rank in importance with the
> dissemination of contemporary material. Nor do we believe that the law of
> defamation need inhibit the responsible maintenance of archives. Where it is
> known that archive material is or may be defamatory, the attachment of an
> appropriate notice warning against treating it as the truth will normally remove
> any sting from the material.
>
> ...
>
> The change in the law of defamation for which the appellants contend is a
> radical one. In our judgment they have failed to make out their case that such
> a change is required.[1]

² *Loutchansky v Times Newspapers Ltd* [2001] EWCA Civ 1805, [2002] QB 783 at [74]-[76].

31.47   Further discussion regarding the desirability of adopting a 'single
publication' rule took place in the Australian case of *Dow Jones & Co Inc v
Gutnick*.[1] Here a story had appeared in the appellant's journal and website which
was allegedly defamatory of the defendant. Proceedings were raised in the
Australian courts. The appellants sought to have these struck out on the basis
that publication had occurred when the material was loaded onto its servers in
New Jersey in the US. The Australian courts were not therefore, it argued, the
most appropriate forum for the action.

¹   [2002] HCA 56, Aus HC.

31.48   Once again the defendant sought to persuade the court to change
traditional practice. The argument was addressed with some sympathy by Mr
Justice Kirby. In the course of a judgment which is replete with useful information
and comment regarding the impact of the Internet on legal rules he stated that:

> The idea that this Court should solve the present problem by reference to
> judicial remarks in England in a case, decided more than a hundred and fifty
> years ago, involving the conduct of the manservant of a Duke, despatched to
> procure a back issue of a newspaper of minuscule circulation, is not immediately
> appealing to me. The genius of the common law derives from its capacity to
> adapt the principles of past decisions, by analogical reasoning, to the resolution
> of entirely new and unforeseen problems. When the new problem is as novel,
> complex and global as that presented by the Internet in this appeal, a greater
> sense of legal imagination may be required than is ordinarily called for. Yet the
> question remains whether it can be provided, conformably with established
> law and with the limited functions of a court under the Australian constitution
> to develop and re-express the law.[1]

Although he recognised that trenchant criticisms could be made of the existing
state of the law he concluded, in line with the remainder of the High Court of
Australia, that change of the nature and extent required was properly a matter
for the legislature rather than the courts. Echoing comments of the Canadian

Supreme Court in the case of *R v Stewart* discussed at para 14.15 above,[2] he concluded:

> It would exceed the judicial function to re-express the common law on such a subject in such ways. This is a subject of law reform requiring the evaluation of many interests and considerations that a court could not be sure to cover.[3]

1   *Dow Jones & Co Inc v Gutnick* [2002] HCA 56 at 92.
3   50 DLR (4th) 1.
4   [2002] HCA 56 at 138.

Conclusions

31.49   The English law of defamation is generally regarded as being considerably stricter than that applying in most other jurisdictions. Assuming the necessary connection with the jurisdiction can be established by a claimant, the general rule applied by the courts to jurisdictional issues was described by Lord Goff in the case of *Spiliada Maritime Corpn v Consulex Ltd*,[1] in the following terms:

> The basic principle is that a stay will only be granted on the ground of forum non conveniens where the court is satisfied that there is some other available forum, having competent jurisdiction, which is the appropriate forum for the trial of the action, i.e. in which the case may be tried more suitably for the interests of all the parties and the ends of justice.

1   [1987] AC 460 at 476.

31.50   Although there will often be considerable practical difficulties in pursuing and enforcing an action against a foreign-based party, the suggestion has been made by one lawyer that:

> Plaintiffs will be able to choose countries with repressive libel laws, like Britain. Anyone with an international reputation will sue here, because, relatively speaking, it's like falling off a log.[1]

1   *Guardian*, 25 April 1995.

31.51   Pending reform of the UK's defamation laws, this may indeed be the case but, as with so many aspects of the topic, we are once again brought to the realisation that national boundaries may be of little effect in the era of the global information infrastructure. As always, however, there may be a significant gap between an individual considering him- or herself or herself to be the victim of defamation finding a claimant-friendly jurisdiction and securing enforcement of any award made in other jurisdictions. It may be considered unlikely, for example, that a US court would enforce an award of damages made against a US citizen by an English court in respect of a defamatory comment posted on the Internet from the US. In the case of *Telnikoff v Matusevitch*[1] the claimant had obtained an award of damages in the English courts following publication of a newspaper article deemed to be defamatory. He took action to enforce the award in the US only for the Court of Appeals for the District of Columbia to rule that the 'cause of action on which the judgment is based is repugnant to the public policy of the State' and refuse to order its enforcement.

[1]   702 A 2d 230 (1997).

Index

All references are to paragraph number.